Affirming Diversity

Affirming Diversity

The Sociopolitical Context of Multicultural Education

Sixth Edition

Sonia Nieto

University of Massachusetts, Amherst

Patty Bode

Tufts University in affiliation with
The School of the Museum of Fine Arts, Boston

Boston   Columbus   Indianapolis   New York   San Francisco   Upper Saddle River
Amsterdam   Cape Town   Dubai   London   Madrid   Milan   Munich   Paris   Montreal   Toronto
Delhi   Mexico City   Sao Paulo   Sydney   Hong Kong   Seoul   Singapore   Taipei   Tokyo

Senior Acquisitions Editor: Kelly Villella Canton
Senior Development Editor: Maxine Chuck
Editorial Assistant: Annalea Manalili
Senior Marketing Manager: Darcy Betts
Production Editor: Paula Carroll

Editorial Production Service: John Shannon
Manufacturing Buyer: Megan Cochran
Electronic Composition: TexTech, Inc.
Interior Design: Anne Flanagan
Cover Designer: Linda Knowles

The book's front cover art is made up of self-portraits from students of art teacher Eve Del Greco and student teacher, Kelly Stoos at Susan B. Anthony Middle School for the Arts, Revere, Massachusetts in 2010: Lucas Chaves, Cheyenne Gibney, Jovan Lamothe, Nelfry Martinez-Bonilla, Mary Ann Perna, Leila Slakovic, Shara Tran, and Charudy Thy.

Library of Congress Cataloging-in-Publication Data
Nieto, Sonia.
    Affirming diversity : the sociopolitical context of multicultural education / Sonia Nieto, Patty Bode.—6 th ed.
    p. cm.
    ISBN-13: 978-0-13-136734-0
    ISBN-10: 0-13-136734-X
    1. Multicultural education–United States—Case studies.   I. Bode, Patty.   II. Title.
LC1099.3.N54 2011
370.1170973—dc22   2011005694

10 9 8 7 6 5   EBM   15   14

www.pearsonhighered.com

ISBN-10: 0-13-136734-X
ISBN-13: 978-0-13-136734-0

This book is dedicated to all the students and teachers with whom we have had the privilege to work.

—S.N. and P.B.

About the Authors

Sonia Nieto is Professor Emerita of Language, Literacy, and Culture, University of Massachusetts, Amherst. She has taught students at all levels from elementary through graduate school and she continues to speak and write on multicultural education, the education of Latinos, and other culturally and linguistically diverse student populations. Other books include *The Light in Their Eyes: Creating Multicultural Learning Communities, Second Edition* (2010), *What Keeps Teachers Going?* (2003), and two edited volumes, *Puerto Rican Students in U.S. Schools* (2000) and *Why We Teach* (2005). She has received many awards for her research, advocacy, and activism, including an Annenberg Institute Senior Fellowship (1998–2000), the Outstanding Language Arts Educator of the Year from the National Council of Teachers of English (2005), the Social Justice Education Award from the American Educational Research Association (2008), and honorary doctorates from Lesley University (1999), Bridgewater State University (2004), DePaul University (2007), and Manhattanville College (2009).

Patty Bode is the Director of Art Education for Tufts University in affiliation with the School of the Museum of Fine Arts, Boston. Her research interests include multicultural theory and practice in teacher preparation, the arts in urban education, and the role of visual culture in the expression of student knowledge. She has published and lectured on retheorizing identity and curriculum, redefining multicultural education, and critical art pedagogy. Years of experience as an activist public school teacher and teacher educator inform her art making, research, and teaching. She has received awards for efforts in antiracist curriculum reform and bridging theory and practice in multicultural education, including the 2010 Art Educator of the Year for Higher Education of the Eastern USA Region by the National Art Education Association, the Massachusetts 2010 Art Educator of the Year for Higher Education by the Massachusetts Art Education Association, and 2005 *Multicultural Educator of the Year Award* from the National Association for Multicultural Education.

Brief Contents

Contents

Setting the Stage: Multicultural Education within a Sociopolitical Context   2

1

Understanding the Sociopolitical Context of Schooling   4

2

Defining Multicultural Education for School Reform by Sonia Nieto   40

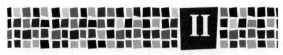

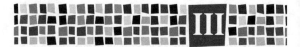

Implications of Diversity for Teaching and Learning in a Multicultural Society   294

Foreword

The 6th edition of *Affirming Diversity* appears at a time when educators in U.S. schools (and schools in many other countries) are increasingly frustrated at the dishonesty and ineptitude of policy-makers whose prescriptions for change are based on evidence-free ideological convictions. Rather than focus on alleviating the well-documented effects of poverty on school performance and ensuring that all students have access to a print-rich environment in school and home, policy-makers have targeted teachers as the cause of the achievement gap between rich and poor. Teachers in schools that are perceived to be underachieving have been fired en masse despite the fact that these schools are frequently dramatically under-funded compared to more affluent schools and typically serve students whose families struggle on a daily basis with the effects of poverty. Standardized tests police the implementation of one-size-fits-all instruction for low-income students with the result that the pedagogical divide between affluent and impoverished communities has probably never been greater.

In this climate of top-down mandates that have pushed equity to the sidelines, *Affirming Diversity* lucidly articulates the inseparability of equity and excellence in any serious and evidence-based attempt at school improvement. The pages of this book resonate with the voices of educators whose vision of education encompasses equal opportunity for all students and whose instruction focuses on expanding minds as the primary means of attaining curriculum goals.

The policies and instructional approaches promoted in *Affirming Diversity* take on added urgency in the context of current global realities. Education can no longer afford to ignore the importance of critical literacy and intercultural communication skills in a world struggling to contain armed conflicts, environmental degradation, and escalating gaps between rich and poor.

The first decade of the new millennium has undoubtedly been among the most turbulent in human history. The 9/11 attacks were quickly followed by the invasions of Afghanistan and Iraq at the cost of hundreds of thousands of lives. The domestic reality of these geographically distant conflicts is constantly present not only in the spiralling toll of American and NATO troop casualties but also in the stringent security procedures that all of us experience whenever we fly from one city to another. Feelings of fragility and unease have been compounded in recent years by the global financial collapse of 2008 and the subsequent recession that has exacerbated the impoverished conditions in which many Americans live. Discord, division, and anger have replaced the brief optimism that greeted the election of the first African American president.

During this same period, in an almost surreal juxtaposition, education in the United States has been pushed further than perhaps ever before into a sanitized and disconnected state. As a result of the high-stakes testing regime ushered in by the federal legislation *No Child Left Behind* (NCLB) passed in 2001, many schools have drawn their blinds and turned their backs on the world outside the classroom. Schooling has been reduced to the transmission of scripted skills and facts to the exclusion of inquiry, critical literacy, and social awareness. In schools across the country, instruction focuses relentlessly on teaching to the test. This is particularly the case in schools in low-income areas, which are considered most at-risk of failing to demonstrate "adequate yearly progress." Ryan Monroe (2006), an ESL teacher in a Maryland public school, calculated that during the 2004/2005 school year, English language learning (ELL) students in the fifth grade classroom where he was assigned took five different standardized tests, some of them more than once. He notes the instructional consequences: "During the course of the year, my students missed 33 days of ESL classes, or about 18% of their English instruction, due to standardized testing." This calculation does not include the extensive time that many schools devote to preparing their students to take these tests.

In addition to the loss of instructional time, a further consequence of the current educational regime is the fact that discussion of issues that matter—for example, students' experiences and perceptions, social realities in communities and the country as a whole, world events, and issues crucial to becoming an informed citizen, such as the roots of conflict and inequality—are assigned to the dubious category of off-task behavior (even recess has been sacrificed on the altar of adequate yearly progress in some school districts).

Affirming Diversity provides us with a powerful set of conceptual tools to push back against current attempts to constrict the instructional space. A central message throughout the book is that *teachers have choices.* Despite the pressures that are being applied to exclude critical literacy and student experience from classroom instruction, we always have at least some degrees of freedom in how we interact with students, how we connect with their cultural experiences and language talents, how we involve parents in their children's learning, how we adapt content to link with students' prior knowledge, and in the levels of cognitive engagement we try to evoke through our instruction. Alternative modes of assessment (such as portfolio assessment) can also present a counter-discourse to the inaccurate and misleading account of student progress and effort often reflected in standardized test scores. In articulating our choices, both individually and collectively, we rediscover our own identities as educators and also become aware of the identity options that our instruction opens up (or shuts down) for our students.

Sonia Nieto and Patty Bode open up a dialogical sphere of both affirmation and resistance: affirmation of student and teacher identity and resistance to coercive and misguided top-down control. When we realize that we *do* have choices, and when we articulate these choices explicitly, we take the first steps towards *empowerment*, which can be defined as the collaborative creation of power. Disempowered teachers are not in a position to create contexts of empowerment for their students. We need to understand, and rediscover, the power that we bring to the classroom, not as an instructional technician who simply transmits the curriculum, but as an *educator* whose instructional choices will exert a dramatic impact on the lives of our students.

Affirming Diversity challenges us, as educators, to make explicit the image of our students and of our society that is implied by our interactions in the school context. What kind of people do we hope our students will grow up to be? What kinds of abilities and knowledge are accessible to them in our classroom? What kind of society do we hope they will create? The answers to all these questions are written in the daily record of our interactions with our students. Our interactions with students and communities constitute a moral enterprise, whether we define it as such or not.

Students' and teachers' voices occupy a central place in this book. They complement and illustrate the theoretical analyses and remind us that the interactions between educators and students dramatically affect not only the acquisition of knowledge and skills but also the creation of both student and teacher identity. Unfortunately in many classrooms, the curriculum has been sanitized such that opportunities for critical reflection on personal and collective identity and on issues of social justice are minimized. The image of our students and society implied by this pedagogical orientation is an image of compliant consumers who will gratefully accept their place within the existing power structure and who can easily be manipulated to exercise their democratic rights to preserve that power structure.

A radically different image is implied by the pedagogical orientations articulated in *Affirming Diversity.* Students are viewed as critical thinkers capable of, and responsible for, creating change through action both in their own lives and in the broader society. Their interactions in school provide opportunities to collaborate across cultural and linguistic boundaries in the generation, interpretation, and application of knowledge. The curriculum orients students towards critical reflection on issues of social justice and of identity (both personal and collective).

The image of students and society implied in these educational interactions is an image of individuals who have developed respect both for their own cultural identity and for the identities of others; who are capable of collaborating with others in the democratic pursuit of social justice; and who see themselves as members of a global community with shared economic, scientific and environmental interests. As such, the directions highlighted in *Affirming Diversity* respond much more adequately to the challenges of the twenty-first century than the introverted xenophobic focus of those who argue, explicitly or implicitly, for a monolingual monocultural education.

The alternative to multicultural education is monocultural education. The history of monocultural education is written in the certainties of the Crusades and the Inquisition, the smug brutalities of slavery, the casual eradication of language, culture, and identity in boarding schools inflicted on Native American children, as well as in contemporary claims of fundamentalist groups, from various religious persuasions, to have exclusive access to ultimate truths. Surely, 9/11 should have brought home to us the destructive power of monocultural fundamentalist belief systems. Surely, it should have been a wake-up call to figure out ways of living together in a global context where cross-cultural contact and population mobility are at an all-time high in human history. Surely, it should have been an urgent reminder that education is a microcosm of the society we hope our students will form. Yet, within our classrooms we see reiterations of *us versus them* (right versus wrong) ideologies, insistence on monocultural certainties as opposed to multicultural inquiry, and frazzled impatience at suggestions that we consider the gap between teaching to the test and education for national and global citizenship. Multicultural education is still as likely to be seen as a threat to fundamental (fundamentalist?) values of our society as it is an invitation to critical self-reflection and dialogue.

Affirming Diversity not only constitutes an eloquent and forceful statement about the importance of multicultural education to our society, it also affirms the central role that individual educators play in nurturing and shaping the lives and identities of our youth. To be a teacher is to be a visionary—as we interact with our students we envisage what contributions they will play in shaping a better society and we orchestrate our classroom interactions to enable them to realize these possibilities. This book encourages us to recognize that power relations in the broader society often operate to constrict our vision of what we can achieve with our students. *Affirming Diversity* challenges us to make choices in our classrooms that will resist the perpetuation of coercive relations of power. It affords both the insight and inspiration to enable us to create interactions with our students that are respectful, intellectually challenging, and empowering for both them and us.

Affirming Diversity not only opens up a world of ideas and the sharing of experiences. It also unlocks an internal switch. It opens a door to dialogue. It is through dialogue that we create understanding and initiate action. As you read this book, talk back to it. As you listen to the experiences and perspectives of the teachers and students who speak from the pages about their educational experiences and the choices they have made, talk back to them about your experiences and choices, those you have made in the past and will make in the future.

Affirming Diversity is both medium and message. The medium of change is dialogue—both internally within ourselves and with our colleagues. Our dialogue, however, must be informed by accurate information. The fact, for example, that NCLB has produced no improvement in students' overall educational progress nor closed the achievement gap across social groups, provides a basis for thinking critically about what alternative educational directions might be pursued. *Affirming Diversity* does not supply prescriptions or formulaic solutions but it does present empirical research and invites us to think and talk about our own identities as educators and the potential and consequences of the choices we make on a daily basis. As such, it represents a powerful source of inspiration, ideas, and solidarity for all of us who see social justice and equity as important core values within our educational systems. *Affirming Diversity* also highlights the fact that our global society can use all of the multilingual and multicultural intelligence it can get. The consequences of squandering the intellectual, linguistic and cultural resources that our students bring to school can be seen in our domestic prisons, in our battlefields abroad, and in the spiritual malaise that afflicts our society. This book does not provide a map, but it does provide inspiration—it breathes new life into those of us who believe that education is important. If we believe that education is fundamentally a spiritual endeavour rather than just an economic or bureaucratic exercise, then this book points the way.

Jim Cummins
University of Toronto

Reference

Monroe, J. R. (2006). Standardized testing in the lives of ELL students: A teacher's firsthand account. Retrieved 25 November 2006 from http://www.elladvocates.org/documents/nclb/Monroe_Standardized_Testing_for_ELLs.pdf

Preface

Why students succeed or fail in school has been the subject of much research and debate, particularly for students whose racial, ethnic, linguistic, or social identity backgrounds differ from that of the dominant group. In this book, we consider these matters in relation to a comprehensive understanding of multicultural education within a sociopolitical context. That is, rather than focus only on individual experience or psychological responses to schooling, we explore how societal and educational structures, policies, and practices affect student learning, and we suggest some ways that teachers, individually and collectively, can provide high-quality education in spite of obstacles that may get in the way. For us, multicultural education needs to consider not just schooling but also the social, economic, and political context of the world in which we live.

In this sixth edition of *Affirming Diversity,* we continue to explore such matters as diversity, equity, and equality, bringing our discussion up to date by considering issues of current policy, practice, and legislation. For example, high-stakes testing, a standardization of the curriculum, vouchers, "choice," charter schools, and a marketization of schooling have had a tremendous impact on public schools in the past decade or more. At the same time, education is increasingly defined by policies far removed from daily classroom life but nevertheless having enormous consequences for teachers, students, and communities. The increasing diversity in our nation and debates over immigration, the U.S. invasion and subsequent wars in Iraq and Afghanistan, the economic recession, interethnic and interracial strife here and abroad, regional wars around the world, global warming, the devastation of the environment, the election of the first biracial president of the nation, his nomination of two more women to the U.S. Supreme Court—one of whom became the first Latina to hold the highest office in the judiciary—all of these are front-page headlines that cannot be separated from schooling. They call for a different way to interact in the world.

Given the situation briefly sketched above, we believe teachers and prospective teachers need, more than ever, to understand how the larger societal context affects students, particularly those most marginalized in schools and in society in general. Why do some students succeed academically while others fail? What do race/ethnicity, social class, language, gender, sexual orientation, ability, and other differences have to do with learning? What is the real significance of the "achievement gap?" How does the societal context influence what happens in your school? Do your school's and your school system's policies and practices exacerbate and perpetuate inequality? Can teachers and other educators turn this situation around? If so, how? *Affirming Diversity* is an attempt to answer these questions—and more— that both new and veteran teachers face every day in increasingly diverse classrooms and in schools that are becoming more bureaucratic and standardized.

 ## About This Book

Affirming Diversity explores the meaning, necessity, and benefits of multicultural education for students from all backgrounds through research that explores:

- Influences on schooling and learning such as:
  - The sociopolitical context of schools and society
  - Racism and other biases and expectations of students' achievement
  - School organization and educational policies and practices
  - Cultural and other differences such as ethnicity, race, gender, language, sexual orientation, religion and social class
- A conceptual framework for multicultural education based on that investigation
- Case studies and snapshots—in the words of a selected group of students from a variety of backgrounds—about home, school, and community experiences and about how these have influenced their school achievement, as well as multicultural teacher stories that exemplify the role of teachers in transforming classrooms and schools.

The book presents data on the multicultural nature of schools and society, including information about different sociocultural groups, their experiences in schools, and the issues and challenges they face. Relevant research and analysis on the success or failure of students in schools is also presented.

Affirming Diversity consists of 10 chapters organized in three parts. Part 1 sets the stage for understanding the *sociopolitical context of multicultural education*. Part 2 develops the conceptual framework for multicultural education, emphasizing institutional and cultural factors in schooling and individual and group responses to diversity. This section explores the multiple forces that may affect the school achievement of students from a variety of backgrounds.

To provide insights into the interrelated roles that discrimination, school policies and practices, and culture play in the education of students in the classroom, we present 16 case studies and 6 snapshots. Incorporated throughout Parts 2 and 3, the case studies and snapshots highlight salient issues discussed in particular chapters, and they provide a concrete means for addressing issues of diversity and success or failure in the schools. We hope that the case studies and snapshots will help you more fully understand the lives and school experiences of a variety of young people who reflect our nation's growing diversity. Parts 2 and 3 also contain a number of Multicultural

Teaching Stories that epitomize what teachers can do, individually and in collaboration with one another, to put into practice some of the theories developed throughout the text.

Part 3 focuses on the implications of the case studies, snapshots, and teaching stories for teaching and learning in a multicultural society such as ours. We use themes that emerged from our interviews with the students and teachers to emphasize conditions that may affect learning for different students. In Chapter 9, three specific curriculum ideas for elementary, middle, and high schools are comprehensively described. These examples embody what the previous chapters have defined as multicultural education, that is, education that affirms diversity, encourages critical thinking, and leads to social justice and action. Chapter 10 offers suggestions for developing environments that foster high-quality education, concentrating on multicultural education as a process. In addition, in Chapter 10 we propose a model of multicultural education that affirms all students.

Each chapter concludes with (1) a series of problems or situations for you to think about and (2) suggestions for classroom activities and community actions. By including these we are not implying that there are immediate or easy answers to the dilemmas you face in schools every day. The purpose of posing particular problems and proposing activities to address them is to suggest that careful attention needs to be paid to the many manifestations of inequality in our schools and that productive resolutions can be achieved when teachers, students, and parents reflect critically on these problems and work together to solve them.

 **New to This Edition**

Previous readers may notice a broad range of changes in this new edition.

- **About Terminology** We have eliminated former chapter 2, titled "About Terminology" so that now instead of 11 chapters, there are 10. Although we continue to believe that issues of terminology are essential to understanding diversity in our nation and the world, we have decided to incorporate the sections that made up this chapter within other chapters as a new feature with the same title. We have placed terms in boxes near sections – generally case studies or snapshots – where they are relevant. It is our hope that doing so will clarify any questions you have about the language we have used in that particular section of the text. For example, the section on "The Conundrum of Race" can now be found in a box in Chapter 3 where racism and discrimination are discussed, while the section on Latinos, Hispanics, and Others is now in Chapter 5 near Yahaira León's case study.

- **Multicultural Teaching Stories** We are introducing a new feature we are calling Multicultural Teaching Stories to highlight the important role of teachers in changing classrooms and schools. There are four such stories in the text: The first one, "The Springfield Renaissance School Anti-Indian Mascot Committee," in Chapter 3 focuses on the actions of a teacher, Marisa Vanasse, and her middle school students in challenging the practice of using Native Americans as mascots for sports teams. In Chapter 4, a story called "Boston Teachers Union School: Teacher

Leadership and Student Achievement" features Berta Berriz and Betsy Drinan who are co-lead teachers of an innovative, teacher-run public school. In Chapter 8, teacher Jarvis Adams is featured in a discussion about teacher care. Chapter 9 provides a teaching story with Bill Blatner about an approach to teaching math through which a diverse range of learners meet with success.

- **A New Case Study** A third major change is the addition of a new case study in Chapter 4. Two siblings, Jasper and Viena Alejandro-Quinn who live in the north-western United States provided insights on their experiences with Native American identity in public schools.

- **Thoroughly updated references** We have gone to great lengths to thoroughly update the vast majority of the references and studies throughout the text.

- *Chapter 1: Understanding the Sociopolitical Context of Schooling.* This chapter has been revised considerably to include the most recent research illustrating five significant tasks of understanding the sociopolitical context of multicultural education: 1) clarifying the goals and key terms of multicultural education, 2) dissolving myths about immigration and difference, 3) naming the social, economic, political, and ideological underpinnings that influence educational structures, 4) studying the current demographic "mosaic" of our nation, and 5) examining the political struggles of legislation and policy in public education.

- *Chapter 2: Defining Multicultural Education for School Reform* remains the anchor of the text, explicating Sonia Nieto's definition of Multicultural Education, which she developed in the first edition of this book in 1992. The definition remains rooted in the seven characteristics while it continues to evolve to address current conditions. Since this conceptual framework was advanced by Sonia when she was sole author, we decided to put Sonia's name on this chapter.

- *Chapter 3: Racism, Discrimination, and Expectations of Students' Achievement* has been thoroughly updated with new research and insights on these topics. Also, a Multicultural Teaching Story on the use of American Indian images as mascots has been added to the chapter.

- *Chapter 4: Structural and Organizational Issues in Classrooms and Schools.* Although the topics in this chapter have remained the same as in the fifth edition, a great deal of new research on the issues has been included. The chapter also includes a Multicultural Teaching Story about the Boston Teachers Union School.

- *Chapter 5: Culture, Identity, and Learning.* This chapter includes more explanation of the history of learning style theory and current critiques than in the previous edition.

- *Chapter 6: Linguistic Diversity in U.S. Classrooms.* This chapter has been significantly updated with new sections on "Understanding Language Issues in a Sociopolitical Context," "Program Models for Teaching English Language Learners," and "Problems and Challenges."

- *Chapter 7: Understanding Student Learning and School Achievement.* Formerly chapter 6, this has been retitled and largely revised in this edition with all new research on caring and deficit perspectives as well as new sections on topics such as Out-of-School-Factors and the School-to-Prison-Pipeline.

- *Chapter 8: Learning from Students* includes a Multicultural Teaching Story about Teacher Caring and a new *What You Can Do* feature that addresses ways to affirm identities of Arabs and Arab Americans in the classroom.

- *Chapter 9: Adapting Curriculum for Multicultural Classrooms* includes a Multicultural Teaching Story about Bill Blatner's Interactive Mathematics Program as well as three new *What You Can Do* features that address the *Welcoming School* curriculum, teaching about religious diversity, and using technology in the curriculum. This chapter was single-authored by Patty Bode, so it bears Patty's name.

- *Chapter 10: Affirming Diversity: Implications for Teachers, Schools, Families, and Communities* has been changed substantially by adding a focus on communities. In addition, a number of topics have been added, including working with families to promote student learning.

- *Student art.* The artwork that appears on the cover as well as in most of the chapter openers and part openers are self-portraits that were created by school students from first through twelfth grade.

 ## Supplements and Learning Aids

Instructor's Manual

The Instructor's Manual includes a wealth of interesting ideas and activities designed to help instructors teach the course. The IM contains a sample syllabus and course suggestions. Each chapter includes the following elements: Overview, Problem Posing, Response Journal Prompts, Whole Class/Group Work assignments, Student as Teacher assignments, a Critical Pedagogy in Action assignment, instructions for projects to be included in student portfolios and used as assessments, handouts to accompany all assignments, and essay questions. (Available for download from the Instructor's Resource Center at www.pearsonhighered.com/irc.)

PowerPoint™ Presentation

Created by Patty Bode, these PowerPoint slides outline the key points of each chapter, and are customizable so that professors may add or delete material as they see fit. Instructors may also download book-specific PowerPoint slides from the Instructor Resource Center at www.pearsonhighered.com/irc. Your local representative can provide a password and instructions for using the IRC.

 ## Pearson's MyEducationLab for Multicultural Education

The Power of Classroom Practice

In *Preparing Teachers for a Changing World,* Linda Darling-Hammond and her colleagues point out that grounding teacher education in real classrooms—among real

teachers and students and among actual examples of students' and teachers' work—
is an important, and perhaps even an essential, part of training teachers for the
complexities of teaching in today's classrooms. MyEducationLab is an online learning solution that provides contextualized interactive exercises, simulations, and other
resources designed to help develop the knowledge and skills teachers need. All of
the activities and exercises in MyEducationLab are built around essential learning
outcomes for teachers and are mapped to professional teaching standards. Utilizing
classroom videos, authentic student and teacher artifacts, case studies, and other
resources and assessments, the scaffolded learning experiences in MyEducationLab
offer pre-service teachers and those who teach them a unique and valuable education tool.

For each topic covered in the course you will find most or all of the following
features and resources:

Assignments and Activities

Designed to enhance student understanding of concepts covered in class and save
instructors preparation and grading time, these assignable exercises show concepts
in action (through video, cases, and/or student and teacher artifacts). They help
students deepen content knowledge and synthesize and apply concepts and strategies they read about in the book. (Suggested answers for these assignments are available to the instructor only under the Instructor Resource tab.)

Building Teaching Skills and Dispositions

These learning units help students practice and strengthen skills that are essential
to quality teaching. After presenting the steps involved in a core teaching process,
students are given an opportunity to practice applying this skill via case studies of
authentic classrooms. Providing multiple opportunities to practice a single teaching
concept, each activity encourages a deeper understanding and application of concepts, as well as the use of critical thinking skills.

General Resources on Your MyEducationLab Course

The *Resources* section on your MyEducationLab course is designed to help you pass
your licensure exam; put together an effective portfolio and lesson plan; prepare for
and navigate the first year of your teaching career; and understand key educational
standards, policies, and laws. This section includes:

*   *Licensure Exams*: Access guidelines for passing the Praxis exam. The *Practice
    Test Exam* includes practice questions, *Case Histories,* and *Video Case Studies.*
*   *Portfolio Builder and Lesson Plan Builder*: Create, update, and share portfolios
    and lesson plans.
*   *Preparing a Portfolio*: Access guidelines for creating a high-quality teaching port-
    folio that will allow you to practice effective lesson planning.
*   *Licensure and Standards*: Link to state licensure standards and national standards.

- *Beginning Your Career*: Educate yourself—access tips, advice, and valuable information on:

  - Resume Writing and Interviewing: Expert advice on how to write impressive resumes and prepare for job interviews.

  - Your First Year of Teaching: Practical tips to set up your classroom, manage student behavior, and learn to more easily organize for instruction and assessment.

  - Law and Public Policies: Specific directives and requirements you need to understand under the No Child Left Behind Act and the Individuals with Disabilities Education Improvement Act of 2004.

- *Special Education Interactive Timeline*: Build your own detailed timelines based on different facets of the history and evolution of special education.

Book-Specific Resources

The book resources section of MyEducationLab includes a Study Plan, Bonus Materials mentioned inside the front cover of this book, and Student Art.

Bonus Materials

The book resources site houses additional case studies, content, and resources that will further enhance students' understanding of concepts and student experiences in multicultural settings.

Student Art

Student self-portraits that are included throughout the book appear in the book resources site in their original, four-color rendering.

Visit www.myeducationlab.com for a demonstration of this online resource.

We end this Preface with a personal reflection from each of us.

 ## Sonia

The first edition of *Affirming Diversity* was published 20 years ago. It helped define my professional career and it had a huge impact on my personal and professional life because it put into words my ideas and values about education, diversity, and social justice. I have been gratified by the enormous and generous response of readers to the text through its first four editions when I was the sole author, and later in the fifth edition when Patty Bode became my co-author. I was thrilled that she joined me in keeping the fifth edition of *Affirming Diversity* fresh, timely, and relevant to our times, and she continues to do so in this sixth edition. Given the challenging times in which we are living—particularly as related to public education—it is my hope that the book will challenge you to think boldly and creatively about what schools can become for all students.

Patty

The first five editions of *Affirming Diversity* played a transformative role in my research, teaching, and worldview. I am honored to be part of this sixth edition and am eternally grateful to Sonia for inviting me to participate in the continual metamorphosis of the book. Through the work on the text, I hear students calling out for teachers who can cross racial, cultural, and social class borders and who can overcome curriculum constraints and resist bureaucratic expectations to create meaningful, high-achieving learning communities. As a teacher, I recognize the struggle that arises from competing messages from academic, political, and popular culture about what counts as knowledge and what defines teaching. The vision we assert in this book hopes to activate antiracist critical pedagogy in classrooms. For all students and their families and teachers, I hope that this new edition of *Affirming Diversity* contributes to creating change.

Acknowledgments

We are deeply appreciative of the many individuals who have helped us with the sixth edition of *Affirming Diversity*. We are particularly indebted to the two students, Jasper and Viena Quinn-Alejandro, who agreed to be interviewed for our new case study, and also to Marisa Vanasse, Jarvis Adams, Bill Blatner, Berta Berriz, Betsy Drinan, and Erik Berg, the teachers who provided inspiring Multicultural Teaching Stories. For their dedicated research assistance and overall commitment to the mission of the book, we thank Brittany D. Henshaw, Cara Wojcik, Bob Moriarty, and Emily R. Yaffe. We also thank those who interviewed students for the case studies and snapshots throughout all the editions: Keonilrath Bun, Paula Elliott, Kristen French, Maya Gillingham, Jason Irizarry, John Raible, Stephanie Schmidt, Vera Stenhouse, Diane Sweet, and Carlie Tartakov. Also, Mari Ann Roberts interviewed one of the teachers in the new feature, Multicultural Teaching Stories. We are also grateful to Kristen French, the author of the Instructor's Resource Manual, a guide characterized by both a critical edge and helpful pedagogical suggestions.

We also thank the art teachers who submitted their students' artwork that appears on the cover and at the opening parts and chapters: Sara Cummins, Eve Del Greco, Nora Elton, Amanda Held, Catherine Lea, Adrienne Roberto, Kelly Stoos, Dawn Southworth, and Alicia Toro. We deeply appreciate the talent and generosity of the students who allowed us to reproduce their art. We are also indebted to the professional artist, Michael E. Coblyn, who contributed his artwork. These art images inform each section and emphasize the role of visual culture in multicultural education.

Professional colleagues who have read and commented on the various iterations of this text have helped to strengthen it, and we are thankful to all of them. For this sixth edition, we thank the following reviewers: Ellen M. Curtin, Texas Wesleyan University; Kathleen Lazarus, Daytona State College; Jonathan Lightfoot, Hofstra University; and Alaric Williams, Angelo State University. Their detailed comments and suggestions for improving the book were enormously helpful. In addition, we wish to acknowledge the helpful comments of Professor Aurolyn Luykx, University of Texas at El Paso, concerning David Weiss's snapshot; Jim Crawford's careful reading and advice on parts of Chapter 6; and Neill Monty's responses to our questions concerning testing (Chapter 4).

At Pearson Education, we are grateful for the tremendous support and encouragement we received from our editor, Kelly Villella Canton, and our development editor, Max Chuck. They have worked tirelessly to help us get this edition out in a timely manner.

Once again, we owe a heartfelt thank you to Jim Cummins, a scholar of rare genius and a wonderful friend, for writing the inspiring foreword to this sixth edition. Jim has been a consistent and enthusiastic supporter of this book for many years. His willingness to write the foreword means a great deal to us.

We would not be where we are without our families. Sonia particularly wants to acknowledge Angel, her partner of nearly 45 years, for his unconditional love and support; Celso, her son-in-law; her daughters Alicia and Marisa; and her granddaughter Jazmyne (our granddaughter/daughter), for teaching her how to be a mother. Her other grandchildren—Corissa, Terrance, Monique, Tatiana, Celsito, Aliya, Clarita, Lucia, Mariya, and Kalil—are another source of joy and inspiration.

Patty wants to thank Mark, her life partner, for his love, humor, and encouragement, and her sons, Bob, Ryan, and Keo for revealing the adventures of life's ongoing journey. Her parents, George and Joann Bode, were her first teachers and continue to provide loving guidance.

Sonia Nieto

Patty Bode

Affirming Diversity

Setting the Stage
Multicultural Education Within a Sociopolitical Context

Picha Choopojcharoen, in Catherine Lea's art class at Bishop Feehan High School, Attleboro, Massachusetts. *Self-portrait*. Graphite drawing, 2010.

"At its best, multiculturalism is an ongoing process of questioning, revising, and struggling to create greater equity in every nook and cranny of school life.... It is a fight for economic and social justice.... Such a perspective is not simply about explaining society; it is about changing it."

—**Rethinking Schools**
15, no. 1 (Fall 2000)

To set the stage for understanding multicultural education within a broad societal context and to help you think about the implications of this context for students of diverse backgrounds, the two chapters in Part 1 introduce a number of foundational concepts. In Chapter 1 we describe key assumptions that undergird this text and define what we mean by the *sociopolitical context of education*. Chapter 1 also introduces other fundamental definitions and parameters of multicultural education and then presents demographic data about both the general population and the population in U.S. schools, with implications of these data for education. We briefly describe a key approach we have employed in this text, namely, the use of *case studies* and *snapshots* that reflect some of the tremendous diversity that currently exists in our schools.

Using the discussion in Chapter 1 as a foundation, Chapter 2 defines *multicultural education* and describes its essential components. Because we view multicultural education as far more than simply altering the curriculum to reflect more Brown and Black faces or adding assembly programs on diversity, Chapter 2 provides examples of what we mean by a *critical* multicultural perspective.

Understanding the Sociopolitical Context of Schooling

Decisions made about education are often viewed as if they were politically neutral. Yet as we hope to make clear in this chapter and throughout the text, such decisions are never politically neutral. Rather, they are tied to the social, political, and economic structures that frame and define our society. The *sociopolitical context* of society includes laws, regulations, policies, practices, traditions, and ideologies.

> "Desegregated schools . . . offer the single most powerful way to reach and prepare the coming generation, which will be the first to live in an America that is truly multiracial and has no racial majority group. It is imperative that we take feasible steps to foster and sustain integration and to deal with the deeply rooted harms of segregation."
>
> **Gary Orfield,**
> *Reviving the Goal of an Integrated Society:*
> *A 21st Century Challenge, 2009*

To put it another way, multicultural education, or any kind of education for that matter, cannot be understood in a vacuum. Yet in many schools, multicultural education is approached as if it were divorced from the policies and practices of schools and from the structures and ideologies of society. This kind of thinking often results in misguided practices such as a singular focus on cultural artifacts like food and dress or on ethnic celebrations that exaggerate exotic attributes of groups. It can become "fairyland" multicultural education, disassociated from the lives of teachers, students, and communities. This is multicultural education *without* a sociopolitical context. In this book, however, we are interested in how the sociopolitical context of the United States, and indeed of our global society, shapes schools and therefore also shapes the experiences of the children and adults who inhabit schools.

Assumptions Underlying this Text

It is important that we begin by clarifying four major assumptions underlying the concepts described in this book. These assumptions advance our goals to (1) connect

identity, difference, power, and privilege; (2) include many differences in multicultural education; (3) counter the argument of "teachers as villains"; and (4) defend quality public education.

Identity, Difference, Power, and Privilege Are All Connected

Race, ethnicity, social class, language use, gender, sexual orientation, religion, ability, and other social and human differences are major aspects of the sociopolitical context that we will address in this book—that is, one's identity frames (although it does not

Larsan Gobeh Korvili, in Catherine Lea's art class at Bishop Feehan High School, Attleboro, Massachusetts. *The Face of Success.* Batik & Mixed Media, 2010. Printed here in respectful memory of Larsan, 1993–2010.

necessarily *determine*) how one experiences the world. Identities always carry some baggage; they are perceived in particular ways by a society and by individuals within that society. Language identity as interpreted by a spoken accent, for instance, may invoke positive or negative images, depending on one's social class, race, country of origin, and variety of language. As a consequence, in the context of U.S. society, someone who is French and speaks with a Parisian accent, for example, is generally viewed more positively than someone from Senegal who also speaks French.

Yet multicultural education does not simply involve the affirmation of language, culture, and broader aspects of identity. Multicultural education not only affirms issues of identity and difference but also assertively confronts issues of power and privilege in society. This means challenging racism and other biases as well as the inequitable structures, policies, and practices of schools and, ultimately, of society itself. Affirming language and culture can help students become successful and well-adjusted learners, but unless language and cultural issues are viewed critically through the lens of equity and the power structures that impede the goals of social justice, these perspectives are unlikely to have a lasting impact in promoting real change. Making explicit connections among identity, difference, power, and privilege can move education toward such transformation.

Multicultural Education Is Inclusive of Many Differences

This book's framework and approach to multicultural education are broadly inclusive: They are based on the belief that multicultural education is for *everyone* regardless of ethnicity, race, language, social class, religion, gender, sexual orientation, ability, or other differences. Multicultural education as a field and in practice is not directed at only one group or certain kinds of students. One book, however, cannot possibly give all of these topics the central importance they deserve. For that reason, this book *uses race, ethnicity, and language as the major lenses* to view and understand multicultural education. While we address other differences in one way or another, we give special emphasis to these. The inceptions of both multicultural and bilingual education were direct outgrowths of the civil rights movement, and they developed in response to racism (discrimination based on race), ethnocentrism (discrimination based on ethnicity and national origin), and linguicism (language discrimination) in education. These inequities continue to exist, especially for American Indian, Latino, African American, Asian, and multiracial youngsters, and they are central to this book's perspective and approach.

Nevertheless, we believe that multicultural education includes everyone, and we have made an attempt in this text to be inclusive of many differences. Having a broad definition of multicultural education raises another dilemma. One reason that multicultural education is such a challenging topic for some educators is that they have a hard time facing and discussing the issues of race and racism. For example, whenever we bring up racism with a group of predominantly White teachers, we find that, too often, they want to move on immediately to, say, sexism or classism without spending much time on racism. Sexism and classism are certainly worthy of study and attention—in fact, they must be part of a multicultural agenda, and many books are dedicated to those topics—but the discomfort of many White teachers in talking about race and racism is very evident. Racism is an excruciatingly difficult issue for many people. Given our nation's history of exclusion and discrimination, this is not surprising, but it is only through a thorough exploration of *discrimination based on race* that we can understand the genesis as well as the rationale for a more inclusive framework for multicultural education that includes language, social class, sexual orientation, gender, ethnicity, religion, and other differences. For these reasons, this book aims to include all students and all teachers in these challenging yet hopeful discussions.

Teachers Are Not the Villains

Another belief that informs this book's perspective and approach is that teachers cannot be singled out as the villains responsible for students' academic failure. Although some teachers bear responsibility for having low expectations because they are racist and elitist in their interactions with students and parents and thus provide educational environments that discourage many students from learning, most do not do this consciously. Most teachers are sincerely concerned about their students and want very much to provide them with the best education possible. Nonetheless, because of their own limited experiences and education, they may know very little about the students they teach. As a result, their beliefs about students of diverse backgrounds may be based on spurious assumptions and stereotypes. These things are true of all teachers, not just White teachers. In fact, a teacher's identity from a non-White ethnic group or background does not guarantee that he or she will be effective with students of diverse backgrounds or even with students of his or her own background. Teachers are often at the mercy of decisions made by others far removed from the classroom; they generally have little involvement in developing the policies and practices of their schools and frequently do not even question them.

Teachers also are the products of educational systems that have a history of racism, exclusion, and debilitating pedagogy. As a consequence, their practices may reflect their experiences, and they may unwittingly perpetuate policies and approaches that are harmful to many of their students. We cannot separate schools from the communities they serve or from the context of society in general. Oppressive forces that limit opportunities in the schools reflect such forces in the society at large. The purpose of this book is not to point a finger, but to provide a forum for reflection and discussion so that teachers take responsibility for their own actions. The book aims to support teachers in their efforts to assert their intellectual and creative prowess in challenging the actions of schools and society that affect their students' education, and in helping bring about positive change.

Quality Public Education Is a Cause Worth Fighting For

Another key assumption of this book is that public education that ensures all students full participation in a democratic society is worth defending and fighting for. In spite of all its shortcomings, and although it has never lived up to its potential, public education remains a noble ideal because it is one of the few institutions that at least articulates the common good, even if it does not always deliver it. Public education remains the last and best hope for many young people for a better life. Yet the public schools have often been a target of scorn and disrespect in the press and among politicians. In spite of this, the public still believes in the promise of public education. The *Public Education Network* conducted a public opinion survey that reported on voter concerns about major issues facing our nation and local communities. A substantial majority of voters agreed that every child has a right to a quality public education and that we owe it to our children to provide them with one (93 percent and 97 percent agree in both cases).[1] The California Teachers Association noted that in the June 2010 primary elections, in a state suffering widespread repercussions of the economic downturn, voters endorsed candidates who supported public education through local taxes and school bonds.[2] Given this unambiguous and overwhelming support for public education, it is clear that public schools can provide all children with a good education and it is within the ability of teachers, administrators, and the public at large to ensure that they do so.

■◢ ◣ ■ Defining the Sociopolitical Context of Multicultural Education

Now that we have explained some of the assumptions underlying this text, we want to define what we mean by the *sociopolitical context of education*. As you will see in the remainder of this chapter, understanding this terminology and the research that undergirds it is crucial to the critical view of multicultural education asserted throughout our book. In what follows, we illustrate five significant tasks of understanding the sociopolitical context: (1) clarifying the goals and key terms of multicultural education; (2) dissolving myths about immigration and difference; (3) naming the social, economic, political, and ideological underpinnings that influence educational structures; (4) studying the current demographic "mosaic" of our nation; and (5) examining the political struggles of legislation and policy in public education.

Clarifying Goals and Terms of Multicultural Education

Depending on one's conceptualization of multicultural education, different goals may be emphasized. In this book, we want to make clear from the outset how we define the goals and key terms of multicultural education, the first task of understanding the sociopolitical context. The major premise of this book is the following: *No educational philosophy or program is worthwhile unless it focuses on the following three primary goals*:

- Tackling inequality and promoting access to an equal education
- Raising the achievement of all students and providing them with an equitable and high-quality education
- Providing students with an apprenticeship in the opportunity to become critical and productive members of a democratic society

Tackling Inequality and Promoting Access to an Equal Education

We believe that multicultural education must confront inequality and stratification in schools and in society. Helping students get along, teaching them to feel better about themselves, and sensitizing them to one another are worthy goals of good educational practice, including multicultural education. But if multicultural education does not tackle the far more thorny questions of stratification and inequity, and if viewed in isolation from the reality of students' lives, these goals can turn into superficial strategies that only scratch the surface of educational failure. Simply wanting our students to get along with and be respectful of one another makes little difference in the life options they will have as a result of their schooling. Students' lives are inexorably affected by economic, social, and political conditions in schools and society—that is, by the sociopolitical context in which they live and learn—and this means that we need to consider these conditions in our conceptualization and implementation of multicultural education. (Further elaboration on the terms *equality* and *equity* is provided in this section under "Defining Key Terms in Multicultural Education.")

Raising Achievement of All Students

Learning is an equally central goal of multicultural education. Unless learning is at the very core of a multicultural perspective, having "feel-good" assemblies or self-concept–building classroom activities will do nothing to create equitable school environments for students. Considering the vastly unequal learning outcomes among students of different backgrounds, it is absolutely essential that achievement of all students through an equitable and high-quality education be placed at the center of multicultural education. (See the subsequent discussion of the "achievement gap" under "Defining Key Terms in Multicultural Education.") Otherwise, if they are not receiving a high-quality, rigorous education, too many young people will continue to face harrowing life choices.

Providing Apprenticeships as Critical and Productive Members of a Democratic Society

Learning to take tests or getting into a good university cannot be the be-all and end-all of an excellent education. A third and equally crucial goal of multicultural education is to *promote democracy by preparing students to contribute to the general well-being of society, not only to their own self-interests*. Multicultural educator Will Kymlicka has asserted this goal of providing apprenticeships in the following way: "We need to continually remind ourselves that multiculturalism is not just about expanding individual horizons, or increasing personal intercultural skills, but is part of a larger project of justice and equality."[3] (This is further discussed in the section on "Social Justice" under "Defining Key Terms in Multicultural Education.")

Defining Key Terms in Multicultural Education

In addition to asserting these goals, the first task of understanding the sociopolitical context also includes defining key terms. These definitions help explain the approach we use in this book and support the three primary goals listed above. These four key terms include: (1) equal and equitable, (2) social justice, (3) the "achievement gap," and (4) deficit theories.

Defining Equal Education and Equitable Education: What's the Difference?

Two terms often associated with multicultural education are *equality* and *equity*, which are sometimes erroneously used interchangeably. Both equal education and educational equity are fundamental to multicultural education, yet they are quite different. As educator Enid Lee has explained, "Equity is the process; equality is the result."[4] That is, *equal education* may mean simply providing the same resources and opportunities for all students. While this alone would afford a better education for a wider range of students than is currently the case, it is not enough. Actually achieving educational equality involves providing an *equitable education. Equity* goes beyond equality: It means that all students must be given the *real possibility of an equality of outcomes*. A high-quality education is impossible without a focus on equity. Robert Moses, who began the highly successful Algebra Project that promotes high-level math courses for urban Black and Latino middle school and high school students, has advanced the idea that quality education for all students is a civil rights issue.[5] The work of Moses exemplifies what James Banks calls "equity pedagogy," which he includes in his description of *five dimensions* of multicultural education. Banks explains that an equity pedagogy exists when teachers modify their teaching to include a variety of teaching styles and approaches that are consistent with the wide range of learning styles and cultural groups.[6] In summary, *equal* education implies we are giving every student the *same* thing and an *equitable* education provides students with what they *need to achieve equality*.

About Terminology

What Should We Call People?

Language is always changing. It is a key barometer of a society at any given time because it mirrors social, economic, and political events. Terms in a language may become obsolete; it could not be otherwise because language is a reflection of societal changes. Throughout the years, the shift in terminology related to groups of people (for example, from *Negro* to *Black* to *Afro-American* and more recently to *African American*) is a case in point. Such changes often represent deliberate attempts by a group to name or rename itself. This decision is political as well as linguistic, and it responds to the need for group self-determination and autonomy. Terms also evolve as an attempt to be more precise and correct. In this sense, the term *African American* implies an identity that includes culture rather than only color. It recognizes that the notion of race, in spite of its significance in a society rigidly stratified along these lines, is not accurate and does not capture the complexity of a people. On the other hand, the term *Black* is more comprehensive because it includes people of African descent from all around the world. Recently, more inclusive terms such as *African Diaspora* or *of African heritage* have been used as well. It is not that one term is always right or wrong, but rather that various terms may be appropriate depending on the situation. This is why we need to think carefully about the context before we use any particular term.

Terminology is particularly important in multicultural education. In our society, we have not always been appropriate or sensitive in our use of words to describe people. In its most blatant form, this insensitivity is apparent in the racial and ethnic epithets that even our youngest children seem to know and use. In more subtle ways, words or expressions take on connotations that may seem positive but in the end may categorize an entire group of people. Such is the case, for instance, with *Blacks* and *rhythm*, or with *Asians* and *science*. Although words per se may not be negative, they can become code words for stereotyping or belittling the experience of an entire group of people and, hence, are disparaging.

How We Made Choices About What Terms to Use in This Book

Language carries great weight in education because it affects the lives of students. As educators, we need to be careful about what terms we use and how because our choices may send negative messages that can have long-term effects. Therefore, we need to pay close attention and be sensitive to the connotations and innuendos of our talk.

We generally use terms related to specific ethnic backgrounds; however, if an overarching term is needed for so-called minorities, we prefer to use *people of color*. The term *people of color* encompasses those who have been labeled *minority*, that is, American Indians, African Americans, Latinos, and Asian Americans, and it emerged from these communities themselves. It also implies important connections among the groups and underlines some common experiences in the United States. We prefer the term *people of color* because *minority* is a misnomer; it is never used to describe groups such as Swedish Americans, Albanian Americans, or Dutch Americans, although, strictly speaking, these groups, which represent numerical minorities in our society, should also be referred to in this way. Historically, the term has been used to refer only to racial minorities, implying a status less than that accorded to other groups. Conversely, using the term *people of color* might imply that Whites are somehow colorless, yet as we know, almost everyone is mixed, including many Europeans. In fact, some individuals who identify as people of color may actually be lighter in color than some European Americans, reinforcing the fact that such terms are political rather than descriptive.

The term *people of color* is not without its problems, however. In spite of the wide acceptance of the term and its use by many people (and by us in this book), we find it increasingly unsatisfactory on several counts. One problem is the implication of a common historical experience among all groups and individuals included under this designation. Aside from a mutual history of oppression at the hands of those in power (not an insignificant commonality), a shared historical experience among these disparate groups is an illusion. A presumed common experience also suggests that there is no conflict among these groups. As we know, such conflicts not only exist; they have resulted in periodic outbreaks of serious interethnic violence. These have emanated not only from a shared oppression and the competition for scarce resources that result from political domination, but also from deep-seated cultural and social differences among the groups themselves.

People of color is also inaccurate when referring, for example, to Latinos of European background, as is the case with many Argentines and Cubans, and light-skinned Latinos in general. When these Latinos refer to themselves in this way, they risk implying that they have experienced the same level of virulent racism as their darker-skinned compatriots.

The point we want to make throughout these segments is that language is always tentative, as are the terminology choices we have made here. New terms evolve every day. Language can capture only imperfectly the nuances of who we are as people, and like multicultural education itself, it is in constant flux. Such is the inexactitude of language that it can never completely capture the complexity of our lives. To be both sensitive and appropriate in the use of language, we prefer some words or terms over others. We are not suggesting that the terms we have chosen to use are "politically correct" or that they are the only ones that should be used, nor do we want to impose our usage on others. Rather, in the About Terminology features throughout the text, we explain our thinking to help you reflect on and decide what terminology is most appropriate for you to use in your context.

Our choice of terms used in this book is based largely on the answers to two questions:

1. What do the people themselves want to be called?

2. What is the most accurate term?

The terms used stem from the answers to these questions, based on our conversations with people from various groups, our reading of current research, and our listening to debates regarding the use of terms.

Defining Social Justice

Frequently invoked but rarely defined, *social justice* is another term associated with an equitable education. In this book, we define it as *a philosophy, an approach, and actions that embody treating all people with fairness, respect, dignity, and generosity*. On a societal scale, this means affording each person the real—not simply a stated or codified—opportunity to achieve her or his potential and full participation in a democratic society by giving each person access to the goods, services, and social and cultural capital of a society, while also affirming the culture and talents of each individual and the group or groups with which she or he identifies.

In terms of education, in particular, social justice education is not just about being nice to students, or about giving them a pat on the back. Nor does a social justice curriculum merely ask students to make posters about their "favorite social issue." Social justice education includes four components:

1. It challenges, confronts, and disrupts misconceptions, untruths, and stereotypes that lead to structural inequality and discrimination based on race, social class, gender, and other social and human differences. This means that teachers with a social justice perspective consciously include topics that focus on inequality in the curriculum, and they encourage their students to work for equality and fairness both in and outside the classroom.

2. A social justice perspective means providing all students with the resources necessary to learn to their full potential. This includes *material resources* such as books, curriculum, financial support, and so on. Equally vital are *emotional resources* such as a belief in all students' ability and worth, care for them as individuals and learners, high expectations of and rigorous demands placed on them, and the necessary social and cultural capital to negotiate the world. It also includes a school environment safe from discrimination. These are not just the responsibilities of individual teachers and schools, however. Beyond the classroom level, achieving social justice requires reforming school policies and practices so that all students are provided an equal chance to learn. This entails critically evaluating policies such as high-stakes testing, tracking, student retention, segregation, and parent and family outreach, among others.

3. Social justice in education is not just about *giving* students resources, however. A third component of a social justice perspective is *drawing on* the talents and strengths that students bring to their education. This requires embracing critical pedagogy and a rejection of the deficit perspective that has characterized much of the education of marginalized students to a shift that views all students—not just those from privileged backgrounds—as having resources that can be a foundation for their learning. These resources include their languages, cultures, and experiences.

4. A fourth essential component of social justice is creating a learning environment that *promotes critical thinking and supports agency for social change*. Creating such environments can provide students with an apprenticeship in democracy, a vital part of preparing them for the future. Much more will be said throughout the text about how to create such a learning environment.

These four components of social justice in education are woven throughout the remaining chapters of the book.

Defining the "Achievement Gap"

Another term that needs defining is *achievement gap*. This term has evolved over the past several decades to describe the circumstances in which some students, primarily those from racially, culturally, and linguistically marginalized and low-income families, achieve less than other students. Although research has largely focused on Black and White students, the "achievement gap" is also evident among students of other ethnic and racial backgrounds, such as Latino and American Indian students.[7]

The problem with the term *achievement gap* is that it suggests that students alone are responsible for their learning, as if school and societal conditions and contexts did not exist. The result is that the problem is defined as a "minority" problem rather than as a problem of unequal schooling. For all these reasons, we use the term *achievement gap* with caution and always in quotation marks.

Yet there is no denying that the "achievement gap" is real: In 2009, the National Assessment of Educational Progress (NAEP) reported that White students had higher scores than Black students, on average, on all assessments. While the nationwide gaps in 2007 were narrower than in previous assessments at both grades 4 and 8 in mathematics and at grade 4 in reading, White students had average scores at least 26 points higher than Black students in each subject, on a 0–500 scale.[8] Reports on Hispanic student achievement are also dispiriting overall. Patricia Gándara's research reveals that by fourth grade, 16 percent of Latino students are proficient in reading, compared to 41 percent of White students, with a notably similar pattern at the eighth-grade level, where only 15 percent of Latinos are proficient in reading compared to 39 percent of Whites.[9] Clearly, the gap between African American, American Indian, Hispanic, and some Asian (particularly Laotian and Cambodian) students compared to White students remains very large. Specifically, the gap is the equivalent of two grade levels or more, almost what it was in 1992. For example, while 41 percent of Whites are reading at grade level, only 15 percent of Hispanics and 13 percent of African Americans are at grade level. The gap worsens through the years: Black and Hispanic twelfth graders perform at the same level in reading and math as White eighth graders.[10] The gap is not only deplorable but is also an indictment of our public education system.

In spite of the fact that the "achievement gap" is a reality, sometimes this term is a misnomer because it places undue responsibility on students alone. As a result, we believe that what has become known as the *achievement gap* can also appropriately be called the *resource gap, the opportunity gap,* or the *expectations gap* because student achievement does not come out of the blue but is influenced by many other factors—that is, student achievement is related directly to the conditions and contexts in which students learn. For instance, because some schools are well endowed in terms of materials and resources, the students in these schools have multiple means to help them learn. On the other hand, schools that serve students living in poverty tend to have fewer resources and frequently employ more inexperienced teachers, and thus they provide fewer opportunities for robust student learning. Gloria Ladson-Billings has argued that the focus on school performance gaps is misplaced and that what must be considered are the historical, economic, socio-political, and moral components of racial stratification that have accumulated over time, amounting to what she has dubbed the "education debt."[11]

Despite the struggle over appropriate terminology, research on the "achievement gap" cannot be ignored because it has uncovered salient differences in the learning outcomes for students of various backgrounds. According to Joseph D'Amico, the two major causes of the "achievement gap" are *sociocultural* and *school-related factors*. Sociocultural factors include poverty, ethnicity, low levels of parental education, weak family-support systems, and students' reactions to discrimination and stereotyping.[12] School-related factors include low expectations, particularly in schools that serve students who are both economically disadvantaged and from ethnic and racial minority backgrounds, as well as other practices and policies that jeopardize student learning.

A common response among educators and the public has been to focus on the first set of factors (that is, on sociocultural "problems" and "deficits") more than on school-related factors. Turning this thinking around would be a better policy because educators can do little to change the life circumstances of students but can do a great deal to change the context of schools. For example, some schools are successful with students of color, students living in poverty, and students who live in difficult circumstances. What makes the difference? Karin Chenoweth's recent book, *How It's Being Done: Urgent Lessons from Unexpected Schools* (2009), provides examples from eight different schools throughout the nation that were selected for the Education Trust's Dispelling the Myth Award, which is given to high-achieving, high-poverty, and high-minority schools. Chenoweth's research shines a light on successful school practices such as teachers' and administrators' collaborative work to set standards and goals, as well as their notable, palpable belief in their students' capacity to achieve. She refers to these schools as "ruthlessly organizing themselves around one thing: helping students learn a great deal." These schools also focus on eliminating teacher isolation by providing time for teacher learning through research-based discussions, which in turn spawns teacher collaboration that expands successful practices to create a collective culture of high achievement for teachers and students.[13]

Chris Zurawsky also examined several school models and programs that have proven consistently successful for most students of color. These programs share two common traits: a demanding curriculum and a strong social support system that values and promotes academic achievement. Zurawsky's research underscores that a rigorous curriculum is not enough. Attention also must be given to the social environment. The role of significant people in students' lives who communicated their value of academic success and effort were evident in the successful programs cited in his study. For elementary students, this translates into committed parental involvement. For older students, the support network expands to include peer groups and mentors.[14]

Clearly, addressing school-related issues alone will not completely do away with the "achievement gap" because life experiences and conditions such as poverty play a large part in the differential learning of students. Paul E. Barton and Richard J. Coley synthesized many research studies and reported on 16 "correlates of achievement" that fall into three categories: school factors, factors related to the home-school connection, and factors that are present both before and beyond school.[15] A similar argument has been made convincingly by several noted scholars, including Jean Anyon, who cites a wealth of research and other data to come to the following chilling conclusion:

> Thus, in my view, low-achieving urban schools are not primarily a consequence of failed educational policy, or urban family dynamics, as mainstream analysts and public policies typically imply. Failing public schools in cities are, rather, a logical consequence of the U.S. macroeconomy—and the federal and regional policies and practices that support it.[16]

Likewise, in a comprehensively researched article on the effects of poverty on learning and achievement, David Berliner makes the argument that out-of-school factors (OSFs) caused by poverty *alone* place severe limits on what can be accomplished through educational reform efforts. He points out that "[i]n the U.S. today, too many OSFs are strongly correlated with class, race, and ethnicity, and too many children are in schools segregated by those very same characteristics."[17] His conclusion is that, to improve our nation's school achievement, a reduction in family and youth poverty is essential. Berliner's recommendation to address the impact of poverty on schooling reflects the complexity and urgency of the problem. He includes the following 11 efforts:

1. Reduce the rate of low-birth-weight children among African Americans
2. Reduce drug and alcohol abuse
3. Reduce pollutants in our cites and move people away from toxic sites
4. Provide universal and free medical care for all citizens
5. Ensure that no one suffers from food insecurity
6. Reduce the rates of family violence in low-income households
7. Improve mental health services among the poor
8. More equitably distribute low-income housing throughout communities
9. Reduce both the mobility and absenteeism rates of children
10. Provide high-quality preschools for all children
11. Provide summer programs for the poor to reduce summer losses in their academic achievement[18]

The suggestion that poverty and other social ills negatively affect learning is unsettling and a reminder that schools alone cannot tackle the inequality and stratification that exist in society. Richard Rothstein, an economist who has studied this issue extensively, has also suggested that school reform efforts alone will not turn things around. He advocates three approaches that must be pursued if progress is to be made in narrowing the "achievement gap": (1) promoting school improvement efforts that raise the quality of instruction; (2) giving more attention to out-of-school hours by implementing early childhood, after-school, and summer programs; and (3) implementing policies that would provide appropriate health services and stable housing and narrow the growing income inequalities in our society. He contends that only by implementing all these measures would poor children be better prepared for school.[19]

Although it is true that the "achievement gap" is strongly related to poverty, race and ethnicity are also prominent issues to consider in understanding the gap. Joseph D'Amico found that the gap may be even greater among students of color with *high* socioeconomic status. In addition, he found that, although the "achievement gap" between Black and White students was reduced by about half between 1970 and 1988, there has been a marked reversal of this trend since 1988, no doubt due to the retrenchment of federal and state policies concerning public education.[20]

Perhaps the most dramatic example of the "achievement gap" can be found in high school dropout rates. Researcher Gary Orfield has cited a few hundred high schools in the nation—all overwhelmingly "minority," low income, and located in urban centers—where the dropout rate has reached catastrophic proportions. He calls these high schools "dropout factories." According to Orfield, the dropout rate of African American and Latino students is a civil rights crisis because it affects these communities disproportionately. Less money per student is spent in these "dropout factories" than in schools in other areas—sometimes a difference of over $2,000 less per student.[21] In other research, Orfield points to failed policies of the recent past that have dismantled civil rights policies and calls for "reviving the goal of an integrated society."[22] The fact that these resegregated "dropout factories" are, for the most part, located in economically strapped communities that serve African American and Latino students, that they employ more inexperienced teachers than those in wealthier districts, and that less money is spent in them cannot be dismissed as coincidence.[23] This is also a significant part of the sociopolitical context of education.

Deficit Theories and Their Stubborn Durability

Why schools fail to meet their mission to provide all students with an equitable and high-quality education has been the subject of educational research for some time. As the "achievement gap" grows, theories about cultural deprivation and genetic inferiority are once again being used to explain differences in intelligence and achievement, and the implications of these deficit theories continue to influence educational policies and practices. Deficit theories assume that some children, because of genetic, cultural, or experiential differences, are inferior to other children—that is, that they have deficits that must be overcome if they are to learn. There are many obvious problems with such hypotheses, one being that they place complete responsibility for children's failure on their homes and families, effectively absolving schools and society from responsibility. Whether the focus is on the individual or the community, the result remains largely the same: blaming the victims of poor schooling rather than looking in a more systematic way at the role played by the schools in which they learn (or fail to learn) and by the society at large. All these factors need to be explored together.

Another problem with deficit theories is their focus on conditions that are outside the control of most teachers, schools, and students. Deficit theories foster despair in educators because they suggest that students' problems are predetermined and thus there is no hope for changing the circumstances that produced them in the first place. Teachers and schools alone cannot alleviate the poverty and other oppressive conditions in which students may live. It is far more realistic and promising to tackle the problems that teachers and schools *can* do something by providing educational environments that encourage all students to learn. This is why school policies and practices and teachers' attitudes and behaviors, rather than the supposed shortcomings of students, are the basis for the kinds of transformations suggested in this book.

Dissolving Myths About Immigration and Difference

The second major task of understanding the sociopolitical context of multicultural education emphasizes that immigration is not a phenomenon of the past. It remains one of today's most contentious issues and offers a particularly vivid example of the sociopolitical context, despite its mythological influence on U.S identity and social ideologies. The current contention is graphically illustrated by legislation such as S.B. 1070, Arizona's law of 2010, one of the strictest measures in years.[24] Even though U.S. District Judge Susan R. Bolton suspended portions of the law while a federal lawsuit challenged its constitutional integrity, this and similar legal struggles illustrate the fervor of anti-immigration sentiment across the nation. President Obama decried Arizona S. B. 1070, which he said threatened "to undermine basic notions of fairness that we cherish as Americans."[25]

Meanwhile, media reports scream about "illegal aliens" and electric fences along the U.S.–Mexico border, and describe self-appointed vigilante Minutemen adamant about guarding our borders, albeit illegally. Many families entering the United States as refugees—who arguably deserve the greatest amount of support and most sincere welcome—may find their children in schools where they endure mockery and intimidation regarding many aspects of their lives, including clothing, food, language, religious observance, and family structure. These oppressive acts and attitudes apparently stem from an ironic social amnesia surrounding the protected legal status of refugees, which was defined in 1951 by the United Nations Convention Relating to the Status of Refugees. According to the formal definition of a refugee in article 1A of that convention, a refugee enters a country legally for protection from persecution "for reasons of race, religion, nationality, membership of a particular social group, or political opinion, is outside the country of his nationality, and is unable to or, owing to such fear, is unwilling to avail himself of the protection of that country."[26] While refugee status was initially limited to protecting European refugees after World War II, the concept of a refugee was expanded by the convention's 1967 protocol and by regional conventions in Africa and Latin America to include persons who had fled war or other violence in their home country. It is worth noting that while European refugees after World War II were not universally welcomed on U.S. soil, the experiences of more recent groups of people of color entering the United States, such as El Salvadorans, Cambodians, Somalians, and Sudanese, have been more negative, puncuated by racially motivated atrocities.

Negative individual perspectives and social ideologies about immigrants, especially those from Latin America, Asia, and Africa, also often influence school policies and practices. It is critical for school curriculum and teacher education programs to underscore that the United States is not just a nation of past immigrants (who are often romantically portrayed) but also a nation of new immigrants who daily disembark on our shores, cross our borders, or fly into our metropolitan areas and are deserving of full participation in a democratic society.

Yet romantic myths about U.S. immigration die hard, and these myths influence some teachers' views of students and their families. For example, the widely accepted notion that immigrants came to North America and "made it," never to return to their countries of origin, is not entirely true. According to Irving Howe, one-third of European immigrants who came to the United States between 1908 and 1924 eventually made their way back home, thus shattering a popular myth.[27] In addition, and in spite of common assumptions to the contrary, most European immigrants did *not* succeed academically. In his research, Richard Rothstein found that, during the immigration period from 1880 to 1915, few Americans succeeded in school, least of all immigrants; immigrants of all backgrounds did poorly.[28] Instead, it was the children and grandchildren of European immigrants who fared well in school, but the myth that first-generation immigrants "made it," at least in terms of academics, is firmly established in the public psyche. Because schools have traditionally perceived their role as that of an assimilating agent, the isolation, rejection, and failure that have frequently accompanied immigration have simply been left at the schoolhouse door.

Facing the ugly fact that U.S. history is also steeped in conquest and slavery, or forced immigration, is essential in developing a multicultural perspective and understanding its sociopolitical context. Millions of descendants of Africans, American Indians, Mexicans, Puerto Ricans, and others colonized within and beyond U.S. borders have experienced political and economic oppression and, in schools, disparagement of their native cultures and languages. But the history of racism and exploitation experienced by so many of our people is rarely taught. Instead, conventional curricula and pedagogy have been based on the myth of a painless and smooth assimilation of immigrants, thereby contributing to the stubborn infrastructure that perpetuates institutionalized racism.

The research reported in our book argues that we need to make the history of all groups visible by making it part of the curriculum, instruction, and schooling in general. By highlighting the complexities of struggle and survival, we do not aim to cast a negative pall on all of U.S. history. Rather, multiple perspectives about the immigrant experience highlight the frailty as well as the heroism in current and historic events. The words of the students in the case studies and snapshots included in this book provide eloquent testimony for the need to do so.

These student examples throughout the book provide a critical understanding of immigration and colonization experiences, which are significant points of departure for our journey into multicultural education. This journey needs to begin with teachers, who themselves are frequently uninformed about or uncomfortable with their own ethnicity. By reconnecting with their own backgrounds and with the suffering as well as the triumphs of their families, teachers can lay the groundwork for their students to reclaim their histories and voices. This book invites you to cultivate a critical perspective on these issues unencumbered by mythology and romanticism.

Naming the Underpinnings of Educational Structures

The third task of defining the sociopolitical context of multicultural education is to name the ideologies underlying educational structures. These exemplify how the sociopolitical context is operational at the school level. Schools' and the larger

■ ■ ■ ■ ■ ■ What You Can Do
Explore Your Own Heritage and the Heritage of Others

No matter what subject matter you teach in schools, your perspectives on American history and of your own heritage influence the ways in which you view your students' heritages and cultural identities. Reading some books and viewing videos that offer points of view often overlooked or covered up in traditional American history books can expand your understanding of your ancestors' experiences *and* the experiences of others. You can approach this as a personal goal for summer reading or by pacing these books throughout the school year.

Allow yourself some introspective time by keeping a journal, a sketchbook, or a blog about your thoughts and questions that bubble up in this journey into rethinking historical understandings. Another approach is to create a teachers' reading group with a cluster of colleagues. Recruit your teacher-friends to develop a book club to discuss your reflections about your own histories and the histories of your colleagues and students. Pay particular attention to the ways in which common assumptions or previously held beliefs are challenged by these well-researched texts. Suggested books and videos: *A Different Mirror: A History of Multicultural America* by Ronald Takaki (New York: Back Bay Books, 2008), with a video on BookTV.org at http://www.booktv.org/Watch/10271/In+Depth+Ronald+Takaki.aspx; *A People's History of the United States: 1492 to Present* by Howard Zinn (New York: Harper, 2010); *Voices of a People's History of the United States,* Second Edition, edited by Howard Zinn and Anthony Arnove (New York: Seven Stories Press, 2009). For film resources, see a documentary called *The People Speak,* produced by the History Channel from the texts edited by Howard Zinn, that weaves archival footage and reenactments of speeches performed by many popular celebrities; it can be found at http://www.history.com/shows/the-people-speak. Also, for inspiration, resources, and guidance for teachers using these ideas in the classroom, see Zinn Education Project at http://www.zinnedproject.org.

society's assumptions about people form a belief system that helps create and perpetuate structures that reproduce those assumptions. For example, if we believe that intelligence is primarily inherited, we will design schools that support this belief. On the other hand, if we believe that intelligence is largely created by particular social and economic conditions, our schools will look quite different. Likewise, if we believe that some cultures are inherently superior to others, our schools will replicate the cultural values that are assumed to be superior while dismissing others.

At a personal level, we take in the ideologies and beliefs in our society and we act on them—*whether we actively believe them or not*. In the case of the ideology of racism, for example, Beverly Daniel Tatum has aptly described racism as "smog in the air."

> Sometimes it is so thick it is visible, other times it is less apparent, but always, day in and day out, we are breathing it in. None of us would introduce ourselves as "smog-breathers" (and most of us don't want to be described as prejudiced), but if we live in a smoggy place, how can we avoid breathing the air?[29]

The "smog" is part of the sociopolitical context in which we live and in which schools exist. This context includes not only racism but also other biases based on human and social differences, including social class, language, religion, sexual orientation, gender, and other factors. Pretending that the smog doesn't exist, or that it doesn't influence us, is to negate reality. A good example can be found in school funding: In their yearly report on funding of public schools, the Education Trust has consistently shown that low-income students and students of color are badly shortchanged by most states, proving once again that race and social class still matter a great deal in our nation. In their 2010 report, the Education Trust argued that Congress could promote funding equity within school district budgets if the political will was demonstrated by closing loopholes in the comparability provisions of Title I of the Elementary and Secondary Education Act.[30] Another investigation by the Center for Reinventing Public Education reveals how school funding policies have consistently given more resources to students who already have more, and less to those who have less.[31] The *Christian Science Monitor* found that the difference in annual spending between the wealthiest and the poorest school districts has grown to a staggering $19,361 per student.[32] Surely, no one can pretend that this difference does not matter.

School-Level Policies and Practices

School funding is generally a state- and district-level issue. How does the sociopolitical context affect policies and practices at the school level? Let's take a very concrete example: States that mandate that their schools enforce an "English-only" policy are, unwittingly or not, sending students a message about the status and importance of languages other than English. In some of these schools, students are forbidden to speak their native language not only in classrooms, but even in halls, the cafeteria, and the playground. To students who speak a language other than English, the message is clear: Your language is not welcome here; it is less important than English. From a multicultural perspective, it goes without saying that if your language is not welcome, your affiliation with your family and culture are also not welcome. While the policy may have been well intentioned and created out of a sincere effort to help students learn English, the result is deprecation of students' identities, intentional or not. In some instances, these kinds of policies are not innocent at all but instead reflect a xenophobic reaction to hearing languages other than English in our midst. In either case, the result is negative and an example of how ideologies help create structures that benefit some students over others.

Another obvious example is the curriculum: If the content of school knowledge excludes the history, science, art, culture, and ways of knowing entire groups of people, these groups themselves are dismissed as having little significance in creating history, science, art, culture, and so on. The sociopolitical context also undergirds other school policies and practices, including pedagogy, ability grouping, testing, parent outreach, disciplinary policies, and the hiring of teachers and other school personnel.

To correct the educational shortchanging of diverse student populations, the curriculum and pedagogy need to be changed in individual classrooms. But on a broader level, changes must go beyond the classroom: Schools' policies and practices and the societal ideologies that support them must also be confronted and transformed. That is, we need to create not only affirming classrooms but also an affirming society in which racism, sexism (discriminatory beliefs and behaviors based on gender), social class discrimination, religious oppression, heterosexism (discriminatory beliefs and behaviors directed against gay men and lesbians), ableism (discriminatory beliefs and behaviors directed against people with disabilities), and other biases are no longer acceptable. This is a tall order, but if multicultural education is to make a real difference, working to change society to be more socially equitable and just must go hand in hand with changes in curricula and classroom practices.

Studying the Demographic Mosaic of U.S. Schools and Society

In the fourth task of understanding the sociopolitical context of multicultural education, we need to study the changes in the United States in the recent past and how these changes have transformed our schools. In what follows, we present a mosaic of the rich diversity of the population in the nation as well as in our public schools as a framework for understanding this context. We focus on population statistics, immigration, language diversity, and other differences that characterize U.S. schools and society in the second decade of the twenty-first century.

We begin with an overview of the U.S. population in terms of race and ethnicity. The U.S. total population from the U.S. Census Bureau in 2010 was 308,745,538. The nation's Hispanic population increased by 3.1 percent from 2008 to 2009, to 48.4 million, making it both the largest and fastest growing "minority" group (more on this terminology throughout the text and in the Book Resources section in MyEducationLab). The next largest group is Blacks or African Americans, at 39,059,000 million (see Table 1.1). Growth among different segments of the population has not, however, been proportionate: According to the U.S. Census Bureau, from 2000 to 2008, the number of Whites increased by 6.4 percent and the African American population increased by 9.4 percent. By far, the largest increases were in the Latino population, which grew by 33 percent, and the Asian population, which grew by 28 percent.[33]

Even more dramatic than current population statistics are projections for the coming years: The U.S. Census Bureau estimates that from 2000 to 2050, the total population will have grown from 282.1 million to 419.9 million. Again, however, the growth will not be even: The White population is expected to grow to 210.3 million, an increase of 7 percent, although it is expected to *decrease* in the decade from 2040 to 2050. People of color, now roughly one-third of the U.S. population, are expected to become the majority in 2042, with the nation projected to be 54 percent in 2050. By 2023, people of color will comprise more than half of all children. Whites are thus expected to comprise only 46 percent of the total U.S. population by 2050, compared with 66 percent in 2008 (see Table 1.2), becoming the new minority.

The African American population is expected to grow to 65.7 million, increasing from 14 percent in 2008 to 15 percent of the total population in 2050. In contrast, the Latino population is projected to nearly triple, from 46.7 million to 132.8 million during the 2008–2050 period. Its proportion of the nation's total population is

TABLE 1.1   Resident Population by Sex, Race, and Hispanic-Origin Status: 2000 to 2008

Characteristic	Number (1,000)					Percent change, 2000 to 2008
	2000[1] (April 1)	2005	2006	2007	2008	
Both sexes						
Total	281,425[2]	295,561	298,363	301,290	304,060	8.0
One race	277,527	290,891	293,533	296,292	298,893	7.7
White	228,107	237,204	238,999	240,882	242,639	6.4
Black or African American	35,705	37,732	38,160	38,622	39,059	9.4
American Indian and Alaska Native	2,664	2,918	2,972	3,028	3,083	15.8
Asian	10,589	12,512	12,865	13,211	13,549	28.0
Native Hawaiian and Other Pacific Islander	463	525	538	550	562	21.5
Two or more races	3,898	4,669	4,830	4,998	5,167	32.6
Race alone or in combination[2]						
White	231,436	241,228	243,168	245,203	247,113	6.8
Black or African American	37,105	39,534	40,047	40,599	41,127	10.8
American Indian and Alaska Native	4,225	4,613	4,694	4,779	4,862	15.1
Asian	12,007	14,244	14,662	15,075	15,480	28.9
Native Hawaiian and Other Pacific Islander	907	1,035	1,061	1,087	1,112	22.7
Not Hispanic	246,118	253,032	254,378	255,818	257,116	4.5
One race	242,712	248,987	250,201	251,504	252,664	4.1
White	195,577	198,037	198,518	199,060	199,491	2.0
Black or African American	34,314	36,068	36,422	36,809	37,172	8.3
American Indian and Alaska Native	2,097	2,240	2,269	2,299	2,329	11.0
Asian	10,357	12,232	12,574	12,910	13,238	27.8
Native Hawaiian and Other Pacific Islander	367	410	418	426	435	18.4
Two or more races	3,406	4,045	4,177	4,314	4,452	30.7
Race alone or in combination[2]						
White	198,477	201,514	202,114	202,780	203,336	2.4
Black or African American	5,499	37,591	38,015	38,477	38,916	9.6

	Number (1,000)					
Characteristic	2000[1] (April 1)	2005	2006	2007	2008	Percent change, 2000 to 2008
Black or African American	5,499	37,591	38,015	38,477	38,916	9.6
American Indian and Alaska Native	3,456	3,686	3,732	3,781	3,828	10.8
Asian	11,632	13,781	14,179	14,572	14,957	28.6
Native Hawaiian and Other Pacific Islander	752	845	863	881	899	19.6
Hispanic[4]	35,306	42,529	43,985	45,472	46,944	33.0
One race	34,815	41,904	43,332	44,788	46,228	32.8
White	32,530	39,166	40,480	41,822	43,148	32.6
Black or African American	1,391	1,664	1,738	1,813	1,887	35.6
American Indian and Alaska Native	566	679	703	729	754	33.2
Asian	232	280	290	301	311	33.9
Native Hawaiian and Other Pacific Islander	95	116	120	124	128	33.7
Two or more races	491	624	654	684	715	45.6
Race alone or in combination[3]						
White	32,959	39,714	41,054	42,423	43,777	32.8
Black or African American	1,606	1,943	2,032	2,122	2,211	37.7
American Indian and Alaska Native	770	927	962	998	1,034	34.4
Asian	375	463	483	503	523	39.6
Native Hawaiian and Other Pacific Islander	155	190	198	205	213	37.4
Male						
Total	**138,056**	**145,465**	**146,946**	**148,466**	**149,925**	**8.6**
One race	136,146	143,163	144,563	145,997	147,370	8.2
White	112,478	117,397	118,374	119,375	120,326	7.0
Black or African American	16,972	17,973	18,189	18,418	18,640	9.8
American Indian and Alaska Native	1,333	1,461	1,488	1,517	1,545	15.9
Asian	5,128	6,065	6,238	6,408	6,574	28.2

(Continued)

TABLE 1.1　Continued

Characteristic	2000[1] (April 1)	2005	2006	2007	2008	Percent change, 2000 to 2008
Native Hawaiian and Other Pacific Islander	235	267	273	279	286	21.5
Two or more races	1,910	2,302	2,384	2,469	2,555	33.7
Race alone or in combination[3]						
White	114,116	119,387	120,438	121,516	122,545	7.4
Black or African American	17,644	18,849	19,109	19,384	19,651	11.4
American Indian and Alaska Native	2,088	2,284	2,325	2,368	2,410	15.4
Asian	5,834	6,931	7,137	7,341	7,541	29.2
Native Hawaiian and Other Pacific Islander	456	520	534	547	560	22.7
Not Hispanic	119,894	123,514	124,235	124,981	125,670	4.8
Hispanic[4]	18,162	21,951	22,712	23,485	24,254	33.5
Female						
Total	**143,368**	**150,096**	**151,417**	**152,824**	**154,135**	**7.5**
One race	141,381	147,728	148,970	150,295	151,523	7.2
White	115,628	119,806	120,625	121,506	122,313	5.8
Black or African American	18,733	19,759	19,971	20,203	20,419	9.0
American Indian and Alaska Native	1,331	1,458	1,484	1,512	1,539	15.6
Asian	5,461	6,447	6,626	6,803	6,975	27.7
Native Hawaiian and Other Pacific Islander	227	258	264	270	276	21.6
Two or more races	1,987	2,368	2,447	2,529	2,612	31.4
Race alone or in combination[3]						
White	117,321	121,841	122,730	123,686	124,568	6.2
Black or African American	19,461	20,685	20,939	21,215	21,476	10.4

Number (1,000)

Characteristic	Number (1,000)					
	2000[1] (April 1)	2005	2006	2007	2008	Percent change, 2000 to 2008
American Indian and Alaska Native	2,137	2,329	2,369	2,411	2,452	14.7
Asian	6,173	7,313	7,525	7,734	7,940	28.6
Native Hawaiian and Other Pacific Islander	451	514	527	540	553	22.6
Not Hispanic	126,224	129,518	130,143	130,837	131,446	4.1
Hispanic[4]	17,144	20,578	21,273	21,987	22,689	32.3

[1]See footnote 3, Table 7.

[2]281,425 represents 281,425,000. As of July, except as noted. Data shown are modified race counts; see text, this section.

[3]In combination with one or more other races. The sum of the five race groups adds to more than the total population because individuals may report more than one race.

[4]Persons of Hispanic origin may be any race.

Source: U.S. Census Bureau, "Annual Estimates of the Population by Sex, Race, and Hispanic Origin for the United States: April 1, 2000 to July 1, 2008 (NC-EST2008-03)" (released May 14, 2009); http://www.census.gov/popest/national/asrh/NC-EST2008/NC-EST2008-03.xls.

projected to double, from 15 percent to 30 percent. If these projections bear out, nearly one in three U.S. residents would be Hispanic. Asians are also expected to increase substantially in number, from 15.5 million to 40.6 million, an increase from 5.1 percent to 9.2 percent of the total U.S. population. While American Indians and Alaska Natives are projected to climb from 4.9 million to 8.6 million (or from 1.6 to 2 percent of the total population), the Native Hawaiian and Other Pacific Islander population is also expected to increase: from 1.1 million to 2.6 million. While there is already a substantial jump in the number of people who identify themselves as being of two or more races, it is projected to more than triple from 5.2 million to 16.2 million.[34]

In addition to the growing U.S. population, legal immigration has grown enormously in the past three decades, as is evident in Figure 1.1 As we can see in this graph, legal immigration hit a peak in 1991 in terms of numbers (although not in terms of percentage of total population, which peaked at the beginning of the twentieth century), reaching more than 1.8 million. By 2009, a total of 1,130,818 persons became legal permanent residents (LPRs) of the United States, still a sizable number.[35]

Another noteworthy indication of the growing diversity in the United States is the current number of foreign-born or first-generation U.S. residents, which in the year 2000 reached the highest level in U.S. history—56 million, or triple the number in 1970. And unlike previous immigrants, who were primarily from Europe, more than half of the new immigrants are from Latin America, and 25 percent are from Asia. In 2009, the following five countries accounted for 35 percent of all new LPRs (in ascending order): Mexico, China, the Philippines, India, and the Dominican Republic.[36]

TABLE 1.2 Projected Change in Population Size by Race and Hispanic Origin for the United States: 2000 to 2050. High Net International Migration Series

Race and Hispanic Origin[1]	(Resident population as of July 1. Numbers in 1000)					
	2000–2050		2000–2025		2025–2050	
	Numerical	Percent	Numerical	Percent	Numerical	Percent
Total Population	**175,971**	**62**	**82,350**	**29**	**93,621**	**26**
One race	163,322	59	77,539	28	85,783	24
White	109,001	48	52,362	23	56,639	20
Black	22,857	64	11,397	32	11,460	24
AIAN	2,948	110	1,421	53	1,527	37
Asian	27,678	259	11,987	112	15,691	69
NHPI	837	180	372	80	465	55
Two or more races	12,649	322	4,810	122	7,839	90
Race alone or in combination[2]						
White	120,600	52	56,705	24	63,895	22
Black	30,354	82	14,054	38	16,300	32
AIAN	4,564	108	2,174	51	2,390	37
Asian	32,682	270	13,910	115	18,772	72
NHPI	1,798	197	777	85	1,021	60
Not Hispanic	**68,097**	**28**	**38,421**	**16**	**29,676**	**10**
One race	57,904	24	34,457	14	23,447	8
White	10,338	5	12,006	6	-1,668	-1
Black	18,950	55	9,801	28	9,149	21
AIAN	1,268	60	732	35	536	19
Asian	26,865	257	11,684	112	15,181	69
NHPI	484	131	235	64	249	41
Two or more races	10,193	297	3,964	115	6,229	84
Race alone or in combination[2]						
White	19,694	10	15,585	8	4,109	2
Black	25,215	71	12,045	34	13,170	28
AIAN	2,201	63	1,218	35	983	21
Asian	31,019	264	13,335	114	17,684	71
NHPI	1,162	154	543	72	619	48
Hispanic	**107,873**	**303**	**43,928**	**123**	**63,945**	**80**

| (Resident population as of July 1. Numbers in 1000) | | | | | |
| Race and Hispanic Origin[1] | 2000–2050 | | 2000–2025 | | 2025–2050 | |
	Numerical	Percent	Numerical	Percent	Numerical	Percent
One race	105,418	300	43,083	123	62,335	80
White	98,663	300	40,356	123	58,307	80
Black	3,907	278	1,596	114	2,311	77
AIAN	1,680	294	689	120	991	79
Asian	813	346	303	129	510	95
NHPI	354	369	138	144	216	92
Two or More Races	2,455	494	846	170	1,609	120
Race alone or in combination[2]						
White	100,905	303	41,118	124	59,787	80
Black	5,140	317	2,010	124	3,130	86
AIAN	2,363	304	956	123	1,407	81
Asian	1,662	439	575	152	1,087	114
NHPI	636	405	234	149	402	103

[1]Hispanics may be of any race.

[2]"In combination" means in combination with one or more other races. The sum of the five race groups adds to more than the total population because individuals may report more than one race.

Abbreviations: Black = Black or African American; AIAN = American Indian and Alaska Native; NHPI = Native Hawaiian and Other Pacific Islander

Note: The original race data from Census 2000 are modified to eliminate the "some other race" category. This modification is used for all Census Bureau projections products and is explained in the document entitled "Modified Race Data Summary File Technical Documentation and ASCII Layout" that can be found on the Census Bureau website at http://www.census.gov/popest/archives/files/MRSF-01-US1.html.

Table 7-H. Projected Change in Population Size by Race and Hispanic Origin for the United States: 2000 to 2050 High Net International Migration Series (NP2009-T7-H)

Source: U.S. Census Bureau, Population Division Release Date: December 16, 2009.

The growth in immigration has been accompanied by an increase in linguistic diversity. Currently, 20 percent of the total U.S. population speaks a language other than English at home. As of 2008, 10.9 million school-age children (ages 5 to 17) spoke a language other than English at home; 7.8 million of these children spoke Spanish at home.[37] While Spanish is clearly the language spoken by well over half of linguistically diverse students, there are also many other languages spoken in U.S. homes. (More information on linguistic diversity is given in Chapter 6.)

FIGURE 1.1   Legal Permanent Residents Flow to United States

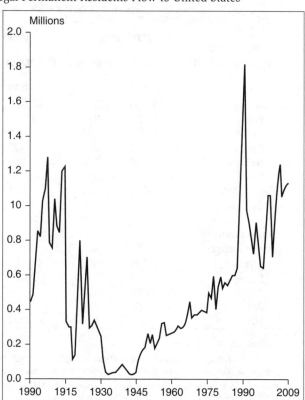

The impact of the growing cultural, racial, national origin, and linguistic diversity is clearly visible in our nation's public schools in several ways. First, the sheer number of students in U.S. public schools is growing: In 2010, 56 million students were enrolled in elementary and secondary schools in the United States, and 89 percent of those were in public schools, an increase of more than 2 million since 2001.[38]

Second, the nature of the student population is quite different from what it was just a few decades ago. In 1970, at the height of the public school enrollment of the baby boom generation, White students comprised 79 percent of total enrollment; followed by African Americans at 14 percent; Hispanics at 6 percent; and Asians, Pacific Islanders, and other ethnic groups at 1 percent. These statistics have changed dramatically: As of 2008, 43 percent of elementary through high school students were students of color. The Census Bureau's population projections indicate that the student population will continue to diversify in the coming years. Third, our public schools' growing diversity is clearly evidenced by the number of students who are foreign-born or have foreign-born parents. As of 2009, over 49 million students, or 31 percent of those enrolled in U.S. elementary and secondary schools, were foreign-born or had at least one parent who was foreign-born.[39]

At the same time that diversity in schools around the country is growing, racial and ethnic segregation has been on the rise. That is, students in U.S. schools are now more likely to be segregated from students of other races and backgrounds than at any time in the recent past. Indeed, according to Gary Orfield, much of the progress made in integrating the nation's schools during previous decades was eradicated by the end of the 1990s. For Blacks, the 1990s witnessed the largest backward movement toward segregation since the U.S. Supreme Court's decision in *Brown v. Board of Education,* and the trend is continuing. For Latinos, the situation has been equally dramatic: Latinos are now the most segregated of all ethnic groups in terms of race, ethnicity, and poverty.[40] Despite this trend, there is growing evidence that schools with diverse student populations are good for students of all backgrounds.[41]

Race and ethnicity have a strong link to poverty due to the history of institutionalized racism. The percentage of all people in the United States living below the poverty level is currently 12.5 percent. The number of children living in poverty increased by 21 percent from 2000 to 2008, which means there are at least 2.5 million more children living in poverty now than a decade ago. Research shows that compared to White families with children, Black and Latino families with children are more than twice as likely to experience economic hardships. About 11 percent of White children live in poverty, while 35 percent of African American, 31 percent of American Indian, 31 percent of Hispanic, and 15 percent of Asian children live in poverty. The poverty rate does not tell the whole story because the equations for the federal poverty level have not been adjusted for inflation since the 1960s. It bears noting that research demonstrates that families require about twice the federal poverty level to make ends meets, and that families who do not meet that figure are considered low-income. In terms of the school-age population, 41 percent of all U.S. children live in low-income families, and over 20 percent live in poor families, which translates into the sobering reality that *more than half of all children in the United States live in some degree of poverty.* It is well documented that food insecurity, lack of affordable housing, and other hardships affect millions of American children, not just those who are officially poor. Even more disturbing, although the number of children living in poverty had declined from 1990 to 2000, it has been rising steadily since then.[42]

At the same time that the number of students of color, those who speak languages other than English, and those who live in poverty has increased, the nation's teachers have become more monolithic, monocultural, and monolingual. For example, as of 2003, 90 percent of public school teachers were White, 6 percent were African American, and fewer than 5 percent were of other racial/ethnic backgrounds.[43]

One implication of the tremendous diversity previously described is that all teachers, regardless of their own identities and experiences, need to be prepared to teach effectively students of all backgrounds. One way to do so is to heighten awareness of the sociopolitical context of students' lives by learning about the social, cultural, and political circumstances of real students in real schools. At the end of the chapter, we briefly discuss the case study approach used in this book to help readers think about how they can best translate the information into their classroom practices.

Examining Political Struggles: Multicultural Education, Backlash, and Legislation

Since its beginnings in the 1970s, multicultural education has been criticized for many reasons. While some of the criticisms have been warranted and have, in fact, helped the field develop a more solid foundation, many of the arguments against multicultural education have been deeply ideological and have ignored both educational research and actual practice. That is, multicultural education has come under fire precisely because it has challenged the status quo, encouraged the emergence of previously silenced and marginalized voices, and championed the transformation of curriculum and the use of alternative pedagogies. The criticisms and detractions of multicultural education are also embedded in the broader sociopolitical context. Three common strategies for trying to destabilize multicultural education include (1) calls for going back to basics, (2) claims of erosion of the educational canon, and (3) political struggles of legislation and policy.

The Back-to-Basics Argument

The backlash against multicultural education has been evident in claims that a focus on diversity is a diversion from the "basics." This has been the case for almost three decades: since the educational reform movement that began in 1983 after the publication of *A Nation at Risk*.[44] One vivid example of the back-to-basics argument is E. D. Hirsch's 1987 book *Cultural Literacy: What Every American Needs to Know*, which he initially developed to combat the "multicultural threat." The book includes a list of several thousand terms and concepts that the author considers essential for every educated person to know or at least to recognize and be familiar with.[45] Many critics have charged that both the book and the list are provincial and Eurocentric, with little attention given to the arts, history, or culture of those from groups other than the so-called mainstream. Yet since the publication of Hirsch's book 25 years ago, several hundred schools around the nation have been structured and organized according to what has been dubbed "core knowledge" and the "cultural literacy" model. Hirsch's work further promulgated a notion of so-called cultural literacy that flies in the face of the rapidly changing demographics—not to mention the rich multicultural history—of our nation. Numerous spin-off publications are targeted toward parents and guardians and focus on different grade levels, making Hirsch's cultural literacy model and ideas a cottage industry that is hard to ignore. In contrast to Hirsch's work, Kristen Buras analyzed the neoconservative evolution and contradictory ideology of this core knowledge school reform movement. She uncovered the conservative leaders and their financially powerful backers, as well as the strategies and campaigns to politicize school curriculum in order to develop a permanent conservative majority—which she dubs the rise of "Rightist Multiculturalism."[46]

The pitfalls of Hirsch's assertions of what counts as literacy are multifold. While many of us might welcome a generally agreed-upon definition of the educated person, this is a complex issue that cannot be solved by a prescribed list, or even a prescribed curriculum. Eugene Provenzo has challenged Hirsch's views by publishing his own book, *Critical Literacy: What Every American Ought to Know,* a critique of both Hirsch and the simplistic ideas behind the cultural literacy model that he promotes.[47]

Eroding the Traditional Educational Canon

The call for back to basics falls under the broader conservative argument against multicultural education as a liberal movement that erodes the traditional educational canon. The claim is that multicultural education can slide into a separatist monoculturalism that pits Europeans and European Americans against people of other backgrounds, creating a divisive "us versus them" mentality. This argument makes two assumptions: that no "us versus them" mentality existed previous to multicultural education and that there already is unity among all people in our country—both clearly erroneous assumptions. There are tremendous divisions among people in the United States, many of which have become increasingly visible since the election of the first person of color to the U.S. presidency, and glossing over these differences will not make them go away. The notion that multicultural education has separatist goals could not be further from the truth. On the contrary, supporters of multicultural education assume that a more pluralistic curriculum is also more complicated and truthful and will, in the long run, help develop citizens who think critically, expansively, and creatively and therefore will be actively engaged in a democratic society.

In terms of its impact on schooling, opponents have been especially nervous about how a multicultural perspective might translate into curriculum changes. Those who fear that the traditional educational canon is being eroded have vociferously criticized it because, they claim, a multicultural curriculum will do away with our "common culture." The ramifications of this stance can be seen in efforts to do away with specific courses at high schools and universities. In the aftermath of September 11, 2001, multicultural education opponents claim that it is now more important than ever to focus on a rigidly defined version of American history. An example of this can be found in the actions of the Texas State Board of Education, which in the spring of 2010 adopted a set of social studies and history standards that dilutes the teaching of the civil rights movement and slavery, while directing teachers to examine America's relationship to the United Nations as a threat to U.S. sovereignty.[48] Another alarming example during the spring of 2010 is the legislation in the state of Arizona, HB 2281, which did away with ethnic studies courses under the claim that such courses promote "the overthrow of the United States government or promote resentment toward a race or class of people."[49]

In countering these arguments, we need to remember that the history of all groups in the United States is not foreign; it *is American history*. Our history was never exclusively a European saga of immigration and assimilation, although that is, of course, an important part of the American story. But our collective consciousness began with—and continues to be influenced by—indigenous Americans as well as by those who were forcibly brought from Africa into slavery. No one in our nation has been untouched by African American, Native American, Mexican American, and Asian American histories and cultures (among many other groups, including women, European American immigrants, and working-class people). The influence of these groups can be seen throughout our history in scientific discoveries, technological advances, popular culture, civic engagement, and the arts. The expansive globalization of communication, commerce, and cultural experiences will continue to increase, and it behooves us to educate our students to participate more fully in multicultural and global social exchanges.

Political Struggles of Legislation and Policy

The sociopolitical context is vividly revealed in struggles over power and privilege in the heart of U.S. policy making. The Elementary and Secondary Education Act (ESEA) has been law for nearly 50 years; since 1965, it has been the federal government's primary legislative vehicle for supporting and influencing K–12 public education in more than 16,000 local school districts across the country. The most recent iteration of the back-to-basics argument has occurred since the passage of the version of ESEA called No Child Left Behind (NCLB) in 2001, particularly because, along with higher standards, the law required that each state have an annual testing program in reading and math.[50] When the NCLB version was enacted, it was particularly damaging on several levels. It marked the most extreme reach of federal policy into state and local school districts in the history of U.S. public education, and that scope was also the most punitive to students and their schools. While NCLB was originally enacted in response to several issues plaguing our educational system, including the deplorable history of educational inequality in our nation, its single-minded focus on standardized tests as the primary criterion for viewing academic progress, as well as the dismal results this focus produced, revealed many flaws in the policy.

In the spring of 2010, the Obama administration released its "Blueprint for Reform," an updated Elementary and Secondary Education Act to overhaul No Child Left Behind. President Obama pronounced that "while the federal government can play a leading role in encouraging the reforms and high standards we need, the impetus for that change will come from states, and from local schools and school districts."[51] This statement directly addressed the overreach of No Child Left Behind and a promise to return more power to states and local school districts. The blueprint also set forth a plan to eliminate the current accountability system, which requires public schools to make adequate yearly progress (AYP) in raising student achievement as measured by state tests and other indicators and replace it with a more comprehensive strategy of measuring growth. The Center on Education Policy also recommends eliminating AYP, one of several recommendations in its 2010 paper, "Better Federal Policies Leading to Better Schools."[52] Yet there are concerns that much of the new blueprint springs from some of the same misguided assumptions that plagued NCLB.

The conveners of the Forum for Education and Democracy, a group of highly respected educators and researchers, have argued that it is necessary to work from a different set of assumptions.[53] They suggest five assumptions based on research and supported by the conveners' experience in the field of education and in the classroom. These assumptions set a foundation for a compelling list of specific recommendations concerning the reauthorization of ESEA. Their assumptions also support the central goals of this book, so they are worth examining here:

1. *Equity:* First and foremost, all public policy must work to ensure that every child has equal access to a high-quality public education. This is a fundamental matter of civil rights.

2. *Teaching:* A high-quality teaching profession is our best guarantee that our schools will be places of excellence. The provision of such is the rightful role of federal and state policy.

3. *Culture:* Young people will do their best work in schools where the culture is one of academic challenge, support, and engagement. Public policy should promote—not hinder—the establishment of such school cultures.

4. *Evidence:* Using multiple sources of evidence to measure student success will help every school community improve its work and create an environment where what matters is not simply data—but how well we respond to it to improve the learning conditions for children.

5. *Community:* As public trusts, our schools work best when the community is engaged, valued, and involved in meaningful decision making.[54]

In light of those five assumptions, their report recommends a range of specific policies and practices and asserts that

> we must restore an appropriate balance of authority, with the federal government taking a more pro-active role in ensuring equitable educational opportunity, and a less heavy-handed, more productive role in supporting states and localities to focus on improving the quality of teaching and learning. This agenda would reclaim and extend the historic federal role in public education: first, by acknowledging education as a civil right that should be made available to all on equal terms; and second, by taking on the critical tasks that demand a strong central role in building the capacity of schools to offer high-quality opportunities responsive to our fast-changing world.[54]

As you will see in demographic data, research studies, and our own case studies throughout this text, educational inequality has been a fact of life for many children in our schools, but especially for students of color and children living in poverty. Parents, educators, and other defenders of public education have long advocated for addressing this inequality through legislation. It is not surprising, then, that many advocates of equal education initially supported NCLB and, while debate about its benefits or injuries to schools continues, it remains popular with some.

At the same time, conspicuous among the most ardent supporters of NCLB are those who support privatization of schools through techniques that include, among others, vouchers, charter schools, and so forth, that frequently exclude the most vulnerable children from their classrooms. Thus, the goals of various groups promoting NCLB are not the same and, in some cases, may be contradictory. In the years since NCLB was first passed, it has lost favor with a great many people for a spectrum of reasons. Researchers Heinrich Mintrop and Gail L. Sunderman of the Civil Rights Project provide an analysis of why the NCLB policy is failing, and also, despite the counterintuitive indicators, why it continues to reap support from policy makers. Their evidence indicts NCLB for causing serious costs to the U.S. education system by keeping schools mired in low-level intellectual work. They reveal how teachers get stuck in test-driven basic skills remediation, pointing out how this is particularly destructive for students who are in the schools NCLB identifies as failing: schools that are overwhelmingly populated by students of color and students living in poverty.[56] They go on to explain that there are what Marshall Meyer and Lynne Zucker call powerful "secondary beneficiaries"[57] of NCLB such as testing agencies, segments of the school improvement industry, and others deriv-ing economic and political benefit from the system—even when it is failing.[58]

These conflicting views and contentious debates are part of the reason that, as this book goes to press, the ESEA has yet to be reauthorized by the U.S. House and Senate. In the interim, while waiting for the new reauthorization of the Obama admin-istrations's blueprint of ESEA, other inititatives were launched such as the 2010 Race to the Top (RTTT). RTTT provides competitive grants to encourage and reward states that are creating the conditions for education innovation and reform as defined by the U.S. Department of Education. The grants from RTTT tap the resources made avail-able through the Education Recovery Act under the broader umbrella of the economic stimulus called American Recovery and Reinvestment Act (ARRA) of 2009.[59]

Some of these initiatives have created concern that the overemphasis on and misuse of standardized testing will continue and may even be buttressed by fund-ing to reward teachers based on student test scores. Calling for revisions to the Race to the Top Fund Guidelines, the research and advocacy organization FairTest has taken a strong stand in opposition to the overemphasis on standardized testing: "By encouraging states to make student test scores a 'significant factor' in teacher and principal evaluation, RTTT will intensify the damage."[60] Educators have turned their attention to the Obama administration's blueprint with particularly focused concentration on how it addresses *teaching to the test* and *high standards*.

Teaching to the Test and High Standards

In the past decade, there has been immense pressure on teachers and administrators to "teach to the test" and to devote a lion's share of the school day to reading and mathematics. The effects have been mixed, at best. While test scores are rising in some districts, the law's pressure on school districts has reduced instructional time for other subjects to make more time for reading and mathematics.[61] Subjects that are not evaluated on high-stakes tests have been reduced or eliminated in some schools. Recess and physical education have also been curtailed in many schools. Although multicultural education is not a subject area, it too has been one of the casualties of this pressure. As a consequence of NCLB, the testing frenzy has had a chilling effect on schools' and teachers' autonomy to develop and implement curric-ula, and this includes multicultural curricula. NCLB mandates have also funneled professional development funding away from any goals that are not test-score driven, further eroding opportunities for teachers to learn about or expand multicultural goals.

Most state standards do not preclude the possibility of including multiple per-spectives in the curriculum. In fact, there is no contradiction between high stan-dards and multicultural education. Quite the opposite is the case: Since its very beginning, one of the major arguments in support of multicultural education has been that some students—particularly students of color and poor students of all backgrounds—have been the victims of an inferior education, often based on their race/ethnicity, social class, first language, and other differences. Multicultural edu-cation, through a rich curriculum and rigorous demands, was an antidote to this sit-uation. Nonetheless, the pressure that teachers and administrators are under to meet AYP, as defined by standardized tests, has resulted in little support for the arts and even for subjects such as social studies and science, much less for innovation and creativity in curriculum and instruction. The potential disaster on the limitations of knowledge for future generations is frightening, and the U.S. standing in the international community is at risk both economically and politically.

For example, the organization Common Core conducted an international analysis of policies related to curriculum standards and its findings revealed that, in their national curriculum, high-achieving countries focus on several topics that the United States has been ignoring. These topics include comprehensive, content-rich education in the liberal arts and sciences such as history, civics, geography, literature, music, visual arts, and sciences. Common Core cautions that this report is "not intended to be an endorsement of the idea of national standards or a national test" because not all of these countries have written national standards and many do not require national tests.[62] Rather, this study focuses on the content taught in schools and found that the common ingredient across these nations "is a dedication to educating their children deeply in a wide range of subjects."[63] The study drew information from nine nations that consistently have outranked U.S. schools on the Programme for International Student Assessment (PISA): Finland, Hong Kong (a territory), South Korea, Canada, Japan, New Zealand, Australia, the Netherlands, and Switzerland.[64]

The undue attention on test scores in the United States also has devastating effects on teachers' sense of professionalism. Many teachers are now reluctant—and in some cases forbidden—to engage in projects outside the prescribed curriculum with their students, or even to collaborate with peers due to possible criticisms, or job-security threats they are likely to receive from administrators who are also under tremendous pressure to keep their schools out of the headlines for failing to meet AYP. The result in many schools around the country is that teachers are expected to follow a rigidly prescribed curriculum, particularly in reading and math, with little room for innovation or collaboration. What are teachers to do?

Teachers' Responsibilities Within NCLB

In terms of teachers' responsibilities, we must once again consider the sociopolitical context of education. Curriculum and pedagogy, along with other school policies and practices, as we shall see in Chapter 4, are as much *political* issues as they are educational issues. The same is true of standards. State standards and curriculum frameworks are not going to disappear, and most recommendations about how to change NCLB include references to strong standards.[65] We make the assumption here that all educators want to hold their students to high standards. Yet every curriculum decision also says something about the values, expectations, and dreams that teachers hold for their students. If this is the case, it becomes the responsibility of teachers to help define the curriculum and not simply to be automatons who implement a rigidly prescribed curriculum.

Christine Sleeter suggests that there is a difference between a *standards-driven* and a *standards-conscious* curriculum. A standards-driven curriculum, according to her, begins with the standards and draws the "big ideas" from them for further design and implementation. A standards-conscious curriculum, on the other hand,

uses the standards as a *tool* rather than as either the starting point or the underlying ideology for the development of big ideas. In her book, *Un-Standardizing
Curriculum: Multicultural Teaching in the Standards-Based Classroom*, Sleeter
provides powerful vignettes of teachers who face the same pressures to "teach
to the test" as do all teachers. In spite of this pressure, rather than following
the standards uncritically, these teachers developed standards-conscious curricula
that are both creative and critical.[66] Another example of using the standards in
inventive ways is Mary Cowhey's *Black Ants and Buddhists: Thinking Critically
and Teaching Differently in the Primary Grades*.[67] A first- and second-grade teacher,
Cowhey uses the standards to develop curriculum that is inspiring, demanding,
and multicultural.

These books, and a growing number of others, are challenging the notion that
standards will necessarily lead to rigid standardization. They provide vivid examples of how powerful learning and imagination can be promoted even within a testing and accountability context that tends to leave little room for these things.

Qualitative Research and Choices in Methodology

An essential element of the sociopolitical context of education concerns students—
who they are, how they identify themselves, what their families are like, how
they live, the values they hold dear, what helps them learn, and their desires and
hopes for the future. Because of the importance of student voices in understanding
the sociopolitical context of education, our research in this book includes case studies and snapshots that provide descriptions and stories of students of diverse backgrounds. (See the Appendix in the Book Resources section of MyEducationLab for
more information about the selection of students for the case studies and snapshots
and the approach to selecting the themes illustrated by these students.)

What Are Case Studies?

The case study approach fits within the social sciences general framework of qualitative research. Sharan Merriam describes the essential characteristics of a qualitative case study as an intensive, holistic description and analysis. She further explains
case studies as *particularistic* (focusing on one person or social unit), *descriptive*
(because the result is a rich, thick portrait), and *heuristic* (because it sharpens the
reader's understanding, leading to discovering new meanings).[68] A case study is also
inductive because generalizations and hypotheses emerge from examination of the
data. In this book, we use *ethnographic case studies,* which include a sociocultural
analysis of each of the students, all of whom are presented contextually, that is,
within their cultural and social environment.

The case studies and snapshots differ in terms of length and treatment: snapshots are short and written mostly in the words of the young people, with a brief
analysis, while case studies are longer and offer more in-depth analysis. Case studies are placed at the ends of Chapters 3 through 8, and snapshots are placed within
various chapters to highlight particular issues discussed in the chapters.

The young people in the case studies and snapshots are actual students who
were interviewed about their experiences in school; the importance of ethnicity, race,

culture, and language in their lives; what they like and dislike about school; teachers who made a difference in their lives; and what they expect to get out of school. The students are described within a variety of settings—home, school, community, and city or town in which they live—because, by looking at each of these settings, we gain a clearer, more complete picture of their lives.

The students represent multiple communities and identities. As young men and women from a number of racial, ethnic, linguistic, social class, and cultural groups, they have had many different life experiences. They live in various geographic locations, from large cities to small rural areas and native reservations. They are first-, second-, or third-generation Americans, or their ancestors may have been here for many hundreds of years or even since the first humans populated this continent. Some are from families in economic difficulty, while others are from struggling working-class, middle-class, or well-to-do families. Most are heterosexual, and others are gay or lesbian. They range in age from 13 to 19. When first interviewed, some of them were almost ready to graduate from high school, a few were in middle or junior high school, and the others were at various levels of high school. They range from monolingual English-speaking youths to English language learners, to fluent bilinguals. Their families vary from very large (11 children) to very small (one child) in both one- and two-parent households. Their parents' educational backgrounds vary as well: from no high school education to postgraduate degrees.

In spite of the vast differences in their experiences and backgrounds, most (although not all) of the students in these case studies share one characteristic: They are successful in school. Although there may be disagreements about what it means to be successful (research by Michelle Fine, for example, suggests that, in some ways, the most "successful" students are those who drop out of school[69]), most of the students have been able to develop both academic skills and positive attitudes about themselves and about the value of education. They generally have good grades, most have hopes (but not always plans) of attending college, and they have fairly positive perceptions of school.

Beyond Generalizations and Stereotypes

We did not include these case studies and snapshots for the purpose of generalization to all students in U.S. schools. No educational research, whether qualitative or quantitative, can do so. The students in the case studies and snapshots in this book are not *samples*, as might be the case with quantitative research, but *examples* of a wide variety of students. Case studies can help us look at specific examples so that solutions for more general situations can be hypothesized and developed. For example, James Karam, the Lebanese Christian student whose case study follows Chapter 5, does not reflect the experiences of all Lebanese students in U.S. schools. However, describing James's experience within its sociocultural framework can help us understand many experiences of other Lebanese students. Whereas quantitative methods can yield some important data about Lebanese students in general (for example, their numbers in the United States or their relative levels of achievement), it is only through a qualitative approach that we can explore more deeply, for example, the impact on James of "invisible minority" status.

No case study of a single individual can adequately or legitimately portray the complexity of an entire group of people. (Neither, of course, can any quantitative approach claim to do this.) Although some Mexican Americans prefer to learn collaboratively, and some African American students may perceive school success as "acting White" (these issues are discussed further in Chapters 7 and 8), many do not. To reach such conclusions contradicts one of the very purposes of case studies, which is to challenge stereotypes.

The case studies and snapshots are meant to encourage you to ask questions rather than to make assumptions about what it means to be from a large family, to be raised by two dads, to be Vietnamese, middle class, lesbian, African American, Cape Verdean, or anything else. It is far easier to pigeonhole people according to our preconceptions and biases, but the deeper struggle is to try to understand people on their own terms. Some of the experiences, feelings, and statements of the young people described in the case studies and snapshots may surprise you and shake some deep-seated beliefs. So much the better if they do. On the other hand, they may reflect some of your own experiences or your knowledge of young people of diverse racial and sociocultural backgrounds. In either case, what these students say should be understood within the context of their particular school, family, and community experiences.

Learning from the Case Studies and Snapshots

We hope that you will read each of these stories critically and with the goal of understanding how the experiences and thoughts of young people can influence classroom discourse and strategies as well as school policies and practices in general. These young people challenge us to believe that all students in our nation's classrooms are capable of learning. Although their stories demonstrate the indomitable strength of youth, they also reveal the tremendous fragility of academic success, which is so easily disrupted by a poor teacher, misguided policies, a negative comment, or an environment that denies the importance of one's experiences. In the end, all their voices challenge us as teachers and as a society to do the very best we can to ensure that educational equity is not an illusion but an achievable goal.

Conclusion

In this chapter, we have attempted to provide a definition and description of the *sociopolitical context of multicultural education*. As described, comprehending the sociopolitical context requires the following: (1) clarifying the goals and key terms of multicultural education; (2) dissolving myths about immigration and difference; (3) naming the social, economic, political, and ideological underpinnings of educational structures; (4) studying the current demographic "mosaic" of our nation; and (5) examining the political struggles of legislation and policy. This fifth effort was considered through a topic that is both current and controversial in schools and communities around the nation: the reauthorization of the federal Elementary and Secondary Education Act and its implications for education in a multicultural society. By rooting these challenges in qualitative research, these issues can be studied through ethnographic "lenses," specifically through case studies and snapshots of students who reflect the tremendous diversity of our school-age population. Such research can help us understand the effect of the sociopolitical context of schooling on various segments of the population as well as on the nation as a whole.

 To Think About

1. Can you describe the sociopolitical context of your own education? For you to become college-educated and to pursue a career in education, what circumstances cultivated both success and challenges for your family and your ancestors?

2. Consider the academic accomplishments of two of your current students: one who earns high marks in school and one who is struggling with grades. Compare what you know about the OSFs described by David Berliner's research. Does this influence the ways in which you and the school might support each student?

3. Consider the various iterations of the Elementary and Secondary Education Act. Compare the more recent Blueprint for Reform of ESEA to the former version, No Child Left Behind. Look specifically at Title I funding and consider how it influences the teaching and learning in your school. Does it influence your school differently than a school in a neighboring district? Does it seem to provide your students with more resources or fewer? What are the implications of federal policy on your local school?

Activities *for Personal, School, and Community Change*

1. Increase awareness in your school culture of the rich mosaic of diverse backgrounds and languages in U.S. society by developing a classroom activity that draws upon the wide array of resources available from the U.S. Census Bureau developed specifically for teachers at http://www.census.gov/dmd/www/teachers.html. Compare the U.S. demographics to your school's demographics. Place emphasis on diversity as an asset rather than as a "problem." Make your students' thinking visible to the entire school through bulletin board displays, presentations during morning announcements, school Web spaces, multimedia projections in the lunchroom, and the like.

2. Has your school responded to test preparation and budget constraints by cutting programming that supports students' multiple ways of knowing and expressing, such as art, music, clothing design, cooking, physical education, technology curriculum, theater, and so on? If so, help organize students, families, cultural workers, community artists, and other educators to provide after-school activities to increase students' multiple intelligence engagement as well as to maintain their attachment to the school environment.

2

Defining Multicultural Education for School Reform

by Sonia Nieto

In discussing multicultural education with teachers and other educators over many years, I have heard comments and remarks (examples in the box) that make it seem as if multicultural education is already "a done deal" or that we do not need it. Nothing could be further from the truth. In fact, statements such as these reflect a profound misunderstanding of multicultural education.

Multicultural education is an essential component of school reform. Nevertheless, when it is mentioned, many people first think of lessons in human relations and sensitivity training, units about ethnic holidays, education in inner-city schools, or food festivals. If multicultural education is limited to these issues, the potential for substantive change in schools is severely diminished. On the other hand, multicultural education, when broadly conceptualized, can lead to more understanding and empathy. It can also help to address the four areas of potential conflict and inequity to be addressed in Part

> "We don't need multicultural education here; most of our students are White."
>
> "I don't see color. All my students are the same to me."
>
> "We shouldn't talk about racism in school because it has nothing to do with learning. Besides, it'll just make the kids feel bad."
>
> "Let's not focus on negative things. Can't we all just get along?"
>
> "I want to include multicultural education in my curriculum, but there's just no time for it."
>
> "Oh, yes, we have multicultural education here: We celebrate Black History Month, and there's an annual Diversity Dinner."
>
> "Multicultural education is just therapy for Black students."
>
> "Multicultural education became irrelevant after 9/11. It's divisive because it focuses on differences. Now, more than ever, we need to stress our similarities."

2—namely, racism and discrimination, inequitable structural conditions in schools and society, the impact of culture on learning, and language diversity.

Why School Reform?

This chapter proposes a definition of multicultural education as an essential element of school reform. The definition is based on the context and terminology discussed

Alex Demarjian, Jorge Piccole, Elliot Thomas, Phoebe Weissblum in Dawn Southworth's art class at Glen Urquhart School, Beverly, Massachusetts. *Self-portraits*. Linoleum prints. 2010.

in the preceding chapters, and it analyzes seven primary characteristics included in the definition, characteristics that underscore the role that multicultural education can play in reforming schools and providing an equal and excellent education for all students. Emerging from the reality of persistent problems in our nation's schools, it especially addresses the lack of achievement among students of diverse backgrounds and emphasizes the context and process of education rather than viewing multicultural education as an add-on or luxury disconnected from the everyday lives of students.

At the same time, we need to stress that multicultural education is not a panacea for all educational ills. Because schools are part of our communities, they reflect the stratification and social inequities of the larger society. As long as this is the case, no school program alone, no matter how broadly conceptualized, can change things completely. Multicultural education will not cure underachievement, eliminate boring and irrelevant curriculum, or stop vandalism. It will not automatically motivate families to participate in schools, reinvigorate tired and dissatisfied teachers, or guarantee a lower dropout rate. Only by addressing inequities in the larger society can we hope to solve these problems.

Despite these caveats, when multicultural education is conceptualized as broad-based school reform, it can offer hope for real change. Multicultural education in a sociopolitical context is both richer and more complex than simple lessons on getting along or units on ethnic festivals. By focusing on major conditions contributing to underachievement, multicultural education, as defined here, permits educators to explore alternatives to a system that promotes failure for too many students. Such an exploration can lead to the creation of a richer and more productive school climate and a deeper awareness of the role of culture, language, and power in learning. Seen in this comprehensive way, educational success for all students is a realistic goal rather than an impossible ideal.

 # A Definition of Multicultural Education

In spite of some differences among major theorists, during the past 40 years since multicultural education first developed, there has been remarkable consistency in the educational field about its goals, purposes, and reasons.[1] But no definition of multicultural education can truly capture all its complexities. The definition I present here reflects one way of conceptualizing the issues; it is based on my many years of experience with students, teachers, researchers, and teacher educators. Although the definition includes seven characteristics that I believe are essential in multicultural education, you might come up with just three, or with 15. The point is not to develop a definitive way to understand multicultural education but instead to encourage you to think about the interplay of societal and school structures and contexts and how they influence learning.

What I believe *is* essential is an emphasis on the sociopolitical context of education and a rejection of the notion that multicultural education is either a superficial addition of content to the curriculum or, alternatively, the magic pill that will do away with all educational problems. In the process of considering my definition of multicultural education, I hope that it will serve to foster further dialogue and reflection among you and your colleagues so that you will develop your own ideas, priorities, and perspectives.

I define multicultural education in a sociopolitical context as follows:

> Multicultural education is a process of comprehensive school reform and basic education for all students. It challenges and rejects racism and other forms of discrimination in schools and society and accepts and affirms the pluralism (ethnic, racial, linguistic, religious, economic, gender, and sexual orientation, among others) that students, their communities, and teachers reflect. Multicultural education permeates the school's curriculum and instructional strategies as well as the interactions among teachers, students, and families and the very way that schools conceptualize the nature of teaching and learning. Because it uses critical pedagogy as its underlying philosophy and focuses on knowledge, reflection, and action (praxis) as the basis for social change, multicultural education promotes democratic principles of social justice.

The seven basic characteristics of multicultural education in this definition are:

Multicultural education is antiracist education.

Multicultural education is basic education.

Multicultural education is important for all students.

Multicultural education is pervasive.

Multicultural education is education for social justice.

Multicultural education is a process.

Multicultural education is critical pedagogy.

Multicultural Education Is Antiracist Education

Antiracism, indeed antidiscrimination in general, is at the very core of a multicultural perspective. The antiracist nature of multicultural education must be kept in mind because, in many schools, even some that espouse a multicultural philosophy, only superficial aspects of this philosophy are apparent. Celebrations of ethnic festivals are the extent of multicultural education programs in some schools. In others, sincere attempts to decorate bulletin boards with what is thought to be a multicultural perspective end up perpetuating the worst kind of stereotypes. Even where there are serious attempts to develop a truly pluralistic environment, it is not unusual to find incongruencies. In some schools, for instance, the highest academic tracks are overwhelmingly White, the lowest are populated primarily by students of color, and girls are nonexistent or invisible in calculus and physics classes. These strategies may claim to be multicultural but they fail to take an explicitly antiracist and antidiscrimination perspective.

Because many people erroneously assume that a school's multicultural program automatically takes care of racism, we stress that multicultural education *must be consciously antiracist*. Writing about multicultural education 30 years ago, when the field was fairly new, Meyer Weinberg asserted:

> Most multicultural materials deal wholly with the cultural distinctiveness of various groups and little more. Almost never is there any sustained attention to the ugly realities of systematic discrimination against the same group that also happens to utilize quaint clothing, fascinating toys, delightful fairy tales, and delicious food. Responding to racist attacks and defamation is also part of the culture of the group under study.[2]

Being antiracist and antidiscriminatory means being mindful of how some students are favored over others in school policies and practices such as the curriculum, choice of materials, sorting policies, and teachers' interactions and relationships with students and their families. Consequently, to be inclusive and balanced, multicultural curriculum must, by definition, be antiracist. Teaching does not become more honest and critical simply by becoming more inclusive, but this is an important first step in ensuring that students have access to a wide variety of viewpoints. Although the beautiful and heroic aspects of our history should be taught, so must the ugly and exclusionary. Rather than viewing the world through rose-colored glasses, antiracist multicultural education forces teachers and students to take a long, hard look at everything as it was and is, instead of just how we wish it were.

Too many schools avoid confronting, in an honest and direct way, the negative aspects of history, the arts, and science. Michelle Fine has called this the "fear of naming," and it is part of the system of silencing in public schools.[3] Related to the fear of naming is the insistence of schools on "sanitizing" the curriculum, or what Jonathan Kozol many years ago called "tailoring" important men and women for school use. Kozol described how schools manage to take our most exciting and memorable heroes and bleed the life and spirit completely out of them because it can be dangerous, he wrote, to teach a history "studded with so many bold, and revolutionary, and subversive, and exhilarating men and women." He described how, instead, schools drain these heroes of their passions, glaze them over with an implausible veneer, place them on lofty pedestals, and then tell "incredibly dull stories" about them.[4] Although he wrote these words many years ago, Kozol could just as well be writing about education in many of today's U.S. schools.

The process of sanitizing is nowhere more evident than in depictions of Martin Luther King, Jr. In attempting to make him palatable to the U.S. mainstream, schools have made King a milquetoast. The only thing most children know about him is that he kept "having a dream." School bulletin boards are full of ethereal pictures of Dr. King surrounded by clouds. If children get to read or hear any of his speeches at all, it is his "I Have a Dream" speech. As inspirational as this speech is, it is only one of his notable accomplishments. Rare indeed are allusions to his early and consistent opposition to the Vietnam War; his strong criticism of unbridled capitalism, and the connections he made near the end of his life among racism, capitalism, and war. This sanitization of Martin Luther King, a man full of passion and life, renders him an oversimplified, lifeless figure, in the process making him a "safe hero."

Most of the heroes we present to our children are either those in the mainstream or those who have become safe through the process of what Kozol referred to as "tailoring." Others who have fought for social justice are often downplayed, maligned, or ignored. For example, although John Brown's actions in defense of the liberation of enslaved people are considered noble by many, in most history books he is presented, at best, as somewhat of a crazed idealist. Nat Turner is another example. The slave revolt that he led deserves a larger place in our history, if only to acknowledge that enslaved people fought against their own oppression and were not simply passive victims. However, Turner's name and role in U.S. history are usually overlooked, and Abraham Lincoln is presented as the Great Emancipator, as if he was single-handedly responsible for the abolition of slavery (and with little acknowledgment of his own inconsistent ideas about race and equality). Nat Turner is not considered a safe hero; Abraham Lincoln is.

A powerful example of reclaiming one's history was recounted by Rebecca Geary, a school administrator in Massachusetts and a former graduate student on whose master's thesis committee I served. In writing about her great-great-grandfather, Moses Hunter, in her master's thesis, she recounts that he

> pounded his fist upon the table when he heard my father sharing his school lesson about how Lincoln "freed the slaves." "Nobody freed me, sir! I earned my freedom with a pitchfork and a knife," he bellowed in frustrated rage at my father's misinformation.[5]

To be antiracist also means to work affirmatively to combat racism. It means making antiracism and antidiscrimination explicit parts of the curriculum and teaching young people skills in confronting racism. A school that is truly committed to a multicultural philosophy will closely examine both its policies and the attitudes and behaviors of its staff to determine how these might discriminate against some students. The focus on school policies and practices makes it evident that multicultural education is about more than the perceptions and beliefs of individual teachers and other educators. Multicultural education is antiracist because it exposes racist and discriminatory practices in schools.

Racism is seldom mentioned in school (it is bad, a dirty word) and therefore is not dealt with. Unfortunately, many teachers think that simply having lessons in getting along or celebrating Human Relations Week will make students non-racist or nondiscriminatory in general. But it is impossible to be untouched by racism, sexism, linguicism, heterosexism, ageism, anti-Semitism, classism, ableism, and ethnocentrism in a society characterized by all of them. To expect schools to be an oasis of sensitivity and understanding in the midst of this strat-ification is unrealistic. Therefore, part of the mission of the school becomes cre-ating the environment and encouragement that makes inequality a source of action. Teaching the missing or fragmented parts of our history is crucial to achiev-ing this mission.

Although White students may be uncomfortable with discussions about race, broaching this discussion can actually be a positive pedagogical approach to help students think about their position in society and their responsibilities to combat racism and other biases. Beverly Daniel Tatum's groundbreaking work on bringing discussions of race out of the closet proposes discussing race and racism within the framework of racial and cultural identity theory. Doing so, she contends, can help students and teachers focus on how racism negatively affects all people and can pro-vide a sense of hope for positive changes.[6]

What about teachers? Because many teachers have had little experience with diversity, discussions of racism often threaten to disrupt their deeply held ideals of fair play and equality. As a result, fruitful classroom discussions about discrim-ination rarely happen because many teachers are uneasy with these topics. If this continues to be the case, neither unfair individual behaviors nor institutional poli-cies and practices in schools will change and students of disempowered groups will continue to bear the brunt of these kinds of inequities. The dilemma is how to challenge the silence about race and racism so that teachers can enter into mean-ingful and constructive dialogue with their students. For example, in research with teachers from around the country, Karen McLean Donaldson found that many teachers were in denial about racism and its effects in schools. On the other hand, those who became active in antiracist projects broadened their understanding and were able to use their new skills in creating affirming learning environments for all their students.[7]

One of the reasons schools are reluctant to tackle racism and discrimination is that these are disturbing topics for those who have traditionally benefited by their race, gender, and social class, among other advantageous differences. Because instruction in, and discussion of, such topics place people in the role of either the victimizer or the victimized, an initial and logical reaction, for example, of European American teachers and students in discussing race is to feel guilty. But being antiracist does not mean flailing about in guilt and remorse. Although this reaction is under-standable, remaining at this level is immobilizing. Teachers and students need to move beyond guilt to a state of invigorated awareness and informed confidence in which they take personal and group action for positive change rather than hide behind feelings of remorse.

The primary victims of racism and discrimination are those who suffer its immediate consequences, but racism and discrimination are destructive and demeaning to everyone. Although not everyone is directly guilty of discrimination, we are all responsible for combating it. This means that working actively for social justice is *everyone's* business. Yet it is often the victims of racism and other kinds of discrimination who are left to act on their own. Everybody loses when a particular group of students is made a scapegoat. Rebecca Florentina's case study, which follows Chapter 5, is a good example. As a lesbian, Rebecca felt the need to personally confront the heterosexual biases in her school, but this should have been viewed as everyone's responsibility. Indeed, we will have come a long way when everybody feels this same obligation.

Multicultural Education Is Basic Education

One of the major stumbling blocks to implementing a broadly conceptualized multicultural education is the ossification of the "canon" in our schools. When multicultural education is peripheral to the core curriculum, it is perceived as irrelevant to basic education. Consequently, given the recurring concern for teaching the "basics," multicultural education must be understood as basic to an excellent education. That is, multicultural literacy is just as indispensable for living in today's world as reading, writing, arithmetic, and computer literacy.

The canon, as generally understood in contemporary U.S. education, assumes that the knowledge that is most worthwhile is already in place. This notion explains the popularity of E. D. Hirsch's series *What Every* [*First, Second, Third . . .*] *Grader Needs to Know*.[8] Geared primarily to parents, this series builds on the fear that their children will not measure up if they do not possess the core knowledge (usually in the form of facts) that they need to succeed in school. According to this rather narrow view, the basics have, in effect, already been defined, and they are inevitably European, male, and upper class in origin and conception. In a thoughtful response to Hirsch's view of cultural literacy, Eugene Provenzo faults Hirsch for a limited and rigid understanding of cultural literacy that is ultimately impoverished, elitist, antidemocratic, and even un-American because it excludes so much that is uniquely American.[9]

The alternative to multicultural education is monocultural education, which reflects only one reality and is biased toward the dominant group. Unfortunately, monocultural education is the order of the day in too many of our schools. Typically, what students learn represents only a fraction of what is available knowledge, and those who decide what is most important make choices that are influenced by their own limited background, education, and experiences. Because the viewpoints of so many are left out, monocultural education is, at best, an incomplete education. In fact, nothing is more harmful or divisive than a monocultural education because it excludes many people and perspectives from schools' curricula and pedagogy. A monocultural education deprives all students of the diversity that is part of our world. What is needed is a true multicultural literacy. In the words of James A. Banks,

> Multicultural literacy consists of the skills and abilities to identify the creators of knowledge and their interests . . . to uncover the assumptions of knowledge, to view knowledge from diverse ethnic and cultural perspectives, and to use knowledge to guide action that will create a humane and just world.[10]

About Terminology

The Conundrum of Race

The concept of race has received a great deal of criticism because, in a biological sense, race does not exist at all. There is no scientific evidence that so-called racial groups differ in biologically or genetically significant ways. Differences that do exist are primarily social; that is, they are based on one's experiences within a particular cultural group. Thus, it is now generally accepted that the very concept of race is a social construction; that is, a racial group is socially and not biologically determined. There is really only one race—the human race. Historically, the concept of race has been used to oppress entire groups of people for their supposed differences.

Although race as a notion is dubious at best, racism is not. Consequently, the problem with using terms that emphasize only culture is that the very real issue of racism in our society is then obscured. Our use of terminology in this text is in no way meant to do so, but rather to stress that the notion of race alone does not define people. For example, African Americans and Haitians are both Black. They share some basic cultural values and are both subjected to racist attitudes and behaviors, but the particular life experiences, native language usage, and ethnicity of each group is overlooked or even denied if we simply call both groups Black rather than also identifying them ethnically.

We have decided to use terms that refer specifically to so-called racial groups when such terms are warranted. In speaking of segregated schools, for example, it makes sense to refer to Black and White students rather than to African American and European American students because color is the salient issue here. In this way, we hope to underscore the fact that there are always differences of opinion about the use of various terms.

We have capitalized the terms *White* and *Black* because they refer to groups of people, as do terms such as *Latino, Asian*, and *African*. As such, they deserve to be capitalized. Although these are not the scientific terms for so-called racial groups, terms such as *Negroid* and *Caucasoid* or *Caucasian* are no longer used in everyday speech or are rejected because of their negative connotations, as well as their inaccuracy. For example, all people with light skin are not from the Caucasus region bordering Europe and Asia.

Because race is a social construction, some scholars who write about it have made the decision to use the term only in quotation marks ("race") to underscore its social construction. We have decided not to do so in this book for several reasons. First, it can be reasonably argued that all differences are socially constructed (social class, gender, ethnicity, sexual orientation, and so on) and that to separate race from the others is arbitrary. The second reason is a more practical one: Because of the many references to race, gender, social class, ethnicity, and other differences in this text, readers would find it disconcerting to confront a flurry of quotation marks around words in paragraph after paragraph about "race," "gender," "social class," and so forth.

The idea that there is a static and sacred knowledge that must be mastered is especially evident in the arts and social sciences. For instance, art history classes rarely consider other countries besides France's, Italy's, and sometimes England's Great Masters, yet surely other nations in the world have also had great masters. "Classical music" is another example. What is called "classical music" is actually European classical music. Africa, Asia, and Latin America define their classical music in different ways. This same ethnocentrism is found in our history books, which portray Europeans and European Americans as the "actors" and all others as the recipients, bystanders, or bit players of history. The canon, as it currently stands, is unrealistic and incomplete because history is never as one-sided as it appears in most of our schools' curricula.

This is not to say that the concern that the canon tries to address is not a genuine one. Modern-day knowledge is so dispersed and compartmentalized that our young people learn very little about commonalities in our history and culture. Nevertheless, proposing static curricula almost exclusively with European and European American referents, does little to expand our actual common culture. The point is that those who have been important in the evolution of our history, arts, literature, and science, yet who are invisible, should be made visible. Recent literature anthologies are a good example of the inclusion of more voices and perspectives than ever before. Did these people become "great writers" overnight, or was it simply that they were "buried" for too long?

If this is the case, no school can consider that it is doing a proper or complete job unless its students develop multicultural literacy. What such a conception means in practice will no doubt differ from school to school, but at the very least, we should expect all students to be fluent in a language other than their own; aware of the literature and arts of many different peoples; and conversant with the history and geography not only of the United States but also of African, Asian, Latin American, and European countries. Through such an education, we can expect students to develop social and intellectual skills that help them understand and empathize with a wide diversity of people. Nothing can be more basic than this.

The curriculum is not the only thing that needs changing for multicultural education to become basic. Even more significant is the context in which students learn, or fail to learn. In an article I wrote a few years ago, I proposed that we need to ask "profoundly multicultural questions," that is, questions that at first blush might not appear to be "multicultural" but that are in fact profoundly and fundamentally multicultural.[11] Among others, these include questions such as "Do all students have access to calculus [physics, or any other high-status course]?" and "Is the bilingual [ESL, special ed, or any other program with low status] in the basement?" These are "profoundly multicultural questions" precisely because they concern *access* and *equity* rather than simply a change in course content. All students deserve a chance at an equitable and high-quality education, and this is what it means when multicultural education is "basic education."

Multicultural Education Is Important for All Students

There is a widespread perception—or rather, misperception—that multicultural education is only for students of color, for urban students, or for so-called disadvantaged or at-risk students. This belief probably grew from the roots of multicultural education: the civil rights and equal education movements of the 1960s. During that era, the primary objective of multicultural education was to address the needs of students who historically had been most neglected or miseducated by the schools, especially students of color. Those who first promoted multicultural education firmly believed that attention needed to be given to developing curriculum and materials that reflected these students' histories, cultures, and experiences. This thinking was historically necessary and is understandable even today, given the great curricular imbalance and learning gaps that continue to exist in most schools.

More recently, a broader conceptualization of multicultural education has gained acceptance: All students are miseducated to the extent that they receive only a partial and biased education. Although it is true that the primary victims of biased education are those who are invisible in the curriculum and whose schooling experiences are inequitable, everyone loses when education is biased. Important female figures, for example, are still largely absent, except in special courses on women's history that are few and far between. Working-class history is also absent in almost all U.S. curricula. The children of the working class are deprived not only of a more forthright education but, more important, of a place in history, and students of all social class backgrounds are deprived of a more honest and complete view of our past. Likewise, there is a pervasive and impenetrable silence concerning lesbian, gay, bisexual, and transgender (LGBT) people in most schools, not just in the curriculum but also in extracurricular activities. The result is that gay and lesbian students, as well as those with family members who identify as LGBT, are placed at risk in terms of social well-being and academic achievement.[12]

Teachers in primarily White schools might think that multicultural education is not meant for their students. They could not be more wrong. White students too receive only a partial education, which helps to legitimate their cultural blindness. Seeing only themselves, they may believe that they are the norm and thus most important and everyone else is secondary and less important. A book that challenges this perception, *What If All the Kids Are White,* provides excellent strategies and resources for teachers working in mostly White communities.[13]

Males also receive an incomplete education because they (not to mention their female peers) learn little about women in their schooling. The children of the wealthy learn that the wealthy and powerful are the real makers of history, the ones who have left their mark on civilization. Heterosexual students receive the message that gay and lesbian students should be ostracized because they are deviant and immoral. Only the able-bodied are reflected in most curricula, save for exceptions such as Helen Keller, who are presented as either bigger than life or as sources of pity. The humanity of all students is jeopardized as a result.

Multicultural education is, by definition, *inclusive.* Because it is *about* all people, it is also *for* all people, regardless of their ethnicity, ability, social class, language, sexual orientation, religion, gender, race, or other difference. It can even be convincingly argued that students from the dominant culture need multicultural education more than others because they are generally the most miseducated or uneducated about diversity. For example, European American youths often think that they do not even have a culture, at least not in the same sense that easily culturally identifiable youths do. At the same time, they feel that their ways of living, doing things, believing, and acting are "normal." Anything else is "ethnic" and exotic.

Feeling as they do, young people from dominant groups are prone to develop an unrealistic view of the world and of their place in it. These are the children who do not question, for example, the fact that everyone, Christian or not, gets days off at Christmas and Easter and that the holidays of other religions are given little attention in our calendars and school schedules. They may automatically assume that all children are raised by heterosexual, biological parents and may be surprised to learn that many children are instead raised by just one parent, adoptive parents, grandparents, foster parents, or lesbian or gay parents. Whereas children from dominated groups may develop feelings of inferiority based on their schooling, dominant-group children may develop feelings of superiority. Both responses are based on incomplete and inaccurate information about the complexity and diversity of the world, and both are harmful.

In spite of this, multicultural education continues to be thought of by many educators as education for the "culturally different" or the "disadvantaged." Teachers in predominantly European American schools, for example, may feel it is not important or necessary to teach their students anything about the civil rights movement. Likewise, only in scattered bilingual programs in Mexican American communities are students exposed to literature by Mexican and Mexican American authors, and ethnic studies classes are only, if at all, offered at high schools with a high percentage of students of color.

The thinking behind these actions is paternalistic as well as misinformed. Because anything remotely digressing from the "regular" (European American) curriculum is automatically considered soft by some educators, a traditional response to making a curriculum multicultural is to water it down. Poor pedagogical decisions are then based on the premise that so-called disadvantaged students need a watered-down version of the "real" curriculum, whereas more privileged children can handle the "regular" or more academically challenging curriculum. But making a curriculum multicultural inevitably enriches, not dilutes, it. All students would be enriched by reading the poetry of Langston Hughes or the stories of Gary Soto, by being fluent in a second language, or by understanding the history of Islam.

Multicultural Education Is Pervasive

Multicultural education is neither an activity that happens at a set period of the day nor another subject area to be "covered." Having a "multicultural teacher" who goes from class to class in the same way as the music or art teacher is not what multicultural education should be about either. If this is a school's concept of multicultural education, it is little wonder that teachers sometimes decide that it is a frill they cannot afford.

A true multicultural approach is pervasive. It permeates everything: the school climate, physical environment, curriculum, and relationships among teachers and students and community. It is apparent in every lesson, curriculum guide, unit, bulletin board, and letter that is sent home. It can be seen in the process by which books, audiovisual aids, and multimedia materials are acquired for the library; in the games played during recess; and in the lunch that is served. *Multicultural education is a philosophy, a way of looking at the world,* not simply a program or a class or a teacher. In this comprehensive way, multicultural education helps us rethink school reform.

■ ■ ■ ■ ■ ■   ## What You Can Do
"Multiculturalize" Your Lessons

Be on the lookout for resources—books, articles, artwork, people, and organizations—that can help you make your curriculum more multicultural. Try to adapt at least one lesson a week and make sure that you do so with all the subject matters you teach, whether language arts, mathematics, social studies, art, a foreign language, science, or other content areas.

What might a multicultural philosophy mean in the way that schools are organized? For one, it would probably mean the end of rigid forms of ability tracking, which inevitably favors some students over others. It would also mean that the complexion of the school, both literally and figuratively, would change. That is, schools would be desegregated rather than segregated along lines of race and social class as they are now. In addition, there would be an effort to have the entire school staff be more representative of our nation's diversity. Pervasiveness would be apparent in the great variety and creativity of instructional strategies, so that students from all cultural groups, and females as well as males, would benefit from methods other than the traditional. The curriculum would be completely overhauled and would include the histories, viewpoints, and insights of many different peoples and both males and females. Topics usually considered "dangerous" could be talked about in classes, and students would be encouraged to become critical thinkers. Textbooks and other instructional materials would also reflect a pluralistic perspective. Teachers, families, and students would have the opportunity to work together to influence the school's policies and practices, including designing motivating and multiculturally appropriate curricula.

In other, less global but no less important ways, the multicultural school would probably look vastly different. For example, the lunchroom might offer a variety of international meals, not because they are exotic delights but because they are the foods people in the community eat daily. Sports and games from all over the world might be played, and not all would be competitive. Children would not be punished for speaking their native language. On the contrary, parents would be encouraged to continue speaking their native language at home, and students would be encouraged to do so at school, and it would be used in their instruction as well. In summary, the school would be a learning environment in which curriculum, pedagogy, and outreach are all consistent with a broadly conceptualized multicultural philosophy.

Multicultural Education Is Education for Social Justice

All good education connects theory with reflection and action, which is what Brazilian educator Paulo Freire defined as *praxis*.[14] Developing a multicultural perspective means learning how to think in more inclusive and expansive ways, reflecting on what is learned, and applying that learning to real situations. Nearly a century ago, educational philosopher John Dewey described what happens when education is not connected to reflection and action when he wrote "information severed from thoughtful action is dead, a mind-crushing load."[15] Multicultural education invites students and teachers to put their learning into action for social justice (for a definition of social justice, see Chapter 1). Multicultural education with a social justice perspective also means learning to question power structures and the status quo. Whether debating a difficult issue, developing a community newspaper, starting a collaborative program at a local senior center, or organizing a petition for the removal of a potentially dangerous waste treatment plant in the neighborhood, students learn that they have power, collectively and individually, to make change. This aspect of multicultural education fits in particularly well with the developmental level of young people who, starting in the middle elementary grades, are very conscious of what is fair and unfair. If their pronounced sense of justice is not channeled appropriately, the result can be anger, resentment, alienation, or dropping out of school physically or psychologically.

Preparing students for active membership in a democracy has frequently been cited by schools as a major educational goal. But few schools serve as sites of apprenticeship for democracy. Policies and practices such as inflexible ability grouping, inequitable testing, monocultural curricula, and unimaginative pedagogy contradict this lofty aim. In some schools, democratic practices are found only in textbooks and are confined to discussions of the American Revolution, and the chance for students to practice day-to-day democracy is minimal. The result is that students in many schools perceive the claim of democracy to be a hollow and irrelevant issue. Henry Giroux, for example, has suggested that what he calls "the discourse of democracy" has been trivialized to mean things such as uncritical patriotism and mandatory pledges to the flag that the 9/11 disaster has exacerbated.[16]

The fact that controversial topics such as power and inequality are rarely discussed in schools should come as no surprise. As institutions, schools are charged with maintaining the status quo, and discussing such issues might seem to threaten the status quo. But schools are also expected to promote equality. Exposing the contradictions between democratic ideals and actual manifestations of inequality makes many people uncomfortable, including some educators. Still, such matters are at the heart of a broadly conceptualized multicultural perspective because the subject matter of schooling is society, with all its wrinkles and warts and contradictions. Ethics and the distribution of power, status, and rewards are basic societal concerns; education *must* address them.

Although the connection between multicultural education and students' rights and responsibilities in a democracy is unmistakable, many young people do not learn about these responsibilities, or about the challenges of democracy and the central role of citizens in ensuring and maintaining the privileges of democracy. Results from a study about the First Amendment, in which over 112,000 high school students were surveyed, is a chilling example of how little students understand about democracy. The project, which was funded by the John S. and James L. Knight Foundation, found that when the First Amendment was quoted to students, more than one-third of them felt that it went too far in the rights it guarantees. The report concluded that "[i]t appears, in fact, that our nation's high schools are failing their students when it comes to instilling in them appreciation for the First Amendment."[17] In this situation, social justice becomes an empty concept.

Multicultural education can have a great impact in helping to turn this situation around. A multicultural perspective presumes that classrooms should not simply allow discussions that focus on social justice but also welcome them and even plan actively for such discussions. These discussions might center on issues that adversely and disproportionately affect disenfranchised communities—poverty, discrimination, war, the national budget—and what students can do to address these problems. Because these problems are pluralistic, education must, of necessity, be multicultural. In fact, addressing such problems is necessary because, according to Homi Bhabha, "[I]t is from those who have suffered the sentence of history—subjugation, domination, diaspora, displacement—that we learn our most enduring lessons for living and thinking."[18]

Multicultural Education Is a Process

Curriculum and materials represent the content of multicultural education, but multicultural education is, above all, a process. It is ongoing and dynamic because no one ever stops becoming a multicultural person and knowledge is never complete. This means that there is no established canon that is set in stone. Second, multicultural education is a process because it primarily involves relationships among people. The sensitivity and understanding teachers show their students are more crucial in promoting student learning than the facts and figures they may know about different ethnic and cultural groups. Also, multicultural education is a process because it concerns intangibles such as expectations of student achievement, learning environments, students' learning preferences, and other cultural variables that are absolutely essential for schools to understand if they are to become successful with all students.

The dimension of multicultural education as a process is too often relegated to a secondary position because content is easier to handle and has speedier results. For instance, staging an assembly program on Black History Month is easier than eliminating tracking: The former involves adding extracurricular content, and, although this is important and necessary, it is not as decisive at challenging fundamental perceptions about intelligence, ability, social class, and race through the elimination of tracking. Another example: Changing a basal reader is easier than developing higher expectations for all students. The former involves substituting one book for another; the latter involves changing perceptions, behaviors, and knowledge—not an easy task. As a result, the processes of multicultural education are generally more complex, more politically volatile, and even more threatening to vested interests than introducing "controversial" content.

Because multicultural education is a process, it must debunk simplistic and erroneous conventional wisdom as well as dismantle policies and practices that are disadvantageous for some students at the expense of others. Nothing short of a complete restructuring of curricula and the reorganization of schools is required. The process is complex, problematic, controversial, and time consuming, but it is one in which teachers and schools must engage to make their schools truly multicultural.

Multicultural Education Is Critical Pedagogy

Knowledge is neither neutral nor apolitical, yet it is generally treated as if it were. Consequently, knowledge taught in our schools tends to reflect the kind of knowledge that is least controversial. Students may leave school with the impression that all major conflicts have already been resolved, but history, including educational history, is still full of great debates, controversies, and ideological struggles. These controversies and conflicts are often left at the schoolhouse door.

Defining Critical Pedagogy

A multicultural approach values diversity and encourages critical thinking, reflection, and action. Through this process, students are empowered both individually and collectively to become active learners. This is the basis of critical pedagogy. Its opposite is what Paulo Freire called "domesticating education"—education that emphasizes passivity, acceptance, and submissiveness. According to Freire, education for domestication is a process of "transferring knowledge," whereas education for liberation is one of "transforming action."[19] Education that is liberating encourages students to take risks, to be curious, and to question. Critical literacy, which developed from critical pedagogy and focuses specifically on language, has a similar goal. According to educational researcher Barbara Comber,

> When teachers and students are engaged in critical literacy, they will be asking complicated questions about language and power, about people and lifestyle, about morality and ethics, about who is advantaged by the way things are and who is disadvantaged.[20]

Critical literacy is, at its core, about understanding and questioning power, a concept that is beautifully articulated in *Literacy and Power,* a recent book by Hilary Janks.[21] Although many of the examples in her book refer to South Africa—both before and after Apartheid—the lessons are universal and certainly applicable to U.S. classrooms.

Critical pedagogy is not new, although it has been referred to by other terms in other times. In our country, precursors to critical pedagogy can be found in the work of African American educators such as Carter Woodson and W. E. B. DuBois.[22] In Brazil, the historic work of Paulo Freire influenced literacy and liberation movements throughout the world. Even before Freire, critical pedagogy was being practiced in other parts of the world. Almost half a century ago, Sylvia Ashton-Warner, teaching Maori children in New Zealand, found that the curriculum, materials, viewpoints, and pedagogy that had been used in educating them were all borrowed from the dominant culture. Because Maori children had been failed dismally by New Zealand schools, Ashton-Warner developed a strategy for literacy based on the children's experiences and interests. Calling it an "organic approach," she taught children how to read by using the words *they* wanted to learn. Whereas basal readers, having little to do with Maori children's experiences, were mechanistic instruments that imposed severe limitations on the students' creativity and expressiveness, Ashton-Warner's approach, based on what children knew and wanted to know, was extraordinarily successful.[23]

■ ■ ■ ■ ■ ■ **What You Can Do**

Learn About, and Practice, Critical Pedagogy

Become familiar with the books and resources mentioned throughout this text. Go to the Teaching for Change (teachingforchange.org) and Rethinking Schools (rethinkingschools.org) websites to get ideas about how to change your curriculum to reflect the ideas discussed in this section. Share your ideas with a colleague and get feedback before using them with your students. Communicate with your students' parents so they know what's happening and why.

As this example illustrates, every educational decision made at any level, whether by a teacher or by an entire school system, reflects the political ideology and worldview of the decision maker. Decisions to dismantle tracking, discontinue standardized tests, lengthen the school day, use one reading program rather than another, study literature from the Harlem Renaissance or Elizabethan period (or both), or use learning centers or rows of chairs (or both) all reflect a particular view of learners and of education. In addition, all the decisions educators make, no matter how neutral or trivial they may seem, can have an impact on the lives and experiences of our students. This is true of the curriculum, books, and other materials we provide for them. State and local guidelines and mandates may limit what particular schools and teachers choose to teach, and this too is a political decision.

Critical pedagogy is also an exploder of myths. It helps to expose and demystify as well as demythologize some of the truths that we take for granted and to analyze them critically and carefully. Justice for all, equal treatment under the law, and equal educational opportunity, although certainly ideals worth believing in and striving for, are not always the reality. The problem is that we teach them as if they are, and were always, real and true, with no exceptions. Critical pedagogy allows us to have faith in these ideals while critically examining the discrepancies between the ideal and the reality.

Some Examples: The Content of the Curriculum

What is excluded from the curriculum is often as revealing as what is included. Much of the literature taught at the high school level, for instance, is still heavily male-oriented, European, and European American. The significance of women, people of color, and those who write in other languages (even if their work has been translated into English) is diminished, unintentionally or not. This is because history is generally written by the conquerors, not by the vanquished or by those who benefit least in society. The result is that history books are skewed in the direction of dominant groups in a society. When American Indian people write history books, they generally say that Columbus *invaded* rather than *discovered* this land, and that there was no heroic *westward expansion,* but rather an *eastern encroachment.* Mexican Americans often include references to Aztlán, the legendary land that was overrun by Europeans during this encroachment. Many Puerto Ricans remove the gratuitous word *granted* that appears in so many textbooks and explain that U.S. citizenship was instead *imposed,* and they emphasize that U.S. citizenship was opposed by even the two houses of the legislature that existed in Puerto Rico in 1917. African American historians tend to describe the active participation of enslaved Africans in their own liberation, and they often include accounts such as slave narratives to describe the rebellion and resistance of their people. Working-class people who know their history usually credit laborers rather than Andrew Carnegie with the tremendous building boom that occurred in the United States and the rapid growth of the U.S. economy during the late nineteenth century and early twentieth century. And Japanese Americans frequently cite racist hysteria, economic exploitation, and propaganda as major reasons for their internment in U.S. concentration camps during World War II.

Textbooks in all subject areas exclude information about unpopular perspectives or the perspectives of disempowered groups in our society. These are the "lies my teacher told me" to which James Loewen refers in his powerful critique of U.S. history textbooks. In a more recent book (*Teaching What Really Happened*), Loewen encourages teachers to get students motivated about history by avoiding "the tyranny of textbooks."[24] For instance, Thanksgiving is generally presented as an uncomplicated celebration in which Pilgrims and Indians shared the bounty of the harvest, but it is unlikely that the Wampanoags experienced Thanksgiving in this manner. One way to counter simplistic or one-sided views is to provide alternative or multiple views of the same topic. A book that does just this, published by the Boston Children's Museum, presents a multiplicity of perspectives on Thanksgiving, including the Wampanoag perspective. Another, *Rethinking Columbus,* from Rethinking Schools, is a treasure trove of ideas to combat the simplistic perspective often presented about American Indians.[25] (For a classroom example in which a middle school teacher and her students challenged the use of Native Americans as mascots, see Chapter 3.)

A major problem with a monocultural curriculum is that it gives students only one way of seeing the world. When reality is presented as static, finished, and flat, the underlying tensions, controversies, passions, and problems faced by people throughout history and today disappear. To be informed and active participants in a democratic society, students need to understand the complexity of the world and the many perspectives involved. That is, all students need to understand multiple perspectives and not only the viewpoints of dominant groups. Unless they do, students will continue to think of history as linear and fixed and to think of themselves as passive and unable to make changes in their communities and the larger society, or even in their personal interactions.

Let us consider some examples: The immigrant experience is generally treated as a romantic and successful odyssey rather than the traumatic, wrenching, and often less-than-idyllic situation it was (and still is) for so many. The experiences of non-European immigrants or those forcibly incorporated into the United States are usually presented as if they were identical to the experiences of Europeans, which they have not at all been. We can also be sure that, if the perspectives of women were taken seriously, the school curriculum would be altered dramatically. The historian Howard Zinn provides one of the few examples of such a multifaceted, multicultural, and complex history. In his classic, *A People's History of the United States* (most recently updated in 2005), we clearly see a history full of passion and conflict with voices rarely included in traditional history texts.[26]

Using a critical perspective, students learn that there is not just one way (or even two or three) of viewing issues. To explain what I mean by "using a critical perspective," let me be facetious and use the number 17 to explain it: Let's say there are at least 17 ways of understanding reality, and, until we have learned all of them, we have only part of the truth. The point is that there are multiple perspectives on every issue, but most of us have learned only the "safe" or standard way of interpreting events and issues.

A multicultural perspective does not simply operate on the principle of substituting one "truth" or perspective for another. Rather, it reflects on multiple and contradictory perspectives to understand reality more fully. The historian Ronald Takaki explained it in this way: "The intellectual purpose of multiculturalism is a more accurate understanding of who we are as Americans."[27] Critical pedagogy thus acknowledges rather than suppresses diversity of all kinds. Thus, in our pluralistic society, teachers and students need to learn to understand even those viewpoints with which they may disagree—not to practice "political correctness," but to develop a critical perspective about what they hear, read, or see.

Critical Pedagogy in Action

Ira Shor has proposed that critical pedagogy is more difficult precisely because it moves beyond academic discourse to reflection and action.[28] Yet the typical curriculum discourages students from thinking critically. In this sense, critical pedagogy takes courage. What does it mean to teach with courage? Some examples are in order. Vivian Vasquez, in her book *Negotiating Critical Literacies with Young Children*, documented her experiences in using a critical literacy approach with 3- to 5-year-olds. Among the many examples she cites, one is about what happened when the children in her class realized that a classmate had not eaten at the annual school barbecue because he was a vegetarian and only hot dogs and hamburgers had been served. On their own initiative—but having learned to confront social injustice—the students drew up a petition about providing vegetarian alternatives and gave it to the event committee. The next year, vegetarian alternatives were provided.

Mary Cowhey, in her book *Black Ants and Buddhists: Thinking Critically and Teaching Differently in the Elementary Grades*, gives numerous examples of how her 6- and 7-year-old students develop a critical perspective. In one case, she recounts that her young students wanted to be involved in a presidential campaign. Knowing that they could not vote until they were 18 years old, they decided that, rather than be passive bystanders, they would instead conduct a voter registration drive. The result was that they educated the community about the importance of voting and in the process registered 37 new voters. They then brought the voter registration cards to the town hall and met with the mayor to tell her about their project. A recent book edited by Cheryl Dozier, Peter Johnston, and Rebecca Rogers and based on their work in Albany, New York, describes in concrete terms how classroom teachers use critical literacy strategies with children about whose success other teachers might have had strong doubts. Another recent book, *Teaching for Joy and Justice*, by Linda Christensen, describes in moving detail some of the English language arts lessons she has done with high school students. These books also affirm that students of all ages, even the youngest, can learn to think critically and positively about their ability to effect change through their actions.[29] In these beautiful and hopeful books, teachers and researchers demonstrate that critical literacy is not about despair and anger but rather about joy and inclusion.

Other approaches that have successfully used the experiences of students are worth mentioning. The superb preschool curriculum first developed over two decades ago by Louise Derman-Sparks and the Anti-Bias Curriculum Task Force is especially noteworthy. Catherine Compton-Lilly, in her role as a first-grade teacher and later as a reading teacher, uses a critical perspective to develop classroom strategies to "change the world" by confronting assumptions about race, poverty, and culture. Instructional strategies based on students' languages, cultures, families, and communities are also included in wonderful books by the educational organizations Rethinking Schools (rethinkingschools.org) and Teaching for Change (teachingforchange.org). These, along with a growing number of other resources for prekindergarten through college, make it clear that critical pedagogy is a significant component of multicultural education for all ages.[30]

 ## Conclusion

In this chapter, I have described how multicultural education represents a way of rethinking school reform because it responds to many of the problematic factors leading to school underachievement and failure. When implemented comprehensively, multicultural education can transform and enrich the schooling of all young people. The definition reviewed in this chapter includes an understanding of multicultural education as antiracist, basic, inclusive, pervasive, and critical.

This discussion leads us to an intriguing insight: In the final analysis, multicultural education, as defined here, is simply good pedagogy. That is, all good education takes students seriously; uses their experiences as a basis for further learning; and helps them to develop into informed, critically aware, and empowered citizens. What is multicultural about this? To put it simply, in our multicultural society, all good education needs to take into account the diversity of our student population. Our world is increasingly interdependent, and all students need to understand their role in a global society, not simply in their small town, city, or nation. Multicultural education is a process that goes beyond the changing demographics in a particular country. It is more effective education for a changing world.

 ## To Think About

1. Why is it important for antiracism and antidiscrimination, in general, to be at the core of multicultural education?

2. How are European American students miseducated if they are not exposed to a multicultural curriculum? How are males miseducated if they do not learn about women in history?

3. Think of a number of curriculum ideas that conform to the definition of multicultural education as social justice. How might students be engaged through the curriculum to consider and act on issues of social justice? Give some specific examples.

4. How do you define multicultural education? Explain your definition.

 ## Activities *for Personal, School, and Community Change*

1. Prepare a public presentation on the benefits of multicultural education for your colleagues, a group of new teachers, or a group of parents. What might you include in your presentation to convince skeptics that multicultural education, broadly defined and implemented, is necessary for your school?

2. Ask to be on your school's hiring committee when the next teaching position becomes available. How can you use your influence to define the job qualifications and job description in a way that includes multicultural education? What should these be?

3. With a group of colleagues, develop an art, science, or math project that builds on multicultural education as critical pedagogy. How would you do this? In what activities would students be involved? How would these activities motivate them to think critically? Discuss the results with your colleagues.

Developing a Conceptual Framework for Multicultural Education

Kenny Blasser, Melissa Campbell, in Amanda Held's art class at Pembroke Community Middle School. Pembroke, Massachusetts. *Self-portraits*. Ink drawing, 2009.

"Educators need to know what happens in the world of the children with whom they work. They need to know the universe of their dreams, the language with which they skillfully defend themselves from the aggressiveness of their world, what they know independently of the school, and how they know it."

—Paulo Freire,
Teachers as Cultural Workers:
Letters to Those Who Dare Teach, 1998

Part 2 develops the conceptual framework for multicultural education. It considers issues such as racism and other biases, school organization and educational policies and practices, and cultural and linguistic differences. Although we cannot say whether any of these factors inevitably leads to students' success or failure, these issues need to be considered to understand how they may influence the educational experiences of students.

The 16 case studies and six snapshots in Chapters 3 through 10 highlight how these factors can influence academic success or failure. Although we have grouped the case studies with particular chapters in Parts 2 and 3 because of common themes, each case study raises numerous issues discussed in other chapters, too. For example, Linda Howard's case study is placed after Chapter 3 because it highlights not only the impact that racism can have on school achievement but also issues of teacher expectations and school climate. At the same time, Linda's case study also explores issues of family involvement, a topic covered in Chapter 4. Besides addressing racism and other institutional barriers to learning, Chapter 3 also explores the influence of the teachers' and schools' expectations on students. In addition, this chapter includes a brief snapshot and is followed by three case studies that underscore these issues.

Chapter 4 considers how school organization, policies, and practices—including tracking, testing, pedagogy, and curriculum—may affect student learning. Case studies that emphasize curriculum and other school-related factors follow Chapter 4.

Chapter 5 explores the relationship between cultural issues and education, and Chapter 6 focuses on linguistic diversity and schools' responses to it. These chapters are followed by case studies that consider the influence of cultural and linguistic diversity on student learning.

The final chapter in Part 2 (Chapter 7) presents a synopsis and critique of various theories and provides a comprehensive perspective for understanding student learning. The case studies at the end of the chapter provide two vivid examples of students whose educational achievement was negatively influenced by conditions both in school and out. Unlike most of the case studies in which students are successful learners (sometimes in spite of school conditions), the last two case studies reflect an important reality for many students.

We hope all the cases in this book challenge readers to think about how changes in classrooms and schools might positively affect student learning.

3

Racism, Discrimination, and Expectations of Students' Achievement

Linda Howard, one of the interviewees whose case study follows this chapter, was directly harmed by racism in school and out, and she developed a sophisticated understanding of it on both an individual and an institutional level. As you will see in her case study, Linda thought very deeply about racism. Regrettably, too many teachers and other educators have not. In this chapter, we explore the impact that racism, other biases, and expectations of student abilities may have on achievement. We focus on racism as an example of bias but also discuss other kinds of personal and institutional discrimination. These include discrimination on the basis of gender (sexism); ethnic group (ethnocentrism); social class (classism); language (linguicism);[1] sexual orientation and lesbian, gay, bisexual, and transgender (LGBT) identities (heterosexism); age (ageism); and discrimination against Jews (anti-Semitism), against Arabs (anti-Arab discrimination), and against people with disabilities (ableism), among other differences.

> "[Racists have power] only if you let them! We'll stick with [the example of] striped shirts: If I go where everyone is wearing solids, and I'm wearing a stripe, and someone comes up to me and tells me, 'You don't belong here; you're wearing stripes,' I'll say, 'I belong anywhere I want to belong.' And I'll stand right there! But there are some people who just say, 'Oh, okay,' and will turn around and leave. Then the racist has the power."
>
> —Linda Howard, interviewee

Racism and Discrimination: Definitions and Dimensions

Although the terms *racism* and *prejudice* are often used interchangeably, they do not mean the same thing. Gordon Allport, in his groundbreaking work of almost six decades ago on the nature of prejudice, quotes a United Nations (UN) document that defines discrimination as "any conduct based on a distinction made on grounds of natural or social categories, which have no relation either to individual capacities or

62

merits, or to the concrete behavior of the individual person."[2] This definition is helpful but incomplete for two reasons. For one, it fails to describe the harmful *effects* of such conduct; for another, it fails to move beyond the individual level. More broadly speaking, *discrimination* (whether based on race, gender, social class, or other differences) denotes negative or destructive *behaviors* that can result in denying some groups life's necessities as well as the privileges, rights, and opportunities enjoyed by other groups. Discrimination is usually based on prejudice, that is, on the attitudes and beliefs of individuals about entire groups of people. These attitudes and beliefs are generally, but not always, negative. Attitudes alone, however, are not as harmful as the behaviors, policies, and practices that result from such attitudes.

In the past decade and a half, a great deal of theoretical work has been done on understanding the sociopolitical and structural foundations of racism. Much of this has been done through the emerging field of critical race theory (CRT). Some of the tenets of CRT include the following: first, that racism is part and parcel of our everyday lives and not an aberration; second, that it serves important material and psychological purposes, that is, that some people inevitably benefit from it; third, that race is a social construct, not a biological one; and, fourth, that people of color have a unique voice and unique experiences that can communicate the reality of people of color in a way that White people cannot.[3]

Michael Coblyn, Professor of Painting in the Department of Art, Architecture and Art History at the University of Massachusetts Amherst. *All Friends.* Watercolor. 2009

Our society, among many others, categorizes people according to both visible and invisible traits, uses such classifications to assign behavioral and cognitive traits to these categories, and then applies policies and practices based on these categories that jeopardize some people and benefit others.[4] In the United States, the conventional norm used to measure all other groups is European American, upper middle class, English-speaking, heterosexual, able-bodied, and male. Classifications based on physical and social differences are omnipresent. Frequently, they result in gross exaggerations and stereotypes: Girls are not as smart as boys; African Americans have rhythm; Asians are studious; Poles are simple-minded; Jews are smart; and poor people need instant gratification. Although some of these may appear to be "positive" stereotypes, both "negative" and "positive" stereotypes have negative consequences because they skew our perception of entire groups of people. There are two major problems with categorizing people in this way. First, people of all groups begin to believe the stereotypes, and, second, both material and psychological resources are doled out accordingly.

Racism and other forms of discrimination are based on assumptions that one ethnic group, class, gender, or language is superior to all others. Discrimination based on perceptions of superiority is part of the structure of schools, the curriculum, the education most teachers receive, and the interactions among teachers, students, and the community. But discrimination is not simply an individual bias; it is, above all, an *institutional practice*. Institutional practice is the reason that individual effort alone is not generally enough to counteract racism and other negative biases. In our society, the metaphor of "pulling yourself up by your bootstraps" is powerful, but it fails to explain how structural inequality gets in the way of individual efforts.

Individual and Institutional Dimensions of Racism and Discrimination

Too often, prejudice and discrimination are viewed by many people as *individuals'* negative perceptions toward members of other groups. Unfortunately, some definitions of racism and discrimination obscure the institutional nature of oppression. Although the beliefs and behaviors of individuals may be very hurtful and psychologically damaging, institutional discrimination—that is, the systematic use of economic and political power in institutions (such as schools) that leads to detrimental policies and practices—does far greater damage. These policies and practices have a destructive effect on groups that share a particular identity, be it racial, ethnic, gender, or other. The major difference between individual and institutional discrimination is the wielding of *power*. It is primarily through the power of the people who control institutions, such as schools, that oppressive policies and practices are reinforced and legitimized. Linda Howard, the young interviewee introduced at the beginning of this chapter, understood this distinction. In her interview, she distinguished between prejudice and racism in this way: "We all have some type of person that we don't like, whether it's from a different race, or from a different background, or they have different habits." But she goes on to explain, as we saw in her quote at the beginning of the chapter, that a racist is someone who has the *power* to carry out his or her prejudices.

Here's another example: Let's say that you are prejudiced against tall people. Although your bias may hurt tall individuals because you refuse to befriend them or because you make fun of them, you can do very little to limit their options in life. If you belong to a group of powerful "nontalls," however, and you limit the access of tall people to certain neighborhoods, prohibit them from receiving quality health care through particular policies, discourage or outlaw intermarriage between "talls" and people of short or average height, develop policies against the employment of "talls" in high-status professions, and place all children who are the offspring of "talls" (or who show early signs of becoming above average in height) in the lowest ability tracks in schools, then your bias would have teeth and its institutional power would be clear. The following discussion focuses primarily on this kind of discrimination, that is, *institutional discrimination*.

Institutional discrimination generally refers to how people are excluded or deprived of rights or opportunities as a result of the normal operations of the institution.

Although the individuals involved in the institution may not themselves be prejudiced or have any racist intentions, or even an awareness of how others may be harmed, the result may nevertheless be racist. Intentional and unintentional racism may differ, but because they both result in negative outcomes, in the end it does not really matter whether racism and other forms of discrimination are intentional. Rather than trying to figure out whether the intent of a discriminatory action was to do harm or not, educators' time would be better spent addressing the *effects* of racism.

The Systemic Nature of Discrimination

When we understand racism and other forms of discrimination as a *systemic* problem, not simply as an individual dislike for a particular group of people, we can better understand the negative and destructive effects it can have. Vanessa Mattison, whose case study is one of those that follow this chapter, provides a good example of a young person struggling to reconcile our country's lofty ideals of equality and fair play with the reality of the injustice she saw around her. Vanessa was committed to promoting social justice, but she saw it primarily as working to change the attitudes and behaviors of individuals. She had not yet made the connection between racism and institutional oppression, and she did not grasp that institutional racism is far more harmful than individual biases or acts of meanness. But she was beginning to see that certain norms existed that were unfair to Blacks, women, and gays and lesbians. In her words, "There's all these underlying rules that if you're not this, you can't do that."

This discussion is not meant to minimize the powerful effects of individual prejudice and discrimination, which can be personally painful, or to suggest that discrimination is perpetrated only by certain groups, for example, by Whites toward Blacks. There is no monopoly on prejudice and individual discrimination; they may be directed at any group and even occur within groups. Members of any group may be prejudiced, and it is everyone's responsibility to work to eradicate individual racism and other biases. In our society, however, interethnic and intraethnic biases and personal prejudices, while negative and hurtful, simply do not have the long-range and life-limiting effects that institutional racism and other kinds of institutional discrimination have.

Prejudice and discrimination, then, are not just personality traits or individual psychological dysfunctions; they are also manifestations of economic, political, and social power. The institutional definition of racism is not always easy to accept because it goes against deeply held ideals of equality and justice in our nation. According to Beverly Tatum, "An understanding of racism as a system of advantage presents a serious challenge to the notion of the United States as a just society where rewards are based solely on one's merits."[5] Racism as an institutional system implies that some people and groups benefit and others lose. Whites, whether they intend to or not, benefit in a racist society; males benefit in a sexist society. Discrimination always helps somebody—those with the most power—which explains why racism, sexism, and other forms of discrimination continue in spite of the fact that everyone claims to be against them.

According to the late Meyer Weinberg, a well-known historian whose research focused on school desegregation, racism is a system of privilege and penalty. That is, one is rewarded or punished in housing, education, employment, health, and in other institutions by the simple fact of belonging to a particular group, regardless of one's individual merits or faults. He wrote, "Racism consists centrally of two

facets: First, a belief in the inherent superiority of some people and the inherent inferiority of others; and second, the acceptance of distributing goods and services—let
alone respect—in accordance with such judgments of unequal worth." In addressing
the institutional nature of racism, he added, "Racism is always collective. Prejudiced
individuals may join the large movement, but they do not cause it." According to this
concept, what Weinberg called the "silence of institutional racism" and the "ruckus
of individual racism" are mutually supportive.[6] It is sometimes difficult to separate
one level of racism from the other because they feed on and inform one another. What
is crucial, according to Weinberg, is understanding that the doctrine of White
supremacy is at the root of racism.

The History and Persistence of Racism in U.S. Schools

As institutions, schools respond to and reflect the larger society. Therefore, it is not
surprising that racism finds its way into schools in much the same way that it finds
its way into other institutions, such as housing, employment, and the criminal justice system. In schools, overt expressions of racism may be less common today than
in the past, but racism does not exist only when schools are legally segregated or
racial epithets are used. Racism is also manifested in rigid ability tracking, low expectations of students based on their identity, and inequitably funded schools, among
other policies and practices.

Racism and other forms of discrimination—particularly sexism, classism, ethnocentrism, and linguicism—have a long history in our schools, and their effects are
widespread and long-lasting. The most blatant form of discrimination is the actual
withholding of education, as was the case historically with African Americans and
sometimes with American Indians. To teach enslaved Africans to read was a crime
punishable under the law, and it became a subversive activity that was practiced by
Blacks in ingenious ways.[7] Another overt form of discrimination is segregating students, by law or custom, according to their race, ethnicity, or gender, as was perpetrated at one time or another against African American, Mexican American, Japanese,
and Chinese students as well as against females. Yet another form is forcing a group
into boarding schools, as was done to American Indian students well into the twentieth century. The result was that children were encouraged to adopt the ways of the
dominant culture in sundry ways, from subtle persuasion to physical punishment
for speaking their native language. All of these examples are bitter reminders of the
inequities in U.S. educational history.

Unfortunately, the discrimination that children face in schools is not a thing
of the past. School practices and policies continue to discriminate against some
children in very concrete ways. Recent studies have found that most students of
color are in schools that are still segregated by race and social class, and the situation is worsening rather than improving. The result is that today students of all races
are less likely to interact with those of other backgrounds than at any time in the
past four decades, that poor children are segregated in inferior schools, and that the
high schools attended by these students are what Gary Orfield has called "dropout
factories."[8] At the impetus of the civil rights movement, many school systems
throughout the United States were indeed becoming desegregated, but less than rigorous implementation of desegregation plans, "White flight" (that is, the movement

■■■■■■ What You Can Do
Make Differences and Similarities an Explicit Part of Your Curriculum

From preschool through high school, you can create a physical environment that affirms differences. This environment might include a variety of pictures and posters, wall hangings from different cultures, children's artwork, maps and flags from around the world, bulletin boards of special days that feature multicultural themes, exhibits of art from around the country and the world, and a well-stocked multicultural library in which all manner of differences are evident. The game corner can include a variety of games, from checkers to Parcheesi, to Mankala, to dominoes. Different languages can also be featured on bulletin boards and posters, with translations in English.

of Whites to rural and suburban areas and to private schools) and segregated housing patterns succeeded in resegregating many schools. Segregation invariably results in school systems that are "separate and unequal" because, in general, fewer resources are provided to schools in poor communities, and vastly superior resources are provided to schools in wealthier communities. The curriculum in such schools is also unequal, offering young people in schools with poor resources few high-level courses that prepare them for postsecondary education. Also, teachers in poor urban schools tend to have less experience and less preparation than those who teach in schools that serve primarily European American and middle-class students. Even when they are desegregated, however, many schools resegregate students through practices such as rigid ability tracking. Consequently, desegregating schools, in and of itself, does not guarantee educational equity.

Manifestations of Racism and Discrimination in Schools

Racism and discrimination are manifested in numerous school practices and policies. Policies that are likely to jeopardize educationally marginalized students are most common precisely in the institutions in which those students are found. For example, studies have found that some policies have especially negative consequences for African American, Latino, and American Indian students. This is the case, for instance, with rigid ability tracking and high-stakes tests.[9]

In an example of how difficult it is to separate racism from individual teachers' behaviors or seemingly neutral policies, Patricia Gándara found in a study of 50 low-income and high-achieving Mexican Americans that most of them were either light-skinned or European in appearance. Few of the sample, according to Gándara, looked "classically Mexican in both skin color and features.[10] Does this mean that teachers intentionally favored these students because of their light skin? Did teachers assume that light-skinned students were smarter? These questions are impossible to answer in any conclusive way, although it is probable that institutional racism and teachers' biases both played a role. The results, however, are clear. In Gándara's study, the light-skinned students were able to derive significantly more benefits from their schooling than their dark-skinned peers.

Thus, it is clear that racism and other forms of institutional discrimination play a part in students' educational success or failure. In general, African American, Latino, American Indian, and poor children continue to achieve below grade level, drop out in much greater numbers, and go to college in much lower proportions than their middle-class and European American peers. Three concrete examples illustrate this point. First, Black and Latino students are chronically underrepresented in programs for the gifted and talented; they are only half as likely as White students to be placed in a class for the gifted, although they may be equally gifted. In a second example, Latino students drop out of school at a rate higher than any other incredibly and unacceptably high rates: in some places, the rate is as high as 80 percent.[11] To comprehend the enormity of this situation, one needs to imagine a school in which *80 of every 100 students* enrolled do not make it to high school graduation. This would be completely unacceptable in middle-class and wealthy communities, yet it is not unusual in poor communities. A third example concerns the fact that schools are frequently unsafe for lesbian, gay, bisexual, and transgender (LGBT) students. Although the situation has improved somewhat in the past decade for high school students, a 2009 report by the Gay, Lesbian, and Straight Education Network (GLSEN) found that middle school LGBT students were significantly more likely to face hostile school climates than were high school LGBT students, yet they had less access to school resources and support.[12]

If educational failure were caused only by students' background and other social characteristics, it would be difficult to explain why similar students are successful in some classrooms and schools and not in others. In his extensive review of schools where the "achievement gap" has narrowed, Joseph D'Amico described a number of differences between schools that primarily serve middle-class or affluent European American students and those that primarily serve students of color and students living in poverty. He found that schools with a narrow "achievement gap" have highly competent, dedicated, and well-trained teachers who have higher expectations for all students; a curriculum that is both culturally sensitive and challenging; and a school community that emphasizes high achievement.[13]

Even when schools are successful at narrowing the "achievement gap," however, they alone cannot solve all the problems created by an inequitable and unequal society. For example, discrimination based on social class is also prevalent in our public schools, and social class and race are often intertwined. In her research, Jean Anyon has found that differences in academic achievement are due primarily to the kinds of schools students attend, the length of time they stay in school, the curriculum and pedagogy to which they are exposed, and societal beliefs concerning their ability. As a result, unequal opportunities to learn can produce significant differences in academic achievement by low-income urban versus affluent suburban students, and the consequences may be dramatic in terms of future life options. Using extensive data from numerous studies, Anyon concluded that compound educational and political inequality in the occupations, salaries, and housing of the urban poor and the affluent reinforce political and economic differences.[14] Her work suggests that while school reform is both important and necessary, what schools can accomplish is limited if larger macroeconomic policies having to do with employment, housing patterns, health, and other issues do not change.

Rather than eradicate social class differences, then, it appears that schooling reflects and exacerbates (or even duplicates) them. This finding was confirmed by

Samuel Bowles and Herbert Gintis in their groundbreaking class analysis of schooling more than three decades ago.[15] Bowles and Gintis compared the number of years of schooling of students with the socioeconomic status of their parents and found that students whose parents were in the highest socioeconomic group tended to complete the most years of schooling. They concluded that schooling, in and of itself, does not necessarily move poor children out of their parents' low economic class. More often, schooling maintains and solidifies class divisions. Tragically, as researchers Jean Anyon, David Berliner, Richard Rothstein, and others have more recently documented, this outcome is still true.[16]

Intentional or not, racism, classism, and other forms of discrimination are apparent in the quality of education that students receive. For instance, even when teachers believe they are being fair, the results may be unfair. A study by Janet Ward Schofield found that teachers who claimed to be "color-blind" suspended African American males at highly disproportionate rates.[17] Another graphic example of discrimination based on both race and class is found in the vastly different resources given to schools, depending on the socioeconomic level of the student population served. As Jonathan Kozol states in his most recent, searing indictment of public education, the resegregation of students of different backgrounds is akin to apartheid, the heinous policy that legally separated people according to race in South Africa (similar to Jim Crow, the racist laws and actions in the southern United States during the late nineteenth century and first half of the twentieth century).[18] Recent research by Gary Orfield and Chungmei Lee support this contention: According to them, African Americans and Latinos are segregated as much by poverty as they are by race and ethnicity, and thus segregation is an overriding contributor to the tremendous standardized test disparities that exist between the races.[19]

The effect of discrimination on students is most painfully apparent when students themselves have the opportunity to speak. For example, Junia Yearwood, a high school teacher of students of diverse racial backgrounds, decided to find out for herself how they experienced school. She asked them to write down the answers to two questions: "What is the best thing a teacher has ever said to you?" and "What is the worst thing a teacher has ever said to you?" What she found through her research is a clear indication of the power of words to either make or break students' attitudes about school. This is part of what Junia wrote:

> There was no dearth of examples of experiences of degradation offered by my students. They said that teachers called them, among many other words, "stupid," "slow," "ignorant," "fat," "dumb," "punk." They said that teachers made comments such as "You'll never amount to anything," "Shut up," "You can't even pass a test," "Even if you study, you'll still fail," "That was a dumb answer," and "You are the worst student." One said that when he failed a test, the teacher said, "I'm not surprised," and another volunteered that his fourth grade teacher had said, "I should put you in kindergarten." Another student said a teacher had told him that in a couple of years, he would be either dead or in jail.[20]

In another example, a study conducted by Karen McLean Donaldson in an urban high school in the Northeast discovered that an astounding 80 percent of students surveyed said they had experienced or witnessed racism or other forms of discrimination in school. She found that students were affected by racism in three major

> "I think I believe in the power of kids even more than I did before."
> —Marisa Vanasse

Because young people often perceive history as little more than boring facts about wars, conquests, and famous men, when Marisa Mendonsa Vanasse began teaching 12 years ago, she was determined to bring to life the bold, exciting, and everyday challenges posed by history. She has endeavored to do this throughout her teaching career. Nothing epitomizes this determination more forcefully than the Anti-Mascot Curriculum that she engaged in with her students during the 2008–2009 school year.

Multicultural Teaching Story

The Springfield Renaissance School
Anti-Indian Mascot Committee

Marisa is a history teacher at the Springfield Renaissance School, a 6th to 12th grade school in Massachusetts (see http://www.sps.springfield.ma.us/schoolsites/renaissance)[1]. A multiracial and multiethnic school, Renaissance reflects the city's population with about 40 percent Latino/a, 35 percent Black (including African Americans and others from the African Diaspora, as well as biracial students), and 25 percent White students. It is a small school with only about 100 students per grade, and for three years, Marisa was the history teacher of the students involved in the Anti-Indian Mascot Project described below.

Using expeditionary learning, The Springfield Renaissance School is based on direct student engagement through research and presentations concerning the core interdisciplinary curriculum. In 2008, the history teachers decided that the 8th grade curriculum should begin with a study of the pre-Columbus era, one that had not previously been included. Given the previous invisibility of Native Americans in the curriculum, they chose the theme of "Silenced Voices." Marisa said, "When we think of genocide, we immediately think outside of our country, that it's never happened on our soil," and she wanted her students to know a more complete and true history. Rather than focus simply on the past, however, Marisa wanted to bring these issues to the present day. This happened serendipitously one day when one of her students brought in an article.

[1] According to the website of the Harborside Expeditionary School in Kenosha, WI, "Expeditionary Learning is a design and program for school improvement that builds on the educational ideas and insights based on the ideas of Kurt Hahn, Outward Bound's founder, 60-year history and craft wisdom, and the ideas and examples of other educational thinkers and leaders from John Dewey to Paul Ylvisaker, Harold Howe, Ted Sizer, Eleanor Duckworth, Howard Gardner, Debbie Meier and Tom James." See http://harborside.kusd.edu/el.html_Additionally, the website http://oak.cats.ohiou.edu/~jw199800/eng305/infopub.htm says that "Expeditionary Learning is a curriculum designed to promote critical thinking, skills and habits, academic achievement, and personal development through the use of in-depth investigations that engage students in community, projects, and service. An expedition brings experts into the classroom, takes students into the field, and engages students in real world learning experiences."

Shortly after they had started the study of pre-Columbian history, this student came to her with an article concerning the use of Native American mascots written by a friend of her parents. Marisa gave it to her students and they got "all fired up" saying things such as, "We never learned this before!" and "I can't believe we're treating them this way!" They were outraged that an entire group of people was being used as mascots for sports teams and they decided to do something about it. Ultimately, as Marisa said, the curriculum "was driven by the students," not by her.

The students learned about resources—people, institutions, and places—in their community and at the state and national levels. They visited the Pequot Museum in Connecticut and interviewed a local member of the Seneca nation and a board member from the Massachusetts Center for Native American Awareness. They found out about the New England Anti-Mascot Coalition and they interviewed its founder. They did research in the library and on the Internet and they read an impressive array of books and articles on the topic. They designed a website and prepared a PowerPoint presentation. They were so energized by this topic that a group of them—about 15, quite a sizable number of the entire grade—decided to meet one day a week after school and on Saturdays.

The students then prepared a document titled "A Proposal to Eliminate Native American Mascots" as the final product of their 8th grade expedition on "Silenced Voices." On the cover of their proposal is the image of an Indian with a feather headdress with a slash through it, saying "No stereotypes in our schools" and "Indians are people, not mascots" on the outside of the symbol. In their comprehensive proposal of 15 pages, they wrote, "Redskins, Warriors, Indians, Braves: the name changes but the effect is the same. Using American Indians as mascots fuels stereotypical images and thoughts through American society." Their goal? To eliminate Native American mascots from schools in Massachusetts, especially in their own city, where one of the high schools uses one. Why? "To remove these mascots from our school systems is an essential step in eliminating both stereotypes of Native peoples and harmful depictions and images for Native youth."

At about this time, the *Springfield Republican,* the local newspaper, printed a story about Turners Falls High School in a neighboring community. The new superintendent of that town had decided to put a stop to the school's tomahawk chop, which he found offensive, and this provoked a great debate in the town. Marisa decided to contact the Turners Falls School Committee to find out what they were doing. After her visit, they contacted her and invited her students to speak before the School Committee. Marisa's students did a great deal of preparation for this presentation—it was, according to Marisa, "a huge undertaking for my kids"—and it turned out to be a tremendous success. She said it was "the scariest moment" she had ever had in her teaching career. Although her students had already done a similar presentation in their school and another at a local university, they were intimidated by the fact that the Turners Falls School Committee would be voting on this issue and they knew their presentation would have an impact, one way or another, on the vote. "It was," Marisa said, "their *best* presentation!" After the students spoke, she and the students ran out to the hall, "high-fiving and fired up." Marisa explained,

> My kids weren't scared anymore. They realized that when you believe in something, even if people don't agree with you, it's okay to share your opinion. And if you've done your research and you can support that, everything's okay.

A month later, the School Committee voted against using the tomahawk chop in their school.

As a result of their work, the students were interviewed for a local television station and they received messages of solidarity from as far away as Minnesota. They decided to continue their research throughout their high school careers, forming an after-school club to which they will invite other interested students. They developed what Marisa describes as "amazing skills" in forming opinions, debate, doing presentations, and writing. They've also become more sensitive to other issues and more open to finding out about other injustices. As for Marisa, this experience also changed her as a teacher. "I wasn't sure I could do this kind of work," she said. "It made me realize that you can do things you thought you couldn't do with a certain age group." It changed the students and also the people they addressed because "when you have 13- or 14-year-olds talking about oppression ('*oppression? What's that?*') and discrimination, talking about issues that they never gave thought to, it stops people in their tracks."

Marisa Vanasse did not set out to be an activist teacher. She simply wanted to help her students think differently about history, to help them develop a different level of awareness and open their minds up to new and different perspectives. She accomplished this and much more. What's next for her and her students? She talked about her desire to use the community as the subject matter of the curriculum. While "big" issues such as the genocide in Darfur are important and necessary for students to know about, she wants to start with the "big" issues that are right in her community and then expand from there.

In terms of the anti-mascot curriculum, she said that the students want to continue studying this issue, one that may take them through their remaining years of high school. Because another high school in the city uses a Native American mascot, their next step is to contact the school and make a presentation there. Beyond that, through their research, the students discovered that there are 42 schools in the state that have mascots or use Native American symbols. As a result, they want to go directly to the state level and ask the governor and the Massachusetts Department of Education to sign a resolution calling for an end to Native Americans mascots, a resolution that other states have adopted. This will make "the fight a little bit larger," according to Marisa. But, as she concluded, "I've got four years with these kids, they have four years of high school ahead of them, and they are not slowing down, and I'm not slowing down either!"

ways: (1) White students experienced guilt and embarrassment when they became aware of the racism to which their peers were subjected; (2) students of color sometimes felt they needed to compensate and overachieve to prove they were equal to their White classmates; and (3) at other times, the self-esteem of students of color was badly damaged.[21] However, self-esteem is a complicated issue that includes many variables. It does not come fully formed out of the blue; it is *created* in particular contexts and responds to conditions that vary from situation to situation. Teachers' and schools' complicity in creating negative self-esteem cannot be discounted.

Racism, Discrimination, and Silence

Well-meaning teachers are sometimes unintentionally discriminatory when they remain silent about race and racism. They may fear that talking about race will only intensify the problem of racism. As a consequence, most schools are characterized by a curious absence of talk about differences, particularly about race.[22] Such silence about racism is sometimes thought to be appropriate because it demonstrates that teachers are "color-blind," that is, fair and impartial when it comes to judging people based on their race. They insist that they see no difference in their students, in spite of their students' obvious differences in race and ethnicity. This patronizing stance facilitates the denial of racism because, according to Pearl Rosenberg, "[P]eople who are colorblind have an optical defect that limits their ability to see."[23] Mica Pollock refers to the purposeful suppressing of words associated with race as "colormuteness." Colormuteness is a result of uneasiness with directly addressing issues of race. She writes, "Given the amount of worrying that race-label use seems to require in America, it is perhaps unsurprising that many Americans have proposed we solve our 'race problems' by talking as if race did not matter at all."[24] In the United States, color blindness and colormuteness begin in early childhood, when children are admonished not to say anything about racial differences, among other differences, because "it's not nice." We learn early on that even admitting that we notice race is wrong. This kind of thinking assumes that the only way to deal with differences is to pretend they don't exist. Yet the reluctance to discuss race can result in overlooking or denying issues of power that are embedded in race. There is ample evidence, for example, that even the youngest children learn about what Debra Van Ausdale and Joe Feagin have labeled "The First R," that is, race and racism, and that they form their opinion about these things before they even begin their schooling.[25] This research is a direct contradiction to the view that young children are immune to the racist messages around them. If this is true, then educators have an important role to play in helping them "unlearn" racism.

Failure to discuss racism, unfortunately, will not make it go away. Racism, classism, and other forms of discrimination play a key role in creating and maintaining inappropriate learning environments for many students. A related phenomenon concerns the impact of teachers' expectations on student achievement.

Expectations of Students' Achievement

Much research has focused on teachers' interactions with their students, specifically teacher expectations. The term *self-fulfilling prophecy*, coined by Robert Merton in 1948, means that students perform in ways that teachers expect, that is, that student performance is based on both overt and covert messages from teachers about students' worth, intelligence, and capability.[26] The term did not come into wide use until 1968, when a classic study by Robert Rosenthal and Lenore Jacobson provided the impetus for subsequent extensive research on the subject.[27] In this study, several classes of children in grades 1 through 6 were given a nonverbal intelligence test (the researchers called it the Harvard Test of Influenced Acquisition), which researchers claimed would measure the students' potential for intellectual growth. Twenty percent of the students were randomly selected by the researchers

■■■■■■ What You Can Do
Start Early

Focusing on human differences and similarities can begin as early as the preschool years, for example, talking about skin color, hair texture, and other physical differences and similarities. Rather than telling White children that it is not polite to say that Black children have "dirty" skin, use this remark and others like it as a basis for making skin differences an explicit part of the curriculum. Use individual photographs of the children; pictures from magazines of people from all over the world; stories that emphasize the similarities in human feelings across all groups; and dolls that represent a variety of races, ethnicities, and genders.

Patty Bode, one of the authors of this text and a former art teacher, uses a color theory lesson to focus attention on skin color. One year, Patty developed a schoolwide activity in which every student and staff member in the school was involved, from cooks to teachers, to the principal and custodian. She had everyone mix the primary colors to match their particular skin color and then make handprints. In the process, they engaged in dialogue about race, the words we use to describe people of different backgrounds, discrimination and racism, and other issues rarely discussed in most schools. When they were finished, Patty hung all the handprints (more than 500) in the halls of the schools. It was a powerful graphic representation of diversity and inclusiveness.

Continue Through the Grades

When used critically, festivals can also become an important element of the curriculum. Although we need to avoid creating a superficial view of diversity based only on festivals, Deborah Menkart has suggested that even using the traditional idea of "heritage months" can become a positive approach in diversifying the curriculum.* In addition to heritage months and festivals, foods can also become a rich resource in the curriculum. Mark Zanger, in a thoroughly researched and excellent resource on foods from around the world, suggests that food can be used as the basis for many creative projects related to culture and immigration.†

In addition, you can work with your students and colleagues in many different ways to develop a "school culture" that truly represents your community. Some activities and rituals, such as selecting local or national school heroes from a variety of backgrounds, can be conducted as schoolwide projects. Other activities could be having all students learn songs,

as "intellectual bloomers," and their names were given to the teachers. Although the students' test scores actually had nothing at all to do with their potential, the teachers were told to be on the alert for signs of intellectual growth among these particular children. Overall, these children—particularly in the lower grades—showed considerably greater gains in IQ during the school year than did the other students. They were also rated by their teachers as being more interesting, curious, and happy and were thought to be more likely to succeed later in life.

Rosenthal and Jacobson's research on teacher expectations caused a sensation in the educational community, and controversy surrounding it continued for many years.[28] From the beginning, the reception to this line of research has been mixed, with both supporters and detractors, but one outcome was that the effect of teachers' expectations on the academic achievement of their students was taken seriously for the first time. Before this research, students' failure in school was usually ascribed wholly to individual or family circumstances. Now, the possible influence of teachers' attitudes and behaviors and the schools' complicity in the process had to be poems, or speeches from several cultures and having all students take part in local history projects that explore the lives, experiences, and accomplishments of many different people. You might develop a "classtory" (i.e., a history of the class) that includes the pictures and biographies of all members of the class, from information about their ethnicity and the languages they speak, to the things they like to do with friends and family.

With older students, focusing on multicultural literature that depicts the reality of women and men of many groups is an effective strategy. Curriculum that discusses the history and culture of particular groups is also helpful, especially when used in an interdisciplinary and cross-cultural approach.

Directly Confront Racism and Discrimination

Focusing on similarities and differences alone does not guarantee that racism will disappear. In fact, a focus on similarities and differences can become an excuse for not delving more deeply into racism. Because racism and other biases are generally hushed up or avoided in schools, they can become uncomfortable topics of conversation. Directly confronting racism and discrimination can be a healthy and caring way to address these difficult issues.

Even young children can take part in discussions on racism and discrimination. Although many teachers believe that young children should not be exposed to the horrors of racism at an early age, they overlook the fact that many children suffer the effects of racism or other forms of discrimination every day. Discussing these issues in developmentally appropriate ways helps even the youngest children tackle racism and other biases in productive rather than negative ways.

The name-calling that goes on in many schools also provides a valuable opportunity for you to engage in dialogue with your students, as well as with other teachers, administrators, and families. Rather than addressing name-calling as isolated incidents or as the work of a few troublemakers, as is done too often, discussing it openly and directly helps students understand these incidents as symptoms of systemic problems in society and schools. Making explicit the biases that are implicit in name-calling can become part of "circle" or "sharing" time or can form the basis for lessons on racism, sexism, ableism, or other biases.

*Menkart, D. J. (1999). Deepening the meaning of heritage months. *Educational Leadership* 56 (7): 19–21.

†Zanger, M. (2003). *The American history cookbook.* Westport, CT: Greenwood Press.

considered as well. For instance, teachers' beliefs that their students are "slow" can become a rationale for providing low-level work in the form of elementary facts, simple drills, and rote memorization. The most compelling implications were for the education of those students most seriously disadvantaged by schooling, that is, for students of color and the poor. Students are not immune to these messages.

Early research by Ray Rist on teachers' expectations is also worth mentioning here. In a groundbreaking study, he found that a kindergarten teacher had grouped her class by the eighth day of class. In reviewing how she had done so, Rist noted that the teacher had already roughly constructed an "ideal type" of student, most of whose characteristics were related to social class. By the end of the school year, the teacher's differential treatment of children based on whom she considered "fast" and "slow" learners became evident. The "fast" learners received more teaching time, more reward-directed behavior, and more attention. The interactional patterns between the teacher and her students then took on a castelike appearance. The result, after three years of similar behavior by other teachers, was that teachers'

SNAPSHOT
Kaval Sethi

Kaval Sethi, a junior in high school at the time of his interview, and his sister, a junior in college, were born and raised in the United States shortly after their parents moved from Bombay, India. They currently lived in a wealthy suburb of Long Island in New York. Kaval, a hopeful and positive young man, had attended school in the same district since kindergarten. He was in honors classes in all subjects and had a 3.7 cumulative average; in addition, he was taking four advance placement (AP) classes. Kaval was active in a number of school activities, including the math club and jazz band. In the community, he was involved in his local Gurudwara, the Sikh house of worship, and he volunteered in the soup kitchen affiliated with the Gurudwara. Besides his native English language, he also spoke Punjabi and Hindi.*

As a Sikh, Kaval wore a Dastaar (turban) and kept a beard, requirements for men who follow the Sikh religion. These things made him visibly different from other young men, and he was sometimes made fun of or singled out by other students.

Kaval Sethi was keenly aware of how his ethnicity and social class affected his life. During his interview, he talked about both the social class and economic privileges he enjoyed as well as the marginalization he experienced because of his religious affiliation. Kaval openly discussed the challenges faced by Sikhs and others after the events of September 11, 2001.

I am an Indian American. My Sikh identity is very important to me. I like to keep my beard and keep my turban, and I don't cut my hair. Sikhism defines my religion, how I act religiously, and how I act in my morals. When I say [I am] Indian American, that is how I am culturally. My cultural character: the food I eat, the kinds of friends I have, the things I do. I am very Indian, but I mix a lot of American values into my culture.

Sikhism defines a lot about my life. I am Sikh, and my religion prohibits cutting hair. I want everyone to know that I am Sikh. I am just as different as everyone else. I am part of your culture—but I'm different as well.

I visited India recently. The life that they live isn't much different from mine. It's a little tougher. I guess it's not as much technology. I was very comfortable in India. [There], they realize you are a foreigner, and *you* realize you are a foreigner. I know that [in the United States], other people see me differently from another person. You don't get that feeling when you walk around India, but as soon as you speak to an American, they know you are an American.

My parents worked hard to get where they are. They owe it all to education. They find it very important. *I* find it very important. My dad came when he was 17, and he went to college in New York. . . . My mom's first time coming to America was when she first got married to my dad. [My parents] also learned a lot of things by living life, not just by going to school. From my family, basically I've learned my whole moral character. My parents have taught me to be morally strong.

Some people are concerned [about Sikhs coming into the school]. I guess that is because they are confused about our affiliations. We are not Muslims. Some people confuse us with terrorists. In our school, some

behavior toward the different groups influenced the children's achievement. In other words, the teachers themselves contributed to the creation of the "slow" learners in their classrooms.[29] In the research by Rist, all the children and teachers were African American, although they represented different social classes, but similar results have been found with poor and working-class children regardless of race.[30]

Some of the research on teacher expectations is quite old. Although it is reasonable to expect that, with the increasing diversity in our schools, it no longer holds true, there are still numerous examples of teachers' low expectations of students. In kids ask me, "Are you Muslim?" And I say, "No, I'm not Muslim. I'm Sikh." Not a lot of people know about it, but I think it's like the fifth largest religion in the world.

A White American in America does not have to deal with the prejudice that Sikhs have. I had a lot of bad experiences as a little child. [Other kids] would make fun of me . . . because I was different. They used to call me names. Some kids did not make fun of me, and I would hang out with them. By the time people understood, they stopped.

Sikhs are singled out because we wear turbans. I am the only kid in my class who wears a turban. I guess originally, at first, on the day [after September 11], some people were feeling kind of prejudiced against me because of Osama bin Laden and how closely Sikhs resemble Osama bin Laden, because Sikhs wear beards and turbans. So originally, people would be kind of antagonistic, but that really subsided very quickly 'cause they understood that I was a Sikh and I wasn't really a harm to them.

Definitely my English and social studies teachers know plenty about Sikhism. My math and science teachers really don't understand it. They *do* ask questions. Over the years, the math and science teachers have asked plenty of questions about Sikhism, and I've answered them. My teachers are [mostly] fair. . . . [S]ome teachers had prejudices against me. I want them to know about my religion, some basic facts, so they can better relate to me. If they relate to me, I can be more open.

I'm very much into music. I play music and trumpet. I'm into economics and business—and science. Probably biology will be my major in college. I'm into environmental topics. I'm part of the Environmental Action Committee. I'm very much into preserving the environment. . . . I'm also into jazz.

I go to Gurudwara [the temple]. I like to help out as much as possible there. I try to help clean up after *langar* (it's like a free kitchen; on Sunday they have it after the religious service). I like helping at that. I like to help out in things that I can help out in.

Now I am confident. A few years ago I would be shy. I am extremely independent. . . . If I want to do it, I will do it. I am very proud of myself—of what I can accomplish.

Commentary

Sikhs, particularly males, have been targets of anti-Muslim and xenophobic sentiments because of their mistaken association with Islam. Sikh Americans have been verbally and physically assaulted, and some even murdered. Many persons with Brown skin endured hostility and threats after September 11, but Sikh males and Muslims women wearing the hijeb have the physical markers in addition to the phenotypic ones that especially make them targets of bigotry and fear. Kaval felt that most teachers were not prejudiced, but he longed for more awareness and understanding from them because, for the most part, they failed to address these issues, either through private conversations or in the curriculum.

*We are grateful to Khyati Joshi, who found and interviewed Kaval. She also provided us with important background information about Asian and Indian Americans in general, and the Sikh American community specifically. Khyati also suggested other sources of information. The Web sites www.sikhcoalition.org and www.sikhmediawatch.org provide up-to-date information about the Sikh American community. For information concerning hate crimes, see the Web site www.aaldef.org. Two additional classroom resources on Sikhs are available in a DVD format: Sikh Next Door (grades 6 to 12, www.sikhnextdoor.org) and Cultural Safari (grades K to 5, www.kaurfoundation.org). The Sikh Next Door has lesson plans in a PDF format. Teachers can use these as guides to introduce the culture and religion of the Sikh community to their classes.

fact, in a 2000 reprint of his classic 1970 study, Ray Rist came to the conclusion that much of the reality of education for Black youth had changed very little during the intervening 30 years. For Rist, the issues of color and class inequality show evidence of the "profound disconnect between the rhetoric and the reality of American society."[31] He concluded the following:

> The sobering reality is that when it comes to both color and class, U.S. schools tend to conform much more to the contours of American society than they transform it. And this appears to be a lesson that we are not wanting to learn.[32]

Given the increasing diversity in our public schools, the problem is even more acute because many teachers know little or nothing about the background of their students. Consequently, teachers may consider their students' identity to be at fault. In a more recent study, Marcos Pizarro interviewed over 200 Chicano students about their experiences in school. The students were a diverse group: Some were successful students, while others had been largely unsuccessful in school; some lived in small towns and others lived in large cities; they represented different social classes; they were high school, community college, and university students; and some were high school dropouts. As a result of these interviews, Pizarro concluded that the students were "profiled"—a more updated term for the expectations of students based on their identities—by their teachers and that this "profiling" had a significant effect on their schooling experiences and outcomes. He found that teachers categorized the students according to skin color, social class, dress, specific behaviors, linguistic abilities, friendship groups, and so on. The result is that teachers judged the students by these characteristics, which usually had little to do with their intellectual abilities. While the profiling might have been unintentional and unconscious, the results could be far-reaching: "Just as the police often use racial profiles to determine who are potential criminals and who does not need to be pulled over, teachers use racial profiles to determine who will and will not benefit from opportunities to excel in school."[33]

In spite of some very negative experiences, however, Pizarro found some students who had been extremely successful. Significantly, the most successful students were those who had been mentored through the various transitions of their schooling by teachers and other authority figures who linked the students' identities with their schooling in more positive ways. That is, when teachers connected the students' identities with success in learning, the result was students who were self-assured in their own identities and dedicated to their schooling.

The issue of labeling is key here. Rubén Rumbaut found that the self-esteem of immigrant students is linked to how they are labeled by their schools. For example, he found that students' self-esteem is diminished when they are labeled "limited English proficient."[34] If this is the case with a seemingly neutral term, more loaded labels no doubt have a much greater impact, but explicit labeling may not even be needed. According to research by Claude Steele, the basic problem that causes low student achievement is what he terms *stereotype threat*, based on the constant devaluation faced by Blacks, other people of color, and females in society. In schools, this devaluation occurs primarily through the harmful attitudes and beliefs that teachers communicate, knowingly or not, to their students. Steele maintains, "Deep in the psyche of American educators is a presumption that black students need academic remediation, or extra time with elemental curricula to overcome background deficits."[35]

Building on this line of research among young children, a more recent confirmation of the importance of affirming students' identities comes from a widely reported, randomized, double-blind study by Geoffrey Cohen and his associates.[36] The researchers asked a randomly selected group of African American and European American students to complete a writing assignment in which they were to choose either their most or least important value among a list that included relationships with friends or family or being good at art. Although the children completed this brief 15-minute assignment near the beginning of the school year, the results were dramatic: The academic performance of the African American students who had written about their most important value was raised and the racial "achievement gap" was reduced by 40 percent. No effect was seen, up or down, among the European American students. In other words, the intervention benefited targeted students without jeopardizing nontargeted students.

Extensive research by Milbrey McLaughlin and Joan Talbert in high schools around the country confirms the importance of having high expectations for students. The researchers described how many of the teachers in the schools responded to "nontraditional" students (including the growing population of students of color) by lowering their expectations and watering down the curriculum. They also found that the teachers who water down the curriculum usually place the responsibility for low achievement squarely on the students themselves. This pattern was most evident in low-track classrooms. On the other hand, the researchers found that teachers who modified the curriculum without lowering their expectations of students, and who worked to establish strong teacher-student relationships, were better able to reach their students, even those who came from economically disadvantaged backgrounds.[37] Similar findings from numerous studies have been reported consistently over the past several years. In a review of these studies, Christine Sleeter came to the conclusion that the research confirms that "students from communities that have been historically underserved can achieve *when the teachers and school believe they can and take responsibility to make it happen.*"[38]

Teachers' attitudes about the diversity of their students develop long before they become teachers. In a review of related literature, Kenneth Zeichner found that teacher education students, who are mostly White and monolingual, generally view diversity of student backgrounds as a problem.[39] He also found that the most common characteristics of effective teachers in urban schools are (1) a belief that their students are capable learners and (2) an ability to communicate this belief to the students. Martin Haberman reached a similar conclusion, identifying a number of functions of successful teachers of the urban poor. Most significantly, he found that successful teachers did not blame students for failure and had consistently high expectations of their students.[40] Rashaud Kates, whose case study follows this chapter, offers compelling evidence of this reality. According to Rashaud, many teachers do not expect Black students to achieve academically. He said, "People are already judging you when you're African American. I would tell teachers about African American students, 'Everybody's not bad; have high expectations.'"

What happens when teachers develop high expectations of their students? In an inspiring example of how changing the expectations of students can influence achievement in a positive direction, Rosa Hernandez Sheets recounted her own experience with five Spanish-speaking high school students who had failed her Spanish class. Just one semester after placing them in what she labele d her advanced class, the very same students, who had previously failed, passed the AP Spanish language exam, earning college credits while just sophomores and juniors. A year later, they passed the AP Spanish literature exam. As a result of the change in her pedagogy, during a three-year period, these Latino and Latina students who had been labeled at risk were performing at a level commonly expected of honors students. They went, she wrote, from "remedial" to "gifted."[41] Another example can be found in the work of Cynthia Ballenger, a teacher of Haitian American children in a Massachusetts preschool. As Ballenger herself states, "I began with these children expecting deficits, not because I believed they or their background were deficient—I was definitely against such a view—but because I did not know how to see their strengths."[42] Through her work with the children and their families, Ballenger documents how her beliefs and practices shifted as she began to build on the strengths and experiences that the children brought to school, strengths that had not previously been evident to her. Clearly, such expectations can have an immense impact on young people.

Research on teachers' expectations is not without controversy. First, it has been criticized as unnecessarily reductionist because, in the long run, the detractors claim, what teachers *expect* matters less than what teachers *do*. Second, the critics say that the term *teachers' expectations* and the research on which it is based imply that teachers have the sole responsibility for students' achievement or lack of it and that this is both an unrealistic and an incomplete explanation for student success or failure. The study by Rosenthal and Jacobson, for example, is, in fact, a glaring indication of the disrespect with which teachers have frequently been treated in research, and it raises serious ethical issues about how research is done.[43] Blaming teachers, or "teacher bashing," provides a convenient outlet for complex problems, but it fails to take into account the fact that teachers function within contexts in which they usually have little power.

Some teachers, of course, have low expectations of students from particular backgrounds and are, in the worst cases, insensitive and racist. But placing teachers at the center of expectations of student achievement shifts the blame entirely to some of those who care most deeply about students and who struggle every day to help them learn. The use of the term *teachers' expectations* distances the school and society from their responsibility and complicity in student failure. The truth is that teachers, schools, students, communities, and society all interact to produce failure.

Low expectations mirror the expectations of society. It is not simply teachers who expect little from poor, working-class, and culturally dominated groups. For example, a state appeals court in New York ruled that youngsters who drop out of the New York City schools by eighth grade have nevertheless received "a sound basic education." This astonishing ruling overturned a 2001 landmark decision that had found the state's formula for funding public schools unfair because it favored those who live in suburban areas. The majority opinion in the 2002 appeals court case, written by Judge Alfred Lerner, said in part that "the skills required to enable a person to obtain employment, vote, and serve on a jury, are imparted between grades 8 and 9." And although Judge Lerner conceded that such a meager education would probably qualify people for only the lowest-paying jobs, he added, "Society needs workers at all levels of jobs, the majority of which may very well be low-level."[44] One wonders if Judge Lerner would want this same level of education for his own children, or if he would think it fair and equitable for them. A message of low expectations delivered to students who should hear precisely the opposite is thus replicated even by those at the highest levels of a government claiming to be equitable to all students.

 ## The Complex Connections Between Diversity and Discrimination

Societal inequities are frequently reinforced in school policies and practices. Let us take the example of language. The fact that some children do not speak English when they start school cannot be separated from how their native language is viewed by the larger society or from the kinds of programs available for them in schools. Each of these programs—whether English as a second language (ESL), English immersion, or two-way bilingual education—has an underlying philosophy with broad implications for students' achievement or failure. As a consequence, each approach may have a profound influence on the quality of education that language minority children receive. However, linguistic and other differences do not exist independently of how they are perceived in the general society or by teachers: A complex relationship exists among a student's race, culture, native language, and other unique characteristics *and* institutional discrimination, school practices, and teacher and societal expectations.

Social class provides another example of the complex links between difference and discrimination. In spite of the enduring belief in our society that social class mobility is available to all, classism is a grim reality because *economic inequality is now greater in the United States than in many other wealthy nations in the world*. Given the vastly unequal resources of families at different socioeconomic levels, it should come as no surprise, then, that social class and educational attainment are strongly correlated.[45] In addition, social class inequality is especially pronounced and severe among children of color. Linked to this reality is the widely accepted classist view among some educators and others that poverty *causes* academic failure. Although poverty *can* have an adverse or even a devastating effect on student achievement, the belief that poverty and educational failure go hand in hand is questionable. We need to reiterate that the economic situation of students of color and other students living in poverty has often been used as an explanation for academic failure, but it is far more productive to investigate how high-achieving students in these groups are successful *in spite of* poverty and discrimination, among other problems. That is one of our goals in the case studies in this book. Examples such as those in our case studies demonstrate that, although poverty is certainly a disadvantage, it is not an insurmountable obstacle to learning.

Lest we fall into the trap of expecting all students and their parents to be heroic in their efforts to succeed in spite of all these obstacles, we should point out that students and their parents, no matter how much they try, cannot tackle all the odds by themselves. Thus, making the honor roll in a substandard school is vastly different from making the honor roll in an academically rigorous school with abundant resources and highly prepared teachers. One major explanation for low academic achievement is the lack of equitable resources given to students of different social classes and racial and ethnic backgrounds. For instance, one of the most disturbing findings concerning students' access to qualified teachers is this: Many more teachers with little academic preparation and little experience are teaching in schools serving poor children than in those serving middle-class children.[46] Thus, it is clear that the sociopolitical contexts of the schools attended by children of different social and economic classes are vastly unequal, and parents, no matter how noble and inspired, cannot change this by themselves. Therefore, schools need to take some of the responsibility for creating conditions that promote active and engaged student learning.

Although, in the ideal sense, education in the United States is based on the lofty values of democracy, freedom, and equal access for all, these examples point out how this has not been the case in reality. Historically, our educational system proposed to tear down the rigid systems of class and caste on which education in most of the world was (and still is) based and to provide all students with an equal education. Education was to be, as Horace Mann claimed, "the great equalizer," but as some educational historians have demonstrated, the common school's primary purposes were to replicate inequality and to control the unruly masses.[47] Thus, the original goals of public school education were often at cross purposes.

In the United States, mass public education began in earnest in the nineteenth century through the legislation of compulsory education, and its most eloquent democratic expression is found in the early twentieth-century philosophy of John Dewey.[48] In his utopian view, schools could be the answer to social inequality. Over time, however, schools have become one of the major sorting mechanisms of students of different backgrounds. The contradiction between Dewey's hope for education as a social equalizer and the actual unequal outcomes of schooling is with us even today. The commitment to educational equity that Dewey articulated continues through policies such as desegregation and multicultural and nonsexist education, and through legislation and policies aimed at eradicating existing inequalities. At the same time, the legacy of inequality also continues through unequal funding; rigid tracking; racial, ethnic, and social class segregation; and unfair test results. As a result, schools have often been sites of bitter conflict.

Race is another pivotal way in which privilege has been granted on an unequal basis. Based on his research, the historian David Tyack asserts that the struggle to achieve equality in education is nothing new and that race has often been at the center of this struggle. He adds, "Attempts to preserve white supremacy and to achieve racial justice have fueled the politics of education for more than a century."[49] On the other hand, those interested in equal education have not sat idly by. Assertive action on the part of parents, students, teachers, and other advocates for social justice has been crucial in challenging the schools to live up to their promise of equality. Schools were not racially desegregated simply because the courts ordered it, and gender-fair education was not legislated only because Congress thought it was a good idea. In both cases, as in many others, educational opportunity was expanded because many people—including parents, students, teachers, and community members—engaged in struggle, legal or otherwise, to bring about change.

Although, in theory, education is no longer meant to replicate societal inequities but rather to reflect the ideals of democracy, we know that such is not the reality. Henry Giroux has described the connection between racism and democracy in this way: "[H]ow we experience democracy in the future will depend on how we name, think about, experience, and transform the interrelated modalities of race, racism, and social justice."[50] If this is the case, we need to acknowledge that our schools, by historically failing to provide an equitable education for students of all backgrounds, have also failed to enact true democracy. The complex interplay of student differences, institutional racism and discrimination, teacher and societal biases that lead to low expectations, and unfair school policies and practices *all* play a role in keeping it this way.

Conclusion

Racism is unfortunately not a vestige of the past. Even in 2005, in the aftermath of Hurricane Katrina—a hurricane with tragic consequences for many people living in New Orleans and other Gulf Coast areas—racism was painfully obvious in how African Americans were treated. A study by the *Washington Post* confirmed the explicit racism in this situation, a racism that likely was not even perceived by those taking part in the study. Shanto Iyengar, director of the Political Communication Lab at Stanford University, asked more than 2,300 individuals to go to a Web site that featured a news article about the effects of the hurricane. The article was accompanied by a photograph of an individual. Unbeknown to the participants, the researcher varied the race, gender, and occupation of the featured person, so that while participants read the same article, it could be about an African American male or female, a White male or female, or a Latino or Latina. After they had read the article, participants were asked to determine how much government aid the victim should receive. If race did not matter, there would be no difference in the allocations. Race, however, *did* matter: Participants were willing to give assistance to a White victim for about a year, but the average for African Americans was a month shorter. In addition, African Americans would receive $1,000 less than Whites, and the darker the skin, the less the victim received. According to the article, the "penalty" for being Black was not just a psychological one but also a monetary one.[51]

Focusing on the persistence of racism and discrimination and low expectations is in no way intended to deny the difficult family and economic situation of many poor children and children of color, or its impact on their school experiences and achievement. The fact that living in poverty families do not have the resources and experiences that economic privilege would give them is also detrimental. Poverty can lead to stressors such as drug abuse, violence, and other social ills as well as poor medical care, deficient nutrition, and a struggle for the bare necessities for survival—and *all* of these conditions harm children's lives, including their school experiences.

However, blaming poor people and people from dominated racial or cultural groups for their educational problems is not the answer to solving societal inequities. Teachers can do nothing to change the conditions in which their students may live today, but they *can* work to change their own biases and the institutional structures that act as obstacles to student learning and to the possibilities for their students' futures. Although some teachers and other educators might prefer to think that students' lack of academic achievement is due solely to conditions inside their homes or inherent in their cultures, racism and other forms of institutional discrimination clearly play a central role in educational failure, as does the related phenomenon of low expectations.

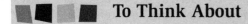

To Think About

1. Let's say that you are a high school teacher and you are having a discussion with your students about the benefits of education. This is your dilemma: Horace Mann's claim that education is "the great equalizer" has been criticized as simplistic or unrealistic. At the same time, a focus on racism, discrimination, and teachers' expectations can be criticized as being overly deterministic in explaining school failure, leading children to lose faith that education can make any difference at all. What is the appropriate approach to take with your students? Should you emphasize the tremendous opportunities that are available in our country? Should you instead focus on the barriers to taking advantage of opportunities, particularly for some segments of the population? Try role-playing this situation: As the teacher, lead your students in an attempt to find the most beneficial and the most realistic stance.

2. Think about schools with which you are familiar. Have you seen evidence of discrimination? Was it based primarily on race, gender, class, language, sexual orientation, or other differences? How was it manifested?

3. How would you go about "erasing stereotype threat" for students of color, as Claude Steele suggests? Think of some strategies in specific situations.

4. Describe a time when teachers' expectations did or did not make a difference in your life.

Activities *for Personal, School, and Community Change*

1. Develop a lesson for your classroom that directly focuses on racism and/or discrimination. If you teach one of the lower grades, you may want to use a children's book. With older students, you can base the lesson on a current event or on a personal experience that one of the students has had. Write and reflect on the outcome of the lesson. Was it difficult for you to plan? To implement? Why? What was the reaction of students? What have you learned from this teaching experience?

2. Ask one of your trusted colleagues to visit your classroom and observe your teaching for several days with the purpose of pointing out how you might unintentionally demonstrate low or high expectations for students. After debriefing your colleague, draw up a plan of action to address any instances she or he may have witnessed.

3. Begin a study group in your school to learn more about the effects of discrimination and racism on students and teachers. Plan to meet regularly for a specific amount of time (half a year, a year, or whatever time frame makes sense in your specific context). Select appropriate books from the references cited in this chapter, and write together about ways to combat these kinds of discrimination.

Case Studies

Linda Howard

Unless you're mixed, you don't know what it's like to be mixed.

Jefferson High School is a large, comprehensive high school in Boston. It has a highly diverse population of students from throughout the city, including African American, Puerto Rican and other Latino, Haitian, Cape Verdean, Vietnamese, Cambodian, Chinese American, other Asian American, and European American students. This is the high school from which Linda Howard, a 19-year-old senior, had just graduated.[1] Linda was the class valedictorian, was awarded a four-year scholarship to a prominent university in New England, and was looking forward to her college education. She was already thinking about graduate school, and although she had not yet decided what she wanted to study, she was contemplating majoring in education or English.

Frequently taken for Puerto Rican or Cape Verdean because of her biracial background (her father is African American, and her mother is European American), she resented these assumptions by those who did not know her. Linda's insistence about being recognized as biracial and multicultural sometimes put her in a difficult situation, especially with friends who pressured her to identify with either her Black or her White heritage. She remained steadfast in proclaiming her biracial identity in spite of the difficulty it caused her. Her friends were a mosaic of the varied backgrounds of her school and of the community in which she lived. Her best female friend was Puerto Rican, and her boyfriend Tyrone was West Indian.

Linda had an uneven academic career. At Tremont School, a highly respected magnet elementary school in the city, she had been very successful. The school's population was diverse, with children of different backgrounds from all over the city. She loved that school and has good memories of the caring teachers she had there. Because she was in an accident and had missed a great deal of school during her recuperation, by the time she reached junior high, she was held back twice, in both seventh and eighth grades. After the eighth grade, Linda transferred to Academic High, which she attended for two years before transferring to Jefferson High. She was a highly successful student, although she felt that Jefferson High was "too easy." The normal load for most students was four academic courses and two electives, but Linda had taken six academic courses per semester.

A gifted student, Linda was also a talented singer and even hoped to someday make a living as a musician. She inherited her love of music from her father, who had given up a career in music. The entire family sang together, and Linda claimed to be the best singer—when her father was not around. She was a member of the school choir and also studied music on her own. Music gave her great solace and motivated her to do her best. Linda was also gifted in language. She frequently wrote poems to express her feelings.

At the time of her interviews, Linda lived with her mother, father, one older brother, and two younger brothers in a middle-class, predominantly Black community in Boston. Her family had moved there from a public housing project 14 years before and bought their first home two years later. She still called the housing project and neighborhood where she grew up "part of my community, part of my heritage." Both of Linda's parents were working professionals, although that had not always been the case. She was proud of the fact that her father had started in the telephone company as a lineman some 20 years earlier and now had a white-collar job. Her mother was a human services administrator.

Being both outgoing and personable, Linda had a great many friends. Showing her more playful side, she told us she and some of them "cruise around, find cute guys, and yell out the window, 'Yo, baby!' That's how we hang!" Her boyfriend Tyrone was her "very best friend." They had known each other for seven years and were actually engaged when she was 15. She broke off the engagement because she felt that she had her life ahead of her and needed to plan for college and a career. One month before being interviewed, they had broken up completely but were still good friends. Linda said that she would do anything in the world for Tyrone.

Linda was very aware of her values and of the role her family played in their formation. Her interviews highlighted a number of issues central to understanding these values: her struggle concerning identity and racism, the importance of teachers' caring and their role in students' learning, and the great value of education in her life and her parents' influence over this factor.

Identity, Racism, and Self-Determination

My parents are Black and White American. I come from a long heritage. I am of French, English, Irish, Dutch, Scottish, Canadian, and African descent.

I don't really use race. I always say, "My father's Black, my mother's White, I'm mixed." But I'm American; I'm human. That's my race; I'm part of the human race.

After all these years, and all the struggling (because when [my parents] got married it was a time right before desegregation), people from all sides were telling them, "No, you'll never make it. You'll never make it. White and Black don't belong together in the same house." And after 20 years, they're still together and they're still strong. Stronger now than ever, probably. That's what I like the most about them. They fought against all odds, and they won.

It's hard when you go out in the streets and you've got a bunch of White friends and you're the darkest person there. No matter how light you are to the rest of your family, you're the darkest person there, and they say you're Black. Then you go out with a bunch of Black people, and you're the lightest there, and they say, "Yeah, my best friend's White." But I'm not. I'm both.

I don't always fit in—unless I'm in a mixed group. That's how it's different. Because if I'm in a group of people who are all one race, then they seem to look at me as being the other race . . . , whereas if I'm in a group full of [racially mixed] people, my race doesn't seem to matter to everybody else. . . . Then I don't feel like I'm standing out. But if I'm in a group of totally one race, then I sort of stand out, and that's something that's hard to get used to.

It's hard. I look at history, and I feel really bad for what some of my ancestors did to some of my other ancestors. Unless you're mixed, you don't know what it's like to be mixed.

My boss, who was a teacher of mine last year, just today said something about me being Puerto Rican. I said, "We've been through this before. I am not Puerto Rican. I am Black and White." I may look Hispanic, but this is what I mean. And this is a person who I've known for a whole year and a half now. [I felt] like I was insignificant. If, after all this time, he didn't know, and we discussed it last year. . . . It was insulting. I usually don't get insulted by it. I say, "Oh, no, I'm not Spanish. I'm Black and White." And people say, "Oh really? You are? I thought you were Spanish."

[Teachers should not] try to make us one or the other. And God forbid you should make us something we're totally not. . . . Don't write down that I'm Hispanic when I'm not. Some people actually think I'm Chinese when I smile. . . . Find out. Don't just make your judgments. And I'm not saying judgment as insulting judgments. But some people, they don't realize that there are so many intermarried couples today. You have to ask people what they are. If you really want to know, you have to ask them. You don't just make assumptions. 'Cause you know what happens when you assume. . . . If you're filling out someone's report card form and you need to know, then ask.

I don't know how to put this . . . race hasn't really been a big factor for me. Because in my house, my mother's White; my father's Black; I was raised with everybody. Sometimes I don't even notice. I see people walking down the street. I don't care what they are; they're people.

My culture is my family. I have an enormous family. I have three brothers, two parents, and my father has ten brothers and sisters, and all of my aunts and uncles have children. That to me is my culture . . . I was born and raised in America. I'm fourth-generation American, so it's not like I'm second generation, where things were brought over from a different country or brought and instilled in me. I'm just American, and my culture is my family, and what we do as a family. Family is very important to us. . . . My family is the center of my life.

I've had people tell me, "Well, you're Black." I'm not Black; I'm Black and White. I'm Black and White American. "Well, you're Black!" No, I'm not! I'm both. It's insulting, when they try and . . . bring it right back to the old standards, that if you have anybody in your family who's Black, you're Black. . . . I mean, I'm not ashamed of being Black, but I'm not ashamed of being White either, and, if I'm both, I want to be part of both. And I think teachers need to be sensitive to that.

I would say I have more Black culture than White . . . because I know all about fried chicken and candied yams and grits and collard greens and ham hocks and all that because that's what we eat . . . . My father had to teach my mother how to cook all that stuff [laughs]. But that's just as far as food goes . . . . But as far as everything else, my family is my culture.

See, the thing is, I mix it at home so much that it's not really a problem for me to mix it outside. But then again, it's just my mother and my grandmother on the "White side," so it's not like I have a lot to mix.

I don't think [being interracial is] that big of a problem. It's not killing anybody. At least as far as I know, it's not. It's not destroying families and lives and stuff. It's a minor thing. If you learn how to deal with it at a young age, as I did, it really doesn't bother you the rest of your life, like drugs. . . .

In the city, I don't think there's really much room for racism, especially anymore, because there's just so many different cultures. You can't be a racist. . . . I think it's *possible,* but I don't think it's logical. I don't think it was ever logical. It's possible. It's very possible, but it's sort of ridiculous to give it a try.

I think we're all racist in a sense. We all have some type of person that we don't like, whether it's from a different race, or from a different background, or they have different habits. But to me a *serious racist* is a person who believes that people of different ethnic backgrounds don't belong or should be in *their* space and shouldn't invade *our* space: "Don't come and invade my space, you Chinese person. You belong over in China or you belong over in Chinatown."

Racists come out and tell you that they don't like who you are. Prejudiced people [on the other hand] will say it in like those little hints, you know, like, "Oh, yes, some of my best friends are Black." Or they say little ethnic remarks that they know will insult you, but they won't come out and tell you, "You're Black. I don't want anything to do with you." Racists, to me, would come out and do that.

Both racists and prejudiced people make judgments, and most of the time they're wrong judgments, but the racist will carry his one step further. . . . A racist is a person that will carry out their prejudices.

[Racists have power] only if you let them! We'll stick with [the example of] striped shirts: If I go where everyone is wearing solids, and I'm wearing a stripe, and someone comes up to me and tells me, "You don't belong here; you're wearing stripes," I'll say, "I belong anywhere I want to belong." And I'll stand right there! But there are some people who just say, "Oh, okay," and will turn around and leave. Then the racist has the power.

I wrote a poem about racism. I despise [racism]. . . .

> Why do they hate me?
> I'll never know
> Why not ride their buses
> in the front row?
> Why not share their fountains
> or look at their wives?
> Why not eat where they do
> or share in their lives?
> Can't walk with them
> Can't talk with them unless I'm a slave
> But all that I wonder is who ever gave
> them the right to tell me
> What I can and can't do
> Who I can and can't be
> God made each one of us
> just like the other
> The only difference is,
> I'm darker in color.

I had a fight with a woman at work. She's White, and at the time I was the only Black person in my department. Or I was the only person who was at *all* Black in my department. And she just kept on laying on the racist jokes. At one point, I said, "You know, Nellie, you're a racist pig!" And she got offended by *that*. And I was just joking, just like she'd been joking for two days straight—all the racist jokes that she could think of. And we got into a big fight over it. She threw something at me, and I was ready to kill her. . . . She started to get down and dirty. . . . She was really getting evil. . . . They locked her out of the room, and they had to hold me back because I was going to throttle her.

She thought I was upset because she tossed the water at me. I said, "You know, Nellie, it's not the water. It's all these remarks you've been saying. And you just don't seem to have any regard for my feelings."

I remember one thing she was talking about. She said, "I'm not racist, just because I was jumped by eight Black girls when I was in the seventh grade, I'm not racist." After [30] years, why was she still saying they were eight *Black* girls? That to me was insulting. That was then; this is now. I didn't do it to you. I didn't jump you. It wasn't my father who jumped you; it wasn't my aunt who jumped you. . . . I told her I didn't want it taken out on me, that's the thing. I don't want anybody's racism taken out on me.

I've got a foot on both sides of the fence, and there's only so much I can take. I'm straddling the fence, and it's hard to laugh and joke with you when you're talking about the foot that's on the other side.

She couldn't understand it. We didn't talk for weeks. And then one day, I had to work with her. We didn't say anything for the first . . . like two hours of work. And then I just said, "Smile, Nellie, you're driving me nuts!" and she smiled and laughed. And we've been good friends ever since. She just knows you don't say ethnic things around me; you don't joke around with me like that because I won't stand for it from you anymore. We can be friends; we can talk about anything else—except race.

Teachers, Role Models, and Caring

My first-grade teacher and I are very close. She's always been there for me. After the first or second grade, if I had a problem, I could always go back to her. Through the whole rest of my life, I've been able to go back and talk to her. She's a Golden Apple Award winner, which is a very high award for elementary school teachers. She keeps me on my toes. When I start getting down, she peps me back up, and I get back on my feet.

All of my teachers were wonderful. I don't think there's a teacher at the whole Tremont School that I didn't like. It's just a feeling you have. You know that they really care for you. You just know it; you can tell. Teachers who don't have you in any of their classes or haven't ever had you, they still know who you are. . . . The Tremont School in itself is a community. I love that school!

I knew [Academic High] would be a hard school, but I didn't know it would be so . . . they're just so rigid. The teachers, there's no feeling. Like I said, the Tremont was a community for me, and I loved it. I'm that type of person; I'm an outgoing person, and I like to be able to talk to anybody and not feel that I can't talk to someone. If I have to spend six hours a day in school, I want to feel that I can talk to my teachers. At Academic, I didn't feel that at all. I hated it, absolutely hated it. They let me know that I wasn't high anymore. I was average. They slapped me with it. My first report card, oh goodness, it was terrible. I don't remember exactly what grades they were; I just do remember it was the first time in my life I had seen an F or a D under my name.

I think you have to be creative to be a teacher. You have to make it interesting. You can't just go in and say, "Yeah, I'm going to teach the kids right out of the book and that's the way it is, and don't ask questions." Because then you're gonna lose their interest. . . . Because I know there were plenty of classes where I lost complete interest. But those were all because the teachers just [said], "Open the books to this page." They never made up problems out of their head. Everything came out of the book. You didn't ask questions. If you asked them questions, then the answer was "in the book." And if you asked the question and the answer wasn't in the book, then you shouldn't have asked that question!

Mr. Benson, he cared; he was the only one of the two Black teachers [at Jefferson High School]. He was not enough. The other Black teacher, he was a racist, and I didn't like him. I belonged to the Black Students' Association, and he was the advisor. And he just made it so obvious . . . he was all for Black supremacy. A lot of times, whether they deserved it or not, his Black students passed, and his White students, if they deserved an A, they got a B. He was insistent that only Hispanics and Blacks be allowed in the club. He had a very hard time letting me in because I'm not all Black. . . . I just really wasn't that welcome there. He never found out what I was about. He just made his judgments from afar. He knew that I was Black and White, and I looked too White for him, I guess. But we never discussed it.

At Jefferson, just about the whole school is like a big community. There are very few White, Caucasian, whatever you want to call them, us [laughing]. There are very few, but they don't cluster together. It's all integrated. . . . Nobody gets treated differently. We're all the same.

I've enjoyed all my English teachers at Jefferson. But Mr. Benson, my English Honors teacher, he just threw me for a whirl! I wasn't going to college until I met this man. He was one of the few teachers I could talk to. Instead of going to lunch, I used to go to Mr. Benson's room, and he and I would just sit and talk and talk and talk. My father and Mr. Benson share a lot of the same values. And every time I've heard Mr. Benson talk, all I could think about was Daddy: "Oh, that's exactly what my father says!" . . . "Education, get your education and go far." "Whether you're flipping burgers at the local joint or you're up there working on Wall Street, be proud of yourself."

'Cause Mr. Benson, he says, I can go into Harvard and converse with those people, and I can go out in the street and "rap with y'all." It's that type of thing. I love it. I try and be like that myself. I have my street talk. I get out in the street and I say "ain't" this and "ain't" that and "your momma" or "wha's up?" But I get somewhere where I know the people aren't familiar with that language or aren't accepting that language, and I will talk properly. . . . I walk into a place, and I listen to how people are talking, and it just automatically comes to me.

Mr. Benson is the same as I am. Well, his mother was Black and his father was White, so Mr. Benson and I could relate on all the problems that you face in the world. Like when you go to fill out any kind of form and they ask you, "Black, White, Chinese, Hispanic, Other." I check off "Other" and I'll write it down. And then Mr. Benson told me that he found out that when you write it down, they put you under "Black" because it all comes back to the old laws about, if you had any Black blood in you, you were Black.

I wrote a poem about it. It was just a bunch of questions: "What am I?" I had filled out a whole bunch of college essays, and I was tired of having to write out "Other: Black American and White American." And I went to him and I said, "Mr. Benson, what do you do when you get all these forms and they ask you 'Black, White, or Other?' And he said, "You might as well just fill out 'Black' because that's what they'll do to you." That just drives me nuts! And we got on this big conversation about it.

He came from the lower class in Chicago and worked his way [up], and he studied every night, six hours a night. He got into Harvard, and he went to Harvard, and now he's back helping the people who needed help. Because the way he sees it, he could go and he could teach at Phillips Academy, and he could teach at Boston Latin, which he did for awhile. But those people don't need his help. That's how he sees it. They're gonna learn with or without him. He wanted to come back to a small community, the underprivileged community, and help those people. That's what made me admire him the most because I like to help people.

The teacher who didn't really help me at all in high school was my computer lit. teacher. Because I have no idea about computer literacy. I got A's in that course. Just because he saw that I had A's and that my name was all around the school for all the "wonderful things" I do, he just automatically assumed. He didn't really pay attention to who I was. The grade I think I deserved in that class was at least a C, but I got A just because everybody else gave me A's. But everybody else gave me A's because I earned them. He gave me A's because he was following the crowd. He just assumed, "Yeah, well, she's a good student." And I showed up to class every day. . . . He didn't help me at all because he didn't challenge me. Everybody else challenges me; I had to earn their grades. I didn't have to earn his grade. I just had to show up.

I *hated* math up until the second time I was in the seventh grade. . . . I despised math until I met Ms. Morgan. And from that point on, I have never received less than a B in math. She turned every math problem . . . every type of math problem was a game, so that school is never, "This is the way it is, and that's just it. Just learn it." I'd make everything exciting and fun, or I'd try to. That makes school enjoyable.

Family Values and Education

In the Tremont and in the Williams [schools], I was the top of my class, well, not top of my class, but I was very high up in the ranks. . . . That all comes from family. My mother's been reading me books since probably the day I was born, up until school age . . . any book with a serious message for children. My mother's always been very big on that, to make sure that reading was important. I still love to read . . . mysteries, human interest stories. It made a difference in elementary school. It really did. And, actually, it made a difference in high school, after I left Academic High, because I graduated first in my class.

The first five years of your life, that's when you develop the most. Before you go to school, you've already got your personality. If you have parents who are showing you the right values (not "*the* right values" because everybody's values to them are right . . .), whatever values they've given you are what you carry for the rest of your life.

That's the way my family has raised me. . . . They really taught me not to judge. You just accept [people] the way they are. With my family, if you go to church, you go to church; if you don't, you don't. My grandmother says, "Jesus still loves you and I still love you, whether you go to church or not." It's that kind of thing. You just learn to accept people.

Sexuality—I don't judge, I try not to, anyway. I'm sure subconsciously I do . . . I don't come out and say, "Ugh, he's gay." My neighborhood is thoroughly mixed and sexually open. And they're my neighbors. I don't differentiate them. And that's something I wish a lot of people would do. Because I think it's wrong. Because if you were to take people and differentiate because of their preferences, be it sexual or anything, *everybody's* different. I prefer a certain type of music; you prefer a different type of music. Does that mean we have to hate each other? Does that mean you have to pick on me and call me names? That's the way I see it.

I'm not going to be exactly like my parents. I grew up with basic values. And I follow those basic values. And if you think about it, the choices I make have something to do with my values. And the only place I got my values from was [home]. So, I may change things around, flip them over, just adjust them a bit. But they still come down to my home values, my basic values, and my basic values came from home.

[My parents] have always taken good care of me. They're always there for me, all the time, if I need to talk. And they make it so obvious that they love me, you know, with these ridiculous curfews that I have [*laughs*]. I know it's for the better, although I can't stand it; I know there's a reason behind it, some twisted reason! . . . Just a regular night out, I have to be in at midnight. If it's a party, I don't have to be in 'til two. All my friends stay out 'til three and four in the morning. But that's because their parents can go to sleep. My parents can't sleep if I'm not home. That's what I like the most about them.

I was reading an article the other day about how the family dinner has sort of been tossed out the window in today's society. My family sits down to dinner together four out of seven nights a week, all six of us. Dinner's at six. If it's late, then everybody waits. You don't just eat on your own. I've noticed a lot of people, my boyfriend, for one, they never eat together. I've had all kinds of friends who always say, "Your family *eats* [together]?" And that's different from other families.

It's very important to my parents, and it'll be important to me. Because that's the time when we sit down and say, "How was your day? What'd you do? How are you feeling? Do you have a headache? Did you have a rough day? Did you have a good day?" You know? And that's about the only time the whole family can sit together and talk and discuss.

I have wonderful parents, although I don't tell them [*laughing*]. [*Do they know?*] Probably. My parents know that the further I go in school, the better life I'll have. Because they had to struggle to get where they are today. They had to struggle to make themselves comfortable. Going to school is going to be a struggle. But as long as I'm in school, my parents will always be there for me. Whereas if I go and get myself a college education, I'm not going to have to start splicing lines if I want to work at the telephone company. I'm going to start with the knowledge that I don't have to splice a line. I could start in the office with my father.

A lot of us [Black kids] just don't have the home life. I really do think it begins when you're a baby! My mother, like I said, I believe she read to me from the day I was born; I'm sure of it. A lot of people just didn't have that. Their parents both had to work; they didn't have anybody at home to read to them. They just sat in front of the tube all day. When they came home from school, their homework was just tossed aside, and they sat in front of the television until Mom and Dad came home. Then Mom and Dad rushed them through dinner, got them to bed, and this and that.

I blew two years. I learned a lot from it. As a matter of fact, one of my college essays was on the fact that, from that experience, I learned that I don't need to hear other people's praise to get by. All I need to know is in here [*pointing to her heart*] whether I tried or not.

It's not the school you go to. It's what you want to get out of it and what you take from it.

If I know I did my hardest, if I know I tried my very best and I got an F, I'd have a beef with the teacher about it, but if that's what I got, that's what I got. If that's seriously what I earned after all my efforts, then I'll have to live with it.

[Grades] are not that important. To me, they're just something on a piece of paper. . . . [My parents] feel just about the same way. If they ask me, "Honestly, did you try your best?" and I tell them yes, then they'll look at the grades and say okay. . . . The first thing my father always looked at was conduct and effort. If all the letter grades in the academic grades said F's, and I had A's in conduct and effort, then my father would just see the F's, and say "Oh, well . . . "

[The reason for going to school is] to make yourself a better person. To learn more, not only about the world and what other people have gathered as facts, but to learn more about yourself. The more that there are opportunities for you to learn, you should always take them. I just want to keep continuously learning because when you stop learning, then you start dying.

I've got it all laid out. I've got a four-year scholarship to one of the best schools in New England. All I've gotta do is go there and make the grade.

If I see the opportunity to become a leader, I'll do it. I'll just go and take over. . . . I like the recognition. I'm ready now. I can face the challenge. I'm ready to go out in the world and let [that] university know who I am!

Commentary

Issues of identity were clearly at the core of Linda's striving to carve out a place for herself in her family, community, and school. Although she had reached quite a sophisticated understanding of race, racial awareness, racism, and identity, some feelings of ambivalence, conflict, and pain were still apparent. Being "mixed," to use Linda's term, is the reality of more and more students in U.S. schools. In fact, it is estimated that in some large urban areas, one in six children is multiracial.[2] In spite of this reality, many schools are unaware of the strains, dilemmas, and benefits that biracial identity poses for children.

It is likely that most people in the United States are a mixture of several racial heritages, but this is either not known or not readily acknowledged. *Miscegenation*, or racial mixing, is far more common than generally admitted in our society. Discomfort with this issue is understandable, given the history of rape and subjugation forced on African American women, especially during slavery. This is an example of the legacy of racism; so is the "one-drop" rule—the idea that one drop of Black blood makes a person Black—to which Linda alluded. In fact, the "one-drop" rule was reaffirmed as late as 1982 in a court decision in Louisiana, in which one thirty-second African ancestry was sufficient to keep "Black" on an individual's birth certificate.[3] This classification, which has not been used in other societies, was not always the case in the United States either. Rather, it emerged some time in the early eighteenth century.[4] The classification benefited the preservation of the institution of slavery because, with this logic, people could still be enslaved even if they were mostly White. Like race itself, this was a social and political construction rather than a biological one.

Although during the first half of the twentieth century, interracial marriages in the United States had declined dramatically from previous centuries, they began to increase again after the civil rights movement, and particularly after miscegenation laws were overturned by the U.S. Supreme Court on June 12, 1967, in the *Loving v. Virginia* case (aptly named because it was about the right of people—regardless of race—to love one another). It is now estimated that about 7 percent of all marriages in the United States are interracial.[5]

Considering the racist underpinnings of group and self-identification in the United States, the dilemmas Linda faced were difficult indeed. According to psychologist Maria Root, the existing psychological models of racial and cultural identity development have not yet caught up with the reality of a rapidly expanding multiracial and multiethnic population. As a result, young people are still adversely affected by mixed-race heritage. If they are of mixed heritage, particularly if that includes European American background, these youngsters are often seen as "less authentic" African Americans, Asian Americans, or Latinos. Thus, she claims, "Authenticity tests are a form of racial hazing and illogically enforce a limited, superficial solidarity."[6] On the other hand, the

About Terminology

Whites, European Americans

What is the appropriate term to use for White people? As the majority in U.S. society, Whites seldom think of themselves as ethnic; they tend to reserve this term for other, more easily identifiable groups. Nevertheless, the fact is that we are all ethnic, whether or not we choose to identify in this way. Because Whites in U.S. society tend to think of themselves as the norm, they often view other groups as ethnic and therefore somewhat exotic and colorful. By using the term *European American*, we hope to challenge Whites to see themselves as ethnic. Although "Whiteness" is an important factor, it hides more than it reveals: There is a tremendous diversity of ethnic backgrounds among Whites, and this is lost if race or color is used as the only identifier.

The term *European American* implies culture, too, although many European Americans lament that they do not have culture. But everybody has a culture, whether clearly manifested in its more traditional forms or not. The term *European American*, like all terms, has its drawbacks. For one, although it is more specific than *White*, it is still overly inclusive of a great many ethnic backgrounds that may have little in common other than race or color. (A similar criticism applies to terms such as *African, Asian*, or *Latin American*.) Another drawback to the use of the term *European American* is that many European Americans are a mixture of several European ethnic groups. A person may be German, Irish, and Italian (they may affectionately refer to themselves as Heinz 57) and not speak any of the languages or follow any of the traditions associated with any of these cultures. It is reasonable to ask, in such

situation is complex because mixed-race identity also has its advantages. As author Rebecca Walker has suggested, the situation for multiracial individuals is complex. According to her, "a new generation, a multiracial president, and a shifting global environment demand that we rethink the old tropes of multiracial identity. It's hip to be multi now.[7]" Thus, in spite of its increasing visibility, multiracial identity is both more complicated and more fluid than it has ever been.

In spite of—or perhaps because of—the relative invisibility of mixed-race people, especially at the time she was first interviewed in 1990, Linda identified most strongly with her family. As she said, "My culture is my family." And because her family was mixed, so was her culture. Hers was a particularly courageous stand in a society that forced an individual to choose one identity over the other or fit a person into one that she or he would not necessarily choose. Linda did not expect all her teachers to be biracial like herself, but she did expect them all to be sensitive and accepting of who she was, rather than imposing their own ideas about identity on her. The teachers who stood out were not only those with whom she could identify culturally but also those who made learning fun, engaging, and challenging.

Linda Howard, an extraordinary young woman, was ambitious, certain of her talents, and ready for the future. No doubt, her strong family bonds, love of learning, cases, why they should be called *European American* when they are essentially "as American as apple pie." Of course, the same can be said of African Americans, Latinos, and Asian Americans whose families have been in the United States for any length of time and for Native Americans, the original inhabitants of the continent. European Americans may never have even visited Europe, for example, or may not identify at all with a European heritage. Nevertheless, we have chosen to use the term *European American* because the traditions, values, and behaviors of White Americans are grounded in European mores and values. Although they may be far removed from their European heritage and may have drastically changed and adapted to U.S. mainstream culture, their roots are still European.

We do not use the terms *Anglo* and *Anglo American,* except when speaking specifically of those with an English heritage, because these are inaccurate terms for referring to Whites in the United States. Many Whites are not English in origin but rather come from a wide variety of ethnic groups from other European societies. Classifying all Whites as Anglos is even more of an overgeneralization than calling them European Americans. If used to contrast English speakers from speakers of other languages, the term *Anglo American* is equally inaccurate because African Americans, among others whose native language is English, are not included in this classification. In addition, it is a term rejected by some, not the least of whom are many Irish Americans, who are often understandably offended at being identified with an English heritage because of the oppression they suffered under the British.

and steadfast identification as Black and White all contributed to her academic success. Her teachers and schools were not always able to understand or support her, which emphasizes the importance of a school's social context and the degree to which it can insulate students from racism and influence their self-esteem.

Reflect on This Case Study

1. Linda Howard insisted on identifying as biracial. She also said that she was just "a member of the human race" and that race was not very important to her. Nevertheless, she obviously spent a great deal of time thinking about race, as some of her anecdotes and poems make clear. Are these assertions contradictory? Why or why not?

2. If you were one of Linda's teachers, how might you affirm her identity? Give specific examples.

3. What can you learn, for your own teaching, from the teachers who have been most influential in Linda's life? What are the implications for curriculum? For pedagogy? For relationships with students?

4. Can issues of race and identity be handled by schools, or are these issues too complicated for them? What skills do you think you need if you are to face these issues effectively?

Rashaud Kates

I am African American. My culture is important to me. It is who I am.

Rashaud Kates, a soft-spoken African American high school student in a midsize town on the southern coast of Georgia, was getting ready to start his senior year of high school at the time of this interview.[1]

Rashaud lived with his mother because his parents had recently divorced, but his father continued to figure prominently in his life. He had older siblings from his mom's first marriage who lived on their own. One sister, with whom he spent a great deal of time, lived nearby. His family lived within very modest means in a neighborhood close to his school that he described as "safe and quiet." His father, a former U.S. Marine, worked for a law enforcement training center. His mother was a housekeeper and also worked at his church.

Rashaud was attending a comprehensive high school for grades 9–12 with approximately 1,600 students. A high-achieving student, he cared deeply about his grades, especially as they reflected his parents' pride and his collegiate future. Co-curricular activities also played a significant role in his school life. He was a member of the after-school club Future Business Leaders of America.[2] Rashaud also played on the school basketball team and looked forward to playing varsity his senior year. The school population was racially diverse: 55 percent White students; 42 percent Black students; and small percentages of Hispanic, Native American, and Asian students. Just under 40 percent of the students were eligible for free or reduced lunch.

Rashaud's school life can be viewed through the lens of the broader context of Black students in U.S. schools. The data on the schooling experience of many African American students, especially young men, reflect the "crisis in Black education" cited by scholars of the American Educational Research Association (AERA) Commission on Research in Black Education (CORIBE).[3] In several studies, the commission documents the overwhelmingly unequal learning opportunities for students of African heritage and calls for a transformative research agenda.[4] Disparities in graduation rates, resources, and access to qualified teachers; racial bias in special education; and cultural alienation in curriculum and instruction are among the many documented characteristics that contribute to systemic inequality for many students of color, especially low-income African American youth.

These realities permeate the lives of many students. Nevertheless, Rashaud, his family, and many of his teachers demonstrated resolve in overcoming institutional discriminatory structures to cultivate a bright future. Rashaud's deep family roots, connections to school, and abiding trust in the promise of education undergird all three themes that emerged in his case study: *determined responsibility, plans for the future,* and *the enduring influence of teachers' expectations,* with which we begin.

The Enduring Influence of Teachers' Expectations

I am African American. My culture is important to me. It is who I am. [But] being an African American student, to me, really it's kinda' tense. People look at you every way, to see if you're doing stuff wrong, but really you don't [do anything wrong]. If you were somebody else, they really wouldn't look at you like that. People are already judging you when you're African American. I would tell teachers about African American students, "Everybody's not bad; have high expectations."

The school does Black History Month. That's about the only time [the school recognizes my culture]. There are mostly White teachers in my school. If a student is trying to do what they need to do, that's all that really matters. It shouldn't matter if the teacher is a different race. The thing that might hold me back from getting a good education, sometimes is that when I first meet a teacher, the teacher thinks I'm bad 'cause I'm Black. I overcome it by just being me, just who I am; then they see me as a regular person.

Sometimes I think it's just the way things are, but you could really do something about it if people would just stop acting up and stuff. Then teachers would be able to understand that everybody ain't bad or whatever. My advice for other African American boys entering our school is, "Don't act like everybody else, like the kids who are acting up. You gotta work hard, study, and stay focused."

I had teachers who I learned a lot from. Ms. Teshek in fourth grade. She joked a lot, she used to have us laughing all the time . . . it was really fun . . . she was really fun. We learned more from her because it made us pay more attention. She taught everything . . . math, reading, science, and everything.

Another teacher in middle school, Ms. Hollis, . . . she was a seventh-grade teacher; she taught math. She was strict. To me, it was good; to other people it might have been bad. It was good because that's how my daddy is about my grades and stuff, so I was just used to it. She used to have a ruler she carried around, and she used to hit the desk all the time to let you know that she was expecting something out of you. A teacher needs to let you know that they expect a lot. It makes you work harder. When a teacher is strict like that, they are doing it because they care about you. I did well in math that year. See, with my daddy, if I get a D or something on my progress report, I get a punishment or something until I get my grades up. Sometimes he gave me a bit of money if I did real good. If I didn't get a good progress report, there would be punishment.

Also, in middle school, Ms. Ketchem, in English—she spent time with me after class, to teach me stuff. In English I did good because she helped me so much. Sometimes after school, sometimes during the lunch break, mostly after school, whenever she could, she would help me know where to put the commas and stuff like that.

Another teacher is from a class I took during tenth-grade year called "Entrepreneurship"; I just really liked it. We made business plans and discussed them, and all this stuff. [We learned about] developing a business; I made a clothing store. I learned so much; I was in FBLA [Future Business Leaders of America]. I joined last year as a junior. It was fun; I felt like a real businessman. We would go and volunteer a lot. We volunteered at Ronald McDonald House in Savannah and we went to a couple of nursing homes. We try to think about how we can help. Mr. Richards runs FBLA, [the] same teacher who taught Entrepreneurship. He helps me think about college.

My favorite subject is math . . . learning about money . . . knowing about money. Maybe Ms. Hollis from seventh grade had something to do with that. If you do well in math you can manage your money better. My least favorite is history. I don't really see a point in knowing what happened in 1720 or whatever . . . all those dates. If I could tell the teacher what I want to learn, I would want to know about the wars. Now they only teach about World War II. We never make it to the subject of the war in Iraq or even the Vietnam War. The war now is never discussed.

If I were principal of the school . . . I would listen to the students' suggestions. We do go to the principal about a lot of stuff. I don't feel like they really listen. For the prom, it was suggested to have a DJ instead of the band, and they didn't listen to that. Then, they only had one pep rally for the whole year. It was for football season. They didn't listen about that.

Some teachers need to be more laid back. Some of them are always on you for the small stuff. Not the way Ms. Hollis was because she was on us to get good grades. Some teachers are just always, always on you for nothing.

Determined Responsibility

I'm an OK student. I messed up my A/B honor roll last year. In ninth and tenth grade I was on the A/B honor roll. But last year in eleventh grade, because of literature class, I messed up at the end of the year. I don't know, I was just slackin'. I got a C. I was disappointed. I do think I'll get back on honor roll senior year because I'm going to work hard. If I feel myself slacking, if my grades start to go, I'll go to the teachers and ask if I can do some makeup work or something.

The way to succeed is through determination. You gotta be determined to do it. If you're not, you won't get it done. Determination means a lot. You need an education to better yourself in life. To get an education, to broaden life, it makes more opportunities and stuff. I think I am accomplishing that.

My parents want to see me successful and get a chance to start my business . . . to be secure financially. My brother didn't graduate from high school. My parents check my grades. They tell me what they are thinking. It matters to me because if they didn't care, I wouldn't care. Since they do, I really do. I really want to make them proud. I think I am getting what I need out of school. Sometimes I wish I could get more out of it. Like some of the classes. Like the literature. I wish I could get more out of the literature. We were learning about allegory and all that, which I liked and then literature class changed. It doesn't seem [to mean] much about anything. There's not really any stories or literature about African Americans in our school.

Plans for the Future

Freshman year I did not play basketball because everybody was telling me it was the hardest year. I was worried about grades, so I didn't play basketball. I did good in school, so sophomore and junior year I played JV. Senior year will be my varsity year. I'd like to play in college.

Guidance counselors are talking about college. They told me to take the SAT test, and I did. They are telling us to take all the tests. They told me I can go to the community college down here, but I really want to go to Georgia State. I have looked at the college application. For financing college, I am going to try to apply for scholarships. I have been on the Internet looking. In the guidance office, I heard about some scholarships. My parents don't say too much about college. They don't really know what to say about it; they haven't been to college. They don't know what it is like. Maybe they worry about money; they just don't talk about college. They want me to go.

If I don't get on the basketball team, I'll still go to college. Sports at college are like this: I would like to play sports so I gotta keep my grades up to be able to play sports, so it helps. But if I don't play sports, I will still be keeping my grades up. The [Georgia State] basketball team is good—I want to play sports, but I gotta keep the grades up, too.

When I am done with college I want to start my own business. I am not too sure yet what business. I am just interested in the business world. I am going to apply to Alabama State, too. That's about all I'm looking at right now. The college here is a community college. A four-year college would be better.

Commentary

Juggling academic achievement with co-curricular activities, part-time employment, family commitments, and participation in a faith community is a balancing act for many American teens, as it was for Rashaud. He enjoyed sports and after-school clubs, and worked at his church, and although he did not have much time for TV, he enjoyed watching sports news shows when he had the chance. He also liked reading mysteries, listening to R&B, and eating chili-cheese-dogs and hamburgers. He cared about school achievement and realized the importance of good grades for his future.

Rashaud knew that he had to overcome the persistence of institutionalized racism in schools. He put it plainly, "The teacher thinks I'm bad 'cause I'm Black." Rashaud's encounters with negative discriminatory expectations echo the experiences of many African American students. The destructive effect of institutionalized racism on students' perceptions of their racial identities is not always obvious to students like Rashaud who develop achievement strategies to counteract the racism. The prevalence of these experiences makes it clear that Rashaud articulated a phenomenon that reaches beyond individual bias; however, he viewed changing this dynamic as the sole responsibility of the students "who act up." The overwhelming social message that individual effort may defeat powerful structural obstacles runs deep. Rashaud did not entertain the possibility that the institutional structures themselves need to be changed.

A study by Ann Arnett Ferguson describes how certain forms of punishment in schools perpetuate the identity of "troublemakers and potential inmates," especially among African American boys, while she makes an argument for changing classroom strategies.[5] Reports by researchers Angel Love and Ann Cale Kruger stress the importance of educating teachers to examine their beliefs related to knowledge, race and culture, teaching practices, teaching as a profession, and expectations of students.[6] The results of such teacher education could change both the students' and teachers' views of the prospects for Rashaud and his peers.

Most students are not taught to assess critically the hierarchies of institutional discrimination and cultural bias that exist in many schools. Rashaud's case shows that he and other students appear to maintain faith in the notion of American meritocracy, believing that determination and hard work alone will bring them success, even when inequities stare them in the face. Research by Prudence Carter noted the persistence of this hopeful yet seemingly contradictory mind-set—that is, that many African American students acknowledge the existence of racism and its influence on their lives and schooling, while at the same time, they are frequently emphatic that their potential success or failures are contingent upon their own personal determination and hard work.[7]

In contrast to the disparaging incidents and situations he faced, Rashaud also remembered a number of teachers who had positively influenced his learning. His description of the warmth and humor of his fourth-grade teacher appeared to be in direct opposition with the seventh-grade math teacher's ruler-banging strategies, yet he said that both styles contributed to his success. We wonder whether the math teacher's rigorous expectations could be developed without the ruler banging, but the point remains that a range of approaches may lead to academic achievement, which is another implication of Angel Love and Ann Cale Kruger's study. They point out that numerous pathways can be followed to teach African American children successfully and that successful teachers may hold an eclectic array of beliefs.[8]

Stories about students like Rashaud underscore the significance of providing curricula, as well as teaching methods, in which students see reflections of themselves and their heritage. Rashaud explicitly yearned for more curriculum, in both social studies and literature courses, that reflected the cultural perspectives of his ancestors as well as his current social and political realities. He may have been edging toward school disengagement with his report of "slackin'" in the literature course, but his resolve to strengthen his grade in the class appeared to draw from a matrix of other support systems. Despite the variety of factors that may have been impeding or promoting his success, Rashaud's sense of self-determination mattered a great deal. His effort to maintain a high level of school engagement may be attributed to a web of intricate factors, not the least of which were his parents' supportive expectations, his views on a productive future, the efforts of many dedicated (if not always culturally responsive) teachers, and his involvement in co-curricular activities.

While Rashaud stated that he was receiving some counseling about the local community college, he appeared to have been left on his own to navigate applying to comprehensive four-year institutions and seeking out scholarships—a high hurdle, to be sure. Several researchers highlight the necessity of mentors to support students of color in this process, which is so vital to socioeconomic upward mobility.[9] Prudence Carter, for example, refers to such mentors as multicultural navigators.[10] Especially for African American males in underresourced schools and communities, multicultural navigators may have an enduring imprint on a student's future. To be guided by an adult who is fluent in the social and cultural capitals of college admissions and scholarship acquisition can make the difference between discouraged confusion and confident assertion for a student. A mentor's sustained support may help a young person to endure the academic rigors of higher education and stay in college and facilitate the youth's passage into independent adulthood.

Rashaud's family was explicitly supportive of his aspirations but may not have had access to the experiences needed to provide multicultural navigation. Rashaud may still have been able to break through the institutional barriers, even in the absence of a specific mentor or a school program or structure to facilitate college entrance. Will Rashaud's commitment to academic achievement, determination to disprove stereotypes, engagement in community service, and athletic skills be enough for him to gain admission to a realm that few people in his daily life have entered? Will he sustain his vision of his future? If so, what resources will he be able to access to pursue his hopeful vision as a successful businessperson? More to the point, how many peers of African heritage will he see in his college classes and in his potential business meetings? Will Rashaud be a celebrated exception or part of revolutionary change? The answers to these questions may depend in large part on the teachers of African American students.

Reflect on This Case Study

1. Rashaud did not see his racial identity or culture reflected in the school curriculum. What may have been preventing the school from being more culturally responsive?

What are some strategies the school administration and teachers could have
implemented to affirm Rashaud's identity and that of his peers?

2. As a teacher, what is your responsibility for ensuring that all students achieve? What
might you do when a student exhibits behavior that Rashaud described as "slackin'"?
Whose responsibility is it to ensure student engagement?

3. What are the respective roles of the school and individual teachers in supporting students through the college admissions process? When does this support begin? How
might this support be shaped for first-generation college-bound students from communities with less experience in the cultural capital of college admissions?

Vanessa Mattison

I don't think that one person should have an easier time just because of the color of their skin, or their race, or 'cause they belong to a particular church or something.

At the time of her interview, Vanessa Mattison was 17 years old. Her family had been in the United States for many gener-ations.[1] European American in background, Vanessa lived in Welborn Hills, a small, rural hill town in western New England, but she had had a number of experiences that helped make her far more worldly than others in her circum-stances. By 17, she had traveled to Africa, the Caribbean, and Mexico. Her travels opened her eyes to some of the realities beyond her small community, which was made up of several diverse groups of people: farm-ing families who have lived in the area for generations; newer families with more formal education and more liberal values who had left urban areas in search of a more rural and simple lifestyle; and working-class families who made their living in the retail and light industries of the surrounding towns and small cities. Although Vanessa's family did not fit neatly into any category, it probably had the most in common with the second group. For example, they read not only *Newsweek* but also *Greenpeace*; they were vegetarians; they listened to Bob Dylan, Joan Baez, and reg-gae and blues music; and they traveled from time to time.

A number of the other families from Welborn Hills also routinely traveled out-side the United States, but others had never even been to Boston or New York, both just a few hours away by car. In the town's only elementary school, as well as in the regional secondary school that the town's students attended, the class conflict between the more liberal and educated families and the families that had lived here for generations was almost palpable.

Only a tiny minority of the residents of Welborn Hills were people of color. The same was true of Hills Regional High School, a school for grades 7 through 12, with a population of approximately 700 students, which served a number of rural towns, including Welborn Hills. For many of the European American students, access to understanding cultural differences and to meeting and being friends with people dif-ferent from themselves depended on class and educational privilege—that is, only students like Vanessa who had had the privilege of traveling had any inkling of the influence of racism or cultural differences on those different from themselves.

Taking classes in Spanish, calculus, sociology, humanities, art, and contem-porary problems, Vanessa was on an academic track. She was successful and engaged in school and was looking forward to being the first in her family to go to college. Socially active and involved in sports, Vanessa was self-confident and open to new ideas. She had many friends, both male and female, from a variety of cultural backgrounds. Soft-spoken and thoughtful in her replies, Vanessa had deeply held beliefs about the value of all people, peace, social justice, and environmental concerns.

Vanessa lived with both parents in a modest home, and she described them in economic terms as lower middle class. Her sister, age 21, lived in a nearby town. Her father, who had been raised in the area, was a craftsperson, and her mother was a paralegal. Although both parents had finished high school, neither had gone to college. Vanessa took pride in the fact that her parents stood up for what they believed in. At the time she was interviewed, their courage of conviction was taking the shape of protest against the first Gulf War, which had just begun.

Having never needed to identify ethnically or racially because she had always been considered the "norm," it became clear from the beginning of her interview that Vanessa was embarrassed and uncomfortable with the issue of identity and culture. In spite of her greater awareness of culture and cultural differences than the majority of her peers, it was a difficult issue for her. She was determined to grapple with it, however. In fact, she agreed to be interviewed precisely because the project sounded "interesting and important," and she made time for it in her busy schedule. *Discomfort with issues of cultural, racial, and linguistic differences* is the major theme that emerged from the interview with Vanessa. The other issues focused on the *promise, sometimes unfulfilled, of education* and on *what teachers can do to make school more fun for students.*

The Discomfort of Differences

[*How do you describe yourself?*] I generally don't. . . . Wait, can you explain that? Like, what do you want to know?

Well, I would [describe myself as White], but it doesn't matter to me, so that's why I said it's a tough question. 'Cause I usually just describe myself as, like, what I believe in or something like that. Rather than, like, what culture I am, whether I'm Black or White. 'Cause that doesn't matter.

[I'm] . . . well, Scottish, French, and German, I guess. My family all speak English at home, though I'm taking Spanish. I guess I'm middle class or lower class. It depends on how you think of it. I guess the German part might have come in the twentieth century. I'm not really sure, that's just a general guess. . . . I wasn't really interested. I don't really know if we have that many connections back to who was where when and what happened. Well, I guess people's backgrounds *do* [matter] because that's what makes them what they are.

I guess . . . obviously I just made it seem like [culture] wasn't [important]. It's just that, like, all the stuff that's happened to people because of their culture, like the slaves and Jewish people. Culture, what you look like, whether you're Black or White could matter less to me. It's the person who you are . . . it's not what your appearance depicts.

People like Blacks still don't have as many rights as the White man. I'm saying "man" because women don't have their rights either. The "superiority game . . . ." 'Cause people just have it stuck in their head that that's the way it is and . . . I don't really know how to change it. . . . I try and change it, speak out against it.

[Other cultures] are not that well represented [in my school] because there's not that many people who live around here. The majority is probably White. But they're represented in a small margin. . . . We've read books, and we've seen movies. I think we saw part of the freedom marches in the South and stuff like that. And we saw *Gandhi,* although that isn't really to this culture.

[Culture] is like a conglomeration of language, the way you speak, the way you are . . . things that are important to you. . . . Well, the culture of the United States is kind of like norms, things that happen a lot. Like if you were to go to another country, it might strike you as weird because you don't do it at home that way.

I don't agree with a lot of our culture. I don't agree with how it's so rushed and how if you're Black, you're supposedly not as good or you're not as fit for the job or something like that. And if you're a woman, it's the same thing. And, like, you can't be gay without being put down. I don't know, there's all these underlying rules about if you're not this, you can't do that.

It seems weird . . . because people came over from Europe, and they wanted to get away from all the stuff that was over there. And then they came here and set up all the stuff like slavery, and I don't know, it seems the opposite of what they would have done. . . . They might not have come over thinking that's what they had in mind, but since that's what they had always known, that's what they did.

Like [the first president] Bush said in his speech a little while ago that "We're doing all we can to fight racism" and blah, blah, blah, when the Supreme Court just made the ruling about schools and busing, which was basically turning back a decision they had made a long time ago.

When I see racism, I often think that I wish I was Black or I wish I was the group that was being discriminated against. You know how some women say, "I hate men"? I don't know, but I'm sure that Black people said this, when they were slaves, like "I hate White people." I don't want to be thought of like that because I'm not against them. I think they're equal. And also after they've been put through so much awfulness, I think that every White person should be in their shoes.

When I was in second grade, there was somebody coming into our class who was going to be Black. He was like a new student and somebody said something about it, and me and a couple of my other friends got really mad at him. "It doesn't matter what color they are. They could be orange or yellow or brown. It doesn't matter, they're just a person."

I don't have any [religious beliefs]. I've never gone to church. We never, like, read the Bible as a family or anything. I think both of my parents used to go to church. I think they were Catholic. . . . They probably didn't think it was as important to their life as the people who had wanted them to go. . . . I don't really know much about it. But if I had a choice, I probably wouldn't want to go to church because I think that I'd rather formulate my own ideas than being told that the Earth was created in seven days and God did this and He did this. I don't know. He seems like just too almighty of a person to me. I just don't believe it.

For strength and inspiration, I usually look to Martin Luther King, Jr. I like Gandhi too, because I believe in nonviolence. And I believe they helped to strengthen the basis for my belief, and they gave specific examples of how it could work. I just believe in nonviolence as a way to get what you want . . . and peace. I don't believe if you punch somebody, then, yeah, they may do what you want them to do, but they're not going to be doing it because they want to. They're just going to be doing it because of fear. I don't think fear is a good policy.

Education and Values

Supposedly education is what this country is built on, but there's no money for it.

Money is being cut out of all the schools. We lost a bunch of programs. We don't have as many teachers. We're going to lose more money, and it seems like the government's always promoting it as this great big deal. Then, where's the money for it? They're not supporting it. . . . [In my school] they still have, for seventh and eighth grade, sewing and cooking and art. Music is still there, and sports was supported by the public this year through bottle drives and a big fundfest. I don't know what's going to happen next year. I hope it's still supported.

[My parents] feel the same way , . . that the government needs to step in and help and that it's sad that it's going downhill. I think they think it's important to learn. Because they want me to be able to do what I want to do, and not, as I said before, get locked in a corner.

I've learned a lot of my morals [from my parents], like nonviolence and expressing myself, and striving for what I want, being able to have the confidence to reach what I want.

They're caring, and they're willing to go against the norm. They're willing to protest, that's a good word for it, for what they believe in . . . . People drive by the [peace] vigils and give us the finger.

I think [Dad] values being able to survive on his own. Like moving away from your family and growing up and having your own job and supporting yourself and being able to get around, and not always having to have people do things for you. . . . He's fun and supportive.

[Mom] also strives for what her goals are and believes in self-support, working for what's yours.

There's a lot of support that I don't see in other families. . . . We don't always go with the flow. You know, like most people supposedly right now are for the [first] Gulf War. We're not, so we stand in the minority. . . . I personally don't believe in violence to solve things. I don't think that killing a zillion million people for oil is a good reason either. And you can't bring peace to somewhere that's not your culture and has a different government, and you especially can't do it through war. That's not going to solve things. And it would take a lot of talking and rearranging their entire society to get them to be like us, which I don't think is what they should be, 'cause they're not and they never have been and probably won't be.

[My parents want me to go to school] so I can be educated and get a job. So I can have options and not get stuck. . . . Probably because they didn't go to college and they'd like me to. That's just a guess . . . [But I would like] a little less pressure . . . like around college and school.

[I want to] go to college to help people. I want to be a psychologist or do social work, work with the environment. I'm not sure.

I guess [grades are important] because they've kind of become that way. . . . I think education is if you learn personally. That's not what the school thinks. It's not like if you get an A or an F, but if you learn. It's not just for the grades. . . . If I get grades that aren't real good, [my parents] are not real excited. And they always make sure that I'm doing my homework. They tell me to get off the phone.

I'm happy. Success is being happy to me. It's not like having a job that gives you a zillion dollars. It's just having self-happiness.

A good education is like when you personally learn something . . . like growing, expanding your mind and your views.

Making School More Fun

[In elementary school I liked] recess, 'cause it was a break between doing stuff. Everything wasn't just pushed at you. And art, which was really fun. . . . It was a safe place, and I liked the teachers and the people that went there. . . . I liked that on Valentine's Day and Christmas and birthdays they had [parties] for us. They mixed school and fun.

I did the work, I understood it, and I was interested.

My favorite [subject] is art because of the freedom to express myself, to paint and draw. Humanities is my worst 'cause it's just lectures and tests.

I'm in a peer-education group. It's a group of 18 seniors who set up programs to educate the other students in the school on issues like alcoholism, drunk driving, stereotyping, a bunch more. It's kind of like, since they're students and they're projecting to a student audience, it's easier for some people to relate.

We did a skit on [stereotyping]. We had jocks, hippies, snobs, burnouts, and a nerd. And we did these little scenarios like the snob liked this guy who was a hippie and all her friends were like, "Oh, my God! You like *him*?! He's such a hippie!" And then, like, the hippie friends said the same thing about the snob, and then, like, everything stopped and the two people who liked each other got up and said, "I wish my friends would understand. . . ." And then the person who was narrating said, "Well, here's one way in which the situation could be fixed." So they went back where they were and said, "Okay, yeah, well, I guess we should give them a chance." Most of the ideas came from us except for the one I just explained to you. Me and two other people basically wrote the whole skit. We just did it for the seventh and eighth grade. We thought that would be the most effective place 'cause that's where it basically starts. They liked it.

It's important for teachers to get to know all the students and know where they're coming from and why they may react a certain way to certain things because then it'll be easier to get through. . . . Maybe if school didn't just start off on the first day with homework, maybe if it started off with just getting to know each other, even if you're in a class that's already known each other.

You could have games that could teach anything that they're trying to teach through notes or lectures. Well, like, if you're doing Spanish, you can play Hangman or something. You can play word games where you have to guess the word. Like they give you a definition and it makes you remember the words. Or if somebody acts out a word, you remember it better than someone just looking it up or writing it down.

Make it more entertaining 'cause people learn a lot from entertainment. If you see a play, you'll probably remember it more than a lecture, [or] if you see a movie, play a game, or something. Work those more into what they're doing. . . . I think that some books should be required just to show some points of view.

Some [teachers], based on [students'] reputation, may not be as patient with some people. [Students get reputations] basically through grades and troublemaking, like if you get in trouble with the system and get detentions.

[Unhelpful teachers are] ones that just kind of just move really fast, just trying to get across to you what they're trying to teach you . . . not willing to slow down because they need to get in what they want to get in.

[Most teachers] are really caring and supportive and are willing to share their lives and are willing to listen to mine. They don't just want to talk about what they're teaching you; they also want to know you.

Commentary

Coming face to face with racial, class, cultural, and other differences was difficult for Vanessa because she had not often needed to consider these things. One gets the sense that, for her, "culture," "ethnicity," and "race" were what *other* people had, and Vanessa sometimes seemed offended at having to talk about them. It was almost as if she considered it rude to broach questions of race and culture—that discussing them meant you were a racist (what Mica Pollock defines as colormuteness).[2] In this, Vanessa was similar to other young people of European descent for whom ethnicity is less important than for young people of color.

Vanessa took the approach that cultural and racial differences are not significant. She was, in fact, simply reflecting the value of being colorblind, which we all have been led to believe is both right and fair. In this framework, differences are seen as a *deficit* rather than as an *asset*. Being White and having Christian heterosexual parents, Vanessa rarely had been confronted with feeling like an outsider. She considered herself the "norm," "just a person." As is the case for most White Americans, she had the privilege of seeing herself as just an individual, an opportunity not generally afforded to those from other groups.

Because Vanessa associated culture, race, and other differences with oppression and inequality, these issues were difficult for her to address. For one, Vanessa viewed cultural and other differences as *causing* oppression ("like all the stuff that happened to people because of their culture, like the slaves and the Jewish people"). For another, she was offended by the unfairness with which differences are treated. The fact that some people are penalized for being who they are, while others are rewarded for it, made it difficult for her to confront differences. Not wanting to benefit from racism, Vanessa found it easier to avoid or downplay the issue. Her growing awareness of sexism, revealed through comments such as, "I'm saying 'man' 'cause women don't have their rights either" may have helped her make the connection between the two issues.[3]

Vanessa was struggling to understand the contradictions between the ideals she had been taught and the discrimination she saw around her. She was beginning to link issues such as peace and social justice with those of racism and other biases. Although she associated herself with her race only when confronted with the example of racism exhibited by other White people, it was at such times that Vanessa clearly saw the need for Whites to stand up and take responsibility. She also understood that being White generally meant having more opportunities, which she resented as unfair.

Through dialogue with Vanessa, it became clear that few of these issues had ever been addressed in any of her classes. When asked if she had learned history and other subject matter in school from the perspectives of different groups of people, she answered that everything was taught from what she called "a general perspective." Because the viewpoints of others are generally invisible or given scant attention in the traditional curriculum, many students think of the one reality that is taught as the "general" reality and the experiences of others as little more than ethnic add-ons to "real" knowledge.

In spite of her lack of awareness of diverse perspectives, Vanessa was becoming keenly aware of, and committed to, social issues. For example, she spoke out against discriminatory statements and in this way tried to change things. Vanessa had exhibited such outspokenness since second grade. Even in that incident, however, she and her friends thought that, by overlooking racial differences, they would be helping the new boy in class. Being colorblind was, to them, the logical response.[4]

Vanessa felt that education, although compulsory, was often not engaging. Although she viewed education as crucial, she wished it were more interesting and interactive. Her perception of schooling as boring and "flat," especially at the secondary level, and her suggestion that teachers should make school more entertaining and fun for all students, corroborate what has been found to be the general attitude of students in many schools around the United States.[5]

Vanessa's parents also understood that education would give Vanessa options they themselves had not had. They were involved in school activities (her mother served on the local school committee, and both parents had volunteered time to the schools), and they also demonstrated their concerns in many other ways. Their involvement, in Vanessa's words, "shows that they care."

Related to the value of education are the other values that Vanessa learned from her parents: self-reliance, self-confidence, and independent thought. These values obviously helped her develop her own persona in a school setting that was both conformist and conservative. A strong and forthright young woman with deeply held values and beliefs, Vanessa, although still uncomfortable with issues of diversity in a comprehensive way, was clearly committed to struggling with them. The interviews themselves seemed to have served as a catalyst to her thinking more extensively about diversity, racism, and identity. Given the strength and support of her family, her searching soul, and her grounding in peace and social justice, she was a wonderful example of a young person ready to, in her words, "expand my mind and my views."

Reflect on This Case Study

1. Why do you think White people in the United States generally do not identify with any particular racial or ethnic group? What can teachers do to help White students identify with their cultural heritage?
2. As a teacher, what is your responsibility for introducing your students to diversity? What strategies and activities might you use? How would these differ in a primarily White school, compared to a more culturally and racially heterogeneous school?
3. What is the role of values in education? Should schools teach values? Why or why not? Should some of Vanessa's family's values be included? Why or why not?

Structural and Organizational Issues in Classrooms and Schools

Nearly a century ago, John Dewey warned, "Democracy cannot flourish where the chief influences in selecting subject matter of instruction are utilitarian ends narrowly conceived for the masses, and, for the higher education of the few, the traditions of a specialized cultivated class."[1] As Dewey feared, our public schools, as currently organized, are not fulfilling the promise of democracy. Certain school policies and practices exacerbate the inequality that exists in society. Although some of these policies and practices have evolved in an attempt to deal more equitably with student diversity, just the opposite may be the result. This is the case with *tracking,* which is often meant to help those students most in academic need yet, as we shall see, results in perpetuating learning gaps. Some practices are so integral to the schooling experience that they are hardly disputed even though there may be little evidence for their effectiveness. This is the case with *retention,* or holding students back a grade. Some may not be official policies but rather unquestioned practices that can lead to disempowerment. This is the case with the limited roles that teachers, students, and parents have in school.

> *"School's really not that challenging to me. . . . Most of my classes are just memorization, and I'm really not learning anything from it. I have found very few teachers who actually teach classes in an interesting way that makes me really want to work."*
>
> —**Nini Rostland, snapshot interviewee, Chapter 7**

Policies and practices can become rigid structures that are difficult to change. Many of these structures, unfortunately, run counter to the grand and noble purposes that Dewey described, yet they have come to define schooling itself. These include the general similarity of curriculum and schedules; particular patterns of resource allocation; and, most recently, an unswerving faith in test scores as measures of ability or potential. The case studies that follow this chapter provide examples of organizational practices and policies that can either help or harm students.

It is legitimate to ask how structural and organizational issues such as school policies and practices are related to multicultural education. The connection is this: When defined comprehensively, multicultural education concerns far more than simply adding ethnic content to the curriculum. Instead, it questions the total context of education, including curriculum, student placement, physical structure of schools, school climate, pedagogical strategies, assumptions about student ability, hiring of staff members, and parent involvement, among other issues. In this sense, organizational structures, policies, and practices are central to the development of a comprehensive multicultural education.

Breanna Burton, Tristan Gonzales, Dionne Nixon, Tshontae James in Nora Elton's art class, Empower Charter School, Brooklyn, NY. *Self-portraits*. Oil pastel drawings. 2010.

Because larger structural issues were discussed in previous chapters, this chapter focuses on school and classroom-based policies and practices that may reinforce social inequities. The focus here is on the classroom and school rather than society, so the impression may be that issues such as school financing, residential housing patterns, unemployment opportunities, racism and other institutional biases, and the ideological underpinnings of education are not as important. On the contrary, as we made clear in Chapter 1, all of these larger structural issues are profoundly implicated in school failure. For example, as highlighted in a report from the National Working Group on Funding School Learning, equitable school financing is central to student learning. Their report begins with the sobering reflection that "[s]tates will never educate all students to high standards unless they first fix the finance systems that support America's schools."[2] We urge you to keep these societal issues in mind to understand how they directly influence inequities at the classroom and school levels.

In this chapter, each of the following school-based policies and practices is briefly described and examined:

- Tracking
- Retention
- Standardized testing
- Curriculum
- Pedagogy
- Physical structure
- Disciplinary policies
- Limited role of students
- Limited role of teachers
- Limited family and community involvement

 # Tracking

One of the most inequitable and, until about four decades ago, relatively undisputed practices in schools is tracking. The term *tracking* generally refers to the placement of students into groups that are perceived to be of similar ability (homogeneous groups) within classes (e.g., reading groups in self-contained classes), into classroom groups according to perceived abilities and subject areas (e.g., a low-level math group in seventh grade), or into groups according to specific programs of study at the high school level (e.g., academic or vocational).[3]

In most schools, some kind of tracking is as much a part of school as are bells and recess. Why this is the case can be explained largely by traditional and static notions of intelligence. That is, some students are thought to "have it" while others do not. If this is the case, so the thinking goes, then it makes sense to provide students considered intelligent with rigorous curricula and other experiences that challenge them, while students who are not considered intelligent often end up with pedagogy that consists of practice, review, and memorization. Yet as Beverly Daniel Tatum has suggested, these ideas run counter to reality as well as to our nation's creed of equal educational opportunity. She cautions,

> If we are really serious about creating learning environments that foster high levels of achievement for all of our students, irrespective of race and class, we have to examine and challenge a fundamental notion central to the educational process—the notion of intelligence.[4]

Tracking may begin at the very earliest grades, and decisions about student placement are sometimes made on tenuous grounds. These can include social indicators such as information provided on registration forms, initial interviews with parents, and teachers' prior knowledge about specific students. Research over many years has confirmed that tracking is frequently linked with racial, ethnic, and social-class differences. In her 1985 pioneering research study of 25 junior and senior high schools around the country, Jeannie Oakes found that the results of tracking were almost exclusively negative for most students. In a more recent edition of her ground-breaking study, Oakes reviewed the field in the intervening 20 years and concluded that tracking as a practice was still largely grounded in ideologies that maintain race and social class privilege.[5]

The effectiveness of tracking is questionable. If the purpose of tracking is to provide access to opportunity for those who have been denied this access the most, it has failed badly. In many instances, it has had the opposite effect because tracking is largely propped up and sustained by social class interests. Because it sorts and classifies students, tracking helps prepare them for their place in the larger society. Students in the top tracks generally end up attending college and having a better shot at becoming professionals; those in the bottom tracks frequently drop out or, if they do finish high school, become unskilled workers. Without lapsing into a mechanistic explanation for a complex process, it is nevertheless true that while a small number of students benefit, most lose because of tracking. As a consequence, tracking decisions are rarely innocent and their effects are not benign; on the contrary, they can have devastating consequences.

The messages children internalize because of grouping practices are probably more destructive than we realize and their effects more long-lasting than we care to admit. Students may develop enduring classroom personalities and attitudes. They may, for instance, begin to believe that their placement in these groups is natural and a true reflection of whether they are "smart," "average," or "dumb." At the high school level, although students may think that they themselves are deciding which courses to take, these decisions may actually have been made for them years before by the first teacher who placed them, for example, in the "Crows" rather than the "Blue Jays" reading group.

A further result of tracking is that students who most need excellent and experienced teachers often have the least access to them. Considering the way in which scheduling decisions are made, teachers with the most experience are frequently given the "plum" assignments, and this usually means teaching high-ability classes. For example, in their research in high schools around the country, Milbrey McLaughlin and Joan Talbert found that teachers assigned to low-track classes were often poorly prepared in their subject matter and new to teaching.[6]

Tracking leaves its mark on pedagogy, too. Students in the lowest levels are the most likely to be subjected to rote memorization and static teaching methods because their teachers often feel that these are the children who most need to master the "basics." As a result, teachers may believe that creative methods are a frill that these students can ill afford until the "basics" are learned. Children living in poverty and those most alienated by the schools are once again the losers, and the cycle of school failure is repeated. The students most in need are placed in the lowest level classes and exposed to the drudgery of drill and repetition, school becomes more boring and senseless every day, and the students become discouraged and drop out.

This is not to imply that students at the top ability levels always receive instruction that is uplifting, interesting, and meaningful. They too are exposed to methods and materials similar to those used for students at the bottom levels. However, if innovative methods and appealing materials exist at all, they tend to be found at the top levels. Knowledge becomes yet another privilege given to those who are already privileged.

According to one report, tracking has remained relatively stable for the past half century: By 2007, 75 percent of the nation's schools tracked eighth-grade math classes and 43 percent tracked eighth-grade English.[7] Although the research on the negative effects of tracking is extensive, the practice is still in place in most schools throughout the United States. The effects of tracking may be contrary to statements about its intended outcomes, but it remains an immutable part of the culture of middle and secondary schools partly because the culture of the school is resistant to change. Once an idea has taken hold in schools, it seems to develop a life of its own, regardless of its usefulness or effectiveness.

If tracking were unanimously acknowledged as placing all students at risk, it would have been eliminated long ago. The truth is that powerful vested interests are at play in preserving it. Although tracking affects most students negatively, it may benefit a few. The evidence is mixed, but there is some indication that high-achieving students benefit from being tracked in honors and high-level classes. It is not surprising, then, that it is frequently the parents of high-achieving students who are most reluctant to eliminate tracking because they perceive it as beneficial to their children. In addition, tracking decisions and race are often linked. This was found to be the case in a three-year longitudinal case study by Oakes and her colleagues. In their review of ten racially and socioeconomically mixed secondary schools participating in detracking reform, the researchers concluded that one of the greatest barriers to detracking was the resistance of powerful parents, most of whom were White. Through strategies such as threatening to remove their children from the school, the parents of students who traditionally benefited from tracking made detracking difficult, if not impossible.[8]

We want to make it clear, however, that grouping per se is not always a negative practice. Good and experienced teachers have always understood that short-term and flexible grouping can be effective in reviewing a particular skill or teaching intensively a missing piece of social studies or math or science. Grouping in such instances can be effective in meeting temporary and specific ends. But because rigid ability-group tracking is linked with, and supported by, particular classist and racist ideologies, grouping of any kind needs to be done with great care.

What are the alternatives to tracking? One approach is to detrack, that is, to do away with tracking based on so-called ability differences. However, detracking alone will do little unless accompanied by a change in the school's culture and norms. In one study of six racially mixed high schools undergoing detracking, Susan Yonezawa, Amy Stuart Wells, and Irene Serna found that the schools' low- and middle-track students, mostly Latino and African American, resisted entering high-track classes even when they were academically capable of taking them because they "hungered for 'places of respect'—that is, classrooms where they were not racially isolated and their cultural backgrounds were valued."[9] Because tracking is supported by a complex set of structures that reinforce cultural assumptions and influence students' identities, the authors concluded that "freedom of choice" for students to select their own classes is, by itself, an empty concept *without* altering the other structures and ideologies that help perpetuate existing track hierarchies. They suggest that, to work, tracking needs to be accompanied by "safe spaces" such as ethnic studies classes that can make students feel valued.

■■■■■■ ## What You Can Do
Become Informed

Use professional days to visit schools that have successfully implemented detracking. Recommend that staff development sessions address directly tracking, detracking, and alternative kinds of grouping. With your colleagues, view the video *Off-Track* (developed by Michelle Fine and her colleagues and available from Teachers College Press). In it, students and staff members address the benefits and challenges of detracking.

Detrack Extracurricular Activities

Tracking also occurs in extracurricular activities. School activities and clubs frequently perpetuate the social class groupings that students develop instead of helping to counter the stereotypes on which they are based. As the case studies and snapshots in this book demonstrate, extracurricular activities were significant in the academic success for most of the students interviewed or described.

Nevertheless, extracurricular clubs or organizations are often seen by students as exclusive and with limited membership. Although the message "You need not apply" is not purposely given, many students infer it from the recruitment policies and activities of some clubs and organizations. You can help make clubs and other organizations appealing to a wider range of students by, for instance, becoming a faculty sponsor for a group and actively recruiting and encouraging students of diverse backgrounds to join. For example, ask yourself, Who is participating in the chess club, and what kind of academic achievement does that reinforce? Who is benefiting and who is losing as a result of participating? Also, you can print recruitment materials in a number of languages, post them in neighborhood centers, and conduct outreach with families of students underrepresented in extracurricular activities to encourage their children to join.

More recent research by Carol Burris, a high school principal; with Kevin Welner, a university professor; and Jennifer Bezoza, an attorney and children's advocate, focused on three case studies: a school in San Diego; a school district in Long Island; and a nation, Finland, to describe how all three have promoted high levels of student achievement by doing away with tracking, or what they call "curricular stratification." Some of the gains were extraordinary: For example, in 1996 at South Side High School on Long Island, 32 percent of all African American and Hispanic students and 88 percent of all White and Asian American students earned Regents diplomas, the most rigorous diploma awarded in the state of New York. Just five years later, 92 percent of all African American and Hispanic students and 98 percent of White and Asian American students entering South Side in 2001 earned Regents diplomas. By June 2009, 95 percent of the school's African American and Hispanic students earned a Regents diploma, far surpassing the rate in the rest of the state. Although Burris, Welner, and Bezoza do not claim that it is an easy or problem-free process, they maintain that the three cases they review offer ample evidence that it is a worthy project because in the three cases, all students benefited from high-level curricula. They also caution that adequate supports are needed and, in their report, they recommend specific supports that can be implemented at all grade levels. These include cooperative learning, peer tutoring, multilevel teaching, shared decision making with students, and deemphasizing the use of textbooks; challenging racist and classist notions of ability can also result in inspired stories of improved learning and intergroup relations.[10]

Although students differ from one another in many ways, and such differences need to be taken into account to provide students with a high-quality education, tracking alone has not proved to be the answer. At the same time, tracking alone cannot be blamed for inequality in learning. Singling out any specific policy or practice as the culprit is an insufficient explanation for schools' lack of success with particular students. Rather, a constellation of factors create school failure. The discussion that follows considers some of these factors.

Retention

Retention, or the practice of holding students back a grade, is another common practice in schools. Like tracking, retention is intertwined with other policies and practices that exacerbate inequality. For instance, it is related to testing because retention decisions are often made as a result of test scores. This is especially evident in the high-stakes testing context of the past several years.

One review of the literature on the effect of retention begins with the pointed question, "Making students repeat a grade hasn't worked for 100 years, so why is it still happening?" Susan Black, the author of the review, goes on to say that, according to some estimates, almost 2.5 million children are retained in U.S. classrooms, and low-income students, boys, and students of color are overrepresented in this number. Aside from a short-term benefit for some students—a benefit that has been found to have no lasting effects—there is no evidence that retention brings children up to grade level. On the contrary, Black reviewed several decades of research that showed retention fails to improve achievement. Also, retention is linked in a very obvious way with dropping out of school: Students who are retained once are 40 to 50 percent more likely to drop out of school than those who have never been retained; for those retained twice, the risk is 90 percent.[11]

Students are typically retained in a particular grade when a determination is made, usually by the teacher (sometimes in consultation with counselors, the principal, and parents) that a student is incapable of performing the work that is required in the coming grade. As in the case of tracking, these decisions are generally made with good intentions: Often, teachers want to protect students from further failure or believe that, during the following year in the same class, students will learn the material that they have not yet learned. But as in the case of tracking, this reasoning is often erroneous. The largest number of students is retained in first grade, although researchers have found that first graders usually benefit the least from the practice. In addition, as more pressure is placed on kindergarten to become more like first grade, there is a related pressure for kindergarten teachers to have their students "ready to learn" in first grade. As a consequence, more retentions are occurring in kindergarten. As one large study found, however, there is no evidence whatsoever that a policy of grade retention in kindergarten improves average achievement in math or reading. In fact, the evidence points in the opposite direction: Children who are retained actually learn less than they would have had they been promoted.[12]

What, then, is the alternative? Considering the widespread public opposition to "social promotion"—promoting students to the next grade even if they have not learned the subject matter of their current grade—it is unrealistic to expect that retention as a policy will be abandoned. It is also unfair to simply move students on to the next grade if they are unprepared for it and to expect them to catch up on their own. Because of this dilemma, more schools are implementing alternative intervention programs such as mandatory summer school and after-school tutoring programs. However, these measures are likely to produce few results unless accompanied by comprehensive schoolwide reform involving other practices and policies. For example, the connection between academic success and co-curricular and extracurricular activities is clear in the case studies in this book, yet poor urban schools, where the need is greatest, have fewer of these activities.

 Standardized Testing

Another practice that impedes equity in schools is the uncritical use of standardized testing, particularly when employed to sort students rather than to improve instruction. Originally designed almost a century ago to help identify children who were labeled "mentally retarded," the use of standardized tests expanded greatly afterward, influenced by the tremendous influx of new immigrants into the country. As a result, the original aims of standardized tests were subverted to include rationalization of racist theories of genetic inferiority.[13] For example, after testing only two American Indian and Mexican American children, Lewis Terman, a psychologist who experimented with intelligence tests at the beginning of the twentieth century, stated with absolute conviction, "Their dullness seems to be racial, or at least inherent in the family stock from which they came. . . . Children of this group should be segregated in special classes . . . they cannot master abstractions, but they can often be made efficient workers."[14] The same reasoning was used on other occasions to explain the "inferior" intelligence of Blacks, Jews, and Italians; practically every new ethnic group that has come to the United States has fared badly on standardized tests.[15]

An extensive review of how test use changed during this period is not called for here, but it should be pointed out that standardized tests have frequently been used as a basis for segregating and sorting students, principally those whose cultures and languages differ from the mainstream. The belief that tests should be used to replicate repressive and racist social theories and policies is not a historical relic. Unfortunately, contemporary examples of this kind of thinking exist.[16] Testing and tracking have often been symbiotically linked. Joel Spring has used a variety of primary sources ranging from real estate publications to newspaper accounts to demonstrate these links.[17]

Although comments today about specific groups tend not to be as blatantly racist as Lewis Terman's, the kind and number of standardized tests to which we continue to subject our students are staggering. This situation is especially related to the testing craze that has swept our nation since the 1983 report, *A Nation at Risk,* followed by testing mandates including No Child Left Behind (NCLB) and, more recently, Race to the Top that mandate standardized testing in various subject areas in elementary, middle, and high school. As a result, students now spend entire days, sometimes weeks, taking standardized tests. On top of the actual testing days, a great deal of time is spent on teaching children *how* to take tests, and in remediation on how to retake tests, time that could be better spent in teaching, and the students' learning, actual content.

The fact that textbook companies and other companies that develop tests earn huge profits from test construction and dissemination is often unmentioned, yet it, too, is a reality. Private testing companies that control the market operate with little or no public accountability, which is ironic considering the calls for accountability in schools. Neill Monty of FairTest, a watchdog organization on testing, has said that determining the exact profits that testing and textbook companies make from tests is difficult because many are for-profit companies with many divisions. He adds that it is hard to find all the companies involved, but clearly it is a lucrative business. According to Neill, "[T]he part of the market that has grown the most involves 'benchmark' and fake 'formative' tests peddled by many commercial operations."[18] In a recent critique of for-profit schemes such as private tutoring for high-stakes testing, Jill Koyama makes the case that such schemes deserve further scrutiny because they end up perpetuating failure.[19] The cost of testing is borne by school districts and state education departments that are already financially strapped and can ill afford it.

A concern for equity is a common reason cited for high-stakes testing, that is, for linking test scores to the success of schools, teachers, and students. Certainly, equity is a significant concern because, as we have seen, schools for poor children of diverse backgrounds are often inferior to others. Nevertheless, there is little evidence to support the contention that standardized tests lead to greater achievement. For instance, despite its purported intent, NCLB has focused little attention on changes in curriculum or instructional practices, on improvements in teacher education, or on equalizing funding for school districts. Richard Elmore, an educational researcher whose work has centered on school improvement, has called this legislation "the single largest—and the single most damaging—expansion of federal policy over the nation's education system."[20] Elmore argues that the work of improving schools should consist instead of improving capacity, that is, the knowledge and skills of teachers, by increasing their command of content and how to teach it.

A number of reviews of testing legislation and practice have concluded that, rather than improving learning outcomes, such legislation is actually having a detrimental impact because gross inequities in instructional quality, resources, and other support services are being ignored. Also, as pointed out in the discussion on retention, because more states are now requiring students to pass a standardized test before they can graduate from high school, dropout rates are actually increasing in some places. Even more alarming, a recent report from the Advancement Project has documented how high-stakes testing policies "funnel youth into the school-to-prison pipeline." Specifically, the report concludes the following:

> Together, zero tolerance and high-stakes testing have turned schools into hostile and alienating environments for many of our youth, effectively treating them as dropouts-in-waiting. The devastating end result of these intertwined punitive policies is a "school-to-prison pipeline," in which huge numbers of students throughout the country are treated as if they are disposable, and are being routinely pushed out of school and toward the juvenile and criminal justice systems.[21]

Standardized test scores are also inequitable because they correlate highly with family income and ethnicity, a situation that belies the myth in the United States about equality of opportunity regardless of social class and race. In a review of abundant national and international studies, Sharon Nichols and David Berliner found overwhelming evidence of a positive and high relationship between social class and test scores.[22] This correlation has consistently been shown to be the case with the Scholastic Achievement Test (SAT), a test that is required for admission to most colleges and universities. Even the College Board, which administers the SAT, found in their own analysis that students whose families make more than $200,000 a year score nearly 400 points more than students whose family income was less than $20,000.[23] Rather than helping to equalize educational opportunity, such tests may in fact aggravate inequality. In affluent schools and neighborhoods, students often learn specific test-taking skills that help them do very well on tests. A recent study found that test coaching, contrary to previous claims, boosted math SAT scores by 18 points.[24]

Affluent families also have the means to pay for tutoring and other classes to help their children do well on tests. Students from less affluent homes, especially if they live in poverty, do not generally have the same kind of access to learning these skills. The very validity of using SAT scores to predict college success has been seriously challenged by researchers Saul Geiser and Maria Veronica Santelices. Their study of 80,000 University of California students found that the students' high school grade point average was actually the strongest predictor of their college success because it was less closely tied to students' family income and ethnicity.[25]

Standardized testing negatively affects equity in other ways, too. For instance, testing may limit teachers' creativity and constrict the curriculum because teachers in schools in which children have poor test scores are often forced to "teach to the test" rather than create curricula that respond to the real needs of learners. The result may be "dumbing down" or restricting the curriculum to better reflect the content and approach of tests. For example, a national survey of 12,000 teachers reported that the extent of curriculum narrowing due to testing was directly associated with the nature of the stakes involved—that is, the higher the stakes, the greater the teachers' focus on tested content.[26] In her review of the damaging effects of poorly designed and administered standardized tests, Linda Darling-Hammond reported that instruction that focuses on memorizing unrelated facts out of context produces passive rather than active learning. She concludes,

> Most of the material learned in this way is soon forgotten and cannot be retrieved or applied when it would be useful later. Students lose ground over time when they are taught in this way, falling behind as intellectual demands increase.[27]

Pedagogy is also negatively affected by standardized testing. Many critics of high-stakes testing have found that when standardized tests were required, there was a decline in the use of innovative approaches such as student-centered discussions, essay writing, research projects, and laboratory work.[28] Because of the unrelenting pressure to raise test scores, teachers may reason that they have little time for innovative approaches. This, in turn, affects teacher autonomy and morale because it moves curriculum decision making from the teacher to the school, district, city, or even state

■■ ■■■ What You Can Do
Be Proactive About Tests

Standardized tests exert a powerful influence on most educational decisions. As we have seen, however, they correlate more with family income than with intelligence or ability. The specific strategies that each teacher, school, and school district chooses to engage in may vary. Two basic strategies can be tried: Either challenge the use of tests, or focus attention on test taking and how to use it to the advantage of the students. In fact, these need not be mutually exclusive strategies. We know of one teacher, for instance, who campaigned against standardized tests because he knew they unfairly jeopardized his students. At the same time, he developed after-school tutorial sessions in which he taught his students specific test-taking skills so that they might be more successful in taking these required tests.

With a group of interested colleagues and parents, you can approach the local school committee and ask that standardized tests be kept to a minimum, that the results be used in more appropriate ways, and that students not be placed at risk because of the results of such tests. Like the previously mentioned teacher, you might decide that, given the pervasiveness of testing and the power it exerts on the options of young people, your energy might be better spent in teaching students how to take tests more critically and effectively. To help even the playing field, you can start an after-school test-tutoring program for students in your school. You might also try to get funding from your school system or parent–teacher association (PTA), or even from a local business.

level. The result is that the further the curriculum is from the teacher and the school, the less it reflects the lives of the students in the school.

Regrettably, the concern for engagement in meaningful activities is missing in many state-mandated testing programs, and students who are most vulnerable are once again the victims. In a vicious cycle of failure, students perceived as needing more help are placed in classes in which the curriculum is diluted, higher levels of thinking are not demanded, and instruction is bland and formulaic. Although standardized tests ostensibly are used to provide teachers and schools with information about the learning needs of students, in fact they are often used to sort students further. John Dewey minced no words in expressing his views of rigid assessments: "How one person's abilities compare in quantity with those of another is none of the teacher's business. It is irrelevant to his work," Dewey wrote. He went on to state, "What is required is that every individual shall have opportunities to employ his own powers in activities that have meaning."[29]

In spite of the shortcomings of high-stakes standardized testing, we need to understand why there is so much popular support for them. For one, many people view standardized tests as highly objective and reliable measures of what students know, even if this is not always the case. In addition, parents whose children attend poor schools have become weary of their children's lack of achievement in such schools. It is true that many teachers who work in poor urban and rural schools are highly competent and devoted to their students; they demonstrate their care through high expectations and rigorous demands. On the other hand, in schools where few teachers know much about the students they are teaching, expectations of student achievement are likely to be quite low. As a result, some children have been chronically underserved for many years. It is little wonder that too many children in these circumstances have failed to learn and that their parents have become staunch advocates of stringent accountability measures, including standardized testing. As we have seen, however, standardized tests alone rarely guarantee equality; in fact, they may intensify inequality.

Nevertheless, reliable and effective assessment of student learning is necessary. Teachers and schools must be held accountable for what students learn or fail to learn, especially in the case of those who have received low-quality schooling. Schools, districts, states, and the federal government need to rethink testing policies and practices so that they are more equitable. One response has been to promote alternative assessments, for example, to replace or at least complement norm-referenced tests with *performance-based assessments,* also called *authentic assessments*. Some examples of more authentic assessment are portfolios, performance tasks, and student exhibitions. These assessments represent an important shift in thinking about the purpose and uses of tests, from sorting and separating students toward ensuring more equitable opportunities for all children to learn at high levels of achievement.

 ## The Curriculum

Broadly defined, *curriculum* is the organized environment for learning. Curriculum concerns *what* should be learned and *under what conditions* it is to be learned. Although it may seem that this is a fairly clear-cut process, it is not. Because curriculum defines what is deemed important for students to know, it also involves the knowledge, attitudes, and traditions valued in a particular society. Thus, curriculum is an inherently *political* matter. To illustrate this point, we turn to curriculum theorist Michael Apple, who has suggested a number of essential questions to keep in mind when thinking about the curriculum—questions that are particularly significant within a multicultural framework. Some of these questions are: "Whose knowledge is it? Who selected it? Why is it organized and taught in this way?"[30] Because only a tiny fraction of the vast array of available knowledge finds its way into state curriculum standards and frameworks, district guides, textbooks, and teachers' instructional manuals, it is obvious that the curriculum is never neutral. Rather, it is deeply ideological and represents what is perceived to be consequential and necessary knowledge, generally by those who are dominant in a society. Furthermore, curriculum decisions in public schools are usually made by those furthest from the lives of students—namely, central and state boards of education—with little input from teachers, parents, and students.

The problem is that the curriculum is often presented as if it were the whole, unvarnished, and uncontested truth. Instead, we should think of curriculum as a decision-making process. If we think of it in this way, we realize that *somebody* made decisions about what to include. For example, it is rare for Black English, also called Ebonics or African American Vernacular English (AAVE), to be incorporated into the established curriculum. Typically, it becomes part of the curriculum only when students who speak Black English are corrected by their teachers. As a consequence, even when present in the curriculum, Black English tends to be viewed in a negative light, and students pick up the powerful message that the language variety they speak has little value in our society. On the other hand, if teachers were to use students' language—including Black English—as a bridge to Standard English or to discuss critical perspectives about the role that language and culture play in their lives, the value of students' identity is affirmed. A good example comes from the work of Bob Fecho, who used his students' vernacular to discuss broader issues about language and power in his urban high school English classroom.[31] Unfortunately, however, talk about such issues is frequently silenced, and in this way, the curriculum serves as a primary means of social control. The curriculum also lets students know whether the knowledge in their families and communities has prestige within the educational establishment and beyond. Many students—particularly those who live in poverty and students from families who are racially and culturally different from the mainstream—find that it does not. As an example, it is not unusual to see urban classrooms in which young children learn about "community helpers" without ever studying about some of the most important people in their own communities. They learn about police officers, firefighters, and mail carriers, all of whom may live outside their immediate communities. They learn about doctors and lawyers and people who own large businesses, but they may never have met one of these people in their own neighborhood. The people that some children do see every day—the owner of the corner bodega, local factory worker, bus driver, or community service provider—are rarely mentioned as community helpers.

Another example: When studying the food pyramid, it is not unusual for children to make up fictitious breakfasts in order to satisfy their teachers. To admit having eaten bread and butter and coffee or cold noodles for breakfast is to admit that they are doing something "wrong," at least in the eyes of the school. Similarly, a teacher with a mandate to teach her second-graders about Holland may struggle to find relevant ways to describe the lives of Dutch children, while at the same time neglecting to include the heritage and backgrounds of some of the children who are sitting in her own classroom. And there is the incongruous but typical situation of Mexican American, Puerto Rican, and other Latin American children who are fluent in Spanish yet being forced to learn Castilian Spanish because their teachers have accepted the premise that it is more "correct." Paradoxically, these same students are often prohibited from speaking Spanish outside Spanish class.

This is not meant to suggest that children should study *only* about themselves and their communities. Doing so would fly in the face of one of the major objectives of education, that is, to broaden students' experiences and perspectives beyond their own particular life circumstances. One of my (Sonia Nieto's) favorite books when I was a child was *Heidi*, a story that was as distinct from my own experience as night is from day. What could I, a relatively poor Puerto Rican child growing up in New York City, possibly get out of the story of an orphan sent to live in the Alps with her cantankerous grandfather? I knew nothing about mountains, had spent little time outside urban Brooklyn, and didn't even have a grandfather. But I understood Heidi because hers was a story of the significance of family relationships and of resilience in the face of considerable obstacles, and I could relate to these things. I could also relate to a girl who loved reading and exploring life. It was precisely because I could identify with these things on a personal level that I was able to benefit from *Heidi*. The point is that a curriculum needs to *build on* rather than neglect students' life experiences in order to broaden their worlds.

Children who are not in the dominant group have a hard time finding themselves or their communities in the curriculum. If they do "see" themselves, it is often through the distorted lens of others. American Indian children may read about themselves as "savages" who were bereft of culture until the Europeans arrived; African Americans often read sanitized versions of slavery; Mexican Americans read of the "westward expansion," with no information about the fact that their ancestors were already living on the lands to which Europeans were "expanding"; working-class children learn almost nothing of their history, except perhaps that the struggle for the eight-hour workday was a long one; and females may be left wondering how it is that half of humanity has consistently been left out of the curriculum. Little wonder, then, that school curricula and real life are often at polar extremes.

In contrast to a traditional approach to curriculum design, James Banks has proposed a *transformation approach* that "changes the basic assumptions of the curriculum and enables students to view concepts, issues, themes, and problems from several ethnic perspectives and points of view."[32] For example, learning how people from different communities feel about a topic such as immigration or war—matters that are paramount in current news stories and in the lives of many students—would help them develop a more nuanced way of understanding the world.

One topic that seems to hold particular saliency for many young people, regardless of their background, is that of biases and discrimination. Yet broaching difficult or conflicting issues in the curriculum and class discussions is something that some teachers, because of their lack of information or experience, are reluctant to do. Michelle Fine has called this *silencing,* that is, determining "who can speak, what can and cannot be spoken, and whose discourse must be controlled."[33] This may be due to several factors: Many teachers are unaccustomed to, afraid of, or uncomfortable discussing discrimination and inequality; they feel pressure to "cover the material," and these topics are not included in the traditional curriculum; they are used to presenting information as if it were free of conflict and controversy; or they may feel that bringing up issues concerning conflict will create or exacerbate animosity among students. In the words of one of the teachers in Michelle Fine's study, discussing such issues would be a mistake because "it would demoralize the students, they need to feel positive and optimistic—like they have a chance," a comment based on the spurious assumption that students are not already demoralized, or that they would have a hard time handling the truth.[34] Racism, discrimination, and other "dangerous" topics, students quickly find out, are not supposed to be discussed in school.

Unfortunately, however, these issues do not simply vanish because they are excluded from the curriculum. On the contrary, quashing them reinforces students' feelings that school life is unrelated to real life. In spite of teachers' reluctance to address issues such as racism, slavery, inequality, genocide, and so on, discussing them can be tremendously beneficial to students if they are approached with sensitivity and care. An example comes from a study in which the researchers found that providing information about racism had a positive impact on the racial attitudes of both White students and students of color.[35] Murray Levin, an educator who taught at Harvard University and Boston University and later at the Greater Egleston Community School in Boston, provides a vivid example. Levin believed that even the most marginalized students learn when education is meaningful to their lives. The title of his book documenting the experiences he had at the school is *'Teach Me!' Kids Will Learn When Oppression Is the Lesson*.[36] We would do well to heed this message.

The relationship between curriculum and democracy is significant, especially in this post-9/11 era. In light of our nation's expressed support for equality and fair play, students need to learn that patriotism means standing up for individual and collective freedom, and this is sometimes unpopular. Actions that we now recognize as patriotic may have been very unpopular at the time they took place. For example, the general public largely reviled the actions of those who took part in the civil rights movement, yet today the view that all Americans deserve equal rights is largely accepted, at least in principle. The same is true of women's rights, considered a radical idea just a few decades ago. The issue of gay rights, still controversial in many quarters, hopefully will follow the same course.

Students need to learn that putting democracy into action may mean taking unpopular stands, and this is something they can learn through the curriculum. A tremendous chasm frequently exists between expounding on democracy and actual democratic actions in schools. Providing students with both the rhetoric and the reality of democracy may help them to become agents of positive social change. Curriculum transformation is needed if we believe that one of the basic purposes of schooling is to prepare young people to become productive and critical citizens of a democratic society. One way for teachers to begin is to develop their own curriculum. An excellent resource for doing so is *Planning to Change the World*, an inspiring teacher's plan book available from Rethinking Schools; it provides weekly planning pages, references to online lesson plans and other resources, and essential questions to spark classroom discussion.[37]

Democratic principles are thwarted by the lack of access to knowledge in other ways, too. Low-income students and students from inner-city and poor rural schools generally have fewer opportunities to learn, and as we have already seen, they also have fewer material resources, less engaging learning activities in their classrooms, and less qualified teachers. While "watering down" the curriculum for socioeconomically disadvantaged students may seem equitable on its face, the truth is that it may instead reflect lower expectations. All children can benefit from high expectations and a challenging curriculum, but some students are regularly subjected to diluted, undemanding, and boring content because teachers and schools do not tap into their strengths and talents. Typically, though, what students want are *more* demands rather than fewer, as you can see in the case studies in this book. In fact, according to an exhaustive review of research concerning the so-called "achievement gap," Linda Darling-Hammond has concluded that unequal access to rigorous courses and a challenging curriculum—rather than student laziness or parent apathy—explains this gap.[38]

Textbooks, a significant component of the curriculum in most schools, may also be at odds with democratic and pluralistic values because women and people of

■■■■■■ What You Can Do
Use the Curriculum Critically

Use your current curriculum as the basis for helping students develop a more critical perspective and better research skills. For example, when studying the Revolutionary War, have students investigate the experiences of African Americans, American Indians, women, working people, loyalists, and others whose perspectives have traditionally been excluded from the curriculum. When studying the Industrial Revolution, ask students to explore the role of the nascent workers' movement and of children and young women factory workers, as well as the impact of European immigration on the rise of cities. Students can also concentrate on the emergence of scientific discoveries through inventions by African Americans, women, and immigrants during the late nineteenth century.

When teaching different mathematical operations, ask students to investigate how they are done in other countries. A variety of materials, such as an abacus and other counting instruments, can be demonstrated. If traditional U.S. holidays are commemorated in the curriculum, try to include other perspectives, too. For example, for Columbus Day, discuss the concept of "discovery" with students so that they understand that this was the perspective of the Europeans, not the Native people. Alternative activities can focus on this holiday as the encounter of two worldviews and histories rather than on the "discovery" of one world by another. (*Rethinking Columbus,** from Rethinking

Schools, is an excellent publication that includes many lesson plans and other resources for classrooms.) Thanksgiving, considered by many American Indians to be a day of mourning, is another holiday that can be presented through multiple perspectives.

Create an emerging multicultural curriculum by using the experiences, cultures, and languages of every student in your class. Encourage them to bring their identities into the classroom, for example, by inviting their parents to teach the class about their particular talent, job, or interest. These talents do not have to be culture-specific: For instance, a parent who is a seamstress might teach the children how to sew a hem. Although a talent may not be particular to a specific ethnic heritage, it helps students to see that people from all backgrounds have skills and worthwhile experiences.

Oral history projects that focus on students and their family experiences are another good way to make the curriculum multicultural. Ask students to collect stories, poems, and legends (either recorded or written down) from their families to create a multicultural library. More elaborate activities might include dramatizations for the school assembly, videotaping parents and other community members reciting poems and stories, and readings by older students to children in the younger grades.

*Bigelow, B., and Peterson, B. (1998). *Rethinking Columbus: The next 500 years*. 2nd ed. Milwaukee, WI: Rethinking Schools.

color are strikingly underrepresented. Generally, textbooks tend to reinforce the dominant European American perspective and to sustain stereotypes of groups outside the cultural and political mainstream.[39] Even in recent textbooks, critical and nondominant perspectives are largely missing. According to James Loewen, most history textbooks are filled with half-truths or myths that are the basis for much of the U.S. history taught in school. In his most recent book, *Teaching What Really Happened: How to Avoid the Tyranny of Textbooks and Get Students Excited About Doing History,* he suggests that teachers go beyond textbooks and use additional resources such as primary documents, camcorders and cameras, guest speakers, and alternative reading material to involve students more directly as "history sleuths" to uncover history.[40]

 ## Pedagogy

Pedagogy refers to the strategies, techniques, and approaches used by teachers in their classrooms, that is, *teachers' practices*. It means more than these things, however. Pedagogy also includes what teachers do to create conditions that help students become critical thinkers and moral human beings. For example, many classrooms, through their practices, reflect the belief that learning can best take place in a competitive atmosphere. As a result, the most prevalent classroom approaches stress individual achievement and extrinsic motivation. These include ability grouping, testing of all kinds, and rote learning. Although learning in such classrooms can be fun or interesting, students may learn other unintended lessons, too: that learning equals memorization, that reciting what teachers want to hear is what education is about, and that independent and critical thinking have no place in the classroom.

The observation that schools are tedious places where little learning takes place and where most students are not challenged to learn is hardly new. It is particularly true of secondary schools, where subject matter dominates pedagogy and classes are too often driven by standardized tests as "gatekeepers" to promotion and/or accreditation. Avi Abramson's case study, that follows this chapter, provides enlightening examples of teachers who, as he says, "teach from the point of view of the kid" or those who "just come out and say, 'All right, do this, *blah, blah, blah.*' "

Avi's impressions are confirmed by research. In his comprehensive and classic study on secondary schools, John Goodlad found that textbooks were used frequently and mechanistically, whereas other materials were used infrequently, if at all; that teaching methods varied little from the traditional "chalk and talk" methodology commonly used over 100 years ago; and that routine and rote learning were favored over creativity and critical thinking.[41] Most students today would likely agree. In a three-year study of students in urban middle schools, Bruce Wilson and H. Dickson Corbett discovered that, more than anything, students wanted teachers who taught content meaningful to their lives and who had high expectations of them.[42] Specifically, students most frequently mentioned projects and experiments as the kind of work they liked doing best and that most helped them learn. Rather than focusing only on teachers' personalities or their sense of humor, students cared about *how* their teachers taught.

In a now classic article, Martin Haberman used the term *pedagogy of poverty* to refer to a basic urban pedagogy that encompasses a body of specific strategies that are limited to asking questions, giving directions, making assignments, and monitoring seatwork. Unsupported by research, theory, or even the practice of the best urban teachers, the pedagogy of poverty is based on the dubious assumption that children who live in poverty and children of culturally, racially, and linguistically diverse backgrounds cannot learn in creative, active, and challenging environments. Suggesting instead that exemplary pedagogy in urban schools actively involves students in real-life situations and allows them to reflect on their own lives, Haberman found that good teaching was taking place when, among other things, the following occur:

- Students are involved with issues they perceive as vital concerns (e.g., rather than avoid controversies such as censorship of school newspapers or dress codes, students use these issues as opportunities for learning).
- Students are involved with explanations of differences in race, culture, religion, ethnicity, and gender.
- Students are helped to see major concepts, big ideas, and general principles rather than isolated facts.
- Students are involved in planning their education.
- Students are involved in applying ideals such as fairness, equity, and justice to their world.
- Students are actively involved in heterogeneous groups.
- Students are asked to question commonsense or widely accepted assumptions.[43]

In a more recent article, Jim Cummins suggested that there are particular "pedagogies for the poor," and these are especially evident in reading programs, approaches, and materials. Focusing specifically on the federal Reading First initiative, Cummins argues that, in spite of the fact that there is minimal scientific support for this approach, it has been mandated in many schools attended by poor children. The result has been a teacher-centered, inflexible way of teaching reading that is not evident in other more affluent communities.[44]

Expanding pedagogical strategies alone, however, will not change how and what students learn in school. Let us take the example of cooperative learning, generally praised as a useful instructional strategy. In reviewing hundreds of studies of cooperative learning over the past three decades, Laurel Shaper Walters concluded that there is a positive correlation between cooperative learning and student achievement.[45] In spite of its commendable qualities, however, cooperative learning should be viewed as no more than a means to an end. It is based on the premise that using the talents and skills of all students is key to designing successful learning environments. If cooperative learning is viewed unproblematically, however, it has little chance of changing the fundamental climate of learning in the classroom. This is a good reminder that particular methods can become disconnected from their educational purposes or sociopolitical context.

Another pedagogical approach growing in popularity is *constructivism*.[46] This approach is based on the notion that students' background knowledge can be enormously significant in their learning and that interpretations of new information are influenced by their prior knowledge and experiences. Through this approach, teachers encourage students to use what they know in order to develop deeper understandings rather than simply to learn random and unrelated facts. Constructivist teaching is characterized by practices such as inquiry activities, problem-posing strategies, and dialogue among peers. In this approach, learning is viewed as an interactive rather than a passive process, and students' creativity and intelligence are respected. Although this sounds promising, constructivism—or any other approach,

■■■■■ **What You Can Do**
Punch up Your Pedagogy!

Go beyond textbooks and use additional resources to make the curriculum more inviting for students. A straight lecture, what has been called "chalk and talk," may be appropriate sometimes, but if it is overused, it treats students as passive learners. This approach is also culturally inappropriate for many students. To help students become more active learners as well as to provide a multiculturally sensitive learning environment, create opportunities for group work, individualized tasks, collaborative research, peer tutoring, cross-age learning, group reflections, dialogue, debates, and action projects in the school and community, among other pedagogical approaches. Also, whenever possible, integrate technology and digital media that taps into the ways of knowing and communicating so common among many youth. Assign video analysis and production; Web-based communication; and, with secondary students, try innovative practices using text messaging and cell-phone based lessons.

for that matter—is not necessarily effective with all students and cannot be simply "applied" as if it is the answer to all learning problems. In a critique of constructivism, Virginia Richardson, who is herself a proponent of the approach, claims that using it indiscriminately may be counterproductive. Richardson writes, "The most serious problem with the use of the constructive pedagogy construct occurs when it becomes valued as best practice for everyone."[47]

We need to view all approaches and methods with a critical eye, even with skepticism, because no method will solve learning problems for all students. This is the problem with any pedagogical approach that is uncritically elevated to the level of "best practice" as if a particular practice is appropriate for all students in all contexts. Lilia Bartolomé suggests that, instead of devotion to a particular instructional strategy, teachers need to develop a "humanizing pedagogy" that values students' cultural, linguistic, and experiential backgrounds.[48] Confirming this view, Jim Cummins cautions that "transformative pedagogy represents a crucial component of any educational reform process that is serious about reversing patterns of underachievement among marginalized groups."[49]

■ ◣ ■ ◥ ■ ## Climate and Physical Structure

Climate refers to the nature of the environment. In schools, the climate can either encourage or stifle learning. In urban areas, and increasingly in some suburban areas as well, for instance, it is not unusual to find schools with police officers standing guard. In some schools, students are frisked before entering. Teachers sometimes feel afraid unless they lock their classrooms. Climate is partially associated with the *physical structure* of schools, that is, the architecture, classroom resources, cleanliness, and order. Climate is also associated, of course, with other policies and practices such as the curriculum, pedagogy, and disciplinary policies, as we have seen above;

with the morale of teachers and administrators in the building; and with family outreach, as we shall see below. The physical structure of schools can also either promote or inhibit educational equity. In some schools, desks are nailed to the floor, halls and classrooms are airless and poorly lit, and shattered glass can be found in courtyards where children play. To understand the connection between climate and physical structures, we turn to Ron Berger, a long-time teacher, who describes how the various elements of a school's culture affect students:

> The aspects of a school that most clearly engrave the school experience on children are often in the "other stuff" category: the physical appearance of the school building, outside and in; the manner in which school property and personal property are respected and cared for in the school; the levels of physical safety and emotional safety that children and adults in the building feel; the way routines of arrival, class transitions, lunch times, and dismissal are handled; the ways authority is exercised; the tone of courtesy, kindness, and acceptance in peer culture; the ways in which students' achievements are shared with the school community and outside of it; the aspects of the school that define it in the larger community. These things are every bit as important as curriculum.[50]

There is indeed a relationship between poor student achievement and the condition of school buildings. These conditions include poor lighting, inadequate ventilation, inadequate or too much heating, school safety, class size, and air quality. In their analysis of the research on school climate, Jonathan Cohen, Terry Pickeral, and Molly McCloskey reviewed a substantial number of studies that confirmed the effect of a positive and sustained school climate in promoting students' academic achievement and healthy development, as well as teacher retention, which in itself enhances student success.[51] One dramatic example was reported by Valerie Lee and David Burkam. Using a sample of 3,840 students in 190 urban and suburban high schools, they found that the structures and organization of high schools can influence students' decisions to stay in school or drop out. Some of the conditions that fostered staying in school were school size of fewer than 1,500 students, a curriculum offering mainly academic courses and few nonacademic courses, and positive relationships between students and their teachers. Lee and Burkam concluded that explanations for dropping out that rely solely on students' social background and school behaviors are inadequate.[52]

School violence is another problem related to the climate for learning, but schools alone are not to blame for violence. Violence in schools is a reflection of the violence that takes place in society, and teachers and administrators often struggle heroically to contain it and to make schools places of learning and joy. Yet it is often students from these very schools who do the damage. Boredom and rage are implicated in these actions, particularly when schools show little regard for students by silencing their voices and negating their identities in the curriculum. Destructiveness and violence by students sometimes represent a clear message that school structures are incompatible with students' emotional and physical needs. For instance, the U.S. Department of Education reported that large and impersonal schools, and those with hostile and authoritarian teachers and administrators, are more likely to be vandalized than schools characterized by cooperation among teachers and administrators and clear expectations for students.[53]

Although school violence in general has diminished in the past several years, it is still a major problem. One aspect of violence that has come under intense scrutiny in the past several years is bullying, which seems to have increased. Students whose identities differ from the mainstream, particularly lesbian, gay, bisexual, and transgender (LGBT) students, or those who are perceived to be, are often the targets of bullying. The negative impact of bullying on the climate of schools is clear. For example, a survey of 32,000 students in 108 urban schools found that 25 percent of those surveyed said they felt uncertain about their safety in school, and fully half indicated that they had seen other students being bullied at least once a month.[54]

The physical resemblance of some schools to factories or prisons is unfortunate but true. In many instances, schools are uninviting, fortresslike places precisely because school officials are trying to protect students and teachers against vandalism, theft, and other acts of violence. The size of schools alone is enough to give them this institutional look. High schools hold sometimes 2,000, 3,000, or even 4,000 students, and it is easy to understand the students' and teachers' feelings of alienation and insecurity that can result. Not all schools are large and impersonal, however. In general, the farther away from urban or poor rural communities, the less institutional the appearance of the school. Suburban schools or schools in wealthy towns tend to look strikingly different from schools that serve the poor. Not only do the former usually have more space, bigger classrooms, and more light, they also have more material supplies and generally are in better physical condition, partly because the level of financing for the education of poor students is lower than for children in more affluent districts. Wealthier schools tend to have smaller classes as well. However, lower budgets do not necessarily have to dictate less imaginative and unwelcoming architecture. Educational vision and political will can lead to more appropriate school environments for all students regardless of their economic situation.

Because school size can make a difference in student learning, many schools are developing schools within schools, teams, or other approaches to encourage more family-like environments and closer relationships among students and teachers. School size may also influence students' feelings of belonging, and thus their engagement with learning, as well as teachers' motivation and engagement. One study, for example, found that facility quality was an important predictor of the decision of teachers to stay or leave, probably even more important than a pay increase.[55] Another study found that elementary schools of fewer than 400 students tended to display stronger collective teacher responsibility for student learning and greater student achievement in math.[56] Small classes also have proven to have a positive effect on student learning. A widely cited study by Jeremy Finn and his associates found that, when students started early and continued in small classes or classes with teachers' aides for at least three years, they performed significantly better in all grades than students in full-size classes or without teachers' aides. In addition, those benefits lasted: Students who attended small classes in grades K–3 continued to perform better in all subjects up to the eighth grade.[57] Although there is some disagreement about the relative effect of small classes on low-achieving students compared with high achievers, a more recent study in London confirmed that student engagement rises as class size falls for both elementary and secondary students, and the benefits at the secondary level were especially strong for the lowest-achieving

■ ■ ■ ■ ■ ■ What You Can Do
Enliven Your Environment

You can do little about some things in your physical environment, but you can change others, both inside classrooms and out.

Make your classroom inviting and comfortable. Ask parents, students, and colleagues to help with ideas and resources. Collect pillows, rugs and colorful fabric swaths for curtains or for covering bulletin boards. In the younger grades, create engaging activity corners, a cozy place to read, comfortable chairs or a couch, and a place for group work. In the older grades, have a quiet place for individual work and a space for collaborative research. From time to time, place seats in a horseshoe arrangement to create a more amenable space for dialogue. From preschool through high school, posters, student artwork, maps, pictures, books, and music help create a sense of community.

Outside the classroom, graffiti and garbage around a school or broken toilets and nonfunctioning science labs give the message that the children who attend that school are not valued. Help organize families, colleagues, and children for clean-up brigades and mural-painting projects. If there are more serious problems, inform parents and other community members about some of the policies and practices that make school uninviting so that they can organize to help solve these problems. These issues can be brought up at parent–teacher association (PTA), school board, and even city council meetings. Letters to the editor can draw a great deal of attention and subsequent action. Unless demands are made to change the negative messages of the school environment, children will continue to be the victims.

students.[58] Class size alone, however, may not be the most important factor in influencing student engagement in learning. Simply making schools smaller will not have a major impact if the emotional climate within schools and negative relationships between students and teachers remain unchanged.[59]

The physical environment of schools can also reflect expectations of students. If students are perceived to be deficient, the educational environment may reflect a no-nonsense, back-to-basics drill orientation. However, if students are perceived as intelligent and motivated and as having an interest in the world around them, the educational environment tends to reflect an intellectually stimulating and academically challenging orientation, a place where learning is considered joyful rather than tedious. Given this reality, we might well ask what would happen if the schools attended by youngsters in poor urban and rural areas were to miraculously become like the schools that middle-class and wealthy youngsters attend. Might there be a change in educational outcomes if all students had access to generously endowed, smaller, and more democratically run schools? We cannot know the answer to this question until we try this approach, but one thing is certain: The physical environment in many schools provides a stark contrast to the stated purposes of teaching and learning. When schools are not cared for, when they become fortresses rather than an integral part of the community they serve, and when they are holding places instead of learning environments, the contradiction between goals and realities is a vivid one. This chasm between ideal and real is not lost on the students.

 ## Disciplinary Policies

Disciplinary policies can aggravate the alienation felt by some students, particularly students who are already marginalized in school. Over two decades ago, in a compelling study using longitudinal data from the national High School and Beyond study, researchers Gary Wehlage and Robert Rutter found that certain conditions in the schools themselves could *predict* the dropping-out behavior of students.[60] They concluded that certain student characteristics *in combination with* certain school conditions can determine the *holding power* of school and, consequently, students' decisions to stay in or drop out of school. In a recent review of related literature, researchers Anne Gregory, Russell Skiba, and Pedro Noguera found that, because schools tend to rely heavily on school exclusion as their primary disciplinary tool, this discipline practice has a disproportionate and negative impact on Latino, African American, and Native American students. As a result, what they call the *racial discipline gap* further exacerbates the racial "achievement gap."[61]

Students living in poverty and students of color are more likely to be suspended and to be victims of corporal punishment. This inequity is frequently related to poor communication among administrators, teachers, and students. For example, in a two-month investigation, the *Seattle Post-Intelligencer* found that Black students were two and a half times more likely to be suspended or expelled than other students. Although common explanations for this situation include poverty and broken homes, the investigation found that Black students were far more likely than others to be suspended or expelled *regardless of their home lives and poverty*. In this case, too, school climate and size make a difference. The report of this investigation cited one school that had become a "small school" by creating a more intimate and sensitive environment. The result was that suspensions and expulsions had been reduced across the board, although a racial gap still existed. "A school culture that prides itself on being color-blind," the report concluded, "might be better off taking a hard look at race."[62]

Interpretations of student behavior may be culturally or class biased, and this poses an additional barrier to enforcing disciplinary policies fairly. For example, students in poor schools who insist on wearing highly prized leather jackets in class may be doing so because of a well-founded fear that they will be stolen if the jackets are left in the closet or a locker. Latino children who cast their eyes downward when being scolded probably are not being defiant but are simply behaving out of respect for their teachers, as they were taught at home. African American students are especially vulnerable to unfair policies if they follow particular styles. For example, in her study of an urban school undergoing restructuring, Pauline Lipman described the case of an African American male student who was given a 10-day in-school suspension for wearing his overall straps unsnapped, a common style among African American males, whereas White students who wore their pants with large holes cut in the thighs, a widespread style among White students, were not even reprimanded.[63]

Discipline can be an issue even among more economically privileged students who are culturally different from the mainstream. For instance, Avi Abramson, the subject of one of the case studies that follow this chapter, pointed out how he was

■ ■ ■ ■ ■ ■   What You Can Do
Create Inclusive Disciplinary Practices

Investigate how disciplinary policies and practices affect students of different groups unfairly by looking at rates of detention, suspension, and assignments to "special" classes or alternative programs in your school. If students in these programs are overwhelmingly from one social or racial group or gender, ask the principal to set up a study or inquiry group to look into this problem. Suggest appropriate steps to address the problem directly.

At the classroom level, think about how to involve all your students as class citizens. For example, have them help design disciplinary policies. At the school level, rather than rely on those who happen to be on the student council—generally a rather limited group of students—suggest a forum in which a broad range of student voices is heard. This forum can include academic classes, assemblies, and other student activities such as sports and clubs.

the subject of several anti-Semitic incidents. Because teachers did not take action, Avi felt that he had to take matters into his own hands. He said, "I went up to the teacher and I said to her, 'I'm either gonna leave the class or they leave.' " This is a good reminder that teachers' actions—not just their words—go a long way toward making students feel safe, or unsafe, in school.

■ ◀ ■ ◢   ## The Limited Role of Students

That many students are alienated, uninvolved, and discouraged by school is abundantly clear. This fact is most striking, of course, in dropout rates, the most extreme manifestation of disengagement from schooling. Students who drop out are commonly uninvolved and passive participants in the school experience.

Usually, schools are not organized to encourage active student involvement. Although it is true that students are nominally represented in the governance structure of many schools, often this representation is merely window dressing that has little to do with the actual management of the school. Rather than being designed to prepare students for democratic life, most schools are more like benign dictatorships in which all decisions are made for them, albeit in what schools may perceive to be students' best interests. They are more often organized around issues of control than of collaboration or consultation. That is, students are expected to learn what is decided, designed, and executed by others. Often, it is not the teacher or even the school that determines the content of the curriculum and the majority of school policies, but some mythical, "downtown" school board or state education department.

In the classroom itself, the pedagogy frequently reflects what Paulo Freire called *banking education,* that is, a process by which teachers "deposit" knowledge into students, who are thought to be empty receptacles. It is education that promotes powerlessness. In a characterization of what happens in most schools, Freire contrasted the expected roles of the teacher and the students:

- The teacher teaches, and the students are taught.
- The teacher knows everything, and the students know nothing.
- The teacher thinks, and the students are thought about.
- The teacher talks, and the students listen—meekly.
- The teacher disciplines, and the students are disciplined.
- The teacher chooses and enforces his or her choice, and the students comply.
- The teacher acts, and the students have the illusion of acting through the action of the teacher.
- The teacher chooses the program content, and the students (who were not consulted) adapt to it.
- The teacher confuses the authority of knowledge with his or her own professional authority, which he or she sets in opposition to the freedom of the students.
- The teacher is the subject of the learning process, while the pupils are mere objects.[64]

What impact does involvement of students have on their school experiences and achievement? Much has been written about how to engage students in their learning, but very little of it has issued from students themselves. In a book focused on the perspectives of secondary students in the United States, England, Canada, and Australia, as well as on the work of teachers, researchers, and teacher educators who have collaborated with a wide variety of students, Alison Cook-Sather and her colleagues focus on student perspectives, articulated in their own words, regarding specific approaches to creating and maintaining a positive classroom environment and designing engaging lessons and on more general issues of respect and responsibility in the classroom. To illustrate how these approaches work in practice, the book includes stories of how preservice and in-service teachers, school leaders, and teacher educators have made student voices and participation central to their classroom and school practices.[65]

In a specific example, researcher Ernest Morrell sought to understand the relationship between apprenticing urban youth as critical researchers of their realities and the development of their academic literacy. In a multiyear, critical, ethnographic study, the students took on the issue of the tremendous inequities that existed in their high school—inequities based on ethnicity and social class background—that effectively made it seem like two separate high schools. Morrell saw students develop from novices to productive writers, researchers, and speakers at national education conferences who published their research as a form of social action. He concluded that, as a result of students' work—including their writings, presentations, conversations, and questions—the decision makers in the school were forced to respond to students' findings about the two-school situation, and indeed to design and implement strategies to address the situation.[66]

In addition, students became more passionate learners. Some who had never dreamed of going to college were so changed by this experience that they decided to do so. As Morrell found, however, such changes cannot be sustained in the absence of a broader political movement in which students, families, and educators mobilize to radically alter the status quo in schools and districts. The message should not be lost on teachers and schools: When students are involved in directing their own education in some way, they are more enthusiastic learners.

The Limited Role of Teachers

As a group, teachers are shown little respect by our society and are usually poorly paid and infrequently rewarded. In school, they are sometimes the victims of physical and verbal threats and attacks, and they feel a lack of parental support and involvement. Teachers are traditionally discouraged from becoming involved in decision-making processes in the schools. As such, they have become alienated in the current climate of reform because it has become obvious that people far removed from the schools are making the decisions about curriculum and instruction, while at the same time accountability is being determined more and more by high-stakes tests and imposed standards. Alienated and discouraged teachers can hardly be expected to help students become empowered, critical thinkers. In contrast, teachers who feel that they have autonomy in their classrooms and in decisions about curriculum generally also have high expectations of their students.

New structures such as teacher-led schools, job sharing, and time, on a weekly basis, for professional development and other activities may help make teachers more active players in their schools. In addition, a number of recent studies have found that, to create a sense of teaching as intellectual work, it is vital to develop schools as professional communities of practice.[67] Changing the nature of professional development in schools so that teachers take more responsibility for their own learning is imperative, but the professional climate in schools is only one aspect of a larger problem. Teachers are disempowered for many reasons, and these do not correspond simply to school structures. Their disempowerment also has a lot to do with their status within the professional hierarchy. Restructuring schools to be more respectful of teachers' professionalism is crucial if they are to become places where teachers feel engaged and empowered.

Nevertheless, restructuring and greater teacher efficacy, by themselves, are no guarantee that schools will become more effective learning environments for students. For this to happen, teachers also need to confront their attitudes and preconceptions of students, particularly students who are different from themselves, and then work to develop positive and caring relationships with their students. In addition, broadening the roles, responsibilities, and status of teachers needs to be accompanied by changes in (1) the general public's attitudes about teachers' professionalism, (2) teachers' beliefs about their own capabilities, and (3) the dynamic possibilities for learning that students' diversity creates. Thus, in spite of the restrictions imposed by high-stakes standardized testing and the bureaucratization of schools, when teachers deliberately choose to work together to promote change, and when they focus on learning about their students' realities, tremendous positive changes can begin to take shape. My (Sonia's) interviews of teachers who move from "surviving" to "thriving" in the classroom and the profession powerfully document this process.[68]

The Boston Teachers Union (BTU) School, a pilot school within the Boston Public School (BPS) system, is an example of a school structure designed to empower teachers because it disrupts the traditional professional hierarchy by emphasizing teacher knowledge and embracing teacher innovation.*

Pilot schools were first launched in Boston in 1994 to serve as sites of educational innovation and research through a collaborative vision shared by the Boston Teachers Union, the mayor, the city's school committee, and the superintendent. The goal of pilot schools was to provide models of effective urban education in Boston. This model also serves as an alternative to charter schools that typically funnel resources and students away from neighborhood schools.

A decade after the initiation of pilot schools, in 2004, the BTU was alarmed by the negative working conditions in some pilot schools that overtaxed and exploited teachers while disregarding the teaching contract. The BTU set out to launch its own pilot school, which opened in September 2009, with classrooms for K1 and K2 and grades 1, 2 and 6. The goal was to add two grades each year until it is a full K–8 school. Founded and democratically led by teachers, the school's emphasis is on bringing teacher knowledge to bear in decision making about how to help kids learn best.[†]

Multicultural Teaching Story

Boston Teachers Union School: Teacher Leadership and Student Achievement

Teachers Union as Educational Leader

A union member and second-grade teacher in Boston, Erik Berg lives and works in the same neighborhood as the BTU School and was instrumental in leading the efforts to create it. He also chairs its governance committee. Erik explained that the union's vision was to embrace teacher knowledge for making decisions about curriculum and school climate in a way that would support all students' achievements, paying particular attention to the needs of the most vulnerable BPS children. The school would fully integrate a broad liberal arts curriculum with rigorous high standards in the arts, history, humanities, and sciences, which have been woefully neglected in many Massachusetts schools since the implementation of high-stakes standardized testing in the 1990s. The test-conscious subjects of math and English language arts would be thoroughly addressed as well, but not at the risk of ignoring or eliminating other content areas, a practice that had been neglecting students' multiple intelligences. Erik expressed that it is important for teacher unions to step forward on educational issues and develop real, achievable opportunities for changing educational experiences for urban kids. He sees the role of the union as pointing out

*For more information on Boston's pilot schools, see http://www.bostonpublicschools.org/node/20
[†]See the Web site of the Boston Teachers Union school at http://www.btuschool.org/

alternatives. He also emphasized that the BTU School model is not a "one-and-only model" for every school, but one among many models. He acknowledged that the BTU School was a work in progress where some of the most prominent features of the structure allowed for teacher-led decision making, robust parent and family engagement, meaningful professional development, and partnerships with teacher educators.

With no principal or headmaster, Berta Berriz and Betsy Drinan are collaboratively responsible for the daily functions of the school as well as for implementing the long-term vision. Berta explained that one of the most distinctive aspects of the school is the way in which teacher knowledge and dedication to student achievement drive decision making:

> Teachers are in charge. That is the most salient aspect of our school. As teachers we are encouraged to bring our knowledge to bear on decisions that are made in our school. We are constantly meeting together and solving problems together to move children forward. In terms of a multicultural organization in a flat decision-making structure, teacher knowledge and shared leadership are prominent. We keep a close watch on children.

Teacher Innovation and Family Participation

In this collaborative model, the BTU teachers use ongoing formative assessment to see how children are doing. For example, in second grade, some children who entered in September were already reading at third-, fourth-, and fifth-grade levels, and many others were reading at a second-grade level. However, there were eight boys who were exhibiting very low skills, and some had no decoding skills. The tendency in many schools would be to refer this cluster of eight boys to special education, and also to provide less attention to those displaying advanced skills. At the BTU School, however, the upper elementary teacher was able to work with the students who were demonstrating mastery of third- through fifth-grade reading. For the eight youngsters who needed to develop early reading skills, the teachers followed a Response to Intervention (RtI) model that seeks to prevent academic failure through early intervention with students who are struggling by giving them targeted support, instead of placing them in special education.

For these eight second-graders, classroom teachers collaborated with the resource room teachers. They engaged the families at every level by preparing take-home literacy packets and working with families on reading activities. This was a much more vigorous outreach than just sending papers home in students' backpacks. Teachers used telephone communication to check with parents and explain ways in which the take-home reading materials could be used. Teachers and staff members also reached out to parents to encourage them to become engaged in activities such as field trips.

By the end of the school year, six of these eight students were able to meet benchmarks and move on to the next grade. Two students were not meeting benchmarks for entering third grade, but they had made significant progress. For example, one of the boys entered the second grade not reading at all in terms of decoding, and he is now at the beginning of second-grade reading level. Berta explained,

> We are thinking about what to do next. He was not picking up the accelerated instruction approach, but he is clearly learning and achieving far more than he was at the beginning of the school year. With all of that—we did that as a team and we did it together using the resources that we had to work with children to teach them how to read. In some schools you might have teachers being blamed, or families being blamed. Part of

this intervention that was so successful included the families and the teachers making resources for families to use at home.

Families in the Fabric of the School

The BTU School corralled a variety of resources to address the needs of these students. The school built its strategies on a solid foundation of family engagement that was already interwoven into the fabric of the school culture.

With creative budgeting, a paraprofessional is now dedicated to family engagement. He works half-time on family engagement and half-time in the kindergarten classroom. He also produces family newsletters and helps to coordinate events. The school holds two all-day conference days when the families come into the school and meet with the teachers. Berta pointed out, "It is not a before-school or after-school thing, or come-when-you-can kind of thing. From the very beginning the families are informed about how the children are doing."

In June, Berta and Betsy explained that they had already met the new families for next year. They have high attendance at events for families because the BTU Family Council is very active. They organized family nights with potluck dinners where the kids performed in the auditorium for the whole school. "We had 148 families—it was wonderful! And the food never ran out!" There are also classroom-parents in charge of communication, ensuring that every parent-guardian receives information in languages they understand (the Web site features English, Haitian Creole, and Spanish) and can voice their questions and concerns directly to teachers.

Teacher Knowledge and Teacher Research

Family connections are a critical piece of the overall BTU School strategy and play a significant role in the teaching and learning of the emergent readers in the second grade. The teachers embrace the skill development of these early readers as an opportunity to reflect on their work and to share their insights with others. The two teachers, who are in the process of writing about their experience with the second-grade readers, will be sharing their knowledge with others through the academic publication process.

Limited Family and Community Involvement

The findings of research on the effectiveness of family and community involvement are clear: In programs with strong family involvement, students are consistently better achievers than in otherwise identical programs with less family involvement. For example, the Harvard Family Research Project studied the influence of family engagement on student achievement. The results were undeniable: Children at all levels of education benefit from family engagement in their schools. Particularly significant was their finding that family engagement helps close educational gaps between children from different racial groups and socioeconomic backgrounds.[69] In addition, students in schools that maintain frequent contact with

This points to another mark of innovation: the way in which professional development is engaged through teachers sharing resources and strategies. On a weekly basis, teachers hold a two-hour meeting after school and they take turn as facilitators. Sometimes they work with the whole group of faculty members and sometimes with smaller groups.

Role of Research, Professional Development, and Teacher Education

Teacher educators from Simmons College in Boston support this teacher-led professional development. While some institutions of higher education claim "partnerships with schools" by merely sending their student teachers, Simmons brings resources to the school in a variety of ways. Professor Theresa Perry rallied from the beginning for Simmons to be a substantive partner in the BTU School. In addition to student teachers, and collaborating with teachers on research and academic publishing, Simmons College provides two Simmons faculty members: Jill Taylor, who works with teachers in the school one day a week, and Roberta Kelly, who contributes to professional development activities and has brought her expertise in educational leadership from the outset. Roberta worked closely with Berta and Betsy as the co-lead teachers to develop their professional relationship, and helped them lay the foundation for shared leadership. Betsy expressed that "being an administrator in the traditional hierarchical model can be really isolating." She said that through the workshops with Roberta, however, she learned many useful strategies for collaborating, communicating, and true democratic leadership.

While teacher-led decision making, robust parent and family engagement, meaningful professional development, and partnerships with teacher educators may not sound new or particularly revolutionary, it is rare for a school to enact these ideals in a democratic process that empowers teachers. The BTU School is an emerging learning community, and everybody involved agrees they have a lot to learn and more challenges to take on.

Berta concluded her remarks by saying that in June, at the end of the school's first year, she was "[e]xhausted but happy. I see it as a liberation project, for teachers, students, and families. It has worked out well with this Freedom-to-Teach approach."

their communities outperform students in other schools. These positive effects persist well beyond the short term.[70]

There are many definitions of parent involvement, and each is more or less effective, depending on the context. Activities such as attendance at parent–teacher conferences, participation in PTAs, and influence over children's selection of courses can help improve student achievement. But involvement of this kind is becoming more and more infrequent in a society increasingly characterized by one-parent families or two-parent families in which both parents work outside the home. Thus, defining involvement only in these traditional ways is problematic. PTA meetings held during the day, parent–teacher conferences held during school hours, and the

■ ■ ■ ■ ■ ■   # What You Can Do
Vigorously Promote Family Outreach

First, recognize and acknowledge that most families are involved in the education of their children through the values they foster at home and in the implicit and explicit expectations they have of their children. At the same time, encourage families to become more involved, as much as they are able, in the day-to-day life of the school.

Most important, communicate with families regularly through a weekly or monthly newsletter, phone calls, meetings at school or home, or a combination of these methods. Mary Cowhey, a teacher we know, visits every family of her students in the two weeks prior to the beginning of school. She says she learns more about her students, about who loves them, and about what's important to them through these visits than any other way.*

When school meetings are to take place, ask administrators to provide childcare, translation of the proceedings into languages spoken by the families, and transportation. Encourage family members to bring activities and materials that are significant to them and their children into the classroom.*

*For a description of her family visits, see Cowhey, M. (2006). *Black ants and Buddhists: Thinking critically and teaching differently in the primary grades.* Portland, ME: Stenhouse.

ubiquitous parent-sponsored cake sale are becoming relics of the past or, at best, the purview of a limited number of families who have the time, the resources, and the inclination to participate in such activities.

It is also true that family involvement is a complex issue, and teachers and other educators are often intimidated by family involvement or are reluctant to reach out to families. For one thing, most educators have had little preparation for working with families. Also, families and school personnel may have little knowledge of one another's realities. One interesting poll found that there was a wide gap in the way parents and principals perceived their relationship: Although 93 percent of the principals said that their relationships with parents were "satisfactory," only 64 percent of the parents polled expressed the same feeling.[71]

Cultural and economic differences influence family involvement outreach in many ways. Families of linguistically and culturally diverse communities and from working-class neighborhoods frequently have difficulty fulfilling the level and kind of parent involvement expected by the school, such as homework assistance and family excursions. Not taking part in these activities should not be interpreted as noninvolvement or apathy, however. Research has consistently found that, contrary to conventional wisdom, families of all backgrounds generally have high expectations and aspirations for their children, although school personnel may not realize this.[72] In addition, teachers and other school staff members often do not understand the cultural values of different families and the goals that parents have for their children; typical involvement strategies may further estrange families who already feel disconnected from the school. The general lack of awareness among many school staff members—from secretaries to teachers and administrators—concerning the cultural and linguistic resources of families of diverse backgrounds can lead to frustration and misunderstanding on the part of both families and educators. Many excellent books provide practical and respectful strategies for engaging families in their children's education; these should be on every educator's bookshelf.[73]

In spite of the challenges of parent involvement—especially when it comes to poor and immigrant families—it still represents a potential avenue for bringing community values, lifestyles, and realities into the school. When families become involved, it also means that their language and culture and the expectations they have for their children can become part of the dialogue, and through dialogue, true change can begin.

Conclusion

The organization and structures of schools often are contrary to the needs of students, the values of their communities, and even to one of the major articulated purposes of schooling—to provide equal educational opportunity for all students. For example, a comprehensive Schott Foundation report on inequities in opportunity to learn reached the shocking conclusion that nationally, students from historically disadvantaged groups have just *51 percent* of the opportunity to learn that White students have.[74] The result of such tremendous inequities is that policies and practices in schools, more often than not, reflect and maintain the status quo and the stratification of the larger society. Too many students, in the words of Kirsten Olson, are "wounded by school."[75] In her insightful book based on autobiographical interviews with over 100 students, teachers, and parents, the author describes the boredom and daily disengagement of students, the drudgery and lack of value in their work, the incessant labeling and tracking based on meaningless tests, and a poor understanding of students and what they really need and want.

But schools by themselves cannot change this situation. Witness the sobering words of Jeannie Oakes and her colleagues. In a longitudinal study of 16 schools around the country undergoing reform, these researchers reached the reluctant conclusion that the educational reforms they studied "did little to interrupt or disrupt the course of the nation's history, flaws, and inequity, its hegemony and racism." They added, "Asking to disrupt a nation is a tall order—one that, we have become convinced, schools will eagerly follow but should not be expected to lead."[76]

In spite of our fondest wishes, therefore, schools cannot, by themselves, become an oasis of equity in a land of inequity. This does not mean, however, that the situation is hopeless. On the contrary, there is much for teachers and other educators to do, both in classrooms and out. This was the subject of this chapter and will continue to be the focus of subsequent chapters.

To Think About

1. Ability-group tracking decisions are often based on ideologies concerning intelligence. The "nature versus nurture" argument in explaining intelligence has been raging for many years: While some people believe that intelligence is primarily dependent on genetic makeup

("nature"), others believe that the environment ("nurture") plays a more important role. What are your thoughts on this debate? Why? What is the basis for your conclusions?

2. Design a school for either the elementary or secondary level that would provide what you think of as an excellent environment for learning. Describe the policies and practices in the school, and explain why you've designed the school in the way you have.

3. Research the disciplinary policies in your district. How do suspensions compare across racial, ethnic, and gender groups? How would you interpret these data? If there are inequities, what can you do—alone, with colleagues, or with parents and other community members—to address them?

 Activities *for Personal, School, and Community Change*

1. Observe a number of similar classrooms, some that are tracked and others that are not. What are the differences among these classrooms? Be specific, citing student engagement with work, expectations of student achievement, level of academic difficulty, and teacher-student and student-student relationships. What are your conclusions about tracking? What can you do about it?

2. Get some evaluation checklists for textbooks at your library or, working with colleagues, design your own. Review and evaluate the textbooks used in your local school. Are they biased against students of any group? How? Give specific examples based on the checklists you have used.

3. With a group of colleagues, prepare a workshop for other teachers on retention and alternatives to it. Present some actual data from your school or district about the effects of retention.

 *Case Studies*

Avi Abramson

Some teachers teach from the point of view of the kid. They don't just come out and say, "All right, do this, blah, blah, blah." They're not so one-tone voice.

Talbot is a small, quiet, and aging working-class town in eastern Massachusetts a few miles from the busy metropolis of Boston. Its total area is a mere 1.6 square miles, and it has a population of approximately 20,000. With the exception of salt marshes and surplus federal installations, there is little vacant land in Talbot.

One gets a sense of the community's aging by its housing. More than half of the dwellings were built near the beginning of the twentieth century, and the population mirrors this aging profile. In the past three decades, the number of youths has been declining, with younger adults and families moving to more prosperous areas. Older residents remain, continuing to live in homes that long ago lost their modern veneer. Both public and parochial school enrollment have been dwindling over the past decades, too. One of the three elementary schools was turned into condominiums. The one high school in town, Talbot High School, has approximately 700 students.

Avi Abramson,[1] the subject of this case study, lived in Talbot at the time of his interview. Talbot was home to many Italians and Irish and to smaller concentrations of other European American immigrants. The percentage of people of color was quite low—only a handful of families. Although there had been a thriving community in Talbot just a generation before, the number of Jewish families was very small at the time of Avi's interview. There were two synagogues in town, one known as the "big synagogue" and the other as the "small synagogue." Many Jewish families had moved to other communities, and the remaining Jews were mostly senior citizens; many of them were religiously observant and went to temple regularly. According to Avi, many people in his community were close to 85 years of age. The high school had no more than ten Jewish students.

Except for a year when his family moved to North Carolina, Avi had lived in Talbot almost all his life. He went to first and second grade in public school, then to a Jewish day school until eighth grade. When interviewed, he was 16 years old and a senior at Talbot High School. As he explained during his interviews, Avi had not always been a successful student. He had a hard time adjusting to public school because the curriculum was so different from what he had experienced in the Jewish day school. His plans were to go to college the following year, and he had given some thought to becoming either a history teacher or a graphic designer.

Avi lived on the water-tower hillside of this quaint old town in a quiet neighborhood of single and multifamily homes. During the Christmas season, his house was easily spotted: It was the only one on the street without Christmas lights. He described his town as peaceful, and he said he enjoyed living there. Avi and his family had good relationships with their neighbors, whom he described with fondness ("Everybody looks out for each other," he said). Nevertheless, he clearly longed to live in a community where he would not be perceived as being so "different."

Avi lived with his mother and a brother who was 10 years his elder. His older sister lived in New York City with her husband and two children. Avi's father had originally come from Israel and had met his Jewish American wife in the United States, where he had remained. He had died after a long illness six years before Avi's interview. He had been a much-loved teacher in various Hebrew schools. Avi's mother was also a Hebrew teacher but, although she loved teaching, there was not much call for Hebrew teachers in the area, so she began studying computers to prepare for a new career.

Exuding a warm glow of familiarity and old, comfortable furniture, Avi's home was filled with the aroma of latkes (potato pancakes) during the Hanukkah season and of many other Jewish foods at other times of the year. Books and artifacts were everywhere, reflecting the family's respect for tradition and history.

In many ways, Avi was a typical American teenager. He had a girlfriend and enjoyed frequent telephone conversations with friends. His bedroom was crammed with posters; comic books; encyclopedias; track team gear; woodworking projects;

Star Trek memorabilia; drawing pads full of his own comics; and, underneath it all, bunk beds. In other ways, however, Avi was different from many other American youths. His serious, wise demeanor was evident in the profound respect and love that he had for his culture and religion. He dedicated every Saturday to leading the last elderly remnants of his community in their Sabbath prayers at the small synagogue (what one might call a "role model in reverse"). He enjoyed speaking Hebrew, loved the Jewish holidays, and devoted a great deal of time to religious and cultural activities. An energetic and thoughtful young man, he enjoyed school as well as sports and other hobbies.

Three basic themes were revealed in Avi's interviews. One was his *sense of responsibility*—to himself, his family, and his community—as well as his persistence in fulfilling this responsibility. This trait was especially evident in the respect and care with which he treated his culture and religion. *The joy and pain of maintaining them* was another theme frequently discussed by Avi. *The role of positive pressure,* from peers and family, and through activities such as track, was the third.

Independent Responsibility and Persistence

I'm fairly religious. I mean, I work in a temple on Saturdays, so I keep myself Orthodox. I try to keep the law, you know, for Shabbat [Yiddish for Sabbath], 'cause I'm reading the Torah [holiest book for Jews], so it would be nice if the person who's reading at least [should follow it]; if you're reading the law, then you might as well follow it. Set an example, in a way. Again, I don't know how much of a role model I can be to 85-year-olds [*laughs sadly*].

I'm currently working, or helping out, in Temple Solomon, with their services. A lot of people here, too, they come to temple but some of them don't understand exactly what they're doing. They come, and if there weren't certain people here, they wouldn't know what to do and they wouldn't come at all, probably. So, I guess one of the reasons why I probably do what I'm doing is . . . well, I enjoy it 'cause I enjoy doing the services. I enjoy being that kind of leader. To help them.

I was going to temple every Saturday when I was little. I didn't follow along, but I just listened to them every time, and I got the tune and everything. It wasn't hard for me at all to learn the service for my Bar Mitzvah 'cause I already knew half of it in my head. Yeah, it's fun . . . it is.

The Price of Maintaining Language and Culture

There were more [Jews] years ago. Yeah, and now everybody has aged, and all the young ones are gone and left. So, there's not too many young ones coming up, 'cause there's not too many families—young families. The average age is probably 50s.

[In school] I'm the only person that I guess follows the [Jewish Orthodox] laws. So I wouldn't go out on a Friday night or something like that. Right now, most people know that I don't usually come out on a Friday night. But when I started high school, people used to say sometimes, "Ya coming out tonight?" I'm like, "No, I can't. . . ." In a way, it brought me away from those people. I mean, I have different responsibilities than most people.

If I miss track and say (cause it's not exactly the holiday, it's the day before) "I have to go home and prepare," most people won't understand. "What do you mean, you have to prepare?" or "I thought the holiday was tomorrow?" Most other religions don't have so many holidays during the year, so there's not that much preparation that they have to do, I guess.

[*How would you feel if you lived in a place where everybody was Jewish?*] [I'd] have a good feeling every day, 'cause everybody knows there's a holiday. It would be fun, 'cause I mean, it wouldn't be boring on Shabbat 'cause when you can't . . . really do anything, there's always somebody around. That's why I go to [Jewish] camp, too.

We just had Simchas Torah here the other day. . . . It was really pathetic. I mean, on Thursday night, there were four little kids there, and there were less than 20 people all together. And then, Friday morning, there were 11 men at the big shul [temple], and there were 10 at the little shul.

When I have kids, I want to bring them up in a Jewish community. And from the looks of it here, there might be a Jewish community. I mean, there is one now, but it's dwindling away, or starting to rebuild itself. But it will probably take a while before it actually becomes a large Jewish community again, when people start coming and bringing their children to the temple and actually doing something. And even if I'm not married, I'd like to be in a place where I could walk to the temple on Saturday, or I could just go down the street and I won't have to travel so far to where I could get some good kosher meat.

If the other people that are out there, if the reason that they don't come [to temple] is also probably 'cause their parents [don't] . . . I was just speaking to a friend of mine last week who's Jewish, and I said to him, "When was the last time you were in temple? I'm just curious." I was just joking around with him, of course. And, he was like, "Yeah, I haven't been there in a while, you know. It's pretty sad. My parents don't follow anything, so I don't," he basically said.

A couple of years ago, I had some anti-Semitic things happen. But that was cleared up. I mean, it wasn't cleared up, but they, I don't know. . . . There's a few kids in school that I still know are anti-Semites. Basically Jew haters.

I was in a woods class, and there was another boy in there, my age, and he was in my grade. He's also Jewish, and he used to come to the temple sometimes and went to Hebrew school. But then, of course, he started hanging around with the wrong people, and some of these people were in my class, and I guess they were making fun of him. And a few of them started making swastikas out of wood. So I saw one and I said to some kid, "What are you doing?" and the kid said to me, "Don't worry. It's not for you. It's for him." And I said to him, "*What?!?*" And he walked away. And after a while, they started bugging me about it, and they started saying remarks and things and. . . . Finally, it got to a point where I had them thrown out of class . . . 'cause I just decided to speak up.

And there was one kid that I didn't have thrown out because I didn't think he was as harmful as they were. But it turned out, as the year went on, I had a little incident with him. too.

It was one of the last days of school, and . . . I came into the class and I said to myself, "This is it. If he says something to me today, I'm gonna go hit him." So I walked in there and I was just walking around, and he started bugging me again, so I did the same thing. I just went up to him and I pushed him, and he must've been 300 pounds. And I just started pushing him and I said, "Come on, let's go already. I'm sick of you." I don't remember exactly what happened, but I know I got pulled away. And he walked by me again and he goes, "You ready for the second Holocaust?" And then I think I had him thrown out. Yeah, you see, I went up to the teacher and I said to her, "I'm either gonna leave the class or they leave."

It was funny 'cause one of the kids I got thrown out actually wasn't that harmful. I don't know, he was just like a little follower on the side. And it turns out last year, I was on the track team and he decided to do track, and I became friends with him. And I got to know him, and . . . apparently his grandfather had converted to Judaism before he died. This year, I'm pretty good friends with him, and every time I'm talking to him, he's always mentioning Judaism. And he's very interested in Judaism and he told me that he would like to convert himself. He just asked me last week if he could come to the temple.

He understands a lot now. So, I mean, he was hanging around with the wrong [crowd]. They didn't care. I mean, they weren't doing anything in the class, anyways. They were just sitting around. Yeah, druggies basically.

[*Do your teachers understand your culture?*] Yeah, when I tell them I'm gonna be out of school for the holidays and they say, "Okay, don't worry. Make it up, don't worry." They know about Rosh Hashanah and Yom Kippur [major Jewish holidays], but they don't know about Sukkot. There's the first day and the last day. After Yom Kippur, I say, "I'm gonna be out these other days" and they go, "Oh, I thought the holidays were over with," and I go, "No, there's a few more." But they're nice about it anyway. I mean, sometimes, once in a while, someone gets a little frustrated. You know, if I come in the next day after a holiday and I'm not ready for the test 'cause I couldn't write or do anything to study for it, but I make up my work in pretty good time. And I don't usually have any trouble.

[*How do you celebrate holidays with your family?*] With pride and tradition! [*laughs*] I usually have to stay around here 'cause I work in the temple. But if we can, we invite somebody over for the Seder [Passover dinner]. It's nice to have people over for the holidays. It makes the holiday more enjoyable.

I like the taste of chicken on a Friday night—that I've waited for all week long. It's just not the same on Wednesday night. You can't even smell it the same. It's different. I like deli stuff: corned beef, a nice sandwich, a little pickle, you know. I like kugel too. All the Jewish food's good. On like Shavuos or Pesach or Sukkot, we usually get special fruits, like the new spring fruits, the first fruits of the harvest.

[Pesach, or Passover] is my favorite holiday. I love the preparation for it. I don't like it after the third day because there's no more seders, and there's nothing left to do except for waiting it out. I mean, it wouldn't be so bad. . . . You see, if I have to go to school, I have to go to school in the middle. But if I didn't have to go to school, then I could sit home and kind of enjoy it. But I have to go to school, and I just say it's not the same when you see other food that you can't eat. I mean, it would be a whole different feeling if you saw so many other people eating matzoth or whatever.

When I went to [Jewish] day school, it was nice to have people who were Jewish around you. I mean, it made you understand. When I came [to public school] in the ninth grade, it was hard 'cause I didn't hardly know anybody, and I didn't know what to expect 'cause it was such a different curriculum.

The Role of Positive Pressure

[Good grades] give you confidence, show you what you're doing . . . and [help you] keep on going.

I haven't done really bad in a while. . . . I mean occasionally, I'll do bad on a test or something, but I'll just bring it back up after, 'cause I'll feel bad after. "Ugh, I really did bad. I should have done really well." And I just try and do it better the next time. . . . Let myself slip a little bit and then I'll go back. I'll take a break and go on.

Growing up at an early age, [my parents taught me] like what was right and wrong and the basics of Judaism. . . . One summer, my mother was teaching me Hebrew. She's fair. . . . She doesn't keep me bound, keep me in. You know, "Stay here; don't go anywhere. You can't go out if you have to." She trusts me. . . . Most of the time, I can see why she wouldn't want me to do some things.

Most [teachers] are understanding. I mean, if you don't know how to do something, you can always just go ask them. And ask them again and again and again. [*He singles out one particular teacher, a math teacher he had in ninth grade.*] 'Cause I never really did good in math 'til ninth grade and I had him. And he showed me that it wasn't so bad, and after that I've been doing pretty good in math and I enjoy it.

There's some teachers that understand the kids better than other teachers. . . . They teach from the point of view of the kid. They don't just come out and say, "All right, do this, blah, blah, blah." I mean, in a way, they like, sometimes joke around with the kid. They try to act like the student. . . . They're not so *one-tone voice*.

[A bad teacher is] one who just . . . for example, some student was doing really bad on his tests, test after test after test. The teacher would just correct them and that's it. Wouldn't say anything to the student. . . .

I try to run [track] as often as I can. I mean, during the season you kinda have to run every day just to keep in shape. But I like to run anyways, 'cause when you run you think about everything and just . . . it gives you time, in a way, [to] relax, and just get your mind in a different place.

I do a lot of drawing. I've been drawing for years. Sometimes it's just doodling or drawing strange designs or things like that. But I enjoy it. It relaxes me to sit down, flip on my radio, anything I want to listen to and just draw away. It just puts you away from the rest of the world.

Some of my friends have an influence on me, too, to do well in school. My friends from [Jewish] camp, I mean, they all do pretty good in school and we're all close friends. Whenever one of us gets in, if we ever got into some sort of trouble, we'd bail each other out of it. Because, well, I mean, we all trust each other, basically. We keep in touch a lot. We'll always be friends.

I run up my phone bill talking to them 'cause they're all out of state. [My mother] tells me to write letters [*laughs*]. But sometimes it's hard 'cause sometimes, in a way, I live off my friends. They're like a type of energy, like a power source.

Commentary

When asked to describe himself, Avi said he was "fun loving and religious," adjectives that might not ordinarily be juxtaposed in this way, yet, curiously, his description was an apt one. Deeply involved in his religion, as was apparent from his earnest and responsible attitude about his work at the synagogue, he was also a gregarious and playful teenager who enjoyed camp, sports, and practical jokes. A little digging may reveal how Avi was able to develop these seemingly divergent qualities.

Because both of his parents were teachers, and given the immense importance of scholarship within religious education in the Jewish culture, it was no surprise that Avi had done well in school. However, the perception that all Jewish children are good students, what has often been called a "positive stereotype," has placed an undue burden on many youths. Like the "model minority" myth surrounding the academic achievement of Asian students, the consequences of this "positive stereotype" are negative because they treat a whole class of students in the same way, without allowing for individual differences.

Avi's enormous commitment to his religious community in the "small synagogue" was evident: He spoke Hebrew and worked hard at it, he studied the Torah, and he was clear about the love he had for his culture and religion. But the price Avi was paying for upholding his religion and culture was often steep. The mismatch of his culture with that of the school was evident in many ways, especially when it came to organizational policies and practices. For example, during his interviews, Avi said that he had accepted that most of his teachers and classmates did not pronounce his name correctly. He appreciated that most of them tried to be understanding about the Jewish holidays, although they usually did not understand what holiday observance meant within the context of Judaism. His days off were always at odds with those of the other students, and the curriculum was at odds with his experience. Because remaining somewhat unassimilated is a hard choice, Avi's desire to move from Talbot when he had his own family was not surprising.

Other problems Avi talked about concerned his social life and the lack of friends in his community. For a teenager, making the decision between staying home on Friday evening with family or going out with friends can be difficult. Incidents of anti-Semitism in school were also painful reminders that being different from the majority can still be dangerous in our society. The decisiveness with which he handled these particular incidents revealed his self-confidence and desire to take control of his life (by "having them taken out of the class"), although in his hesitant explanation, it was also evident that he felt powerless ("But that was cleared up. I mean, it wasn't cleared up, but they, I don't know . . ."). The incidents also revealed his own stereotypes and social class biases about those he called "druggies."

Straddling two worlds, Avi was constantly confronted with the need to accommodate the outside world. This is a challenge historically faced by most immigrants. As expressed by Stephan Brumberg in describing the experience of Jewish immigrants in New York City at the turn of the twentieth century, "In the immigrant world, learning to live simultaneously in two worlds may have been required for successful adaptation."[2] What is unique in Avi's case is that this balancing act was increasingly taking place with those who had been here for more than one or two generations, not simply with new arrivals.

Jewish culture is intertwined with religion and tradition, rather than with nationality as in other groups, and this can make maintaining cultural ties difficult. Although our society claims to be secular, clearly it is not. Rather, it is openly a Christian nation, as can be seen in the abundance of Christian symbols and artifacts, from the daily prayer in Congress to the crèches that adorn small towns in New England, where Avi comes from, at Christmas. Added to this is the weight of centuries of oppression, minority status, and marginality to which Jews have been subjected. Even in societies where they have been assimilated, Jews have often been victimized and treated as scapegoats.[3] Given this long history of oppression, Jews throughout the world have had to think long and hard about the balance between the degree of accommodating to host societies and maintaining their cultural traditions. The results have ranged widely—from becoming completely assimilated and losing all traces of their roots to remaining within religious and cultural enclaves removed from any but the most basic and necessary exchanges with non-Jews.[4]

Pressure toward assimilation and the accommodations made to it are only one reflection of the diversity in the Jewish community in the United States, which has often been portrayed in a one-dimensional manner. However, Jews differ in religiosity, tradition, political viewpoints, language, and social class, among other characteristics. The religious tenets in Judaism itself—that is, Orthodox, Reform, and Conservative elements—reflect this diversity. In addition, some Jews who are not religious at all—secular Jews—are still profoundly Jewish in terms of cultural values. Some Jews speak Hebrew and others speak Yiddish, although others speak neither. Jews also differ in their viewpoints on relations with the Arab world and on Zionism.

Besides his religion and track, another source of positive pressure for Avi was his Jewish friends, who are, in his eloquent phrase, "a type of energy, like a power source." That peers can have this kind of influence on young people is often overlooked by schools and parents, yet it is the very reason for the existence of such institutions as Portuguese American schools, Hebrew camps, and Saturday culture schools in the Chinese community.

Avi Abramson was straddling two worlds, trying to be both an American and a Jew. He was maintaining a difficult balancing act between complete assimilation into the mainstream of U.S. life and holding onto his religion and culture. This is not easy, even for seasoned adults. For Avi, it meant not giving in to assimilationist forces while also accommodating those parts of his life to U.S. society that would not compromise his values. When we last checked in with him, Avi had moved to Israel and had become a rabbi.[5]

Reflect on This Case Study

1. Do you think Avi's school life would be different if he were not on the track team? How? What implications can you draw from this for schools?
2. The United States officially supports "separation of church and state," but is it possible for teachers to affirm Avi's culture and background without bringing religion into the school? Think about some ways this might be done.
3. Friends are, in Avi's words, "like a power source." How can teachers use this power source to advantage? Think of strategies that teachers and schools might develop to build on positive peer pressure.

Jasper and Viena Alejandro-Quinn

Jasper and Viena Alejandro-Quinn[1] are brother and sister who live with their parents on an American Indian reservation in Northwest Washington near the border with Canada. When asked how they identify themselves ethnically and culturally, they both said, "Filipino and Native." Jasper replied, "Technically, Native American," and they each named their tribal affiliations as Paiute, Swinomish, and Visayan. Then Jasper added "[A]nd probably like one-eighth Irish, maybe less—like a drop." When discussing cultural identity, they included reflections about spiritual practices learned from family as well as their journey navigating religious and nonreligious beliefs and practices. Jasper was exploring atheism; Viena was planning to become baptized a Catholic, like her cousins, uncles, aunts, and grandparents.

Jasper at age 13, who was finishing the seventh grade and Viena, age 16, who was just completing her sophomore year of high school, have a great deal in common with many young U.S. teens. They both like watching movies and listening to hip hop, R&B, and rock. Among their favorite foods, they both list adobo (Filipino cuisine) and fried bread, along with other dishes that have become more familiar to many American teenagers, such as burritos, various vegetarian dishes, chicken, and steak. Viena's favorite books are the *Twilight* series[2] and she likes playing soccer. She plans to go to college to be a pediatrician. Jasper likes to read fiction—he reported reading Sherman Alexie's *The Absolutely True Diary of a Part-Time Indian* at least ten times.[3] He said, "I could connect with the character. I connected as Indian. Also, it was Indian humor—telling jokes about white people. That kind of thing." He is cultivating his interest in filmmaking and considering it as a future profession.

Jasper and Viena's parents are professionals in the field of education who are deeply involved in their children's education. They are also both in graduate school at the local state university. Their dad works there as the director of a student center that focuses on the needs of college students of color and is also a doctoral candidate in the program of Educational Leadership and Policy Studies. Their mom, a former teacher, is currently earning her masters degree in education, with a focus on Indian Education. Growing up with parents who are college-educated has exposed Jasper and Viena to a world of ideas, conversations, and opportunities that may not be typical for many Native students, or for other teens their age. Yet having parents involved in their education did not protect them from the challenges that many Native students face in their schooling experiences.

The schools where Viena and Jasper are currently enrolled are comprised of mostly White students, what the U.S. Department of Education Office of Indian Education (OIE) calls "low-density" public schools, where less than 25 percent of the student body is American Indian/Alaskan Native (AIAN).[4] The elementary school they attended enrolls approximately 25 percent Native students, while Jasper's current middle school enrolls 15 percent, and Viena's current high school enrolls only 8 percent Native students. Both the middle and high school demographics are listed as 80 percent White. This is a dramatic shift from the school Viena attended in kindergarten, which was a Bureau of Indian Education (BIE) school on the reservation that serves Native students almost exclusively.[5] However, their parents moved them out of the BIE schools because they found the academic expectations to be too low, which they attributed to the faculty being staffed by mostly White teachers who had little experience with Native students and Native ways of knowing.

Jasper's and Viena's descriptions of their experiences are consistent with some of the students who provided information about themselves, their families and communities, and their school experiences to the National Indian Education Study (NIES) of 2009. The two-part study, conducted by the National Center for Education Statistics (NCES) for the U.S. Department of Education, OIE reported on the educational experiences of American Indian and Alaska Native students in grades 4

About Terminology

American Indians, Native Americans, Indigenous People

As is the case for other groups, what to call the original inhabitants of what is now the United States has been a contested issue for many years. Should we refer to them as *Native Americans, Indians, American Indians, Native people, Indigenous people,* or some other term? It is important to emphasize that Native people also wrestle with terminology, and different people make different decisions about what they want to be called. Some adamantly oppose the use of *Native American,* while others reject the term *Indian.* During the 1960s, *Native American* became the preferred term because it reflected a people's determination to name themselves and to have others recognize them as the original inhabitants of these lands. During the late 1980s and 1990s, the use of this term declined, and *American Indian* and *Native people* became more common. Although the term *Native American* has recently become popular again in some quarters, many Native people reject this term because it is sometimes used by European Americans whose early ancestors came from Europe and who see themselves as native to this land. When speaking among themselves, some Native people prefer to use the term *Indian;* however, *Indian* also refers to people from India, so if we use this term, we usually add the qualifier *American.*

Given all these considerations, we have favored the terms *American Indian, Indian,* and *Native people* in this book because we have noted that people from these groups generally use them most often.

There are many commonalities among all indigenous groups, just as there are among most Latino groups or people of African descent. These may include a worldview, a common historical experience, and shared conditions of life. At the same time, each nation has its own unique history, traditions, language, and other differences. We should also point out that the names of most American Indian nations generally translate to "the people." Most Native people prefer to use the name of their specific tribe or nation, and we have followed their lead in this book. However, it is not always possible to do so because overarching terms such as *Native American* and *American Indian* are generally used, both in the research and in reports. In addition, much of the research literature documenting the experiences of American Indian groups does not distinguish the different ethnic groups. As a result, we are sometimes obliged to use a generic term in spite of our preference to distinguish along ethnic lines.

and 8.[6] The study was designed in consultation with American Indian and Alaska Native educators and researchers from across the country, and one of its goals was for Native students to report on their knowledge and schooling experiences. This study reinforces what many researchers have found: American Indian/Alaskan Native student experiences are not consistent in U.S. schools.[7] For example, while it is worth celebrating the fact that over 50 percent of the students surveyed planned to attend college, it certainly begs the question: What is happening to the other 40 or more percent? It also underscores research by the National Indian Education Association, which reveals the national graduation rate for American Indian high school students was 49.3 percent in the 2003–2004 school year compared to 76.2 percent for White students.[8] These data are consistent with research by Susan C. Faircloth and John W. Tippeconnic III indicating the urgent concern about Native student high school graduation rates. In the seven states with the highest percentage of AIAN students, as well as five states in the Pacific and Northwestern regions of the United States, less than 50 percent, on average, of Native students graduate each year.[9]

These alarming statistics inform Jasper's and Viena's family commitment to holding their children to rigorous educational standards, and this dedication appears in Jasper's and Viena's high academic achievement, despite some of the difficulties they described. Their comments were laced with hopefulness and punctuated with what Jasper calls "Indian humor." The three themes that emerged from their interview point to some of the triumphs and struggles that many American Indian/Alaskan Native students face in U.S. schools: *navigating home culture versus school culture, preserving identity with the support of family,* and *fighting the perpetuation of false assumptions.*

Navigating Home Culture Versus School Culture

JASPER: My culture? I honor my elders and community members whenever they are praying, like the Native way, like drumming, that kind of thing. My culture is as important as it can be—as much as I am exposed to it. My parents take me to events and that kind of thing with my grandmother or whatever. I guess just the kind of things—the day-to-day things that sort of happen. Like whenever people thank the Creator for the food and stuff. That's important to me. I have also learned a lot from my cousins and from the University Center for Students of Color—what it means to be Native: the kind of jokes you tell, the way you talk, the slight distrust of the government, that kind of thing—you take up mannerisms from your family.

VIENA: Being around the people who are the same as you—you pick up the mannerisms from food to religion to clothes—it is just there.

JASPER: [About the fifth-grade student group called Tribal Council] My teacher who started the Tribal Council said that someone approached her and said the Natives were not being represented (in the school). I got into Council because I was Native. . . . It was a fun thing to do. I designed a mural. We painted it! You just need to do something that breaks away from the monotonous habit of the school day—that makes it exciting and interesting. That's why I liked it, it was different. I was getting a better day than the rest of the kids who were not Native because they were not getting to go to council. It was fun.

VIENA: The school district just says you come to school to learn and they don't teach about [cultural identity], but they don't forbid it. Recently in my honors English class, this book was called *Bless Me Ultima.*[10] We worked in groups. I was in one group and we had to answer all these questions about our beliefs and everything. That's when [cultural identity] comes into play in school, when there's an actual study on it.

In the mostly White schools [off the reservation], the Native kids sit together. All the Mexican kids sit together—everyone's comfort zone is with the people they can relate to the most. I notice how different it is when I leave the reservation—the people there are so different. I learned how to get along with both kinds of people when I was young. I have friends from both. I am one of the only persons who can go back and forth . . . . [A]t my high school the majority are White. When I was at the reservation school, it was an all-Native school and then going to the public school off the reservation and seeing nobody who looks like me. . . . The school I am at right now, they do not really accept people who are different.

JASPER: I hang out with the Native kids at my school—I know them better than the rest of the people there. Just cuz you know them better. And we have the same humor. The teachers who I know—they do not understand my culture. Because I do not really expose it. I would say to teachers, be able to understand it or know about it . . . admitting that you don't know it. Take the information you get from the person. Show an interest in it, but do not put people on the spot if you don't want to talk about it. One time, I had a substitute teacher, he was probably the only ethnic teacher I have ever had. It was just for one day. It wasn't like an in-depth occasion. Actually, there was not much of a connection because it would take longer to identify with him . . . but I was excited because he was the only teacher who was ethnic. Just for one day.

Preserving Identity with the Support of Family

JASPER: During the summer sometimes we go to Powwows, and I used to dance and I am going to start dancing again. When I am there, it is really cool. It is more of an experience that I have always been around. That's one of the places my parents take us. They also take us to Filipino cultural night at the university. That kind of thing. My father took me to Hawaii and I met all those Filipinos there . . . also Powwows, events that have Natives and Filipinos present. Seeing speakers at the university or community: we go to lots of [those] kinds of events. I do not think school and identity are connected. Not really. . . . Identity is just part of my life.

VIENA: I think my family wants me to go to school because they see education as an opportunity to express yourself, but right now in high school it is not really where they do intense critical thinking on things that I think are important to learn about—regular math, science, English—until you get into college. Racism or sexism or anything: They do not even face that in high school—they don't address it in class. I think the teachers get kind of surprised by how much I know about stuff like that. They do not expect me to know anything about racism or anything—and growing up around the Center for Students of Color [at the university]—when I bring it up in school my teachers just change the subject so they do not have to involve the rest of the class in the conversation. I think my parents have filled in that gap that my school does not do. We have conversations with my parents about things that really happen in the world; the school should be teaching about it. If kids were exposed to it at an earlier age other than college, it might make a change in life. Like if you grow up in a certain kind of village, you are pressured to think a certain way about people. I have not been forced at all to do that. My parents let me make my own choice and they give me the whole picture to look at.

I am going to go to the university and study pediatrics and then I am going to countries where they need more doctors and help the kids there . . . and then make a lot of money and get a big house . . . and I really want to make a difference.

JASPER: My ambitions are to be a movie director or write scripts like a storyteller with movies. If filmmaking was part of school, it would be better. I watch a lot of movies and read a lot of books. I have been in a video workshop with *Native Lens*[11] . . . being a storyteller with movies. School is for preparing people to be part of our society . . . part of the society of America that we live in. My purpose for going to school—cuz my parents tell me to do it, [and] I want to feel that I am learning things.

Fighting the Perpetuation of False Assumptions

VIENA: Most of the time I feel comfortable in school, unless the teacher talks about something that is not accurate. I do not know if I am supposed to raise my hand and say, "That is not true."

JASPER: I don't really feel comfortable in school. Things have happened to make me feel uncomfortable, so it just doesn't really matter to me. In fifth grade we had this big study-thing on Native Americans . . . and the teacher spelled one of the tribal names wrong, and I said, "One of the spelling of the tribes was wrong." I was annoyed. Then my mom told the teacher how to spell it—and the teacher said, "I saw it this way in the book." So it was really difficult for her to admit that a book could be wrong and a Native person could be correct—so the teacher left both ways of spelling it on the board so kids would see both ways to spell it.

VIENA: The teachers, when they first get to a community, they should not automatically think the students are going to warm up to them and they should not act like they know what they are doing. They should get to know the place a little bit and get to know the children a little more before they start making assumptions or accusations. I know here on the reservation the students are not going to warm up to you [as a teacher]—it's going to be tough. I live here—we are not used to having a lot of change. We have had the same things for years now; if there is just a new person coming in—the parents and grandparents won't be like "Hey welcome!" They will be nice, but not *trusting* automatically. Here on the reservation, [the teachers] come in and automatically think we need help or something, or they think we are the disadvantaged kids or whatever. There was a time, I was in third grade, there was a film about Native Americans, something in the movie I knew wasn't right and I came home really sad about the Paiute. The movie said the so-called pioneers came westward. They were in some fort and their fort was encircled by the Paiute and burnt to the ground. The whole class got to watch that film. The class was saying how horrible the Paiute were. My mom went in and talked to the teacher; she said to the teacher, "Did you know Viena is Paiute?" She could not deal with it. She could not deal with the fact—the European Americans did bring diseased blankets, how many people died. You cannot just say one side. Eventually, my mom made the teacher apologize to me. The teacher said something like, "What do you expect me to do, apologize every time we teach about slavery? Every time we teach about these things?" She needed a reality check. Our people did not just attack people for no reason. It is true that Indians did burn down forts, but it is the way in which the story has been told [that bothers me]. Why did they have to defend themselves in this way?

           . . . When people ask about your identity, there is sometimes a genuine wanting to know, and then there are those who put you in an awkward situation. They have asked me about my background. Let's say we were learning about a certain tribe or something. There is a teacher at my high school right now, and there is a Cambodian girl in my class and a Thai girl in my class and whenever there is anything about Asia at all, they expect them to know the answers about Asia! Even if they have never been to Asia or as if they would know about everything Chinese or something. Stupidity. Stereotyping. Even though I am Native, and I know about my tribe, I am not going to know about the Cherokee tribe or something. I would ask my teachers not to do that.

My teachers don't understand my culture. I don't have any teachers that really know anything about my culture at all. They really never experienced any of the cultural things we do. They should educate themselves more about the minority students who go to our school. I feel like they throw all of the minority kids into a group and say they are all the same; they are just a minority. There are so many different cultures; I think the teachers should really focus and learn more about them.

Commentary

Viena and Jasper sincerely expressed wanting to learn new things while reflecting on schooling experiences that are unique to their circumstances. Yet at the same time, some aspects of their schooling are parallel to findings from reports about Native students. Of the approximately 624,000 AI/AN students in the U.S. K–12 school system, about 93 percent attend public schools, while only 7 percent attend Bureau of Indian Affairs schools.[12] Jasper and Viena's parents faced a difficult dilemma when navigating home culture versus school culture and selecting their schools; their mother explained, "I am happy they survived another year. In some ways there are two choices: the Tribal School and the local public school district. One offers a cultural link, the Tribal School, but not very high academic standards. The other offers no cultural links and a little bit higher academic standards." When families are forced to choose between maintaining cultural links and striving for rigorous academic challenge, our education system is surely failing them, no matter which choice they make. Students cannot flourish academically or culturally in an environment where they merely "survived another year."

The history of centuries-long injustices wrought upon Native communities is reflected in the multifaceted story of Indian education. Yet a resilient spirit of self-determination and resistance to colonization has been documented by researchers Donna Deyhle, Karen Swisher, Tracy Stevens, and Ruth Trinidad Galván.[13] This resistance reverberates in Viena's and Jasper's assertion of the Native perspective as a counternarrative to the school perspective. With the support of their parents, Viena and Jasper *fought the perpetuation of false assumptions* through retelling historical events and acknowledging Native languages through accurate spelling; their family also battled the legacy of low expectations and segregated schooling. Their mother reported, "It is frustrating because I keep going in there and making all these meetings and making all these calls," to question the public school about admission into the Gifted and Talented program, from which Jasper and Viena were excluded. Their parents also found that the school counselors did not recommend Jasper for more advanced classes such as algebra. Yet another teacher expressed that Jasper needed to be challenged; she thought he was bored in school. In addition to the perpetuation of institutionalized racism, these competitive and exclusive practices of tracking are in stark contrast to traditional values held by many Native communities. For example, in a report on Indian education by researchers from the Clearinghouse on Native Teaching and Learning, the topic of gifted and talented education was addressed from a Native viewpoint:

> Indian education dates back to a time when all children were identified as gifted and talented. Each child had a skill and ability that would contribute to the health and vitality of the community. Everyone in the community was expected and trained to be a teacher to identify and cultivate these skills and abilities. The elders were entrusted to oversee this sacred act of knowledge being shared. That is our vision for Indian education today.[14]

This comprehensive study and action plan, developed by Native researchers and educators, indicts educational neglect by the government. It advances specific "achievement and success goals" in four areas to empower Indian communities in their educational future. These goals include (1) "teachers, administrators, school boards, and tribes" about the critical need to develop relationships between school districts and tribes; (2) "health and well-being": to monitor the health and well-being of Native American children, youth, adults, and families, with culture-based prevention programs; (3) "academic achievement and educational attainment" advocating for Native students' proficiency in reading, writing, and math at various grade levels and at high school graduation; and (4) "assessment of learning" that is, supporting Native students by offering more intervention and direction to students and families to improve student learning.[15]

It is notable that all four goals of the report engage tribes and families in the solutions to academic achievement. Researcher Sandy Grande concurs with this stance in her theory of "Red Pedagogy," which reimagines schools as sites of social transformation, honoring the principles of sovereignty, emancipation, and equity.[16] Throughout this text, we have noted that an essential component of multicultural education includes authentically involving families in classrooms and schools. Researchers K. Tsianina Lomawaima and Teresa L. McCarty argue that, for many Native families who bear the burden of centuries of broken promises with government entities and the haunting collective memory of American Indian boarding schools, it a matter of urgency for schools and teachers to cultivate collaborative, respectful relationships with families that draw upon their knowledge and values.[17]

Jasper and Viena told us about a wealth of activities that affirm and *preserve their identity with the support of family*. Yet most of those experiences were completely unrelated to school. Jasper said it plainly: "I do not think school and identity are connected." Many questions emerge out of the glaring gap between Jasper's and Viena's home culture and school culture. Robust academic, arts, and athletic experiences are the rights of *every* child in both reservation schools and public schools. How can these essentials of education be connected and respectful of cultural identities? For example, if more of their White teachers were fluent in multicultural education and Indian education theories of pedagogy, how might it change their relationship to schooling? How might Jasper's engagement in school differ if he had memories of more than one day with one person of color as a teacher? How can the development of more teaching professionals of AI/AN heritage be supported by teacher education programs?

Reflect on This Case Study

1. With supportive parents who are familiar and comfortable with the communication systems of public schools, Viena and Jasper were vocal about misrepresentations and inaccuracies about Native life. Other students may have knowledge to add to the class-room, but they may feel much more inhibited. What can you do to make the voices and knowledge of students, parents, and elders more audible and visible in the school?

2. A statement by the National Education Association (NEA) in the *NEA Closing Achievement Gaps: An Association Guide* (2006) purports, "We will never accept that American Indian or Alaska Native students, or Asian or Pacific Islander students, can-not handle the demands of a college preparation program." If this is the case, what are teachers' unions doing to stand behind that statement? How can you engage your local union to be proactive about college preparation and career counseling for all youth in your school? Do you think Viena's goals to pursue a career in medicine will be cultivated by her high school teacher and her coursework?

3. Consider Viena's comments: "I don't have any teachers that really know anything about my culture at all. They should educate themselves more about the minority students who go to our school." How can you educate yourself more about your students? What steps can you take to, as Sandy Grande advocates, "decolonize your curriculum"?

4. Given Jasper's engagement with Sherman Alexie's book *The Absolutely True Diary of a Part-Time Indian* (2007), what can teachers learn about their approaches to selecting literature and supporting their students' choices in literature? Considering the role that literature plays in affirming the identity of students, how can teachers develop activi-ties around reading to help make students' identities more visible?

Culture, Identity, and Learning

Young people whose languages and cultures differ from the dominant group often struggle to form and sustain a clear image of themselves. In addition, they struggle to have teachers understand who they really are—to help teachers "understand something inside our hearts," in the poignant words of Hoang Vinh—because teachers and schools commonly view students' differences as defi-

> "[Teachers] just understand some things outside, but they cannot understand something inside our hearts."
>
> —Hoang Vinh, interviewee

ciencies. The case studies of Yahaira León, James Karam, Hoang Vinh, and Rebecca Florentina that follow this chapter provide diverse and moving examples of how students' identities may be devalued. In spite of being proud of themselves and their families and communities, at one time or another, all of these young people felt the need to hide or deemphasize their identity, culture, or language in school. Yet this deemphasis may have had negative consequences for their learning. This chapter explores the influence that culture and identity may have on student learning, and it reviews a number of promising pedagogical and curricular adaptations that teachers and schools can make.

Many teachers and schools, in an attempt to be color-blind, do not want to acknowledge cultural or racial differences. "I don't see Black or White," a teacher will say, "I see only *students*." This statement assumes that to be color-blind is to be fair, impartial, and objective because to see differences, in this line of reasoning, is to see defects and inferiority. Although it sounds fair and honest and ethical, the opposite may actually be true. If used to mean *nondiscriminatory* in attitude and behavior, *color blindness* is not a bad thing. On the other hand, color blindness may result in *refusing to accept differences* and therefore accepting the dominant culture as the norm. In the case of lesbian, gay, bisexual, and transgender (LGBT) students, this attitude may be expressed as "I don't care what they do in their private lives; I just don't want them to broadcast it." This may be touted as accepting and nondiscriminatory, but the same statement is not generally made about heterosexual

students. In both cases, these attitudes result in denying the identities of particular students, thereby making them invisible.

A good example of using the concept of color blindness to deny differences was provided by the U.S. Supreme Court in the *Lau* decision of 1974.[1] The San Francisco School Department was sued on behalf of Chinese-speaking students who, parents and other advocates charged, were not being provided with an equal education. The school department countered that they were providing these students with an equal education because the students received *exactly the same* teachers, instruction, and materials as all others. The U.S. Supreme Court, in a unanimous decision, ruled against the school department. The Court reasoned that giving non-English-speaking students the same instruction, teachers, and materials as English-speaking students flew in the face of equal educational opportunity because Chinese-speaking students could not benefit from instruction provided in English. The dictum "Equal is not the same" is useful here. It means that treating everyone in the same way will not necessarily lead to equality; rather, it may end up perpetuating the inequality that already exists. Learning to affirm differences rather than deny them is what a multicultural perspective is about. In contrast, the general tendency throughout U.S. history (and this is also true of the histories of most countries) has been to attempt to do away with differences, an approach based on the notion that unity creates harmony, whereas diversity breeds instability and discord. Color blindness has often meant viewing everyone as "the same," but "equal is not the same," as established in the Lau decision.

Pichaya Choopojcharoen, in Catherine Lea's art class, Bishop Feehan High School, Attleboro, Massachusetts. *Self-portrait.* Scratchboard-drawing, 2010.

What are the educational implications of "Equal is not the same"? First, it means *acknowledging the differences that children bring to school* such as their gender, race, ethnicity, language, social class, sexual orientation, religion, abilities, and talents, among others. The refusal to acknowledge differences often results in schools and teachers labeling children's behavior as "deficient" or "deviant." In other cases, it results in making students "invisible," as happened with James Karam, one of the students in the case studies following this chapter.

Second, it means *admitting the possibility that students' identities may influence how they experience school* and, hence, how they learn. Being aware of the

157

connections among culture, identity, and learning should in no way devalue children's backgrounds or lower our expectations of them, yet this is precisely why so many educators have a hard time accepting "Equal is not the same." That is, they are reluctant to accept this notion because they may feel that, in doing so, they must lower their expectations or "water down" the curriculum so that all children can learn. Yet neither of these practices is necessary; on the contrary, it is imperative to raise the bar for all students.

Third, *accepting differences also means making provisions for them*. When students' cultural and linguistic backgrounds are viewed as strengths on which educators can draw and build, pedagogy changes to incorporate students' lives. This approach is based on the best of educational theory: that individual differences must be taken into account in teaching and that education must begin "where children are at." Unfortunately, these ideas are often overlooked when it comes to cultural and linguistic differences. The fact that Yahaira León, whose case study immediately follows this chapter, was fluent in two languages was rarely viewed as anything but a liability by most of her teachers. If we are serious about providing all students with educational equity, then students' cultures and identities need to be seen not as a burden, a problem, or even a challenge, but rather as assets upon which to build.

Defining Culture

Before we can ask schools to change in order to teach all students, we need to understand the differences that students bring with them to school. Culture is one of these differences, and we define it as follows: *Culture consists of the values, traditions, worldview, and social and political relationships created, shared, and transformed by a group of people bound together by a common history, geographic location, language, social class, religion, or other shared identity*. Culture includes not only tangibles such as foods, holidays, dress, and artistic expression but also less tangible manifestations such as communication style, attitudes, values, and family relationships. These features of culture are more difficult to pinpoint, but doing so is necessary if we want to understand how student learning may be affected.

Power is implicated in culture as well. That is, members of the dominant group in a society traditionally think of dominant cultural values as "normal," while they view the values of subordinated groups as deviant or maybe wrong. The difference in perception is due more to the power of each of these groups than to any inherent goodness or rightness in the values themselves. For instance, U.S. mainstream culture stresses the necessity for youngsters to become independent at an early age, whereas other cultures emphasize interdependence as a major value. Neither of these values is innately right or wrong; each has developed as a result of the group's history, experiences, and needs. However, people with a U.S. mainstream frame of reference may view as abnormal, or at the very least curious, the interdependent relationships of Latino children and parents, for instance. They may characterize Latino children as overly dependent, too attached to their parents and siblings, and needing more attention than other children. For their part, Latino families may view U.S. mainstream culture as strange and cold for its insistence on independence at what they consider too young an age. The difference in these perceptions is that the values of Latinos do not carry the same weight, status, or power as those of the dominant group.

In this text, we are concerned primarily with the *sociocultural* and *sociopolitical* dimensions of identity rather than with individual psychological identity formation. Thus, we focus on issues such as *power, institutional arrangements in schools,* and *the impact of ideology on culture* as well as *students' lived realities and experiences in families and communities*. This is not to dismiss the importance of individual identity development. On the contrary, teachers should understand how children develop their social and cultural selves and how this process interacts with issues of race, ethnicity, gender, and other variables. The work of scholars such as Beverly Daniel Tatum, Gary Howard, Charmaine Wijeyesinghe, and Bailey Jackson, and others focuses specifically on such matters. All teachers should become familiar with these theories as well as the sociocultural and sociopolitical perspectives underlying this text.[2]

We are always on shaky ground when considering cultural differences. The danger of considering culture lies in overgeneralizing its effects. Overgeneralizations can lead to gross stereotypes, which in turn may lead to erroneous conclusions concerning entire groups of people, not to mention the abilities and intelligence of individual students. We have all seen some of the more disastrous consequences of overgeneralizations: checklists of cultural traits of different ethnic groups, the mandate to use certain pedagogical strategies with students of particular backgrounds, and treatises on "indisputable" student behaviors. Culture, in such instances, is treated as a *product* rather than a *process,* and it is viewed as unchanging and unchangeable. Viewing culture in this way can also lead to *essentializing* culture—that is, ascribing particular immutable characteristics to it. This may result in thinking of culture as inherent in individuals and groups. Kris Gutierrez and Barbara Rogoff describe it as believing that individuals and groups are "carriers of culture—an assumption that creates problems, especially as research on cultural styles of ethnic (or racial) groups is applied in schools." They suggest using instead a cultural-historical approach that recognizes the histories and valued practices of cultural groups. Rather than thinking of culture as "pure," unadulterated, and unaffected by other circumstances and contexts, they view learning as a process that takes place within ongoing activity. Gutierrez and Rogoff thus distinguish between *understanding cultural practices* and *locating cultural characteristics* because the latter can be problematic.[3] Using the previous example, we would be in error to view Latino culture as *always* interdependent, regardless of the situation. Culture is too complex and too varied for us to conclude that all those who share a particular background behave in the same way or believe the same things.

■ ■ ■ ■ Hybridity: Another Way of Understanding Culture

One problem with a static view of culture is that it fails to recognize that our society is more heterogeneous than ever. As you can see in the case studies and snapshots of young people in this chapter, many of them have multiple identities: Rebecca is not only a lesbian but *also* Italian American; Yahaira is Dominican *and* Puerto Rican; James is Lebanese and a bike rider. In the case of these young people, *all* of their identities are significant to them. With multiple identities of this kind becoming more and more common, it is impossible to speak about culture as it is lived today, in this context, as if it were unitary. A major premise of this book is that a static view of culture contradicts the very notion of multicultural education as presented here.

This brings us to a discussion of *hybridity,* that is, the fusion of various cultures to form new, distinct, and ever-changing identities. Growing up amidst a range of cultural influences that substantively shape one's development and worldview contributes to cultural hybridity, which is a reality in our own country as well as internationally. It refers not simply to mixed-race and ethnic identity because the conceptual understandings of hybridity have grown with the awareness of the limitations of racial categories. This is evident at the institutional level of the U.S. Census Bureau, which provides the following statement on its Web site and census forms:

> The racial categories included in the census questionnaire generally reflect a social definition of race recognized in this country, and not an attempt to define race biologically, anthropologically or genetically. People may choose to report more than one race to indicate their racial mixture, such as "American Indian and White." People who identify their origin as Hispanic, Latino, or Spanish may be of any race. In addition, it is recognized that the categories of the race item include both racial and national origin or socio-cultural groups. You may choose more than one race category.[4]

Of the 2010 U.S. population of 308,745,538 (estimated), approximately 1.7 percent reported two or more races in their responses to the U.S. Census. Clearly, what has been called mixed-race, multiracial, biracial, and multiethnic identity is certainly a growing reality. About 4 percent of youth under age 18 in the United States are of mixed heritage, and the number is growing rapidly. Alejandra Lopez-Torkos argues that we need to learn to talk about identity in different ways, "allowing for fluidity and multiplicity in racial-ethnic identification."[5] But understandings of hybridity go far beyond listing more than one racial category.

Some examples can help explain this kind of fluidity. In an ethnographic study of a large, urban, and culturally diverse high school, Laurie Olsen described how immigrant students felt "caught in the middle," not really fitting into any category. She found that the "sides" were constantly shifting: While identity was sometimes defined in terms of nationality, at other times it was defined in terms of culture, religion, race, or language and sometimes as a combination of these.[6] In another example, Pedro Noguera's research with Mexican American students in East Oakland illustrates how context influences identity. When they were in elementary school, the Mexican American children were described by African American classmates—and frequently referred to themselves—as "White." However, in the new social contexts of adolescence and middle school, they began to view themselves as Mexican Americans, among other identities.[7] Daniel Yon's research in a Toronto high school illustrates similar complexities: He found, for example, that a Serbian identified as "Spanish," while a White male identified strongly with Guyanese. Yon refers to the shifting notions of identity as "elusive culture," that is, a view of culture as an ongoing process that includes not only race and ethnicity but also popular culture.[8]

Hybridity, then, also refers to *how* people identify, regardless of which ethnic, cultural, or racial group they may belong to. It recognizes that there are many other identities besides race and ethnicity; these may include gender, sexual orientation, geographic location, and professional affiliation, among many others. That is, hybridity refers to Nadine Dolby's point that identity is not "an absolute state of being" but rather a variable that is constantly shifting and changing.[9] For example, urban youth often identify with a culture that is an amalgam of various ethnic, racial and other identifications. Researchers Nikola Hobbel and Thandeka K. Chapman argue for conceptualizing identity as *process* and as *category,* calling attention to the signs of alliance across unlikely borders. They emphasize, "No single aspect of the expression of identity can fully account for cultural and historical context, even given the fact that race has consistently assumed a central role in America's history and imagination."[10] Hip hop culture is a good example of this: Incorporating music, dance, visual culture, as well as working-class and often marginalized urban perspectives, hip hop represents a unique culture that is not tied to any one ethnic or racial group. In fact, it is not unusual in many suburban, primarily White middle schools and high schools to see young people identifying principally with urban hip hop culture, even though many of these young people have never lived in cities or known people of color. Recognizing the complexity in culture allows us to understand the many and varied identities taken on by young people.

Influence of Culture on Learning

Learning is at the core of our discussion of culture. That is, we are not interested in exploring culture simply for the sake of developing awareness of cultural differences or developing sensitivity to students of diverse backgrounds. These are also important goals, but considering the troubling history of underachievement and marginalization of students of particular backgrounds in our schools—especially students of color and poor students of all backgrounds—educators must first examine how culture may influence learning and achievement in school.

While culture is integral to the learning process, it may affect individuals differently. In other words, *culture is not destiny.* Given differences in social class and family structure, individual psychological and emotional differences and experiences, birth order, residence, and a host of other individual and social distinctions, it is folly to think that culture alone accounts for all human differences. Anyone who has children can confirm this truth: Two offspring from the same parents, with the same culture and social class, and raised in substantially the same way, can turn out to be as different as night and day. Hence, culture is neither static nor deterministic; it gives us just one way in which to understand differences among students. The assumption that culture is the primary determinant of academic achievement can be oversimplistic, dangerous, and counterproductive because, although culture may *influence,* it does not *determine* who we are.

Everyone has a culture, but many times, members of the culturally dominant group of a society do not even think of themselves as cultural beings. For them, culture is something that other people have, especially people who differ from the mainstream in race or ethnicity. The problem with conceptualizing culture in this way is that it tends to "exoticize" those people who are not in the cultural mainstream. A more complicated view of culture is needed, especially among teachers whose classrooms are becoming more diverse every day. There are vast differences among learners within ethnic groups, and these differences may be due not just to culture but also to social class, language spoken at home, number of years or generations in the United States, and simple individual differences.

Let us take the example of social class, an aspect of identity that may be as important as ethnicity in influencing learning. Because membership within a particular social group is based on economic factors as well as cultural values, the working class may differ from the middle class not only in particular values and practices but also in the amount and kinds of economic resources they have at their disposal. Because of these differences, gross generalizations may be made, thus perpetuating what has been called "the culture of poverty," that is, a view of poverty that sees the poor as having no culture or having a culture that is without any merit whatsoever. Thus, the "culture of poverty" pathologizes the values and actions of working-class and poor people.

An example of this deficit view can be found in the work of Ruby Payne, an educator whose self-published ideas on poverty have been propagated throughout the country.[11] Her framework for understanding poverty, which runs counter to the message of this text, has been wholeheartedly accepted by some and harshly criticized by others. Jawanza Kunjufu challenges Ruby Payne's theories by pointing to successful examples in schools that serve low-income students; he asserts that teacher expectations, time on task, and the principal's leadership are the main factors in determining educational outcomes.[12] Paul Gorski, another educational researcher, has critically analyzed Payne's framework.[13] According to him, Payne fails to base her arguments on creditable research; she also neglects to address issues such as the root causes of poverty and the tendency for students living in poverty to become the victims of substandard schooling. While Payne asserts that people in poverty do not value education—a claim unfortunately voiced by other educators who work with poor children—Gorski reviews research that refutes this claim. A major problem with Payne's analysis is that it supports a deficit perspective of students and families living in poverty. Such a perspective leaves little hope for students' academic success or for high expectations of them on the part of teachers and schools. Far better analyses of poverty, which educators need to become acquainted with, are grounded in an understanding of the larger structural issues that create and sustain poverty.[14] Rather than rely on frameworks such as Payne's, teachers would do better to reject deficit perspectives and work to create learning environments that are as challenging and nurturing for students living in poverty as they are for more economically privileged students.

Notwithstanding these caveats about overdetermining its significance, we want to emphasize that culture *is* important. One reason for insisting on the significance of culture is that some people, primarily those from dominated and disenfranchised groups within society, have been taught that they have no culture. This has resulted in, among other things, what Felix Boateng has called *deculturalization,* that is, a process by which people are first deprived of their own culture and then conditioned into embracing other cultural values.[15] This is how the patronizing term *cultural deprivation* has come to imply that a group is without culture altogether, although in reality what it means is that some people do not share in the culture of the dominant group. The research cited in this chapter underscores one of the central tenets of multicultural education: Everybody has a culture—that is, everybody has the ability to create and re-create ideas and material goods and to affect their world in a variety of ways.

Multicultural education is one way of counteracting the notion that culture is reserved for the privileged. For example, Hoang Vinh, although only 18 years old when he was interviewed, had a more sophisticated understanding of culture than many adults do. As you will see in his case study, Vinh described Vietnamese cultural values, behaviors, and expectations without falling into simplistic explanations for complex phenomena. He was also very accurate in pointing out cultural differences between his teachers in Vietnam and the United States: He said that one of his teachers, Ms. Mitchell, expected all students to do things in the same way but that people from other countries "have different ideas, so they might think about school in different ways. . . . So she has to learn about that culture." As one example, he described how his English teachers praised him for his fluency in English, although he felt that instead they should have been telling him to study more. He concluded, "But that's the way the American culture is. But my culture is not like that."

Cultural differences in learning may be especially apparent in three areas: *learning styles* or *preferences, interactional* or *communication styles,* and *language differences*. Examples of the first two areas are explored next in this chapter. Language and language issues are considered more fully in Chapter 6, although it should be understood that language is a major component of culture and is also part of the discussion here.

Learning Styles and Preferences

Learning style is usually defined as the way in which individuals receive and process information.[16] Exactly how culture influences learning and learning style is unclear. For example, an extensive review of scholarship on models of learning styles found the field to be wide-ranging and conceptually confusing. There are many and diverse approaches to defining, measuring, and describing learning styles. Many scholars assert that a reliable measure and categorization of learning styles has not yet been found. One report cautioned that considering learning styles as a fixed trait "might lead to labeling and the implicit belief that traits cannot be altered. It may also promote a narrow view of 'matching' teaching and learning styles that could be limiting rather than liberating."[17]

The concepts asserted in early research on learning style were intended to support educators in meeting students' needs. But too often, in the decades that have ensued, these complex theories have been boiled down into labels and lists in school classrooms, often with detrimental results. Researcher Herman A. Witkin's concepts regarding field-independent and field-dependent learners spawned several decades of educational scholarship that investigate learning-style differences. Subsequent research by Manuel Ramierez and Alfredo Casteñeda used these categories in an effort to provide insight into how best to support academic achievement of Mexican

American and American Indian students. Yet these studies were often misinterpreted, resulting in the perpetuation of stereotypes about particular groups of children.[18]

In spite of the advances made in understanding how culture might influence learning, the linear process implied by this theory is not convincing. In fact, some of the early research in this field concentrated on ethnic and racial differences in learning, a perspective that can skirt dangerously close to racist perceptions of differences in IQ. It also flies in the face of cultural hybridity and negates the vast pool of learners who adapt to multiple learning situations and to a range of cultural experiences.

A focus on rigid learning styles is problematic because of its tendency to dichotomize learning; it is doubtful that a process as complex as learning can be characterized as having only two poles, four quadrants, or five characteristics, whatever the theory may assert. Hence, we use the term *learning preferences* because it is a more flexible way of approaching differences in learning. A good example is the case of Hoang Vinh, who loved working in cooperative groups, a learning preference that is not usually associated with Vietnamese students. Joel B. Stellwagen also warns against misapplying learning-style concepts by classifying students in certain categories. He argues that misapplication of these theories can "lead to stereotyping and prejudicial labeling of people."[19] Thus, although learning-style research can be helpful in identifying learning differences related to ethnicity and culture, its misapplication also runs the risk of oversimplification and stereotyping and can be used as a rationale for poor or inequitable teaching.

How learning-style theory can be misapplied is evident in a comprehensive review of research on American Indian and Alaska Native education. In their review, Donna Deyhle and Karen Swisher concluded that learning-style research can point to meaningful adaptations that may improve the educational outcomes of these students, but they also warned of the detrimental consequences of viewing learning-style research uncritically. Specifically, they pointed out that the depiction of the "nonverbal" Indian child is reinforced when teachers read that American Indian students prefer observation to performance. Deyhle and Swisher conclude:

> The power relations in the classroom, rather than the Indian child as culturally or inherently "nonverbal," are central to understanding the nonparticipatory behavior observed in many Indian classrooms. In these "silent" classrooms, communication is controlled by the teacher, who accepts only one correct answer and singles out individuals to respond to questions for which they have little background knowledge.[20]

Furthermore, Navajo researcher Kathryn Manuelito has underscored the importance of incorporating Native American epistemologies in schooling for Indigenous students while indicting the power relations that can impede Native students' educational achievement.[21]

An example of debilitating power relations can be seen in the case study of James Karam that follows this chapter. Although the Arabic language and Lebanese culture were very important to James, they were essentially invisible in his school. As a result, he learned to deemphasize them in the school setting. This kind of "invisibility" of Arab Americans and their culture was reversed after the events of 9/11. A new type of harmful visibility experienced by many Arab Americans in school involves "racial profiling" by peers, where some students—and even some adults—may disparage their culture, language, appearance, and religion and make unfounded, prejudicial accusations. In such a climate, the learning of all students is negatively affected.

Thus, the sociopolitical context, as well as a constellation of factors such as child-rearing practices and cultural experiences, wield substantial influence on students' learning preferences. Circumstances such as power relationships and status differentials are also at work, and these may be even more substantial than child-rearing practices. These power differentials are evident in Rebecca Florentina's comments, summarized in her case study following this chapter. Quite astute in understanding how curriculum and pedagogy can malign students' identities, Rebecca suggested that the major problem in health class was the curriculum and that one way to address this problem was to "get the health teachers to put better curriculum for teaching about same sex, transgender, anything, you know?"

Although not specifically asserted as a discussion of cultural differences or even as related to multicultural education, Howard Gardner's theory of multiple intelligences (MI) from the field of cognitive science and education has implications for culturally compatible education.[22] According to this theory, each human being possesses eight or nine relatively independent forms of information processing, and each is a specific "intelligence." These intelligences include logical-mathematical, linguistic (these first two are the most emphasized in school success), musical, spatial, bodily kinesthetic, interpersonal, naturalistic, intrapersonal, and the ninth—about which Gardner continues to speculate—existential. Accordingly, Gardner defines *intelligence* as the ability to solve problems or develop products that are valued in a particular cultural setting. The salience of cultural differences in intelligence is evident. Gardner's research has demonstrated that individuals differ in the specific profile of intelligences that they exhibit, and these differences may be influenced by what is valued in their culture. Because a broader range of abilities is acknowledged in this conception of intelligence, previously discounted talents of individuals can be considered in a new light.

However, MI theory can also be misapplied. Gardner reports that he "objected strenuously" to a statewide educational intervention "that described major racial and ethnic groups in Australia in terms of the intelligences that they purportedly had and the ones that they purportedly lacked." In a paper released on the twenty-fifth anniversary of the publication of his groundbreaking book *Frames of Mind: The Theory of Multiple Intelligences,* he addressed some of the myths and misunderstanding of MI theory—for example, confusing an intelligence with a learning style, or asserting that all children are strong in at least one intelligence. He asserts that any serious application of MI ideas should entail at least two components: (1) an attempt to individuate education as much as possible and (2) a commitment to convey important ideas and concepts in a number of different formats.[23] Gardner has recently branched into the policy arena to focus not only on how human beings should be *understood* by scientific study, but also on how they should be *nurtured* by educational institutions. His more recent theory, articulated in his book *Five Minds for the Future,* describes these five minds as (1) the disciplined mind, (2) the synthesizing mind, (3) the creative mind, (4) the respectful mind, and (5) the ethical mind.[24]

The theories of multiple intelligences and of five minds may have significant implications for multicultural education because these theories go beyond the limited definition of intelligence valued in most schools. For one, Gardner's theories break out of the rigid definition of intelligence narrowly defined as book knowledge or doing well on standardized tests. As a result, these theories may be particularly helpful in challenging current assessment practices that focus almost exclusively on logical-mathematical and linguistic intelligence and provide guidance in reconsidering the role that schools play in cultivating participation in a democratic society. The danger, as always, lies in extrapolating from individual cases to an entire group. Although it may be true, for example, that a certain culture—because of its social, geographic, or political circumstances—is more highly developed in one kind of intelligence than other cultures, educators should not conclude that all the group's members will manifest this intelligence equally. They should also not assume that individuals from this culture are *primarily* or *only* intelligent in one way and therefore unable to develop intelligence in other areas.

 ## Communication Style

Cultural influences can be found in interactional or communication styles, that is, the ways individuals interact with one another and the messages they send, intentionally or not, in their communications. According to Geneva Gay, communication is much more than the content and structuring of written and spoken language. She states,

> Sociocultural context and nuances, discourse logic and dynamics, delivery styles, social functions, role expectations, norms of interaction, and nonverbal gestures are as important (if not more so) than vocabulary, grammar, lexicon, pronunciation, and other linguistic structural dimensions of communication.[25]

If teachers and schools are unaware of these differences and the impact they can have on learning, the result may be cultural conflict that leads to school failure. School failure, in this case, can be understood as the product of miscommunication between teachers and students and a rational adaptation by students who are devalued by schools. Following this line of thought, unless changes are made in learning environments, school failure may be inevitable.

On the basis of his extensive review of culturally compatible education, Roland Tharp concluded that when schools become more attuned to children's cultures, academic achievement improves.[26] Tharp has suggested at least four cultural variables related to communication that may be at odds with the expectations and structures of schools: *social organization, sociolinguistics, cognition,* and *motivation*. An example will suffice to demonstrate the complex interplay among them. For instance, in the area of sociolinguistics, Tharp explains how short wait times (that is, the length of time teachers wait for student responses) may be disadvantageous for some students, and he specifically cites American Indian students, who generally take longer to respond to teachers' questions because their culture emphasizes deliberate thought.

Tharp and Stephanie Stoll Dalton with the Center for Research on Education, Diversity and Excellence (CREDE) realized the limitations of classrooms organized

■ ■ ■ ■ ■ ■   **What You Can Do**
Respect and Affirm Student Differences

Learning how to understand cultural differences does not mean simply learning about culture. Knowing about *Cinco de Mayo* in the Mexican American community or about health practices among Vietnamese will do little to prepare you for day-to-day experiences with students of diverse backgrounds. Because culture is constantly changing, we cannot view it as static and unvarying. A more promising approach is to reflect on how cultural differences may affect your students' learning and to be open to changing your curriculum and pedagogy accordingly. Therefore, when facing cultural differences, always ask yourself the question "Who does the accommodating?" Is it always students from nonmajority cultures?

Here are some specific strategies:

1. To accommodate the learning preferences of all your students, plan a variety of activities so that all students' preferences are reflected. Students who are comfortable working in groups should have the opportunity to do so, and so should students who are not used to this style of working. The point is not to segregate students according to their preferences but rather to have all students develop skills in a broad range of activities.

2. Investigate out-of-school activities in which your students are engaged (e.g., art, performances, music, athletics, after-school employment, caring for family members). As much as possible, use such experiences in the school to motivate students to learn school-related subjects.

3. Learn to think of yourself as a life-long learner. Listen to and watch a variety of news sources, read books about different cultural and racial experiences, and be open to other experiences that will broaden your outlook beyond your town, cultural group, and nation.

according to culturally compatible education; for example, what happens when you have a classroom demographics comprised of students representing a range of diverse groups such as Navajo, African American, Cambodian, Irish American, and Greek? The exponential growth of classrooms that hold a range of multilingual, multiethnic, multiracial, and multicultural learners, in the ensuing 25 years since Tharp's initial research, led Tharp and Dalton to offer "five standards for effective pedagogy" that can guide teachers in meaningful practice for students of all cultural backgrounds: (1) teachers and students producing together, (2) developing language and literacy across the curriculum, (3) making meaning—connecting school to students' lives, (4) teaching complex thinking, and (5) teaching through instructional conversation. In summary, their five standards guide what they call a "pedagogy system" that includes both collaborative group and individual work; activities linking curriculum to the strengths, needs, and interests of local communities; and the rich dialogic language environments of multiple, simultaneous classroom activity settings.[27]

How relationships between students and teachers can be either improved or damaged by their interactions is another pertinent area of research on culturally responsive classrooms. As an example, students and teachers from the same background are often on the same wavelength simply because they have an insider's understanding of cultural meanings and therefore do not have to figure out the verbal and nonverbal messages they are sending. Michele Foster examined how a shared cultural background or shared norms about how language is used in African American communities can benefit classroom interactions. She found that, in classrooms of African American students taught by African American teachers, there are subtle but significant interactional differences from other classrooms. For example, she documented the positive classroom effect of one African American teacher who used Standard English to regulate student behavior, but "performances" (i.e., what Foster described as stylized ways of speaking that resemble African American preaching style) to relate the everyday life experiences of her students to more abstract concepts.[28] Another example of communication style comes from more recent research on urban youth culture: Ernest Morrell and Jeff Duncan-Andrade used their students' involvement with hip hop culture to successfully engage them in literacy learning.[29]

Carol Lee's research on the literacy practices of African American high school students also showed that cultural resources support learning. In analyzing students' everyday practices, Lee found that African American students who speak Ebonics, or what she calls African American Vernacular English (AAVE), consistently use irony, satire, and symbolism in their everyday talk, especially in the speech genre *signifying,* that is, ritualistic insults and other word games. Because of their creative use of language, Lee reasoned that building on this kind of knowledge and skills would be an effective basis for a literature curriculum because, in Lee's words, "[u]se of rhythm, alliteration, metaphor, irony, and satire are routine in the language practices of this speech community."[30] As a result of this understanding, Lee developed the Cultural Modeling Project, a four-year literature curriculum that has been implemented in a large midwestern city. The result: Students at all grade levels have achieved beyond what their standardized reading scores predicted.[31]

Cultural differences likely influence students in more ways than we can imagine. For example, take the case of Susan, a new teacher who was attending a workshop being given by me (Sonia) many years ago. Susan was a young teacher of English as a Second Language to Puerto Rican students. Although she was sincerely committed to her students' achievement, she was unaware of many aspects of their culture. The Puerto Rican children, most of whom had recently arrived in the United States, used the communication style typical of their culture. For example, many Puerto Ricans wrinkle their noses to signify "What?" When Susan would ask the children if they understood the lesson, some would invariably wrinkle their noses. Not understanding this gesture, Susan simply went on with the lesson, assuming that their nose wrinkling had no meaning.

Two years after first being exposed to this behavior, Susan attended a workshop in which we discussed Puerto Rican gestures and the work of Carmen Judith Nine-Curt in the area of nonverbal communication. She learned that nose wrinkling among Puerto Ricans was a way of asking "What?" or "What do you mean?" or of saying, "I don't understand."[32] From then on, Susan understood that, when her students exhibited this form of nonverbal communication, they were asking for help or for

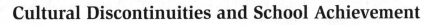

What You Can Do
Research "Families' Funds of Knowledge"

Explore who your students are, what makes them "tick," and the values and life skills of their families. Doing so will help you understand the strengths that families have, rather than focusing on assumed weaknesses or deficits.

If you are an elementary level teacher, make it a point to visit your students' families at least once a year. Focus on learning about what Norma Gonzalez, Luis Moll, and Cathy Amanti have called "families' funds of knowledge"—that is, their skills and competencies—and think about how you can use these in your curriculum. To learn more about doing such research, see their book.*

Considering the large number of students they teach, it is unrealistic to expect secondary school teachers to engage in such research. However, there are other projects that can help you, as a secondary school teacher, become familiar with your students' cultures and identities. Oral histories

are an excellent way to learn about your students' family histories, challenges, and triumphs, and oral histories do not need to be confined to the English or social studies class. Math, health, science, art, and other subject matters are fertile ground for case studies. You'll be surprised at how much you can learn—and use in your curriculum—from conducting this kind of project.

Another approach is called Biography-Driven Culturally Responsive Teaching and is explained in a book of the same title by Socorro Herrara.[†] This practical, hands-on, how-to resource guides teachers in classroom practices that are rooted in well-researched theory.

*Gonzalez, N. E., Moll, L. & Amanti, C. (Eds.) (2005). *Funds of knowledge: Theorizing practices in households and classrooms*. Mahwah, NJ: Lawrence Erlbaum.

[†]Herrera, Socorro. (2010). *Biography–Driven Culturally Responsive Teaching*. New York: Teachers College Press.

further clarification. We all laughed about it that day in the workshop, but this humorous anecdote is not without its serious consequences. Students whose culture, verbal or nonverbal, is unacknowledged or misunderstood in their classrooms are likely to feel alienated, unwelcome, and out of place.

Promoting teachers' familiarity with communication differences would go a long way in helping them transform their curriculum to address their students' backgrounds more adequately. The communication styles explored here are only the tip of the iceberg, but they help to point out the sometimes subtle ways that culture, if it is not understood, can interfere with learning.

Cultural Discontinuities and School Achievement

Cultural discontinuities, that is, the lack of congruence between home and school cultures, may cause numerous problems for students from culturally marginalized groups. A review of some of the literature on culture-specific educational accommodations can pinpoint how discontinuities between schools and students may lead to negative academic outcomes.

A classic research study that paved the way for numerous other studies by anthropologists, sociolinguists, and educators was done by Shirley Brice Heath in the Piedmont Carolinas during the 1970s.[33] In exploring the language of Black children at home and at school, she found that different ways of using language resulted in tensions between the children and their mostly White teachers in the classroom. For example, the children were not accustomed to answering questions concerning the attributes of objects (color, size, shape, and so on), the kinds of questions that typically occur in classroom discourse as well as in middle-class homes (i.e., "What color is the car?" "How many dolls are there?"). Instead, the children generally used descriptive language at home for storytelling and other purposes. The result was a communication breakdown, with teachers believing that many of the students were "slow" and students perceiving a lack of support from teachers. Through research coordinated by Heath, the teachers began to experiment with different ways of asking questions. The result was that teachers helped children bridge the gap between their home and school experiences and thus the children's language use in the classroom was enhanced. Heath continues to bring critical reflections of these findings in her current research in which she considers the implications of contemporary social conditions that are creating changes in family interaction and discourse. Emerging technologies and lifestyle shifts create changes in language use, which influence what we refer to as family literacy. She makes the case for placing value on community literacies in texts of all forms: oral and written, visual and verbal, that comprise projects of joint work and play.[34]

The culture and language children bring to school are often disregarded and replaced, and this situation can have dire consequences. In the words of Geneva Gay, "Decontextualizing teaching and learning from the ethnicities and cultures of students minimizes the chances that their achievement potential will ever be fully realized."[35] A teacher's best intentions may be ineffective if students' cultural differences are neglected in curriculum and instruction, and this is underscored by another classic ethnographic research study. Susan Philips's research on the Warm Springs Reservation is a powerful example that points out the problems that can emerge when teachers are not familiar with their students' culture.[36] In the case of American Indians, the core values of respect and value for the dignity of the individual, harmony, internal locus of control, cooperation, and sharing inevitably influence students' reactions to their educational experiences. Philips found that students performed poorly in classroom contexts that demanded individualized performance and emphasized competition. On the other hand, their performance improved greatly when the context did not require students to perform in public and when cooperation was valued over competition. As Philips's study demonstrated, cooperative learning, which is compatible with the values of many American Indian families, is an approach worth exploring in classes with American Indian children but is helpful in other settings too.

Cultural discontinuities do not develop, however, simply because of differing cultural values among groups. There is often a direct connection between culture and the *sociopolitical context of schooling*. One example of the link between sociopolitical context and culture is the remarkable academic success of South Asian students in U.S. schools. The prevailing explanation for their success is that the cultural values of South

Asian students are congruent with the academic culture of schools. Although this may be true, it alone is not sufficient to explain their success. The fact that the parents of South Asian students are the most highly educated among all immigrants is also a factor. For instance, on average, Asian Americans have a higher level of education than any other ethnic group in the nation: In 2000, 44 percent of Asian Americans age 25 years or older had a college or professional degree, compared with 28 percent of the White population. However, the level of education depends to a great extent on ethnicity: Only about 12 percent of Hawaiians and 10 percent of other Pacific Islanders had achieved a bachelor's degree or more, and among Cambodians, Hmong, and Laotians, almost two-thirds had not completed high school.[37] As we can see, culture cannot easily be separated from other issues such as social class, parents' level of education, and students' access to higher education.

Stacey Lee's research points to the limits of the cultural explanation of academic success among Asian American students. First, it does not account for within-group differences in achievement. She points out that the cultural theory seems plausible for high achievement, but it does not explain low achievement, neglecting the question of why some Asian American students do poorly in school. Other problems with the cultural explanation include considerations of why some Asians struggle with academic achievement in their own country where they are engulfed in their home culture, and why studies of specific Asian ethnic groups show low achievement in some countries but not in others. Lee's work also sends a strong caution against the model-minority stereotype that falsely perpetuates the assumptions that all Asian and Asian American students do well in school. She points out that the stereotype is used to silence claims of racial inequality, and it hides the problems faced by some Asian American students. It also influences the way many Asian students view themselves and their achievements.[38]

The sociopolitical link is embedded in the history of U.S. schooling as illustrated by the practice, in the late nineteenth and early twentieth centuries, of sending American Indian students to distant boarding schools. Attending such schools meant that students were physically separated from their parents and consequently from their cultural connections. The very purpose of these boarding schools was to eradicate students' native language and culture in an attempt to "Americanize" them.[39] The dropout rate among these students was very high because of the school-related social and emotional problems they experienced. Although the dropout rate of American Indians remains catastrophically high in some areas, as documented by the Civil Rights Project, it has been reduced dramatically in cases where secondary education has been returned to local communities.[40]

Becoming aware of the sociopolitical context of education is important for other reasons, too. For instance, in their research on American Indians, Deyhle and her colleagues have expressed the concern that educators sometimes use the cultural discontinuity theory to argue only for a culturally compatible curriculum to solve the dropout problem.[41] In so doing, educators may neglect to confront other more pressing problems in American Indian and Alaskan Native schools, such as the lack of equitable financing and appropriate resources. The same concerns apply to students from other nonmainstream backgrounds, as pointed out by Tyrone Howard's book in which he illustrates case studies of three schools where educators increased understanding of race and culture and have been successful with rigorous academic achievement for young people of color.[42] Another example of the enduring messages and complexity of school culture can be found in the case of LGBT students who may not do well in school. The problem is likely not lack of intelligence or a cultural mismatch with the school, but rather the rejection they experience in school as a result of the school's unwelcoming climate. Changing the curriculum would probably help, but in some cases, LGBT students may decide that dropping out of school is the only recourse they have. Rebecca Florentina, in the case study that follows this chapter, mentions a number of friends who felt the need to do so.

These examples demonstrate that cultural incompatibilities are varied and complex. Research concerning them is vital if we are to grasp how children from different cultural backgrounds respond to teachers' behaviors and what teachers can do to change how they teach. However, no single solution will bridge the gap between the school and the home cultures of all students.

Culture-Specific Educational Accommodations

Various approaches and programs have been designed to provide for the particular educational needs of students from specific cultural groups, and some of these programs have proved to be extremely successful. A number of examples of modifications to make instruction more culturally appropriate reveal the reasoning behind the approach known variously as *culturally compatible, culturally congruent, culturally appropriate, culturally responsive,* or *culturally relevant instruction.*[43]

The Kamehameha Elementary Education Program (KEEP) in Hawaii, a program that was in existence from the late 1970s to the mid-1990s, provides a robust example of using a culturally specific approach in teaching.[44] KEEP was begun when perceived cultural discontinuities in instruction were identified as a major problem in the poor academic achievement of Native Hawaiian children. As a privately funded, multidisciplinary educational research effort, KEEP's purpose was to explore remedies for Hawaiian children's chronic academic underachievement by changing certain educational practices: changing from a phonics approach to one emphasizing comprehension; from individual work desks to work centers for heterogeneous groups; and from high praise to more culturally appropriate praise, including indirect and group praise. The KEEP culturally compatible kindergarten through grade 3 language arts program met with great success, including significant gains in reading achievement. One explanation for the success of the program is that instruction was modified to match more closely the children's cultural styles. The move from phonics to comprehension, for instance, allowed the students to contribute in a speech style called the talk-story, which is a familiar linguistic event in the Hawaiian community. Other instructional changes, including a preference for cooperative work and group accomplishment, were also compatible with Native Hawaiian culture. Roland G. Tharp and colleagues revisited the KEEP standards and pedagogical structures in light of two subsequent decades of research. They remain convinced that teaching must respond to local, particular learners, but that KEEP's standards of pedagogy can serve as guidelines.[45]

There are other challenges in Native Hawaiian education, however, and these often have more to do with the sociopolitical context than with the children's learning preferences. According to Margaret Maaka, "[i]n Hawai'i, a place of many cultures, the English-only ideology is firmly entrenched in all levels of the education system."[46] In the past three decades, a major focus of Native Hawaiian education has been language preservation. In 1896, the Hawaiian language was outlawed as the language of instruction and, as a result, there are fewer Native Hawaiian speakers each year. In 1984, the movement to preserve the Hawaiian language began with the opening of the first Punana Leo Hawaiian language immersion preschool. In addition, the Kamehameha schools, serving students in grades K–12, are recognized for their language-based immersion program to preserve both the Native Hawaiian language and the Hawaiian culture. According to Sarah Keahi, a Native Hawaiian educator, "[a]s indigenous educators, we know that a culture and its language are inseparable, for the language is the vehicle by which the culture is transmitted."[47] This is supported by research reported in a special journal issue dedicated to Hawai'i Creole (Pidgin), local identity, and schooling, in which various scholars advanced critical understandings of Hawai'i Creole, or Pidgin, and its place in the education of the youth of the islands.[48]

Sometimes, new teachers of students of culturally marginalized backgrounds assume that they cannot expect very much of their students, especially if these students are also economically poor, yet the opposite is true. Research on the pedagogy of teachers of students of diverse backgrounds provides convincing illustrations of how teachers use cultural knowledge and experiences to overcome some of the debilitating and negative messages of schools and society. It also documents how the most effective teachers challenge students rather than let them "slide." Jacqueline Jordan Irvine and James Fraser describe culturally responsive teachers of African American students as "warm demanders," that is, teachers who are affectionate and loving while they are tough and rigorous in their expectations.[49] Gloria Ladson-Billings's research of effective teachers of African American students also documents how successful teachers use students' culture as a bridge to the dominant culture. The pedagogy of the effective teachers she describes is empowering because, rather than simply teach students blind acceptance of the inherent values of the dominant culture, these teachers encourage students to think critically and work actively for social justice.[50] H. Richard Milner's edited text highlights the critical importance of teachers understanding the context of their students lives and the implications of their own identities and their students' identities when building productive relationships for learning. The authors in this collection emphasize the good news that teachers of all backgrounds can learn to be culturally responsive.[51] In addition to considering the competencies of teachers who are successful with African American students, these studies document additional effective practices, including teachers' use of interactive rather than didactic methods, and the high standards they set for students.

An illustration in which teachers are effective with students of color, despite the fact that the cultural identities of teachers and students were not always the same, is found in research by Jason Irizarry. Drawing on a larger ethnographic study in the Northeast, he highlighted Mr. Talbert (a pseudonym), an African American teacher who had been recommended by parents, community leaders, and other educators as effective with Latino students. Irizarry found that Mr. Talbert used a variety of practices, including community connections (sharing personal stories, living in the same community, and knowing what went on in the neighborhood), language (that is, supporting various uses of written and spoken language of students, including Ebonics, or Black English), and music (particularly rap) to relate to his students, while he also demanded high-quality work from them. Although Irizarry was particularly interested in what might work for Latino students, what he found instead was a predisposition on the part of Mr. Talbert and the other teachers he studied (who were of Latino, White, and African American backgrounds) to engage with students and their families, to learn about their realities—including how they identify, and to shift their pedagogy accordingly. As a result, the culture of Mr. Talbert's class was negotiated and co-constructed. In the many moving examples provided by Irizarry about how teachers of various backgrounds relate to Latino students, one senses that culturally responsive pedagogy is, more than anything, about *making connections with students*. To describe the practices of particularly effective teachers such as Mr. Talbert, Irizarry coined the term *culturally connected teachers*. As one Latino student explained, "[Mr. Talbert] is the first teacher to ever care about where I'm from and what I'm about. That's love."[52]

Another example of developing culturally congruent teaching practices is reported in research by Cynthia Ballenger. A teacher of preschool Haitian children and the only non-Haitian educator in the school, Ballenger documented how she learned to be a culturally responsive teacher from the children themselves. Initially unfamiliar and even uncomfortable with their ways of learning, Ballenger recounts how she expected to see deficits in the children, not because she thought their background was deficient but because she did not know how to appreciate their strengths. After listening to and learning from the children and other staff members, Ballenger began to adopt some of the styles of the Haitian teachers. She relied on the children's responses to her practices and concluded, "I can tell when I have it more or less right because of the way the children pay attention."[53] The lesson is clear: Heeding what children do and say can make a difference in how teachers interact with them and consequently in how well children learn.

These dramatic examples focus on one cultural group in a school, but changes in instruction and curriculum that reflect the multicultural character of most schools are also possible. For example, most schools favor a highly competitive and individualistic instructional mode in which only some of the students may be successful. By combining this style with a more cooperative mode, the learning and cultural styles of all children can be respected and valued. The lesson is that, although all schools cannot become *culturally compatible* because of the range of diversity in the student body, they can become *multiculturally sensitive*.

A Critical Appraisal of Culture-Specific Accommodations

In spite of their usefulness, culture-specific accommodations are limited by several factors. First, the diversity of the student population in most schools mitigates culture-specific modifications. Many schools are multicultural, with students from diverse ethnic, social class, and linguistic backgrounds. There are few totally homogeneous schools, and designing a school to be culturally compatible with just one group of students, even if it is the most numerous group, might jeopardize students of other backgrounds—that is, if schools change their instructional strategies to be compatible with students from just one ethnic group, these strategies might be the opposite of what students from other backgrounds need.

Another problem with making educational choices that are solely culturally compatible is that it may lead to segregation being posited as the most effective solution to educational failure. Although segregation might sometimes be warranted, the truth is that our history has amply demonstrated that it often leads to inequality. When speaking of culturally dominated groups, "separate but equal" is rarely that; on the contrary, segregation generally means that powerless groups end up with an inferior education because they are given the fewest material resources for their education. Nevertheless, although U.S. courts in the second half of the twentieth century upheld integration as a positive goal to strive for because it purportedly leads to increased educational equality, we know that this is not always the result. In fact, segregation is today more prevalent than it has been in decades. Even when schools are desegregated in name, sometimes they are segregated in other ways, especially through tracking in gifted and talented, special education, and other such programs.

We need to distinguish among different kinds of segregation. Segregation imposed by a dominant group is far different from the self-segregation demanded by a dominated, subordinate group whose members see through the persistent racism behind the veneer of equality in integrated settings. This is the reasoning behind Afrocentric, American Indian, Latino, or other culturally based schools. Even in these cases, however, culturally separate schools may effectively isolate themselves from receiving some of the benefits of the public school system that might help them meet the needs of the children they serve. Although qualitatively different from segregated schools because they are developed by disempowered communities, culturally homogeneous schools are not always effective. There are numerous cases of students of culturally diverse backgrounds who have been successfully educated in what might be considered culturally incompatible settings. Other factors unrelated to cultural conflict must be involved.

Another problem with culturally congruent education is the implication that all students from a particular group learn in more or less the same way. This assertion is problematic because it essentializes culture, which can lead to generalizations and stereotypes that get in the way of viewing students as individuals as well as of members of groups whose cultures are constantly evolving.

In spite of all these caveats, it must be recognized that our public schools are not providing many students—particularly Latino, African American, and American Indian students living in poverty—with the education they deserve. Until they do so, we need to find ways to help these students succeed, and culturally responsive pedagogy, even in segregated settings, is certainly one such approach. Nonetheless, if such programs or schools are based on the notion that culture is unchanging, they are bound to face problems.

Conclusion

This chapter discussed how culture can influence learning in crucial ways. Using learning-style research, educators began to understand how students of different backgrounds might differ in their learning preferences. While learning-style frameworks must be used with caution, more recent methodologies of ethnographic investigation have yielded important findings that can also help teachers and schools recognize the possible impact of culture on learning. Modifications can be made in communication style, program design, and instruction to support the learning of students of diverse backgrounds. Because using only a cultural analysis concerning learning is limited, however, the chapter ended with a critical analysis of some of the problems with culture-specific accommodations. For one, these accomodations often negate the reality of hybridity, an increasingly diverse and complex student body.

Ultimately, however, culture matters. Learning cannot take place in settings where students' cultures—broadly defined to include race, ethnicity, social class, language, and other elements such as urban and adolescent identity—are devalued and rejected. Teachers who want to provide all students with a caring and stimulating environment for learning have to take into account their backgrounds and identities. This means learning *about* and *from* their students and those closest to them, and making the accommodations necessary to promote their learning.

To Think About

1. What do we mean when we say, "Equal is not the same"? To help you consider this question, think about some of the students you know.

2. Can you identify any pedagogical strategies that have seemed to be successful with particular children? How can you use these with students of various cultures?

3. Given the contradictory messages that children receive from their home and school environments, it is possible that they will end up rejecting their parents' culture and way of life. What can teachers and schools do to minimize this situation?

Activities *for Personal, School, and Community Change*

1. Observe three different students in a classroom. How would you characterize their learning preferences? How do they differ? Do you think these differences have something to do with their gender, race, ethnicity, social class, or other difference? Why or why not? What are the implications for teaching these children?

2. What steps can you take to make your classroom more culturally compatible with the student body? Consider changes in curriculum, organization, use of materials, and pedagogical strategies. Try some of these and keep a journal of your reflections on the effect they have on students.

3. Think of some of the ways your school can become a culturally welcoming place for students of various backgrounds. For example, what kinds of schoolwide rituals can be

developed that would make all students feel that they belong? What about parent outreach? What can be done in the hallways and on bulletin boards? Suggest some of these changes to your principal or department head.

Case Studies

Yahaira León

It's easier to be myself culture-wise.

Fifteen-year-old Yahaira León,[1] who was finishing ninth grade at Frontier High School in Philadelphia when she was interviewed, described herself as "half and half" Dominican and Puerto Rican. She continued, "And I guess I could say I'm American, too. I was born here." Her parents were also both born in the United States, specifically in New York City, while her grandparents were all born in either Puerto Rico or the Dominican Republic. Yahaira's cultural identity and academic perspectives are influenced by her family life, educational experiences, and sociopolitical history.

The migration of Puerto Ricans and Dominicans from their island nations to New York and the northeastern United States is part of a larger pattern of migratory experiences among many Latino communities in the United States. In spite of sharing the Spanish language, a Caribbean heritage, and the quest for economic opportunities, there are distinct forces at play within each group's political, social, economic, and familial experiences.

The Dominican population in the United States is over 1.3 million, making it the fifth largest population of Hispanics living in the United States, and 2.8 percent of all U.S. Hispanics. Like Yahaira's family, the vast majority of Dominicans, nearly 80 percent, live in the Northeast, and half live in New York. Almost one-third of the growth in the Dominican community is from births in the United States, as in the case of Yahaira and her parents, while the remainder is from immigration. As of 2008, nearly half of Dominican immigrants (47.4 percent) were U.S. citizens.[2]

The share of Dominicans who live in poverty, 23.2 percent, is nearly double the rate for the general U.S. population, and higher than most Hispanics (20.7 percent).[3] The struggle to combat poverty marks the daily realities of many Dominican and Puerto Rican families. Due to their reliance on goods-producing industries in the Northeast that have suffered from deindustrialization, both Puerto Ricans and Dominicans struggle with unemployment in far greater numbers than other Hispanic groups. In 2008, the mean annual per capita household income of the Dominican population in the United States was $20,571, lower than the median earnings for Hispanics, which stood at $21,588, or less than half the per capita income of the average U.S. household.[4] Unemployment is a common plight within the Dominican community, and the immigration status of some workers keeps them in the lowest

About Terminology

Latinos, Hispanics, and Others

The terms *Latino* and *Hispanic* refer to people whose heritage is from Mexico, Central and South America, and the Spanish-speaking Caribbean islands. Some people have definite and strong preferences for the terms *Latino* and *Hispanic,* arguing that one is far more accurate than the other. The debate is complicated by the tremendous diversity within the Latino/Hispanic community itself. *Hispanic* is more widespread and well known, while *Latino* is preferred in some areas of the country over others. Unlike the terms *European, African, Latin American,* or *Asian, Hispanic* does not refer to a particular continent or country (i.e., there is no continent named Hispania). The term *Latino,* on the other hand, has the disadvantage of having a sexist connotation when used to refer to both males and females together.

Although Latinos share a great many cultural attributes, they are also quite different from one another. A Peruvian and a Dominican, for example, may both speak Spanish, practice the Catholic religion, and share deeply rooted family values. However, the native language of some Peruvians is not Spanish, and Dominicans have an African background not shared by most Peruvians. These differences, among many others, often go unacknowledged when we speak simply of *Latinos* or *Hispanics*. Within the context of the U.S. experience, Latinos differ in many respects, including race, social class, level of education, and length of time in this country. Each of these factors may make a dramatic difference in the school achievement of children from distinct groups.

We generally prefer the term *Latino,* but we have used both terms more or less interchangeably. When the more specific ethnic name is available, we use neither *Latino* nor *Hispanic.* For example, none of the Latino students in the case studies in this book refer to themselves as *Latino, Latina,* or *Hispanic*: Alicia Montejo defines herself as *Mexican*; Paul Chavez uses both *Chicano* and *Mexican American*; and Yahaira León identifies as both

income bracket. Dominicans have slightly higher levels of education than the general Hispanic population, with 16 percent of those 25 and older having obtained at least a bachelor's degree, compared with 12.9 percent of other Hispanics. Ramona Hernandez and Francisco L. Rivera-Batiz describe this as an "explosive increase of the educational attainment" of U.S.-born Dominicans.[5]

The Dominican Republic's long history of political unrest has left its mark on the economic circumstances, political perspectives, and cultural solidarity of the people. As it became more difficult to make a living at farming in the Dominican Republic, people migrated to northeastern cities in the United States to work in factories and tourist industries. Many Dominicans in the United States are referred to by social scientists as transnational migrants, that is, those who organize many aspects of their lives—family, religious, political, and economic—across national borders.[6] While assimilating into the country that receives them, transnational migrants often also sustain strong ties to their homeland.[7] The transnational dynamic

Dominican and *Puerto Rican*. Whenever possible, these distinctions need to be made; otherwise, fundamental differences in ethnicity, national origin, self-identification, and time in this country are easily overlooked.

Chicano, a term popular in the late 1960s and early 1970s, is preferred by some people of Mexican origin, while *Mexican American* is preferred by others. *Chicano* is an emphatically self-affirming and political term reflecting the culture and realities of urban, economically oppressed Mexican Americans in U.S. society, and it grew out of the 1960s Brown Power Movement. Although used by many scholars and activists, the less political term *Mexican American* is more common in other segments of the community.

Puerto Ricans, the second largest Latino group after Mexicans, also use different terms for specific situations to describe or refer to themselves. For example, while *Puerto Rican* is the general term used by most people, a growing number of second- and third-generation Puerto Ricans prefer the term *Nuyorican* (an amalgam of *New Yorker,* the preferred destination of Puerto Ricans in the early to mid-twentieth century, and *Puerto Rican*). More recently, the term *Diasporican* has gained popularity because it acknowledges two realities: First, most Puerto Ricans in the United States no longer live in New York but are dispersed throughout the Northeast and increasingly throughout the country; and second, the immigration of Puerto Ricans represents a true diaspora because more Puerto Ricans currently live in the United States than on the island of Puerto Rico.* The term *Boricua,* derived from *Boriquén,* the name given to the island by the Taínos, its original inhabitants, is an affectionate term for *Puerto Rican* and is also used quite often.

*Diasporican has been popularized by Nuyorican poet Mariposa. See J. M. Valldejuli and J. Flores (2000), New Rican voices: Un muestrario/A sampler at the millennium, *Journal of the Center for Puerto Rican Studies* 12 (1): 49–96.

of these immigrants has implications for both the home country and the host country. For example, as the Dominicans in the United States began to send money back to communities in the Dominican Republic, the standard of living on the island nation improved substantially.[8] However, due to visa and immigration status concerns, U.S. Dominicans may not be able to return to the Dominican Republic as frequently as they desire.

In contrast, Puerto Ricans are U.S. citizens and can travel freely, so patterns of what has been called circular migration are not unusual for Puerto Ricans, who frequently move back and forth from the island to the mainland U.S. and back to the island. This kind of migration stems primarily from the economic dependence of Puerto Rico on the United States. To explain the formidable economic subordination of the island, it is often said that "when the United States sneezes, Puerto Rico catches cold."

Between 1940 and 1970 alone, about 835,000 Puerto Ricans moved to the United States, reflecting one of the most massive outmigrations in the century.[9] In fact, currently more Puerto Ricans live in the United States than in Puerto Rico: According to the U.S. Bureau of the Census, 4.2 million Hispanics of Puerto Rican heritage live in the United States, while 4 million reside in Puerto Rico.[10] Also, although New York City was the primary destination for Puerto Ricans until the 1960s, currently only about 26 percent of Puerto Ricans living in the United States are in New York; most of the others reside in the Northeast, but a growing percentage (about 28 percent) live in the South, primarily in Florida. In addition, Puerto Ricans are increasingly living in relatively small cities such as Holyoke, Massachusetts, the city where Yahaira was born and where she frequently visits her father's side of the family.

As a result of the Spanish-American War, Puerto Rico became a colony of the United States in 1898, which helps explain some of the differences between Puerto Rican migration, or (im)migration, and Dominican immigration.[11] In 1952, Puerto Rico officially attained commonwealth status, although some people maintain that this is a camouflage for what is, in reality, a colony. After 1900, U.S. absentee landlords—and later large corporations—dominated the economy, displacing small farmers and creating the island's economic and political dependence on the United States. Puerto Ricans were made U.S. citizens in 1917—some say, to coincide with the need for soldiers in the armed forces during World War I, for which Puerto Rican men were recruited en masse.

Yahaira's family confronts many hardships against the backdrop of these sociopolitical histories of Dominican and Puerto Rican communities in the United States. Due to the constant search for adequate, affordable housing and better employment by Blanca, her single parent, Yahaira had attended eight different schools by ninth grade. Blanca's unwavering hunt for a safe environment, with access to quality education for Yahaira and her sisters, was a Herculean task because of the stratification of U.S. schools by neighborhood real estate taxes. Yahaira recalls frequent transitions as a pervasive part of her childhood: "We moved around a lot. I don't know why, we just moved around a lot. We just had to keep moving."

Yahaira has navigated these challenges while achieving steady academic success. While the number of transitions to different schools would impede many students, Yahaira was consistently upbeat. She said, "I just have a lot of fun learning 'cause I just liked to learn. I loved school." The three themes that emerged from Yahaira's interview all point to the reasons for her school success: *stability within transition, cultural identity and connection with Mom,* and *cultural connection and academic challenge.*

Stability Within Transition

School is, like, my home, well, my second home. But I just love being there. I love reading and learning and everything about it. School was the main place I could read and write without having to worry about anything.

I went to school a lot of places (*laughs*). The high school now—the name is Frontier. It's in downtown Philadelphia. It's a very good school. It's for advanced students. It's just, like, advanced for all areas. I'm learning a lot of new things that I didn't know and I'm advancing on the things I did. I am meeting more and more people who I can connect with and I make a lot more friends. I just have a lot of fun learning. 'Cause I just liked to learn. I always loved school. And well, you don't hear many kids saying that, but I do (*laughs*).

The reason for going to school is to educate your mind. So far, yeah, I am accomplishing that. It is important to me because nowadays, in this economy, you don't get nowhere if you don't have an educated mind. Without that, I can't do nothing. And without an educated mind, I can't get a job, which [means] I can't get money, and I can't support myself when I get older.

Cultural Identity and Connection with Mom

I'd say I'm Puerto Rican and Dominican because, well, my mom's Dominican and my dad's Puerto Rican. My culture is important because in school they mostly teach us about the English society, the American society. They don't teach us the Hispanic culture or stuff like that, so it's important that I at least know some type of my cultural background, something from there. So whatever I can, I learn from either my family or I try and research it myself.

[What I would like teachers to know about Puerto Rican and Dominican kids is that] we're not the same as every other culture or ethnic group. We have our own ways that should be expressed. We have our own beliefs and customs. If schools would teach about Puerto Rican and Dominican culture, what I would like to learn is, basically, the history and how life is over there now. How it is for the people who have lots of money and compare it to the people who have harder lives. How the Dominican Republic and Puerto Rico came to be what they are today—from the different main events that have happened in the history of the countries. I learned a little—just a little bit about it—from my mom and my grandmother but nothing about it in the schools. As a Puerto Rican and Dominican teenager, I'm more educated about my culture. Kids my age who are not Puerto Rican and Dominican might not have the same knowledge of [my] culture.

[The school] does value my culture. In the school I'm going to now it does . . . on certain levels. Every culture is valued in the school. They have African American clubs, Hispanic clubs, but it's not just clubs. The Hispanic club is not just for the Hispanic kids. Anybody could be in the club. 'Cause when we went to the student orientation for the high school, one of the teachers was saying that in the African American group there's a Hispanic president for the group. It's like they're all mixed in and it's not a problem. They all get along together. I'm gonna try to join a club. Probably the Hispanic one and the African American one.

In ninth grade I was in Mock Trial Club. I didn't have time to join the cultural clubs in ninth grade because I was so busy with Mock Trial Club. We met once a week at the beginning of the year, and then when the competition started, it was twice a week and on Saturdays. Also, I have chores at home and responsibilities to babysit my sisters—they're 12 and 7—'cause my mom works all the time and I'm the one that has to watch the girls while she works. Next year I'm gonna do Mock Trial again and try softball.

So far, I've seen a lot of my friends who are not as successful as I am. I know a lot of people who, at my age, don't really care about school anymore and they're, like, "whatever." I would just tell [new Puerto Rican and Dominican students] to work hard and worry about getting the work done. Don't worry about what's going on with everybody else at school . . . don't be up all in the gossip and just stick to the work and they'll do fine.

[Now, at the high school] I have all really different friends from the type of friends I had last year. They are all really into school. They are all really dedicated to school work and getting things done. They think about college, too.

From my family I've learned that not much of my family has graduated. Because, I mean, that just makes it better for me to graduate and shows the family that it can be done. I mean it just takes hard work, and that helps a lot because then all my younger siblings and younger cousins and nieces and nephews . . . they can see that if they work hard enough, they can do anything.

My mom is involved in my school. She tries her hardest to find out everything that goes on. Every time there's a parent–teacher meeting, she goes. When we go to get our report card, she's always asking my teachers how I'm doing and exactly what I do in school. She gets very involved. She likes to know what's going on. My mom tells me repeatedly about school . . . doesn't leave me alone about it. Like everything I do, whether it's good or bad, she tells me and tells me over and over again. "Just fix it, you could do better." If it's something good, "You did great. Don't worry about it." 'Cause sometimes it gets annoying, her being so involved. But, yeah, it does matter, 'cause, I mean, without her, I probably wouldn't have been so into school and I wouldn't have liked it so much.

My mom is the person I admire the most in the world 'cause without her, I wouldn't be where I am. Without her, I wouldn't even be able to be independent or work out things on my own. I wouldn't be as determined as I am. I think that's enough to make her the most important person in my life.

I have always been living with mom, without dad, since I was 4. I live with my two youngest sisters—they are 7 and 12—and my mother. I am the biggest sister. They look up to me. I want to teach my sisters to always try their hardest at everything else they do—to never settle for less.

Cultural Connection and Academic Challenge

I think my favorite was my fourth-grade teacher. She was really nice and she connected very well with the kids in the class. She wasn't the type of teacher that just gives you the work, tells you to do it, leaves it at that. Or the type that doesn't give you enough work and you're, like, sitting there the rest of the day doing nothing. She gave you the right amount of work, let you have the right amount of fun, but still got everything in all together.

I guess teachers understand my culture. Most of my teachers have either been African American or Caucasian. So I really haven't had any Hispanic teachers [until ninth grade] to understand really the culture—but they understand some of it, so that's enough. In the school I went to in eighth grade, almost every teacher spoke Spanish because almost all the kids there were Hispanic—so they spoke Spanish. Every teacher knew at least some words in Spanish but they also spoke English. That helped because the kids who were just learning English—it was easier for them to communicate with the teachers. In some schools teachers acknowledged Spanish language and in some schools they didn't.

[Something teachers could do better is] involve the culture more into the learning. Like the strategies they use, the methods. If there was more learned or taught about the different cultures, that might help. Like my science teacher [in ninth grade], whenever we had projects, he would bring in movies for us to watch; he would bring in cultural movies that would help us learn what we were being taught in the class as well as being able to understand it better through our culture, help us understand the concepts. My science teacher, each day in the class, he takes time to get to know the kids in the classroom a little bit more. He'll sit down and talk with us on a normal basis. Not teacher-to-student but as in a friend-to-friend role. His sister-in-law is Dominican, so we had that in common and I think he knew some Spanish.

The Mock Trial coach—he builds relationships. [The Mock Trial coach and the science teacher] learn how to talk to the students. They take the time to learn how life is for each student in the world we are living in. They learn how each student is different and they support each different thing about each student.

Of all my teachers, I think my eighth-grade teacher [has been the most helpful] 'cause he was, like, every time I needed something that had to do with school, any time I needed help with anything, he found a way to get me help. Whether it was his subject or not, he'd find somebody to help me and he'd ask my mom—if I needed to—if it was OK to stay after school and get help. In his class I always got top grades 'cause it was my favorite class because it was the reading. That helped a lot.

In my high school, this is a more diverse school. There's more Hispanic kids around. It's easier to be myself culture-wise. A lot of the teachers are more used to working with the Hispanic kids and Black kids, so it's better. They're helping us learn—make it easier by helping us learn within our culture.

I mean that's how school's supposed to be; it's supposed to be hard, not easy. I was in the advanced class in my eighth grade—and we was doing algebra and math and just the basics in reading, science, and social studies. But the math was a little bit ahead— well, we got more work than the other classes, so that kind of made it harder, but I still kept my grades up so it was all right.

The first year at the [advanced] high school was actually kind of easy. I just got through the work really easily; it wasn't as hard as I thought it would be. But that is just normal for me. I wish the teacher would challenge me a little bit more. I think they should make the work a little harder. I guess it's kind of hard [for teachers] 'cause I'm the only one in the class that has it so easy, so it's kind of difficult to make things harder for just me and then have the rest of the class have a problem with it.

I don't really read magazines 'cause I just think they're based on nothing. Most of the magazines now are talking about how girls are supposed to be skinny and pretty and their faces are supposed to be a certain way and all this crap, and it's annoying because the beauty you see when you look at people, it's not much. You have to look inside to know, actually know, what the person is. You can't just tell by looking at them. So I don't really look at magazines.

I'm most happy when I'm in my room reading one of my books or watching . . . no not watching . . . just reading one of the books or drawing or writing or something.

I've thought about [what I want to be]. When I was younger, everybody used to tell me be a lawyer because I like to argue and I always have to have the last word. But as I grow older, I think I'd rather be a teacher because, by being a teacher, I can do something that I really love doing and I can still work hard and get what I need to survive. Reading, English language arts are my favorite 'cause there's reading and writing and I love to read and write. That's kind of why I want to be a teacher, so I can be a reading or writing teacher. Since being in Mock Trial at the high school, I'm thinking maybe a lawyer. Probably a lawyer.

All the teachers and counselors are talking to us about college. It was very interesting. I am thinking about being a lawyer and Harvard. I just heard from people that it is the most challenging college. I figured since every other grade in school has been easy, I think I should pick a hard college. 'Cause everybody says it's one of the best schools. I don't know. I've just wanted to go there since I was, like, four.

Grades are important to me because with grades—with better grades—I get more successful results. And with even better grades, I can get scholarships to college. My mom thinks grades are important. She looks for mostly A's or B's. She'll settle once in a while for a C but mostly A's or B's.

[To be successful later in life] I need to keep doing what I'm doing now. Working hard to get through whatever I gotta get through.

Commentary

Y ahaira's ideas echo themes that Carmen Rolón found in her study of Puerto Rican girls who achieved academic success.[12] In Rolón's study, it was first, parents—in particular, mothers—who were vehicles of encouragement and achievement. Second, teachers who respected and affirmed students' cultural and linguistic diversity were also significant. Third, Rolón found that all her participants defined college education as their primary educational goal. In Rolón's study, in René Antrop-González's research and in Yahaira's words, we hear Latinas describe school as a "second home," or as a "sanctuary".[13] In Yahaira's case, caring, supportive teachers and a determined mother motivated her to shape school as an oasis where she could "read and write, without having to worry about anything."

Because Yahaira entered kindergarten fully bilingual in English and Spanish, she was never enrolled in English language learning programs and achieved well in all school subjects. Despite her fluency in English, she emphasized the link between teachers' "understanding the culture" and affirming Spanish language, whether the teacher knew "at least some words" or was fluent, and "speaking to kids and parents." She described teachers who supported her efforts after school and pointed her toward college. She also noted culturally relevant teaching methods and the importance of relationships among teachers and students.

Yahaira's words resonate with Jason Irizarry's research that describes teachers who are successful with Latino students as "culturally connected." Irizarry describes cultural connectedness in teachers as a framework for understanding that takes into account the development of hybrid identities that emerge as a result of members of various cultural communities negotiating their identities and forging new socioculturally situated identities. It also highlights the potential for teachers who are not members of the same racial or ethnic group as that of their students to become "connected" and improve their practice.[14] Significantly, Irizarry points out that teachers do not have to racially match their students in order to develop a cultural connection with them.

Although not all Yahaira's teachers were "culturally connected," Yahaira was flexible in her expectations. Even more important to Yahaira were teachers' high expectations. Her desire for rigorous work is congruent with Patty Bode's study of urban schools. She found that students felt that teachers should hold high expectations for them. The students articulated an appreciation of teachers who challenge them by pushing them hard and refusing to let them quit.[15] This student attitude is especially salient in discussions about urban schools where most of the students are labeled as "failing," "underperforming," or "below standard" by state mechanisms such as high-stakes standardized testing and federal policies and laws such as No Child Left Behind (NCLB).

Yahaira's efforts to achieve academically deserve commendation because her success could have been disrupted by her family's struggles and the frequent school transitions. The numerous moves may have been less bearable if not for the close-knit extended family to which Yahaira made frequent affectionate references. Collectively, Yahaira's extended family shaped her strong identification with her Spanish language and Puerto Rican and Dominican roots as well as her vision of the future. Her family's nurturing relationships and challenges with hardships formed her perceptions of limitations and possibilities. Despite the emotional support of extended family on both sides, Yahaira still faced many of the tensions of urban life in the difficult socioeconomic circumstances common to many Latino families. Her father's long periods of absence—due to his difficulties with the law—rendered his presence in Yahaira's and her sisters' lives elusive.

Hard work and determination are, in many ways, Yahaira's anchors in a tumultuous ocean of school transitions. She viewed hard work as the way to graduate, gain admission to college (preferably Harvard), and achieve career goals. On the subject of her family members and friends who had not graduated from high school, she said, "I mean it just takes hard work." While hard work is an essential ingredient for academic achievement, Yahaira's statement seems to overlook the sociopolitical conditions in which many Puerto Ricans and Dominicans live. Yahaira seems to have accepted the myth of meritocracy; this is no surprise because it seems to have worked in her case.

The complicated forces at play within Yahaira's educational experiences should not be oversimplified as binary perspectives of a cooperative, communal, and so-called Latino perspective in opposition to a utilitarian, competitive American mainstream perspective. Her mother instilled in Yahaira an obvious sense of hard work and determination to achieve and to never settle for less; many of Yahaira's teachers drew upon cultural knowledge as a means to academic achievement. An elaborate web of academic culture and family culture is woven into her perspective.

Yahaira expressed her Latina identity in intangible but fundamental ways: her deep feelings for her family, respect for her parents, and her desire to uphold important traditions such as being with family. She also bore a larger share of family obligations than a great many young people from other cultural backgrounds. This is what is referred to in many Latino cultures as *capacidad,* or a combination of maturity, sense of responsibility, and capability. It is a valued cultural trait that Latino parents work hard to inculcate, particularly in their daughters.

Yahaira is very much a product of the intersecting and multiple influences of Puerto Rican, Dominican, and U.S. culture (especially youth culture). She, and many young people like her of various immigrant backgrounds, have created a new culture, one that has elements of the native culture but is also different from it. Yahaira was successfully negotiating the mixed and often conflicting messages of home culture, school culture, and youth culture. Questions remain, however, about the cost to cultural identity and becoming more fully human when academic accomplishment is perceived primarily as individual hard work.

For the most part, Yahaira and her mother were left on their own to tap into some appropriate resources to construct Yahaira's road to academic success. From many indicators, she appeared to be well on her way to a successful future. When we last checked in with her about her activities after freshman year, she was attending a summer institute at Yale sponsored by the Junior Statesman Foundation.[16] The program develops political and scholarly skills through college-level coursework and enrichment activities. Yahaira gained admission to the highly competitive program through a convergence of her Mock Trial coach's dedication, her mother's assertiveness to obtain a scholarship for the costly summer program, and

Yahaira's unflagging determination. Such an experience will certainly provide Yahaira a window into her target—an Ivy League college career. As a result of such experiences, navigating higher education may be easier for Yahaira than for other students who do not have a parent or parents with the single-minded determination of Yahaira's mother or the consistent support of teachers like Yahaira's who saw great promise in her.

Reflect on This Case Study

1. Yahaira's perception is that her school mostly teaches about the "English society, the American society." If she were describing your school or your classroom, would you be satisfied with that portrayal? If not, how might you change Yahaira's experience?
2. How can teachers and schools take advantage of students' desires to learn more about their cultural heritages and histories? For example, Yahaira cited her desire to learn more about "[h]ow the Dominican Republic and Puerto Rico came to be what they are today—from the different main events that have happened in the history of the countries." What could be some responses to such a desire?
3. Yahaira fondly remembered one school where every teacher knew "at least some words in Spanish." What are the implications for educators regarding language and learning? How do you feel about trying to pronounce a few words in languages other than English, even if you are far from fluent? What are some classroom strategies for affirming multiple languages in the school?
4. The Mock Trial after-school program built on Yahaira's interests and appears to have deeply influenced her choices about her future. What does this tell us about the role of after-school programs in student achievement? What is the role of after-school programs in your school?
5. Yahaira yearns to be challenged more. Can you think of some strategies to encourage her academic prowess and challenge her intellectual curiosity? How can teachers assess whether they are challenging all students?

James Karam

I'd like to be considered Lebanese.

Poised between childhood and adulthood, James was a pleasing combination of practical, responsible, wise adult and refreshing, spirited, eager kid.[1] Sixteen years old and a junior in high school when he was interviewed, his maturity was due in no small part to his role as the responsible male in the household. His mother and father were separated, and he was the oldest of three children, a position he generally enjoyed, although he admitted it could be trying at times.

Lebanese Christian, or Maronite, James explained that his father was born and raised in the United States. His father met his mother while visiting Lebanon and brought her back to the United States as his bride. She had lived here for almost 20 years and had become fluent in English. Although James's parents were separated, both were close to their children and continued to take an active part in their upbringing and education.

According to the U.S. Census Bureau, Arab Americans are people who can trace their heritage to 22 countries in North Africa and the Middle East. The 2000 census

counted approximately 1.2 million Arab Americans, a sizable increase in comparison to the 1990 census number of 870,000. However, the Arab-American Institute
Foundation estimates that as many as 3.5 million Americans can trace their family
lineage to an Arab country.[2] (As of this writing, the results of the 2010 U.S. Census
were not yet available). The problem, however, is that there was no box for
Americans of Arab descent to check off their ethnic heritage; most had to check
"Other" or "White," making them even more invisible than they already are, a common theme in James's case study.

The Lebanese community, part of the larger Arab population in the United States,
is little known to the general U.S. population. It is, in this sense, an "invisible minority," about which more is discussed later. There are scattered communities of
Lebanese throughout the United States, with large concentrations in several cities,
including Springfield, Massachusetts, where James lived. A study of the Arab community in Springfield, conducted more than four decades ago, reported that the first
Arab settlers from Lebanon arrived in the 1890s. Most were laborers and worked in
the city's factories, for the railroad, or in peddling businesses. They were both
Christian and Muslim Lebanese and there was little animosity between them. On
the contrary, there was a genuine sense of solidarity and cohesiveness in the entire
community.[3]

James had attended a Catholic school from kindergarten until third grade but
had subsequently gone to a public school. He was held back in third grade because
his family moved out of the state and he lost a good deal of school time (this still
bothered him a great deal, as he said when he was interviewed). Despite this setback, at the time of his interview James was a successful student who gave a lot of
thought to his plans after high school. He worked at keeping his grades high so that
he could get into a good college and was fairly certain that he wanted to become a
mechanical engineer. His fantasy was to become a professional bike racer, but even
if able to pursue this dream, he wanted a college education.

Springfield is a midsize metropolitan city. It is culturally, racially, and economically diverse. At the time of his interview, James was attending one of the high
schools in the city, which he described as almost "a little college," and he liked all
his classes. His classmates reflected many of the cultures and languages of the world,
and the school system was intent on incorporating this cultural diversity into the
curriculum in many ways, some more successful than others. When James was interviewed, bilingual education was still going strong in Massachusetts (it was eventually eliminated), so the school system offered a number of bilingual programs for
the Spanish-speaking, Portuguese, Russian, Vietnamese, and Khmer communities.
Some of the other activities, such as cultural festivals and international fairs, although
a promising start, proved to be somewhat superficial attempts at acknowledging the
rich cultural diversity of the city, as James made clear in his interview.

Although he had never studied Arabic formally in school, James was fluent in
both English and Arabic because both languages were spoken at home. His family
attended the Maronite church in the city; the church was established in 1905 and was
influential in encouraging the use of Arabic and the maintenance of Lebanese culture in the community. The church's role was not merely to provide a place for worship; rather, it has served as a haven for cultural pride and observance of traditions.

Indicative of the church's role, the Reverend Saab, pastor for more than 50 years, made the following statement concerning his parishioners during his investiture as monsignor: "I did not want them to forget their Lebanese heritage because this is a wonderful thing."[4] Even when assimilation was generally perceived to be a great value in U.S. society, the Lebanese community was definitely bucking the tide. This was apparent in the large percentage of second- and even third-generation Lebanese in Springfield, both Christian and Muslim, who still spoke Arabic.

In many other ways, however, the Arab American community has acculturated to the U.S. mainstream. In Springfield, Arabic surnames are now almost nonexistent because many family names have been Anglicized. Actually, were it not for the influence of the church, and to a lesser extent other social and religious organizations and clubs, assimilation might have proceeded much more rapidly. The social class structure has changed, too. The Lebanese community in the city started out as working class, but it is now primarily middle class. In the first decades of the twentieth century, the Arab community was similar to many other immigrant communities. It was characterized by large families (an average of ten children); overcrowded flats; congested sidewalks and doorsteps; and dirty, unpaved streets.[5] Most Arabs in the city now own their own homes and live in middle-class communities.

This was true of James and his family, too. He, his mother, 14-year-old brother, and 9-year-old sister lived in a quiet residential neighborhood in the city. His community, primarily European American, was much more homogeneous than the city itself. He said the difference between his neighborhood and the city proper was that there were many trees ("Believe me, I know! I have to rake the leaves every year," he said).

Themes that emerged in James's interview include James's perception of himself as a *good student,* as "smart," and his role as *apprentice within his family*. The most important theme to emerge, however, was the *invisibility* of James's Lebanese American culture in his high school, which is the theme we will address first.

The Invisible Minority

[My elementary school teacher, Mr. Miller] I just liked him. . . . He started calling me Gonzo 'cause I had a big nose. He called me Klinger—he said 'cause Klinger's Lebanese. You know, the guy on *M.A.S.H*? And then everybody called me Klinger from then on. I liked it, kind of . . . everybody laughing at me. Yeah, it doesn't bother me. I don't care if somebody talks about my nose.

We had a foreign language month in school. They had posters and signs and everything. Spanish, French, Spain, Italy—they had all these signs and posters and pictures and stuff all over the school. There was Chinese; they had Japanese; they had Korean. They had lots of stuff.

[*Why didn't they have Arabic?*] I don't know. . . .

[Another time] they made this cookbook of all these different recipes from all over the world, and I would've brought in some Lebanese recipes if somebody'd let me know. And I didn't hear about it until the week before they started selling them. They had some Greek. They had everything, just about. I asked one of the teachers to look at it, and there was nothing Lebanese in there.

[Another time, at the multicultural fair], there was Poland, there was Czechoslovakia, there was Spain, there was Mexico, there was France. There was a lot of different flags. I didn't see Lebanon, though.

I guess there's not that many Lebanese people in . . . I don't know; you don't hear really that much. . . . Well, you hear it in the news a lot, but I mean, I don't know, there's not a lot of Lebanese kids in our school. There's about eight or nine at the most.

I don't mind, 'cause, I mean, I don't know, just, I don't mind it. It's not really important. It *is* important for me. It *would* be important for me to see a Lebanese flag. . . . But you know, it's nothing I would, like, enforce or, like, say something about. If anybody ever asked me about it, I'd probably say, "Yeah, there should be one." You know, if any of the teachers ever asked me, but I don't know. . . .

Some people call me, you know, 'cause I'm Lebanese, so people say, "Look out for the terrorist! Don't mess with him or he'll blow up your house!" or some stuff like that. But they're just joking around, though. I don't think anybody's serious 'cause I wouldn't blow up anybody's house—and they know that. I don't care. It doesn't matter what people say. I just want everybody to know that, you know, it's not true.

On Being a Good Student

I'm probably the smartest kid in my class. It's just, like, usually I can get really into the work and stuff. But everybody else, you know, even the people that do their homework and assignments and stuff, they just do it and pass it in. You know, I like to get involved in it and learn it.

If you don't get involved with it, even if you get perfect scores and stuff, it's not gonna, like, really sink in. You'll probably forget it. You can memorize the words you know, on a test. But you know, if you memorize them, it's not going to do you any good. You have to *learn* them, you know?

I want to make sure that I get my college education. I want to make sure of that. Even if I do get into the career that I specialize in college, I still want to get a college education. . . . I'd love to be an engineer, but my real dream is to be a bike racer. Yeah, it's my love. I love it.

When things go bad, I go ride my bike. That's what I did [once] in the middle of the night. The faster I ride, the harder I pushed, the more it hurt. It made me keep my mind off [things].

[I think I didn't do well in school one year] just because I didn't try. I thought it was too easy so I didn't try. I don't think [Mom] liked that too much. I said, "Mom, I wanna go to summer school, you know, just to bring up my grade." So she paid for it.

In a lot of the things that I do, I usually do good. I don't like it when I don't finish something or when I do real bad. It makes me want to do better. If I ever get a bad grade on a test, it makes me want to do better next time.

Some teachers are just . . . they don't really care. They just teach the stuff. "Here," write a couple of things on the board, "See, that's how you do it. Go ahead, page 25." You know, some teachers are just like that.

Maybe it's not that they don't care. It's just that they don't put enough effort into it, maybe. . . . I don't know.

I like going over it with the class, and you know, letting everybody know your questions. And, you know, there could be someone sitting in the back of the class that has the same question you have. Might as well bring it out.

[Teachers should] make the classes more interesting. . . . Like, not just sit there and say, "Do this and do this and do this." You know, just, like, explain everything, write things on the board.

Apprenticeship Within the Family

I speak a mixture of both [Arabic and English]. Sometimes it's just, like, some words come out Arabic and some words come out English. . . . Whichever expresses what I want to say the best, I guess, at the time.

We go to a lot of Lebanese parties and gatherings. We go to Catholic-Lebanese church every week. I always want to go to church. Most of my friends don't go to church. A lot of them do, but most of them don't.

My mother's really proud to be Lebanese, and so am I. First thing I'd say is "I'm Lebanese." I'm just proud to be Lebanese. If somebody asked me, "What are you?" everybody else would answer, "I'm American," but I say "I'm Lebanese," and I feel proud of it.

Even though somebody might have the last name like LeMond or something, he's considered American. But you know, LeMond is a French name, so his culture must be French. His background is French. But they're considered Americans. But I'd like to be considered Lebanese.

My mother's really old-fashioned: "You gotta be in early." "You gotta be in bed at a certain time." That kind of stuff. I guess it'll pay off. When I'm older, I'll realize that she was right, I guess. But right now, I wish I could stay out, like, a little later. I don't mind it 'cause I don't think I'm really missing much. There must be a reason why. I know a lot of kids that can stay out and, you know, they go out till 12 o'clock, 1 o'clock in the morning. They don't come back home, and their mothers don't even ask them, you know, where they've been or whatever. [My parents are] really loving and caring. . . .

[My parents] basically taught me to be good to people. You know, I've never really been mean to anybody. I don't like fighting. My mother taught me that, mostly. [I] wouldn't want to be a part of any other family, put it that way.

Commentary

Until the events of September 11, 2001, Arab Americans were largely an invisible minority in the United States. James was interviewed in 1989, and at that time, invisibility was a mark of the community. This became clear not only through discussions with James but also through a review of the literature. Whereas much has been written about numerous other ethnic groups in the United States—even those fewer in number—very little was available about Arab Americans, their culture, school experiences, or learning preferences. This situation has changed considerably since 9/11, when Arabs, including Lebanese, inaccurately became linked with extremism and terrorism by many. Compared with most other groups, for whom volumes of information are available (although not necessarily accurate, understood, or used appropriately), Arab Americans still represent a unique case of invisibility because, when represented at all, it is generally in negative ways.

The reasons for this invisibility are varied. For one, the majority of Arabs did not come in a mass influx as the result of famine, political or religious persecution, or war, as have other refugees. Although many Arabs have indeed come to this country under these circumstances in the recent past, previously their numbers had not been conspicuous: Until 2001, Arab immigration to the United States was a relatively "quiet" one. In addition, Arabs' problems of adjustment, although no doubt difficult, had not, until recently, caught the public imagination as had those of other immigrants. Their children have not faced massive failure in the schools, as is true of the children of other immigrant groups, and for this reason, Arab American children have not been the focus of studies as others have been. Finally, Arabs are not always a racially visible minority, as is usually the case with Asians, African Americans, or many Latinos. A good number of Arab Americans—although certainly not all— can "blend in" with the European American population if they so choose.

Nonetheless, considering the number and diversity of Arabs in the United States and the news events surrounding the time when James was interviewed in 1989— when Lebanon was frequently in the news—is reason enough for more information about Arab Americans. Beyond the issue of conflict, the reality of the diverse histories and cultures of the approximately 300 million Arabs worldwide deserves some mention on its own merit.

Although it encompasses different religions, socioeconomic classes, and national origins, the Arab community is one of the most heterogeneous in the United States. It is also one of the most misunderstood—shrouded in mystery and consequently in stereotypes. The popular images of Arabs as rich sheikhs, religious zealots, or terrorists are gross stereotypes that do little to create a sense of community among Arabs and non-Arabs in the United States, yet this is sometimes the only "information" the general public has. These are also the images that James and other Arab American children have to struggle against every day. Yet Arab Americans do not fit the stereotype: They have a higher level of education than the general population (46 percent hold a bachelor's degree compared to 28 percent of Americans at large); their household income is higher ($59,012) than that of the general population ($52,029); and 73 percent are employed in managerial, professional, sales, or administrative fields.[6] Although racist stereotypes of Arabs as barbaric, treacherous, and cruel still persist, teachers have few resources to deal with these issues. The American-Arab Anti-Discrimination Committee has excellent educational resources and information on the Arab American community (lesson plans for teachers on discrimination and stereotypes, facts about Arabs, contributions of Arabs to civilization, and many more).[7]

James experienced firsthand some of the stereotypes of Arab Americans. He had alternately felt invisible or referred to in only negative ways. Because Mr. Miller (the teacher who called him Gonzo) joked in the same way with many of the other students, and because he allowed them to "make fun" of him, too, James liked this attention. It made him feel special in the sense that his background was at least acknowledged. In spite of what he said, however, the stereotypes about his background had probably taken their toll on James. Although he was quite active in school activities, he was vehement about not wanting to belong to student government. "I hate politics," he said simply.

James was acutely aware of being a good student. He was very confident about his academic success, and his perception of being a successful student was important to him. He was proud, for example, of being persistent, a quality he defined as his best characteristic. At the beginning of his junior year, after summer school, James had broken his foot while playing sports. It had required surgery, and he had been on crutches for several weeks. Because he had missed two weeks of school, he stayed after school every day for a number of weeks, making up labs and quizzes and other assignments. He was struggling with both schoolwork and crutches, but his attitude was positive. "I can't wait to be done with all my makeup work," he said, with a touch of frustration. He got through it, though, as with everything else that he had to do.

James's favorite teacher was his geometry teacher, the one who he said "takes the time" and who went over everything in class. She was also the faculty adviser for the Helping Hand Club, a community service group in the school and neighborhood. James was quite involved in this group, which helped raise funds for individuals in need, and for charitable organizations. "I like doing that kind of stuff," he said, "helping out."

Other activities also seemed to give James the energy and motivation to keep up with schoolwork. He played soccer and baseball and was on the swim team. He became most enthusiastic, however, when talking about his favorite activity, biking. This sport energized James in many ways. Biking gave him the opportunity to learn about many things: how "practice makes perfect," how to develop and use leadership skills, how it feels to have a setback and not let it be a permanent loss, how to use a hobby to help relieve stress, and how to hone his interpersonal skills. Biking was not just a physical challenge but also an important motivation. James's room was filled with biking magazines, and he said that the person he most admired was Greg LeMond, at the time the only U.S. racer who had ever won the Tour de France and the world championship. "I want to be just like him," he said.

James's family played a significant role in the value he placed on education and the need to persevere. Like other parents, James's parents had taught him the values and behaviors they believed most important for his survival and success. In the case of a family culturally different from the mainstream, this role is especially crucial. Teaching children their culture can be called an apprenticeship. It is a role that is particularly evident among immigrant families who attempt, often against great odds, to keep their native culture alive. For families of the dominant culture, their apprenticeship is usually invisible because their children are surrounded by and submerged in the culture every day. They hear the dominant language, see dominant culture behaviors, and take part in all the trappings of everyday life—that is, in mainstream culture. For immigrant families, or even for third- or fourth-generation families who have chosen to retain ethnic ties and traditions, the task of their children's apprenticeship is appreciably more difficult. The language they speak at home is not usually echoed in the general population; their values, traditions, and holidays are often at odds with those of the dominant culture; and even the foods they eat or the music they listen to may be absent in the outside world. Because their culture is simply unacknowledged in many ways, these families are engaged in a terribly difficult balancing act of cultural adaptation without complete assimilation.

Although certainly not immune from the difficulties inherent in this role, James had been quite successful at this balancing act. He had a strong and healthy self-image, not only as a student but also as Lebanese. James loved Lebanese food, and he had even learned to cook some of it. The only thing he seemed to dislike, in fact, was Lebanese music, which he called "boring." His house was filled with Lebanese artifacts. A Lebanese pennant was prominently displayed in his room, and his bike-racing helmet had a Lebanese flag on it. James had never been to Lebanon, but he definitely planned to go "when this war is over," as he explained. For the most part, James felt comfortable in two worlds. His apprenticeship had been a largely successful one. He was proud of his culture; he was bilingual; generally he was not embarrassed or ashamed about appearing "different." He considered his family to be "the average American family" in some ways, and he probably considered himself to be an "all-American" kid because he liked to do what he called "normal teenager stuff."

In sum, James Karam was successful in forging his family, culture, language, hobbies, church, friends, and schoolwork into a unique amalgam, which resulted in a strong self-image and a way of confronting a society not always comfortable with or tolerant of diversity. This achievement had not made him immune, however, to the different and distressing issues that arose because of his ethnic minority status. He had learned, for example, to hide hurt feelings when his culture was disparaged. He was quiet, preferring to accept invisibility rather than risk further alienation or rejection. He also learned not to demand that his culture be affirmed. Nevertheless, it was evident that the uncompromising strength of his family, the support he received from his extracurricular activities, and his enduring faith in himself would probably help make the difference between surviving the tension or succumbing to it.

Reflect on This Case Study

1. What invisible minorities are you aware of? Why would you classify them in this way? In terms of visibility, how would you classify Arab Americans since 9/11?
2. Why do you think James was reluctant to bring up his feelings of exclusion from school activities?
3. What advice do you think James would give new teachers about being successful teachers? Why?

Hoang Vinh

For Vietnamese people, [culture] is very important. . . . If we want to get something, we have to get it. Vietnamese culture is like that. . . . We work hard, and we get something we want.

At the time he was interviewed, Hoang Vinh was 18 years old.[1] Born in the Xuan Loc province of Dong Nai, Vietnam, about 80 kilometers from Saigon, he had lived in the United States for three years. Vinh's hands moved in quick gestures as he tried to illustrate what he had to say, almost as if wishing that they would speak for him. Vinh[2] was very conscious of not knowing English well enough to express himself in the way he would have liked and he kept apologizing, "My English is not good." Nevertheless, his English skills were quite advanced for someone who had been in the United States for just a few years.

When he came to the United States, Vinh first went to Virginia and then to New England, where he currently lived in a modest house in a residential neighborhood of a pleasant, mostly middle-class college town with his uncle, two sisters, and two brothers. Everyone in the family had chores and contributed to keeping the house clean and making the meals. In addition, the older members made sure that the younger children kept in touch with their Vietnamese language and culture. They had weekly sessions in which they wrote to their parents; they allowed only Vietnamese to be spoken at home; and they cooked Vietnamese food, something that even the youngest was learning to do. When Vinh and his siblings received letters from their parents, they read them together. Their uncle reinforced their native literacy by telling them many stories. Vinh also played what he called "music from my Vietnam," to which the entire family listened.

Because Vinh's father had been in the military before 1975 and worked for the U.S. government, he was considered an American sympathizer. As a result, educational opportunities for his family were limited after the war. Although Vinh's parents could not leave Vietnam, they desperately wanted their children to have the opportunity for a better education and a more secure future. Consequently, they sent Vinh and his brothers and sisters to the United States during what has been called the "second wave" of immigration from Indochina; that is, they came after the huge exodus in 1975.[3] Although Vinh and his family came directly from Vietnam, most of the second-wave immigrants came from refugee camps in Thailand, Malaysia, and elsewhere. This second wave was generally characterized by greater heterogeneity in social class and ethnicity, less formal education, fewer marketable skills, and poorer health than previous immigrants. During the 1980s, when Vinh and his family came to the United States, the school-age Asian and Pacific Islander population between the ages of 5 and 19 grew by an astounding 90 percent. About half of the 800,000 Asian refugees who arrived between 1975 and 1990 were under 18 years of age.[4] The Asian population has grown dramatically since that time. The Census Bureau, in its 2006 survey, estimated the Asian population in general to be 14.9 million, and the Vietnamese population to be 1.6 million.[5]

Vinh's uncle worked in town and supported all the children in every way he could, taking his role of surrogate father very seriously. Because he wanted to make sure that all the children benefited from their education, he constantly motivated them to do better. During the summers, Vinh worked to contribute to his family here in the United States and in Vietnam, but during the school year he was not allowed to work because of the importance that his parents and uncle placed on his studies ("I just go to school, and, after school, I go home to study," he explained). He used the money he made in the summer to support his family because, he said, "we are very poor." They rarely went to the movies, and they spent little on themselves.

Vinh was starting his senior year in high school at the time he was interviewed. Because the number of Vietnamese speakers in the schools he attended had never been high, Vinh was never in a bilingual program. Although he had done quite well in school, he enjoyed the opportunity to speak his native language and would no doubt have profited from a bilingual education. Some teachers encouraged Vinh and his Vietnamese classmates to speak Vietnamese during the English as a Second Language (ESL) class to improve their understanding of the curriculum content, but other teachers discouraged the use of their native language. All of Vinh's other classes were in the mainstream program for college-bound students: physics, calculus, French, music, and law. His favorite subject was history because he wanted to learn more about the United States. He was also interested in psychology.

Homework and studying took up many hours of Vinh's time. He placed great value on what he called *becoming "educated people,"* one of the central themes in his case study. Other themes concerned his *demanding standards,* his attempt to *understand other cultures,* and the *strength he derived from family and culture.*

Becoming "Educated People"

In Vietnam, we go to school because we want to become educated people. But in the United States, most people, they say, "Oh, we go to school because we want to get a good job." But my idea, I don't think so. I say, if we go to school, we want a good job *also,* but we want to become a good person.

[In Vietnam] we go to school, we have to remember *every single word*. We don't have textbooks, so my teacher write on the blackboard. So we have to copy and go home. So, they say, "You have to remember all the things, like all the words." But in the United States, they don't need for you remember all the words. They just need you to understand. But two different school systems. They have different things. I think in my Vietnamese school, they are good. But I also think the United States school system is good. They're not the same. They are good, but good in different ways.

When I go to school [in Vietnam], sometimes I don't know how to do something, so I ask my teacher. She can spend *all the time* to help me, anything I want. So, they are very nice. My teacher, she was very nice. When I asked her everything, she would answer me, teach me something. That's why I remember. But some of my teachers, they always punished me.

[Grades] are not important to me. Important to me is education. I [am] not concerned about [test scores] very much. I just need enough for me to go to college. Sometimes, I never care about [grades]. I just know I do my exam very good. But I don't need to know I got A or B. . . . I have to learn more and more. Sometimes, I got C, but I learned very much. . . . I learned a lot, and I feel very sorry, "Why I got only C?" But sometimes, if I got B, that's enough. I don't need A.

Some people, they got a good education. They go to school, they got master's, they got doctorate, but they're just helping *themselves*. So that's not good. . . . If I got a good education, I get a good job, not helping only myself. I like to help other people. . . . I want to help other people who don't have money, who don't have a house. . . . The first thing is money. If people live without money, they cannot do nothing. So even if I want to help other people, I have to get a good job. I have the money, so that way I can help them.

Sometimes, the English teachers, they don't understand about us. Because something we not do good . . . like my English is not good. And she say, "Oh, your English is great!" But that's the way the American culture is. But my culture is not like that. If my English is not good, she has to say, "Your English is not good. So you have to go home and study." And she tell me what to study and how to study to get better. But some Americans, you know, they don't understand about myself. So they just say, "Oh! You're doing a good job! You're doing great! Everything is great!" Teachers talk like that, but my culture is different. They say, "You have to do better." So, sometimes when I do something not good, and my teachers say, "Oh, you did great!" I don't like it. I want the truth better.

Some teachers, they never concerned to the students. So, they just do something that they have to do. But they don't really do something to help the people, the students. Some teachers, they just go inside and go to the blackboard. They don't care. So that I don't like.

I have a good teacher, Ms. Brown. She's very sensitive. She understands the students, year to year, year after year. She understands a lot. So when I had her class, we discussed some things very interesting about America. And sometimes she tells us about something very interesting about another culture. But Ms. Mitchell, she just knows how to teach for the children . . . like 10 years old or younger. So some people don't like her. Like me, I don't like her. I like to discuss something. Not just how to write "A." . . . "You have to write like this." So I don't like that. She wants me to write perfectly. So that is not a good way because we learn another language. Because when we learn another language, we learn to discuss, we learn to understand the word's *meaning,* not about how to *write* the word.

I want to go to college, of course. Right now, I don't know what will happen for the future. If I think of my future, I have to learn more about psychology. If I have a family, I want a perfect family, not really perfect, but I want a very good family. So that's why I study psychology. When I grow up, I get married, I have children, so I have to let them go to school. . . . I have good education to teach them. So, Vietnamese want their children to grow up and be polite and go to school, just like I am right now. . . . I just want they will be a good person.

I don't care much about money. So, I just want to have a normal job that I can take care of myself and my family. So that's enough. I don't want to climb up compared to other people because, you know, different people have different ideas about how to live, so I don't think money is important to me. I just need enough money for my life.

Demanding Standards

I'm not really good, but I'm trying.

In Vietnam, I am a good student. But at the United States, my English is not good sometimes. I cannot say very nice things to some Americans because my English is not perfect. Sometimes the people, they don't think I'm polite because they don't understand my English exactly. I always say my English is not good because all the people, they can speak better than me. So, I say, "Why some people, they came here the same year with me, but they can learn better?" So I have to try.

When I lived in Vietnam . . . so I go to school and I got very good credit [grades], but right now, because my English is not good, sometimes I feel very sorry for myself. [My uncle] never told me, "Oh, you do good" or "Oh, you do bad." Because every time I go home, I give him my report card, like from C to A, he don't say nothing. He say, "Next time, you should do better." If I got A, okay, he just say, "Oh, next time, do better than A!" He doesn't need anything from me. But he wants me to be a good person, and helpful. So he wants me to go to school, so someday I have a good job and so I don't need from him anymore.

He encourages me. He talks about why you have to learn and what important things you will do in the future if you learn. I like him to be involved about my school. I like him to be concerned about my credits.

Some people need help, but some people don't. Like me, sometime I need help. I want to know how to apply for college and what will I do to get into college. So that is my problem. I have a counselor, but I never talk to him. Because I don't want them to be concerned about myself because they have a lot of people to talk with. So, sometimes, I just go home and I talk with my brother and my uncle. If I need my counselor every time I got trouble, I'm not going to solve that problem. So, I want to do it by myself. I have to sit down and think, "Why did the trouble start? And how can we solve the problem?" Sometimes, I say, I don't want them to [be] concerned with my problem.

Most American people are very helpful. But because I don't want them to spend time about myself, to help me, so that's why I don't come to them. One other time, I talked with my uncle. He can tell me whatever I want. But my English is not good, so that's why I don't want to talk with American people.

I may need my counselor's help. When I go to college, I have to understand the college system and how to go get into college. The first thing I have to know is the college system, and what's the difference between this school and other schools, and how they compare. . . . I already know how to make applications and how to meet counselors, and how to take a test also.

Sometimes I do better than other people, but I still think it's not good. Because if you learn, you can be more than that. So that's why I keep learning. Because I think, everything you can do, you learn. If you don't learn, you can't do nothing.

Right now, I cannot say [anything good] about myself because if I talk about myself, it's not right. Another person who lives with me, like my brother, he can say something about me better than what I say about myself. Nobody can understand themselves better than other people.

I don't know [if I'm successful] because that belongs to the future. I mean successful for myself [means] that I have a good family; I have a good job; I have respect from other people.

Trying to Understand Other Cultures

I am very different from other people who are the same age. Some people who are the same age, they like to go dancing, they like to smoke, they want to have more fun. But not me. . . . Because right now, all the girls, they like more fun [things] than sit down and think about psychology, think about family. I think it's very difficult to find [a girlfriend] right now. If I find a girlfriend who not agree with any of my ideas, it would not be a good girlfriend. I don't need [her to be] very much like me, but some . . . we would have a little in common. It is not about their color or their language, but their character. I like their character better.

I think it's an important point because if you understand another language or another culture, it's very good for you. So I keep learning, other cultures, other languages, other customs.

Some [Black] people very good. Most Black people in [this town], they talk very nice. Like in my country, some people very good and some people very bad. I have Chinese, I have Japanese, I have American, I have Cambodian [friends]. Every kind of people. Because I care about character, not about color.

Strength from Culture and Family

Sometimes I think about [marrying] a Vietnamese girl because my son or my daughter, in the future, they will speak Vietnamese. So, if I have an American girlfriend, my children cannot speak Vietnamese. Because I saw other families who have an American wife or an American husband, their children cannot speak Vietnamese. It is very hard to learn a language. In the United States, they have TV, they have radio, every kind of thing, we have to do English. So, that why I don't think my children can learn Vietnamese.

When I sleep, I like to think a little bit about my country. And I feel very good. I always think about . . . my family . . . what gifts they get me before, how they were with me when I was young. Those are very good things to remember and to try to repeat again.

I've been here for three years, but the first two years I didn't learn anything. I got sick, mental. I got mental. Because when I came to the United States, I missed my fathers [parents], my family, and my friends, and my Vietnam. So, every time I go to sleep, I cannot sleep, I don't want to eat anything. So I become sick. I am a very sad person. Sometimes, I just want to be alone to think about myself. I feel sorry about what I do wrong with someone. Whatever I do wrong in the past, I just think and I feel sorry for myself.

I never have a good time. I go to the mall, but I don't feel good. I just sit there. I don't know what to do. Before I got mental, okay, I feel very good about myself, like I am smart, I learn a lot of things. But after I got mental, I don't get any enjoyment. I'm not smart anymore. After I got mental, I don't enjoy anything. Before that, I enjoy lots. Like I listen to music, I go to school and talk to my friends. But now I don't feel I enjoy anything. Just talk with my friends, that's enough, that's my enjoyment.

My culture is my country. We love my country; we love our people; we love the way the Vietnamese, like they talk very nice and they are very polite to all the people. For Vietnamese, [culture] is very important. I think my country is a great country. The people is very courageous. They never scared to do anything. If we want to get something, we have to get it. Vietnamese culture is like that. We work hard, and we get something we want.

Every culture . . . they have good things and they have bad things. And my culture is the same. But sometimes they're different because they come from different countries. America is so different.

[My teachers] understand some things, just not all Vietnamese culture. Like they just understand some things *outside*. . . . But they cannot understand something inside our hearts.

[Teachers should] understand the students. Like Ms. Mitchell, she just say, "Oh, you have to do it this way," "You have to do that way." But some people, they came from different countries. They have different ideas, so they might think about school in different ways. So maybe she has to know why they think in that way. Because different cultures, they have different meanings about education. So she has to learn about that culture. I think they just *think* that they understand our culture. . . . But it is very hard to tell them because that's our feelings.

When I came to United States, I heard English, so I say, "Oh, very funny sound." Very strange to me. But I think they feel the same like when we speak Vietnamese. So they hear and they say, "What a strange language." Some people like to listen. But some people don't like to listen. So, if I talk with Americans, I never talk Vietnamese.

Some teachers don't understand about the language. So sometimes, my language, they say it sounds funny. And sometimes, all the languages sound funny. Sometimes, [the teacher] doesn't let us speak Vietnamese, or some people speak Cambodian. Sometimes, she already knows some Spanish, so she lets Spanish [speakers] speak. But because she doesn't know about Vietnamese language, so she doesn't let Vietnamese speak. From the second language, it is very difficult for me and for other people.

I want to learn something good from my culture and something good from American culture. And I want to take both cultures and select something good. If we live in the United States, we have to learn something about new people.

[To keep reading and writing Vietnamese] is very important. So, I like to learn English, but I like to learn my language, too. Because different languages, they have different things, special. [My younger sisters] are very good. They don't need my help. They already know. They write to my parents and they keep reading Vietnamese books. . . . Sometimes they forget to pronounce the words, but I help them.

At home, we eat Vietnamese food. . . . The important thing is rice. Everybody eats rice, and vegetables, and meat. They make different kinds of food. The way I grew up,

I had to learn, I had to know it. By looking at other people—when my mother cooked, and I just see it, and so I know it.

We tell [our parents] about what we do at school and what we do at home and how nice the people around us, and what we will do better in the future to make them happy. Something not good, we don't write.

They miss us and they want ourselves to live together. They teach me how to live without them.

Commentary

Hoang Vinh's experiences in the United States closely parallel those of other Asian refugees in some respects, but they were quite different in others. His case study gives us many lessons about teachers' expectations, demands on Asian students, and the anguish of cultural clash and language loss.

Vinh was emphatic about wanting to become "educated people," which he explained as wanting to know about other people and about the world, and also wanting to be able to get along with, and help, others. Grades were not as important to Vinh as doing "the best you can." He was convinced that there is a big difference—not just a semantic one, but a cultural one as well—in what it means to be "educated" in the Vietnamese sense and in the United States. His explanation is a good example of what many Asians believe to be one of the main differences between U.S. and Asian cultures. Although U.S. culture is rich materially, it often lacks the spirituality so important in most Asian cultures. In one of the very first resources on Vietnamese culture prepared for teachers after the end of the Vietnam War, Tam Thi Dang Wei wrote, "A very rich man without a good education is not highly regarded by the Vietnamese."[6]

Although Vinh remembered his teachers in Vietnam with some fear because they were strict and demanding, he also recalled them with nostalgia. He noticed many differences in the educational system in the United States—some positive, others negative. He appreciated, for example, being allowed to use his native language in class and the individual help he received from teachers. Mostly he talked about how he loved working in groups. He mentioned one ESL teacher, his favorite teacher, who often had students work in groups, talking among themselves and coming up with their own solutions and answers. Most of the topics they discussed were related to their lives in the United States, their culture, and their adaptation.

Much of the conventional wisdom concerning the traditional learning styles of Vietnamese students emphasizes their passivity and reliance on rote memorization, but Vinh's case dramatizes how important it is to interpret such ideas cautiously. For one, there is great diversity among all Asian groups and even within groups. Vinh's predilection for group work, for example, may demonstrate how the *form* of education is not as important as the *process*. That is, group work in this case is the *means* used to facilitate dialogue, which is so important in learning a second language and learning in general. However, as Vinh's case study indicates, the process may be the crucial factor because it is based on the students' own experiences and engages them meaningfully in their education.

Vietnamese and other Southeast Asian immigrants generally have a substantially higher level of education than other groups, even well-established ones. Their high literacy rate has a significant impact on their schooling in this country. Asians in U.S. schools typically spend much more time on homework than other groups, and literacy and educational activities are undertaken at home as well as at school. The effects of Vinh's family background and early school experiences were evident in his attitudes toward school and in his study habits.

To avoid giving the impression that all Vietnamese students are as concerned with educational success as Vinh was, it must be noted that Vinh was quick to point out that one of his best friends, Duy, was "very lazy." Vinh said that Duy did all of his homework but only at school and in a haphazard way. Vinh stated that, although Duy was very smart and had a "very good character," he did not care about learning in the same way as Vinh did. Duy had long hair, spent many hours listening to music or thinking about girls, wanted to be "cool," and acted in what Vinh said was "an American way." Unlike Vinh, Duy had a job after school and liked to spend his money at the mall.

Both Duy and Vinh, in different ways, shatter the "model-minority" stereotype. According to this image, all Asian students excel in school, have few adjustment problems, and need little help. This stereotype is widely resented by many Asians and Asian Americans. It is not only inaccurate but can also lead teachers to believe that all Asian American students are cut from the same cloth (notwithstanding the fact that the Asian American community in the United States is extremely heterogeneous).[7] The model-minority myth is often used as a standard against which all other groups are measured, and it may contribute to the interethnic hostilities, already common in schools, that are occurring with more frequency in communities, too. This myth also helps to discredit the legitimate demands for social justice made by other, more vocal groups. The model-minority stereotype also overlooks the great diversity among Asian Americans, diversity that is apparent in ethnicity, class, and language, as well as their reasons for being in the United States and their history here. It may place severe demands on students, through teachers who have unreasonable expectations of their academic abilities.

Vinh was extremely hard on himself, and much of this self-assessment was tied to his limited English. The use of the English language as a standard by which to measure one's intelligence is not unusual among immigrant students, who often feel frustrated and angry by the length of time it may take to learn the language. Vinh did not consider himself to be a successful student, often contrasting his academic success in Vietnam with his struggles as a student in the United States.

The tremendous traumas refugees suffer when leaving their country and facing the challenges of a new society are well known. One of the results has been a dramatic incidence in mental health problems among refugees. There is evidence that refugees who are unaccompanied minors like Vinh are especially at risk because they experience more depression and other problems, such as withdrawal or hyperactivity. These problems may be caused by guilt, homesickness, alienation, and loneliness, which are sometimes aggravated by the hostility and discrimination they face as immigrants. Considering the pivotal role of the family in Vietnamese culture, particularly the importance of parents and elders in general, Vinh was bound to suffer mental distress when, at the improbable age of 15, he had the formidable task of relocating, along with his siblings, to a foreign country and culture and assuming the role of an "elder" in dealing with a new society. The result was almost inevitable:

He became sick. He talked about this period of missing his parents and extended family members and "my Vietnam" with great melancholy.

Although his culture and family provided tremendous emotional support for Vinh, they were largely unacknowledged by the school. Vinh felt that teachers needed to learn about his culture and be sensitive to the difficulty of learning a second language at an older age. Adjusting to his new country posed many challenges for Vinh: learning a new language and writing system; becoming familiar with a new and very different culture; and grieving the loss of parents who, although still living, were no longer with him. In such cases, even an apparent adjustment may be deceiving. For example, a study of a group of Cambodian refugee children found that, as they became more successful at modeling the behavior of U.S. children, their emotional adjustment worsened. In addition, the feeling of being different from other children increased with time in this country.[8] The problems of adolescence are aggravated by immigrant and minority status. Young people like Vinh have a double, sometimes triple, burden compared with other youth. Continuing to rely on his culture was one way Vinh tried to survive this difficult adjustment.

Newcomers must also learn to live in a country that is extremely pluralistic, at times uncomfortably so. The result can be confusion and uncertainty about other cultures outside the mainstream. Immigrants are quick to pick up messages about the valued and devalued cultures in the society. Their preconceived notions about racial superiority and inferiority may also play into this dynamic. The lack of awareness and knowledge of other cultures and their experiences in the United States can worsen the situation. Given no guidance by schools through appropriate curricula or other means, new students are left on their own to interpret the actions of others. In addition, immigrants are often the target of racist attitudes and even violence by other students.

All these factors help explain how some attitudes brought by immigrants and then nurtured by prevailing racist attitudes and behaviors in society are played out in schools and communities. Vinh was no exception. His experience with African Americans is an example. He explained that, on several occasions, he was jumped and robbed when he lived in Virginia. Being a newcomer to the United States, he was perplexed and frustrated by this behavior and came to his own conclusion about why the incidents occurred. Vinh saw differences between the Black students in the first school (in Virginia) and those in the mostly middle-class town (in New England) in which he lived at the time he was interviewed. The former, he said, were "very dirty, smoked a lot, and played their music very loud." When asked why he thought this was so, he reflected, "I think that depend on the culture. . . . I don't understand much about Black culture." He added, "Not all Black people [are dirty and loud]. . . . There are good and bad in every group," a cliché often used to soften the impact of gross stereotypes. Vinh was obviously grappling with the issues of race and stereotypes and tried very hard to accept all people for "their character" rather than for the color of their skin or the language they speak. In spite of some of his negative experiences, he had made friends with some of the African American students in the New England school ("Some of them is very cool and very nice").

Schools are expected to take the major responsibility for helping children confront these difficult issues, but often they do not. Given the changing U.S. demographics and the large influx of new immigrants, the rivalry and negative relationships among different groups of immigrants and native-born students will likely be felt even more in the coming years. Interethnic hostility needs to be confronted directly through changes in curriculum and other school policies and practices. Students such as Vinh clearly need this kind of leadership to help them make sense of their new world.

Reflect on This Case Study

1. Does Vinh's definition of "educated people" differ from yours? If so, how?
2. Vinh resented the false praise he received from some of his teachers. Some students, however, seem to need more praise than others. What does this situation imply for teaching in culturally diverse schools?
3. Vinh had trouble asking his teachers and counselors for help. Knowing this, what can schools do to help students like Vinh?
4. In light of Vinh's interethnic experiences and his perceptions of other cultures, what can schools do to help students from different ethnic and racial groups understand one another better?

Rebecca Florentina

And all we can do is hope to educate teachers because there's kids in middle school getting beat up in the hallways because of it, you know?

Rebecca Florentina, 17 and a senior in high school, wore her green hair very short.[1] Sporting pierced ears and pride rings, from time to time she also wore a T-shirt that said "I'm not a dyke, but my girlfriend is." Rebecca identified as butch lesbian and "came out" in her high school five months before she was interviewed.[2] It wasn't a big public announcement, according to Rebecca. Instead, she came out when she and her girlfriend Stephie started going out. She said, "We would just walk up to somebody and say, 'This is my girlfriend now.' So that's how I came out. I didn't come out like, 'Hey, I'm lesbian!' I came out as 'Hey, this is my girlfriend. Now figure it out.'" Rebecca was just as direct about everything else in her life.

As one of two children (her sister was a sophomore in college) living with a divorced mother, Rebecca appreciated her mother's open-mindedness about her identity, her grades, her decisions about college, and her life in general. "Do whatever you want as long as you are happy" is the advice she said that her mother always gave her.

A life-long resident of West Blueridge, a small city in Massachusetts known for its liberal attitudes about sexuality, Rebecca didn't contemplate ever moving. She felt safe there, she said, especially as a lesbian. She could hold hands with her girlfriend as they walked down the street and nobody noticed, or at least they didn't say anything. For almost a year, she had been involved in Rainbow Youth, a place where LGBT youths went to talk and socialize, a place where, according to Rebecca, she could hang out with her "second family kind of friends."

Rebecca said she also felt safe in her high school, which she characterized as "mostly accepting." A large comprehensive high school with nearly a thousand students, the school is primarily White and middle class: About 10 percent of the students are Latino, and fewer are African American. According to Rebecca, most of the graduates from her high school went to college.

Rebecca was particularly close to a several teachers in her high school because they had been great supporters of the Gay/Straight Alliance (GSA) student group. This club, which had been in existence for several years, is just one of an estimated 200 throughout Massachusetts formed as a result of the Massachusetts' Governor's Commission on Gay and Lesbian Youth. The movement has spread to many other states: According to the Gay, Lesbian, and Straight Education Network (GLSEN), there are now over 4,000 GSA groups around the country.[3] The Massachusetts Commission was formed by then-governor William Weld in reaction to a federal report on the epidemic of youth suicide among lesbian, gay, transgender, bisexual, and questioning youths. An alarming statistic unearthed by the 1989 federal report was that one-third of all youth suicides were carried out by gay and lesbian youths.[4] Feeling safe in school for LGBT youth has been largely influenced by the presence of GSAs. One large study found that LGBT students in schools with GSAs were three times as likely to feel safe being "out" at school and were much less likely to hear homophobic remarks, compared to students in schools without GSAs.[5]

The Massachusetts' Governor's Commission issued its landmark report in 1993.[6] The first of its kind in the nation issued by a state's department of education, it made many recommendations for making schools safe and welcoming for gay and lesbian youths. Four of the recommendations were adopted by the Massachusetts Board of Education:

1. Schools are encouraged to develop policies protecting gay and lesbian students from harassment, violence, and discrimination.
2. Schools are encouraged to offer training to school personnel in violence prevention and suicide prevention.
3. Schools are encouraged to offer school-based support groups for gay, lesbian, and heterosexual students.
4. Schools are encouraged to provide school-based counseling for family members of gay and lesbian students.

Also, in Massachusetts, students cannot be discriminated against on the basis of sexual orientation if they want to start a GSA, and schools must respond to all requests for the formation and funding of GSAs as they do to requests to form other extracurricular clubs. As a result of these recommendations, many high schools have received training and support for both students and staff members, and they have started to make a positive difference in the climate of high schools throughout the state. The GSA in Rebecca's school was quite active, providing gay and lesbian students with a nurturing environment at the high school. Unfortunately, several years later in 2002, Jane Swift, the acting governor of Massachusetts, eliminated funding for this program due, she said, to severe budget constraints and a bad economy. Given this sociopolitical climate, it is no surprise that an obvious theme in Rebecca's interview was the *mixed messages* she received about safety. It was clear that she was always on guard and that the greater safety she so yearned for was at times elusive. Other themes that emerged were Rebecca's *sense of responsibility to educate others,* her *perseverance and personal motivation,* and her *"invisibility" as an Italian American.*

Mixed Messages

I wouldn't want to be anywhere else. I feel safe here. I feel exceptionally safe here. I take pride in West Blueridge, so it's my community, I guess. It's where I feel the safest. It is what I love. I wouldn't dare move somewhere else. I love it here, but I also don't feel as safe when I go other places, no matter where I go. So even the town down the road, you know? I'll think twice about holding my girlfriend's hand on the streets there. But when I do it in West Blueridge, there's no questions asked. We do it. I mean, who would want to leave a place that makes us feel that safe? There's no fear.

I just think that because it's West Blueridge we get treated so much better than people in other schools. I mean it's obvious, you know? People have gotten killed. [In other places] the comments are like, "Go somewhere else." And people doing double takes and looking at us and giving us weird faces.

I'm in the school's GSA [Gay-Straight Alliance], and that's one reason, you know? The school has a GSA. On a regular basis, there's probably six who go every Friday, which is when we meet, but there's another six or seven who come whenever they can. Not all the time. There's no trans people as far as we know. I think there's two guys, and the rest are female. Our GSA is having a speaker come in. It's an optional thing. We couldn't make it mandatory. If anybody wants to come, there's going to be a speaker. We're doing a whole week on gay rights and awareness. It's our Awareness Week. It's going to be during the school. So we'll have rainbow voices. We'll have pins, things like that. We're doing "101 good things about being gay" kind of thing. We're not doing health class–type things. We're doing positive outlook. We're not saying, "This percentage are into drugs; this percent have AIDS." It's kind of like all the good things. We're just making it a happy time. . . . I don't think [any parents have objected]. I think, in West Blueridge, if you don't approve of the lifestyle, you don't say it because you're going to be offending a heck of a lot of people.

We've gone around and asked teachers to put "Safe Zone" stickers on their door[s]. The majority of them actually have them on their doors. And the teachers don't mind. There's a couple that are kind of iffy. [But] everybody's like "It's West Blueridge." That's all you have to say, so you don't really get too much [criticism]. . . .

I have a psychology teacher who says "heterosexually speaking," so he's not implying that everybody's straight. He's the only person who does it. It made me feel so much safer when I had a different teacher say, in his class the first day, "There will be no swearing, there will be no slurs like 'faggot' or whatever in my class." I have two teachers in four years of high school that have ever said something like that, and that was both this year. I have my band director who says, "All you should be in this room is happy. And leave everything outside. This is a safe place. Let's be happy. Let's play music."

[When we "came out"] I don't think we had a bad reaction. My friends were awesome. I didn't lose a single one, you know? So it was pretty cool.

[In the high school], the climate is like, if you're generally like everybody else, you're fine. But if you're totally opposite of what everybody else looks like and acts, you'll get shoved into a locker or something, or told to shut up. But when I walk down the halls, it's fine. There are some groups of people that, you know, you'll walk more quickly by. I don't like to call them cliques, but there are people who congregate in little sections of the hallway. But who doesn't, you know? I do it, too.

But our school is, like, it's West Blueridge, so it's accepting. That's what I like about it. Most of the teachers are great. It's very open.

[Students] never say slurs. [They don't say "that's disgusting" or anything like that], but you can tell they're thinking it. You can just tell. And we're, like, okay. But that doesn't . . . that happens like once every two weeks. It's not a big deal, you know? And we're not going to stop being who we are.

I'm in band, and everybody there knows about me and my girlfriend because we're both in band. And they're all cool with it. And if they're not, they don't say anything. But, like, I wear my sweatshirt all the time. And I'll be reluctant to wear this [t-shirt that says "I'm not a dyke, but my girlfriend is"] in the halls; like, if I'm walking in the halls and some guy who's got his hat twisted up all weird and baggy pants, I'm gonna be reluctant to do that, I think, alone. Because if I go in the bathroom or something, I don't wear this shirt when I'm alone in school.

I don't feel totally safe. But I feel like I have the privilege of feeling more safe than everybody else does. So I'm thankful for what I have, and I just take precautions because that's just me.

You hear ["faggot"] and, like, you can't do anything about it really. It gets said; I probably hear it once every week. I don't know if the teachers hear it. Some girl said, "Oh you faggot" in one of my classes. But I don't know if he heard or not. . . . I think if you had to hold your tongue in class without saying that stuff, it would help a little bit. But when you get out in the halls, it's a totally different atmosphere. People act basically the opposite of how they act in class. It's, like, second nature, you know? They kind of just say it all the time. It makes me angry. I mean, there's nothing you can do, really. I don't think they could do anything. You're not going to stop the kids from doing something they want to do. If I'm in the hall and some other kid's in the hall, and there's no teachers, he can hit me if he wants. Or she.

I think that's all we can do, and I don't think for some people it will help because if you have this one mind-set, you're not going to change it if you don't want to.

[*What advice would you give to a new lesbian student in your school?*] "Join the GSA!" Here are my friends. They're nice, you know? You'll definitely have accepting people who will never turn anybody away. That's why I love them so much. (*pause*) I don't know. Just don't broadcast it, you know? I think we go as far as any straight couple, speaking of myself and my girlfriend. But we don't make out in the halls. That's our personal whatever . . . we don't want to do that. But I don't think we would even . . . because we would get crap for it. I'd just say, "Be who you want to be, and if they don't like it, that's their problem." But most of the people won't mind it.

Educating Others

[I want teachers to know that LGBT students] are just like everybody else. I mean, everybody sees it as somebody who's different and not normal. But it's just your sexuality. I don't identify myself as, like, "Hi, I'm Rebecca and I'm a lesbian." It's, like, this is me, and this is my sexuality. That's as far as I'm going to go with it. I mean, I'll wear a shirt or something. I'm proud of who I am.

It's the teacher who wants to learn from the students, and not just the students who learn from them, that makes a great teacher, and I love that. I would fire the teachers who yelled at their students because I have teachers who refuse to do that, and the environment is much better. Patience is just taught by being patient yourself. And (*pause*) I have such great teachers right now I can't think of anything bad [to say about them].

My girlfriend and I were mentioned in a newspaper article about gay and lesbian students. And my history teacher, who is just this guy who goes skiing, kind of a jocky guy, said, "That was a great article. I'm happy about you guys." I like the teachers who pay attention to what you're doing, no matter who you are. They're, like, "I saw you in the paper." They're not just there to give you a grade, like, "Here's a test." They actually get involved, not to the point of obsessed, but just enough. It was a great feeling because now I know he doesn't discriminate against me, and he accepts me and he thinks I'm a good person. That's incredible to have.

My psychology teacher's class . . . I'm the third [lesbian student], and we've opened his eyes. Now he's this amazing person. Before he was ignorant. Now he's incredible.

And all we can do is hope to educate teachers because there's kids in middle school getting beat up in the hallways because of it, you know? I think with high school, it's just more accepting, and when you go to middle school before high school, it's awful for some reason. Kids are just more active.

The health class, at least in the high school, looks at same sex whatever or queer whatever in a derogative way. The curriculum says, "Here's these lesbian people, and we should accept them," something like that. It's not, like, "Here's the great things about being gay." It's, like, "Here's all the things that happen and that people think of them." And I don't even think it's that accepting. It's just, like, "There are people who are gay." And that's the whole curriculum.

So I think if you want to educate people better, it's get the health teachers to put better curriculum for teaching about same sex, transgender, anything, you know? Because it's looked at in a negative way instead of a positive way.

The psychology book refers to obese people as abnormal. Our teacher actually commented on that and said it was awful. But we don't have enough money for new books. So we can't get new ones. It makes a lot of rude comments. There's two things about homosexuality in the psychology book. One is we don't know if it's a choice or not, and I don't know what the other one is. You know, "There are these people" and that's it for psychology. It's sad.

I came out to my psychology class to make an educational thing out of it. Prior to that, they knew me . . . they're not my friends, but they've known about me. And then I told them this, so how can they judge me? I've got a lot of kids who—when my psychology teacher goes, "your little friend"—turn around and make a face at me and say [whispering] "Why can't he just say lesbian?" And I never had that before, and I think it's great. And I have people leaning across from me in the class say [whispering] "My mother's a lesbian." And I don't think they would do that without [my] coming out. And I think it's great that they can tell somebody. If I can help them, I think that's what I want to do. So if this makes things more normal for them, and more commonplace, then do it, you know?

My English teacher lets the kids read books that are very liberal and very queer friendly [for example, with lesbian characters]. And I think that's great . . . or a poem that's written by a lesbian author . . . and giving kids books . . . you know? But he's one [teacher] out of a lot.

[Advice for teachers?] Be open-minded, I think, and be inclusive of everybody. It's hard to be politically correct in everything, every second, in every word you say. But there are some teachers you just don't want to approach sometimes because they are very closed.

Perseverance and Motivation

I like the fact that my mother said, "Do whatever you want as long as you are happy." Because even though I kind of messed up in high school and middle school and couldn't get into a really great college, I still was self-motivated, and I found it in myself to do what I wanted to do, instead of her telling me what to do. So I respect that. I think that's a great way to raise a kid.

[In elementary school] behavior-wise [I was good]. Interested in work, no. I wasn't interested in working hard. That didn't happen until later on in high school. That was always my issue. I was always in for recess because I didn't do my work.

I'm in ensembles outside of school, and I do all that. The school doesn't offer very much music education, so I kind of find my places elsewhere. Since that's what I'm interested in, rather than playing sports, I have to find [it] somewhere else.

Right now I'm looking at college. The only reason I started doing well in school was because I went to the state university and I heard their band. I realized that I wanted to do that. So in order for me to get there, I would have to pick up my academics. [I realized this] at the very beginning of my junior year. That was my fuel for getting through the next two years. If you want to play music, you need to do this. It's not me necessarily interested in academics because I'm not. I just have a different mind-set, you know? Artist-type people have that. And they'd rather be doing something else. Intellectual people would rather be sitting there with their books. And so, I see it as a way to do what I want, so I have to get through it in order to do it.

I think I did it on my own. I mean, if you go in the guidance office, they're like, "Take the SATs, and do good in school, bye." Whatever happens, happens. Teachers at least in my high school, you get whatever grade you want. They don't care; if you get an F, you get an F. They're not saying, "You need to go to college. And you need to do this. Here's how much effort you put into this." I got scared about not being able to go to college. I knew I wasn't going to have much of a future if I didn't. So I scared myself.

And I did it all myself. I can honestly tell you that cuz I did. And nobody told me I would get into the state university, but I did. Nobody told me I could get into the department of music, and I'm on the waiting list for that. I wasn't rejected. I did it myself because I wanted to. The school—it didn't help. The school says, "Do whatever you want. We're not responsible for you in that way. Get whatever grades you want. Let your parents deal with it." They're not, like, "Here's what has to happen." I don't know if they have the time, though. I don't know if I want to blame them for that. They have so many kids, you know?

[I'm successful] because I had a guidance counselor tell me, "There's no way in hell" basically—she didn't say that, but you could see it in her eyes—"You're never going to make it into the state university. You don't even have a shot. Go to community college." You could read it in her face. She was, like, "I don't think this is going to happen here." And from day one of junior year I said, "I'm going!"

[Recently] I called the admissions office, and they sent me a letter not rejecting me from the music department, which meant that I had to get into the university first, in order for them to send me that letter, so it means I got in. I haven't got my acceptance letter, but I basically know they're not messing with me. They sent that because I got in. And the second thing is that I wasn't supposed to walk into the music department at the state university, which is very, very good. And to be able to pull it off and be worthy of them at least putting me on the waiting list because they can only take 12 people. They only took, like, five because they already had a certain amount in their studio. I wasn't supposed to do that. I've been playing for three and a half years. I've been playing seriously for nine months. And I did that, and I think that's cool, and I did it all by myself, and that's why [I'm proud] (laughs).

As my psychology teacher puts it, I'm very self-actualized. He said I'm one of the people he's ever met at my age who's so self-actualized. This shouldn't be happening. I should be conforming to everybody else. He admires me and tells me I'm great because I can be who I want to be and not care what anybody else thinks. I like that because I'm happier because of it. Everybody else is hiding something.

Ethnic Invisibility

[*How do you identify racially or culturally?*] White, or what are you talking about?

Well, my culture, I mean, I'm Italian. I don't know if you want that. I mean, that's important to me. It's important to me and my mother, and my grandfather. [But it's not important in my school]. [*Is there an Italian student group in your school?*] No! (*laughs*) Definitely not! You're not going to find something like that. (*pause*) I wish there was.

The only thing I can tell you is that when my psychology teacher told me—I told him that I was Italian—he told me he loved me because he's Italian! I mean he'll speak Italian in class.

[For holidays], we'll just make the basic eggplant parmesan, stuffed shells, or mani-cotti [*pronounced in a distinctly Italian accent*]. It's fun. My mom's into that.

My grandfather was a sheepherder in Italy for, like, seven years. [I admire] my grandfa-ther because he was an orphan. Both of his parents died when he was, like, three. Put in an orphanage, never got a formal education, but still remained happy and healthy. He's still doing construction work at age 82. He made the best out of what he had. I'll always admire somebody for that. And he loves being Italian. He loves everything about his culture.

He's the only one in my family who would say, "I like your [green] hair." He's 82, and he's telling me that.

Commentary

Being gay or lesbian in school today is not as daunting a challenge as it once was. For one, more people are writing about what it means to be gay in school (as either a teacher or a student), and there are far more resources than ever.[7] Also, since the 1990s, there has been more legal recourse to counteract the discrim-ination faced by LGBT students.[8] This does not mean, however, that it is easy, and it is clear in Rebecca's case study that, no matter how "safe" and how "accepting" a school or even an entire town might be, there is ample reason for LGBT students to feel insecure or even in danger. For example, the Gay, Lesbian, and Straight Education Network (GLSEN), in its most recent report on safety in U.S. schools, found that nearly nine out of ten LGBT students experience harassment in school. On the other hand, they also reported that supportive school staff members, more inclusive policies and practices, and Gay-Straight Alliances all made a positive dif-ference, both in creating a safe environment and in promoting higher achievement among LGBT students.[9]

Rebecca's inconsistent comments about the use of slurs in her school are a good indication of mixed messages about safety. Although she felt quite privileged compared to LGBT students in other places, she was still careful about whom she came out to. She appreciated the efforts of some of her teachers to support gay and lesbian students and the GSA, but she was also clear that some teachers were "iffy" about supporting them. Although she mentioned that most people in her school were fairly nonchalant about LGBT students, she was aware of the strong negative feelings some of them had about gays and lesbians. Even in describing what was a relatively painless "coming out," Rebecca was quick to point out that she didn't lose *even one friend* as a result—something she wouldn't have to point out if she had "come out as Italian," for example. So, in spite of her constant references to "It's

West Blueridge, so it's accepting," Rebecca would tell a new student not to "broadcast it." Clearly, she knew that, in many ways, it was still unsafe to be a lesbian.

Related to the issue of LGBT identity in school was Rebecca's commitment to educate others. Ironically, Rebecca had reversed roles with some of her teachers, becoming in essence their teacher, at least as far as LGBT issues are concerned. One teacher, she said, was "ignorant," but he had become "incredible" and "amazing" because she and other lesbian students had been able to reach him. Although it is admirable that Rebecca had taken on this role, it is also an indication of how far schools and teachers still need to go in understanding LGBT students. It is reminiscent of the role, often unwelcome, played by students of color who feel they must educate their teachers about their identities.

Calling herself "self-actualized," Rebecca was clearly proud of herself and of what she had accomplished. She got into the college of her choice by her own wits and determination without relying on teachers, guidance counselors, or anybody else to help her. In fact, it was precisely because of a guidance counselor's skepticism about her ability to get into college due to her grades that Rebecca had decided to prove the counselor wrong.

Rebecca was confused when asked about her cultural identity. "White, or what are you talking about?" was her initial response. Unlike Rebecca, most young people of color immediately identify in racial or cultural terms. In this, Rebecca is typical of many other White students who have not had to identify racially because they are perceived as "the norm." Nonetheless, as quickly became apparent later in the interview, Rebecca was proud of her Italian heritage and wished that it, too, could be part of her school experience, demonstrating that being safe relates not just to sexual orientation but to all aspects of identity. Rebecca's interview, however, also underlined the complicated nature of ethnic identity. Half Italian and half Polish, Rebecca identified strongly as Italian; her sister, however, identified as Polish. In Rebecca's words, "She took to the Polish side, and I took the Italian side."

It is imperative that teachers develop a more nuanced understanding of culture in terms of sexual orientation, ethnicity, race, social class, disability, language, and other markers of identity. As in the case of Rebecca, it is evident that, as our schools become more aware of the presence of LGBT students, we have a great deal to learn about being responsive to a large number of students who, until recently, have felt the need to remain "in the closet." Young people with courage and willpower like Rebecca are making a difference in many schools. As more teachers become advocates for all students, we will not need to count as much on students like Rebecca to learn to do what is right.

Reflect on This Case Study

1. What responsibilities do teachers have to their LGBT students? Does this responsibility extend to elementary schools as well? Why or why not? What do you or what would you say to people who say that LGBT issues have no place in the school?
2. What are the advantages of a GSA? If you teach at a secondary school, does it have a GSA? If not, would you consider starting one? Why or why not?
3. Do you know of any LGBT students in your school? What is your perception of how they do academically? How do they feel? How do you know?

6

Linguistic Diversity in U.S. Classrooms

Language is intimately linked to culture. It is a primary means by which people express their cultural values and the lens through which they view the world. It should come as no surprise, then, that the language practices that children bring to school also invariably affect how and what they learn. Yet in multicultural education, native language issues are frequently overlooked or downplayed.

> *"Being Latino, it's good 'cause a lot of people tell me it's a good advantage for me to know two languages. I like that."*
>
> —Alicia Montejo, interviewee

This situation is apparent in, for instance, the lack of terms concerning linguistic diversity in the field. Terms that describe discrimination based on race, gender, and class are part of our general vocabulary (*racism, sexism, ethnocentrism, anti-Semitism, classism*), but until a couple of decades ago, no such term existed for language discrimination, although this does not mean that language discrimination did not exist. Tove Skutnabb-Kangas, by coining the term *linguicism* to refer to discrimination based specifically on language, helped to make the issue more visible.[1]

This chapter explores the influence that language differences may have on student learning. How teachers and schools view language differences; whether and how they use these differences as a resource in the classroom; and different approaches to teaching language-minority students, that is, those whose first language is not English, are all addressed in the discussion that follows.

Definitions and Demographics

There are numerous terms to identify students who speak a language other than English as their native language. The term currently in vogue is *English Language Learners (ELLs)*. This term has become popular as a substitute for the more contentious *bilingual* (more on the controversies surrounding bilingual education later in the chapter), although *bilingual* itself was a misnomer because most students to whom this

label was applied were not really bilingual but rather *monolingual* in their native language, or *becoming bilingual* in their native language and English. Some students are *multilingual* when they arrive to school, but they have not yet added English to their multiple fluencies. The terms *ELL* or *ESL* (English as a second language), on the other hand, focus only on students' need to acquire English rather than on the fact that they already possess language, although it may not be English.

A decade or two ago, the most common term was *limited English proficient (LEP)*, an unfortunate acronym to which many people objected; it has now been largely abandoned, although it is still in use in some federal government documents. Another term used for this population is *language minority students*, which reflects the fact that they speak a minority language in the United States. Although no term is completely accurate or appropriate, in this text we have chosen to use either *English language learners* (or *ELLs*) or *language minority*

Monica Hampe, Connor Sheehan, Tyler Levesque, Marissa Dakin in Amanda Held's art class, Pembroke Community Middle School. Pembroke, Massachusetts. *Self-portraits.* Ink drawing, 2009.

students to refer to students who are learning English as a second or additional language.

Who are the ELLs to whom we refer in this chapter? In the United States, the population of those who speak a language other than English as their native language has increased dramatically in the past several decades. In 2010, the U.S. Census Bureau reported that the number of people age 5 and older who spoke a language other than English at home had increased by 140 percent in the previous 30 years, currently reaching 20 percent of the entire population, while the nation's overall population grew only by 34 percent.[2] The number and variety of languages spoken in the nation is over 380—from Urdu to Punjabi to Yup'ik—although by far the largest number (about 60 percent) speak Spanish. Table 6.1 enumerates the most widely spoken languages in the nation.

TABLE 6.1   Detailed Languages Spoken at Home and Ability to Speak English for the Population 5 Years and Over for the United States

	Release Date: April 2010			
	Number of speakers	Margin of Error[1]	Spoke English less than "Very Well"	Margin of Error[1]
Population 5 years and over	280,564,877	7,708	24,252,429	67,280
Spoke only English at home	225,488,799	83,368	(X)	(X)
Spoke a language other than English at home	55,76,078	81,124	24,252,429	67,280
Spoke a language other than English at home	55,076,078	81,124	24,252,429	67,280
Spanish and Spanish Creole	34,183,747	52,633	16,120,772	54,213
Spanish	34,183,622	52,636	16,120,749	54,210
Latino	125	98	23	38
Other Indo-European Languages	10,347,377	49,301	3,405,878	26,398
French	1,358,816	14,743	292,422	5,842
French	1,304,758	14,891	284,809	5,734
Patois	28,475	2,268	4,835	982
Cajun	25,583	1,550	2,778	463
French Creole	621,135	13,313	273,888	7,401
Italian	807,010	10,810	231,736	5,267
Portuguese	678,334	11,600	289,899	7,246
Portuguese	676,963	11,509	289,771	7,251
Papia Mentae	1,371	673	128	109
German	1,120,670	12,812	196,957	4,113
German	1,119,963	12,808	196,929	4,111
Luxembourgian	707	237	28	37
Yiddish	162,511	5,616	50,957	2,997
Other West Germanic Languages	269,600	7,680	62,711	3,558
Pennsylvania Dutch	117,547	5,840	38,494	2,884
Dutch	132,191	4,206	22,358	1,715
Afrikaans	18,943	1,653	1,781	384
Frisian	919	324	78	60
Scandinavian Languages	132,956	3,989	17,474	1,384
Swedish	56,713	2,979	6,842	856
Danish	29,728	2,126	4,025	641
Norwegian	41,197	2,287	5,781	655
Icelandic	5,170	849	798	476
Faroese	148	100	28	47

Release Date: April 2010				
	Number of speakers	Margin of Error[1]	Spoke English less than "Very Well"	Margin of Error[1]
Population 5 years and over	280,564,877	7,708	24,252,429	67,280
Greek	**340,028**	**9,204**	**90,360**	**3,633**
Russian	**846,233**	**13,514**	**430,850**	**8,004**
Polish	**632,362**	**12,763**	**274,693**	**6,910**
Serbo-Croatian Languages	**273,729**	**9,634**	**115,165**	**5,050**
Serbocroatian	152,331	6,705	71,216	3,743
Croatian	57,565	3,663	19,912	1,626
Serbian	63,833	4,113	24,037	2,239
Other Slavic Languages	**318,051**	**8,552**	**122,058**	**4,305**
Bielorussian	1,363	436	716	257
Ukrainian	142,711	6,414	68,487	3,641
Czech	55,382	2,336	13,253	1,228
Lusatian	189	133	78	113
Slovak	32,227	2,364	8,666	1,063
Bulgarian	57,016	3,514	21,129	1,659
Macedonian	22,134	2,294	7,715	1,185
Slovene	7,029	988	2,014	549
Armenian	**220,922**	**7,558**	**98,041**	**4,096**
Persian	**359,176**	**9,536**	**137,765**	**4,990**
Hindi	**531,313**	**10,495**	**114,070**	**4,656**
Gujarati	**301,658**	**8,943**	**108,352**	**5,093**
Urdu	**335,213**	**9,621**	**102,364**	**4,602**
Other Indic Languages	**619,954**	**14,103**	**238,583**	**7,599**
India n.e.c.[2]	81,125	5,875	29,167	2,688
Bengali	190,090	6,733	79,837	3,695
Panjabi	208,387	7,698	91,416	4,614
Marathi	54,223	2,599	7,610	1,055
Bihari	151	144	115	129
Rajasthani	464	286	103	80
Oriya	4,790	845	1,013	401
Assamese	1,215	449	56	56
Kashmiri	833	368	202	151
Nepali	34,139	2,990	14,857	2,047
Sindhi	6,907	1,034	1,398	423
Pakistan n.e.c.[2]	13,092	2,184	5,560	1,334
Sinhalese	22,278	2,330	6,904	1,200
Romany	2,260	775	345	216
Other Indo-European Languages	**417,706**	**10,116**	**157,533**	**5,868**
Jamaican Creole	19,872	3,141	5,870	2,324
Krio	6,900	1,358	1,839	631
Hawaiian Pidgin	108	101	(B)	—

(Continued)

TABLE 6.1   Continued

	Release Date: April 2010			
	Number of speakers	Margin of Error[1]	Spoke English less than "Very Well"	Margin of Error[1]
Population 5 years and over	280,564,877	7,708	24,252,429	67,280
Pidgin	2,527	691	390	268
Gullah	352	361	18	32
Saramacca	112	112	46	71
Catalonian	1,917	505	292	158
Romanian	146,840	6,050	58,351	3,126
Rhaeto-romanic	39	64	(B)	—
Welsh	2,452	517	262	135
Irish Gaelic	22,279	1,670	3,455	629
Scottic Gaelic	1,445	353	31	33
Albanian	125,220	6,363	57,358	3,605
Lithuanian	42,306	2,545	14,331	1,473
Lettish	16,149	1,622	3,794	687
Pashto	15,788	2,400	5,849	1,044
Kurdish	12,982	2,291	5,564	1,050
Balochi	268	376	18	30
Tadzhik	150	134	65	80
Asian and Pacific Island Languages	**8,267,977**	**30,947**	**4,041,963**	**24,276**
Chinese	**2,455,583**	**20,609**	**1,370,874**	**12,506**
Chinese	1,554,505	16,654	848,358	11,270
Hakka	1,086	386	537	251
Kan, Hsiang	291	342	(B)	—
Cantonese	437,301	10,320	273,042	7,005
Mandarin	381,121	10,132	199,507	6,442
Fuchow	2,671	730	2,282	630
Formosan	76,131	3,306	45,426	2,302
Wu	2,477	557	1,722	460
Japanese	**457,033**	**7,972**	**211,017**	**5,822**
Korean	**1,048,173**	**13,449**	**610,340**	**8,799**
Mon-Khmer, Cambodian	**182,387**	**6,650**	**98,764**	**4,369**
Hmong	**185,401**	**5,616**	**88,556**	**3,655**
Thai	**139,845**	**4,572**	**72,998**	**3,157**
Laotian	**147,865**	**6,238**	**74,772**	**3,481**
Vietnamese	**1,204,454**	**17,809**	**731,555**	**12,113**
Other Asian Languages	**644,363**	**11,834**	**192,046**	**5,903**
Kazakh	1,006	513	404	276
Kirghiz	131	135	53	60
Karachay	698	331	248	193
Uighur	3,190	911	2,069	797
Azerabaijani	1,282	458	492	218
Turkish	107,405	5,588	44,045	3,103
Turkmen	221	261	14	23

Release Date: April 2010				
	Number of speakers	Margin of Error[1]	Spoke English less than "Very Well"	Margin of Error[1]
Population 5 years and over	280,564,877	7,708	24,252,429	67,280
Mongolian	8,430	1,528	5,164	1,055
Tungus	326	271	198	219
Dravidian	2,146	708	274	189
Gondi	76	64	(B)	—
Telugu	171,495	5,658	35,703	2,040
Kannada	35,902	2,307	5,229	964
Malayalam	112,378	4,849	35,254	2,399
Tamil	130,731	5,047	22,220	2,150
Munda	2,334	771	587	339
Tibetan	9,764	1,679	6,096	1,364
Burmese	35,281	3,910	22,295	3,121
Karen	3,924	1,182	3,596	1,134
Kachin	178	154	109	127
Miao-yao, Mien	17,421	1,974	7,996	1,140
Paleo-siberian	44	32	(B)	—
Tagalog	**1,444,324**	**16,857**	**455,975**	**9,514**
Other Pacific Island Languages	**358,549**	**9,464**	**135,066**	**4,853**
Indonesian	60,657	3,805	28,111	2,145
Achinese	32	53	(B)	—
Balinese	272	159	108	70
Cham	891	479	376	262
Javanese	441	218	268	178
Malagasy	935	404	243	196
Malay	12,440	1,566	4,191	804
Bisayan	23,644	2,185	8,981	1,491
Sebuano	10,027	1,190	3,321	638
Pangasinan	2,144	648	1,088	441
Ilocano	76,896	4,252	40,764	2,825
Bikol	812	347	210	121
Pampangan	5,432	1,226	1,884	564
Micronesian	5,514	1,397	3,035	951
Carolinian	187	236	14	21
Chamorro	17,985	1,664	2,856	573
Gilbertese	173	124	102	100
Kusaiean	1,056	564	526	360
Marshallese	10,739	1,930	5,672	1,329
Mokilese	448	282	205	196
Mortlockese	40	63	40	63
Palau	4,153	1,175	1,491	590
Ponapean	2,347	720	981	393
Trukese	5,434	1,465	2,728	801

(Continued)

TABLE 6.1 Continued

	Number of speakers	Margin of Error[1]	Spoke English less than "Very Well"	Margin of Error[1]
Release Date: April 2010				
Population 5 years and over	280,564,877	7,708	24,252,429	67,280
Ulithean	39	71	39	71
Woleai-ulithi	51	62	(B)	—
Yapese	795	392	282	186
Melanesian	973	369	464	304
Polynesian	723	468	163	141
Samoan	57,368	3,813	14,396	1,328
Tongan	26,322	2,865	8,411	1,251
Niuean	17	28	(B)	—
Tokelauan	290	275	193	208
Fijian	3,701	987	1,226	400
Marquesan	605	500	392	412
Rarotongan	124	137	(B)	—
Maori	659	278	115	85
Nukuoro	141	154	(B)	—
Hawaiian	24,042	2,094	2,190	405
All Other Languages	**2,276,977**	**29,341**	**683,816**	**12,172**
Navajo	**170,822**	**4,710**	**39,724**	**2,566**
Other Native North American Languages	**203,127**	**4,352**	**32,140**	**1,874**
Aleut	1,236	374	235	134
Pacific Gulf Yupik	8	13	(B)	—
Eskimo	2,168	391	552	164
Inupik	5,580	616	1,453	254
St Lawrence Island Yupik	993	256	392	171
Yupik	18,626	927	6,896	606
Algonquian	288	146	57	65
Arapaho	1,087	366	13	22
Atsina	45	35	(B)	—
Blackfoot	1,970	577	217	149
Cheyenne	2,399	567	77	62
Cree	951	392	83	66
Delaware	146	123	37	67
Fox	727	195	161	143
Kickapoo	1,141	293	476	160
Menomini	946	381	375	248
French Cree	75	71	53	66
Miami	168	275	85	139
Micmac	230	159	25	28
Ojibwa	6,986	867	788	277
Ottawa	312	174	34	43
Passamaquoddy	982	254	60	46

Release Date: April 2010				
	Number of speakers	Margin of Error[1]	Spoke English less than "Very Well"	Margin of Error[1]
Population 5 years and over	280,564,877	7,708	24,252,429	67,280
Penobscot	144	98	8	13
Abnaki	86	89	(B)	—
Potawatomi	824	271	82	67
Shawnee	321	203	20	35
Yurok	491	387	8	17
Kutenai	200	124	65	70
Makah	176	96	53	51
Kwakiuti	85	62	21	32
Nootka	10	18	(B)	—
Clallam	146	143	2	5
Coeur D'alene	174	126	(B)	—
Columbia	17	27	(B)	—
Cowlitz	110	179	91	146
Salish	1,233	362	282	178
Okanogan	284	215	31	51
Puget Sound Salish	207	119	99	103
Quinault	128	202	(B)	—
Haida	118	72	23	38
Athapascan	1,627	351	318	148
Ahtena	18	27	(B)	—
Ingalit	127	164	(B)	—
Koyukon	58	53	7	11
Kuchin	1,217	422	302	189
Tanaina	11	24	(B)	—
Chasta Costa	84	101	5	10
Hupa	174	175	(B)	—
Apache	14,012	1,527	495	185
Kiowa	1,274	466	122	72
Tlingit	1,026	277	84	55
Mountain Maidu	319	176	22	38
Northwest Maidu	32	53	32	53
Sierra Miwok	216	261	(B)	—
Nomlaki	38	49	(B)	—
Wintun	24	26	(B)	—
Foothill North Yokuts	407	204	111	113
Tachi	45	74	26	43
Santiam	50	81	(B)	—
Siuslaw	6	9	(B)	—
Klamath	95	73	26	44
Nez Perce	942	329	114	83
Sahaptian	1,654	589	102	67

(Continued)

TABLE 6.1 Continued

	Number of speakers	Margin of Error[1]	Spoke English less than "Very Well"	Margin of Error[1]
Release Date: April 2010				
Population 5 years and over	280,564,877	7,708	24,252,429	67,280
Upper Chinook	58	54	6	10
Tsimshian	68	66	(B)	—
Achumawi	68	61	(B)	—
Atsugewi	15	26	(B)	—
Karok	700	373	38	44
Pomo	648	318	96	95
Washo	227	152	22	30
Cocomaricopa	44	49	10	16
Mohave	330	193	21	25
Yuma	172	97	55	59
Diegueno	228	138	139	123
Delta River Yuman	483	191	110	98
Havasupai	90	101	47	79
Walapai	458	197	22	19
Yavapai	139	90	(B)	—
Chumash	39	69	39	69
Tonkawa	29	36	(B)	—
Yuchi	4	10	(B)	—
Crow	3,962	523	261	202
Hidatsa	806	341	36	38
Mandan	104	96	40	57
Dakota	18,804	1,363	1,855	402
Chiwere	60	52	(B)	—
Winnebago	1,340	357	84	67
Kansa	7	10	(B)	—
Omaha	457	192	9	13
Osage	260	153	53	59
Ponca	131	96	9	14
Alabama	165	88	33	39
Choctaw	10,368	1,180	2,430	582
Mikasuki	188	131	43	63
Koasati	59	53	4	8
Muskogee	5,072	708	995	226
Chetemacha	89	64	19	32
Keres	13,073	1,181	810	234
Iroquois	76	71	(B)	—
Mohawk	1,423	494	166	99
Oneida	527	335	309	295
Onondaga	239	180	7	14
Cayuga	6	12	(B)	—
Seneca	1,353	446	152	97
Tuscarora	179	152	18	27

Release Date: April 2010			
	Number of speakers	Margin of Error[1]	Spoke English less than "Very Well"	Margin of Error[1]
---	---	---	---	---
Population 5 years and over	280,564,877	7,708	24,252,429	67,280
Cherokee	12,320	1,264	2,012	488
Arikara	103	83	(B)	—
Caddo	51	64	12	21
Pawnee	122	111	20	28
Wichita	242	175	39	49
Comanche	963	341	102	114
Mono	349	362	(B)	—
Paiute	1,638	568	193	104
Northern Paiute	12	21	(B)	—
Chemehuevi	15	27	(B)	—
Ute	1,625	467	85	53
Shoshoni	2,512	435	182	83
Hopi	6,776	1,473	1,274	385
Cahuilla	139	148	(B)	—
Cupeno	11	20	(B)	—
Luiseno	327	203	14	26
Serrano	5	10	(B)	—
Pima	8,190	1,297	1,204	436
Yaqui	425	158	43	40
Tiwa	2,269	604	73	78
Tewa	5,123	864	707	361
Towa	2,192	578	606	225
Zuni	9,432	1,996	1,341	944
Chinook Jargon	644	736	114	119
American Indian	8,888	1,076	1,487	382
Jicarilla	455	155	66	61
Chiricahua	457	313	(B)	—
Spokane	20	25	8	15
Hungarian	**94,125**	**3,675**	**27,473**	**1,825**
Arabic	**760,505**	**15,845**	**263,704**	**8,573**
Hebrew	**216,615**	**7,104**	**40,291**	**2,704**
African Languages	**710,214**	**15,252**	**234,509**	**6,819**
Amharic	146,337	6,535	64,140	3,196
Berber	1,475	550	455	222
Chadic	5,091	1,254	1,533	673
Cushite	90,434	5,808	50,577	3,806
Sudanic	8,966	1,835	5,728	1,391
Nilotic	4,964	1,399	1,577	507
Nilo-hamitic	525	357	223	180
Nubian	129	124	34	56
Saharan	19	30	(B)	—
Khoisan	19	32	(B)	—

(Continued)

TABLE 6.1   Continued

	Number of speakers	Margin of Error[1]	Spoke English less than "Very Well"	Margin of Error[1]
Release Date: April 2010				
Population 5 years and over	**280,564,877**	**7,708**	**24,252,429**	**67,280**
Swahili	72,404	4,763	15,897	1,793
Bantu	42,098	3,028	11,507	1,977
Mande	27,657	3,314	11,719	1,747
Fulani	22,469	2,407	10,544	1,569
Gur	849	494	225	242
Kru, Ibo, Yoruba	267,174	9,400	54,983	3,218
Efik	5,497	1,091	613	239
Mbum	340	394	127	149
African	13,767	1,970	4,627	1,076
Other and Unspecified Languages	**121,569**	**6,870**	**45,975**	**3,512**
Finnish	25,806	1,589	4,782	618
Estonian	5,938	734	1,484	348
Lapp	23	31	5	8
Other Uralic languages	31	51	31	51
Caucasian	6,870	1,607	3,294	897
Basque	1,649	473	527	216
Syriac	61,272	5,133	25,099	2,476
Aztecan	1,327	485	1,035	389
Sonoran	63	62	(B)	—
Misumalpan	127	201	127	201
Mayan languages	6,832	1,277	5,257	1,084
Tarascan	470	395	414	381
Mapuche	214	289	36	60
Oto - Manguen	2,596	947	2,147	878
Quechua	935	420	437	241
Aymara	63	76	20	32
Arawakian	1,960	641	614	331
Chibchan	48	58	24	40
Tupi-guarani	456	306	248	163
Uncodable Entries	4,889	621	394	153

[1]Data are based on a sample and are subject to sampling variability. The degree of uncertainty for an estimate arising from sampling variability is represented through the use of a margin of error. The value shown here is the 90 percent margin of error. The margin of error can be interpreted roughly as providing a 90 percent probability that the interval defined by the estimate minus the margin of error and the estimate plus the margin of error (the lower and upper confidence bounds) contains the true value. In addition to sampling variability, the ACS estimates are subject to nonsampling error (for a discussion of nonsampling variability, see Accuracy of the Data). The effect of nonsampling error is not represented in these tables.

[2]N.E.C. stands for not elsewhere classified. These are languages where respondents indicated they spoke either INDIAN or PAKISTAN. For Indian, it cannot be determined if the respondent spoke a native American language or spoke a language from India. For Pakistan, respondents wrote in Pakistan but it cannot be determined which one of the languages spoken in Pakistan is actually being spoken. To distinguish these languages, n.e.c. is used to indicate they are not classified in any other language code.

A "(B)" entry in the estimate column indicates that either no sample observations or too few sample observations were available to compute an accurate count.

An "(X)" entry in any column indicates that the question does not apply.

An "—" entry in the margin of error column indicates that either no sample observations or too few sample observations were available to compute a standard error and thus the margin of error. A statistical test is not appropriate.

Source: U.S. Census Bureau, 2006-2008 American Community Survey.

There is a need to differentiate between *language minority students* and the larger category of *immigrant students*. Not all immigrant students are limited in their English proficiency nor are all students who are English language learners immigrants. In fact, there are many English language learners who are citizens (Puerto Ricans, for example, or others who are second or even third generation); there are also immigrants for whom English is a native language (Jamaicans, for instance). Native language and national origin are therefore different concepts.

The growth of the population that speaks native languages other than English is also reflected in public school enrollments. There are over 5 million ELLs enrolled in grades pre-K through 12, roughly 10 percent of total public school student enrollment, and nearly 80 percent of ELLs are Spanish-speaking.[3] Among the states, California enrolled the largest number of English language learners, followed by Texas, Florida, New York, Illinois, and Arizona.[4] At the same time, the greatest growth in the percentage of students with limited English proficiency was in states that had previously had very low numbers of such students. Most of the states with the greatest growth in ELL students are in the Southeast and Southwest. The population of children of immigrant families is growing more rapidly than any other segment of the population, but most are U.S. citizens: nearly 80 percent of language-minority students were born in the United States.[5]

The demographic changes indicated by these statistics are part of a larger trend of immigration to the United States, which, since the late 1970s, has been responsible for a remarkable shift in our population. The reasons for this trend are varied, from a worsening economic situation in many countries with concomitant increases in economic opportunity in the United States, to a rise in the number of refugees from countries where the United States was involved in aggression (as has been the case in Central America, Southeast Asia, and the Middle East). Unlike the earlier massive wave of immigration at the turn of the twentieth century, the greatest number of immigrants is now from Asia and Latin America. These changes in the population of the United States have profound implications for education.

A Brief Overview of the History of Language Diversity in U.S. Schools

In our nation, linguistic diversity has commonly been viewed as a temporary, if troublesome, barrier to learning. As a result of this thinking, the traditional strategy in most schools historically has been to help students rid themselves as quickly as possible of what is perceived as the "burden" of speaking another language. After students learn English, the thinking goes, learning can then proceed unhampered. Forgetting their native language is seen as a regrettable but necessary price to pay for the benefits of citizenship.

The notion that children who do not yet speak English lack language altogether is a prevalent one in the United States, and it is linked with the mainstream perception that cultures other than the dominant one lack significance. Nevertheless, school policies and practices concerning language have by no means been uniform. Rather, they have ranged widely from "sink or swim" policies (i.e., immersing language minority students in English-only classrooms) to the imposition of English as the sole medium of instruction, to allowing and even encouraging bilingualism. By 1900, for example, at least 600,000 children, or about 4 percent of students enrolled in public and parochial elementary schools, were being taught in bilingual German/English bilingual schools. Smaller numbers were taught in Polish, Italian, Norwegian, Spanish, French, Czech, Dutch, and other languages.[6]

Generally, however, language use and patriotic loyalty have been linked. Being fluent in another language, even if one is also fluent in English, has been viewed with suspicion, at least in the case of immigrants. Where language issues are concerned, everyone has gotten into the fray. James Crawford quotes President Theodore Roosevelt, a spokesperson for the restrictive language policies at the beginning of the twentieth century that were a response to the huge influx of primarily East European immigrants to the United States, as saying: "We have room for but one language here, and that is the English language; for we intend to see that the crucible turns our people out as Americans, of American nationality, and not as dwellers in a polyglot boardinghouse."[7] Roosevelt's views were widely shared by people who felt threatened by the new wave of immigrants.

Unfortunately, such views are not limited to the past. Negative views of language diversity still hold sway today for any number of reasons, from the massive number of new immigrants crossing our borders to the incidents of September 11, 2001. For instance, in 2010, Ana Ligia Mateo, a school secretary in the Charlotte-Mecklenburg Schools in North Carolina lost her job for speaking Spanish. Although she had been hired as a bilingual secretary, when a new principal took over, she prohibited faculty and staff members from speaking Spanish to parents, this in spite of the fact that 43 percent of the students in the school were Hispanic and that the school's theme was the "Academy of Cultural and Academic Diversity."[8]

As a result of negative views and policies concerning the use of languages other than English in the United States, the language rights of substantial numbers of people have been violated, from prohibiting enslaved Africans from speaking their native languages to the imposition of "English Only" laws in a growing number of states.[9] Restrictive language policies have also found their way into schools. Joel Spring provides compelling historical examples of the strategy of linguistic "deculturalization" used in the schooling of Native Americans, Puerto Ricans, Mexican Americans, and Asian Americans.[10]

Language Diversity, the Courts, and the Law

Although frequently addressed as simply an issue of language, it can be argued that using students' native language in instruction is a civil rights issue because without it, millions of children could be doomed to a future of educational underachievement and limited occupational choices. Contested and often contradictory issues—for example, the U.S. creed of equal educational opportunity for all, alongside the fear that English might be supplanted as our national language—have made the choice of appropriate strategies for teaching English language learners difficult for teachers and administrators. The zigzag of support for native language instruction in the United States reflects this tension, and this has been the case since before the

United States became a nation. For a fascinating history of language diversity in the nation and efforts to deal with it, see James Crawford's many books and monographs on the topic, as well as his informative Web site (http://www.language policy.net).

How language diversity has been addressed, nationally and internationally, says a great deal about the status of nondominant languages in particular societies. The proposal for a Universal Declaration of Children's Linguistic Human Rights places linguistic rights on the same level as other human rights.[11] This proposal includes the right to identify positively with one's mother tongue, to learn it, and to choose when to use it. Although these rights may be self-evident for language majority children (in the United States, "language majority children" means native English speakers), they may not be so apparent for those who speak a language that carries a stigma, as is the case with most language minority students in the United States.

As our nation has become more diverse, issues of language have become even more salient. Due to the efforts and advocacy of families, community members, and educators, the Bilingual Education Act of 1967, signed by President Lyndon Johnson, provided financial incentives to school districts to help English language learners. Some of the first programs to be awarded these funds initiated programs in bilingual education. The funds were limited, however, and the number of English language learners was increasing, creating a need for support in other cities and towns. A few years later, in 1974, the U.S. Supreme Court recognized the connection between native-language rights and equal educational opportunity. In 1969, plaintiffs representing 1,800 Chinese-speaking students sued the San Francisco Unified School District for failing to provide students who did not speak English with an equal chance to learn. They lost their case in San Francisco, but by 1974, they had taken it all the way to the Supreme Court. In the landmark case *Lau v. Nichols,* the Court ruled unanimously that the civil rights of students who did not understand the language of instruction were indeed being violated. Citing Title VI of the Civil Rights Act, the Court stated, in part:

> There is no equality of treatment merely by providing students with the same facilities, textbooks, teachers, and curriculum; for students who do not understand English are effectively foreclosed from any meaningful education. Basic skills are at the very core of what these public schools teach. Imposition of a requirement that, before a child can effectively participate in the educational program he must already have acquired those basic skills is to make a mockery of public education.[12]

Although the decision did not impose any particular remedy, its results were immediate and extensive. By 1975, the Office for Civil Rights and the Department of Health, Education, and Welfare issued a document called *The Lau Remedies,* which served as the basis for determining whether school systems throughout the United States were in compliance with the *Lau* decision. This document provided guidance in identifying students with limited proficiency in English, assessing their language abilities, and providing appropriate programs. Bilingual programs became the common remedy in most school systems around the country.

The Equal Educational Opportunities Act (EEOA) of 1974 was also instrumental in protecting the language rights of students for whom English is not a native language. This law interprets the failure of any educational agency to "take appropriate action to overcome language barriers that impede equal participation by its students in its instructional programs" as a denial of equal educational opportunity.[13] In both the *Lau* decision and the EEOA, bilingual education emerged as a key strategy to counteract the language discrimination faced by many students in the schools and, in fact, it became the preferred model for teaching language minority students in the 1970s and 1980s.

The first state to mandate bilingual education was Massachusetts, which in 1971 passed the landmark Transitional Bilingual Education (TBE) Law, which required all school districts to provide students who did not speak English with native language instruction as well as English as a Second Language (ESL) for a maximum of three years, as long as there were at least 20 students who spoke the same language. Many states followed suit, modeling their law after the Massachusetts law. In 1980, President Carter proposed regulations requiring bilingual education, but shortly after becoming president, Ronald Reagan's administration canceled the proposed regulations and began reducing federal aid to the education of language minority students. A period of retrenchment in both financial and moral support for bilingual education followed, and for the first time since the Bilingual Education Act of 1967, funding for bilingual education was reduced yearly.[14]

By the 1990s and certainly in the new millennium, a backlash had resulted in eliminating many bilingual programs. Closely related to the issue of bilingual education has been the equally contentious issue of whether English should be the official language of the United States, a topic that has been in and out of the news for the past 30 years or so. During this time, the U.S. English organization was founded and, as a result of its lobbying efforts, during the 1980s and 1990s, many states passed laws making English the official language. In spite of this opposition, the federal bilingual education law was reenacted in 1994, under the Democratic administration of Bill Clinton. In 1998, the controversy surrounding native-language use resulted in the passage of California's Proposition 227, in which bilingual education was replaced with structured English immersion (SEI), a program in which students are separated from their English-speaking peers and placed in classrooms where they learn English, including some of their academic content in English. Arizona followed suit with Proposition 203 in 2000, and Massachusetts with Question 2 in 2002. (A similar proposition failed in Colorado in 2002.)

When President George W. Bush took office, he signed the No Child Left Behind law in 2002, in effect repealing the Bilingual Education Act of 1967. The Office of Bilingual Education was renamed the Office of English Language Acquisition, Language Enhancement, and Academic Achievement for Limited English Proficient Students. Many state and city departments of bilingual education were also renamed, usually to Department of English Language Learners, reflecting a rejection of bilingual education as the sole or preferred approach to educate students for whom English is a second language.

The number of students in bilingual programs dropped precipitously during these years: after the passage of Proposition 227 in California, for example, the number of English language learners in bilingual programs went from 60 to 8 percent.[15] Nevertheless, research has generally found that the elimination of bilingual education has led to further erosions in student learning. A recent text by Patricia Gándara and Megan Hopkins, featuring contributions from well-known educators and scholars in bilingual education, pulls together the most up-to-date research on the effects of restrictive language policies in California, Arizona, and Massachusetts. It refutes the claim that bilingual education inhibits student learning and instead concludes that such policies often create a chilly climate for the learning of English language learners.[16]

After a decade in remission, the campaign for "Official English" flared up again in 2006 as an amendment to immigration legislation. Passed by the Senate on May 18 of that year, it designated English as the "national language." The measure also sought to restrict access to government services in any language other than English and, although the proposal ultimately failed, it was a reminder that language is always a hot-button issue.[17]

The most recent court case with implications for English language learners is *Horne v. Flores*.[18] Brought by Nogales, Arizona, parents of ELLs in 1992, the case dragged on for many years before making its way to the U.S. Supreme Court. The suit charged that the state had violated the Equal Educational Opportunities Act (EEOA) by neglecting the education of ELL students. Subsequent rulings mandated increased funding for ELL students, but state education officials protested, claiming that the mandates were too rigid and were not keeping pace with changing policies, including No Child Left Behind (NCLB). In 2009, the Supreme Court, in a sharply divided decision, overturned the decision and sided with state education officials, agreeing that the state should determine its own requirements regarding the instruction of ELLs. This decision has been seen by advocates of immigrant and ELL students as a setback, although not necessarily as a total loss. According to James Crawford, the decision muddied the law where EEOA is concerned, and it held that changed circumstances in the form of NCLB and Proposition 203 may have satisfied the state's obligation to take appropriate action to overcome language barriers. Crawford wrote,

> But on the brighter side, the 5–4 majority remanded the case to federal district court, which must now look specifically at Arizona's English-only programs and judge whether they are effective. By expanding the scope of the litigation from per pupil funding to a review of all aspects of ELLs' educational experience, the court may have opened the door to a decision outlawing the state's policies (which include not only the SEI mandate but also a four-hour English block each day, to the exclusion of other subjects, and an arbitrary 2-year limit on enrollment in SEI programs).[19]

The ultimate outcome of the case, as of this writing, is still to be determined.

Although not directly linked to language diversity, other court cases have focused on immigrant issues, a closely related issue. For instance, in 1982, in the *Plyler v. Doe* decision, the U.S. Supreme Court struck down a Texas statute denying funding for education to children who were illegal immigrants and, at the same time, struck down a municipal school district's attempt to charge an annual tuition fee for each undocumented student. In a 5–4 decision, the Court ruled that the law violated the Equal Protection Clause of the Fourteenth Amendment, which guarantees all people in the nation, regardless of status, equal protection under the law.[20] This means that all children in the United States—native or foreign-born, legal or undocumented—have a right to an education in our schools.

 **Linguistic Diversity and Learning**

All good teachers know that learning builds on prior knowledge and experiences. In the case of language minority students, this means that their native language can be a strong foundation for future learning. If we think of language development as the concrete foundation of a building, it makes sense that it needs to be strong to sustain the stress of many tons of building materials that will be erected on top of it. This is analogous to what takes place when English-speaking students enter school: they use the language they know as a foundation for learning the content of the curriculum. Because they know the majority language, this is usually a seamless process. For English language learners, however, not knowing English is a tremendous disadvantage, not because their native language is ineffectual for learning but because schools do not generally view languages other than English as a resource for learning. Extending the metaphor further, it would be as if the strong foundation that had been created were abandoned and the building materials were placed on top of a sand lot across the street. Needless to say, the building would crumble quickly.

As a rule, because bilingualism is often viewed in a negative light, school policies generally focus on transitioning to English as soon as possible. In fact, in the United States, the prevailing view about knowing languages other than English is that, among culturally dominated groups, bilingualism is a burden, yet among middle-class and wealthy students, it is usually seen as an asset. It is not unusual to find in the same high school the seemingly incongruous situation of one group of students having their native language wiped out while another group of students struggles to learn a foreign language, a language most of them will never use with any real fluency.

In contrast to negative perceptions of bilingualism, a good deal of research confirms the positive influence of knowing more than one language, and these benefits begin very early in life. In studying seven-month-old babies raised in bilingual households, Agnes Kovacs and Jacques Mehler at the International School for Advanced Studies in Trieste, Italy, found that bilingual babies are precocious decision-makers who demonstrate enhanced cognitive control.[21] At the other end of the life span, neurologists have found that bilingual brains stay sharp longer than monolingual brains. Specifically, a team of Canadian researchers studied people being treated for dementia and found that those who were bilingual reported a later onset of the symptoms of dementia—specifically, about four years later—than those who were monolingual.[22]

A recent metareview of the benefits of bilingualism concluded that bilingualism is reliably associated with increased attention control, working memory, metalinguistic awareness, and abstract reasoning, all of which, naturally, can contribute positively to academic success.[23] Also, in their review of research studies concerning the adaptation and school achievement of immigrants of various backgrounds, Alejandro Portes and Rubén Rumbaut came to a striking conclusion: students with limited bilingualism are far more likely to leave school than those fluent in both languages. That is, rather than being an impediment to academic achievement, bilingualism can promote learning. In addition, native-language maintenance may act as a buffer against academic failure by simply supporting literacy in children's most developed language.[24]

In spite of such evidence, schools may disregard language minority students' native languages and cultures for what they believe to be good reasons: because they link students' English language proficiency with prospective economic and social mobility, teachers and schools may view English language learners as "handicapped" and thus urge students, through both subtle and direct means, to abandon their native language. For example, teachers and administrators often ask parents to speak English to their children at home, they punish children for using their native language in class, or they simply withhold education (by teaching them only English and no other content) until the children have mastered English, usually in the name of protecting students' futures. The research contradicts the common advice given to language-minority parents to "speak English with your children at home." This leads us to reflect on the innate wisdom of many immigrant mothers, including my (Sonia's) mother, who ignored teachers' pleas to speak to us in English. Had it not been for my mother's quiet but obstinate resistance, my sister and I would probably now be monolingual English speakers rather than fluent bilinguals. Abandoning one's native language leads not only to individual psychological costs and communication breaches within one's family, but also to a tremendous loss of linguistic resources to the nation.

Understanding Language Issues in a Sociopolitical Context

Language diversity needs to be placed within a sociopolitical context to understand why speaking a language other than English is not itself a handicap. The problem of language minority children has often been articulated as a problem of not knowing English, as if learning English were the solution to all the other difficulties faced by language minority students, including poverty, racism, poorly financed schools, and lack of access to excellent education. Lack of English skills alone, however, cannot explain the poor academic achievement of language minority students because confounding English language acquisition with academic achievement is simplistic at best. For example, a study of a rural high school in northern California by Rebecca Callahan found that English proficiency was not the most salient influence on the academic achievement of language minority students. Specifically, *track placement* proved to be more significant because many English learners were enrolled in low-track curricula that do little to prepare them for college and other postsecondary school opportunities. More than anything, then, teachers' and schools' perception of the abilities of English language learners may get in the way of student achievement. In Callahan's words, "[c]onstructions of English learners as deficient, bilingual programs as compensatory, and ESL classrooms as linguistic rather than academic speak to the marginalization of English learners in U.S. schools."[25]

Learning English is, of course, important and necessary for all students; this is a given. But rather than supporting the suppression or elimination of native language use at home and at school, the research reviewed here supports promoting native-language literacy as a way to enhance learning English more effectively. If this is the case, the language dominance of students is not the real issue; rather, *the way in which teachers and schools view students' language may have an even greater influence on their achievement.*

SNAPSHOT

Liane Chang

Liane was a ninth-grade student at a comprehensive high school in a midsize town in the Northeast. With a European American father and a Chinese mother, Liane felt fortunate that her efforts to learn Chinese, her mother's native language, were supported in her school. Her experience points to the power of a school experience that can support students in maintaining or reclaiming their family language.

If I look at how my different ethnicities have influenced my education, I would have to say that it has impacted my confidence in expressing my cultures to others. When people ask me to tell them how I identify, I reply, "Eurasian" [and] their reaction is always a very positive comment, the sort of thing that could start a whole conversation. I think that being Eurasian is about the coolest identity a person could have. Many might think that it would be embarrassing to be anything other than what is said to be "American," but through my teachers' and peers' influence, I see it as an opportunity to be an individual.

Now I am learning Chinese in school. I felt that, since I am Chinese, I should learn the language so that, when my mom and I go to China, I can understand and speak the language also. My love of the Chinese language has always been great throughout my childhood. I used to dream and wonder what it

would be like for me to speak a different language, and my inspiration came from my mother's conversations with her Chinese friends, either on the phone or in person. Late at night, right before I was tucked into bed, my mother would always say goodnight to me in Chinese.

My lesson on how to say "Thank you" in Chinese was useful when I went to Chinese restaurants or people's homes. Many trips yearly to New York City's Chinatown were also a great inspiration in my early childhood. This language and culture inspired me to choose to learn the language through my middle and high school world-language programs. Now that I'm learning Chinese, it's like I'm more related to my mom. It gave me more of a personal connection with my mom . . . something that I'll always share with her. She can help me because she understands it, and [it is] just something between her and me . . . very special. It can be very, very difficult at times because, when she corrects me, it doesn't seem like I know the language very much. But she helps me in a way that I can't be helped at school, and she gives me a new outlook on the language. It's a neat experience.

My grandparents on the European side of me are the only grandparents I have ever known. They have taught me hard work ethics and frugality that they learned through their daily lives. From these cultures, I have received what my grandparents learned through

Consequently, we want to emphasize that educating English language learners is not simply a question of following a set of prescribed strategies. Although learning new approaches and techniques may be very helpful, teaching students successfully means, above all, changing one's attitudes toward the students, their languages and cultures, and their communities. In the words of Lilia Bartolomé,

> As progressive educators, we must not forget that our work with linguistic-minority students—most of whom are not White and come from low socioeconomic status backgrounds—is political work and not purely a pedagogical undertaking.[26]

generations and have passed down to my parents and myself. And because these were the only grandparents I have ever known during my life, their stories and memories were also passed to me to treasure and to pass on to other generations. Through their hardships growing up in Europe during World War II and their few choices, I feel that I can appreciate my opportunities here to receive a good education. During World War II, my grandpa in Poland was captured by the Germans and forced to do manual labor, but he did not have to go to a concentration camp. When he got out, he went to France because he couldn't return to Poland. Then he married my Grandma, so my dad is French-Polish.

Somewhere else, people might think I'm not American because I don't look like the typical American, but here, in this school system, it's sort of the opposite. Being different makes you cool, and you can have your own individuality and you can differentiate yourself from different people. It's sort of a good thing, here, to be different—and I've never had someone be racist about my different cultures—except when you are really little, you know, the rhyme when they pull back their eyes? But that's little-kid stuff.

In seventh grade, I went to China with my Chinese teacher. It was a really good chance to see it . . . to be in an environment where I was actually a minority—being American—instead of being in an environment where everybody's similar, you feel not part of their culture because it is so different from what you are used to. My language skills were new then. I knew basic questions of survival. The experience was really overwhelming at times, but really exciting, too. We went to visit a Chinese high school, and we were each set up with a Chinese student, and we tried to communicate with, and ask them about their life. Actually it was the school that my mom's dad went to when he was in China. Isn't that neat?

In seventh-grade art, I completed a project about myself, expressing various symbols that had meaning [for me]. Though I did not have many symbols, each of them represents a lot about my life and heritage. For example, the flags that I put on my collage symbolize more than my heritage. They symbolize the people who come from there and are a big part of my life.

In my picture, I have the flags of my heritage flowing out of my fingernails like smoke. There are a total of three: the Chinese, French, and Polish flags. The Chinese flag represents my heritage on my mom's side. Both of her parents were born in China and immigrated to Taiwan during the Chinese Revolution. On the other hand, in my painting, my dad is both French and Polish. Polish and French are a big part of my family. Last of all, I have an American flag for the background of my project. This, of course, represents the place my sister Jillian and I were born. Since it is the biggest part of my life, it is the largest in the collage. I am proud to be American and that is the most important thing of all that I symbolized in the project.

Commentary

Liane's snapshot can help us think about what it might mean to have more school systems support students' identities by offering language courses from various language groups and even trips to the countries where those languages are spoken. Although not every language can be offered and trips are out of the question for many schools, it is intriguing to see how Liane's experience was made so much more positive by studying Chinese. Not only was it one of the languages of her heritage, but learning Chinese also promoted a closer relationship with her mother. We can adapt this approach for language minority students in our schools: those who enter school without English but are our future leaders.

This means understanding the sociopolitical context of society and education because anything short of this will result in repeating the pattern of failure that currently exists. Fortunately, as Jim Cummins has eloquently stated, "[G]ood teaching does not require us to internalize an endless list of instructional techniques. Much more fundamental is the recognition that human relationships are central to effective instruction."[27]

Bilingual education has always been controversial, but the major issue may be more about power than about language. This approach challenges conventional U.S.

educational wisdom that native language and culture need to be forgotten in order for students to be academically successful. In addition, bilingual education generally represents the class and ethnic group interests of traditionally subordinated groups and, in principle, it comes out on the side of education as an emancipatory proposition. Thus, the issue is not so much whether bilingual education works, but rather the real possibility that it *might*. As a result, in spite of its sound pedagogical basis, bilingual education is, above all, a political issue because it is concerned with power relations in society.

Although bilingual education is a political issue, we need to emphasize that it is *also a pedagogical issue*. Successful bilingual programs have demonstrated that students can achieve academically while they learn rigorous content through their native language.[28] This achievement contradicts the conservative agenda, which calls for a return to traditional curriculum and pedagogy. In fact, fluency in English, although necessary, is no guarantee that students of language minority backgrounds will succeed in school or later in life. If this were the case, all language minority students who have never been in bilingual programs or who were mainstreamed into regular classes years ago would be doing quite well academically, but as we know, this is far from the case. Research by Alejandro Portes and Rubén Rumbaut found that the students they studied from nationalities that speak English best (including West Indians and Filipinos) are not necessarily those who earn the highest incomes or have the highest number of managers and professionals among their ranks. On the other hand, Chinese and other Asians and Colombians and other Latin Americans, with relatively low fluency in English, earn considerably more. English language fluency, then, is not the only explanation. In some cases, according to Portes and Rumbaut, the way in which immigrants have been received and incorporated into the society also matters a great deal.[29]

Approaches to Teaching Language Minority Students

Given the dramatic increase in the number of English language learners in the country over the past several decades, every classroom in every city and town has already been, or will soon be, affected. This reality belies the conventional wisdom that only specialists need to know about and teach these children. This responsibility can no longer fall only on those teachers who have been trained specifically to provide bilingual education and ESL services but must be shared by *all* teachers and *all* schools.

What do all classroom teachers need to know to help them be better teachers of language minority students? How can you best prepare to teach students of different language backgrounds and varying language abilities? Fortunately, more attention is being paid to these questions than has been the case in the recent past. Several excellent resources can help teachers who are ESL or bilingual education specialists, as well as regular classroom teachers who teach young children or adolescents, and who teach everything from reading and writing to content knowledge.[30] In the following sections, we suggest a number of steps that teachers and schools can take to educate English language learners effectively.

About Terminology

Asians/Pacific Islanders

An incredibly diverse array of groups is included in the category of Asian American and Pacific Islander, including Chinese, Japanese, Vietnamese, Cambodian, Filipino, Native Hawaiian, Pakistani, and Indian, among others. One designation could not possibly be sufficient to cover them all because they differ not only in history and culture but also in language and national origin. Asians also differ in social class, length of time in the United States, immigrant experience, and educational background and experiences, and these differences invariably influence the educational achievement of the children in these groups. The term *Pacific Islander* is now used together with *Asian* to provide a more specific overarching term for a number of groups. It is preferred by most Asians and Pacific Islanders to the outdated and exotic term *Oriental* or even *East Indian*, but still fails to account for all differences.

It is also common to hear Asian groups referred to by regional labels that attempt to subdivide groups according to both geographic roots and culture. For example, *East Asian* typically refers to Japanese, Chinese, and Koreans while the term *South Asian* usually includes Indians and Pakistanis. Furthermore, *Southeast Asian* distinguishes Vietnamese, Filipinos, Cambodians, Thai, Laotian, as well as ethnic minorities in the region such as the Hmong. These categories can be useful in an attempt to reclaim cultural heritage and to resist mainstream U.S. habits of lumping the whole population under the term "Asian." However, these regional labels can also be problematic and cause overgeneralizations. For example, the subregion of East Asia holds 38% of the Asian population, which is also 22% of all the people in the world. Clearly, there are wide spectra of diversity within each national border and cultural cluster. Language, religion, family structure, social class, educational opportunities, and social mores are endlessly varied.

These labels also fail to account for mixed-race or mixed-heritage students. This language is limiting when referring to the experience of multiple cultural experiences in Asia, such as Chinese-Cambodian families or Korean-Japanese families. It is also inaccurate for U.S. students such as Lianne Chang, who identifies as *Eurasian* as a result of her mother's Chinese background and her father's Polish and French ancestry. We have met other students with mixed Asian and European backgrounds who describe themselves as *Amerasian* or *Asian American*. Other students in our case studies and snapshots express their Asian identities in various ways: Gamini Padmaperuma called himself "Sri Lankan by nationality" and "an American." Savoun Nouch names himself as "Cambodian and proud," but notes his difference from "somebody living in Cambodia" and "difference from other American families." Our classrooms also hold students whose hybrid ancestry includes Puerto Rican and Cambodian or Thai and Greek.

The key here is to refuse to think of all students of Asian heritage as a monolithic group. Furthermore, it is unfortunately still common for some teachers in U.S. classrooms to describe children of Asian heritage as all "looking alike" and to perpetuate the model minority myth, both very damaging practices. Learning about students' backgrounds and how they identify their heritages can help teachers use the most appropriate terminology and also reinforce awareness about each student's unique learning strengths and needs.

Understanding Language Development and Second-Language Acquisition

All teachers need to understand how language is learned—both native and subsequent languages. This knowledge is often reserved for specialists in bilingual and ESL education, but it should become standard knowledge for all teachers. For example, Stephen Krashen's important and classic work on second-language acquisition and his recommendation that teachers provide students for whom English is a second language with *comprehensible input*—that is, cues that are contextualized in their instruction—is useful for all teachers who have language minority students in their classrooms.[31] Likewise, related knowledge in curriculum and instruction, linguistics, sociology, and history are all helpful for teachers of language minority students. Consequently, all teachers should have:

- Familiarity with first- and second-language acquisition.
- Awareness of the sociocultural and sociopolitical context of education for language minority students.
- Awareness of the history of immigration in the United States, with particular attention to language policies and practices throughout that history.
- Knowledge of the history and experiences of specific groups of people, especially those who are residents of the city, town, and state where you are teaching.
- The ability to adapt curriculum for students whose first language is other than English.
- Competence in pedagogical approaches suitable for culturally and linguistically heterogeneous classrooms.
- Experience with teachers of diverse backgrounds and the ability to develop collaborative relationships with them to promote the learning of language minority students.
- The ability to communicate effectively with parents of diverse language, cultural, and social class backgrounds.[32]

Unfortunately, however, many teachers have not had access to this kind of knowledge during their teacher preparation or even in their professional development after becoming teachers. If this has been your experience, you may need to acquire this knowledge on your own. You can do this by attending conferences in literacy, bilingual education, multicultural education, and ESL; participating in professional development opportunities in your district and beyond; subscribing to journals and newsletters in these fields; setting up study groups with colleagues to discuss and practice different strategies; and returning to graduate school to take relevant courses or to seek an advanced degree.

Developing an Additive Bilingual Perspective

Additive bilingualism refers to a framework for understanding language acquisition and development that *adds* a new language rather than *subtracts* an existing one.[33] This perspective is radically different from the traditional expectation in our society

■■■■■■ What You Can Do

Accept Students' Identities

Even little things can make a big difference. For example, learn to say each child's name correctly. Don't change *Marisol* to *Marcy* or *Vinh* to *Vinny*. As simplistic as it may sound, this basic rule of respect is violated daily in classrooms across the nation. Given the pressure to conform that all students face, some of them readily accede to having their names changed so that they can fit in. Although learning many names in different languages may be time consuming for teachers, it is a first step in demonstrating respect for students' identities.

that immigrants need to shed their native language as they learn their new language, English. Many educators and others are now questioning whether it needs to be this way. Additive bilingualism supports the notion that two is better than one—that English *plus* other languages can make us stronger individually and as a society.

The challenge is that many teachers do not speak the native languages of their students. Nevertheless, all teachers, even those who are monolingual English speakers, can create a learning environment that supports and affirms the native languages of their students. A good example comes from researchers David Schwarzer, Alexia Haywood, and Charla Lorenzen, who suggest, for example, that teachers tap into some of the resources available in students' native languages by creating a multiliterate learning community with the help of students, their families, elders, and other community members. Some of the ideas they suggest for doing this include:

- Creating a multiliterate print environment in the classroom.
- Using literature in students' native languages.
- Learning some key words in students' first languages.
- Creating audio recordings of greetings, simple conversations, songs, and stories in students' first languages.[34]

Additional ideas for developing an additive perspective that benefits all learners, not just English language learners, can be found in a helpful edited book by Yvonne Freeman, David Freeman, and Reynaldo Ramirez, *Diverse Learners in the Mainstream Classroom.*[35] In these chapters, researchers and teachers share their ideas about using technology, multiple intelligence theory, mathematics, and social studies, among other resources and content, to develop an additive perspective in teaching mainstream, ELLs, and gifted students, as well as those with special needs. Nurturing native-language literacy is supported by research demonstrating that the skills students develop in their native language are usually transferred easily to a second or third language.[36] This being the case, how can we continue to view bilingualism as a deficit?

Consciously Fostering Native-Language Literacy

According to extensive research, native-language literacy is a resource that should be cherished.[37] Teachers can, for example, make a commitment to learn at least one of the languages of their students. When they become second-language learners, teachers develop a new appreciation for both the joys and the struggles experienced by language minority students—including exhaustion, frustration, and withdrawal—when they are learning English. This was what happened to Bill Dunn, a veteran teacher who decided to, in his words, "come out of the closet as a Spanish speaker." He realized that, after teaching for 20 years in a largely Puerto Rican community, he understood a great deal of Spanish, so he decided to study it formally and to keep a journal of his experiences. Although he had always been a wonderful and caring teacher, putting himself in the place of his students helped him understand a great many things more clearly—from students' grammatical errors in English to their boredom and misbehavior when they did not understand the language of instruction.[38] As a result, he developed more targeted pedagogical strategies for teaching them as well as a renewed respect for the situation of students who are learning English.

The responsibility to create powerful learning environments for English language learners should not rest on individual teachers alone, however. Entire schools must also develop such environments: for instance, they can make a conscious and concerted effort to recruit and hire bilingual staff members who can communicate with parents in their native languages. They can provide professional development opportunities, and rewards, so that teachers are motivated to learn a second language. Another important strategy is for administrators to support respectful outreach efforts to the families of English language learners.

Program Models for Teaching English Language Learners

Most language minority students receive some level of service to help them learn English, although it is still the case that in too many classrooms, children are left to "sink or swim" if they do not speak English. This happens especially in cases where language minority students have not previously been part of the school's population, or where the school system has no specialized staff members.

Structured English Immersion (SEI)

The prevalent model for teaching language minority students is some version of ESL, or English as a Second Language. Students are either separated from their peers in "newcomer" classes, or they are removed from their regular classrooms to receive ESL instruction for part of the day. Often they are omitted from specialized classes such as art and music where, ironically, they might be able to express their learning on a more level playing field. Although they are learning English, students in ESL programs may be languishing in other subject areas because their education consists mainly of learning English until they can function in the regular English language environment. *Structured English immersion (SEI)* has become a widely used model for teaching English language learners. In this model, students are usually placed in a separate classroom where they learn all their content in English until they are proficient enough to be "mainstreamed" to a regular classroom.

Bilingual Education

There is a dizzying array of models and definitions of bilingual education,[39] but in general terms, *bilingual education* can be defined as an educational program that involves the *use of two languages of instruction* at some point in a student's school career. This definition is broad enough to include many program variations. For example, a child who speaks a language other than English, let's say, Vietnamese, may receive instruction in content areas in Vietnamese while at the same time learning English as a second language. In the United States, a primary objective of bilingual education is to develop proficiency and literacy in the English language.

Transitional Bilingual Education

In spite of fervent opposition to bilingual education in some places, various models of bilingual education can still be found in schools throughout our nation. *Transitional bilingual education* is probably the most common model. In this approach, students receive content-area instruction in their native language while learning English as a second language. As soon as they are deemed ready to benefit from the monolingual English language curriculum, they are "exited" or "mainstreamed" out of the program. The rationale behind this model is that native-language services should serve only as a transition to English; consequently, there is generally a limit on the time a student may be in a bilingual program—usually three years.

Developmental or Maintenance Bilingual Education

This model is a more robust version of dual-language instruction because it is both comprehensive and long-term. As in the transitional approach, students receive content-area instruction in their native language while learning English as a second language. The difference is that the primary objective of this approach is to develop students' fluency in both languages, or *biliteracy*, by using both for instruction. Thus, there is generally no limit on the time students can be in the program. The longer the students remain in the program, the more functionally bilingual they can become and therefore the more balanced the curriculum to which they are exposed. The students can eventually receive equal amounts of instruction in English and their native language.

Two-Way Bilingual Education

Two-way bilingual education, also called *two-way immersion (TWI),* is an approach that integrates students whose native language is English with students for whom English is a second language. The goal of this approach is to develop bilingual proficiency, academic achievement, and positive cross-cultural attitudes and behaviors among all students. Because all students have considerable skills to share with one another, this approach lends itself to cooperative learning and peer tutoring, among other collaborative strategies. There is generally no time limit, although some two-way programs are part of existing transitional programs and therefore have the same entrance and exit criteria, at least for the students who are learning English. Two-way programs hold the promise of expanding our nation's linguistic resources and improving relationships between majority and minority language groups. Given the fact that the majority of language minority students in the United States are Spanish-speaking, most are Spanish/English programs.

Results of the two-way model have been very positive. In a longitudinal study of students who had been in two-way immersion (TWI) Spanish/English programs, researchers Elizabeth Howard, Donna Christian, and Fred Genesee found impressive levels of performance in reading, writing, and oral language in both English and Spanish. Students, both native English speakers and native Spanish speakers, had very high levels of English fluency, and while native English speakers scored lower on reading Spanish than native Spanish speakers, their oral Spanish proficiency was quite high.[40]

Another study of a two-way program found that a high number of high school students who had been enrolled in a two-way program throughout elementary school had positive attitudes toward school and expectations of attending college. Many of the Hispanic students in the study credited the two-way program with keeping them from dropping out of high school. The researchers, Kathryn Lindholm-Leary and Graciela Borsato, pointed to the development of a sense of "resiliency" among the Hispanic students in the study, especially those who were from low-income families.[41]

All of the program models detailed above have been reviewed and investigated for many years. Most of the research over the past several decades has found that bilingual education is generally as or more effective than other programs, such as ESL alone, not only for learning content through the native language but also for learning English. This finding has been validated by many studies and meta-analyses over the years.[42] This apparently counterintuitive finding can be understood if one considers that students in bilingual programs are educated in content areas *along with* structured instruction in English. Students in bilingual education programs are building on their previous literacy, but this may not be the case in English immersion programs that concentrate on English grammar, phonics, and other language features out of context compared to the way in which real, day-to-day language is used.

Bilingual programs may have secondary salutary effects, which include motivating students to remain in school rather than dropping out, making school more meaningful, and in general making the school experience more enjoyable. This was certainly true for Manuel Gomes, whose case study follows this chapter. Because of the close-knit relationships between his Crioulo-speaking teachers and their students, Manuel's transition to English was far easier than it might otherwise have been. A related phenomenon may be that bilingual education reinforces close relationships among children and their family members, promoting more communication than would be the case if they were instructed solely in English.

Bilingual education, ESL, and structured English immersion each have their proponents as the best way to educate English language learners. One recent longitudinal study comparing students in TBE classes with those in SEI classes found that both learned equally well. The first randomized study of its kind, this research is significant because it moves the debate from whether bilingual education or SEI is a better approach to considering the quality of instruction, shared beliefs about the capability of students, and the resources provided to the program.[43] Along the same lines, a report from the Pew Foundation found that the states with the largest concentration of English learners also had the most crowded urban schools and the largest number of students living in poverty. The report also found that the achievement gap was narrowed in less segregated schools, regardless of the program model used.[44]

 ## Problems and Challenges

Providing quality education to English language learners poses a number of serious problems and challenges. One is that many teachers have not received adequate preparation for teaching these students. One recent study, for example, found that, while 76 percent of new teachers said that teaching in ethnically diverse classrooms was "covered" in their teacher education courses, more than half still felt unprepared to teach students of diverse backgrounds, particularly language minority students.[45]

Another problem with bilingual programs has to do with the manner in which they usually define success. Bilingual programs, particularly weak models with a transitional focus, are meant to self-destruct within a specified time, generally three years. Success in these programs is measured by the rapidity with which they mainstream students. Therefore, their very existence is based on a compensatory education philosophy. Students' knowledge of another language is considered a crutch to use until they master what is considered the real language of schooling, English.

Low expectations of ELL students on the part of teachers and schools is also a problem. Even in bilingual programs, for example, if there is an emphasis on low-level rote and drill, little learning takes place. In contrast, researchers Luis Moll and Elizabeth Arnot-Hopffer suggested that when schools exemplify "educational sovereignty"—that is, when they challenge the arbitrary authority of the dominant power structure, in this case, manifested through English-only and high-stakes testing policies—English language learners are successful. In a longitudinal study of a dual-language school in Arizona, they found that all students in the school, regardless of their sociocultural characteristics, became literate in both languages. This success was due to several factors, including a highly qualified and diverse teaching staff; close and caring relationships between teachers and students; and the teachers' ideological clarity in understanding that teaching is, above all, a political activity. Consequently, the school is not only successful in producing biliterate students, a rare achievement in U.S. schools, but it is also successful despite the heavy ideological and programmatic pressures of the state to dismantle bilingual education, a consequence of the state's English-only policy, and the current emphasis on high-stakes testing, also conducted only in English.[46]

What is troublesome for some school districts is that in their student population, they have numerous language groups called *low incidence populations,* that is, students who speak a particular language for which there may not be a sufficient number of speakers to entitle them legally to a bilingual program. This is often the case with Asian languages and some European languages. Providing a bilingual program for each of these small groups would be not only impractical but impossible. In this situation, the most common programmatic practice is some kind of ESL or SEI.

Both bilingual education and SEI programs separate students from their peers for instruction. This is a particularly thorny issue in a society that claims to value

■ ■ ■ ■ ■ ■   ## What You Can Do
Accept Students' Language

Accept students' language, including language used by both new speakers of English and those who speak another variety of it. Overcorrecting can jeopardize learning. Although all students need to learn Standard English, especially those who have been traditionally denied access to higher status learning, it is equally crucial that

teachers accept and value students' native languages or dialects. Rather than always directly correcting students' language, model Standard English in your responses or statements so that they pick up the message that there are different ways of saying the same thing and that some are more appropriate than others in certain settings.

integration rather than segregation. Nevertheless, it should be remembered that a great deal of segregation of language minority students took place *before* there were bilingual programs (and it continues even more strongly today in sheltered English and ESL pullout-type programs). In fact, Latino students, who represent by far the highest number in bilingual programs, are now the most segregated population in U.S. schools, and bilingual education has nothing to do with this.[47] Instead, "White flight," that is, the tendency for Whites to move to suburban or other residential areas when African Americans and Latinos move into the neighborhood; a retrenchment in busing policies (the dismantling of busing children to different schools for purposes of racial integration); and segregated residential housing patterns are largely to blame. It is also true, however, that both bilingual and SEI programs have numerous opportunities for integrating students more meaningfully than is currently the case. For example, they can be placed in the same classrooms for art, physical education, and other nonacademic classes with their English-speaking peers.

Finding qualified personnel has been another major problem. Bilingual and ESL teachers often bear the burden of the "bilingual" label in the same way as their students. These teachers are suspected of being less intelligent, less academically prepared, and less able than nonbilingual teachers—this in spite of the fact that those who have been adequately prepared are often fluent in two languages and have developed a wide range of pedagogical approaches for teaching a diverse student body. In fact the case can be made that bilingual teachers, who are often from the same cultural and linguistic backgrounds as the students they teach, bring a necessary element of diversity into the school.

■ ■ ■ ■   ## Conclusion

Language differences may affect students' learning in numerous ways. These differences are not necessarily barriers to learning, but the history of linguicism in our society has resulted in making them so. As we have seen throughout this chapter, there is no single best approach or panacea for the education of English language learners. Nevertheless, bilingual education—whether TBE, maintenance, or two-way—has proved to be an effective program for students for whom English is a second language because it is based on a fundamental critique of the "assimilation equals success" formula on which much of our educational policy and practice is based. In the words of researchers Patricia Gándara and Frances Contreras, "When our approach to language education involves eradicating a student's native language in an effort to transform their identities, the results are predictably negative."[48]

Although bilingual education represents a notable advance over monolingual education, it is a mistake to view it as the silver bullet for all the educational problems of language minority students because even with bilingual education, many children are likely to face educational failure. The same is true of SEI because no approach or program can remedy all the problems, educational and otherwise, facing language minority students. Essential issues such as poverty, racism, reception and incorporation into the society, and structural inequality also are implicated. The reality is that many ELLs receive an inferior education—whether "sink or swim," SEI, or bilingual education—simply because they happen to live in poverty and attend poorly resourced schools. A more promising approach to this problem is exemplified in a recent publication from the California Department of Education: rather than focus on whether bilingual or SEI should be mandated, the text considers what we know about the education of English language learners, what teachers need to know to be effective with them, and how to close the "achievement gap."[49]

We have also pointed out some of the problems that arise when programs for English language learners have low status and when these students are separated from other students for instruction. The previously mentioned study by Moll, for example, makes it clear that, while there is no magic solution for all the educational problems of English language learners, a good place to begin would be to honor and affirm students' native languages, their families, their communities, and the resources they bring to their education. In the cases at the end of this chapter, we see the positive impact that doing so can have on their learning.

To Think About

1. Research the English-only movement. Do you consider it an example of linguicism? Why or why not?

2. The argument "My folks made it without bilingual education; why give other folks special treatment?" has often been made, particularly by descendants of European American immigrants. Is this a compelling argument? Why or why not?

3. If you were the principal of a school with a large population of language minority students, how would you address this situation in your school? What if you were a parent of one of those children, or a teacher? What if you were a language minority student?

Activities *for Personal, School, and Community Change*

1. If you do not currently speak a language other than English, enroll in a course to learn one (preferably a language spoken by a number of your students). Keep a journal of your reflections, noting what you're learning, what it feels like to be a learner of another language, whether your relationship with your students changes, and if and how your teaching strategies change as a result.

2. Ask your students to do a "language inventory"—that is, ask them to find out how many members of their families speak or used to speak another language or language variety; what language or languages they speak or spoke; and, if they no longer speak it, why they do not. Encourage them to interview family members and even to record them, if possible. Have them bring the results to class and use these recordings as the basis for a lesson or unit on language diversity in the United States.

3. Investigate your school's policies concerning the use of languages other than English in the classroom, on the playground, and in other areas of the school. If there is an "English Only" policy in any of these contexts, find out how the policy came to be. Ask other staff members and families what they think about it. If you disagree with the policy, develop an action plan to address it.

Case Studies

Manuel Gomes

It's kind of scary at first, especially if you don't know the language.

The first thing you notice about Manuel is that he is constantly on the move, as if the engine had started and he was ready to shift to fourth without moving through the other gears. Of slight stature and with a somewhat rumpled look, Manuel had an infectious and lively sense of humor and a generally positive attitude about life.

Manuel Gomes[1] emigrated to Boston with his family from Cape Verde when he was 11 years old. When he was first interviewed, Manuel was 19 years old and was to graduate from high school that year. In many urban high schools, 19 is no longer a late age to graduate for immigrant and refugee students because they are more likely to be retained in-grade, to be inappropriately placed in special education, and to be placed in low academic tracks. That Manuel was soon to graduate from high school is noteworthy because foreign-born students tend to have a very high dropout rate: while foreign-born students make up just 11 percent of the total population of students in this age group, they make up 33 percent of the dropout population.[2]

Even before gaining its independence from Portugal in 1975, Cape Verde, an archipelago of ten large and several smaller islands off the West Coast of Africa, had a huge out-migration of its population. Official documents estimate that close to 180,000 Cape Verdeans emigrated voluntarily between 1970 and 1973, some 20,000 to the United States alone. The process of emigration had begun with the arrival of North American whaling boats from New England in the late seventeenth century, so that by the end of the nineteenth century, there was already a sizable Cape Verdean community in Massachusetts. Currently, well over twice as many Cape Verdeans reside abroad than live at home. As of 2010, over 500,000 Cape Verdeans lived in the United States (about equal to the number who reside on the islands), representing the largest Cape Verdean community outside Cape Verde.[3]

Having suffered from more than 400 years of colonial neglect under Portugal, Cape Verde was left in poor economic and social condition. For example, the literacy rate in 1981 was 14 percent, a dramatic indication of the lack of educational opportunities available to the majority of the people. After independence, the situation improved significantly, and by 2009, the literacy rate was 83 percent, one of the highest in Africa, according to the United Nations Office for the Coordination of Humanitarian Affairs.[4] Although the official language of the islands is Portuguese, the lingua franca is Crioulo, an Afro-Portuguese Creole.

Most Cape Verdeans in the United States live in New England, primarily in Rhode Island and Massachusetts, with one of the largest concentrations in Boston. Manuel's family, like most, came to the United States for economic reasons. Although formerly farmers in Cape Verde, they quickly settled into the urban environment. Manuel's father found a job cleaning offices downtown at night, while his mother stayed home to take care of their many children. In Boston, they lived in a three-decker home with apartments occupied by other members of the extended family. The neighborhood, once a working-class Irish community, had become multiracial, with a big Catholic church close by and Vietnamese and Cape Verdean restaurants up the street. The older homes, the din on the street, and the crowding all added to the sense of an aging but still vibrant urban community.

Manuel was the youngest of 11 children, and he would be the first in his family to graduate from high school. For several years he had been in a bilingual program where the language of instruction was Crioulo. The State Assembly of Massachusetts passed legislation in 1977 distinguishing Crioulo as a language separate from Portuguese and required that Crioulo-speaking students be placed in separate programs from those for Portuguese-speaking students. The result was a scramble to find Crioulo-speaking teachers and aides and to develop appropriate materials because few or none existed.

The rationale for placing Cape Verdean students in a separate program was that students should be taught in the language they speak and understand, not in their second or third language. A benefit of separating the program was that a strong sense of community among teachers, students, and parents developed. Some of the teachers and other staff members in the program were intimately involved in the life of the community, and the separation that often exists between school and home, especially for immigrant children, was alleviated. Manuel's participation in the bilingual program proved to be decisive in his education because it allowed a less traumatic transition to the English language and U.S. culture. Nevertheless, he constantly referred to how hard it had been to fit in, both in school and in society in general.

Boston, like most big cities in the United States, is a highly diverse metropolitan area. It is not unusual to walk from street to street and hear languages from all over the world, smell the foods of different continents, and hear the music of a wide variety of cultures. In spite of this diversity, and perhaps in part because of it, the city is not without its tensions, including diverse economic vested interests and interethnic hostility. These tensions are evident in many arenas, including the schools. The attendant problems of segregation, with a long and tumultuous history in the city, are still apparent. The city's schools, for example, experienced a vast decrease in the percentage of White and middle-class students beginning with court-ordered desegregation in the mid-1970s. Although the Boston city schools were once highly regarded, they have lost both resources and prestige.

Manuel's plans for the future were sketchy, but when interviewed, he was working in a downtown hotel and wanted to use the accounting skills he learned in high school to find a job at a bank. His positive experience in a theater class as a sophomore, along with his great enthusiasm and expressiveness, sparked his desire to continue in the act-ing field. He also talked of continuing his education by attending a community college.

Manuel was excited and proud of graduating from high school but reflected on *the pain and fear of immigration*. This is the major theme that characterized Manuel's experiences, both as a student and as an immigrant to this society. *Role reversals within the family* is another central theme that emerged. Finally, the *mediating role of bilingual education* in his success as a student was evident. Each of these themes is further explored in the following sections.

The Pain and Fear of Immigration

We have a different way of living in Cape Verde than in America. Our culture is totally different, so we have to start a different way of living in America. It's kind of confusing when you come to America, you know.

I liked going to school in Cape Verde 'cause you know everybody and you have all your friends there. In our country, we treat people different. There's no crime. You don't have to worry about people jumping you, taking your money, or walking at night by your-self. There's no fear for that. In Cape Verde, you don't have to worry about something happening to your child, or you don't have to worry about using drugs.

My father and mother used to work on plantations. We used to grow potatoes; we used to grow corn; we used to grow beans and stuff like that. We had a lot of land. Every season, we farmed. We had cows. Me and my brother used to feed the cows and take them to walk and give them water to drink and stuff like that. We used to sell our milk to rich folks, and I used to deliver [it]. It was kinda fun. These rich people, every time I'd go there, they'd feed me, which I liked very much [*laughs*]. They used to give me cake and stuff like that, cookies. We'd have a lot of crops and we'd give some away to poor people, those that don't have any. We had a lot of friends and stuff like that.

When we came to America, it was totally different.

In Cape Verde, they have this rumor that it's easier to make a living up here. So every-body wants to come up here. They have this rumor that once you get here, you find money all around you, you know. So, when you're, like, coming up here, they make a big commo-tion out of it: "Oh, you're going to America, rich country," and stuff like that. So they think once you come here, you got it made . . . you're rich. People in our country actually think that we're rich here, that we are filthy rich, that money surrounds us—we eat money!

I was disappointed in a lot of ways [when we came here], especially with the crime, especially with the kids. They don't respect each other; they don't respect their parents. It's very different here. It's very tough.

I was afraid. I had people jumping me a few times, trying to take my wallet and stuff like that. It's a scary situation. It didn't really bother me, but like what got to me, is, if they try to start a fight with you, you go to tell, like, a teacher, they couldn't do nothing about it. That's what got to me, you know?

It was a few students. I know this kid, this big Black kid. He tried to fight me, like, three times. Then I had a brother that was going to the same middle school, so he had a fight with my brother, my big brother. After that, it calmed down a little bit, you know?

Kids might try to stab you if you probably step on them. That happened to me once. I stepped on this kid's sneaker once, and he tried to fight me. He said, "What you doing?" I said that I'm sorry and he said, "That's not enough," and he tried to punch me. He didn't, but he was very furious.

You gotta get used to it. That's why a lot of Cape Verdean kids, when they get here, they change. They become violent, like some of the kids in America. So, it's sad. It's very hard for the parents. The parents are not used to that, and it's happening [to] a lot with parents in our neighborhood. It's happening to our family. I have a cousin, and his mother tried to commit suicide because her son was dealing drugs and hanging with the wrong crowd, with all these hoods. The son almost died because someone beat him up so bad. And it's sad, you know?

They try to be strict about it, you know. But with kids, they try to copy kids that were born here. They try to be like them. They try to go out and do the stuff that *they're* doing. It's like teen pressure, you know? So, it's very hard, you know? You want to fit in. You like to fit in with the crowd. If you hang with the wrong crowd, you're going to be in big trouble. You just change . . . and you're going to be a person that you don't want to be. You'll probably end up in jail.

I been here eight years, and I never hang with the wrong crowd. I've never used drugs in my life. I've never *smelled* cigarettes. So, I really hate when I see other kids doing it. It's sad when you see especially your friends doing it. So I had to say, "Go away. I don't want that life." So I had to separate from them. I had a hard time finding friends that wasn't doing that stuff like they were doing. It's very hard if you hate what your friends are doing.

Start learning the language was hard for me. And then start making friends because you gotta start making new friends. When American students see you, it's kinda hard [to] get along with them when you have a different culture, a different way of dressing and stuff like that. So kids really look at you and laugh, you know, at the beginning.

It was difficult like when you see a girl at school that you like. It's kind of difficult to express yourself and tell her the way you feel about her, you know? When you don't even know the language, it's kind of hard. I had a hard time. It's kind of scary at first, especially if you don't know the language and, like, if you don't have friends there. Some people are slow to learn the language and some just catch it up easy. It wasn't easy for me . . . like, the pronunciation of the words and stuff like that. Like, in Portuguese and in English, they're different. It's kinda hard, you know?

I don't think I want to be an American citizen. To tell you the truth, I don't like America at all. [Well], I *like* it, but I don't like the lifestyles. It's different from my point of view. What I'm thinking of doing is work in America for 10 years and go back to my country because America's a violent country. It's dangerous with crime, with drugs.

Role Reversals Within the Family

Because they don't speak English, I have to go places with [my family] to translate and stuff like that. So I'm usually busy. We have a big family. I have to help them out.

If I felt like I had support from my family, if they only knew the language. . . . If they were educated, I could make it big, you see what I'm saying? I would've had a better opportunity, a better chance.

I'm very happy about [graduating]. It means a lot to me. It means that I did something that I'm very proud [of]. It feels good, you know? And I'd really like to continue in my education because, you know, I'm the first one. And I want to be successful with my life. I just wanted to help them, you know? I wanted to be the one to help them. They didn't support me, but I wanted to support them.

I took [my father] to the hospital. Then I found out that he had cancer. I didn't wanna tell him. The doctor told me that he had cancer. I didn't wanna tell him because he hates to get sick and he hates to die! He hates to die. If you tell him he's gonna die, he'll kill you before he dies!

This happened when I was in school, so I was missing school a lot. I was the only one that was able to understand the language. It actually got to the point that *I* had to tell him. It was, like, sad when I had to tell him because it's very hard to tell him that he had cancer.

My mother's proud of me. My father is, too. It was tough for me when I found out that my father had cancer because, you know, I really wanted to graduate. I just want to show him that I can be somebody, you know? I actually did this, try to graduate from high school, for him.

Bilingual Education as Linguistic and Cultural Mediator

A Cape Verdean person is usually, he looks like he's a nice person, educated, you know? Not all of them, but like 70 percent of Cape Verdeans, they look educated. They're not violent. You can tell someone is Cape Verdean . . . if he starts pointing at you. That's a sign that he's Cape Verdean automatic. If he starts staring at you, he's Cape Verdean. We have problems when we look at American people. They might think we are talking about them and stuff like that, so we have to change that behavior. We have to get used to not pointing at people and not looking at them very much because American people are not used to people staring at them.

What we do in our country, we *observe* people. It don't mean nothing to us Cape Verdeans. It's just normal. But if we do it to an American person, it makes that American person nervous, I guess, and he would ask you, "What are you looking at?" or "Why are you looking at me?" and start questioning and probably start trouble with you.

It's normal to us. That's why other people got to understand that not everybody has the same culture; not everybody is the same. So some people don't understand. Like a Spanish [Hispanic] person, what he usually do, they use their body in a different way. With [Hispanic people], what they do, they point with their lips. They go [*demonstrates puckering of the lips*]. So, that's different. Other cultures, they might use their head; they might use their eyebrows.

It's good to understand other people's culture from different countries. America is made up of different countries, and we all should know a little bit about each one's cultures.

I think [teachers] could help students, try to influence them . . . that they can do whatever they want to do, that they can be whatever they want to be, that they got opportunities out there. Most schools don't encourage kids to be all they can be.

What they need to do is try to know the student before they influence him. If you don't know a student, there's no way to influence him. If you don't know his background, there's no way you are going to get in touch with him. There's no way you're going to influence him if you don't know where he's been.

You cannot forget about [your culture], you know? It's part of you. You can't forget something like that. . . . You gotta know who you are. You cannot deny your country and say, "I'm an American; I'm not Cape Verdean." That's something that a lot of kids do when they come to America. They change their names. Say you're Carlos—they say, "I'm Carl." They wanna be American; they're not Cape Verdean. That's wrong. They're fooling themselves.

I identify myself as Cape Verdean. I'm Cape Verdean. I cannot be an American because I'm not an American. That's it.

[*Describe yourself as a student*] I'm not a genius [*laughing*]! [But] I know that I can do whatever I want to do in life. Whatever I want to do, I know I could make it. I believe that strongly.

Commentary

Manuel was eloquent in expressing his concerns as an immigrant and student, concerns related to his academic success and his motivation for graduating and possibly continuing his education. But behind the sometimes forced enthusiasm he displayed, Manuel's voice was also tinged with sadness at what might have been. His expression changed when talking about his early experiences in Cape Verde. In spite of the obviously difficult circumstances of going to school (where he was in a crowded, one-room schoolhouse with many other students of all ages and where he said that corporal punishment was a common practice), Manuel had, over the years, idealized his experiences there. He seemed to have forgotten the harsh life he had in Cape Verde, although he did admit that he did not like farming. In spite of the difficulties, life there was, at least when he reflected on it years later, easier and more predictable. Manuel often contrasted the crime and violence in the United States with his romanticized memories of a bucolic childhood in Cape Verde.

With obvious pain, Manuel described what it was like being perceived as different by his peers when he first arrived in the United States. For example, other kids would call him names and ridicule him. The situation had changed after he reached high school, but those first years were indelibly etched in his memory.

The distress caused by immigration is multifaceted. Not only do immigrants leave behind a country that is loved and an existence that is at least familiar, if not comfortable, but they also leave a language and culture that can never find full expression in their adopted country. In addition, they are coming into a situation that, although it may offer many exciting possibilities, nonetheless is often frightening and new. Hence, Manuel was ambivalent about his experience in the United States.

Several of the painful incidents that Manuel described focused on interethnic rivalries and violence. This situation is a guarded secret, especially at many urban schools. School officials, perhaps fearful of being labeled racists, are reluctant to confront the prejudicial behaviors and actions of one group of students toward another, yet the issue is real and becoming more apparent all the time. Racial stereotypes and epithets are commonplace, voiced by even the most seemingly sensitive students. For example, Manuel's comment about a "big Black kid" reinforces the negative stereotype of African Americans as frightening and violent.

Manuel was the linguistic and cultural broker in his family because his was the public face that interacted with the greater community. Immigrant children routinely experience role reversals with their parents as a result of their parents' lack of English fluency and knowledge of U.S. customs. Based on their extensive studies of immigrant children, Alejandro Portes and Rubén Rumbaut explain: "This role reversal occurs when children's acculturation has moved so far ahead of their parents' that key family decisions become dependent on the children's knowledge."[5] Manuel's role as translator was especially prominent when his father developed cancer a few years before and he was placed in the extraordinary position of being the one to tell him that he had cancer. This experience had a great impact on Manuel, especially because the cancer was considered terminal. Although his father recovered from the cancer against all the odds, the experience left Manuel shaken. His grades also suffered during that period.

When immigrant students play the role of family interpreter and arbiter, the result may be the transfer of authority and status from parents to children, which in turn can lead to further deterioration of traditional roles and therefore produce conflict at home. In addition, teachers not accustomed to this kind of adult responsibility often interpret students' absences and lateness as a sign that their parents do not care about education or that the students are irresponsible. Frequently, just the opposite is true. Immigrant parents are not oblivious to the benefits of education, but they often need support in attending to their basic needs. Here is where the school, as an advocate of children and their families, can come in. The school can help locate needed services or suggest ways to attend to family needs without keeping the children out of school.

There may also be different perceptions of family involvement among immigrant parents. Manuel's parents, for example, rarely visited his school. This is not surprising: parent involvement in schools in most countries is minimal because, in these countries, the feeling is that, after children begin school, it is the school's responsibility to educate them. The parents, in essence, hand over their children to the school, trusting that the school will take over, at least in terms of their education. To jump to the conclusion that these parents do not care about education is to misread the families' intentions.

Manuel said that the bilingual program at the high school provided a safe environment for him and other Cape Verdean students. It was a rather large program, much larger than the one at the middle school, and most of the teachers and some of the other staff members were Cape Verdean, too. Cape Verdean students in the city had a strong identification with this high school and looked forward to attending it. In fact, it was always one of the more constructive and distinguishing characteristics of this particular urban school. That the bilingual program acted as a linguistic and cultural mediator was evident in many of Manuel's comments. For example, Manuel was extremely perceptive about culture and its manifestations. This perceptiveness is a common by-product of bilingual programs, in which culture and language become a natural aspect of the curriculum. The description of how his Latino classmates use their lips to point rather than their fingers demonstrates Manuel's sensitivity and sophistication in understanding nonverbal cues. Many teachers, even those who work with students from different cultures, fail to pick up these sometimes subtle cues.

The significance of the bilingual program in Manuel's life cannot be overemphasized, and this has been true for many Cape Verdean and other language minority students. The bilingual program helped Manuel retain his language and culture and, with it, ties to his family and community. It gave him something to hold on to.

Even this kind of program, however, is not enough if it is not part of a larger whole that affirms the diversity of all within it. It and other bilingual programs like it become tiny islands in a sea of homogeneity and pressure to conform.

Unfortunately, Massachusetts voters eliminated bilingual education in 2002. As a result, immigrant students such as Manuel can no longer count on the kind of support that bilingual education provided in the past.

Manuel also spoke fondly of the theater workshop that he took as a sophomore (a project that was also, sadly, eliminated shortly thereafter). Although it was not part of the bilingual program and all the skits were in English, it focused on issues that were relevant to immigrant and language minority students. Manuel recalled with great enthusiasm a monologue he did about a student going to a new school, a situation he could identify with because it was so reminiscent of his own experiences.

One of the ways Manuel dealt with finding a place to fit in was by joining and becoming very active in a fundamentalist Christian church. As Manuel so eloquently expressed it, "That's the place I belong to. I fit there. I felt that God had moved there. Jesus got hold of me. He said, 'Calm down.'" A number of issues were apparently influential in leading Manuel to this particular church. It was about this time that his father developed cancer and Manuel was immersed in his role as "the man of the family." It was also around the time that he decided to drop some of his friends (as he said, "It's very hard if you hate what your friends are doing"). In looking for something to keep him on track, as the bilingual program and other cultural supports had done previously, he looked toward the church community. Although Manuel had been raised a Catholic, the local Catholic church was unappealing to him because it had made few accommodations to its newest members, many of whom were immigrants who spoke little or no English. His new church, however, seems to have gone to great lengths to welcome Cape Verdeans, and Manuel felt he had finally found a place to fit in.

The tension of fitting in was well articulated by Manuel when he pitted being Cape Verdean against being American. He did not perceive the possibility that he could be *both* Cape Verdean *and* American. That is, if he identified with being American, he felt he was abandoning his culture and country; on the other hand, if he chose to remain Cape Verdean, his possibilities in U.S. society might be limited. These are hard choices for young people to make and are part of the pain of living in a culture that has a rigid definition of "being American."

Reflect on This Case Study

1. Consider some of the ways in which Manuel's experiences as an immigrant were frightening and painful. What can teachers and schools do to help?
2. What can account for Manuel's highly developed sensitivity to cultural differences? What can teachers and schools learn from this?
3. It is probable that school authorities and teachers assumed that Manuel's family was wrong in keeping him home to attend to family business during his father's illness. What do you think? What could the school have done to accommodate his family's needs?
4. Do you understand why Manuel felt reluctant to identify himself as "American"? How would you approach this issue if he were one of your students?

Alicia Montejo

[M]y sister uses the word Hispanic or Latina; I'm Mexican: I am really Mexican.

When she was first interviewed, Alicia Montejo[1] was finishing ninth grade at Red Rock High School in greater Denver, Colorado. After her mother's death three years earlier, she had moved several times. For about 18 months Alicia had lived with her stepfather, who served as her legal guardian, in the midsize Texas border city where she was born and raised. She later moved to Colorado with her older sister, who became her legal guardian just six months before this interview.

Being Mexican, speaking Spanish, and experiencing economic struggles were inseparable realities central to Alicia's life, both at home and at school. Alicia attended preschool through sixth grade in a south Texas school district with a student population of 98 percent Hispanic and 93 percent economically disadvantaged. The district also lists the K–12 population as 51 percent limited English proficient.

The school that Alicia attended for her freshman year is a public high school that had been created during massive districtwide reform as part of the Colorado Small Schools Initiative (CSSI),[2] which was funded by a grant from the Bill & Melinda Gates Foundation.[3] The school district, serving 5,700 students, transformed one large high school into seven distinct, small high schools, offering students a choice of enrollment. In Alicia's case, Red Rock High School met some of the district's objectives to create "personalized secondary learning environments that challenged and engaged students, supporting high standards for all."[4] However, it fell short in challenging Alicia to her fullest potential. The built-in option to transfer to one of the seven new high schools within the district appealed to Alicia, who said that she hoped to move to another school where she "could be pushed harder."

That Alicia was doing well in school demonstrates that she was beating the odds for English language learners living in poverty. Poverty has been, and continues to be, a major problem among Latino youths, including Mexican Americans. As of 2008, 29 percent of Latino/Latina children lived in poverty, a percentage that most likely increased during the severe recession of 2009–2010.[5] Complex socioeconomic circumstances, combined with severely unequal schooling conditions from preschool through high school, create devastating and enduring consequences for Mexican American and other Latina/Latino youth. Among many factors that conspire to perpetuate this situation are teachers' low expectations and brutally underresourced schools.[6] English language learners are especially vulnerable: For example, according to the National Center for Education Statistics, ELLs are woefully behind their peers, even among former ELLs, in reading and math.[7] In addition, a report from the Pew Hispanic Center found that, even though the number of Hispanic college graduates has reached an all-time high, about 41 percent of Latinos 20 years of age and older in the United States do not have a regular high school diploma, compared with 23 percent of African American adults and 14 percent of White adults.[8]

When examining data of those who make it through high school, the dropout rate—or what some activists and researchers have called the *pushout rate*—is holding steady.[9] Tara J. Yosso's analysis of the data on the K–12 educational pipeline revealed that, for every 100 Chicana/Chicano students entering elementary school, only 44 graduate from high school. Her study also showed that for every 100

Chicana/Chicano students, only seven graduate with a bachelor's degree, two earn a masters, and one earns a doctorate degree.[10]

Within this sociopolitical context, three themes emerge from Alicia's case study. These three themes tell us a great deal about her perspective on language, education, and her Mexican heritage. The role of Spanish language in shaping her identity is pervasive throughout these themes: *interconnectedness of language, identity, and learning; family, respect, and expectations*; and *desire for academic challenge*.

Interconnectedness of Language, Identity, and Learning

My dad and my mom, they came from Mexico. They moved here before I was born, but I was born here; Mexican American. All I say is that I am Mexican; my sister uses the word *Hispanic* or *Latino*; I'm Mexican: I am really Mexican.

Being Latino, it's good 'cause a lot of people tell me it's a good advantage for me to know two languages. I like that. Sometimes it's frustrating. I know English, but not perfect English. Sometimes it gets frustrating that you don't know what something's called in English.

By the time I was in first grade, I already had all my English. The school did have a program [for English language learners], but I didn't have to go to it. It worked out for me pretty good. Nobody at home taught me. I just learned from my friends in preschool and my teachers. My parents, they didn't speak English, so I guess I pushed myself really hard to learn English. My parents were pushing me really hard to learn English, they were, like, "You gotta learn it!"

I remember my pre-K teacher 'cause she helped me a lot. She taught me English. She spent time with me after school and everything. I had no friends then, and my teachers made me feel good. They were there for me and they helped me out. There was this one time where I didn't really know much English, but my friend next to me, she had to do her homework and she spoke pure Spanish [meaning only Spanish, no English], and I helped her out. That made me feel really good that I helped other people out with what they didn't know and what they did know. But still, I get frustrated sometimes when my friends need help or whatever and I don't know to help them out.

Now, in Colorado my friends are a little different. There are a lot of Mexican people here, but not as much as there were in Texas. There's mountains. You could see some of the mountains from here. There's different kinds of people, like African Americans, Latinos, White people, Asians. In Texas, I had friends from other kinds of groups, but mostly Mexican. In Texas, almost everybody spoke Spanish. Here in Colorado, some people speak Spanish, but lots don't. Here the Mexicans come from lots of different [regions in Mexico]. In Texas, everybody was from the same place. Here, even some of the Mexicans don't speak Spanish.

A lot of White people do not know Spanish. White people don't know how to pronounce stuff in Spanish, or they don't know Spanish at all. And they have a hard time communicating. Then there's some kids at our school that know pure Spanish, and they want to communicate with them but they can't. It's probably frustrating for them to not be able to talk to each other—communicate to other people that know a different language or something. But I can talk to everybody.

[If I could give advice to the school] I would tell teachers to help the Mexican kids who don't speak English. Help them a little but don't leave them behind, and don't do the work for them. Have a special class for them at one point in the day at least, but mostly regular classes. Then have a time when they can learn and use Spanish, and flash cards with the different languages—and learning how to speak better English—and learn in English and Spanish, both languages in school.

If a new Latino student came to our school, I would tell them not to give up. I mean, if they only know Spanish, not to give up. Just to try and understand as much as you can, or try to ask somebody that speaks both languages. It might be frustrating for them not to understand what their teachers are saying, but don't give up.

What I would advise teachers is to learn Spanish so they can teach [ELL Latino students]. Latinos that know pure Spanish, they get frustrating just to sit there and not be able to know what the teacher's talking about. They just sit there and they get a worksheet. They don't know what to do with it and they have to ask somebody. It would be frustrating. And then the [bilingual] students [in the bilingual program] might not be able to explain to them right, and they get frustrating. Tell teachers just not to get frustrated with students that speak Spanish or other languages. Just try your best to communicate with them. The school does have teachers come in and translate the lessons for the Mexican kids, but all I saw was one for that one class.

When teachers understand our culture, they speak to us in Spanish. Mr. Thomas, my humanities teacher, he knows Spanish 'cause he's married to a Mexican woman. He talks to everybody in Spanish! The people that know Spanish come to him and he tells me to translate to them something that I need to help them with, like a worksheet. You can tell if a teacher understands our culture by other stuff, too. Like in the art room, there's, like, Mexican stuff put up and all that: Mexican flag, Mexican paintings.

To get to know my culture, I would tell teachers to understand my language. Take a course or something; take courses. The other way they can learn about our culture is by asking us about it. Ask us.

Family, Respect, and Expectations

The person that I most admire is my sister. She went through a lot when she was small. She married a good husband. He doesn't do drugs, he don't cuss, he don't smoke or nothing. He's got a nice job. He's respectful to her. She made a lot of good choices. Like when she was a teenager, she didn't get pregnant or anything 'til now that she's married and she got a nice job. She really made a lot of good choices. Her and her husband. They act like my parents.

My mom talked to me about me growing up and having a good life. Not to let myself go with any guy or whatever, not to have sex: to protect myself. Nothing is holding me back from getting a good education, unless I get pregnant, which I probably won't. I'm scared for that. But nothing's keeping me back. I'm more into school than that. Right now, I wouldn't be ready for a kid. I want to go on in school. I want to go straight to college and get a career and after I have a career and then maybe have children. One of my friends just had a baby and she's really struggling. I wouldn't want to be like that. I'm gonna do the same thing my sister did. I'm gonna wait till I grow up, have a nice job, and then think about babies.

My family taught me just to value school. Value what I have. All my family is positive about school. Since my dad was Mexican, he didn't really have many chances—he's like a construction [worker] or something like that. He told me that Mexicans don't have a lot of choice in work 'cause they're not legal from the United States. Doing good in school is to get a chance to do stuff that most of my family hasn't been able to do: to get a good job and have money, be able to raise a family.

From my family, I learned respect and manners. Well, my mom passed away in 2002; she's not here with us anymore. But she was really positive about school. My dad, he works—he's still alive but he's working off in a place [far from here]. They just tell me to get an education, to grow up and have a good job and a good family.

I was a good student when I was younger and I still am. My family, they taught me well. How to be respectful and everything, and how much school is important. Sometimes I think about ditching, but I don't, 'cause I'm a really good student. I have to do my work 'cause school is important to me. I know I complain a lot, but it is important to me. I'm friendly. I am respectful, most of the time. I help other people when they need help and if I know how, I'll help them. Pretty much, I'm responsible. Not all the time, but I'm responsible. But when I'm having a bad day, or when teachers really get on my nerves, that's when I'm not that respectful. I talk back or I ignore them. I just tell them, "Leave me alone," "Don't talk to me," or I'll just don't talk to them. I'll listen to them, but I won't talk to them. And you can tell right away whenever I have that look or whenever I roll my eyes.

My sister, she's very positive about me going to school. She wouldn't want me to drop out or anything like that. Her husband, he's the same way. They're really positive about school. He tells me stories, like, to get a good job. 'Cause not a lot of people have that chance to get an education and have a good job. People [who drop out] are usually [working] at Burger King or McDonalds or something, or a grocery store.

My sister is involved in the school. She works at a school. She's a teacher's aide with four-year-olds in the preschool. She likes it. She's thinking of getting a degree and her own job, I mean her own classroom for herself where she's teaching. She wants me to go to college. She's told me before and she talks to me about it a lot. [She asks about] what colleges do I want to go into, or whatever. My sister and her husband, they're there whenever I need help. They're fun to be around. But my sister's a little bit uptight because she's never had to take care of a teenager.

Grades are important to me. I don't like a C or below. I love to make my family happy. Making them feel good, letting them know that I do good in school and that I try to keep my grades up high. Grades are important at home. My sister and her husband, they would want a B or above. They would prefer an A. They'll talk to me and they'll help me out with whatever I need, but they would rather an A. But they're not too happy with the C's. I mean they're OK with it, but they would rather an A.

Desire for Academic Challenge

School ended up pretty good freshman year [at Red Rock High School]. It was pretty good; it could have been a lot better. I liked how we actually could go out in fieldwork and actually learn stuff, not in school but the actual place where history happened. I wouldn't mind getting pushed a little bit harder. When there was a little bit more of a challenge, I did good. I got A's, B's, and C's. I only got one D in my whole life. When I got that D, me and the teacher, we kinda knocked heads. We didn't work together. I could do better. I could be pushed more.

I want to go to Mountain Academy—they push you a little harder there. They don't really get to go out on field trips as much, but I want a new environment. I want something that's going to help me a little bit more—push me a little harder. Mountain Academy is more challenging. I want to be pushed harder. I want to meet new people. I want to see what's better for me.

I think [the teachers at Red Rock High School should] maybe get it to the next level. Mainly, when we wrote stuff, they don't push you hard. For your last final grade for the trimester, they would just pick your highest grade and give you that. Other kids passed when they were just not really doing the work in class. I feel like I slacked off a bit. I am a talkative person and sometimes I talked too much.

[In school] we have talked about what we want to do or be, but we don't talk much about college. In the future, I see me being a person that actually has nice work that's got money. I could support my kids that I have and the family. Help my family out and everything. Just a nice future. I am thinking of going into the medical field when I graduate, or the law enforcement field. Nobody is talking with me about helping me choose classes. [I am hoping to become] a doctor for children, a pediatrician or else law enforcement, border patrol. . . . I am not interested in law enforcement as much as I was when I lived in Texas, but I am still thinking about it. When I lived in Texas, I lived near the border, and I saw the border patrol trucks all over the place. Now I am thinking a doctor—helping children.

Commentary

The fusion of language and cultural identity became obvious during Alicia's interview. Her family and home community deeply influenced the intertwined relationship of her mother tongue and distinctive way of life. She seemed shocked to discover that in Colorado, there are Mexicans who don't speak Spanish. As she changed communities and geographic region, the role of her bilingualism changed. Her perspective grew from taking her bilingualism for granted as intrinsic to everyday life, to perceiving her language skills as a precious asset, realizing that "some kids lose their Spanish, their own language." Although she had been academically bilingual since first grade, Alicia referred to Spanish as her language and equated knowing it with knowing her culture.

Notably, Alicia referred to the monolingual Spanish-speaking Mexican students as "knowing pure Spanish," meaning that they spoke only Spanish. At no time in the interview did she use deficit labels commonly heard in school policies and practices such as "non-English-speaking," "students without English," or "limited English proficient." She consistently referred to those peers as "pure Spanish speakers" and supported bilingual education, even though she herself did not participate in such a program.

In terms of advice for teachers, Alicia urged them to get to know her culture by learning to understand her language. She emphasized the importance of being patient with pure Spanish speakers and recommended offering support while still providing challenge. In addition, she encouraged teachers to "ask the kids." Her statements echo my (Patty's) research findings that urban students continually urge teachers to "just ask kids about their culture."[11] Alicia's insistence on being challenged academically also resonates with a great deal of research that has found that many students view school curriculum as not challenging enough, which contributes to decisions to drop out. For example, in a broad survey of more than 500 students who did not complete high school, 47 percent cited boredom and irrelevant curriculum as reasons for dropping out, challenging the myth that these students may be incapable of the work.[12]

Alicia's refusal to settle for limited opportunities and to accept stereotypical messages contributed to the construction of her "counterstory." Alicia's words resonate with the work of researcher Tara J. Yosso, who writes about the "very serious leaks" in the Chicana/Chicano educational pipeline. The harmful stereotypes stem from a majoritarian story that assumes all people have access to equal education and that faults Chicana/Chicano students for not taking advantage of that equal opportunity.

In Yosso's work, counterstories point out the bias in the majoritarian story and reveal the structural, practical, and discursive influences that facilitate the high dropout (pushout) rates along the Chicana/Chicano educational pipeline.[13]

Supporting and working for family and strong identification with, and solidarity among, family members are qualities that are held in high esteem in most Mexican communities.[14] Because of the centrality of the role of family in Mexican culture, and Alicia's perspective as a contemporary Latina and an academic high-achiever, she may have been zigzagging through multiple cultural intersections in trying to negotiate statements about what is expected of Mexicans. Straddling the realms of race, class, and gender are especially challenging for a youth in her position.

Despite the various social and institutional structures that can impede academic success, Alicia was committed to continuing her academic achievement by trying to enroll in a different high school that would push her a little harder. Her statements about the importance of school and grades express her family's values and teachings of *respeto*. Linking the completion of high school with a "nice future," she said that she had aspirations to go to college and become a professional: either a medical doctor or a border patrol officer. While the latter may seem an ironic choice for a second-generation Mexican American, the social context reveals a great deal. In her economically strapped community on the Texas border, one of the only professional opportunities to which she was exposed was driving a border patrol truck. Her imagined engagement in border patrol also indexes what Ricardo D. Stanton-Salazar refers to as "playing host to the system." He argues that, for many Mexican-origin urban youth, the diminished pool of resources, lack of institutional support, structured segregation, and cultural alienation lead community members to reproduce the unequal, hierarchical relations of the racialized, patriarchal, capitalist society.[15]

Alicia's goals are visibly tied to making her family proud and her hope to adequately provide for a future family. These perspectives point to the urgency of wide-ranging curriculum choices and the role of expansive career and college counseling, especially for youth who are first-generation college-bound students. Their parents and/or guardians may be unfamiliar with the complexities of the U.S. educational system. The cultural capital and social fluency required to be admitted to, and eventually succeed in, a quality college cannot be underestimated.

Alicia certainly demonstrated agency through her efforts in planning her educational future by, for example, actively seeking supportive institutional structures. It remains to be seen if the structures and cultural processes at her new school provide the robust academic challenge and collaborative relationships that would help her succeed.

Reflect on This Case Study

1. How can you support students who speak "pure Spanish" (or any other language), even if you don't speak the language or don't teach ESL?
2. It is obvious that Alicia's identity is important to her. Besides the examples she gave of an art teacher's support for her identity and another teacher's Spanish-language ability, what other ways can you think of to support her pride in her culture?
3. Alicia mentioned that there isn't much conversation in school about going to college. What can you do, as a classroom teacher, to encourage these conversations?

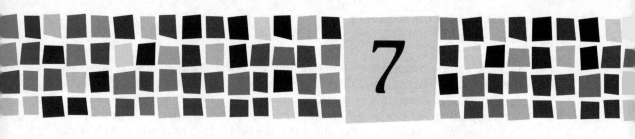

Understanding Student Learning and School Achievement

As improbable as it might sound, the words in this quote are those of a young man who was suspended and expelled from school on many occasions. A gang member with a difficult family life, Paul Chavez had managed to be accepted into an alternative school, where he was experiencing academic success for only the second time in his life. As you will see in his case study, which follows this chapter, Paul was resolute about continuing his education and becoming a teacher or counselor to help young people like himself. Given his background and experiences, however, few people would have believed that he was capable of learning. Conventional theories of academic success or failure do not explain cases such as Paul's.

"There's so much to learn and that's all I want to do is just learn, try to educate my mind to see what I could get out of it."

—**Paul Chavez, interviewee**

This chapter examines a number of theories about the complex conditions that may affect school achievement and then considers how these conditions can collectively influence the academic success or failure of students. After the discussion of these theories, the case studies of two students who have *not* been successful in school, Paul Chavez and Latrell Elton, are presented. Both of these young men were written off by their respective schools and teachers as incapable of becoming successful students. Their cases demonstrate that learning can take place even in the most difficult personal and societal circumstances.

In what follows, we review explanations of school success or underachievement through theories that address the following issues: *caring, deficit perspectives, economic and social reproduction, cultural incompatibilities, out-of-school factors, resistance and the school-to-prison pipeline, cultural-ecological theories,* and *complicating theories of identities within school structures.* The chapter concludes by pointing out the need to develop a comprehensive understanding of student learning, rather than relying on only one theoretical explanation.

Caring

An essential component in promoting student learning is what Nel Noddings has called the "ethic of care."[1] Noddings's impressive contribution to the conversation concerning student engagement with schooling cannot be overemphasized. For her, educators' caring is just as important—and in some cases, even more so—than larger structural conditions that influence student learning. Noddings postulates that whether and how teachers and schools care for students can make an immense difference in how students experience schooling. Her research is corroborated by a nationwide survey of several hundred 13- to 17-year-old students who were asked whether they work harder for some teachers than for others. Three out of four said yes, and they explained the reason was because these were the teachers who cared most for them. The survey authors concluded that effective schooling relies almost entirely on creative and passionate teachers.[2]

Angela Valenzuela, in a three-year investigation of academic achievement among Mexican and Mexican American students in a Texas high school, provides compelling examples of care among a small number of teachers.[3] Teachers showed they cared through close and affirming relationships with their students, high expectations for students' capabilities, and respect for students' families. This was the case in spite of the general context of the school that provided what Valenzuela called *subtractive schooling*, that is, a process that divested students of the social and cultural resources they brought to their education, making them vulnerable for academic failure. Her research led Valenzuela to equate the problem of "underachievement" not with students' identities or parents' economic situation but with school-based relationships and organizational structures. Nilda Flores-Gónzales, in a study among Latino students in Chicago, came to similar conclusions.[4] For these researchers, care was shown to be of immense significance.

More examples of the ethic of care can be found in the burgeoning body of research on the topic. Rosalie Rólon-Dow, in a study of Puerto Rican middle school girls, proposes that what is needed is *critical care* that responds to historical understandings of

Kevin. N. Costa, in Sara Cummins art class, Cameron Middle School in Framingham, Massachusetts. *Self-portrait.* Charcoal. 2010.

students' lives and to the institutional barriers they encounter as members of racialized groups. In this way, Rólon-Dow examines caring at both the individual and institutional levels.[5] In another study, Rubén Garza investigated the perceptions of Latino and White high school students' reporting on teacher behaviors that convey caring. He found five dominant themes that described what students appreciated about the strategies their teachers used: Teachers (1) provided scaffolding during a teaching episode, (2) reflected a kind disposition through actions, (3) were always available to the student, (4) showed a personal interest in the students' well-being inside and outside the classroom, and (5) provided affective academic support in the classroom setting. Garza examined both the similarities and the unique experiences between the two student ethnic groups and suggested ways that teachers can evaluate their own practices of culturally responsive caring.[6]

Another example comes from a study that focused on students of Mexican descent in California. In this migrant education program, researchers Margaret Gibson and Livier Bejínez discovered that staff members facilitated students' learning in various ways: caring relationships, access to institutional support, and activities based on students' cultural backgrounds. The researchers concluded that caring relationships were at the very heart of the program's success. Specifically, in spite of students' vulnerable status (including their migrant status, poverty, and the fact that only 7 percent had parents who had completed high school), there was a remarkably high degree of school persistence. Nearly halfway through their senior year, 75 percent were still attending high school. As in other research highlighted here, the researchers explain *caring* not just as affection but as close and trusting relationships that, most important, create a sense of *belonging* in the school community. This sense of belonging is especially meaningful, they conclude, for Mexican American and other students of color because of the power differential that exists between them and people of the dominant society.[7]

In research focused on African American communities in a southeastern state, Mari Ann Roberts investigated how the ethic of care was practiced among a group of eight African American teachers of African American students. She found that expressing concern for students' future with candor and support dispels the color-blind equal opportunity myth that is often perpetuated in schools. She posits a framework of *culturally relevant critical teacher care* that provides a counternarrative to current discussions of teacher care as color-blind actions that try to help all students or are considered just part of good teaching.[8] Hence, *care* does not just mean giving students hugs or pats on the back. Care means loving students in the most profound ways: through high expectations, great support, and rigorous demands.

These ideas resounded in two distinct research projects we (Sonia and Patty) each conducted. When I (Sonia) asked teachers to explain why they teach, I found five qualities that describe caring and committed teachers: *a sense of mission, solidarity with and empathy for students, the courage to challenge mainstream knowledge, improvisation,* and *a passion for social justice.*[9] All of these qualities are rooted in caring and committed practices, but here we focus on the second quality: *solidarity with and empathy for students.* Solidarity and empathy can also be described as love, although *love* is not a word that one hears very often when discussing teaching. Within the context of schools, love means that teachers have genuine respect, high expectations, and great admiration for their students. *Solidarity* means remembering what it was like to be a child, and forming a community of learners. The combination of empathy and solidarity is demonstrated in numerous ways, including valuing students' families, understanding what life is like for children of diverse backgrounds, and anticipating the various worlds they encounter.

Patty's study echoed Sonia's. When I (Patty) interviewed students in urban schools, I asked them what teachers needed to know to be effective in diverse classrooms. Their answers consistently pointed to solidarity with, and empathy for, students. One of the implications that my study asserts is that reconceptualized multicultural teacher education may need to consider ways to educate preservice teachers in what were previously called *unteachable qualities* such as solidarity, empathy, and compassion to influence high academic achievement.[10] Frameworks on care that require teachers to take a positive, proactive approach to their students' achievement provide a useful backdrop when examining the other hypotheses about causes of academic success or school failure discussed in this chapter.

Deficit Perspectives

The theory that genetic or cultural inferiority is the cause of academic failure has been a recurrent theme in U.S. educational history. Throughout the past several decades, much of the research on school failure focused on what was assumed to be the inadequacy of students' home environment and culture. In an early review of research concerning the poor achievement of Black children, for instance, Stephen and Joan Baratz found that most of the research they achieved was based on the assumption that Black children were deficient in language, social development, and intelligence. This assumption resulted in blaming students' failure to achieve on their so-called deficits. Singled out for blame were children's *poorly developed language* (more concretely, the fact that they did not speak Standard English); an *inadequate mother* (the assumption being that low-income Black mothers were invariably poor parents); *too little stimulation* in the home (that Black children's homes lacked the kinds of environments that encouraged learning); *too much stimulation* in the home (their homes were too chaotic and disorganized or simply not organized along middle-class norms); and a host of other, often contradictory hypotheses. Baratz and Baratz found that the homes and backgrounds of Black children and poor children, in general, were classified in the research as "sick, pathological, deviant, or underdeveloped."[11] Such caricatures, which continue to exist, are of little value to teachers and schools who want to provide their students with a high-quality education.

The case studies of Paul and Latrell, which follow this chapter, are compelling examples of life in difficult circumstances: both lived in poverty with families headed by single mothers, both had been involved in antisocial and criminal behavior, and both had had negative school experiences. One might be tempted to write them off because of these circumstances, but as their case studies demonstrate, both Paul and Latrell began achieving academic success in alternative schools. Deficit explanations of school achievement cannot explain their success.

Although more comprehensive explanations of academic achievement have been proposed in recent decades, theories of genetic inferiority espoused during the 1920s eugenics movement and theories about cultural deprivation popularized during the 1960s have left a mark on the schooling of children living in poverty and of children of color. These theories are not only classist and racist but are also simply inadequate in explaining the schooling experiences of many students. Although the social and economic conditions of their communities and families *can* be significant contributing factors in the academic failure of students, they alone are not the cause of student failure or success. As an early critic of deficit theories, the late William Ryan turned the argument of cultural deprivation on its head by claiming that it was a strategy to "blame the victim." In a book that had a great impact in challenging the theory of cultural inferiority during its heyday in the 1960s and 1970s, Ryan was eloquent in his critique:

> We are dealing, it would seem, not so much with culturally deprived children as with culturally depriving schools. And the task to be accomplished is not to revise, amend, and repair deficient children, but to alter and transform the atmosphere and operations of the schools to which we commit these children.[12]

Students' identities—that is, their sense of self based in part on their race, ethnicity, social class, and language, among other characteristics—can also have an impact on their academic success or failure, but it is not these characteristics per se that *cause* success or failure. Rather, it is the school's *perception* of students' language, culture, and class as *inadequate* and *negative,* and thus the devalued status of these characteristics in the academic environment, that help explain school failure. In Paul Chavez's case, his early gang affiliation had had a decided negative effect on teachers' academic expectations of him. To underscore the essential role of teachers' perspectives, Ronald Ferguson describes two instructional conditions that are especially significant in classrooms where children of color are in the majority *and* are academically successful. These are teaching styles that he calls *high help* and *high perfectionism.* High help is when the teacher communicates convincingly that she likes it when students ask questions and that she loves to help them when they are confused or making mistakes. High perfectionism is when the teacher consistently and continually presses students to strive for both understanding and accuracy in their assignments.[13] Ferguson points out that the combination of *high help* and *high perfectionism* communicates high expectations to students. Unfortunately for many children of color and those in economically strapped communities, deficit perspectives have dominated how they are viewed. The result has been low expectations on the part of educators.

That the behaviors of middle-class parents of any race or ethnic group tend to be different from those of poor parents is amply documented. Parents living in poverty either may be unaware of the benefits of what middle-class parents know by experience or may be unable to provide certain activities for their children. Middle-class parents, for example, usually speak Standard English. They also tend to engage in school-like prereading activities much more regularly than working-class parents. Schools deem other activities in which middle-class parents and their children participate as essential to educational success: going to the library on a consistent basis, attending museums and other cultural centers, and providing a host of other experiences that schools and society have labeled enriching.

Whether these activities are, in fact, enriching is not in question; the problem is that the activities of poor families, some of which may also be enriching, are not viewed in the same way. For example, many poor families travel either to their original home countries or to other parts of the United States from where they originally came. Children may spend summers "down South" or in Jamaica or Mexico, but what they learn on these trips is usually ignored by the school, in spite of its potentially enriching character.

I (Sonia) recall, for example, that it never occurred to me that my own experience of visiting family in Puerto Rico between fifth grade and sixth grade might be of interest to my teacher or classmates. My teachers never told me this directly, but I had already gotten the message that issues of consequence to my family carried no great weight in school. When I think of the giant tarantula I caught, froze, and brought home, or of the many things I learned about living on a farm, or of how my Spanish substantially improved that summer, I can only conclude that these things might have been as interesting to my teacher and classmates as they were enlightening for me. I never shared them, however, believing that they were not related to school life.

Learning to affirm the culture of students in their education can make the difference between failure or academic achievement in many schools, especially where parents are expected to provide help in ways they may be unable to do. Some parents are unaware of how to give their children concrete support in areas such as homework, but this lack of support, in itself, does not necessarily produce school failure. Blaming parents or children for academic failure begs the question, for the role of schools is to educate *all* students from all families, not only the most academically gifted students from economically advantaged, mainstream, English-speaking, European American families. Students' home and family situations are seldom subject to change by the school. Because schools cannot change the living conditions of students, the challenge is to find ways to teach children effectively in spite of the poverty or other disabling conditions in which they may live. Instead of focusing on students' life circumstances, it makes sense for schools to focus on what they *can* change: school culture and school structure.

However, genetic and cultural inferiority theories are unfortunately not a thing of the past. While these misguided notions are closely related to the history of the 1920s and 1930s eugenics movement, which asserted a biological basis for White supremacy, remnants of such ill-founded theories are still evident. For the past 20 years the writings of Richard Herrnstein and Charles Murray have been resurrecting the argument that genetic inferiority was the root cause of academic failure among African American students.[14] Although widely discredited by serious scholars as both ethnocentric and scientifically unfounded, genetic and cultural inferiority theories have survived because they provide a simplistic explanation for complex problems.[15] That is, by accepting theories of genetic and cultural inferiority, the detrimental effects of structural inequality, racism, poverty, and inequitable schooling on student learning are left unexamined.

To examine such structural inequities, we need to understand the power of what has been called the *cultural capital* of dominant groups. According to Pierre Bourdieu, cultural capital can exist in three forms: dispositions of the mind and body; cultural goods, such as pictures, books, and other material objects; and educational qualifi-

■ ■ ■ ■ ■ ■ **What You Can Do**

Rely on Research to Expand Perspectives of Success

In conversations with fellow teachers—both casual chats and formal faculty meeting discussions—the topic of children's family lives frequently arises. Too often these comments link family home life and culture to underachievement. Often made with an air of authority, or by people in positions of authority, these statements are difficult to challenge and confusing to understand. However, you can challenge prejudicial assumptions without alienating yourself from your peers or losing your job. Rely on research. In a conversational tone that is both courteous and professional, ask about the research that shows evidence linking family culture to underachievement. Simultaneously, offer to share research that affirms students' cultural identities and cites strategies for teachers to promote school achievement. Use the wide range of scholarship cited in this chapter to assist you.

Teachers are smart and intellectually curious by nature. Their intellectual prowess deserves to be cultivated and supported. Teachers may also be overworked and have too much to read, so finding ways to integrate the most current research into school discussions can be helpful. Some strategies are described in two other What You Can Do features in this chapter.

cations. In all three forms, transmission of cultural capital is, according to Bourdieu, "no doubt the best hidden form of hereditary transmission of capital."[16] That is, the values, tastes, languages, dialects, and cultures that have most status are invariably associated with the dominant group. As a consequence, the weight of cultural capital cannot be ignored. To do so would be both naive and romantic because it would deny the reality that power, knowledge, and resources are located in the norms of dominant cultures and languages. As a result, to imply that working-class students and students from dominated groups need not learn the cultural norms of the dominant group is effectively to disempower the students who are most academically vulnerable. However, Bourdieu's concepts of reproduction are useful to counter the notion that cultural inferiority is the cause of academic failure; the curriculum should also be relevant to the cultural experiences and values of students from subordinated groups. A complete education needs to include *both* the norms and canon of the dominant culture and those of the dominated cultures because including culturally relevant curriculum is a valuable way to challenge a monocultural canon.

■ ■ ■ ■ ## Economic and Social Reproduction

The argument that schools reproduce the economic and social relations of society and therefore tend to serve the interests of the dominant classes, articulated first during the 1970s by scholars such as Samuel Bowles, Herbert Gintis, and Joel Spring, placed schools squarely in a political context.[17] According to this theory, the role of the schools was to keep the poor in their place by teaching them the proper attitudes and behaviors for becoming good workers and to keep the dominant classes in power by teaching their children the skills of management and control that would presumably prepare them to manage and control the working class. Schools, therefore, reproduced the status quo; they not only reflected structural inequalities based on class, race, and gender but also helped to maintain these inequalities.

Economic and social reproduction theorists maintain that the *sorting function of schools,* to use a term coined by Spring, is apparent in everything from physical structure to curriculum and instruction. For example, the schools of the poor are generally factory-like fortresses that operate with an abundance of bells and other controlling mechanisms, whereas the schools of the wealthy tend to be much more open physically and psychologically, allowing for greater autonomy and creative thinking on the part of students. Likewise, relations between students and teachers in poor communities reflect a dominant–dominated relationship much more so than in middle-class or wealthy communities. The curriculum also differs. More sophisticated and challenging knowledge is generally taught in wealthy schools, whereas the basics and rote memorization are the order of the day in poor schools. The sorting function of the schools results in an almost perfect replication of the stratification of society.

This thinking revolutionized the debate on the purposes and outcomes of schools and placed the success or failure of students in a new light. The benign, stated purpose of U.S. schooling to serve as an "equalizer" seriously questioned by these theories. For example, following the logic of this thinking, it is no accident that so many students in urban schools drop out; rather, it is an *intended outcome* of the educational system. That is, some students are intentionally channeled by schools to be either fodder for war or a reserve uneducated labor force. According to this theory, schools do just exactly what is expected of them: they succeed at school failure.

The arguments of the social reproduction theorists are compelling, and they have had an enormous impact on educational thinking since the 1970s. By concentrating on the labor-market purpose of schooling, however, these theories tended to offer static, oversimplified explanations of school success or failure. According to these theories, school life is almost completely subordinated to the needs of the economy, leaving little room for the role that students and their communities have in influencing school policies and practices. These analyses assume that schooling is simply imposed from above and accepted from below but, in reality, schools are complex and perplexing institutions, and things are not always this neat or apparent.

Because they place schools in a sociopolitical context, economic and social reproduction theories provide a more persuasive analysis of academic failure than either genetic and cultural inferiority or cultural incompatibility theories. Nevertheless, these analyses are incomplete because they can fall into—or can be misinterpreted as—mechanistic explanations of dynamic processes, assuming a simple cause-and-effect relationship. Such theories fail to explain, for example, why students from some culturally dominated communities have managed to succeed in school or why some schools in poor communities are extraordinarily successful in spite of tremendous odds. By emphasizing only the role of social class, these social and economic reproduction theories fail to explain why schools are also inequitable for females and for students of racially and culturally subordinated communities who do not necessarily live in poverty. In addition, these theories overlook the lengthy struggles over schooling in which many communities have been historically involved, for example, struggles about the desegregation of schools; bilingual education; multicultural education; and access to education for females as well as for lesbian, gay, bisexual, and transgender (LGBT) students and students with special needs. If education were simply imposed from above, these reforms would never have found their way, even imperfectly, into schools. Some theorists, such as Michael Apple, have suggested that schools are the product of conflicts among competing group interests and that the purposes of the dominant class are never perfectly realized in the schools but, rather, are resisted and modified by the recipients of schooling.[18]

Economic and social reproduction theories help explain how academic failure and success are not unintended outcomes but rather are logical results of differentiated schooling. They also help move the complete burden of failure from students, their families, and communities to the society at large, and they provide a macroanalytic, or societal, understanding of schooling. Social reproduction theories are also incomplete, however, because they generally fail to take cultural and psychological issues into account.

 ## Cultural Incompatibilities

Another explanation for school failure is that it is caused by cultural incompatibilities—that is, because school culture and home culture are often at odds, the result is a "cultural clash" that produces school failure. According to this explanation, it is necessary to consider the differing experiences, values, skills, expectations, and lifestyles children have when they enter school and how these differences, in being more or less consistent with the school environment, affect their achievement. The more consistent that home and school cultures are, the reasoning goes, the more successful students will be. This line of reasoning asserts that the opposite is also true: The more that students' experiences, skills, and values differ from the school setting, the more failure they will experience.

This explanation makes a great deal of sense, and it explains school failure more convincingly than simple deficit theories. That some students learn more effectively in cooperative settings than in competitive settings is not a problem per se. What makes it a problem is that many schools persist in providing *only* competitive environments. Given this reality, cultural differences begin to function as a risk factor. This reasoning turns around the popular concept of "children at risk" so that the risk comes not from within the child but develops as a result of the interaction between the sociopolitical realities of some students and particular school policies, practices, and structures.

Likewise, the fact that some students enter school without speaking English is not, itself, a satisfactory explanation for why some of them fail in school. Rather, the interpretation of their non-English-speaking status and the value, or lack of value, given to the child's native language also matter. Whereas in some schools a student might be identified as non-English-speaking, in another school that same child might be called Khmer speaking. The difference is not simply a semantic one. In the first case, the child is assumed to be missing language, but in the second case, the child is assumed to possess language already, even if it is not the majority language. And because language ability is the major ingredient for school success, how schools and teachers perceive children's language is significant.

The cultural mismatch theory is more hopeful than deterministic explanations such as genetic inferiority or economic reproduction theories because it assumes that teachers can learn to create environments in which all students can be successful learners. It also respects teachers as creative intellectuals rather than as simple technicians. Teachers are expected to be able to develop a critical analysis of their students' cultures and to use this analysis to teach all their students effectively. In terms of the kind of knowledge teachers need to know about their students' realities, the late Paulo Freire eloquently described their responsibility:

> Educators need to know what happens in the world of the children with whom they work. They need to know the universe of their dreams, the language with which they skillfully defend themselves from the aggressiveness of their world, what they know independently of the school, and how they know it.[19]

Gloria Ladson-Billings, in coining the term *culturally relevant teaching,* has suggested that this kind of pedagogy is in sharp contrast to assimilationist teaching, whose main purpose is to transmit dominant culture beliefs and values in an uncritical way to all students. In the same vein, Geneva Gay's work in defining and explicating what she calls culturally responsive teaching has also been tremendously significant.[20]

Although the cultural mismatch theory is more comprehensive than deficit theories and is without their implicit racist and classist overtones, the cultural mismatch theory is also insufficient to explain why some students succeed and others fail. The extraordinarily high dropout rate among American Indian and Alaska Native students (higher than all other racial or ethnic groups in the United States) is a case in point. According to a comprehensive report by Susan Faircloth and John Tippeconnic from the Civil Rights Project, this crisis demands immediate action at the federal, state, local, and tribal levels. Providing "opportunities for students to be immersed in their Native language and culture and develop and implement culturally appropriate and relevant curricula" is one of the 12 strategies recommended in the report. This recommendation emphasizes that addressing cultural discontinuities through the curriculum can help, but this strategy alone is just a partial solution because the structural inequality that produces enormous poverty is left untouched.[21] The report includes cautions about making assumptions about what it means to be culturally relevant and culturally appropriate because of the wide range of cultural and linguistic diversity represented among the American Indian and Alaska Native student population, as well as diversity in the size, location, and type of schools they attend. Such diversity lessens the effectiveness of a one-size-fits-all approach. Rather, a variety of comprehensive yet flexible approaches are needed to decrease the dropout rate and in turn increase the number and percentage of Native American students who graduate from high school.[22]

Newer research points to a major weakness in the theory of cultural discontinuity: insufficient attention is given to cultural accommodation, biculturation, and hybridity experienced by immigrants and by multi-ethnic and multiracial students. No culture exists in isolation, and a rigid interpretation of the theory of cultural

■ ■ ■ ■ ■ ■   # What You Can Do
Build Collegial Relationships for Solidarity Rooted in Research

You may have the experience of a colleague saying something that rings of stereotyping and misinformation, for example, "Well, you know, Puerto Ricans, as a culture, do not value education." As upset as you may be, a full-blown confrontation will not solve the problem. Let your colleague know that you are uncomfortable, but that you want to talk more about the issue. Her perspective has been developed over time and thus will take some time to change. It is also unlikely that any single retort or conversation will change her view, so start with little things, such as, "Oh, I am surprised to hear that point of view. It doesn't match up with the families that I know. Did you read about that somewhere? Because I would like to know more."

Try to keep your conversations rooted in research and experience. For example, at an opportune moment, share some anecdotes about your positive experiences with Puerto Rican families in the school. At another time, share your excitement about, for example, the children's literature and cultural resources created by Edwin Fontánez of Exit Studio as great curriculum supplements.* Many teachers learn a great deal of cultural information from the children's resources they use in their classrooms. At another time, bring up some educational research that helps teachers support the academic achievement of Puerto Rican students, such as the book *Puerto Rican Students in U.S. Schools* edited by Sonia Nieto.[†] Also refer to work that examines the education of Latinos more broadly, for example, *Latino Education: An Agenda for Community Action Research,* edited by Pedro Pedraza and Melissa Rivera, and *The Handbook of Latinos and Education,* edited by Enrique Murillo.[‡]

*See Edwin Fontanez's Web site, at http://www.exitstudio .com/, for books, CDs, and videos about Puerto Rican culture from Exit Studio.

[†]Nieto, S. (Ed.) (2000). *Puerto Rican Students in U.S. Schools*. Mahwah, NJ: Lawrence Erlbaum.

[‡]Pedraza, P. & Rivera, M. (Eds.) (2005). *Latino Education: An Agenda for Community Action Research*. Mahwah, NJ: Lawrence Erlbaum; and Murillo, E. G., Jr. (Ed.) (2010). *Handbook of Latinos in Education: Theory, Research, and Practice*. New York: Routledge.

discontinuity presupposes that all children from the same cultural background experience school in the same way, yet we know this is far from true. The result of a cultural discontinuity perspective is that individual and family differences, school conditions, and the broader sociopolitical context that also influence learning may be disregarded. In fact, a rigid interpretation of this theory hovers dangerously close to stereotyping students from particular cultural groups, resulting in *limiting* views of them and thus *limited* educational opportunities for them. Because these constructed meanings have evolved from notions such as "the culture of poverty" asserted by Oscar Lewis and Michael Harrington in the 1960s, they may become rigid.[23]

Gloria Ladson-Billings notes that the way the concept of culture is used by some teachers and students in preservice teacher education can exacerbate the problem and perpetuate stereotypes. She points out that a growing number of teachers use the term *culture* as a catch-all for a wide variety of behaviors and characteristics when discussing students and parents who are not White, not English speaking, or not native-born U.S. citizens. For example, some teachers muse that "maybe it is part of their culture" for groups of students to be noisy or for parents to be absent from open house night. Not only are these assessments inaccurate, they also turn attention away from socioeconomic reasons or school policies and practices that might precipitate such behaviors. Parents may be absent from open house night for any number of reasons. For example, they may be working a night shift or caring for younger children, they may have no transportation, they may feel isolated or unwelcome in the school, or they may not have had a translation of the open house information into their language. Groups of children may be loud simply because they are groups of children, not because of their skin color or another reason related to "their culture."[24]

Another problem with the cultural discontinuity theory is that it cannot explain why students from some cultural groups are academically successful, even though, according to these theories, one might assume they should not be. This reality has been well documented by many scholars,[25] which leads us to other explanations, some of which we discuss below.

Out-of-School Factors (OSFs)

Examining social and economic inequities, and their resulting negative educational consequences, can assist in ascertaining how schools are effective or ineffective within the broader social picture. Richard Rothstein's research asserts that, outside school, myriad factors related to social class and how families in some groups are stratified in society profoundly influence learning in school. He advocates three approaches to pursue if progress is to be made in narrowing the "achievement gap": (1) promoting school improvement efforts that raise the quality of instruction; (2) giving more attention to out-of-school hours by implementing early childhood, after-school, and summer programs; and (3) implementing policies that would provide appropriate health services and stable housing and narrow the growing income inequalities in our society.[26] Likewise, David Berliner makes the argument that out-of-school factors (OSFs) caused by poverty *alone* place severe limits on what can be accomplished through educational reform efforts. His comprehensive list of eleven recommendations are made in light of the fact that "America's schools are so highly segregated by income, race, and ethnicity, that problems related to poverty occur simultaneously, with greater frequency, and act cumulatively in schools serving disadvantaged communities."[27] Making the case that schools in these economically depressed communities face greater challenges than schools in economically stable communities, Berliner asserts that efforts to improve educational outcomes are unlikely to succeed unless policies are implemented to address six OSFs that significantly affect learning opportunities: (1) low birth-weight and nongenetic prenatal influences on children; (2) inadequate medical, dental, and vision care; (3) food insecurity; (4) environmental pollutants; (5) family relations and family stress; and (6) neighborhood characteristics.[28]

An example of addressing OSFs simultaneously with school achievement can be found in the work of Geoffrey Canada, president of the Harlem Children's Zone (HCZ).[29] HCZ, which is funded mostly by private donations, infuses social, medical, and educational services for free to the 10,000 children and their families who live within the 10 blocks of the HCZ. The specific intent of HCZ is to raise academic achievement for every child. Canada's reluctance to wait for governmental funding for comprehensive reform led him to integrate private funding with public programs. The HCZ's rates of success have been a model to public social service and public school reformers throughout the nation and point to what the possibilities can be for government officials with the will and the resources to back such programs.[30]

Undeniably, many students face a multitude of difficult problems, and the school cannot be expected to solve them all. To address this reality, the Economic Policy Institute convened a task force that drafted a statement titled *A Broader, Bolder Approach to Education* to inform legislators and the general public. The task force concluded that "school improvement, to be fully effective, . . . must be complemented by a broader definition of schooling and by improvements in the social and economic circumstances of disadvantaged youth." To continue to close achievement gaps, their report calls for (1) continued school improvement efforts; (2) developmentally appropriate and high-quality early childhood, preschool, and kindergarten care and education; (3) routine pediatric, dental, hearing, and vision care for all infants, toddlers, and schoolchildren; and (4) improvement of the quality of students' out-of-school time.[31] Pedro Noguera consistently argues that, because poor children typically attend schools that are overcrowded, underfunded, and staffed by inexperienced teachers, schools need to be viewed as an integral part of social solutions. Noguera emphasizes that "reducing poverty and improving schools should not be treated as competing goals."[32]

The research on OSFs is helpful in explaining how the lack of health care, inadequate nutrition, inadequate housing, and unstable family life impinge on school experiences. These arguments assertively address social supports that are required for schools to be successful in educating all children. This scholarship ties social and economic factors together *with* effective school reform rather than separating social reform efforts from school reform agendas. Graphically illustrated in his aptly titled book, *Five Miles Away, A World Apart,* James E. Ryan, a scholar of education law, presents a comprehensive case comparison of two schools in Virginia that exemplifies the multifaceted historical missteps in policy that have led to ingrained segregationist mind-sets and practices, creating the crisis of high-poverty schools. Ryan urges reform efforts to address *simultaneously* both educational policies to support schools *and* social policies to support families.[33]

The conclusions of the research reviewed in this section emphasize the powerlessness of schools to achieve educational equity on their own without concomitant massive social reforms. The research also argues that educational reform efforts that do not take into account the social and economic conditions outside schools can be only partially successful. Considered in this way, OSFs must be addressed in order to affect student learning and school achievement.

Resistance and the School-to-Prison Pipeline

Resistance theory, as articulated by scholars such as Henry Giroux, Jim Cummins, and Herbert Kohl, adds another layer to the explanation of school failure.[34] According to this theory, not learning what schools teach can be interpreted as a form of political resistance. Frederick Erickson maintains that, whereas cultural differences may cause some initial school failures and misunderstandings, it is only when they become entrenched over time that *not-learning,* a consistent pattern of refusing to learn, becomes the outcome of schooling.[35]

Resistance theory is helpful because it attempts to explain the complex relationship between disempowered communities and their schools. Students and their families are not only victims of the educational system, they are also actors. They learn to react to schools in ways that make perfect sense, given the reality of the schools, although some of these coping strategies may be self-defeating and counterproductive in the long run. On the other hand, Herb Kohl, describing "not-learning" as the response of students who refuse to learn, has concluded, "Over the years I've come to side with them in their refusal to be molded by a hostile society and have come to look upon not-learning as positive and healthy in many situations."[36]

There are numerous examples of students' resistance, and they range from innocuous to dangerous: inattention in class, failure to do homework, negative attitudes toward schoolwork, poor relationships with teachers, misbehavior, vandalism, and violence are all illustrations of students' resistance. However, rather than venerate self-destructive or delinquent behavior, Giroux's research distinguishes between resistance that is oppositional (deviant behavior) and resistance that is strategic (conscious and meant to achieve a common good).[37] We see many of these manifestations of resistance in the case studies of Paul Chavez and Latrell Elton, which follow this chapter.

Students who develop a critical consciousness may end up resisting education. Such students are often branded and punished as loudmouths and troublemakers. Although some drop out, others choose to stop participating actively in the "game" of school. They might still show up, but they may adopt a passive or passive-aggressive stance. Others end up cutting many of their classes. Students who do continue coming to class may "dumb down" their own critical responses to the curriculum or to their teachers' pedagogy because they know instinctively that being seen as too smart or too much of a leader is potentially dangerous. Teachers, on the other hand, are often frustrated by apparently disinterested youth who look bored and disengaged even in honors classes, or who allow themselves to engage only minimally and only with the more interesting and inventive strategies used by creative teachers. As a result, many capable and critically aware students are intellectually "on strike" even though they may be physically present in school.[38]

The lifelong deleterious effects of schools' responses to resistance can have irreversible consequences in these times of hypersurveillance of youth, resulting in what has come to be known as the school-to-prison pipeline. Marian Wright Edelman and the Children's Defense Fund have thoroughly documented that young Black men in the United States are incarcerated in the juvenile justice system at four times the rate of White youth.[39] Several studies have pointed out how school disciplinary policies such as zero tolerance have contributed to the astonishing rate at which young people are funneled from classrooms into incarceration.[40] The situation has only worsened in the past decade, since 2000, when the Harvard Advancement Project and Civil Rights Project, in consultation with attorneys, psychiatrists, academicians, educators, and children's advocates, published a multidiscipline review that reported that zero tolerance is unfair and contrary to the developmental needs of children and often results in the criminalization of children.[41]

In addition to studies that examine the discipline policies of K–12 schools, Sabina Vaught articulated the constellation of forces in schools and courts that place blame on the youth, their families, and their communities.[42] John Raible and Jason Irizarry reach beyond critiquing the K–12 school structure; for example, they argue that pre-service teachers need to be educated about the crisis and to examine the role of teacher surveillance of youth through classroom management strategies as one of the factors that pushes students out of school and into the penal system.[43] Johanna Wald and Daniel J. Losen cited three specific themes that emerged in the research about the connections between school-life and prison-life for youth. These three themes are summarized here: (1) failure to provide appropriate behavioral interventions [in schools] may be contributing to delinquency among students with disabilities; (2) following removal from school, many students experience enormous difficulty in reentering; and (3) effective interventions and programs that reduce risk and enhance protective factors for youth at risk for delinquency do exist. The conclusions of Wald and Losen point to the political will urgently required to expand and replicate models of preventive measures for youth.[44]

Pedro Noguera and Chiara M. Cannella address such preventive measures by analyzing youth agency and activism and by suggesting public policy that would support youth civic activism. By examining the various ways in which youth who have been marginalized and maligned have taken action to resist—against all odds—the forces that have constrained their lives, Noguera and Cannella (following Giroux) emphasize *strategic resistance* and distinguish it from some forms of delinquency and defiance that may not only be self-destructive, but may also be a form of conformity to societal norms and reinforce stereotypes perpetuated by the media and marketplace. They call for five principles for public policy to advance as social justice youth policy: (1) a bill of rights for young people, (2) representation of young people in the formulation and development of policy, (3) investment in the capacity of youth leaders, (4) increased accountability of public institutions to disenfranchised youth and communities, and (5) counteracting the prevalence—and impact—of misconceptions and distortions about youth. They admit that developing such policy might be complicated, but they also point to the urgency with which these issues must be addressed, particularly when seen in the light of the cumulative effects of past policies that have divested attention away from youth.[45]

What causes students to resist education and otherwise engage in behaviors that might ultimately jeopardize their chances of learning or increase their chances of involvement with the law? There is no simple answer to this question, but one element that contributes to the constellation of reasons is a school climate that rejects students' identities and fails to engage them in meaningful work. This is nowhere more evident than in the case studies that follow this chapter. Both Paul and Latrell were eloquent in describing how their backgrounds were not reflected in the school structures and curriculum. Latrell, especially, had perceived few positive messages in his school experience.

What You Can Do
Engage in Collaborative Research to Promote Teaching as Intellectual Work

In addition to building personal, collegial relationships, take action for building schoolwide awareness among your peers. Suggest to your principal, department chair, or curriculum director that a forthcoming faculty or department meeting be dedicated to reading some educational research about student achievement. It is most effective to allow time for reading and discussion within the meeting time frame because many teachers may not have time to read in preparation for the meeting. This chapter is filled with citations of books, chapters, and articles about particular topics. You may choose a single article or a book chapter. For a more comprehensive view, such as the one provided by this chapter, break the faculty into small groups and assign each group a short article or portion of a chapter to read. Regroup the whole faculty and ask each group to report on the findings of the article or chapter section and what the implications may be for your particular school community, thereby co-constructing a wider range of group knowledge.

Even if this seems like an untenable request of your administration, ask anyway. How do you know unless you try? If the first level of administration, let's say, the principal, rejects the idea, try another level (department head, grade-level chair, team leader, districtwide curriculum director, or superintendent). If your attempts to organize "sanctioned" in-school study-group discussions fail, try an after-school voluntary group. Whether the study groups are voluntary or assigned, be sure you document the time and get professional development points or credits for all participants. These strategies may be applied to a range of educational research topics.

Cultural-Ecological Theory: Immigration, Minorities, and "Acting White"

A traditional argument used to explain differences in academic achievement is that (in the common parlance of public schools) it takes students from certain cultural groups who are not doing well in school a generation or two to climb the ladder of success, just as it took all other immigrants to do so. While this argument may be true for some European immigrants (but by no means for all), it is a specious argument for others because it fails to explain the educational and historical experiences of African Americans, American Indians, Asian Americans, and Latinos, which are markedly different from those of European ethnic groups. For one, American Indians, African Americans, and many Mexican Americans can hardly be called new immigrants. Many have been here, on U.S. soil, for generations, and some for millennia. Also, some Asians have been here for four or five generations, and although many do well in school, others are not as successful.

In an alternative explanation of school failure and success, the late John Ogbu and colleagues developed what he called a cultural-ecological theory, which goes beyond cultural discontinuities. Ogbu and Herbert Simons suggested that it is necessary to look not only at a group's cultural background but also at its situation in the host society and its perceptions of opportunities available in that society.[46] Ogbu classifies most immigrants in the United States as voluntary immigrants, and racial minority group immigrants as either voluntary or involuntary minorities, that is, those who come of their own free will as compared with those who were conquered or colonized.[47] The latter groups, including American Indians, Africans, Mexicans, and Puerto Ricans, among others, were incorporated into U.S. society against their will. According to Ogbu, voluntary immigrants include all European and some Asian, African, and Central American immigrants, among others. The distinction is not always true, of course, because those who appear on the surface to be voluntary immigrants may not be so at all, and vice versa. Witness, for example, the current situation of millions of Mexicans who not only come to the United States voluntarily, but risk their lives to do so. Those who arrive here as refugees, whether from Cambodia, Sudan, Somalia, or Afghanistan, do not fit neatly into voluntary or involuntary categories because many were forced from their homelands. Nevertheless, the categories, imperfect as they are, are used in cultural-ecological theory to explain the present condition and educational experiences of some groups.

Ogbu concluded that students from particular backgrounds experience a great variability in academic performance, and this variability can often be explained by the sociopolitical setting in which they find themselves. The visions, hopes, dreams, and experiences of voluntary and involuntary minorities also need to be kept in mind. According to Ogbu, most voluntary minorities have a "folk theory" of school success: They see the United States as a land of opportunity where one gets ahead through education and hard work. According to this view, even a relative newcomer with few skills and little education can succeed economically, and their children can experience even more success if they work hard in school, largely because these immigrants have great faith in the "American dream." As a result, they apply themselves to achieve it. They understand that, to achieve success, they may have to endure, for example, racism, economic hardships, and working at several menial jobs at the same time. These are accepted as the price they have to pay for success. Immigrants coming from war-torn countries or refugee camps and those who have experienced the death of loved ones may not consider living in an economically depressed neighborhood and engaging in backbreaking work to be a severe hardship.[48]

On the other hand, claims Ogbu, because of the long history of discrimination and racism in U.S. schools, involuntary minority children and their families are often distrustful of the educational system. Children in these communities have routinely been subjected to what Jim Cummins calls identity eradication,[49] whereby their culture and language have been stripped away as one of the conditions for success. These negative experiences result in their perception that equal educational opportunity and the folk theories of getting ahead in the United States are myths. The folk theories, however, are readily accepted by immigrants who have not had a long history of discrimination in this country. Given this situation, Ogbu claims that it is not unusual for students from what he called caste-like minorities to engage in *cultural inversion*, that is, to resist acquiring and demonstrating the culture and cognitive styles identified with the dominant group. He asserts that these behaviors, considered "White," include being studious and hardworking, speaking standard English, listening to European classical music, going to museums, getting good grades, and so on. Instead, involuntary minority students may choose to emphasize cultural behaviors that differentiate them from the majority and are in opposition to it—that is, to demonstrate what Ogbu calls *oppositional behavior*. Such behaviors include language, speech forms, and other manifestations that help to characterize their group but are contrary to the behaviors sanctioned and promoted by the schools.

Even extremely bright students from involuntary minority groups may try just to get by because they fear being ostracized by their peers if they engage in behaviors that conform to the mainstream culture. They must cope, according to Signithia Fordham and John Ogbu, "with the burden of acting White."[50] These students, assert Fordham and Ogbu, see little benefit from academic success, at least in terms of peer relationships. Those who excel in school may feel both internal ambivalence and external pressures not to manifest such behaviors and attitudes. In research conducted in a predominantly African American high school, Fordham and Ogbu found that successful students who were accepted by their peers also were either very successful in sports or had found another way (for example, by being class clown) to hide their academic achievement. According to Ogbu, involuntary minority parents, who themselves have a long history of discrimination and negative experiences at school, may subconsciously mirror these same attitudes, adding to their children's ambivalent attitudes about education and success.

Cultural-ecological theories have been helpful in explaining differences in the school experiences of students of various backgrounds. Ogbu's explanation of oppositional culture has been criticized as being dangerously close to the old concept of the culture of poverty. The theories have come under great scrutiny and criticism for being incomplete, ahistorical, and inflexible in allowing for individual differences. For example, Ogbu's theory may result in placing an inordinate responsibility on students and families without taking into account conditions outside their control that also affect learning. In addition, Ogbu's theories do not explain the long struggle of African American and other involuntary minorities for educational equality, nor do they explain the tremendous faith so many of these communities have had in the promise of public education.

Some scholars and educators have found Ogbu's theories too dichotomous and deterministic. For example, the typology does not neatly fit all groups, such as Mexican Americans, who share elements of both voluntary and involuntary minorities. Also, recent studies—most notably, one by Margaret Gibson—have found that the second generation of voluntary minorities is experiencing as much school failure as more established involuntary minorities because they do not wholeheartedly accept the folk theory of success like their parents did. They are also less likely to perceive the long-term benefits of hard work and study.[51]

Another criticism has to do with the role and influence of oppositional culture. As viewed by Ogbu, oppositional culture is detrimental to academic success because, in rejecting behaviors and attitudes that can lead to success, students are, in effect, jeopardizing their own futures. The possibility that African American students could be *both* oppositional *and* academically successful is not presented as a possibility in Ogbu's theory. David Gillborn, who has studied youths of

SNAPSHOT

Nini Rostland

Nini Rostland[1] is a 15-year-old freshman at Avery High School in a midsize college town in the Midwest. She describes herself as racially and ethnically mixed. Her mother is Black South African and her father is Polish American. Her family moved from South Africa to the United States when she was in kindergarten, so most of her education has been in U.S. public schools. This snapshot of Nini emphasizes that many students of mixed heritage negotiate labels, assumptions, and expectations with friends and teachers in school settings.

It kind of makes me mad that they always try to put people into a certain box. You have to check a box every time you fill out a form. I don't fit in a box. Especially these days, more people are getting more and more racially mixed. I don't identify myself as Black or as White. I usually put "both" or "other," because I'm not either; I'm both.

My cultural identity is really important to me. It makes me mad when people say, "Oh, you are not White." Well, I know I'm not White. I'm not Black either. People automatically assume that I'm not Caucasian, and they are automatically, "You're Black." And I'm, like, "Not necessarily." It makes me mad sometimes.

Being of mixed heritage is kind of difficult sometimes because it's hard finding where you fit in. For me, for a while I didn't really know what kind of people would accept me. Now I find people who accept me just as I am, not for trying to be like them. Now I try to hang out with people who are of all different races. I hang out with the Black people, the mixed people, the White people, Asian, everything. I don't like to be classified as a certain thing. The Black people treat me like I'm one of them. I find that Black people are more accepting of people in their group. More of the White people are, like, "You're not rich and you're not White, so you can't be in our group." Most likely, if you are mixed with some Black, the group of Black people will accept you.

Some of my friends would say that you can be attracted to both, that White people can like you, mixed people can like you, and Black people can like you. My closest group of friends, there's a foursome of us, and we all became really close over the summer at this camp for people of mixed heritage or of other ethnic backgrounds. And over that camp we have become really, best friends. That was in seventh grade. So for two years now, we've all been really close. And three of my friends are . . . like me: mixed with Black and White, and my other friend is African.

It's difficult because you don't really fit anybody's expectation. I think expectations may be holding me back a little bit. I think when people see me, they assume, "Oh, she's Black." They automatically assume, "Oh, she's not going to achieve well." That is kind of holding me back because it's sort of like a psychological thing where you think, "Well, if that's what people expect you to achieve," then you kind of think, "Oh, I might achieve that." I'm trying to turn that around, and be, like, "Well I can achieve anything I want to."

I think school in some ways is kind of like mainstreaming. It's what we are all forced into doing when we're young: You have to go to school, you have to get an education, you have to go to college so you

various backgrounds in Great Britain, suggests that the dichotomy between resistance and conformity is too simplistic because it overlooks the great complexity of students' responses to schooling. That is, accommodation does not guarantee that success will follow, nor is it the only way to be academically successful; similarly, can get a good job. But really, I think if you look back at history, the people who went out of the way of the expectations of society, they were the ones who went on to be really great. I understand that there is a good reason why I should go to school because I don't want to be working at McDonald's my entire life. But I also think that it's important that I be able to explore other things.

School's really not that challenging to me. One of the classes that I actually learn something in and enjoy is art class because I am learning a lot of new techniques. But most of my other classes are just memorization, and I'm really not learning anything from it. I have found very few teachers who actually teach classes in an interesting way that makes me really want to work. But when I see all the stuff that my mom did, it makes me feel like my mom went through a lot harder stuff than I have went through, so I should try my hardest at what I'm doing right now. One way that I think school is really important is through my mom. Because I have seen that to get to where she came from, she had to put in a lot of effort and go through a lot of high-level schooling just so that she could come to the U.S.

Both of my parents taught me about each of their heritages. I can just identify with that because that's me. I learned about my dad's Polish background because his parents are Polish and they make a lot of Polish dishes. We even went to a traditional Polish dinner where they made Polish meals and stuff like that. My dad has told me about some of the traditions they had when he was younger. Also, from my dad I've learned about social issues and what's going on in the world. I learn so much about government and that kind of stuff from my dad. From my mom I've learned ethnic pride. I'm really proud of my heritage. My mom is South African and she came through a lot just so that she could be here. I know a lot of history about what happened in South Africa and what my mom and my brother both lived through. They've told stories about what happened to them and stuff like that. But my parents don't really know what it's like to be of mixed heritage.

Commentary

Racial, ethnic, and cultural identities are constantly under construction, and adolescence is an especially vulnerable time for this formation. Messages from peers, family, popular culture, and school strongly influence a young person's perspectives on his or her cultural heritages, identities, and school engagement. In spite of the challenges presented by mixed heritage, Nini appears to possess a strong sense of identity and an appreciation for her background. Her parents provide her with familial, historical, and cultural knowledge, and she has formed powerful bonds, through a summer camp experience, with a small group of peers with similar roots. Simultaneously, she struggles with feelings of acceptance within certain groups and the threat of negative anticipations. The tensions she experiences around racial identity extend beyond peer groups and are felt in teacher expectations, too. Can schools offer the level of affirmation that the summer camp provided while simultaneously creating a robust academic atmosphere? Can we develop learning communities that help students and teachers cross racial boundaries to cultivate more full individual selves within deeply connected communities? If, as Nini says, "[t]hese days, more people are getting more and more racially mixed," what are the implications for developing learning communities that affirm multiple histories and multiple forms of cultural knowledge?

[1]We appreciate the work of Dr. Carlie Tartakov, who interviewed Nini and provided background information for the snapshot, and that of John Raible, who helped transcribe the interview.

opposition does not necessarily lead to failure.[52] To understand these issues more clearly, we advise examining the complexity of students' identities and developing a broad perspective of the many factors that may influence learning and achievement within schools.

About Terminology

Mixed Race/Multiracial/Multicultural/Multiethnic

Many young people and their families are refusing to accept rigid categorizations based on one culture, race, or other kind of social grouping. The hybridity that we discussed in this chapter is a growing phenomenon in the United States and, indeed, around the globe. The great increase in the number of mixed race, biethnic, multiethnic, biracial, and multiracial people, and their insistence on identifying as such, is a reminder that words cannot totally describe the multifaceted identities of human beings. Of the 2010 estimated U.S. population of 308,745,538, approximately 1.7 percent reported two or more races in their responses to the U.S. Census.

While racial, ethnic, and cultural groups have been intermingling throughout history, in the recent past it was common to hear biracial and multiracial labels applied only to individuals of African American and European American heritage, and often those labels were demeaning and oppressive. Institutionalized racism and the social stratification of race embodied in the one-drop rule dictated that individuals with any African ancestry be categorized as Black. Now, as a result of the civil rights movement and subsequent legislation, it is much more common for students and families to proudly claim their multiple ancestries. In the snapshot about Nini Rostland, she refers to herself as "racially and ethnically mixed," with her Black South African mother and her Polish American father. Elsewhere in this book, we have featured other students who illustrate the porous boundaries of racial labels and identify as racially mixed. Linda Howard describes herself as biracial, naming her parents as "Black and White American." Also, Yahaira León identifies as "half and half," referring to her Dominican and Puerto Rican heritage. She points out how important it is to recognize both portions of her ancestry. Liane Chang calls herself Eurasian, and Jasper Quinn describes his combined Native American ancestry as "Paiute, Swinomish, [and] Visayan." Yet the 2000 U.S. Census was the first one in history where individuals were instructed to "mark one or more boxes" when identifying their racial heritage, even though laws against interracial marriage were struck down in 1967. While teachers should always take cues from their students on what language is most descriptive and precise to describe the students' identity, it is especially critical that teachers listen carefully to students of mixed heritage. Many multiracial students and their families have been discouraged from embracing their multiple heritages or, at worst, have been made to feel ashamed. Acknowledging students' multiple backgrounds allows students to be more fully themselves and to be affirmed in their totality. Choosing terminology that students and their families claim is a step in affirming their entire identity.

Complicating Theories of Identities Within School Structures

Dissatisfied with the cultural-ecological explanations of school failure such as those of Ogbu and Fordham on "acting White," and likewise unconvinced by resistance explanations, some alternative theories are emerging from scholars such as Prudence

Carter, Gilberto Conchas, and others.[53] These scholars present research in which students' perspectives, voices, and experiences are centered. Both Conchas and Carter take a sociological view of the ways in which culture and identity are understood and enacted by urban students. Conchas warns, for example, that minority group categories used in cultural-ecological theoretical frameworks do not allow for variations in the school experiences of racial minorities.[54]

Likewise, Carter cautions against creating master narratives that try to speak about all members of involuntary minority groups as if each student in these groups had identical experiences and perspectives.[55] For instance, she points out that recent research has shown that African Americans subscribe to the basic values of education as much as Whites do, or in some cases, even more so. Nearly all of the participants in Carter's study agreed that education is the key to success. They believe in the so-called American dream that education may bring good jobs, home and car ownership, and intact families.

After interviewing 68 youth from low-income communities who identified as African American or Latino/Latina, Carter challenged the framework of oppositional culture. She paid close attention to the ways in which culture was discussed and how it influenced student engagement and achievement:

> Students use culture as a vehicle to signal many things, ranging from the stylistic to the political. The oppositional culture framework, however, ignores the full spectrum of why and how culture becomes a social and political response to schooling by discounting the positive values and functions of these students' culture.[56]

Carter highlights the positive cultural assertions of youth that contribute to their success, and she argues that their ethno-racial cultures are not adaptations to the limits created by a dominant culture. She maintains that focusing on a student's culture as a maladaptive response to social marginalization ignores the roles and values of nondominant cultural practices in the lives of minority youth.

Carter also found that gender is enacted in specific ways that affect school achievement within the lives of female and male students in marginalized communities. So much of the focus has been on disparities among racial and ethnic groups that the gender story *within* the groups has gone untold. That girls and boys take up academic achievement by developing attachment and committing to engagement in differing ways is often ignored in research about low-income students of color. The students in Carter's study, both girls and boys did not equate academic achievement with "acting White." Instead, students recognized the unfairness in, and were critical of, the representation of what counts as knowledge, and the linking of intelligence (or what it means to be smart) with certain styles that are defined in "White" middle-class ways.

Asserting that culture *does* matter in the achievement of African American and Latino students, Carter notes that students draw upon both dominant cultural capital and nondominant cultural capital to construct academic success. Three forces—race/ethnicity, class, and gender—dictate much about how "acting Black," "acting Spanish," or "acting White" is integrated into the identities of students. She is clear that African American and Latino students need tools to make them literate, self-sufficient, politically active, and economically productive. Educators cannot disregard the value of different groups' cultural repertoires; instead, they need to build on the powerful cultural dynamics permeating the school.[57]

Conchas's study also holds implications for how educators address the cultural identities within schools. He is emphatic about the different ways that students (in his study, those who identified as African American, Latino, and Vietnamese) embraced and asserted their cultural and academic identities within and between groups. By examining and comparing specific programs that follow the structural model of school-within-a-school, Conchas addressed institutional mechanisms that create alienation among some successful students of color. Examining students' ideology in such programs revealed that they "embraced the importance of individualism and meritocracy, while simultaneously downplaying the significance of race, class, and gender equity."[58] Conchas found mechanisms in some programs that acted as a "mediating force against racial disparity," specifically by supplying youth with both cultural and social capital, and encouraging cooperative experiences of academic achievement.[59]

Nurturing, mentoring relationships within schools are significant for students' development of multiple forms of social capital that may contribute to educational success. As such, Conchas suggests that concentrated efforts are needed to reduce ethnic segregation and equalize the access that all students have to mentoring and encouragement. He also points to structural models that support sociocultural processes that can develop a high-achieving academic culture of success, citing the benefits of smaller, intimate school-within-a-school structures and small learning communities. His findings note that school structures directly contribute to differing patterns of school adaptation within and between racial groups. Some institutional arrangements are much better at creating a supportive cross-ethnic community of learners, while the sense of exclusion and competition in other programs contributes to racial tensions in schools.

Conchas's description of a culture of academic achievement, the social capital created by school relationships, and the call for small learning communities echo the assertions made by D. Bruce Jackson. Jackson points out that students who are successful in school take on and sustain what he calls "academic identity".[60] Academic identity is an understanding of self within the context of school, in which intellectual activities within and outside school are valued. Jackson acknowledges that many forces influence student identity but argues that, despite the range of theories about student success or failure, success depends on what students decide to do or not do. Although teachers can influence those decisions, ultimately it is students who really direct how they spend their time. They are critical agents in their own education.

The theories developed by Carter, Conchas, and Jackson stem from a range of research projects conducted from diverse perspectives, but they share a concern for the ways in which students' identities intersect with school cultures. They all maintain that, while sociocultural factors and discriminatory histories may influence students' perception of their academic identities and their academic achievement, these factors do not *predetermine* academic success. These scholars are optimistic about the opportunity to tap into youths' dynamic, multiple ways of shaping self and their diverse means of expressing cultural identities. Given the complexity of adolescent identity, which researcher John Raible has documented in writings with Sonia, it is imperative that educators note how race, sexual orientation, ethnicity, gender, and other markers of identity are intricately entangled while profoundly influencing students' school lives.[61] Within this lively interplay lies the potential for taking up academic identity and multiple strategies for success. It would be naive to assert that simply wanting to succeed magically grants one an academic identity. That is why the focus of these theories holds particular promise: Rather than designing a particular road map to success, their focus is more like a global positioning system for teachers and students to view the multifaceted aspects of identity and the web of structures that support academic achievement.

 ## Conclusion

No simple explanation accounts for student achievement or failure. As we have seen in this chapter, each theory holds helpful analysis, but most explanations have been inadequate or incomplete. Some have failed to consider the significance of culture in learning; others have not taken into account the social, cultural, and political context of schooling; and still others have placed all the responsibility for academic failure or success on students and their families. Even the persistence of racism and discrimination, the presence of unjust policies and practices in schools, and the role that schools play in reproducing existing societal inequities do not fully explain school failure.

The significance of caring relationships among students and their teachers has taken on great significance in the recent past. Awareness of the tremendous difference that teachers—and the school climate in general—can make in the lives and futures of young people is growing. Teachers and schools that affirm students' identities, believe in their intelligence, and accept nothing less than the best have proved to be inspirational for young people, even if they live in otherwise difficult circumstances. In fact, the case can be made that such relationships are one of the most important elements of student learning.

The discussion in this chapter leads us to the conclusion that school achievement can be explained only by taking into account multiple, competing, and dynamic conditions: the school's tendency to replicate society and its inequities; cultural and language incompatibilities; the unfair and bureaucratic structures of schools; the nature of the relationships among students; students' multiple and dynamic ways of asserting ethno-racial, gender, and cultural identities; teachers' relationships with the communities they serve; and the political relationship of particular groups to society and the schools. It is tricky business, however, to seek causal explanations for school success and failure. Understanding how numerous complex conditions are mediated within the school and home settings can also help explain students' academic success or failure. Understanding all these conditions contributes to a more comprehensive explanation of the school failure of many students.

It is clear that no single explanation of academic achievement is sufficient to explain why some students succeed in school and others fail. Rather, we need to understand school achievement as a combination of *personal, cultural, familial, political, relational,* and *societal* issues, and this requires an understanding of the sociopolitical context in which education takes place.

To Think About

1. What did William Ryan mean by "culturally depriving schools"? Can you give some examples?

2. Think about schools and classrooms with which you are familiar. Have you noticed examples of student resistance in these contexts? If so, what are they, and what is their effect?

3. You and a group of your colleagues need to determine why a particular student has been doing poorly in your classes. What will you examine? Why?

Activities *for Personal, School, and Community Change*

1. If you teach in an elementary school, plan a visit to the homes of your students to get to know their families. Use the occasion to find out about the children: what they like and what motivates them to learn. Ask the families about some of the culturally enriching activities they are engaged in within their communities. If you teach in a middle or high school class in which you have many students, thus making home visits difficult, ask students to describe some of the activities they do with their families. How can you use what you've learned to create a more culturally affirming classroom?

2. Think about a teacher who has made a difference in your life. Try to get in touch with her or him. Tell that person how she or he influenced you, and ask for advice on how you can have the same impact on your students. How can you apply what you have learned from this to your own teaching?

3. Get together with a group of colleagues to discuss how students in your school display "resistance" behaviors. Describe these behaviors. Are they getting in the way of students' engagement with school? Are students displaying *strategic* resistance that makes efforts toward social change? Decide on a plan of action for your classrooms to assist students in civic action to help them accomplish their goals in a productive way.

Case Studies

Paul Chavez

I don't want to speak too soon, but I'm pretty much on a good road here.

Speaking in an earnest and intense tone, Paul Chavez[1] thought carefully before sharing his thoughts about the importance of school, the "hood," and his family. Paul was 16 years old at the time of his interview, and he had already lived a lifetime full of gang activity, drugs, and disappointment. The signs were evident, from his style of dress to the "tag" (tattoo) on his arm, to his reminiscence of "homeboys" who had been killed. Describing himself as Chicano and Mexican American, Paul was the third generation in his family to be born in Los Angeles. He did not speak Spanish but said that both his mother and grandmother did, even though they too were born and raised here.

Paul lived with his mother, two brothers and two sisters. Another brother, 21, was not living at home. His mother was trying to obtain her high school equivalency diploma; she had failed the test once but was studying hard to pass it the next time. She and Paul's father had been separated for about four years, and Paul described the entire family as "Christian." His mother was a church leader, and his brother was a Bible study leader. Even his father, a recovering alcoholic, who had lived on the streets for years and spent time in prison, was living in what Paul called a "Christian home," probably a halfway house.

The one-family homes in Paul's East Los Angeles neighborhood mask the poverty and despair that are easier to see in other economically depressed neighborhoods, with their high-rise tenements and projects. Here, the mostly Latino families struggle to maintain a sense of community in the well-kept homes on small lots. However, signs of gang activity are apparent in the tags on buildings and walls. Paul said that an outsider suspected of belonging to another gang was likely to get jumped merely for walking down the street.

School problems began for Paul when he was in third or fourth grade, and he had been suspended on numerous occasions for poor behavior. The problem was not lack of ability (his teachers always felt that he was smart) but rather lack of interest. He was more interested in belonging to a "school gang," a group of young boys looking for boys in other classes to fight. In spite of the lure of gangs, he remembered fifth grade as the best year he had had in school, and he attributed this to Ms. Nelson, the most caring teacher he had until he went to his current school. Paul already wore gang-affiliated attire, and he had a reputation as a troublemaker, but she did not let this get in the way of her high expectations of him. It was in her class that he became interested in history, and he recalled being fascinated by the American Revolution.

By the time Paul began junior high school, peer pressure, family problems, and street violence brought the situation to a head. Seventh and eighth grades were his worst years. He was expelled in eighth grade, and he was told by school authorities to attend an alternative school in another district. But he refused to go and instead stayed home for six months. By ninth grade, he was heavily involved in gang activity, joining the 18th Street Gang, a gang with thousands of members not only in Los Angeles but also in other cities and even in other states. Thirteen of his cousins were or had been in the same gang, as was his older brother, so the role of gang as "family" was even more relevant in his case. An uncle and a cousin had both been killed as a result of their gang activity.

Encouraged by his mother, Paul tried to enroll in another program but was again expelled after a few months. Then he heard about and applied to the Escuela de Dignidad y Orgullo (School of Dignity and Pride), a high school for students who had dropped out of other schools. With a large Chicano population, the school was characterized by a multicultural curriculum with a focus on Chicano history, and it relied on student and staff involvement in its day-to-day operations. All talk of gangs was discouraged, and the staff tried hard to create a different kind of community, one not affiliated with gang culture. The staff included counselors, a psychologist, a probation officer, and several teachers. Paul had not been formally arrested, but because of his previous problems, he agreed to a voluntary placement with the probation officer, just to "keep me on the right road," he said.

The new road Paul had taken was far from easy for him, however. He had also been expelled from Escuela de Dignidad y Orgullo, and it was only after trying another program and then spending several months on the street that he had realized he wanted to return. All of his friends had quit school, and he feared ending up like them. He had been accepted at Escuela once again and had done well since returning two years before. At the time he was interviewed, Paul was spending most of his time at school, doing homework every day when he got home, and working after school at the local city hall, a job that the school had found for him. Paul described Escuela as different from any other he had attended because all of the staff members cared about and encouraged the students and because Chicano culture and history were central to the curriculum, making it a more exciting place to learn.

Paul's philosophy at this point was to take life one day at a time because the lure of gang life was still present. He had not yet quit the gang, and it was obvious that he was at a crossroads in his life. The next several months might determine which direction his life would take: either an escalating life of crime on the streets or a promising future of education and work.

Paul's case study highlights two goals he had had for a long time: *to be respected* and to make something of himself, two goals that are frequently at odds. Another theme is his determination to *"make it better,"* and the third is the *importance of family support*.

"Everybody's Gotta Get Respect"

I grew up ditching school, just getting in trouble, trying to make a dollar, that's it, you know? Just go to school, steal from the store, and go sell candies at school. And that's what I was doing in the third or fourth grade. I was always getting in the principal's office, suspended, kicked out, everything, starting from the third grade.

My fifth-grade teacher, Ms. Nelson, she put me in a play and that, like, tripped me out. Like, why do you want *me* in a play? Me, I'm just a mess-up. Still, you know, she put me in a play. And in fifth grade, I think that was the best year out of the whole six years [of elementary school]. I learned a lot about the Revolutionary War, you know? The fifth grade was a grade I'll always remember. Had good friends. We had a project we were involved in. Ms. Nelson was a good teacher. She just involved everyone. We made books, this and that. And I used to like to write, and I wrote two, three books. She did pretty nice things. She got real deep into you, just, you know, "Come on, you can do it." That was a good year for me, the fifth grade.

My most troubled years [were] my junior high years. Seventh grade, first day of school, I met this guy and then, from there, we started to form. And every junior high, you're gonna have a group, okay? You're gonna have a group that you hang around with. And it got to we just started always starting trouble in classes. Whatever period we had, we just started trouble in. And me, I have a great sense of humor, right? I can make people laugh a lot. So then I was always getting kicked out of the classroom. And so what that got me was kind of, I guess popular, right? Where girls were always around me. I had a big group. But I was always the one clowning, getting in trouble. So it kind of like set a path for me where I was, like, all right, so I clown and get popularity. All right, I understand now the program.

I [wasn't] in a gang, but I was dressing pretty . . . still gang affiliated. And so people looked like, "Well, where you from?" "I ain't from nowhere." And that kind of like got me to want to be from somewhere so I could tell 'em, "Well, I'm from here. . . ." Those were the years in seventh grade, and I was fighting with eighth graders. I'd be in a dance, a little Oriental kid would come up to me and she goes, "I know you, you're Paul," this and that. They would know me. It made me feel good.

Being in a gang, you think about who you're retaliating, you know, just another Chicano brother. And that's kind of deep. Well, why you're gonna be from a neighborhood [gang], have pride, this and that, and take out your own *Raza*,[2] you know? So that kind of always caught me in my mind. You see a lot of your own people just going down because of your neighborhood. And it's a trip. And you got a lot of homeboys that come out from the system, the jails, and it's real segregated in there, you know, the Blacks and Chicanos. And they even got the border brothers, the ones from Mexico who don't speak no English. They're even separated from the Chicanos, the Sureños, that's right from South L.A. Okay, they're paranoid in there, and everybody is, like, "What's up with the Blacks? It's on, it's on. We're gonna have a war." And everybody, then they turn little things into big things. So it's really just a race war going on in the inside, and they bring it out to us.

It has a great hold on you, and it's, like, I talk to my cousin. He's still into it real deep. I'm not really. Don't get me wrong: I'm from the neighborhood, but I'm not really deep into it. You know what I mean? But it's, like, I talk to 'em. "Yeah, we were with the homeboys on the Eastside, blah, blah, blah, this and that," and I'll be like, "Damn," and I think, "I wish I was there getting off on drinking and shit."

I had a cousin, he was 16 when he passed away. He was my cousin . . . family . . . from [the] 18th Street [gang], too. And what happened, see, he passed away and that's another tragedy. It's just, you see so much. I'm 16, and I see so much. First his dad passed away and then my cousin . . . my uncle and my cousin. And you think, "Man, all this because of a gang!" And there's times when you just sit and you think, you sit and you think, and you say, "Why? Why? Why? What is this?" But you don't know why, but you have it so much inside of you. It's hard; it's not easy to get rid of. I don't want to get rid of it, but you just got to try to focus on other things right now. I'm from a gang and that's it, and just 'cause I'm from a gang doesn't mean I can't make myself better.

But me, I *do* care. I have a life, and I want to keep it. I don't want to lose it. I have two little sisters, and I want to see them grow up, too, and I want to have my own family. So, I got the tag. I got a big 18 on my arm where everybody could see it, and that's the way I was about a year ago. You know, man, if you would be talking a year ago I'd be, like, "I'm from the neighborhood." I'd be talking to you in slang street, all crazy, you know? Now I'm more intelligent.

I try not to get influenced too much . . . pulled into what I don't want to be into. But mostly, it's hard. You don't want people to be saying you're stupid. "Why do you want to go to school and get a job?" I was talking to my homeboy the other day, so [he said] "[S]chool? Drop out, like. . . ." "Like, all right, that's pretty good. Thanks for your encouragement" [*laughs*]. See, they trip like that, but they just mess around. That's just a joke, but it's, like, you just think about things like that. I guess your peers, they try to pull you down and then you just got to be strong enough to try to pull away.

I got to think about myself and get what I got to get going on. Get something going on, or else nobody else is going to do it. It's where you're starting to think a little different. You sort of know what's happening. All they're thinking about is partying. Nothing wrong with it, but I got to try to better myself.

Making It Better

I guess in a lot of ways, I *am* [successful] . . . a lot of things I'm trying to achieve. Starting something, already you're successful, you know? But finishing it, it's gonna make you more complete . . . successful and complete. Got to have your priorities straight. Get what you got to get done, and get it done, and just be happy when you're doing something.

I came to this school, and it was deep here. They got down into a lot of studies that I liked, and there was a lot going on here. But see, I was me, I was just a clown. I always liked to mess around, so they gave me chance after chance. I took it for granted, and they kicked me out. They booted me out, right? So I went back to that other school and it was like, "This thing is boring. Nothing going on." And so I called over here and I go, "I need another chance to get back into school." So they gave me another chance and that's why I'm here right now, 'cause they gave me a chance.

They get more into deeper Latino history here, and that's what I like. A lot of other, how you say, background, ethnic background. We had even Martin Luther King. We had Cesar Chavez. We had a lot of things. I never used to think about [being Chicano] before. Now I do . . . being Brown and just how our race is just going out. You know, you don't want to see your race go out like that.

[Mexican American], it's what you make it, you know? Let's say I'm Chicano and I dress like a gang member. They're gonna look at you like one of those crazy kids, you know, Mexican kid, Chicano kid. But if you present yourself nice or whatever, it really depends how your outer appears. Like, people say it's just *from the inside,* but it's really what's *on the outside* . . . how you look on the outside, like tattoos and that. So it's, like, I get discriminated because of a lot of things, and I can't really pinpoint it. So it's, like, I don't really know if it's 'cause I'm Brown or if it's 'cause of my gang tattoo, so I can't really pinpoint. But for me, as far as me being Chicano, it's prideful, it's pride of your race, of what you are.

[Chicano young people] have some pretty trippy insights of life. It's like they know how to talk to people, and they know how to give presentations, you know what I mean? Like what we're doing right now [*referring to the interview*]. A lot of the things they say is pretty deep.

[In this school], they just leave the killings out and talk about how you can make it better, you know what I'm saying? Try to be more of the positive side of being a Brown person, that's what I'm talking about. A lot of the other alternative schools you can't go because of your gang. It's all gang affiliated. Every single alternative school is gang affiliated. This is the only one where it's all neutral.

[To make school better I would] talk about more interesting things, more things like what *I* would like, students would like. And I would just get more involved . . . get more people involved. Get things going, not just let them vegetate on a desk and "Here's a paper," . . . teach 'em a lesson and expect them to do it. You know, get all involved.

Put some music in the school. I mean, put some music and get some like drawings. Get a better surrounding so you feel more like the 'hood, you could learn more, you'll feel more comfortable. This [school] is pretty good, but if you had somebody kicking it, put like a character on the wall or something . . . yeah, like a mural or something, it would be more like a more comfortable setting to work.

Try to find out what we think is important. Try to do the best you can to try to get it. The kids want it, they're gonna use it. If they don't want it, they're not. I remember the *Diary of Anne Frank*. I was pretty deep into the Nazis and Jews, and so that was pretty cool.

I think [multicultural education] is important because that goes back to segregating. You got to get to know everybody more better. If you understand them better, you're gonna get along better. So, yeah, I think that would be good.

I'm getting out all I can get out [from this school]. There's so much to learn and that's all I want to do is just learn, try to educate my mind to see what I could get out of it. Anything I can, I'm gonna get out of it.

I was here when they barely opened this school. I brought my mom and my dad, and we had a couple of kids here and the staff here. What we did was wrote all the rules, just made an outline of how the school was gonna be: People are gonna get treated right, what you could wear. Everything was done with each other, you know? It wasn't just talked about with the staff and brought to the students. It was the students *and* the staff.

[*What would have made school easier for you?*] If you had asked me that question a year ago, I would have said, "No school!" School would have been made easier if it wasn't so early in the morning [*laughs*]. But school, it will be better if more activities [are] going on. People wouldn't just think of it as a routine. People got into it really where it really meant something. But it's both on the students' part and the teachers' part. It takes both.

The classes [should have] more better learning techniques. It's an advanced age. We got a lot of computer things going on. Get a lot of things going with computers and a lot of things that are going to draw the eye. Catch my eye and I'm gonna be, "Oh, all right," and gonna go over there and see what's up.

I think they should get more of these aides, assistants, to be parents, okay? 'Cause the parents, I notice this: A parent in a school is more, like, they got love. That's it, they got love and they give it to you. They give it back to more students. I think they should get more parents involved in the school to teach. Get more parents involved in the classroom, too. Parents have a lot of things to say, I would think, about the schools.

[Teachers should] not think of a lesson as a lesson. Think of it as not a lesson just being taught to students, but a lesson being taught to one of your own family members, you know? 'Cause if it's like that they get more deep into it, and that's all it takes. Teach a lesson with heart behind it and try to get your kids to understand more of what's going on. And don't lie to your students, saying, "Everything is okay and 'just say no to drugs'; it's easy." Let them know what's really going on. Don't beat around the bush. Let them know there's gangs, drugs. "You guys got to get on with that. That's for kids. Do what you got to do and stay in education." They're starting to do that more now. Try to get a dress code going on. I never used to like that, but that's a pretty good idea, you know? But not really a strict dress code, but just where you can't wear gang attire.

Now I take every chance I get to try to involve myself in something. Now it's like I figure if I'm more involved in school, I won't be so much involved in the gang, you know? . . . It's what you put into it, what you're gonna get out of it. That's just the kind of person I am, where if I can't do something just to trip myself up, I want to do this. You know, just so I can learn it more real good and show 'em that I can . . . try to make an example out of myself, of everything I do.

[Good grades] make you feel good, getting A's. See this gang-member-type man getting A's. I get pretty good grades. I get A's, B's, and C's. That's better than all F's on report cards that I used to get, all failures in all six subjects.

After, when I get my diploma, it's not the end of school; it's the beginning. I still want to learn a lot more after that. I basically want to go to college. That's what I want to do. Get more schooling so I could learn more.

Probably I would want to be either a teacher, a counselor, something like working with youngsters to share my experience with them, you know? 'Cause I know there's a lot of people out there who talk down to youngsters, you know what I'm saying? Instead of talking *with* them. And just try to understand what they're going through.

I mean, you can't get a teacher, put 'em in a classroom with a bunch of kids from the neighborhood, and the teacher lives in [another neighborhood] and expect to understand. I have problems at home, a lot of problems. And to come into school and for a teacher to come with a snotty attitude, I'm gonna give it back. That's the way it is.

I don't want to speak too soon, but I'm pretty much on a good road here. I'm pretty much making it. Trying to make something out of myself. I'm on that way, you know . . . I'm going that way.

You can't talk about next month, at least at this time. I'm just today, get it done. That's it. The best I can.

And I just, I'm tripping out on myself. I don't believe I'm doing this. But I don't really like to build myself too high . . . because the higher you are, the harder you're gonna fall. I don't want to fall.

Family Support: "I Had a Love That Kept Me Home"

I like kids. I like kids a lot. They see me and, "Gee, that guy is scary. He's a gang member. . . ." This experience the other day when I was at work: I was working in [a daycare center], and I walked in and the kids were looking at me like and whispering. And this one kid, this Oriental kid, came up and we started playing. The next thing I know, she was sitting on my lap and all these kids just started coming towards me. And they know: They could feel I love kids.

You need to educate your mind. Somebody gets born and throw 'em into the world, you know, they're not gonna make it. You get somebody, you born 'em, you raise 'em, you feed 'em and encourage 'em, and they're gonna make it. That's the reason for going to school. A lot of it, of my going to school, is 'cause of my mom. I want her to be proud and to say that I made it.

My mom used to run with gangs when she was young. My mom and my father both belonged to gangs. They're out of it. They don't mess around no more.

I learned a lot of morals from my mother. Respect, how to respect people. If my mom wasn't in church, she wouldn't be there for us, I don't think. She would be trying to find a way to seek to comfort herself, you know what I mean?

My mom, she's real strong and real understanding. Not strict, but more understanding, you know? She don't really compromise with me. Usually what she says is what she says, that's it. My mom, I wouldn't change nothing, nothing [about her]. My dad, I would just have him be there for me when I was younger. I could have turned out different if he was there, you never know.

It's hard for me to talk to my mom or my dad, but I talk to my mom about a lot of things like girlfriends, things that happen. Like when homeboys die, I don't go talking to nobody else but my mom. My homeboy just passed away about a month ago or two months ago, and I just remember I was in my mom's room. My mom was ironing and I just started crying, and I don't cry a lot. I started crying and I started telling her, "I hurt, Mom. I don't know why, but I hurt so much." 'Cause I had been trying to, how do you say, run from it, I'd been trying to put it off, like my homeboy's gone, 'cause we were pretty close. So I was like, "It hurts, Mommy." She said, "I know, in your gut." So we talked. We get pretty much into it.

She dropped out in the tenth grade, and she was pregnant. And she says, "I want you to do good. Don't be like me, going back to school when it's already kind of late, you know?" It's never too late, but you know what I'm saying. She was like, "Just learn now, Paul. Do it the first time right and you won't have to do it again."

My mom wants me to go to school basically so I could have a good house and home when I build up my family, and so we won't have to be five people living in a three-bedroom home, with not that much money to live on, you know?

My mom makes a good living, not in money but in moral standards. We're happy with what we've got and that's just the bottom line. So I go to school for my mom, try to help her and try to help me.

My mom, she's not really [involved in school]. She's too busy doing her own thing. She gets out of school, makes dinner, cleans the house, goes to church, comes home, irons for my two sisters. She doesn't really have time for all this. She'll come in and she'll talk to my probation officer, talk to Isabel [a staff member], different people, yeah, pretty much involved when she can be.

You're gonna realize that you got to learn from day one and education will never end. It's only when you stop it. I realize that now. But see, me, I never really had somebody to push me. My mother pushed me, and my mom, she just got tired. "Paul, you're too much for me." My father, he never really pushed me. He talked to me. That was, like, "Education, Paul, education," you know? And getting letters from my dad in jail, "Stay in school," and that's all. He said some pretty deep things, understanding things to me. And my dad always knew the right words to say to me that kind of encouraged me. And my mom. They both encouraged me.

If it wasn't for the family, the love I get from my family, I would look for it in my homeboys. I never had to do that. I just wanted my homeboys to party. A lot of my friends, they go to homeboys to look for just to kick it with somebody. See, me, I had a love that kept me home, that kept me in my place.

I remember I used to just take off from Friday night to Monday morning, come home. My mom be worrying all night, "Where is this guy?" and I was in the street. And that was like every weekend. 'Til now, I stay home every day and I'm just going to school. . . . I come from work, do my homework, whatever. Go to work, come home, go to church, 'cause I go to church with my mother.

My mom, she's really proud of me. My friend was telling me that she was at church, at Bible study, a gathering at home of church people. And [my mom] was crying. She was proud. [My friend] said, "Your mom was talking about you, and she was crying. She's real proud." And that's my mom, she's real sensitive. I love my mom so much it's even hard to explain. And she thinks . . . she tells me, "You don't care about me, Paul," this and that, 'cause like it's hard for me. . . . It's hard for me to show my feelings.

Commentary

Luis Rodríguez, author of *Always Running, La Vida Loca: Gang Days in L.A.,* whose experiences parallel Paul's in many ways, describes gangs as young people's search for a sense of belonging.[3]

Looking back on his own youth and fearing for the future of his son, who was following the same path, Rodríguez wrote his book to encourage people to understand that gangs, in spite of providing belonging, respect, and protection to their members, represent an unhealthy and self-destructive response to oppression. Gangs emerge when communities are deprived of basic human rights. According to Rodríguez, few young people would choose gangs if they were given decent education, productive jobs, and positive channels for social recreation.

Schools may unwittingly contribute to young people's gang involvement by failing to provide the strong cultural identity and support that students need. In fact, James Diego Vigil has suggested that neighborhoods and schools interact in ways that can interfere with the learning of many Chicano students. According to him, understanding this connection can help educators create a more positive school experience for Chicano students. Vigil suggests that schools can develop a balanced strategy of prevention, intervention, and suppression.[4] For example, *prevention* would focus on strengthening families and addressing some of the conditions that lead children to street life and gangs. *Intervention* would address students' behavioral problems, and *suppression* would confront the most destructive behavioral aspects of gang culture. However, suppression can also unintentionally lead to creating school dropouts. For instance, dress codes may appear to be neutral rather than targeted at only gang members, but these dress codes may drive gang members out of school. Even in the early grades, when Paul began to dress like a gang member, teachers' negative reactions—if not specific dress codes—made him feel that school was not a place for him. That is why he so vividly remembered Ms. Nelson, the one teacher who treated him kindly despite his attire.

The yearning for respect, which is, after all, just another word for a sense of competence, is what Paul described when he talked about joining first what he called a "school gang" and later the full-fledged street gang. Young men and women in desperate economic straits are turning, in ever larger numbers, to *la vida loca*, or the crazy life of gangs. In 1991, when Paul was interviewed, Los Angeles alone was estimated to have 100,000 gang members in 800 gangs. In that peak year for gang activity, nearly 600 youth were killed, mostly by other youth.[5]

Constance L. Rice, co-director and civil rights lawyer for the Advancement Project, a policy, communications, and legal action group, has called for policies and actions to move away from suppression and incarceration-only approaches to a comprehensive public health approach that reduces the attractiveness of gang ideology and to holistic wraparound safety programs that keep children out of the reach of gangs and other dangers. As this book goes to press, however, the regions of Los Angeles neighborhoods that are gripped by gang activity, known as hot zones, are far reaching.[6] In Los Angeles County, of the 850,000 children living in hot zones, 90 percent report exposure to serious violence as victims or witnesses. Rice reports that "[a]fter spending $25 billion in a thirty year 'war on gangs,' and after locking up 450,000 youth 18 and under in the last decade alone, Los Angeles had six times as many gangs and twice as many gang members. Estimates for the County are 800 to 1,000 gangs and anywhere from 70,000 to 90,000 gang members, only a small minority of whom are violent."[7]

The rage felt by young people when their dreams are denied or suppressed is turned inward, resulting, for example, in drug abuse or suicide, or it is turned outward. The unspeakably violent actions of Chicanos against their own *Raza,* so poignantly expressed by Paul, is an example of the latter. Rodríguez describes this violence as emanating too often from the self-loathing that is the result of oppression: "And if they murder, the victims are usually the ones who look like them, the ones closest to who they are—the mirror reflections. They murder and they're killing themselves, over and over."[8]

Nevertheless, blame for gangs and for other manifestations of oppression in our society cannot be placed on schools. The issues are too complicated for simplistic scapegoating; they include massive unemployment, a historical legacy of racism and discrimination, and a lack of appropriate housing and health care, among others. In addition, families struggling to survive on a daily basis can seldom do much to counteract the lure of gangs and drugs, with their easy money and instant popularity, that influences so many of their children. As Paul said, his mother, try as she might, just got tired: "Paul, you're too much for me," she said.

Although schools can neither do away with gangs nor put a stop to the violence taking place in communities across the United States every day, they can make a difference. Paul was quick to place the responsibility for his past on his own shoulders rather than blaming teachers. When he thought more deeply about it, however, he also recognized that particular teachers and schools *did* make a difference. This is nowhere more evident than in the case of Ms. Nelson or the teachers in his alternative school.

Chicano parents and their children often have high aspirations, but unless these are somehow incorporated into the culture of schools, they will make little difference. For instance, Alejandro Portes and Rubén Rumbaut, in their extensive research on various immigrant communities, found that the strengths of these communities are frequently disregarded by schools. In the specific case of Mexican Americans, they concluded that "[i]n many Mexican families, the *only* thing going for the children is the support and ambition of their parents. These aspirations should be strengthened rather than undermined."[9] This finding compels us to shift the focus to the context and structure of schools rather than only on the shortcomings of students and their families. In other words, policies and practices need to be reviewed to make education more engaging and positive for all students. Schools need to develop strategies that use a more culturally congruent approach rather than an approach based on culture as a deficit.

Paul's suggestion that his school hire more parents as school aides because they "got love and they give it to you" reminds us of the powerful influence of family on Hispanic/Latino culture. Even families in difficult circumstances want the best for their children but often are unaware of how to provide it for them. His father's insistence on "Education, Paul, education," if unaccompanied by structural support to help him stay in school, is of little help. Paul clearly understood this when he said that, although his parents supported him, they never really pushed him.

Paul Chavez was fortunate to be in the alternative school he was attending, and it seemed to be serving as a safeguard to keep him at some distance from his gang. The policies and practices of his school were geared toward creating a positive learning environment: There was no tracking, staff interactions with students were positive and healthy, students were involved in the school's governance, there were high expectations and demanding standards of all students, and their languages and cultures were an integral part of the school's curriculum. Nevertheless, an insightful observation by Vigil is worth noting here. Alternative schools, he says, may replicate street gang culture by concentrating a critical mass of gang members in one place. Thus, these schools can act as "temporary warehouses," or in the words of some of the gang members quoted by James Vigil, as "preparation for prison."[10]

One cannot help but remember, however, that at the time of his interview, Paul was only 16 years old, a tender age, and he had so many difficult situations and easy temptations still facing him. In spite of Paul's strong motivation and eloquent insights, his school's caring, his mother's love and strict discipline, and his growing realization that gang life is no solution to the problems facing Chicano youth, he still had a long and hard road ahead of him.

Reflect on This Case Study

1. What can teachers and schools learn from Paul's fifth-grade teacher, Ms. Nelson? Give specific suggestions.
2. What support services do you think are needed in schools such as those in Paul's neighborhood? Why?
3. Look at the recommendations that Paul made to improve schools. Which do you think make sense? Why?
4. Why do you think Paul never thought about being Chicano before? What kinds of ethnic studies would be important for students at different levels?

Latrell Elton

I wanna do positive stuff now. I wanna do something positive with my life.

At the time he was interviewed, Latrell Elton,[1] a 16-year-old African American young man, was finishing his sophomore year of high school in Atlanta, Georgia. After starting at his local high school, the district transferred him to Bowden County Alternative High School, a school for students who had been expelled from their home schools. While the alternative school claimed to develop self-esteem, self-discipline, trust, lifelong learning, and respect for others, Latrell's description of his experience there raises many concerns about the gaping divide between a school's mission and the messages, both explicit and implicit, that students receive from the school's policies and practices.

Latrell reported that the alternative school is 100 percent segregated: "The school is—all it is—is Black. The students are all Black and the teachers are all Black," aligning it with Jonathan Kozol's description of apartheid schools.[2] Within this environment, Latrell's narrative pointed to three distressing themes: *his school experience as resembling prison, the detrimental messages about his racial identity,* and his *low expectations for the future.*

Prison Analogy

We're in school, but it ain't like the regular school. When you go in the school, they check you tucked in your shirt. And then you gotta go through the metal detectors. When you go through the metal detectors, they search you. After they search you, you go on to the cafeteria—you sit down. Goin' through metal detectors at school, I don't feel uncomfortable with it. Well, truly it shouldn't be happenin' but I don't be feelin' uncomfortable with it, you know what I'm saying? Every day we go in school, they searchin' us like we prisoners and stuff. I put my own self in a predicament to go to that school. I didn't really wanna go. But they were, like, "Well Mr. Elton, we can't let you in school until you go and do a year in there." And I was, like, "All right. I'll do what I gotta do." The main thing I'm focused on is trying to get up out that school. As soon as I get up out that school I'll be a happy person.

We ride on a bus that have two Bowden County motorcycle mans right here. They have marked police in the front, one in the middle, and one in the back, and they have each marked police on each bus. Man, make me feel like I'm in jail. Like I'm just a prisoner, like I'm a bad person. My bus have burglary bar windows. They got cameras on there. You can't get up out your seat.

Detrimental Messages and Racial Identity

I'm African American. Y'all don't want to hear what I got in my blood. I got the N-word in my blood. 'Cause I'm just, I just don't like sitting down, I can't stay seated. I just wanna run around, get my energy out. It's negative. Right now I'm trying to control it at school. When I was in [my previous] school, I used to run around, can't sit down in class, sit on top of the desk, cut. But now I don't. I sit down.

I feel like Black folk these days, we doin' stupid stuff, we wanna kill each other over little stupid stuff like a car. We wanna go out here and break into houses. To tell you the truth, the whole jail system is made for us only. That's why they build jails and welfare: for Black people. 'Cause they know what we're gonna do. [Black people] put themselves in a predicament, I ain't gonna lie.

Say, for instance, a Black person would have got shot right here and we call the ambulance. You know how long it's gonna take them? About an hour to 35 minutes just to come. Just to come. Oh, this Black person, they got shot. That's one less Black person we got to worry about on the street. One person we ain't got to do nothing for. But if it's like a mixed person being shot, they be on the scene in less than five minutes. You hear the sirens and everything. You got helicopter, news, and everything.

About my neighborhood, I would tell you: Be safe. Be careful. Don't trust nobody around here. People around here, they steal, they'll lie to you. Everything. They'll do everything around here. People around here, they just don't care. Like, you trying to cross the street, they won't slow down. They'll just keep flying by you. Just go on.

The community people are all Black folk. That's what all it is. That's what I said, nothing but black folks all on the street. They like this because they ain't been in no real life, you know what I'm saying? With people who got quieter streets, who like respect, like neighborhood watch. We ain't got no neighborhood watch. It's just people out there doing stupid stuff. Where I'm from, when we had neighborhood watch, they wouldn't be doing what they doing now.

Future Expectations

I hope when I get out of Bowden Alternative School, I can go ahead and go back to regular school. And when I get on to regular school, first thing I'm gonna be looking for is basketball tryout. When I find out when they having basketball tryout, I'm gonna stay after school. I'm just gonna play basketball. And when I play basketball, I'm gonna try and go pro. I'm trying to go to the top. Trying to be the best I can be in basketball. My teacher told me I could be a comedian. I got jokes. I got some jokes. I could joke. I'm gonna try and be a comedian, too, if basketball don't happen.

I see all these folks out here, they be like, "Yeah cous', do this, selling drug gonna get money." Selling drugs ain't gonna get you nowhere. Drug money don't last long. And then drugs get you locked up and stuff. I wanna do positive stuff now. I wanna do something positive with my life. I don't wanna keep on doing no negative stuff. Can't keep on doing that. It just ain't right. 'Cause I see all this money, there's money out here. I tell people, there's money out here. You got cars you can wash—you even got—even yards to cut grass all day, you know what I'm saying? I don't like cutting yards, but I cut 'em. Only why I cut 'em is because, sometimes when I'm feeling broke and I got more to cut.

It make me feel good about myself [to have a job cutting grass] 'cause I know I ain't gotta go out here and ask nobody for no money, you know what I'm saying? 'Cause I don't want my momma see me in a couple more years on the street asking folks for 50 cents. I want her to see me coming in a car. So clean. With a big old house, with a bag full of money. Just say, "Momma, for all the years of hard work you put me through, there you go, right there. There you go, a brand new set of car keys, there, got you some house keys, there you go." See my momma there, up in the house. I got big plans for when I get out of school.

'Cause if I keep on putting my mind on right things, positive things, I ain't got to worry about no nigga still trying to get through my brain and trying to make me mess up. 'Cause right now, since I been in these sports and stuff, it's helped me out a lot. Because I know I'm with safe people. People who I really can trust. People who I ain't gotta worry about got illegal drugs. I know I ain't gotta worry about all that. I'm on the right track. I can do this and that to make my life positive.

Now, since I'm in the alternative school, they've been helping me out a lot, a way, way lot. 'Cause I've got after-school tutorial, and we got more help after school. I'm a good student right now. I consider myself a good student. [What makes me a good student right now is] my behavior, the way I done calmed down. Going to school on time. Getting A's. Passing all my classes. I ain't got to worry about none of this. Last year, [at my previous school] I didn't have nothing but stress. I didn't know what to do with my work. Until I met this lady named Miss Kathy. So when I met her, I showed her my report card and I talked to her about getting me a mentor. And then when she had found me this mentor, and ever since, I been coming home with good grades, passing. Look, yo, I show her every Tuesday, look at my progress report. You see, I done did good. I done finally learned something. I don't worry about falling asleep in class, not doing no work. I used to fall asleep every day in class.

In literature class now, my average is a D. It's between a C and a D. By the end of the semester, I'm hoping to have A's, A's, A's, A's, A's by paying attention, doing what I'm doing every day all day. Working. Trying not to go to sleep.

The school I went to before, I went there and I just kept causing trouble. I had so many friends that I knew from middle school, you know what I'm saying? They trying to tell me, "Do that. Go do that, mess with that right there." But like I told my mom when I get out that school system and stuff I ain't got to worry about it. Gotta be a grown man. I can make my own decisions, do what I wanna do. I ain't gotta worry about people telling me what to do, and I just be free.

Commentary

Latrell is a bright, perceptive young man who was painfully aware of the ravages of institutionalized racism in his community. His poignant comments address both the responsibilities of school structures and the limits of the school's reach within underresourced and overexploited communities. Latrell said he was "not uncomfortable" about entering the school through metal detectors, implying that he viewed it as a necessary reality.

He equated having the "N-word in my blood" with struggling to conform to classroom expectations, apparently having absorbed the bigoted message that staying seated and overcoming restlessness are racial traits. It is evident that Latrell's perspective of his racial identity and cultural group had become skewed by experiences of racism, marginalization, and violence.

While Latrell's hopeful outlook on the future was courageous, it also pointed to a lack of adequate guidance and academic preparation for professional goals. In the overwhelming shadow of American popular culture, it has become the norm for many young people, especially young men of color, to dream of becoming professional athletes or entertainers. While these are noteworthy possibilities that should not be dismissed, both are exceptionally competitive careers, considering the percentage of individuals who actually secure personal and financial success in such pursuits. Strong guidance and career counseling services in some schools help students with such aspirations follow their hearts *and* prepare for a collegiate trajectory that supports their vision. For example, thoughts of pursuing a career that might be related to his interests in comedy and sports such as sports medicine, sports management, physical education, theater studies, entertainment management, or entrepreneurial endeavors did not even appear in Latrell's vocabulary. Regrettably, he is not alone.

In Gilberto Conchas's research of successful programs for urban youth of color, he found a common thread among the low-income African American males in the school that he studied. Even in a highly successful program that boasted strong graduation rates and consistent levels of matriculation into two- and four-year colleges, low-income African American males placed higher value on athletic fame than on their collegiate path. Conchas writes, "They knew college was important but they really wanted to play football or basketball or perhaps become entertainers."[3] Conchas's research illustrates that, although these particular low-income African American males were provided with the social and academic support systems essential for college, "their perceptions of social mobility were seemingly no different than the general stereotype."[4] Despite the tenacious power of negative stereotypes, Conchas concludes that schools can take steps to counteract the negative consequences of linking racial identity and academic performance. He insists, "We must remain critical of larger historical and structural forces that impact African American youth's perceptions of the opportunity structure."[5]

By indicting systemic social injustices, Latrell was perceptive about the opportunity structures that limit students' life options. He linked standard-of-living disparities to institutionalized oppression. In his daily life, he witnessed the slow response of emergency services as a reflection and reinforcement of the pervasive messages about the disposability of Black people. He perceived the lack of cooperation among members of his community as a response to the constraints of living immensely unequal lives.

Many urban schools recognize the toll that inhumane socioeconomic conditions have taken on minority students' perceptions of themselves and their racial identities. Some school administrations have implemented self-esteem programs and attempted to include culturally affirming curriculum. While such efforts may be commendable, they are insufficient shields against the forces of historically rooted racist beliefs and structures of racism. Reflecting on the myriad methods of self-esteem-building tactics that have become commonplace in many urban schools, Jonathan Kozol asserts,

> We are in a world where hope must be constructed therapeutically because so much of it has been destroyed by the conditions of internment in which we have placed these children. It is harder to convince young people that they "can learn" when they are cordoned off by a society that isn't sure they really can.[6]

Kozol's assessment concurs with Latrell's: "They like this because they ain't been in no real life." Yet this *is* Latrell's real life, and it is the real life of his family, his peers, and his neighbors.

The poetic nuance of Latrell's phrase exposes his feeling that having a different kind of life was unrealistic or even otherworldly. Despite his indictment of institutional inequities and community challenges, Latrell's perspective is explicitly hopeful. He recognized that mowing lawns pays less than selling drugs, but he deliberately chose cutting grass as a means of resisting the prevalent opportunities for drug dealing. He saw the analogies to prison in his school structures but yearned for academic success. He revealed an awareness of his responsibility in achieving higher grades, but it is unclear whether the adults in his world were hearing his hopeful voice. What will it take for Latrell and his peers to attend a U.S. urban school where the notion of metal detectors seems foreign and out of place? Why does it seem only imaginary for Latrell to engage in a rigorous curriculum that promotes fluency in multiple academic disciplines, with participation in co-curricular activities that promote healthy athleticism and artistic accomplishments and with teachers and guidance counselors supporting achievable, fulfilling academic goals?

Reflect on This Case Study

1. Conchas's research suggests ways that schools can create structures to counteract the negative consequences of the linkage between racial identity and academic performance. How might a small group of dedicated teachers embark on changing structures in schools? Identify the stakeholders the group would have to bring on board to effect change.

2. What perceptions do you think most teachers would have of Latrell? What information would you share with those teachers to advocate for Latrell's participation in rigorous academics, arts, and athletics? What support structures would you build to help Latrell be successful?

3. Imagine you are Latrell's teacher. How does your memory of your high school experience compare to Latrell's? How do the communities and neighborhoods in which you grew up compare to Latrell's? What can you do as a teacher to learn about the realities of your students' daily lives? Does it matter?

Implications of Diversity for Teaching and Learning in a Multicultural Society

Myko Noel, Alica James, Jahkeema Johnson in Nora Elton's art class, Empower Charter School, Broolyn, NY. *Self-portraits*. Oil pastel drawings. 2010.

"We want our classrooms to be just and caring, full of various conceptions of the good. We want them to be articulate, with the dialogue involving as many persons as possible, opening to one another, opening to the world."

—**Maxine Greene**

"The Passions of Pluralism: Multiculturalism and the Expanded Community," Educational Researcher, *1993*

Part 3 analyzes the experiences of the young people in the case studies and snapshots by placing their stories in the broader sociopolitical context of schools and society. It also reviews some of the changes that can be made in schools and classrooms, based on the lessons young people can teach us through their experiences and insights. Students, although rarely consulted, are eloquent in expressing their own needs, interests, and concerns. It is in this spirit that their stories, desires, hopes, and goals are presented.

Chapter 8 explores conditions and experiences that students in the case studies and snapshots perceived as central to academic and social success. This exploration describes how young people, in their own words, define success; what they believe helped them achieve; and what held them back. The major purpose of this discussion is to explore what teachers and schools can do to provide successful academic environments for all students.

Chapter 9 presents three case studies of curriculum in a wide array of structural models that deal with a range of grade levels, content, topics, and skills. The chapter honors teachers' ingenuity and intellectual prowess in developing curriculum specific to their learning communities. Rather than advocating any one single model, the examples are presented in the hope that educators will find inspiration to design their own units. Two additional curriculum cases are on the companion Web site, at www.ablongman.com/nieto5e. One of the cases on the Web site documents a teacher's response to Hurricane Katrina and demonstrates how students analyze images from the news media. The other case on the Web site explains how one middle school math teacher tackled the issue of detracking the seventh- and eighth-grade math program in his school. Chapter 8 also features a multicultural story about a high school math teacher who believes every student can succeed.

Chapter 10 addresses three major conditions that promote learning among students: maintaining and affirming cultural connections, supporting extracurricular activities and experiences, and developing positive learning environments in schools. In this chapter, the seven characteristics that define multicultural education are developed further in a model ranging from tolerance to affirmation, solidarity, and critique.

Three major ideas are addressed in Part 3. One is that *complete assimilation as a prerequisite for success in school or society is a dubious notion at best, and a counterproductive one at worst*. The stories of the students in the case studies and snapshots are striking examples of this tension. These young people embody tremendous strength and resilience, and they want to do well and succeed in spite of sometimes overwhelming odds. But the conflicting experiences they have had in school also attest to the difficulties they have encountered.

A second significant idea discussed in Part 3 is that *schools need to accommodate their policies and practices to students' needs and realities if they are to be safe and nurturing learning environments*. When schools do not provide the structures needed for learning and affirmation, they can become places of defeat and despair.

The third significant idea illustrated in Part 3 is that *classroom curriculum can affirm students' identities while rigorously advancing academic achievement in preparation for life in a multicultural society*. Myriad models of curriculum design can be adapted within the multicultural perspectives asserted in this book, as demonstrated by the three curriculum examples described in Chapter 9.

8

Learning from Students

The voices of the students in the case studies and snapshots in this book are testimony to the vitality and spirit of youth. Despite a variety of conditions that might severely test the mettle and aspirations of others in similar circumstances, these youth have demonstrated a staunch determination to succeed in school and in life. Most define themselves as successful students, and they are proud of this fact, so understanding the insights of these particular students can be enlightening for educators interested in providing effective learning environments for all young people. Students who have not been as fortunate also have important messages for us because they challenge our prevailing assumptions about learning and teaching.

> *"To keep us from forgetting our culture's language, schools could still have reading sessions in our culture's language. I think that would help the Asian students."*
>
> —Savoun Nouch, interviewee

In this chapter, four major issues that emerged from the case studies and snapshots are reviewed:

1. A redefinition of success and achievement
2. Pride and conflict in culture and language
3. The key role of activities outside academics in sustaining students' enthusiasm and motivation for school
4. The intertwined roles of family, community, and school in providing environments for success

 ## Redefining Success and Achievement

Many young people have a conception of education that is distinct from that commonly held by schools. For instance, the role of hard work in becoming educated was mentioned by most of the students. During his interview, Kaval Sethi said that

intelligence rather than hard work was rewarded in his school. He said, "I don't think school is fair for people who are not as intelligent as other people. . . . It is very rigid." Others also made it clear that intelligence is not an innate ability or immutable quality—something that one is born with—as it is often defined in U.S. society. Intelligence is, in fact, something that one cultivates, studies hard to attain, and eventually achieves. Being smart is a goal, not a characteristic. Being smart is also the result of family and community support and the quality of care shown by teachers and schools. In this sense, intelligence is within everyone's reach.

Grades are a major indicator of academic success in our schools, and their importance is increasing in the current climate of accountability and high-stakes standardized tests. Grades were significant for most of the students we interviewed, but contrary to what many teachers and schools might believe, academically successful students may not consider grades to be as meaningful as other manifestations of their success. Many of the students we interviewed mentioned being satisfied with a grade for which they worked hard even if it was not the best grade. Yahaira Léon's science classes, which were far more demanding than other classes but in which she did not get as high a grade, were nevertheless her favorites. Many students exhibited a desire to fulfill their potential as human beings and as family members more often than concern about the quality of their future jobs. For Hoang Vinh, going to school had one purpose: to become educated. He considered a good job to be secondary. Yahaira said, "The reason for going to school is to educate your mind."

A word needs to be said, however, about the vague or romantic ideals some female students tend to have regarding their future. Alicia Montejo and Linda Howard talked about dual and seemingly contradictory career goals.

Youngeun Ahn in Adrienne Roberto's art class at The ArtRoom, a fine art studio and gallery in Topsfield, Massachusetts. *The Glare.* Oil pastel. 2010.

Alicia wanted to be either a medical doctor or a border patrol officer; and Linda, a teacher or a world famous singer. Particularly for females, the reality of limited choices in the past, and the continuing sexualization of their identities, have an impact. Most of these young women selected what seems to be a glamorous choice or one that could wield social power. Besides culture, language, and social class, gender also mediates what students may consider realistic goals for their future.

Pride and Conflict in Culture and Language

One of the most consistent, and least expected, outcomes to emerge from our interviews was the resoluteness with which young people maintained pride and satisfaction in their culture and the strength they derived from it. This does not mean that their pride was sustained without great conflict, hesitation, and/or contradiction. Because young people's positive sense of cultural identification challenges the messages and models of an essentially assimilationist society, it creates its own internal conflicts, but the fact that almost all of the students mentioned a deep pride in their culture cannot be overlooked. Students volunteered that their culture helped them in many ways and that they felt proud of who they are. Vanessa Mattison was an exception; she was uncomfortable even describing herself in ethnic terms. She reflected pride and shame in her cultural background, but for a different reason: because of the unfair privilege she derived from it as a White person.

Many of the young people understood that their culture was not what they *do*, but who they *are*. They seemed to understand intuitively that their heritage informed and enriched them, but they were also clear that it did not define them. For many, strong self-identification was understood as a value. "You gotta know who you are," is how Manuel Gomes expressed it. At the same time, they resisted essentialist notions of identity. They understood, to a much greater extent than most adults, that they were *cultural hybrids*. "I mix a lot of American values into my culture" is how Kaval described this hybridity.

We have written elsewhere, with colleagues Eugenie Kang and John Raible, about young people's growing awareness of the multiple influences on their identities and cultures. These influences draw from categories of race and identity but do not adhere to stable, fixed notions or labels.[1] The young people described in the case studies and snapshots defined culture as an active, dynamic interplay of their home, school, youth, traditional and contemporary cultures, and more, as created and re-created identities. Within this theme we noted four ways in which students spoke about pride and conflict: (1) conflict and ambivalence, (2) self-identification and conflict, (3) creating new cultures, and (4) identity and learning.

Conflict and Ambivalence

Pride in culture was neither uniform nor easy for these young people. In Eugene Crocket's Snapshot, he speaks about the difficulty of being "out" concerning his gay dads when he was in middle school: "I wasn't ashamed, but more embarrassed. I don't know . . . I didn't want people to think of me as different." He went on to explain the conflict: "At home everything is normal, like everyone else's family. Going out in public is a little more different." The experiences of other students in the case studies and snapshots are similar in their negotiation between love for family and comfort in family culture, and confrontation with mainstream expectations. As Jasper Alejandro-Quinn said in his interview, "The teachers who I know—they do not understand my culture."

Pierre Bourdieu's theory of cultural capital and of the role of schools in determining what knowledge has greatest status is helpful here.[2] This theory postulates that because schools primarily reflect the knowledge and values of economically and culturally dominant groups in society, they validate and reinforce the cultural capital that students from such groups already bring from home. This validation takes place through the overt and covert curriculum and the school climate. According to Bourdieu, the confirmation of the dominant culture's supremacy results in a symbolic violence against devalued groups. The cultural model held up for all is not within easy reach of all, and only token numbers of students from less-valued groups can achieve it. If they learn and take on this cultural capital—abandoning their own culture, language, and values—they may succeed. In this way, although few students from dominated groups are permitted to succeed, the myth of a meritocracy is maintained.

Some examples of the symbolic violence suffered by the students we interviewed help illustrate this point. James Karam's Lebanese culture was missing from all school activities, although other, more "visible" cultures were represented. Rashaud Kates longed for the presence of African American historical figures in his school curriculum. Nadia Bara, a Muslim American, and Kaval, a Sikh, both mentioned that their cultures were nearly nonexistent in their schools before September 11, 2001. After that date, they became visible, but mostly in negative ways. The invisibility of Native American content in Jasper's and Viena's school curriculum is another example of the devaluation of knowledge. Students may perceive that what is not taught is not worthy of learning.

In contrast, the language and culture of Manuel was highly evident in his schools, and teachers often referred to them explicitly both in curricular and extracurricular activities, giving them even more status. Liane Chang, whose middle school offers classes in Chinese, felt affirmed in her desire to become fluent in the native language of her mother. In her mind, teaching a language visible in the community makes a statement about the importance of that language to the *entire* community. The schools of these two students demonstrate, in a concrete way, respect for students' identities. In the case of Manuel, the bilingual program was at least partly responsible for his success. Savoun Nouch, whose case study is at the end of this chapter, and Paul Chavez, although originally not successful in school, became empowered by the multicultural curriculum at their alternative schools.

Although they learned to feel proud of themselves for many things, including their culture, their dexterity in functioning in two or more worlds, and their bilingualism, several of the students interviewed also learned to feel ashamed of their culture and of the people who reflect it. They faced what they saw as irreconcilable choices: denying or abandoning their identity to succeed, or holding onto it and failing in school and society.

Sometimes, students blame their families and communities for perceived failures while absolving the school of almost all responsibility. Latrell Elton sometimes used words to describe his community that either victimized or blamed people for their failure: "They [Black people] put themselves in a predicament," and "doin' stupid stuff," some of the very words used by those outside the African American community to criticize it. Although demanding accountability from one's own community is necessary, the critical analysis that must accompany it is missing. Latrell's case, however, is complex. For instance, he did not place all of the responsibility on his own community. He also considered the role that social structures, schools, and teachers play by having low expectations of Black students. Nini Rostland's comments concurred with Latrell's perspective: "I think expectations may be holding me back a little bit. I think when people see me, they assume, 'Oh, she's Black.' They automatically assume, 'Oh, she's not going to achieve well.'"

Nini's snapshot provides a window into negotiating identity as a multiracial youth. In school, she often felt that both her Polish American identity and her African heritage were not recognized. Assumptions based on her appearance were exacerbated by institutional racism. The strong influence of her family, friends, and summer camp environment supported her assertions of multiple perspectives, but her interview also revealed the weight of always being a boundary crosser and cultural bridge between groups. Some students who are not supported as strongly as Nini may try to ignore or disregard cultural identity, an unfortunate and ultimately counterproductive strategy.

Vanessa's case is especially notable and poignant. Because she was actively opposed to racism and other forms of discrimination (note her actions beginning in elementary school and her stand against heterosexism), she attempted to distance herself from the privileges she earned simply as a result of her ethnic background. Vanessa knew that she had benefited because of being White, but she thought this was unfair. Consequently, she took the position that one's culture and race are unimportant, accepting color blindness as the ultimate expression of fairness.

Others for whom the conflict is simply too great drop out, either physically or psychologically, or are expelled. Paul and Savoun both dropped out of school. For many students who drop out, the reason is not that they are incapable of doing the work, but that the school is an unaffirming place. For example, in an extensive review of literature on the education of American Indian students, Donna Deyhle and Karen Swisher concluded that the major reason for leaving school was students' perceptions that the school curriculum was not disconnected from their lives.[3] Although they were also committed to completing their educational journeys, this was certainly the case for Jasper and Viena Alejandro-Quinn. In terms of the education of American Indians, Sandy Grande proposes what she calls Red Pedagogy, that is, a pedagogy that pays particular attention to contemporary students' multifaceted identities in order to assertively address their realities while also providing a cogent analysis of colonialism. Thus, Grande argues for an examination of the ways in which "power and domination inform the processes and procedures of schooling and develop pedagogies that disrupt their effects."[4]

As we have seen, most of the young people in the case studies have struggled to remain true to themselves, but the process of fitting into a culture different from their family culture is a complex one. The students are also challenging the dichotomy between being culturally different from the majority and succeeding academically. This dilemma has been aptly described by Laurie Olsen in her comprehensive study of a highly diverse urban high school in California. One young woman interviewed by Olsen talked about the pressure from peers and teachers to stay within strictly defined cultural borders. She observed, "They want to make you just their culture and if you try to be who you are, and try to be both American and yourself, forget it. It won't work. It's not allowed."[5]

Self-Identification and Conflict

Like the student in Olsen's study, another conflict that some of the students in the case studies and snapshots expressed was an inability to identify both as American and as belonging to their cultural group. Their sense of pride in culture precluded identification with the United States because, for some of these students, claiming both meant denying their background or being a traitor to it. Why some young people make this choice is no mystery. Ethnicity in the United States, according to Stanley Aronowitz, has been "generally viewed as a temporary condition on the way to assimilation."[6] This being the case, it is no surprise that Manuel, for example, was emphatic about saying, "I'm Cape Verdean. I cannot be an American because I'm not an American. That's it."

Later in this chapter, Christina Kamau marked out her identity when she said, "I'm not Black American, I'm African and I came from Kenya." Yahaira, who was born in the United States, as were her parents, stated, "I'd say I'm Puerto Rican and Dominican" she continued, "And I guess I could say I'm American, too. I was born here." Our society has forced many young people to make a choice, and the students in the case studies and snapshots sometimes made it in favor of their heritage and family culture. Considering their youth and the negative messages about ethnicity around them, this is a courageous stand, but it can also be a limiting one. The consequences of such a choice probably affect what they think they deserve and are entitled to in our society. Having no attachment to the dominant society, they may also feel they have no rights, including the right to claim their fair share of society's power and resources or even to demand equality within it. Exclusive identification as a member of their cultural group may also exacerbate the conflict of feeling separate, different, and, consequently, powerless.

But are these the only choices? Fortunately, recent research is pointing in a healthier direction. In their longitudinal research among young people of various immigrant backgrounds, Alejandro Portes and Rubén Rumbaut came to the conclusion that the most positive path to identity was what they called *selective acculturation*, that is, a process by which children of immigrant backgrounds acculturate to the host society in a measured and careful way while at the same time maintaining ties with their ethnic communities. Portes and Rumbaut explain that preserving fluent bilingualism is linked with higher self-esteem, higher educational and occupational expectations, and higher academic achievement. They emphasize that children who learn the language and culture of their new country while maintaining their home language develop a better understanding of their place in the world. These understandings prevent them from clashing with their parents as often or feeling embarrassed by them because they are able to bridge the gap across generations and value their elders' traditions and goals.[7]

SNAPSHOT
Gamini Padmaperuma

At the time of his interview, Gamini was an eighth-grade student in a midsize town in the Northeast. His parents speak Singhalese, their native Sri Lankan language. In spite of his youth, Gamini powerfully articulated the struggle to learn Singhalese in the United States, a society with a strong and growing monolingual stance. In his snapshot, he pondered the problems and promises of crossing cultures in U.S. schools.

In art class, we have been working on a portrait of our hands as a painting, in unison with curriculum of other classes. Our hand paintings are supposed to give a visual image of how we identify ourselves.

As one first looks at my painting, they will see the following: an American flag on the left side of a road, on the other side of the road is the Sri Lankan flag, and handle bars of a bike with my hands on it. The handle-bars of the bike with my gloved hands on it represent my passion for biking. I like biking because it's a place where I can get away from everything and just concentrate on one thought, whatever that may be, while still paying attention to the road ahead.

My cultural background has played an influence on my educational experience since the beginning of my schooling: Sri Lankan by nationality, I have seen how it has made me more conscious about my culture. I realize who I am, what makes me different from many of my peers, and how that relates me to my surroundings.

Being Sri Lankan hasn't really affected how my teachers treat me but rather what is expected of me from myself and my family. In Sri Lanka, when I was traveling there, I realized how valued academics and an education are. There, it is the highest priority of any

child, not sports, not being popular, but totally focused on learning. My parents didn't leave those values behind; they still would expect me to succeed in school, which is an expectation of myself as well. But in Sri Lanka, a given student's social status, in school (that is, how "cool" or popular), isn't important. But in the American culture, kids tend to take school for granted, and they're more concerned about what they wear and how popular they are.

When I look at my parents, I see how far they have come. Coming from Sri Lanka to America is a big thing, so I should not shame my parents—they've worked so hard. If I blow off school, it would really upset them. This poses a problem between myself and my parents, for they have trouble understanding how important it is to spend time with friends, and doing school work. Well, I can do both. The schools my parents had gone through—the school that my dad went to was an all boys' school since he was in kindergarten through high school, and the school that my mom went to was an all girls' school. So my parents aren't so comfortable with how in America we have boys and girls going to the same school. Like, sometimes when I have a girl over, just like as a friend, they aren't as comfortable as the other American parents. But my parents are working really hard for us. My mom has a long ride to work because the job is better paying so she and my dad can earn enough to send me and my other two brothers to go to college. They work so hard for us.

I've lived in the U.S. all of my life, and I consider myself an American, but the Sri Lankan culture has been weaved into my life since I was young. Every so often my family will have religious ceremonies so my brothers and I can experience the traditions from the

The preservation and intersection of languages, cultures, and identities were also salient themes advanced by the 26 immigrant youth interviewed by Judith Blohm and Terri Lapinsky. Their book emphasizes the diverse ways in which students claim their identities inside and outside the home, and it offers curriculum and activities to affirm them.[8] Another example of the tension felt in making choices can be seen in the following snapshot of Gamini Padmaperuma, who sometimes felt pressure to

"Old Country." I can't speak Singhalese, which is the official language of Sri Lanka, so when I travel there I generally can't speak to some of the kids who haven't learned English yet. When I traveled there two summers ago, it was the first time I was surrounded by people who are like me, but I could not really communicate with them. I got to stay with my relatives, and I actually spent a day in the Sri Lankan school [co-ed now] where my mom had gone. It is a very big difference. I really noticed how teaching is a lot stricter there and the kids take it a lot more seriously. But I also now see how we take for granted the things we have in our school here, like lots of textbooks, and even the classroom and the building. It also taught me so much about cultures and societies. Educationally, I feel like I should start working harder and live up to my parents' expectations. It made me think a lot.

I have been trying to learn the language. I can understand what my parents are saying because they talk [Singhalese] to one another, and I have picked up words, but I feel ashamed that I can't speak [it]. Especially when I see some of my other friends who speak their language with their parents. It makes me feel that I should really work on that. There are kids who are born here, and they can speak their parents' language.

See, when I was younger, I knew English, and I didn't care about my parents' language. I wouldn't want to go to the grocery store and start talking to my mom in Singhalese, like if she asked me to go get milk. I knew what she was talking about, but I felt embarrassed, I felt weird because people start looking at you and wonder about your language and stuff. But now I see my cousin, who lives in England, but he lived in Sri Lanka for a year, and he is learning the language. I am pretty amazed because he can come back and speak Singhalese. It makes me wish I could do something like that. A lot of Sri Lankan kids tend to lose the language when they go to American, English-speaking schools. You speak it at home, but then you go to school in kindergarten and it just goes out the window.

But if you look at my painting, you see that the road I'm headed on splits, one towards America, one to Sri Lanka, and one in the middle. It represents a choice I have to make. Should I turn onto the road and take a bite of Americana? Should I turn towards Sri Lanka, continue Buddhism, learn about the language, have the culture take a larger portion of me? Or should I take the middle path? I don't know where it leads. Is it rough? Is it tough? I don't know.

Commentary

Most students, particularly adolescents, make choices about how much of their culture and language to embrace and how much to be influenced by those around them while shaping a self-image. They may do so consciously or subconsciously, but they do choose. Do Gamini's choices have to be "rough" or "tough"? Can we create a school environment and a society where Gamini and other students like him feel proud to speak their family's language—where they can create a new road rather than face difficult choices between America or home culture, or try to forge a path between the two on their own?

identify in one way or the other. Gamini wrote about his identity for a project done in my (Patty Bode's) art class, in which students developed identity portraits, both in writing and graphically. Gamini's portrait accompanies his words.

The way the young people in our case studies and snapshots sustained culture is fascinating and enlightening to educators. In more than one case, they maintained their "deep culture," particularly values and worldviews, although they may have abandoned more superficial aspects such as food and music preferences. These modifications are a function not only of clashing messages from school and home but also of young peoples' involvement with a peer culture, with its own rituals and norms. Although peer culture acts as a primary assimilating structure of our society, we should not assume that individuals have completely abandoned their family's culture simply because they act like other young people their age.

Creating New Cultures

Identity is constantly being negotiated and renegotiated by young people. Gamini Padmaperuma presents a good example of this negotiation. His snapshot and his accompanying painting demonstrate in a graphic way how complicated identity can be, but even adolescents of similar backgrounds have starkly different senses of their personhood. For instance, a volume co-edited by Clara Park, A. Lin Goodwin, and Stacey Lee advances a comprehensive perspective of how "American identities" are shaped by Asian and Pacific Americans.[9] Similarly, an exploration of how adolescents negotiate their multiple identities, and what teachers and schools can learn from them, is described in a book edited by Michael Sadowski.[10] Throughout the chapters in the book, various authors demonstrate why identity matters so much to adolescents.

That young people are involved in creating new cultures is evident in the remarks of the students in the snapshots and case studies. Their native cultures do not simply disappear, as schools and society might expect or want them to. Rather, aspects of the native culture are retained, modified, reinserted into different environments, and recast so that they are workable in a new society.

In creating new cultures, young people also need to choose from an array of values and behaviors, selecting those that fit in the new society and discarding or transforming others. The process is neither conscious nor planned. This is not just a phenomenon in the United States. For example, in an extensive study of over 7,000 immigrant youth from diverse cultural backgrounds living in 13 countries, researchers investigated how immigrant adolescents adapt at the intersection of two cultures. They found that most youth adapt in different ways, following four distinct patterns during their acculturation: an integration pattern, in which youth orient themselves to, and identify with, both cultures; an ethnic pattern, in which youth are oriented mainly to their own group; a national pattern, in which youth look primarily to the national society; and a diffuse pattern, in which youth are uncertain and confused about how to live interculturally.[11]

Those whose values and behaviors differ from those of the mainstream are inevitably involved in this transformation every day. Whether children or adults, students or workers, they are directly engaged in changing the complexion, attitudes, and values of our society. In the process, they may experience the pain and conflict that the young people in our case studies and snapshots articulated so well.

The point to remember is that U.S. society does not simply impose its culture on all newcomers. The process is neither as linear nor as straightforward as those who claim complete success for the process of Anglo-conformity might have us believe,[12] but neither has the result been a truly pluralistic society. Although the

United States is, in fact, multicultural, it is sometimes so in spite of itself; that is, it is not always the result of a conscious goal. For the most part, our society still reflects and perpetuates European American values and worldviews, but it has always also reflected, albeit at times poorly or stereotypically and against its will, the values of less respected and dominated groups, too. Latino heritage, for instance, can be seen in innumerable ways, from architecture in the Southwest to the myth of the cowboy. Jazz, widely acknowledged to be the greatest authentic U.S. music, is primarily African American in origin rather than European American.

What is "American" is neither simply an alien culture imposed on dominated groups nor an immigrant culture transposed indiscriminately to new soil. Neither is it an amalgam of old and new. What is "American" is the result of interactions of old, new, and created cultures. These interactions are neither benign nor smooth. Often characterized by unavoidable tension and great conflict, the creation of new cultures takes place in the contexts of the family, the community, and the schools.

Creating new cultures is made even more complicated by schools that, consciously or not, perceive their role as needing to shape all students to fit the middle-class, European American model. "They want to *monoculture* us," says a student in a video of successful Hispanic students in a Boston high school speaking about their identities and their schooling.[13] As we can see in the case studies and snapshots, students of diverse backgrounds respond in numerous ways to the pressures of an assimilationist society that is attempting to do away with differences. By refusing to accept either assimilation or cultural rejection, they force us to look at new ways of defining success.

Identity and Learning

Students pick up competing messages about language and culture from teachers, schools, and society. This was evident in the remarks of the students in our case studies and snapshots. One of the messages to emerge can be stated as follows: *Culture is important,* something that most of the students are proud of and maintain. However, students also learn that *culture is unimportant* in the school environment.

The notion that assimilation is a prerequisite for success in school or society is contested both by the research reviewed here and by the case studies and snapshots. The experiences of these young people call into question the often-cited claim that students who are not from European American backgrounds have poor self-images and low self-esteem. It is not that simple. In fact, schools and society may be complicit in *creating* low self-esteem. That is, students do not simply develop poor self-concepts out of the blue; self-concepts are also the result of policies and practices of schools and society that respect and affirm some groups while devaluing and rejecting others. Although young people might partially internalize some of the many daily negative messages about their culture, race, ethnic group, class, sexual orientation, and language, they are not simply passive recipients of such messages. They also actively resist negative messages through more positive interactions with peers, family, and even school. The mediating role of families, communities, teachers, and schools helps to contradict detrimental messages and to reinforce more affirming ones.

■ ■ ■ ■ ■ ■ What You Can Do

Become Knowledgeable About Arab and Arab American Students

Creating classrooms that affirm and expand understanding of students' cultural identities is essential. For example, the effort to learn more about Arabs and Arab Americans is especially necessary, considering the dilemmas faced by the Arab American students in the case studies: James, a Lebanese American, and Nadia, a Syrian American. Peers and teachers misunderstood their identities, and Nadia was explicit about the devastating stereotypes after the events of September 11, 2001. Because the discrimination and bigotry faced by Arab Americans has increased in the ensuing years, it is clear that *all* students in *all* classrooms will benefit from expanding their understanding of Arabs and Arab Americans and well as learning more about Muslim communities. As you will see in Nadia's case study, however, the identity of Arabs is complex and often misconstrued. Keep in mind the research of Gary C. David and Kenneth

K. Ayouby, which articulates the following three areas of concern in the portrayal of Arab Americans in classroom materials: *conflating, essentializing,* and *normalizing. Conflating* occurs when ethnic-racial and religious categories that should be distinct are used interchangeably, such as conflating the Middle East with the Arab world. The Middle East includes non-Arab countries such as Iran, Israel, and Turkey. The League of Arab States includes 22 countries. *Essentializing* occurs when some cultural, social, or religious trait mistakenly defines all Arabs. *Normalizing* is a twofold process that presumes to "rehabilitate" Arab Americans (1) to become just like everyone else and (2) to embody positive traits. The problem here is that it is rooted in a premise of negative assumptions that fail to recognize the marginalization of Arab Americans by mainstream culture. David and Ayouby recommend selecting materials that limit their scope to address one topic at a time: Arabs, Arab Americans, or Islam, not all three at once.

The conclusion that sustaining native language and culture nurtures academic achievement turns on its head not only conventional educational philosophy, but also the policies and practices of schools that have done everything possible to eradicate students' identities, they maintain, so that all students can succeed in school. We suggest that the opposite is true: School policies and practices that stress cultural knowledge, build on students' native-language ability, and emphasize the history and experiences of the students' communities would be much more productive.

 ## Beyond Academics

In nearly all the case studies and snapshots of students who were successful in school, significant involvement in activities beyond academics emerged as a key component. Whether through school-related organizations, hobbies, religious groups, or other activities, students found ways to support their learning. Although the activities promoted learning, they often had little to do with academics. Students spoke about activities beyond academics in four meaningful ways: (1) keeping on track, (2) shielding against peer pressure, (3) developing critical thinking and leadership skills, and (4) creating a sense of belonging.

Materials that try to cover all topics tend to conflate or essentialize the groups.*

Graphic Novels

High school teachers of social studies and English language arts can integrate graphic novels into the curriculum to provide engaging content and historical overviews in first-person narrative with compelling illustrations. Teens of all backgrounds and religious affiliations find these books spell-binding and informative. *Arab in America* by Toufic El Rassi is an eye-opening auto-biographical view of life as a middle school and high school student growing up in U.S. classrooms.[†]
A suggestion for a comparative graphic novel is *Persepolis: The Story of a Childhood,* by Marjane Satrapi. It is an autobiography of her life as a young girl under the Islamic Revolution in Iran (a non-Arab state).[‡]

Videos and DVDs

Every teacher of elementary and middle school knows the power of multimedia in the classroom. It is critical, however, to use sources that provide accurate information in an engaging way. *Cultural Safari,* by the nonprofit Kaur Foundation, is a 17-minute video aimed at educating schoolchildren, teachers, and school administrators about what it means to be a Sikh American. It comes with a resource guide.[§] One of the characters in the DVD asks, "Did you know the word *Sikh* means 'student—seeker of knowledge'?" The DVD is scripted to answer questions raised by teachers about Sikh Americans. It was made after extensive research of educators and administrators at the national level. Go to http://www.kaurfoundation.org/about-DVD.php.

*Gary C. David and Kenneth K. Ayouby (2005). Studying the exotic in the classroom: The portrayal of Arab Americans in educational source materials. *Multicultural Perspectives* 7 (4): 13–20.

†Toufic El Rassi. (2007). *Arab in America*. San Francisco: Last Gasp Publications.

‡Marjane Satrapi. (2003). *Persepolis: The Story of a Childhood*. Pantheon.

§Kaur Foundation. (2008). *Cultural Safari*. DVD. http://www.kaurfoundation.org/

While such activities take place in a range of settings, from organized or structured formal programs to extended family gatherings or neighborhood settings, the role of organized after-school programs for youth development cannot be overstated. A burgeoning field of research is documenting the influence of these community activities on young people's lives. Robert Halpern's research describes the historical development of after-school programs and emphasizes their critical role, especially in the lives of children from economically strapped communities.[14] In another study, Barton J. Hirsch studied six Boys and Girls Clubs across the country and, through the voices of students, documented how recreation and relationship building create a "second home" for these urban youth.[15] Similarly, in a study of a math and science enrichment program, Annie Bouie outlined the successes that can spring from focusing on the inherent strengths and resilience of young people's cultures and communities.[16] The research and practice of these community workers and others points to the growing importance of after-school programs and their relationships to schooling.

Keeping on Track

One way in which activities outside school help is by keeping students on track. That is, nonschool activities focus students' attention on the importance of school

■■■■■■ What You Can Do
Widen Horizons by Acknowledging What You Do Not Know

Think about the students who you are currently teaching, and ask yourself: Do any of them have cultural experiences or backgrounds with which you are unfamiliar? Pick two students who may represent groups of which you have little knowledge. For the purpose of example, we'll use two groups that Eugene mentions in his snapshot in Chapter 10: Tibetans and lesbian, gay, bisexual, and transgender (LGBT) people.

Make a KWL chart for each of the two students you have selected: what I *k*now, what I *w*ant to know, what I *l*earned. Make a plan to fill in the charts within one month. Use at least one print source as resources: read a book or an article. Also, take at least one field trip that immerses you in each family's culture: visit a community event, a performance, or the students' family. Perhaps you can also visit an arts event, go to a Tibetan cultural gathering, attend a political rally or meeting to support gay marriage rights, or take each student's family out for ice cream or another family favorite treat.

After you fill in "what I learned," choose two other students' families and start with two new KWL charts. Continue throughout the year.

while simultaneously providing some relief from it. This finding is consistent with other research. For instance, Jabari Mahiri's research on the literacy activities of 10- to 12-year-old African American males during participation in a neighborhood basketball association found that this sport had immense motivational value in inspiring them to engage in literacy activities.[17]

In the case studies and snapshots, extracurricular activities also had a definitive influence, and these extended beyond simply sports. Rashaud, for example, spoke about his membership in Future Business Leaders of America. This after-school group engaged in community service in children's hospitals and nursing homes. In addition to a sense of fulfillment, these activities provided a framework for understanding the role of the business leader beyond that as somebody who focuses on making money. Involvement in the Gay/Straight Alliance was significant in carving out a place where Rebecca Florentina and other LGBT students could feel at home. Melinda Miceli's research documents the social and political impact of the Gay/Straight Alliance. She emphasizes the role of the first student leaders who created these organizations within their communities as vehicles of change within schools.[18] Such after-school activities taught Rashaud, Rebecca, and their peers essential life skills, and it also gave them the impetus and energy to educate others.

Many researchers have documented the important role of the arts in co-curricular, extracurricular, and after-school activities in developing rich multicultural student expression. A collection of essays by Maxine Greene provides a critical account of the role of the arts in social change. She argues that releasing students' imagination and artistic expression asserts multicultural student voices while developing skills in academic disciplines.[19] To illustrate the power of arts in after-school communities, Shirley Brice Heath and Laura Smyth, in collaboration with researcher Milbrey

Mclaughlin, created a documentary film and guidebook. The film and book present four case studies of high-quality after-school arts programs that defy stereotypical public perceptions of urban youth.[20] Other projects directly integrate school curriculum with after-school life through the arts. An example can be found in the inspiring work of a project called Through Students' Eyes (TSE), which was founded by experienced teachers in urban schools who collaborated with photographers and community activists. Students in the TSE project use "photovoice" and visual sociology methods to document their answers to three questions: (1) What is the purpose of school? (2) What helps you succeed in school? and (3) What gets in the way of your school success? This image-based activity about their after-school lives helped engage students in writing activities in their English language arts clasroom.[21]

Shields Against Peer Pressure

The negative peer pressure to which students are subjected can be very difficult to resist, but most of the students in the case studies were successful in doing so. One reason was the activities in which they were involved, which, for some, shielded them against negative influences. This was described vividly by Paul, who had not yet totally succeeded in resisting the pressure to be in a gang but nevertheless said, "Now it's like I figure if I'm more involved in school, I won't be so much involved in the gang, you know?" As you will see, Savoun also explained the role of peers in his former choices: "I was unwilling to focus on my education life. I chose friends over education, and one thing led to another and I dropped out there."

For other students as well, involvement in community activities took up non-school time, acting as a preventive strategy for discouraging less productive, although at times more alluring, activities. This was the reason, for example, that Manuel dropped some of his friends; at just about the same time, he joined a church in which he became deeply involved. Jasper's enthusiasm about attending powwows, Linda's devotion to music, and Avi's insistence on honoring the Sabbath can be understood in this way, too.

Developing Critical Thinking and Leadership Skills

Extracurricular, co-curricular, after-school, and community activities also contribute to the development of important skills such as critical thinking and leadership qualities. Through a theater workshop based on students' experiences and ideas, Manuel was able to analyze and critique his own experience as an immigrant to this country. This workshop gave him a place to reflect on his experiences more deeply and to articulate consciously and clearly the pain and fear that he felt in his first years here. Other examples of empowering activities include Yahaira's work with the mock trial after-school program, and Jasper's video workshop with Native Lens. These activities tapped into and expanded their academic interests, which in turn influenced their choices about school coursework, future college paths, and possible careers.

James's involvement with bicycle racing, his self-acclaimed first love, consumed both his time and attention. Before his bike accident, he was riding 40 miles per day. James's involvement in bicycling extended beyond racing itself, however. He subscribed to all of the related magazines, got his racing license, and was actively recruiting others interested in the sport to start a biking club. He was also planning to approach local bicycle merchants with the idea of obtaining financial support to sponsor the team. Gamini expressed a similar attachment to biking, an activity that helped him sort out his thoughts.

Avi's work in the synagogue is another powerful example of how extracurricular activities can develop leadership skills. Not only did his involvement in the temple require a great deal of study and sacrifice, but it also made him a role model for others in his community. The same was true of Nadia's involvement in her mosque and of Kaval's work in the Gurudwara, the Sikh house of worship. Vanessa's work with a peer education group helped her develop important leadership qualities and a growing critical awareness of and sensitivity to issues of exclusion and stratification.

Belonging

The feeling of belonging, so important for adolescents, is also a benefit of participating in extracurricular activities. Young people seek to fit in and belong in any way they can. Some meet this need by joining gangs or taking part in other harmful activities where they feel part of a so-called replacement for family. For many young people, the satisfaction of belonging is particularly evident in activities related to their ethnic group. Paul and Savoun were notable exceptions to participation in outside-of-classroom activities. Transportation, finances, and obligations to care for his sisters prevented Savoun from joining the football team at his former school. Paul and Savoun succumbed to the lure of some of the only "extracurricular" activities in their neighborhoods—gangs and criminal activity—yet when provided with more positive outlets, they blossomed.

The role of faith communities in young people's lives also needs to be understood in a cultural context. For many people with deep connections to religion, their spiritual lives are not an add-on or an extracurricular activity. The youth groups or committees that emerge from religious communities may be extracurricular but, in many cases, they have inextricable connections with cultural identities. Khyati Joshi's research on the experiences of second-generation Indians offers a framework for understanding the relationships of ethnicity and race to religion in the United States. Joshi argues for educational curricular reforms and, more broadly, for recognition of religion as a form of social identity.[22] In this context, young people's activities in their religious communities may be significant factors in their identity development.

These are valuable illustrations of how extracurricular activities in school, as well as activities outside school, including hobbies and religious and cultural organizations, support student learning. Rather than detracting from students' academic success by taking time away from homework or other school-related activities, such involvement helps young people by channeling their creative and physical energy. In some cases, the activities may also have academic benefits.

Family, Community, and School Environments for Success

Successful students are surrounded by messages that encourage success, including direct and indirect support from family and friends; activities that enhance, rather than detract from, success; and teachers and other school staff members who demonstrate their care. Students noted two major strands when explaining environments for success within the intertwined roles of family, community, and school: (1) the crucial role of family and (2) teachers, schools, and caring.

The Crucial Role of Family

The ways families support children in their learning are complex and sometimes not what one might expect. Non–middle-class families, in particular, may not have much experience with academic involvement or achievement, but they do what they can to help their children in other ways. One way that families demonstrate their support for academic success is through high expectations. Education was highly valued by the families of all these students, regardless of their economic background. In fact, in some instances, working-class parents and parents living in poverty had even *more* hope in education than middle-class parents, for obvious reasons.[23] They could not always help their children with homework or in learning English, and because they often lacked the "cultural capital" valued in society at large, they could not pass it down to their children. As a result, the ways they manifested high expectations were sometimes indirect, but the messages they verbalized to their children were clear. Vinh said his uncle supported him by saying, "Next time, you should do better." Alicia explained, "Doing good in school is to get a chance to do stuff that most of my family hasn't been able to do." Rashaud told us about his parents' concern: "It matters to me because, if they didn't care, I wouldn't care. Since they do, I really do. I really want to make them proud."

Family messages that communicate high expectations, although powerful, are not always enough. Many of the young people described in the case studies and snapshots had great respect and appreciation for their families and understood the sacrifices that had been made on their behalf. Nevertheless, this appreciation did not always make their school experiences any easier or more tolerable. Because their parents were not always able to give them concrete help and tangible guidance, students sometimes lacked a sense of direction. Manuel put it most poignantly when he said, "If I felt like I had support from my family, if they only knew the language. . . . If they were educated, I could make it big, you see what I'm saying?" Although parents' inability to speak English is not a liability in itself, it can become one if the school does not provide alternative means for student learning through structures such as bilingual programs and homework centers.

Given the kind of help middle-class parents are able to provide for their children, Manuel was absolutely right when he concluded, "I would've had a better opportunity, a better chance." A good example comes from Barbara Comber's research that focused on early literacy experiences of children in Australia. Comber explains that children's families do not just "disappear" when the children start school. On the contrary, children bring with them their privileges and disadvantages and everything they have learned prior to beginning school. Discussing three specific children, she argued that children's lives aren't simply "background" information for teachers, and in describing Mark, one of the children, she explained:

> At home, Mark did not have a collection of books and nobody read him bedtime stories. But he did have knowledge and dispositions, which counted for quite a lot in making the transition to school. He knew how to be a "good boy." He knew what counted as important practices in the classroom (e.g., looking after books, answering questions).[24]

Families who lack formal education and have limited experience with the means for achieving academic success frequently do a great deal to prepare their children for school. They often compensate by providing other critical support to their children. In the case of students from different linguistic backgrounds, parents and other family members frequently maintain native language use in the home, despite contrary messages from school and society. Such language use helps students develop literacy and prepares them for school. The more students are able to use language in a variety of ways and in diverse contexts, the more they replicate the literacy skills necessary for successful schoolwork.

Maintaining native-language communication at home also implies nurturing cultural connections through activities such as family rituals and traditions, not to mention the even more meaningful underlying cultural values that help form young people's attitudes and behaviors. Savoun put it plainly: "I would never want to leave my culture or my language; I always want to learn more." "Apprenticeship" in their families, and the consequent learning of culture, language, and values, is a primary way in which children receive and internalize the message that they are important. This is a crucial message for teachers to understand. Although the children in their classrooms might not have the specific skills called for in school, they *do* have attitudes, skills, and capabilities that can be tapped to advance their learning.

Encouraging communication within the family is another way parents support the academic success of their children. The importance of talking with their parents about issues central to their lives was mentioned by a number of young people. Alicia recalled significant conversations with her mother, when she was still alive, about "protecting herself," sexual responsibility, and the importance of school. Yahaira stated that she talked to her mother about "almost everything," including school achievement. As you will see in Nadia's case study, Nadia described each member of the family as forming a piece of the "puzzle" and communication as central to maintaining this close connection. For Vinh, even long-distance communication was meaningful. He wrote to his parents weekly and was in turn revitalized by their messages. Linda's description of shared dinnertime in her family is a moving expression of the value of communication.

In numerous ways, academically successful students in the case studies and snapshots made it clear that they dedicated their school success to their parents, almost as a way of showing their gratitude for the sacrifices their parents made for them. These young people frequently mentioned that their parents were the motivating force behind their success, even if the parents did not always completely understand or appreciate what it meant. For example, Paul was inspired to return to school by his mother's own return to school. Gamini said that he wanted to do well for his family because of all they had sacrificed for him and his brothers. More than one student mentioned making her or his parents *happy*. This focus on parents' happiness, not what one might expect from contemporary, sophisticated adolescents, is a theme that emerged time and again.

Students in the case studies and snapshots often described their parents in remarkably tender and loving ways. From Yahaira's "my mom is the person I admire the most in the world," to Vanessa's "they're caring and they're willing to go against the norm," students made it clear that they had warm, close-knit relationships with their parents, which had a significant influence on their lives and the formation of values. Viena told us, "I think my parents have filled in that gap that my school does not do." Savoun described his affection for his family thus: "It's been great to be a member of my family. Sometime they don't understand me, but I still love them." Linda said that her parents were "always there for me, all the time" and even that she understood the "twisted reasons" for their rules and limits.

This is not to say that parents whose children are not successful in school have *not* provided affirming environments. There are a multitude of complex reasons why students are successful in school, and a close and warm relationship with parents is only one of them. Notwithstanding the caring and loving environments that parents may provide their children, their children may still be rebellious, alienated, or unsuccessful in school. A good example is Paul, who maintained that, "If it wasn't for the family, the love I get from my family, I would look for it in my homeboys. . . I had a love that kept me home." While earnestly stating this, Paul was still engaged in the gang. Latrell expressed his sincere desire to avoid drug dealing and "negative stuff" so he could make his mother proud. His interview demonstrated the many forces that he had to negotiate to accomplish his goal of a positive future.

Other issues also influence academic success. What Carlos Cortés called the *societal curriculum*, that is, influences of the general society—including the mass media, gender-role expectations, anti-immigrant hysteria, and rampant violence—are another layer of the sociopolitical context of education that needs to be considered.[25] Additional factors that may affect school achievement include rank within family, other family dynamics such as relationships among siblings, and simple personality and idiosyncratic differences. It appears, however, that a close and open relationship between children and their parents or guardians is necessary but insufficient for school success.

Although relationships with their parents and other family members were obviously prominent in the academic success of these students, their families were not always involved in the school according to the traditional definition of parent involvement. There were some exceptions, such as Viena's and Jasper's parents, who were very vocal in their children's schooling. However, most of the students' families did not go to school unless called, did not attend meetings or volunteer in school activities, and were not members of parent organizations. This was somewhat surprising,

■ ■ ■ ■ ■ ■   What You Can Do

Expand the Comfort Zone for You and Your Students

The students in the snapshots and case studies told us about crossing cultural boundaries and negotiating multiple worlds. How often do you consider the many realms that students are required to juggle to meet school success? Here is a little experiment to help you consider life through the eyes of students whose lives may not be easily integrated into mainstream cultures.

Your Comfort Zone: Two Weeks in the Life of a Teacher

Week One: Consider your daily routines, environments, and communications as a teacher and also as a member of your community. For one week, keep brief journal entries that describe these experiences: What is your usual journey to and from work? Where do you purchase your food? How do you take care of your laundry? Who are the people you see in these events? Do you have a regular stop in your weekly routine: visiting a neighbor or family member; stopping at a coffee shop, an exercise class, or a library; escorting young ones to activities or elders to appointments? What language do you speak when you engage in these activities? Write down the mundane and the ordinary.

Week Two: Change your daily routine. Try a different route to get to work. Purchase your food from a merchant you have never or rarely visited.

---

considering the research on the relationship between parental involvement and children's academic achievement. The fact that some of these parents did not speak English, that they themselves had not always had positive experiences in schools, and that they were inhibited by the impersonal and unreceptive nature of schools may be partial explanations. Conflicting work schedules, child-care needs, and other situations also help explain their noninvolvement.

Teachers, Schools, and Caring

Many of the students in the case studies and snapshots mentioned particular teachers, programs, and/or activities in school that helped them succeed. The key role that teachers play in the achievement of their students is not surprising. The most important characteristic students looked for in their teachers was caring. Students evaluated their teachers' level of caring by the amount of time they dedicated to their students, their patience, how well they prepared their classes, and how they made classes interesting.

Students are empowered not only by studying about their *own* culture but also by being exposed, through a variety of pedagogical strategies, to different perspectives. Numerous students mentioned this, including Paul, who was empowered when he read *The Diary of Anne Frank* in elementary school. It was not only the subject matter but also how it was taught that made history come alive for him. Viena mentioned her classroom study of *Bless Me Ultima,* the story of a young Chicano boy in the 1940s, as an avenue into learning about others. Several students mentioned the desire to learn

Cook a recipe or purchase prepared food you have never tasted. Fold your laundry in a different way. Travel to an unfamiliar neighborhood. Change the day of some routines that do not have prescribed schedules. Learn at least two sentences in a language you have never spoken. Keep brief journal entries. What did you notice? How did you feel? How well did you function? Did these changes have positive aspects? Did they have negative aspects?

Everyday experiences such as getting to work, purchasing food, and folding laundry are not necessarily cultural events, but cultural life *is* enacted and comprised of everyday experiences. To cultivate empathy for, and solidarity with, students who are perceived as different—or perceive themselves as different—it is useful to reflect on how familiarity and routine create comfort. You don't necessarily have to plan a heritage festival to develop awareness of how identities are asserted and affirmed in our daily lives.

This exercise will help you imagine how students might feel when their perspectives and identities are negated or ignored. In turn, the significance of the little things that make a difference in students' school day—such as a warm smile, an extra moment of patience in an explanation, or acknowledgment for even small accomplishments—take on fresh meaning. Imagine a classroom where all the students and teachers work from such a perspective.

Your Students' Comfort Zones

Adapt this activity for your students, but do not assign it until you have done it yourself!

more about world regions and the cultural groups involved in current events. Several mentioned wishing they were taught more about the war in Iraq and Afghanistan and expressed a desire to learn about the experiences of people in those two countries as well as about Islamic traditions.

Teachers of the same background as students also make a difference. Jasper wondered what it would be like to have a person of color as a teacher for more than the one and only day that he had a substitute teacher of color. Several recent studies have pointed to the positive influence that same-group identity between a teacher and students can have. A study by Sabrina Zirkel, for instance, found that students with race- and gender-matched role models had better academic performance, had more achievement-oriented goals, and thought more about their future, compared to students who did not have such matched role models.[26] However, the fact that the teachers and other staff members who understand and call on the students' cultures are often from the same background does not mean that only educators from the students' ethnic group can teach them or be meaningful in their lives. Having teachers from students' ethnic backgrounds cannot be underestimated, but students in the case studies also named teachers *not* from the same background who had made a difference in their lives. These teachers had either learned the students' language or were knowledgeable about, and comfortable with, the students' cultures, or they were simply sensitive to the concerns of young people.

What can teachers and other educators learn from the experiences of the students in the case studies and snapshots? For one, it is apparent that how educators view their role in relation to their students can make a powerful difference in the

Multicultural Teaching Story

Mr. Jarvis Adams on Teacher Care

Researcher Dr. Mari Ann Roberts asked parents of high school students to name teachers who help Black students achieve.* A high school teacher of twelfth-grade economics, Mr. Jarvis Adams was named by many parents and guardians at Martin Luther King High School near Atlanta, Georgia. Mr. Adams spoke to Dr. Roberts about the historical role of African American teachers' care as an essential ingredient in helping African American students achieve.

I know I teach from the Afrocentric perspective. I do talk a lot of self-pride, self-love. Telling them more, "it's okay to love yourself." That doesn't mean you hate anyone else.

Then, it's the economics [class] and it's Martin Luther King High School and we all Black, I talk to them a lot about economic equality. One of the projects—see that project there, the Smoothie King? They had to research a franchise and see what it takes to open up a franchise. You know, if Publix and Kroger leave, and Wal-Mart leaves, where are we going to buy groceries? Why are we dependent on other people? You go down Buford Highway, they've got Mexican grocery stores everywhere. I talk to them a lot about everything—economics, how you can apply it with our community.

I just think, from looking from a historical perspective, we learn through oral tradition—so that's the way we need to teach. The Koreans, and the Jews, they teach their kids the way that they learn. They take their culture as part of the way they learn and they teach towards their culture, but for some reason, the African American school system, we kind of forget.

Care in relationship to adult/student, not "I'm an adult and I'm your friend." Care is "I'm going to chastise you when you're doing wrong. I'm not going to embarrass you. I'm not going to degrade you. I'm not going to call you dumb. I'm going to be here to offer you extra help, but if you don't want to do it, then it is what it is." I think caring [about] in that way, almost like a parent does.

Mr. Adams expressed many of the components of teacher care that we heard from students and other researchers: holding students to rigorous, high expectations by giving strong messages and skill support for academic achievement; communicating care through a watchful eye and attitude that refuse to let kids fail; and a heightened awareness of cultural ways of knowing. Mr. Adams also discussed his role in the athletic lives of the youth as a football coach and how he transferred the ethic of hard work from sports to academics:

I always tell my linebackers. "I never coach your effort. Either give me 110 or just go elsewhere." Now, if you put forth the effort, and I tell my students now, "It's my job to teach you. Don't let me not do my job because I'm not going to let you out of here unless you pass my assessment." So, if they want to learn and they don't get it, it's my job to make them get it. They'll hold me up. . . .

When you coach football, you run a play, you don't run it right, you don't just move on. We're going to run it again, we're going to run it again. So, [in the classroom] we have

20-something QCC—33 for this subject. We're going to get the QCCs right. We'll at least understand what the QCC, the nutshell, what it means. Then, we can move onto a new QCC and then when it comes to the end of course test, just like coaching football, when it gets to game day, you give your speeches. You put a whole other mood on. You get into their psyche then. You get them focused.

Mr. Adams also reflected on his role in the community and his relationship to the neighborhood. He is what Jason Irizarry has called a "homegrown teacher" who uses community connections (sharing personal stories, living in the same community, and knowing what goes on in the neighborhood) to demonstrate care and to support academic achievement.[31]

I live in the area. . . . my third-grade teacher, Ms. Connell; second-grade, Ms. Graham; Ms. Smith for fourth-grade teacher; Mr. Davis, my fifth-grade teacher, they all lived in my neighborhood. Now, I lived in a housing project and they lived in houses. I'd go to the grocery store and I would see them. They knew my mom. Ms. Smith and Ms. Connell, they sung in the choir with my mom. I just kind of feel like staying in the area. A lot of teachers think opposite. . . . But, growing up—that's the way it was when I was growing up and it made a difference. . . .

I think if you didn't care, you wouldn't teach. I think you have to care for them and that's why you would teach. It's not a great paycheck. It's not bad. I . . . come here and teach because that's why they came here, to learn. They didn't come here to do—some people out here, they play cards every day. You can't care about the kids if you let them play cards [in school]. It's Black on Black crime, really, because you're making them lazy and I know boys. . . .Boys tend to do better in my class and the reason is Black males are logical thinkers. Love debate, love confrontation. Love just the whole [thing]—because that's how we are. You go to the barbershop and they're going to debate whether you should snatch the pen off or twist it off and it's going to be a heated discussion, and even if you're not into it, you're going to pick up on it and you're going to walk away with, "Man, you just answered—," and you're going to have a reason why you should do it because that's our nature as a people. I think that, without being a Black male, how we act in a barbershop, how we act when we're shooting pool, how we act at the back of the church when there ain't nobody around. You just have to know how we learn with each other.

Teaching should cause you to look for doors to open that you don't know exist [yet], to go out and seek something else that you don't even know [yet] that's there. Definition of teacher care: Holding a child accountable. Holding a student accountable. That's what I believe.

"Knowing how we learn with each other," is another trait of successful teachers of African American students examined in Gloria Ladson-Billings' work on culturally responsive teachers.[31] Mr. Adams's word as demonstrate the qualities that many researchers have found in teachers who bring students to reach high academic achievement.

*We are grateful to Mari Ann Roberts, who conducted the interview with Mr. Jarvis Adams as part of her research about teacher caring. We are also very grateful to Mr. Adams for agreeing to share his words in this text.

lives of students. This role definition is not about strategies as much as it is about attitudes. In the words of Jim Cummins, "The interactions that take place between students and teachers and among students are more central to student success than any method for teaching literacy, or science or math."[27]

In a related area, the lesson that relationships are at the core of teaching and learning is reinforced through the case studies. Students mentioned teachers who cared about them and how these teachers helped to make them feel that they belonged. In an investigation by Brandelyn Tosolt about teachers' caring behaviors, one teacher demonstrated what Tosolt calls a mixture of interpersonal caring and academic caring behaviors, as explained by a student in the study: "[W]hen we get off task, she says, 'I care about you, but that's not what we're talking about right now.'"[28] When students feel connected to school, they identify as learners, and they have a far greater chance of becoming successful students. When they feel that they do not belong, identifying as a learner is more difficult.

Finally, educators can learn that there are many ways to show caring. Accepting students' differences is one way; another is to have rigorous and high expectations of them. Also, becoming what Ricardo Stanton-Salazar has called *institutional agents*, providing social networks for students, is equally meaningful. These networks, from information on college admissions to securing needed tutoring services, are generally unavailable to culturally marginalized students or those living in poverty, but they can make the difference in achieving academic success.[29] Prudence Carter builds on that notion by calling for "multicultural navigators" who are fluent in the social and cultural capital of college admissions, scholarship acquisition, and the like, yet do not totally acculturate, or give in, to the establishment. According to Carter, navigators are needed who can demonstrate:

> how to overcome poverty with critical, self-loving, and other respecting perspectives, who do not make [students] ashamed of who they are but rather proud of how far they will go.[30]

Whether they are in traditional or alternative schools, whether they are from mainstream or nonmainstream backgrounds, whether they speak students' native languages, *all* teachers can make a significant difference in their students' lives. The young people in our case studies and snapshots have provided much information about how teachers can make this significant difference.

Conclusion

Cultural and linguistic connections can play a key role in students' academic success. In most of these cases, language and culture have been reinforced in the home and sometimes in the school, too. When reinforced in both settings, the message that language and culture are valued is clear and powerful. If they are valued only in the home, students may develop conflicted feelings about them.

The larger society also plays a key role in student learning. If young people see their culture devalued in things such as political initiatives (e.g., propositions to abolish bilingual education or to ban gay marriage), they are certain to develop conflicted attitudes concerning their ethnic group, family, and social culture. In spite of sometimes harsh attacks on their culture, however, many successful students have been able to maintain considerable pride in their ethnic group, family culture, and community. In the process, they reject both the pressure to assimilate and the pressure to give up. They are transforming culture and language to fit in, but on their own terms.

To Think About

1. What characteristics do you think define academic success? Do these characteristics differ from how you think most teachers define it? Do you think your cultural values influence your definition? How?

2. If it is true that pride in culture and language are important for academic success, what does this mean for school policies and practices? Discuss policies and practices related to culture and language that you think schools should reconsider to promote educational equity for all students.

3. Caring on the part of teachers, schools, and parents was highlighted by a number of students. What might schools do to give students the message that they care? How would these practices compare with current practices?

Activities *for Personal, School, and Community Change*

1. The crucial role of families in providing environments for success was highlighted by many of the students in the case studies, but their families' roles were often different from that which schools traditionally define as parent and/or family involvement. Come up with an action plan for working with parents and/or guardians to develop environments for success while also respecting their specific contexts. For example, not all families have computers, so requiring that they provide them for their children is unrealistic. Likewise, not all families speak English fluently, and asking them to do so might be counterproductive. What can you do in such cases to encourage families to motivate their children to become academically engaged?

2. Lead a professional development activity to view the video *Breaking the Silence: Asian American Students Speak Out,* a conversation facilitated by Dr. Roberta Wallitt. Engage your colleagues in reflection about the messages from the youth in the film and in developing an action plan to address these messages in your school. The DVD is available from Teaching for Change at http://www.teachingforchange.org/node/408, where you can download a free study guide to accompany your discussion of the film.

3. If you don't already do so, begin a weekly "Letter to Parents" in which you highlight some of the classroom activities their children have been doing. You can ask for their advice on curriculum issues, encourage them to volunteer in the classroom, and so on. You might also include children's work in the letters from time to time.

Case Studies

Nadia Bara

I could never really stand in other people's shoes but now … I kind of feel for the people that had racists against them because now I kind of know how they feel.

I n some ways, it's hard to believe that Nadia Bara[1] was just 14 years old when she was first interviewed. Talking about school, her family, her religion, or the joys and difficulties of being different, she was at once a wise older spirit and a teenager.

A ninth-grader in a high school known throughout the state as an excellent school, Nadia lived with her mother and father in Linden Oaks, a comfortable, upper-middle-class suburb in the Midwest that boasts the highest yearly median income in the state. Her sister Layla, 18 years old, was a first-year student at the state university, also a well-regarded institution in the Midwest. Layla lived on campus a couple of hours from home but frequently returned home on weekends. Nadia's mother, Sarah, and her husband, Omar, both physicians, had lived in the United States for nearly two decades. Sarah was born in the United States, but while still a child, she had returned with her family to Syria, where she was raised and completed her education, including her medical training. Omar was born in Kuwait and attended medical school in Egypt. They met and married in Kuwait and came to live in the United States shortly before the birth of their first daughter, Layla.

The entire family visits Syria for at least two weeks every year to see family and friends and reconnect with their roots. During these trips, they usually visit at least one new place, too. They had recently been to Holland, Germany, Austria, and Maui. These trips had increased Nadia's motivation to travel, which she loved, because, as she said, "I love seeing all the different types of people anywhere." During her interview, Nadia spoke fondly about her experiences in Syria, while also describing her status as an insider/outsider both in Syria and the United States.

The Bara family is a close-knit and fairly religious one. They belong to a relatively sizable Muslim community in Linden Oaks, and they try, in the midst of the fast-paced and postindustrial society of the United States, to live as Syrians and Muslims. This is not always possible, and Nadia and her sister both spoke of the tribulations they have faced because of their identities.

Nadia and her family are part of a growing Arab and Muslim presence in the United States. In 2000, a few years before Nadia was interviewed, the U.S. Census Bureau counted 1.2 million Arabs in the United States, or about 0.4 percent of the U.S. population, although Muslims continue to arrive in the United States, and a growing number of non-Arabs in the United States are converting to Islam.[2] Arabs are a remarkably diverse group, hailing from some 20 countries in the Middle East and Northern Africa. Most Arabs in the world are Muslims, but Arabs are only 20 percent of all Muslims in the world (estimated to be more than 1 billion in number). In fact, Islam is the fastest growing religion in the world.[3] Nevertheless, only a quarter of Arabs in the United States are Muslim. Arabs live in many parts of the United States, settling in places that would surprise many people. According to Diana Eck, for example, about a century ago, three small communities in North Dakota were home to an early group of Muslim immigrants, and one of the first mosques in the country was built in 1920 in the town of Ross, North Dakota. In addition, the Muslim community in Cedar Rapids, Iowa, goes back more than 100 years. Thus, from the start, the Midwest has been a destination for Muslims from various countries.[4]

Reasons for making the United States their destination vary greatly, but economic and political reasons account for why many come. Although Arabs are not new to the United States, the challenges they face have become more apparent in the recent past. These challenges include negative stereotyping, racism, discrimination, and misinformation about their history and culture, a theme echoed by Nadia. Schools are some of the places where these problems are most visible.

The Bara family chose public schools for their daughters. This decision was not an easy one to make, particularly because of differences in religion and religious practices. Both Nadia and Layla have done very well in school. Layla, for instance, graduated with a 4.0 grade point average (GPA) from the same high school that Nadia was attending. Nadia loved school and was also doing well academically, having received a special award for earning straight A's in eighth grade. She was involved in many nonschool activities, especially sports (soccer, tennis, track, and volleyball), as well as school activities, including student council, theater productions, and the school newspaper.

As pointed out in the case study of James, the Christian Maronite student, Arabs and Arab Americans were often "invisible" in schools—until recently. This invisibility disappeared after the events of September 11, 2001, when Arabs and Arab Americans became all too visible. This point is corroborated by Amaney Jamal and Nadine Naber in their thorough research about the racialization of Arab Americans.[5] Nevertheless, Arabs are still frequently invisible in curricula and in other school policies and practices. Consequently, Islam is the religion about which most Americans have the least information and the most biases.[6]

In the case study that follows, we see a young woman who reflects on these issues in a thoughtful and mature way. The major themes that surfaced in Nadia's interviews were: *the centrality of family, the call to activism,* and *belonging and the challenge of difference,* with which we begin.

"I'm Torn Right in the Middle": Belonging and the Challenge of Difference

I'm Nadia. I'm 14 years old, and I am a freshman at Linden Oaks High School. I speak Arabic, English, and I've been in Spanish since first grade. One of my best friends is Jewish, and a lot of my friends are Protestant and Catholic, and I have many Black, White, everything [background of friends] . . . it's good.

I think the thing I like the most about myself is, I guess, how I can be funny and make people feel better. All my friends, they say I can cheer people up. I would much rather be laughing than thinking about bad stuff. I think that's a good thing, being optimistic.

I'm Arabic, and my parents are both Syrian. When I come here, you know I feel like I belong and . . . I mean I feel American, but I also go back to my race, you know? But when I go to Syria, for some strange reason, I feel like I belong even more. I'm, you could say, the only Syrian at my school right now, but there's lots of other people from the Middle East. But it's never been a problem, and I don't know, at first, after September 11th it was a little shaky, and I didn't want to tell people that I was Arabic because you got the weird looks, or when I went to camp someone asked me, they said, "Are you . . . you kind of look Afghani?" That's when it's a bit of a burden, just when you get singled out. People look at you different when they find out you're Arabic, especially now. Before it wasn't [that way] at all. But now, especially when we're in restaurants or something as a family, my parents are talking Arabic, the waitresses will come and [ask], "Where are you from?" My parents will tell them, and they all give us weird looks like it's scary.

But I love going back to Syria. It's one of the greatest places in the world, and I love to be there, and I love my religion. I love it. I mean it's just there's times when it's a little hard, but it's no big deal. Before, I never thought about it very much. Going to Syria makes it all much better. It's so fun because you don't have to hide anything about your religion there, and you can be completely religious. It's great because everyone's the same.

Being Muslim and being American is hard because, here, I guess you know how the traditional Muslims, they wear the *hajab* over their head? There's a lot of stuff that I guess we're not too religious about, and it's really hard to be that religious here when you have friends. I mean, I don't have a boyfriend. Lots of my friends are dating, and they all go and that's what's a little hard about it. You feel kind of different and singled out. Sometimes if I wanna go out with friends and stay 'til eleven [my parents] won't let me. All my friends stay out 'til twelve, and I come home at ten. My parents are a lot stricter than all my other friends' [parents] and I don't date and I don't talk to boys on the phone. I'm not allowed to do that. Like, it's a lot stricter, but sometimes I think it's for the better but other times . . . I mean, I get frustrated a lot with it because these are the times when everyone is dating and everyone is going out, and I'm not allowed to go out, like, every day of the weekend. But I pray and I fast during Ramadan, and we give to charity and everything like that. It's just lots of stuff is hard to keep up with when you're a teenager growing up in America, trying to be Muslim, and trying to be Arabic, and trying to be American. Sometimes it's a lot but . . . I love everything.

A lot of my friends or just people at my school, they're not that religious, and they don't really have much to fall back on. And I guess it's very humbling maybe, just to go back and be at home and know that, even if you don't belong at school or even if that didn't work out, you have your religion and you have your culture and you know that *that's* never gonna change. And that makes you who you are.

Going back to Syria, I feel very much at home. But there's also times in Syria when I feel like I don't know as much as everyone there knows and I guess especially now, this year, when I went back there's a little more hostility towards . . . I mean, not my family, but people that we would see on the street if they heard us talking English. Just because of everything that's going on in Palestine, there's a little more hostility towards Americans I guess. And that's when it becomes a little hard, because I'm torn right in the middle, you know? But going to Syria, being Muslim, in a Muslim group, I'm not the strongest, most religious Muslim, but I have the beliefs. When you're in Syria, sometimes it makes you feel bad because I look around I'm like, "Wow, I'm not religious enough and when I go home I'm going to be very good," but then, when you get home, you don't know what to do because it's a back-and-forth thing really.

[In school], the weird thing was they never really asked us our nationality or anything until [after 2001]. They would ask you in every class, and you had to raise your hand [saying] what you were and they went through every culture except they didn't have Middle Eastern. And so I never raised my hand, and they're, like, "What *are* you?" And I [would say], "Arabic," and then they would um . . . I mean the teachers, they never gave me, like, weird looks or anything like that. It's just sometimes kids are . . . especially after September 11th, everyone's shaky.

The thing that was really cool is my friends have stuck with me through and through. They know who I am and they know my family and they've known I'm Arabic and they haven't changed at all. My friends have stayed the same. My teachers don't care at all. It's just every now and then you'll get a weird look or you'll get a weird feeling . . . kind of feel singled out sometimes, but it's nothing too big at all.

We were on a field trip one time. We were coming back on the bus, and there's another boy who goes to my mosque, and he's made fun of a lot. I don't really know why. And a boy that's normally my friend, he made fun of the other boy that's Muslim and he told him (this is after September 11th), he told him something like, "Well at least, I don't believe in blowing planes into buildings," and I felt bad because Khallid, the boy that goes to my mosque, he didn't really say anything, and I was infuriated, so I yelled at my friend. Which was really an uncomfortable feeling because I hated to yell at my friend, but I was so sad and hurt that he would say something like that. And I just told him, "How could you say something when you don't know?" Now he kind of held a grudge about it, and we're kind of friends, but it was just really an uncomfortable feeling to be in that situation because Khallid didn't say anything, and I think he was really just too scared to get into it.

Most of the time I just tell myself, especially with that boy, he doesn't know any better. I feel bad because he's uneducated . . . it's kind of like looking at a German and saying, "Oh, they're a Nazi." It's just stereotypes, and I think that's horrible and I just try to tell myself, "Don't get mad, don't let it get to you. Just tell him that that's not right and try to educate him that that's completely wrong."

I think now, after the events of September 11th, it's become more of an issue. And the weird thing was when we would learn about racism and just stuff like that, I never really knew what it felt like, and I could never really stand in the people's shoes, but now I kind of feel for the people that had racists against them. People that I know have been discriminated against, but I haven't myself as much. I think now I just have a bigger . . . I'm trying to think of the word, like I feel for them, I guess, a little more. I kind of know how they feel, and I'm more understanding because I've been through it, I guess.

I know adults are a lot more smart about the whole thing, and they know that not all Arab people are terrorists, and I just wouldn't want [teachers] to associate everything that I say or do with my ethnicity or with my religion, and I'm not a representative of it. I know I'm a representative of it *to an extent,* but what I do does not portray what every other Arabic Muslim would do. We're all different, and no one is the same.

My friend Chelsea, she's Jewish, Russian. All our lives we never even *thought* about me being Muslim and her being Jewish and how anywhere else that would have been such a big deal, and we never thought about it, and we've been best friends since, like, second grade, and she's such a great person. Now, after September 11th, when we hear about all this stuff and when we hear about the fights going on in Israel and Palestine, it's really hard. But her mom is so open-minded. I love our friendship because it's against what everyone would say in the Middle East. It proves that it doesn't matter where you're from or what religion you are, you can still be getting along well.

The Call to Activism

Just a couple of weeks ago I was confronted by one of the leaders of the mosque to see if I could teach the little kids, the ones that don't know . . . like the ones from Bosnia and the ones that don't know Arabic hardly at all, if I could teach them Arabic. I haven't heard from the lady again, but that sounds like fun. My sister did that before she went off to college, and she said it was really fun. I like kids.

My dad came to me, and one of his friends had asked him [to speak to me]. They were having a rally for peace in the Middle East. It was just a lot of people from our mosque trying to put something together, and they wanted a youth speaker, and I jumped at the chance 'cause I like speaking and I like writing. So I wrote a speech up in, like, the end of May, and the rally was in the beginning of June, and so I went and I gave a speech, and it was really great. I got interviewed for the newspaper, and a different lady came from this world newspaper. She interviewed me, and so we got a copy of those. It was really fun. I like to get really involved.

Most of the time I hate hearing about what's going on in Palestine [and] Israel you know, 'cause it's heart wrenching. We can't do much over here to help, and I feel like the littlest thing [can help]. Just do whatever you can to help, so I jumped at the chance to do that.

I love being in front of people. Like I love doing speeches, and just being in front of a crowd is fun for me. When they asked me if I would do that speech, I wanted to do it so bad, but then I was also, like, "This could be kind of weird, if I'm in the newspaper and someone sees it." And I was really hesitant sometimes, but just to give people a good feeling of what it is to be Arabic and what it is to be Muslim. And just to show them that we're not all terrorists and we're not all radicals.

The Centrality of Family

My parents are very family-oriented, and they always want us to have a family dinner hour. Like, especially on Sundays, we all come together, and we just do something together just like how they grew up. Everything's family-oriented. We celebrate [holidays], especially since there's not very much of our family here. Everyone's in Syria. We get as much as we can, especially during our holiday. My parents try to make it a very big deal, since me and my sister aren't that religious. They try and make it a very big deal, so we can get close to our religion, at least for that part of time. A while ago we had to drive to Florida, and it was a 17-hour drive, very long drive. I learned so much in that 17 hours in the car with my parents, them talking about their backgrounds with their families and everything. I guess they taught [my culture] to me in a way that I think I won't ever forget it. Instead of a teacher teaching it to you. They love their culture, and they love going back to Syria, as do I. And so, pretty much everything I know came from them, and all my religious beliefs came from them.

My sister, I followed in her footsteps a lot. Pretty much, we're almost the exact same, but there's so many things about her that I love. . . . I'm pretty good at looking at the bright side of things, especially with my sister. So if I'm having a horrible day, she can just cheer me up right away and the same with [me]. I can cheer her up in a second. [My parents] want to hear about friends. It's good to tell them, but once again you can't tell your parents everything. . . . I tell lots of stuff to my parents, and I tell lots of stuff to my sister. It's good to have that, I guess.

I have learned lots of things [from my parents], most of them when I was younger, but one of the main ones was be proud of who you are and be confident. Because when I was younger . . . I mean now I'm starting to not have as much insecurities, but I've always had lots of insecurities, and they were always there just to make me feel a lot better about myself and bring the self-esteem up and just make you feel very good. You know, they always say, "Don't be afraid of who you are—be confident. No one's better than you, but you're not better than anyone else."

I'm the youngest and I've always had my spot. I guess we're all like a puzzle. Without one of us, it's not the same. Like especially now with my sister gone, it's a little harder, so we're all trying to make up for it, and so I'm trying to mature a little more because I know that my mom, especially my mom, she's having the hardest time with it. They're not used to that 'cause, where they grew up, you go to college [and] you come home at the end of the day and you stay at your house. So they're not used to this at all, and so it's hard on them. I guess, like I said, without every piece of the puzzle, it doesn't go together. So we're all trying to work together a bit more, and I'm sympathizing with my parents more, and I'm not fighting with them as often. I know that I'm needed in the family just as everyone else is. It really feels good to have that spot, and you know it's never gonna go away. . . . We all make a difference.

When we're all together, we talk about pretty much anything, especially now we mostly talk about, like, my sister's college and how everything's changing. A lot of the times we talk about what's going on in the Middle East, although it hurts. I don't like to talk about that stuff very much because I feel so helpless, and I can't do anything, and my parents get so frustrated, and they watch like the Arabic news 'cause we have Arabic channels. Arabic news show a lot more. They show like a dead person, and they show like what happened when someone got shot. It's so, so heart wrenching, and you feel so helpless, and it's horrible. So sometimes I get very frustrated, and I don't want to talk about it, but it's always gonna be there, I guess, and so you have to face it. And we talk about school and we talk about doctor stuff a lot. My parents always have funny stories about patients, and so it's fun.

I think that lots of happiness doesn't just come from grades, but [from being] with friends and with family.

Commentary

In Nadia's voice, we hear some of the complexities involved in finding a way to manage family, school, religion, and other activities. Nadia wore a necklace with "God is good" written on it; at the same time, she played soccer and spoke publicly against racism and bigotry. This is a complex balancing act for a young person of Nadia's age, but she was nevertheless managing admirably.

It was clear throughout the interview with Nadia and her family that she was deeply attached to her religion and culture. She was simultaneously living with the challenges of fitting in and belonging in two very distinct cultural worlds. As a result, she felt, at times, both comfortable and uncomfortable in one or the other. Generally, Nadia was comfortable in her school and in her city. At other times, she felt the sting of discrimination, something that, prior to September 11, 2001, she said that she had not really experienced. When she and her family traveled to Syria, Nadia sometimes was more at home there than in the United States, while at other times, she felt like an outsider. Her musings about fitting in were poignant, and they reflect the experiences of numerous young people of diverse backgrounds in our society.

School could be a place where these differences are negotiated, but this has not been the case for Nadia. She mentioned that, before September 11th, no one had even mentioned Syria or Muslims. Afterward, being Muslim became a negative thing. When she said "teachers don't care" that she's Muslim, she said it in a positive way, meaning that they didn't discriminate on the basis of her background. But neither did they make it part of the curriculum, something that might have helped Nadia feel more included while also educating other students about her community.

There are several ways in which Nadia was negotiating these dilemmas of diversity. For one, as we saw, diversity was not an empty concept to Nadia. Her best friend was Jewish, and she also had an African American friend who was teaching her to cook soul food. In addition, even at this young age, Nadia was becoming outspoken about justice and fair play. This was evident in her participation in Heart Connection at school. She had also agreed to teach Arabic to young Muslim children. Her willingness, even eagerness, to speak publicly at a rally condemning bigotry against Muslims was another indication of her commitment to social justice.

But it was through her strong family connections where Nadia and her sister were able to negotiate their identities most powerfully. The Bara family was a close-knit and loving family that insisted on maintaining certain cultural and religious values as a foundation for their daughters' futures. Nadia didn't like all her parents' rules, but it was obvious that, even though she would rather have stayed out later with her friends, or to have the opportunity to talk to boys on the phone, she was grateful for her parents' values. The metaphor of a puzzle, and of each piece having a particular and crucial place in the puzzle, is a fitting one. She wanted to "fit in" but not in a cookie-cutter way. Nadia is a unique piece of our American puzzle, and it is young people like her who can make it work.

Reflect on This Case Study

1. What do you think Nadia meant when she said that she was "torn right in the middle"? As a teacher, what could you do about this?
2. Since September 11, 2001, have you noticed any changes in your students' perceptions or actions concerning Muslim students? One way to address these issues in the curriculum is to read the book *Muslim Voices in School: Narratives of Identity and Pluralism* (edited by Ozlem Sensoy and Christopher Darius Stonebanks). Use some of these narratives in classroom curriculum or faculty meeting discussions.
3. If you were one of Nadia's teachers and had seen the newspaper article in which she was featured, would you have said or done anything about it? Why or why not? If so, what would you have done?

Savoun Nouch

When people look at me as an Asian I say, "No I'm not Asian, I'm Cambodian." There are other Asian kids, but I am the only Khmer kid.

Savoun Nouch[1] said that he had "traveled quite a distance" to start his senior year at Watershed High School in Providence, Rhode Island. His mother arrived in New England as a refugee from Cambodia, and Savoun was born in New England, but he and his mother migrated to California when he was a small child. He said, "I think of California as my actual home." His mom chose Stockton, California, because of its sizable Cambodian community (over 10,000 in a city of 285,000 in 1990 when they moved there). A friend welcomed them into her home when they arrived there.

In Stockton, Savoun attended a large city high school with 2,500 students. The student population was diverse, and according to Savoun, almost 25 percent of the student body was Asian, primarily Cambodian. The school also included a small percentage of Native American and Filipino students and more sizable percentages of White, African American, and Latino students. About 8 percent of the students were English language learners. Just over half the students participated in meal-assistance programs.

The school community struggled with racial tensions that played out in harmful ways. Savoun described how school gangs dominated his early high school experiences: "My school was very segregated, basically Asians. We Cambodians, we were the Asians. We got together and we were feuding with other nationalities. Almost every single day we would get into arguments and it would escalate into a fight with Blacks and Latinos. Every day. Mostly fistfights, but a few times there were some weapons. Some people outside of school got wounded or lost their lives."

The Cambodian population in U.S. schools today is a diverse group in terms of religious practices, language, education, and more. Some are first-generation immigrants, recently arrived from Cambodia or Thailand, where many refugee camps were located. Others are second- and third-generation Americans, with the perspectives and language common to mainstream American teens. Some Cambodian families hold Buddhist beliefs close to their daily lives, others are secular, and still others practice Christianity or other religions.[2] In spite of their varied experiences, the Khmer community shares a common tormented history and a determined resiliency.

More than thirty years have passed since the genocide carried out by Pol Pot's regime of the Khmer Rouge. The four years from 1975 through 1979 saw the death of 1.7 million people by execution, starvation, disease, and overwork in labor camps. The Khmer Rouge's "Democratic Kampuchea," a horrific campaign of social, ethnic, and racial cleansing, wiped out a large percentage of Cambodia's population (estimates range from 20 percent to 48 percent). Pol Pot tried to exterminate the Cham, Vietnamese, Thai, and Lao minorities in Cambodia.[3] For many Cambodians in America, the tragedies of that holocaust and the efforts to sustain cultural memory persistently influence daily life.[4]

The political struggles that created the Cambodian diaspora and the resulting widespread post-traumatic stress among Cambodians are notable. Political analysts from the 1970s through today assert that President Richard M. Nixon's bombing campaign of Cambodia, which was implemented without congressional approval, set the stage for civil war–torn Cambodia to be relinquished to Pol Pot's regime.[5] Estimates are that between 100,000 and 600,000 civilians lost their lives, and 2 million were rendered homeless by the U.S. bombings, ostensibly done to push the communist North Vietnamese away from the Cambodian border. Instead, the Vietnamese moved deeper inside Cambodia, and the U.S carpet bombings followed, inflicting greater devastation on the peasant civilians. To escape the violent chaos of internal civil war and the bombings, hundreds of thousands of Cambodian people fled their country to seek refuge in neighboring countries. These horrendous experiences led to more than 235,000 Cambodian refugees resettling overseas between 1975 and 1992; 180,000 resettled in the United States.[6]

Escaping violence was a theme that shaped Savoun's life in many ways. His parents' escape from the Khmer Rouge in Cambodia was echoed by his deliberate break away from racially motivated gang violence in California. He dropped out of his large high school and twice made efforts to re-enter school through different alternative programs. But the gang activity persisted, as he explained:

> [I]t was a very rocky road, and I decided that this was not the way life should be for me. I realized if I stayed, there was nothing there for me. I finally decided to drop everything and leave.

With the company and moral support of a good friend, Savoun got on a bus headed for the East Coast and got off by mistake in Providence, Rhode Island. Because he had a cousin in Providence who welcomed him "with open arms," he stayed with her and enrolled in a new high school, with a fresh start.

Because of the history of violence that had affected Savoun and his family, the major theme that reappeared many times in his interview was a *determination to escape violence*. Just as powerful were the themes of *family pride and academic achievement*, as well as *cherishing culture and language*.

Cherishing Culture and Language

It's great to be Cambodian; I'm proud of it. I love this culture, love everything about it. You have your culture to "represent"—to cherish. I am different from somebody in Cambodia; I have the opportunity to learn English and to have more hope and to have a better life, but I have not been to Cambodia. Identity and culture [are] important to me. I am proud of my culture because of where I was born from. Being Khmer has been a big part of my upbringing. I have learned from my parents my culture, how I was brought up, everything. They have been through a whole lot of devastating moments back in Cambodia. So what we have now, we should cherish it. The people in Cambodia don't have what we have now. [My parents] really don't talk about it because it brings bad memories for them. So I ask them myself, so they answer my questions, but I have to ask.

My mother carried the Cambodian culture a lot with her when she came to the United States. They worked in the past, grew crops back in Cambodia, near Phnom Penh. But there's not a lot of Khmer farmers around here. She wanted to stay in the Cambodian environment; my neighborhood in California was all Cambodian people.

Every single day she could be there and talk with her friends, just chat with Cambodian people. They are very isolated from the world. They don't really go out that much unless they go to their friends. Mostly all their friends are Cambodian. They do not interact with other cultures very much.

We are different from other American families. We don't celebrate holidays as much as other cultures. That's a big difference. We do celebrate some, like Thanksgiving and Christmas, now—and birthdays. Cambodian New Year is the only Khmer holiday. For me, for my birthday, I would just get a present—no cake; no friends come over; I did not invite people over. My parents were not into inviting people over. It was like, "We keep it really simple. Here's your gift and don't ask for more." We have our family—we have how our family acts—how we are brought up different . . . So, we act different, we cook different, things like that. For Thanksgiving, my parents do cook American food. So on a Thanksgiving dinner table, it is a mixture of Cambodian food and American food: Turkey, with stuffing, and we have mashed potatoes, Cambodian soup . . . all those things together.

When I was in California, my parents take me to temple [to] get some blessings, and we participate in Cambodian activities. My parents would take me there, see the monks to get my blessings. I would ask them why. They would tell me to "vanish all the bad things." I went to temple once a year. My parents would go much more often to the temple. I did not like to go for the prayers that much when I was younger, but when it was Cambodian New Year, I was always there! In the future, definitely, I would like to go to the temple more on my own, to be more involved in my parents, to get a good feel for why they go to the temple. . . .

The first person I learned from was my parents . . . to speak Cambodian. I don't know that much, but I know enough to speak it. Mom speaks Khmer at home. When I got to school, [learning English] was a process between elementary school and toward junior high. I just had to figure out. There were teachers' assistants who translated English for kids who did not know English. At times, we had reading sessions where she would actually read in Cambodian, teach the lessons so we could learn in Cambodian *and* English. There was a balance of Cambodian and English when I was growing up. I would never want to leave my culture or my language; I always want to learn more.

I got the hang of English ever since I hit junior high. I was speaking, like, intermediate English. I was actually speaking a balance of Cambodian and English, but at junior high there was no more reading sessions, no more culture lessons. None of it. Basically, I was speaking all English throughout the junior high and the high school. There was no more of my culture's language in the school. The only time I would speak my language was to my family members and with some friends.

As I learn more and more English, I am forgetting my culture's language right now. To keep us from forgetting our culture's language, schools could still have reading sessions in our culture's language. I think that would help the Asian students. Reading sessions would help . . . because a lot of the students right now, they are forgetting their culture's language and they really do not know how to speak as much as they used to. We would love to learn more. We wish we would. I just try to speak as much Cambodian at home as possible. When I am at home and speak to the other people and older people, I only speak Cambodian.

When I lived with my parents, I did a lot of translation. It was hard for me because I don't speak Cambodian that well, and when you translate back and forth, there are words in English that do not translate into Cambodian. I talked to my parents pretty well. They can understand me. It's been great to be a member of my family.

Sometime they don't understand me, but I still love them. Growing up, it was a problem. It was hard for them to know what I've been through. They think it is very easy for me because I was born in America, I had the opportunity to go to school. [But] I had to deal with all these peer pressures. Gang stuff. Stuff they don't know anything about. They think it's a perfect world out there. They seen hard stuff back in Cambodia.

Determination to Escape Violence

I would describe my neighborhood I live in now [in Rhode Island] as a pretty good community . . . no violence, a lot of nice people, a lot of Hispanic. But at my old school [in California] what I remember most was—there was a lot of violence. A lot of racial issues between we Asians and other cultures such as African American and Hispanics. You can say that it was gang related. It's more about who is the boss of the school, who won the school. I was part of a gang. It's all about what you are going to say and who is going to kick whose ass. I had my peers with me. I had my friends, so I felt very comfortable. I would say 90 percent of my friends in California dropped out of school because of gangs and violence. A few got shot, a few ended up in the hospital, a few got locked up. Only a few are still thinking about life.

Everything got rough for me because I was in a gang. I did not really have the support that I needed. I was the type of kid . . . I always wanted to play sports, but, money-wise, the football uniform, and transportation from practice . . . it was very hard, it would be too hard, and my sisters, I had to look after them after school. I didn't have the support from my family, so everything was a big whole downfall for me because, during my junior year, my average was like less than a 2.0 GPA. I stopped going to school. One thing led to another and I dropped out of my junior year at Avery High School.

I wouldn't say [the school administrators and teachers] didn't try to help me. It wasn't really that. They didn't really have any interventions to help students with the whole bureaucracy to get kids through. All you had to do was go to the guidance counselor and they would transfer you. I went to two different high schools. The first one was a model alternative school. The same thing happened. My friends were there, and there wasn't a lot of support. I was unwilling to focus on my education life. I chose friends over education, and one thing led to another and I dropped out there.

They are my friends, but they have different goals in life. I feel bad for them. I moved out here to change. I would hope the same thing for them. I would hope they could move out here with me. I can't control another person's life. When you are in the gang, [you don't realize there are] more things than being in a gang. I think about the future. Like what does life bring to you. There are things like life and education. You got to get your education, think more about life . . . than gang bangin' 'cause that's not gonna get you nowhere in life.

To get to Watershed High School now, in Providence, my cousin talked to the co-founder of the school and asked for me to get an interview. I went there and they interviewed me and ever since then, I fell in love with it. I fell in love with it because [of] the diversity, how personal the teachers get with you. It is no typical school. At the interview there are not teachers who interview you; it was students. That breaks that barrier, like kids-to-kids. I talked to a few kids. There was no Asians at all, only one girl. Everyone else was different nationalities and I was so surprised and the way they welcomed me, I was like, "This school must be very great and there is no one feuding or fighting or nothing." I was so surprised there was no one feuding or anything. I was the only Asian kid, and the diversity was really great because even though I was the only Asian (and lots of—majority was Spanish and African American), [there were] no racial problems at all. Nobody feuding. I just loved it!

It has changed my whole perspective about school. Going to school here, because the teachers are so involved with you either at school or at home—always there for you, ready to talk to you and everything—about your education. They call me up at home to talk to me.

Family Pride and Academic Achievement

You got to have an education. It is important. In order to pursue your dream, what you want in life, get your education first. For my family, my parents, it is important for other people to see their reputation, how they raised their child to be, to go to school, and it is the opportunity America gives to you, so get that opportunity and make it useful. They make a great deal about their reputation, their reputation for the son they're raising. They don't want to have a son who is a bad kid, with other people talking about them. They want you to be good. If you do bad things, the community will hear about you. They will often spread rumors, the gossip in the Khmer community.

My parents support me being here in Providence 100 percent, and my cousin supports me being here with her 100 percent. My cousin welcomed me with open arms. I believe in education 100 percent. My parents want to hear good things, like if I'm getting my work done, how I'm getting my work done, all the details. My adviser contacts them and tells them the things they need to know and what I need to know. I never had my parents back in California participate in what the teachers had to offer, so this is a very new experience.

It is important to me to be Cambodian in my school. Definitely I stand out from the crowd because I am the only Cambodian person at my school. One of the teachers, she tried to learn more about my culture, so then I did a book report and everything. I wanted to do it on Cambodian and Khmer, on my culture. She tells me she is very fascinated by my culture. She knows something about the Khmer Rouge genocide, a little something about it.

The way the school works, they wouldn't just pass out work and have it just turned in. It has to be completed and 100 percent revised. So every time she handed out an assignment, we would continually revise it until it reached its perfection. We went through that whole process for the whole entire junior year and senior year. The way she was, the way she treated us, the way she made that connection—it made me work. She would contact me, out of school, to see what I was doing. We would have conversations, like friend to friend. That made us bonded very well and then I opened up.

To improve schools, if they could change the system, the way they teach, that would be [a] great idea, but even if they can't change the system, have a good relationship with the students and be in contact with them, always be in contact with them. Call them up. And, of course, I would love to learn more about my culture. If the teachers would make, like, an elective about my culture, that would be it. Learn more about the history, the war, the whole South East Asian history. The politics, who and what—a lot of information that is hard to get if you don't learn it in school. My mother told me about her escape from Cambodia. It was hard living in Cambodia. She lived in a refugee camp for a while. That's about it. But she did not tell me much about the war.

My adviser helped me plan my future—give me prep for college, looking for scholarships, looking for college, everything—the whole nine yards. What would help me be successful into the future is: be more involved with me—I tend to procrastinate a lot.

I need someone there telling me I need to get stuff done. My advisers are very hard on me. They call me up at home. But that makes me successful.

[In the future,] I definitely want to go back to California to be closer to my mom. The person I most admire is my mother because of what she's been through in the past and how she's got me here. I want to go to college first for four years. So I can at least support my mom when I go back. I don't want to leave with nothing and go back with nothing.

Commentary

Maintaining and reshaping cultural traditions is a work in progress for Savoun. Throughout this text, we caution about the pitfall of essentializing culture and the importance of understanding culture as an evolving process rather than as a static product. A cultural-historical approach, as defined by Kris Gutierrez and Barbara Rogoff, illustrates the flexibility of cultural identity in Savoun's life.[7] Savoun's identity has evolved through a process of amalgamation of his parents' perspective as Cambodian farmers and refugees from civil and international warfare, transplanted to Stockton, California, and living in a primarily Khmer-speaking neighborhood; his multiple perspectives in urban youth cultures, with the expressiveness of hip hop; his experiences in and out of gang affiliations; and then eventually his reinvogorated affiliation with academic achievement in his new school. For Savoun, his culture was something to be "cherished," and yet he seemed to be unfamiliar with much of its history, traditions, religious and practices. While certain Cambodian practices and beliefs may be lost to Savoun, other new understandings are gained.

A study by Yoonsun Choi, Michael He, and Tracy W. Harachi on intergenerational cultural dissonance (ICD)—a clash between parents and children over cultural values—found ICD to be a frequent issue for youth in Vietnamese and Cambodian immigrant families.[8] However, Nancy Smith-Hefner's research reveals the efforts of Khmer Americans to maintain and reinvent culture in the aftermath of the violence of the Pol Pot holocaust. In her ethnographic study of Cambodians residing in metropolitan Boston, Smith-Hefner portrays the attempts to preserve Khmer Buddhism by the elders in the community. Her study provides a context for understanding how cultural heritage may influence the performance of Khmer children in U.S. schools.[9] Other researchers found that the philosophy of Buddhism provided strong support to Cambodian families in ongoing recovery from the unspeakable expereinces and losses they had endured in Cambodia.[10] Roberta Wallitt suggests that, in addition to gaining insights from such studies, more contemporary research is needed. As the Cambodian population in the United States ages, cultural values and influences will fluctuate.[11]

Issues of cultural identity dominated Savoun's school experiences. He moved from a school where about 25 percent of the student body was Cambodian to being the only "Khmer kid" at Watershed High School. As much as Savoun appreciated his new school, with its personalized approach and supportive infrastructure, he was conscious of his isolation as the only Cambodian student. The isolation was underscored by his own—and his teachers'—lack of knowledge about his cultural history. His comments point out how the refugee experience is often invisible or misrepresented in school curriculum. Similarly, in Roberta Wallitt's study, she found that "one of the greatest sources of alienation was the absence of their history and culture in the curriculum."[12]

Despite the absence of other Cambodians and of a culturally specific curriculum in his current high school, Savoun was deeply affirmed and felt a strong sense of solidarity with his peers and teachers at Watershed. There, he was pleasantly surprised to learn that racial diversity does not necessarily lead to violence. The importance of cultivating a safe learning environment that develops racial inclusion is articulated in Savoun's affectionate description of his new school life: "No racial problems at all. Nobody feuding. I just loved it!"

In terms of academic achievement, Savoun compared his new school to his old school and proudly noted that his teachers expected nothing less than perfection in his final drafts of schoolwork. Teacher communication was another hallmark of his experience at Watershed. On multiple occasions, he mentioned that his teachers "call me up at home." Likewise, another recommendation from Wallitt's study concerned the essential role that teachers, advisers, and mentors can play when they develop cultural competency and reach out to support students through home visits, phone calls, navigation of college applications, and attending cultural events.[13] The effort to reach out to Savoun outside school hours left an enduring legacy of caring support and high expectations for him.

When we last checked in with Savoun, he had just graduated from Watershed High School. He was ecstatic about making his family proud through his accomplishments and was looking forward to starting community college in the fall "and then transferring credits to a bigger college." With the support of his adviser, he transformed his interest in car repair and auto mechanics into a goal of achieving a degree in business, with the hope of eventually opening his own car dealership. The outcome of this vision is still a few years away, but his willfulness to make sound educational choices, combined with his sincerity to "represent his culture" by providing for his mother and a future family of his own, appears to have pointed him toward success.

Reflect on This Case Study

1. Savoun said, "To keep us from forgetting our culture's language, schools could still have reading sessions in our culture's language." That may not have been possible because Savoun was the only Cambodian student in his school, but what are some strategies that could have been implemented in the school to affirm and cultivate his language?

2. Receiving phone calls from teachers left a lasting impression on Savoun. What are the implications of this information for your classroom practice? How can you integrate such personal communication with students before and/or after the school day?

3. Almost every school has students who may feel that they are "the only one" of a cultural, religious, ethnic, language, sexual orientation, class, or ability group. How can you and your colleagues affirm the students' identities in meaningful ways that make them feel more "visible" and understood while also challenging them academically?

4. Gang activity affects the school lives of countless students and families in U.S. schools. What can we learn from Savoun's case study about the teacher's role in helping students resist gang activity?

Christina Kamau

If you could just have a chance to go to some countries that are suffering and see the difference . . . you will be so shocked.

As a 16-year-old junior in high school, Christina Kamau[1] expressed viewpoints common to many immigrant teens in the United States. At the same time, her individual perspectives, based on personal life experiences, are evident. Christina's family is from Kenya, where she attended school until fifth grade. They moved to Botswana, where she attended middle school in her early teens. At the beginning of her freshman year of high school, her family immigrated to the United States—to Shephardstown, a midsize college town surrounding a large state university in the heart of the Midwest.

Christina's family is much like many of the over 1 million African immigrants currently living in the United States. The U.S. Census Bureau reports over 50 percent of this population arrived between 1990 and 2000, making African immigrants significantly more visible in U.S. schools in recent years.[2] In the 1990s, the highest numbers came from Nigeria, Ethiopia, and Ghana.

The influence of African immigrants in the United States is evident in the cultural, linguistic, political, business, and religious life of big cities and small towns throughout the country. Larger urban areas such as New York, Washington, DC, Houston, Atlanta, and Chicago are home to the largest numbers of recent African immigrants, but small towns and suburbs, especially in the Midwest, are more and more often the destination for families such as Christina's.

Because culture, language, religion, and political frameworks are so diverse within the continent of Africa, the sociopolitical contexts of African immigrants vary greatly. Media coverage of African immigrants often focuses on refugees. The difficulties faced by immigrant refugees cannot be underestimated, but within the broad scope of African immigrant demographics, refugees account for only 10 percent of the immigrant population admitted to the United States in the 1990s. Of these, more than 40,000 were Somalis, and approximately 21,000 came from Ethiopia, while 18,500 arrived from the Sudan.[3] The children of refugee families bring values such as a vibrant connection to family and religious communities, steadfast determination to maintain multiple languages, and strong traditions. In addition, they often have vivid memories of human suffering in their homelands, which have continuing strife due to civil wars, human rights abuses, political unrest, corrupt governments, natural disasters, and the ravages of economic policies gone awry under globalization.

The detrimental effects of these struggles should not be diminished, but there is a propensity in the West, especially in the United States, to view Africa condescendingly, and as if it were a monolith. The widespread misinformation about Africa affects mainstream U.S. perspectives on immigrants from the African continent. For instance, most people in the United States do not know that the majority of immigrants from Africa are highly skilled professionals who intend to establish permanent homes in the United States.[4] Christina's father, for example, is a university professor, and her mother is a medical student. While the influx of highly educated immigrants continues, their employment in the United States does

not always match their talents. Their opportunities are limited for a variety of reasons, including immigration documentation and the fact that university degrees
from overseas are often not recognized here. Many with prestigious credentials
work as cab drivers, restaurant servers, or parking lot attendants, striving for the
American dream through any opportunity that may be available. Frequently, it
is more than economics that motivates this community. In his comprehensive
assessment of contemporary African immigrants, Joseph Takougang points out,
"The new African immigrant is no longer just interested in making money; they
are also interested in building stronger communities and organizing themselves
in order to become a more powerful political and economic force in their respective communities."[5]

Racism also influences wages and job opportunities. Despite their hard work
and determined outlook, Takougang reveals that, not surprisingly, many African
immigrants encounter racism. Other research corroborates this, pointing out that
many African immigrants do not have a history of experience with race relations in
the United States and are naive about the confrontations with institutional racism
and negative stereotypes.[6] The 1999 killing of Amadou Diallo, an African immigrant
from Guinea, by New York City police officers is a tragic illustration of racist violence and has become a metaphor for the way African immigrants are perceived and
treated by some law enforcement authorities.[7]

Christina entered U.S. schools in ninth grade within this challenging yet hopeful and complex social, political, economic, and cultural matrix. Relocating several
times into vastly diverse cultures and language communities, she cultivated her
perspectives on friendship, learning, and the meaning of academic achievement.
The viewpoints she expressed during her interview highlight three themes: *adapting
to new cultures and school structures, preconceptions and stereotypes,* and *educational
achievement for social action.*

Adapting to New Cultures and School Structures

After being in Kenya my whole life, Botswana was difficult. I started to go to a Christian,
American type of school. And the school was way different for me, honor roll and all
this stuff I didn't understand. There was no corporal punishment, you understand.
[I did not know] what detention was. In Kenya, you get beaten by the teacher and you go
home, even though you didn't do anything wrong. [Teachers] call your parents most of
the times.

But I got used to Botswana. Our teacher was never like one-to-one, and she would
teach a whole class and just gives you books to help yourself. Never checked to see who
was correct, just give you points for completion. I didn't understand that because in
Kenya [there is] step by step and explaining. You know what [you need] to know. When
I went to the American-type school in Botswana, I found it very different to be trying all
these different things. The funny thing was, in my math class, they let us use calculators,
which I never did in Kenya. You had to know your times tables and your subtraction and
addition and all your facts. You have to do that on your paper. You can't use a calculator
to solve those problems. So in sixth grade I was introduced to a calculator. I was, like,
"I don't know how to do this!" I found it strange and exciting, too. It made my life easier in

school terms because I can do homework much faster and go play and go do something else. So it was different for me for awhile.

Then, in seventh grade I moved to another school. It was, like, a private school and it had from elementary all the way to high school. That was different because I couldn't speak the same language as everybody else because each country in Africa has their own languages and their own native language. I spoke Swahili, and then in Botswana, you speak Botswanan. I couldn't speak Botswanan. I had to get used to learning how to interact with other students without them making fun of me trying to say things. I had to speak in English all the time. That made me practice my English a lot because I couldn't communicate with them in any other way except in my English.

To make friends and do all those other things were hard for me because all the other students were, you know, cliquish. Because they had their own languages and they knew how to talk to each other without having to speak English, which I had to do all the time. But school became easier for me because my teacher could talk to me all the time in English and try to teach me a little bit of Botswanan and interpret the other students. So that was pretty nice.

When I came here [to the United States] I was really shocked by the high school. We entered the parking lot, I kept asking Mom, "Are all these cars for the teachers or all for the students?" She was, like, "Yeah, all for the students." I couldn't believe how many students have such nice cars, so many cars, it was so crazy. Also the building was, like, wow, I always thought high school [was like] in TV and stuff in movies. I always wonder what it would be like to go to school in America.

School was crazy in the U.S. at first. First, projectors. I have never seen a projector before in my whole life. I got used to that, I guess, even the markers. Writing on the board in Africa, we used chalk, chalkboards in Africa. I miss that. I wish we had that here. Because markers smell strange, I don't know; it's hard for me to see up there with the projector. So I couldn't understand how you could look there at your answers, to check your answers to see if your answers are correct.

And at the beginning of the first semester, it was my world studies class, the teacher says we have to go to the media center, and I don't know where the media center is, and I didn't know what that was. So all of us go, open the door, and it's a bunch of kids and computers everywhere! I was, like, cool, 'cause I never seen so many computers before! It was really hard for me to get used to going to Microsoft and going, oh, check tool, and check spell, check all these stuff. First day at school, my teacher said, "You have to research on different regions;" it's like research on Hinduism because we're studying India. He said, "Okay, log on, get your password and get your stuff and get to the Internet and go to Google and start searching." I didn't know I *had* a log name. I could see other kids looking at me, wondering, "Why she is not knowing all these things?" We didn't have all these stuff. So I started looking for the Internet, so many programs—Microsoft Excel, PowerPoint, school printing, and all these stuff. All by myself, was trying to get to the Internet. So the other teacher kind of sees me sitting. "Okay, I can help you." By the way, he is Laotian, he is from Laos, so he told me that he had a hard time. He knows how I feel.

I noticed that on the next day, for my English class, all we did was type up papers, like every week. Every Friday, double-spaced pages of essay. So I was used to writing with my hand, all my rough drafts, I could write them. Handwriting, you have really good handwriting, good grammar in Africa. But the first paper, I didn't know how to type, so I asked. She at least took half of the points off because it wasn't typed. I tried to explain to her, I was still learning. But she was, like, "You need to get a move on because you have to catch up with these people." Now I'm pretty good at typing and stuff and I'm trying to encourage my sister to get that stuff done because it's a big deal when it comes to high school. If you don't know how to use computers you are in a big trouble because that's all we use all the time to research for classes. It is really big deal for us.

Preconceptions and Stereotypes

When I couldn't get that computer stuff, some girls were calling me an "African girl" because "an African girl doesn't know anything." That's not really nice of you to say that. Even the teacher went to her and said, "That's not really nice for you to say. It's not like you who have the privilege to go Internet everyday and get all these things. She's still getting accustomed to all these stuff."

I guess some other people really help me. Like the way my best friend was to the lunch lady. So I go to the line to get my food first day. I couldn't understand how this huge cafeteria, all of us could sit and talk, so noisy! Everybody's trying to get food and huge line. She told me, "You gotta move on, you know, you have to get your food." I go to line and have my ID card and going to my line and get my food. She tells me to swipe my card so that we can get my food and get out. And I swiped my card and it didn't go through. She was like, "Wait, your card is not yet activated." I have no idea how to do that; it was my first day! She was really mean, I could tell. Maybe she didn't have a good day. So some girls behind me, some African girls behind me, heard my accent, "Oh, are you from Africa?" I was, like, "Yes!" They say, "Okay, we will pay for you." I am like, "Really? That's so sweet of you." They paid for me, and got out. We sat down and they were, like, "Is this your first day? We could tell, because the same thing happened to us!" I was like, "Okay" [*giggle*]. So we have something common, that's only my best friends, they are from Ghana. We are good friends now.

I really have a big deal with people calling me *Black American*. I don't like being called that because I noticed that people in our school use that to get a sympathy from other people. "Oh yeah, my ancestors struggle for this and that" and you know what? That's gone. It's gone, so you can't use it now to defend yourself. Because you are creating another stereotype for you. In our school, there is very few Black people. And I'm sad for the fact that I'm not being able to interact with them that well 'cause they are not open to me. They always say, "Oh that's African culture." I think that I have more White friends than Black friends. I can still talk to them and I always say hi. I always say, "I'm not Black American, I'm African and I came from Kenya."

All the teachers are really nice to me. They all are interested about Africa. Africa is really cool. [They] always ask me, "Is it how we see on TV?" I tell them, "No, it's no way. [On TV] it's like a jungle place. We have CDs, we have cars and computers; it depends on what level class you come from." They all are interested, and for my English class that's all I did, my life comparing to American and African. Yeah, even in my speech class, that's all I did. My teacher was like, "Let's learn about Africa," all the time.

I joined track as an after-school activity. That's because my coach was, like, "Are you from Africa, from Kenya?" I was, like, "Yes." "Well, you have to join the track [team] for me." The funny thing is that I have never run before. [*laughter*] He found out that I couldn't run that well, but he taught me, and pushed me, and it was fun. I met a lot of people; it was a good experience for me.

Educational Achievement for Social Action

Freshmen year, it was not good for me, even my GPA reflected that, and my parents were disappointed. I was really disappointed myself because less than 3.0 GPA was a really big shock for me. All my teachers told me, "You have a lot of potentials, just try to get used to the school." And so, in my sophomore year, I tried really hard; I did all my homework and always ask questions. Even after school—I went to school earlier and stayed later than everyone and my GPA was able to go higher, to 3.8. That was really good thing for me. I'm hoping to do the same thing this year—try to even get 4.0 GPA.

I just want to get my degree and go help people somewhere. I want to be somewhere in Africa or somewhere in China. Somewhere where I know I am useful to help people. For me right now, going to school is a really big deal because I want to help people. That's the only way for me to get that education through school. For me, that is the reason for going to school. For me, it's getting a better education. I have seen in Africa that people give up. You know, here you can drop out of school and go to try your GED after a while. In Africa you don't get to do that. When you drop out of school, it's a failure; it's like an embarrassment to your family.

Also this year, Mr. Gervisay is recommending me to join the model UN, like a club. I'm really opinionated. Especially like in Mr. Gervisay's class, he encourages you to talk about politics, what's going in the world. Most people would be not interested, [they say] "Oh, the war, it's not in the U.S." How could you be so ignorant about something that happened to you? It's gonna affect you for the rest of your life, you know. If you could just go, to have a chance to go to some countries that are suffering and see the difference. You are so sheltered here that you can't step away; you will be so shocked.

I have the privilege of being here. For me, being here, my parents always say, "The land of opportunities, take them." You know, it's really hard, for many people dream to be here. And some of the best schools are here, like the state university. [My parents] want me to go to school because I can be a better person. I can help them raise [my] little sisters, you know, when they are older, look after myself, and I wouldn't get that chance if I didn't have that education to be able to get a job. Be better myself and be independent.

[For my future] I'm really battling between being a doctor or UN advocate, like maybe a lawyer. To see the wrongs of all the countries' policies and those stuff. I wish I could be, not a secretary general of the United Nations, but just trying to see a way of being able to tell other countries, you know, if you did something wrong, you have to face the consequences. Right now, in the world, any country, as long as you have the power, you don't face up to what you did wrong. Because my parents punish me, you know, when I get something wrong—always have the consequences, you always have to face it. I notice that other countries don't do that, and I always believe in the UN. Bunch of countries always together, you know, try to make the world a better place. But being a doctor for me would be fine, to do like doctor's organizations, Doctors Without Borders. Maybe in Africa, help a bunch of orphan kids and that would be a good thing. I don't know—it's a hard one, maybe a pediatrician. Because I like kids. But I don't know.

I guess being the fact that I am an international student, I have to push myself harder. I have to work harder and to prove that I do have the intelligence as everybody else and I should get the same opportunity as everybody else, especially with college. You can be anything. It doesn't matter what color you are and what shape, what country, what language you speak.

Just push yourself into being the best you can be, and try to strive the best you can be. Just remember where you came from. You know, remember your origin in Africa. You're not American; you're African first. Always keep that in mind.

Commentary

Christina demonstrated remarkable resilience in adapting to school structures in various countries and cultures. When she described each school experience, she eloquently noted a range of approaches to curriculum, instructional methods, and homework practices. She compared administrative policies regarding student behavior, parent involvement, dress code, and more. She analyzed her school achievement the first year in Shepardstown High School, considering all those factors, and made explicit adjustments in her approach to her studies, such as staying after school for help and practicing technology skills.

The importance of having peers in school who share some perspectives was evident throughout Christina's interview. From her description of the language differences in Botswana and the lunch line rescue by the Ghanaian students in the U.S. high school, it was clear that immigrant students are often isolated in facing the academic and social realms of school. Unlike many immigrant students, however, Christina already spoke English, which established a common ground in academics and social endeavors. Yet Christina's language of origin, nationality, African identity, and more influenced her integration into the school. She emphasized that there were very few Black students in her school, highlighting racial identity concerns. Some students feel desperately alone despite spending their day in a school building with hundreds, or even thousands, of other students and adults.

The issue of cultural isolation affects students' views of school life, and it has curricular and structural implications. The more teachers get to know students through the curriculum, the more insight they may gain into students' perspectives, thereby cultivating authentic connections in relationships and in curricular adaptations. Judith Blohm and Terri Lapinsky provide several examples of "linking classroom to community" in a book that includes interviews with more than two dozen teen immigrants.[8] As structural remedies, some schools create buddy systems, ambassador programs, and other safety nets to assist new students, especially immigrants, in navigating the mystifying structures of the school. Too often, the quick-fix approach is used. For example, Christina told us, "I had an ambassador at the first day at school to show me all the classes, and she did help me, but, like, the second day of the school, she left."

In addition to the challenge of establishing peer groups, adapting to new technologies and teaching methods, and navigating surprising new institutional structures, fighting bias was a major theme in Christina's school life. The perceptions of some teachers and peers about the capabilities of an "African girl" did not sway Christina's determination to achieve academically, but it did make her feel that she had to prove herself. Simultaneously, she spoke affectionately of most teachers' efforts to learn about her heritage and to weave her experiences in Africa into her schoolwork. When confronted with a so-called positive stereotype—that all Kenyans are talented runners—she laughed. She demonstrated a graceful capacity to recognize the damaging implications of stereotypes while overcoming the limits of prejudicial encounters. Such wisdom and stalwart determination is to be commended, but it most certainly added tremendous weight to the challenge of adapting to a new school and new culture.

By emphasizing markers of her identity as a Kenyan, and more broadly as an African, Christina distinguished her language and her continent of origin as powerful affinities, but she also differentiated herself from her African American counterparts. She stressed that she had a "big deal . . . with people calling me Black American," pointing to the differences in historical heritage between recent African immigrants and African Americans. The dynamic between African American communities and African immigrant communities is a complex and multilayered phenomenon.[9] A report from the New York Public Library Schomberg Center for Research in Black Culture observes that for many immigrants from Africa,

> [I]dentity as "black" is often perceived as a negation of culture and origin, which Africans regard as the most important elements of identity. They are keenly aware that they encounter racism and discrimination as black people; but they generally reject the imposition of an identity they feel does not completely reflect who they are.[10]

Despite confronting racism and the implications of being Black in America, Christina holds a classic view of the American dream. "You can be anything. It doesn't matter what color you are and what shape, what country, what language you speak," she asserts. For Christina, this may well be true because of the combination of her family's social class advantage, their expectations that education will make her a better person, and their model of academic achievement, among other factors. Her peer support helps navigate the confusing cultural conflicts, and the dedication of many teachers advances her academic achievement. From these sources, and clearly based on her own strength, Christina had resolved to get her degree and "go help people somewhere." Christina's accomplishments and determination raise the question about how schools can support rigorous academic engagement of students who are culturally, linguistically, and racially different: Specifically, how might schools influence *all* students to view successful education as a means to serve others and to help fight injustice?

Reflect on This Case Study

1. Christina described some examples of teachers' and students' demonstrating solidarity with and empathy for her. How might a school encourage these gestures by staff members and students, especially toward students who are culturally, racially, and linguistically different from the majority?
2. What do you think about Christina's differentiation between African Americans and Africans? What tensions are revealed in her statements? What is the role of the school in recognizing and taking action regarding these tensions?

3. The practical aspects of daily school life can be a struggle for any new student. What makes some of these challenges particularly difficult for international students? How could Christina's first experiences with the media center, cafeteria, locker combinations, and the like, be made more welcoming? If such welcoming strategies are not in place in your school, what might you and your colleagues do to call attention to the need for them and what suggestions for effective change might you make?

Adapting Curriculum for Multicultural Classrooms

by Patty Bode

A question that we hear time and time again is "What does a truly multicultural curriculum look like?" Teachers are swamped with data about achievement and models of so-called "best practices." It can be difficult to sort out trendy jargon from effective teaching.

When considering the implications of the previous chapters, it is clear that multicultural education is a multifaceted, complex process. Nowhere is this process more visible and palpable than in the curriculum teachers implement in their classrooms. Many teachers in pre-K–12 classrooms acknowledge the need to adapt the curriculum and their practices to meet the needs of their increasingly diverse student populations. They face many challenges, however, in developing a multicultural curriculum.

> "The curriculum is never simply a neutral assemblage of knowledge, somehow appearing in the texts and classrooms of a nation. It is always part of a selective tradition, someone's selection, some group's vision of legitimate knowledge."
>
> —**Michael Apple**
>
> "The Politics of Official Knowledge," Teachers College Record, 1993

In keeping with our commitment to making curriculum culturally relevant to specific learning communities, we do not provide specific lesson plans or "canned" curriculum in this book. Instead, in this chapter we present three cases of curriculum change that have been successful and engaging. There are myriad ways in which curriculum may be conceived and designed. We do not advocate any one, single model. The three approaches described in this chapter include concrete, hands-on examples to provide educators with both inspiration and ideas for developing a parallel unit on a similar or different theme or to spin off an activity and add their own creative questions in a range of content areas. The three cases include:

1. An Interdisciplinary Unit Focusing on Specific Cultures and Geographic Regions Across Middle School Content Areas: A study of Cambodia and the Cambodian American Experience.

2. Expanding Definitions of Family: A thematic approach in first grade and seventh grade.

3. Gay and Lesbian Literature: Expanding topics for inclusive high school content.

In addition to the three cases described here, two more examples can be found on the Companion Website at www.ablongman.com/nieto6e. One of these curriculum cases on the Web site focuses on teaching about current events in a unit called "Hurricane Katrina and the Opportunity for Change" and the other follows the efforts of a middle school math teacher in a case titled "Transforming Pedagogy by Detracking Math."

One approach to transforming curriculum through a more multicultural perspective is the strategy of teaching about a specific geographical region and the cultural experiences of its people. This approach can develop rich, robust questions and understandings about specific groups, their histories, and their traditions. However, if the topic of a certain cultural group is approached as merely "adding color" to the curriculum, teachers run the risk of stumbling into any one of a number of pitfalls that run counter to the critical multicultural approach we have advanced in the previous chapters. Such pitfalls include perpetuating stereotypes by painting a group of people with a broad brush; "exoticizing" the "other" through a shallow "tourist" approach; or, even more damaging, developing new pigeonholes by reinforcing a limited understanding of the experiences of a group of people. Out of concern for these pitfalls and fear of the unfamiliar, teachers may shy away from presenting a unit about specific cultural groups.

Mariah Aviles, Aaron A. Feliciano in Alicia Toro's visual arts class, Bronx Charter School for the Arts, The Bronx, NY. *Self-portraits*. Charcoal. 2006.

On the other hand, using a problem-posing approach and constructing curriculum with students on topics that both teachers and students want to explore creates an authentic learning experience. This is not to suggest that teachers enter blindly into creating curriculum on a random topic or subject area. Some preparation is always necessary. When teachers announce their own curiosity and model their own struggle with ignorance, students are empowered to ask previously hushed questions and uncover misconceptions. An example of such an approach is illustrated in the first curriculum case.

Curricular Adaptation 1: A Study of Cambodia and the Cambodian American Experience

When teachers use a problem-posing approach, students who are unfamiliar with a particular topic, say, Cambodia and the Cambodian American experience, may feel sanctioned to voice confusions that they might otherwise feel inhibited to ask—for example: "I thought Cambodians and Vietnamese kids were the same. How are they different?" "Why did Cambodian families move here to our community?" Or some students may point to social discrepancies that they feel uncomfortable about voicing: "I'm Cambodian and all my relatives are Cambodian, and we all live together with our relatives in the apartments in town. Why don't most White kids live with their relatives?"

Students' questions can reveal how social structures create stereotypes and lack of information that may lead to tension, alienation, and conflict. Attentive teachers can invite those questions and affirm a classroom culture that creates trustful, respectful dialogue. Such dialogue reveals that many of us are wondering about these questions and issues, and it also reveals why it is so crucial to use our academic skills to demystify them. By modeling an inquisitive mind-set that takes a social justice stance, educators can encourage students to express their curiosity. Teachers can do this by making statements such as "There is a growing Cambodian community here in our town. The first Cambodian families immigrated here in the 1970s, yet over 40 years later, we study very little about the Cambodian culture or the experience of Cambodian American families in our school. Do you think it is worth exploring this community?" Dialogue can help promote academic rigor directed by a classroom community's curiosity.

The example of curriculum that follows was developed by a team of teachers of middle school students in an effort to stimulate intellectual growth, deepen understanding, support curiosity, and affirm the identities of students from all backgrounds. In addition to describing the curriculum that the team of teachers developed, this example also provides suggestions for expanding it.[1] We hope this sample curriculum will be viewed within the framework of critical pedagogy and multicultural education. It is one of many models that can be transferred and expanded to other curriculum units of regional studies and cultural groups, and it lends itself to continual adaptation by teachers for their specific learning communities.

What We Don't Know

This team of seventh-grade teachers known as Team C was driven to develop and implement this curriculum about Cambodia by their concern about the academic achievement of their Cambodian students. The team included teachers of science, math, social studies, English, and art and about 100 seventh graders. These teachers noticed that, while there was a small population of Cambodian students (an average of 8 to 10 in a school of about 630 students), the Cambodian students expressed their culture in several distinct ways. Team C teachers also noticed, with distress, that many of the Cambodian students in the school were experiencing low academic achievement. The individual teachers on the team brought a range of philosophies and perspectives to their classrooms, but something on which they all agreed was that they lacked knowledge about Cambodia and the Cambodian American experience.

Preparation

Supported by the school system's staff development funds, the team of teachers met during the summer to study the topic of Cambodia. They enrolled in a course called Cambodian Culture, American Soil: Conflict, Convergence and Compromise, which was co-taught by a Cambodian teacher in their district and his colleague, an activist in the community.[2] In addition to taking the course, the principal also provided each teacher with copies of the book *First They Killed My Father: A Daughter of Cambodia Remembers* by Loung Ung.[3]

While many school districts may not support such in-depth staff development, an alternative approach to a study group could be for teachers to read primary sources and have book discussions. Such an approach requires commitment of considerable time and energy, but the results can be transformative.

Whether preparation for curriculum development comes through coursework, reviewing literature, or field research, there is rarely a moment when teachers think they know everything they should to embark on creating a curriculum. On the contrary, thoughtful teachers are intensely aware of the seemingly endless boundaries of knowledge on any given subject. Rather than avoid the unknown, a problem-posing teacher launches into the topic by asking the students stimulating questions. Herein lies the tension between overpreparing structured curriculum, which may exclude student voices, and including student questions in the actual development of the curriculum. Teacher preparation as a foundation is essential, and setting some goals for framing students' questions is helpful.

Goal Setting

When setting goals from a multicultural perspective for a curriculum unit about a geographical region or specific cultural group, teachers need to think beyond content, facts, and figures to consider the unit of study as intellectual and cultural work. Teachers who plan curriculum with a social justice mindset bring far-reaching goals to the curriculum design by considering what ideas will endure long after the books are closed and years after the students leave their classrooms. Grant Wiggins and Jay McTighe refer to these concepts as "big ideas" or "enduring understandings" and assert that depth of understanding is developed if these concepts are articulated clearly in the classroom when embarking on a unit of study, as opposed to content presented as only to be tested at the end.[5]

A multicultural curriculum with enduring understandings based on a social justice perspective can help motivate teachers and students to work together toward social change. A unit about Cambodia and the Cambodian American experience could be designed with the following enduring understandings:

- Knowledge about historical events can help us understand current social conditions.

- War, genocide, and forced migration deeply influence people's lives for many generations.

- Recovering, preserving, and renewing cultural identity is an ongoing process of education, artistic expression, and cultural exchange.

- Awareness of the oppression and resistance experienced by a group of people can motivate them, and others, to work toward social change.

These enduring understandings could be taught through many content areas within a range of thematic topics, and they are transferable to other cases of war and displacement. Note that none of these understandings mention the word *Cambodia*; rather they assert knowledge that is transferable and relevant to life-long learning. In this way, overarching goals such as the ones listed above can serve as guidelines when teachers get into the nitty-gritty work of planning objectives for their daily lessons and activities to uncover more specific content.

Team C teachers formulated the following specific objectives for the unit:

- All students will understand the history of Cambodia and its relationship to the United States.

- All students will develop inquiry about the Cambodian presence in western Massachusetts: What do we know? What do we wonder? (What is our knowledge? What are our questions?)

- All students will engage in direct involvement with the Cambodian community: at the Cambodian community garden, at the Buddhist temple with the monks, with high school "buddies" from the Cambodian club, and through other community events.

- The curriculum will affirm the identity of Cambodian students and families.

- The curriculum will build understanding among all students of all backgrounds.

The first two objectives are traditionally academic in nature, pointing to understanding history and current events. The academic achievement *embedded in* the overarching enduring understandings and in the specific objectives underscore that multicultural education is *basic education,* as emphasized in this book's definition of multicultural education. Likewise, the editors of *Rethinking Schools* have consistently asserted that multicultural curriculum and classroom practice must be academically rigorous.[6] The deliberate intellectual grounding of this unit disputes the misperception that multicultural curriculum is just about making people feel good, as detractors may claim. Each of the objectives addresses academic engagement in a variety of ways. Throughout this curriculum, you will see many opportunities for students to develop and increase academic and life skills.

The Work of Learning

One of the first questions teachers often ask is "How long should I spend on this unit?" The unit about Cambodia and the Cambodian American experience was developed and operated as three different schedule plans: (1) events throughout the school year, (2) intensive study for one to three weeks, and (3) the focus group week. We will give examples of the activities for the three different schedule plans.

Events Throughout the School Year

While the major framework and implementation of the unit work happened within a one- to three-week schedule, many other experiences reinforced the overarching, enduring understandings throughout the year. Team C teachers had a great deal of other curriculum on many other topics to teach, yet they viewed the entire school year as having opportunities for teaching and learning about the Cambodian experience unit. Some of the activities throughout the year included visitors and field trips.

Visitors

A Community Member   The social studies teacher invited, Mr. Mao, a teacher in the school and member of the Cambodian community, to visit her classes for four different sessions. The students were captivated by Mr. Mao's memories of his childhood, his family, his village, and his strategies for survival when captured by the Khmer Rouge. He showed the students how he had to trick the Khmer Rouge soldiers into believing he was a peasant farmer by demonstrating that he knew how to make rope from raw fibers. Mr. Mao's visits emphasized the grim tragedies of surviving genocide as well as the resilience of human nature. His warm nature and sparkling wit overcame the seventh-graders' discomfort with the difficult topic of genocide, creating a community of honest questioners. The personal accounts Mr. Mao related to the class were reinforced by a series of videos which the students had viewed previously about the history of Cambodia and the devastation caused by Pol Pot's regime.

High School Khmer Culture Club   Other guests included high school students from the district's Khmer Culture Club. The high school students shared their experiences as Cambodian American teenagers. They discussed the challenges of negotiating multiple cultural perspectives and the tension between traditional Cambodian family structure and mainstream U.S. teen culture. Many of the high school students had never been to Cambodia; they were born in the United States or had emigrated as very young children from refugee camps. Their experiences of Cambodia were vicarious, derived from collective memories of the elders in their families. Some teens were second-generation Cambodian Americans. Some were fluent in Khmer and English and some spoke no Khmer. They articulated the responsibilities of being bilingual youth in a culture in which most of the adults with literacy skills had been murdered in the genocide. The challenge of becoming assimilated into the U.S. mainstream while simultaneously maintaining cultural solidarity with their families had often been compounded by their struggles against institutionalized racism and poverty.

The teens also shared and taught traditional art forms, such as Cambodian folk dance and poetry, to the middle school youth. In addition, they talked about their favorite music and forms of entertainment in U.S. popular culture. The high school students' visits provided a dialogue and demonstration of the perspectives of many postmodern youth who are fluent in family language, hip hop culture, Standard English, and multiple ways of expressing their academic and artistic knowledge. By making multiple perspectives visible and embodied, these encounters expanded the notion of what it means to be Cambodian American.

Master Musician   Another visitor, provided through the Cambodian Masters in the Classroom Program, played traditional Cambodian music and demonstrated traditional musical instruments to the whole team.[7]

Field Trips

Cambodian Community Garden   In the early fall, the entire team took a trip to the local Cambodian Community Garden. The vegetables grown in the garden were sold to restaurants and farmer's markets to raise funds for rebuilding temples and schools in Cambodia. The whole team picked vegetables to contribute to the community effort.

Khmer Dance Performance   A combination of serendipity and resourcefulness brought Team C to a performing arts event at a nearby university. The Asian Dance Program was hosting a performance of the award-winning Cambodian Angkor Dance Troupe from Lowell, Massachusetts.[8] Because the teachers were alert to gleaning from the community all available knowledge related to the Cambodian experiences, and because they were energetic enough to write grants to fund the trip, all seventh-graders, including Team C students, attended the dynamic dance performance. The Angkor Dance Troupe features teen Cambodian dancers who are mastering the classical Cambodian traditional dance forms as well as developing hybrid performances that integrate break dance and other hip hop forms into their movements. One of the seventh-graders, Eric, made this observation about the performance: "I wish I was a Cambodian dancer. Those guys can break dance mad-cool and then they know their culture, too. I wish I had something like that."

In lieu of a lucky coincidence of a live performance within walking distance of one's school, teachers can use videos, DVDs, and Web sites projected onto a large screen to bring the performing arts to their students. For example, *Monkey Dance* is a recent documentary film about three teens from the Angkor Dance Troupe coming of age in Lowell, Massachusetts. The Web site about the film explains: "Children of Cambodian refugees inhabit a tough, working class world overshadowed by their parents' nightmares of the Khmer Rouge. Traditional Cambodian dance links them to their parents' culture, but fast cars, hip consumerism, and good times often pull harder."[9]

The Peace Pagoda and the Nipponzan Myohoji Sangha Buddhist Temple   Teachers made connections with the monks at the nearby Buddhist temple[10] in Leverett, Massachusetts, where many of the Cambodian families gather for prayer and meditation as well as for education and celebration. A field trip was planned in early April so that Team C students could help clean the grounds and plant flowers in anticipation of the annual Cambodian New Year celebration. Snowfall is not unusual during spring in New England, and it snowed several inches on the day of the field trip; the gardening plans turned into a snow-shoveling project, which also included a snowball battle with the monks! In addition to learning about the humor and snowball skills of the monks (qualities that can be gained only through the spontaneity and dynamism of a field trip), Team C students learned about many of the symbols in the physical space of the temple and about the role of Buddhism in many Cambodian families.

Team C scheduled these visitors and field trips between September and June. The teachers witnessed a sustained interest in the topic of Cambodia and the Cambodian American experience long after the one- to three-week immersion study. Giving the students some breathing room to consider the topic and the questions that emerged throughout the school year reinforced the intellectual depth of the study.

One- to Three-Week Unit

The teachers developed an intensive classroom unit of study that can last from one to three weeks. These time frames are flexible, depending on how often teachers meet with their classes and the depth of study on the topic. Because this curriculum was enacted in a middle school, each Team C teacher taught in a specific discipline.

English Class   The English teacher led an in-depth investigation of Cambodian and Southeast Asian folktales. Students read from children's picture books (traditional prose translated into English from the Khmer source) and saw videos of storytellers. Specific attention was focused on how folktales use humor and metaphor to teach lessons. These activities met the state's framework standards and were integrated with a wider body of literature about cross-cultural folktales in the English department curriculum. Students could draw similarities and differences about the literature while viewing the Cambodian folktales as a means for reclaiming and reinvigorating cultural symbols that had been threatened by extinction in the aftermath of the genocide.[11]

Science Class   During the two years that this curriculum was implemented, there were two science teachers. One year, a science teacher led an investigation of endangered species in Southeast Asia. Students developed research projects on specific animals and species. They expressed their findings in text and artistic forms to create oversize classroom books. The books of illustrated scientific research were donated to the local elementary school, which served a large population of Cambodian students. In addition, the seventh-graders created bookmarks depicting a synopsis of their research. They sold the bookmarks in a fund-raising effort to purchase protected areas of rainforest acreage in Southeast Asia.

Another year, a science teacher integrated his science curriculum with a study of the local Cambodian Community Garden. While at the garden, the science teacher led groups in measuring the space with global positioning satellite (GPS) devices;

students worked with partners to map the surface area while learning about technology and computation. At school, they went to the computer lab and learned how to download and analyze the data. These science activities met the state's framework and standards for studying ecosystems and using technology for collection and analysis of data.

Social Studies Class   The social studies teacher engaged the students in an exploration of the refugee experience. They scrutinized the legal and social implications of refugee status, giving specific attention to the ravages of war and the conditions that cause a population to be forcibly displaced and become refugees. They developed questions about the plight of people in many regions, from Afghanistan and Cambodia to the United States. In addition to studying groups from abroad who have been named political refugees under U.S. policy, they also critically examined the history of American Indian groups and compared their status in their native land as similar to the refugee experience.

Math Class   The math teacher worked with concepts of ratio, proportion, and scaling to compare and contrast the amount of space used in a typical house in Cambodia with the amount of space in a typical house in the United States. The math teacher worked with the Cambodian community teacher, who provided lots of photographs and illustrations of houses in Cambodian villages and cities. The students designed a scale model of a house that reflected the typical size and shape of a Cambodian house. Meeting the seventh-grade math standards, they worked from their individual design of a flat net that could be folded into a three-dimensional structure.

The math teacher also worked closely with the science teacher on a map activity. Students divided the maps into sections and analyzed Cambodia's ecosystems in science class. In the math activity, they developed an analysis of the total Cambodian population compared to the population densities in specific areas of the country. Using computational skills, they created a visual graph to illustrate their understanding of how people are dispersed regionally. This activity was integrated with the social studies investigation of the refugee experience to learn what the population looked like before and after the war.

Art Class   In art class, the seventh-graders studied the history, architectural design, and sculptural relief work of the temple of Angkor Wat. Studying the twelfth-century temple as an example of architectural accomplishment and cultural endurance helped bring alive the intersection of spiritual beliefs, political struggles, and environmental changes in Cambodia's history. Students explored Cambodia's cultural junctions of India and China through the presence of Hindu and Buddhist traditions, multiple language influences, and the stories illustrated by the seemingly endless sculptural murals of the temple.

By studying the symbolism, stories, and astonishing technical prowess demonstrated in the construction of the temple, the seventh-graders gained insight into the depth of history and the significance of the temple in present-day Cambodia. One student exclaimed, "No wonder they put it in the middle of their flag!"

Continuing with the art exploration, the students, using clay and plaster, created their own relief sculptures depicting the animals they studied in science class and the folktales they explored in English. When some students asked about copying illustrations of the goddesses that are carved on Angkor Wat, they engaged in a group discussion about religious iconography and who had the right to appropriate religious imagery. They imagined what it might be like for a classroom to produce 25 crucifixes or 25 images of the Star of David. They also looked at the work of some contemporary artists who use religious imagery in their work—whether reverently or irreverently—and noticed that most of these artists have a personal connection with the religious images they use. Such open discussions helped students make informed, deliberate decisions about whether they chose to imitate the statues of the goddesses of Angkor Wat.

Focus Groups

After their intensive one- to three-week studies in the separate disciplines—visiting each teacher throughout their school day as middle school students usually do—Team C students chose a focus group in which to work. Each focus group worked in a single discipline for a full school week. Students spent the entire day with one teacher, working in depth on a single project. After reflecting on the power of spending a whole week in one classroom with one teacher and the same group of peers, one seventh-grader said (enthusiastically) that it was "just like elementary school!" Each focus group visited the art room daily to work on a visual art component of the focus group project. Students chose from the following focus group activities:

- The English teacher led a focus group of students to dramatize the folktales the team had studied. Students made collaborative decisions while directing plays, memorizing lines, creating costumes, and managing props and scenery. In art class, they worked on scenery and props for the plays inspired by illustrations from the picture books and by their study of Angkor Wat.

- The science teacher led a focus group in the construction of a scale model of the Cambodian Community Garden. Students used the data from their GPS activity to re-create the plot of land they had visited on the field trip. To investigate how to grow certain vegetables, they compared the climate and environmental conditions in Cambodia with the conditions in their hometown. In art class, they used materials and techniques to develop the three-dimensional effect of the scale model garden.

- The math focus group expanded the scale-model house design and built three-dimensional houses to reflect their study of the typical architecture of Cambodian houses. They carried their house to and from the art room each day, adding structural and technical details, surface design, and texture to try to depict an authentic-looking Cambodian house. In art class, they compared U.S. houses to Cambodian houses and used images from the book *Material World: A Global Family Portrait,* by Peter Menzel, Charles Mann, and Paul Kennedy, to consider the implications of consumerism in the United States.[12]

■■■■■■ **What You Can Do**
Teach for Interreligious Understanding in Your Multicultural Curriculum

When students have questions about religious diversity, many teachers shy away from such inquiries by changing the subject or by stating, "We do not talk about religion in school because of separation of church and state." Our book certainly does not advocate teaching students a religious doctrine or suggesting to them how or what they should believe because that *would* be a violation of separation of religion and state in a public school. However, questions about religious difference can be fodder for academic study and scholarly research. Bringing questions about religious difference out of secrecy and into classroom discussion can promote interreligious understanding, expand perspectives about religious freedoms in a democratic society, engage students in school by affirming identity, and build community. Students do not have to wait to get to high school or college to take a course in comparative religions.

Work with a group of colleagues in a collaborative discussion to make several lists on chart paper:

1. Questions about religious diversity that we have heard from students and teachers.

2. Epithets or hurtful, prejudicial comments we have heard from children and adults in our school.

3. Worries or concerns we have as teachers about approaching this topic.

Then make an action plan to gather resources, gain education, and implement some activities in your classroom and school. Some resources can be found at the Web site for the Tanenbaum Center for Interreligious Understanding: www. tanenbaum.org/. The goal of this center is to foster interreligious education and dialogue. They have an exciting new resource for grades K–5 called *Religions in My Neighborhood,** and it is filled with unit plans and hands-on activities rooted in "big ideas" and essential questions. This book and others can provide teachers with practical means for integrating topics of religious diversity into daily discussions that also support academic achievement.

*Religions in My Neighborhood: Preparing Students for a Multicultural and Multireligious World, published by Tannenbaum Center (2010).

- The social studies focus group decided to write and perform vignettes to demonstrate various refugee experiences throughout the world. Some students took on the role of the United Nations. Others took on the role of the Red Cross and the Red Crescent, some wrote and performed the parts of the refugees, and some took on the role of military guards in refugee camps. In art class, they worked on scenery, props, and costumes informed by their research projects and news media images.

Demonstration Day

At the end of the focus group week, Team C students and teachers hosted Demonstration Day to illustrate their knowledge, understanding, and questions about Cambodia and the Cambodian American experience. All families, friends, and school personnel were invited. On a rotating schedule, visitors could enter each classroom to get a sense of what the students had learned. The science focus group set up their garden model in the art room, and the math focus group placed their houses in the garden to create a scale model of a Cambodian village. The students welcomed visitors and held discussions about contrasting and comparing the environments and houses in Cambodia to those of the New England valley where they lived. The English focus group performed miniplays inspired by the Cambodian folktales but adapted by the seventh-graders as "fractured fairytales" to reflect the intersection of U.S. popular culture, ancient stories, middle school humor, and symbolism of the Cambodian tales. The social studies focus group also performed their vignettes to pull their audience members into the experiences of refugees. After each vignette, the group held a question-and-answer session with the audience, drawing upon their research findings.

The seventh-grade students of Team C completed Demonstration Day with a feeling of fulfillment and accomplishment. Each student participated fully in the work of the intensive unit and individually evaluated his or her work. Each seventh-grader engaged in self-directed participation within a collective group goal in his or her focus group. The students increased their skills in every academic content area, yet the teachers and students realized that there was still much to learn. Team C teachers asked the students to evaluate the learning experiences. Students wrote many statements about their challenges, accomplishments, and achievements. One Cambodian student, Prasour, wrote, "I liked this part of school when we studied my own culture. I thought it was awesome. The kids who aren't Cambodian thought it was awesome. It just makes you feel awesome to be Cambodian."

Curricular Adaptation 2: Expanding Definitions of Family

Another approach to transforming a curriculum is the strategy of examining a particular theme from a variety of perspectives. In the curricular adaptation that follows, we offer a glimpse into a study of *family* as the theme. The concept of family has always been both deeply political and intimately personal. The political framework for defining family has become a contentious issue in recent years because of the lesbian, gay, bisexual, and transgender (LGBT) community's struggle to gain legal marital status. The voices of political parties and special interest lobbying groups that claim ownership of the definition of *family values* have punctuated the controversy.

This case is divided into descriptions of two approaches to curricular adaptation. The first case examines the topic of family in a first grade, and the second portion of this case presents a middle school setting.

Why the Topic of Family?

The topic of family is an attractive theme for teachers because it offers many promising possibilities. The promise lies in the idea that every student, from preschool through high school, may be able to tell a story about family and relate to ideas about family change. Such stories and ideas provide ways for teachers and students to collaborate and involve every student in the curriculum. If these attributes are not approached with a critical multicultural perspective, however, a curriculum about family can prove to be problematic—even damaging—to students. What is often thought to be a "universal" theme requires acknowledgment of multiple experiences and perspectives, with specific attention to deep-seated myopic views of the definition of *family* that may work to support institutional oppression of some people.

Who Is Included?

For example, families who are headed by lesbian, gay, bisexual, and transgender people have been the specific target of recent oppressive political campaigns, and they are frequently ignored or deliberately silenced in school curricula. Also, families headed by adults who are not married, whether homosexual or heterosexual, are excluded from traditional definitions of family, and the children of these families may be questioned about the validity of their family structure. Families headed by single parents and grandparents raising children are still not affirmed in many curricula. Students who have family members who are incarcerated rarely see a welcome opportunity to share their story, and they are silenced by some teachers if they attempt to raise the topic. Families caring for members with mental illness may be reluctant to participate in a classroom invitation to share stories from home. The perspective of children of adoption is frequently omitted in classroom discussions about heredity and family trees. There are as many pitfalls in approaching family as a theme as there are families in our schools. How does a teacher develop a curriculum about family that draws from the strength of one of the most elemental human experiences and simultaneously lead students to fight oppression, develop critical thinking skills, and affirm all community members?

When teachers embark on the study of family with clarity about the long-term goals of the unit, it helps students tap into the shared understanding of human experience. Long-term goal setting may help avoid activities that exclude some students from the classroom community. In its most effective form, a curriculum rooted in big ideas or enduring understandings will lead students to advocate for human rights for all families.

Avoiding Pitfalls

A common activity in curriculum about family includes students' researching the history of their names. While this can be a powerful community-building activity, it is also rife with difficulties, especially when it is not grounded by an overarching long-term goal. Many students may know the family story of their name or may have easy access to it by asking family members who are eager to share the story. However, many children may not. Children of adoption and children in foster care may not know the origin of their name and may feel that such an assignment will lower their status as a classroom community member. Other students may have painful associations with the history of their name, such as one student we met who reported that he was named after a family member who had been incarcerated for abusing him.

Rather than discard the assignment about researching one's name and relegate such potentially robust activities to the "untouchable" category, teachers may develop a menu of various assignments from which students can choose. For example, if the big idea of the assignment is to *engage in research skills related to naming and personal history,* the menu of activities might include the following:

- Research the name of the street on which you live (or the name of the building, housing community, or neighborhood; or the building in which your faith community worships; or the land on which your tribal community lives). Find out when it was named and why. Tell us something about its history, and if you choose the place where you live (building, street, housing community, or tribal community land), find out when your family moved there or started living there. Some family moves are exciting and celebratory. Other family moves may be a response to family and community difficulties such as economic strife, divorce, abuse, natural disasters, or political oppression. Tell us only what you and your family would like to share.

- Research the name of our school and compare it to the name of another school in our district that you have never attended. Tell us something about the history of the school between the time it was named and the time you began attending the school.

- Research the name of an important person in your family, your religious community, your tribal community, or your cultural community. Tell us something about what the name means. Tell us something about the history of the person between the time she or he was named and the time you were born.

- Research your name and its origins. Find out who chose your name and why. Tell us something about what your name means. Tell us something about the history of your family between the time you were named and the time you began attending this school.

A culminating activity may involve each student creating an artistic representation of his or her own name to display as a heading for his or her research presentations. The artistic representations may provide another way for students to demonstrate knowledge while simultaneously bringing a unifying activity to a classroom where students have been engaged in an assortment of research projects.

The pitfalls and promises of the history-of-your-name activity are examples of why it is critical to begin a curriculum with big ideas or enduring understandings rather than simply planning activities. This curricular activity also exemplifies the delicate balance inherent in a teacher's role. Even the most thorough multicultural curriculum cannot solve the personal crises that some children face. When students reveal painful memories or dangerous situations, it is critical that teachers tap into the resources in the school and community through guidance counselors and social workers to keep their students healthy and safe.

What follows are examples of curriculum for two different grade levels: one created by first-grade teachers and students, another created by a middle school team of teachers.

First-Grade Curriculum Based on Big Ideas in Gina Simm's and Susie Secco's Classrooms

The first-grade curriculum about family stems from the following four big ideas or enduring understandings and essential questions developed by first-grade teachers Gina Simm and Susie Secco:

1. There are all kinds of families:
    *   What is a family?
    *   How do we know a group of people make up a family?

2. Families have wants and needs:
    *   What do families need? (Food, water, clothing, shelter, love.)
    *   What is the difference between a need and a want?
    *   What are some things that you must have to survive?
    *   Is money a want or a need? Are some things "in between"? Do all families need a way to exchange goods?

3. Responsibilities:
    *   What are the responsibilities that parents and guardians attend to while kids are at school?
    *   What are the responsibilities of each child in the family?

4. Experiencing *change* is common to all families. Examples of change are marriage, divorce, getting older, moving, illness, getting well, death, birth:
    *   Does change happen in all families?
    *   Why do we like or dislike change?
    *   Can we prepare for change in families?

With these enduring understandings in mind, the first-grade teachers start each school year with the integrated social studies unit on family and spend approximately six weeks incorporating these big ideas into all aspects of the curriculum. As the year unfolds, they also study other units in specific content areas that reinforce and revisit many of the enduring understandings that were established during the unit on family. The other units in the social studies and science curricula are anchored in the big ideas concerning the family unit throughout the year.

All Kinds of Families

The teachers deliberately take an antibias approach throughout the six-week unit on family, as well as throughout the school year, by teaching first-graders that there are all kinds of families. Through children's literature, the daily calendar, math problems, and other activities of classroom life, the students consistently see images of, and learn about, family diversity. Specific attention is given to affirming the particular families of the children in the classroom while simultaneously expanding the students' views of what family can be. Some of the many examples of "all kinds of families" include families headed by gay dads and lesbian moms; families experiencing divorce; families created or expanded through adoption; single-parent families; families struggling with financial resources; multiracial families; foster families; families experiencing illness or death; families in which the grandparents are raising the children; families with stepparents and stepsiblings; families from a wide range of different racial, ethnic, and religious backgrounds; and families that may be defined as nuclear or traditional families.

Families in the Classroom

In many schools, the practice of bringing family members from all walks of life into the classroom as helpers and experts has had more support in recent years. In a unit about family, this is certainly a dynamic component. Teachers can develop many creative means for parents, guardians, and extended family members to be present. However, making *all* families "visible" and honoring the diversity of their life experiences are challenging endeavors. To explore the big idea about families and responsibilities, one teacher developed an activity that meets the challenge.

At the beginning of this activity, the classroom community discusses the idea of responsibilities. The students complete a series of assignments to explore and document the responsibilities of adults and children in the family. The assignments are designed to raise awareness of responsibilities but also to make every child's family visible in the classroom. The students in the class make a list of responsibilities that they have in school or "jobs" they need to accomplish. This simple task expands the notion of what it means to have a "job" beyond a place of work where one gets paid. Especially for children in families struggling with unemployment, this broad view of jobs and responsibilities affirms the work of all family members. The class also makes a list of jobs that kids do at home, such as making their beds, walking the dog, carrying their plates to the sink, helping to carry groceries, folding towels, etc.

After developing their understanding of responsibilities, each first-grader conducts a family survey by interviewing the adults in the family, asking questions such as "What responsibilities do you have while I am at school?" "What jobs do you do, either at home or away from home?" These interview questions allow for a range of replies to be respected, which may not be true of the more limiting question that children frequently hear: "Where do your parents work?" The first-graders learn more about what their caregivers do and about the assortment of possibilities of adult responsibilities; the teacher gains a better view of the complex workings of each student's family. The assignment results in adults' replies such as caring for younger children or elders, searching for employment, cleaning or fixing up the home, taking care of the yard, volunteer work, going to school, resting to go to the night shift at work, and many more. The students hear about a variety of places that people call work: the office, the school, the fire station, the bakery, the construction site, the chemistry lab, the home, the sandwich shop, the hospital, grandma's house, the cafeteria, the hotel, and more.

Part of the interview requires the students to ask the adults what they have to be good at to accomplish their responsibilities. This kind of questioning affirms the multiple intelligences required for everyday life. Children hear about skills such as talking to people, knowing when the baby is hungry, using special tools, keeping things organized, being a good listener, making food taste good, knowing different kinds of plants, figuring out when a burning building might fall down (in the case of a parent who is a firefighter), and so on. The assignment continues with students' researching the jobs for which all the children in their home have responsibility. Eventually, they investigate what the adults in their families imagined they would be when they grew up and how this compares to the adult responsibilities they now have. Finally, the students spend time drawing, writing, and presenting their investigations, culminating in imagining several kinds of responsibilities they would like to have when they grow up.

The work of multicultural education is not only to affirm students about who they are, but also to challenge them about who they may become. This variation on a common early childhood activity of "What do you want to be?" is designed to provide multiple models, unleash the imagination, and expand the possibilities these first-graders envision for themselves. All the while, every family "comes to life" in the class, even if the adults in the family could not enter the classroom door.

Children's Literature

The first-grade teachers use children's literature to emphasize that there is not one "normal" way to experience family, but rather that *diversity is normal*. While reading lively and engaging children's literature such as *1,2,3: A Family Counting Book*, by Bobbie Combs and illustrated by Dannamarie Hosler, students see paintings that depict families headed by gays and lesbians, including two dads reading a bedtime story to their children, two moms sharing popsicles with their children on the porch, and several families gathered in community activities.[13] Using children's literature that includes encounters with families with same-sex parents deliberately combats heterosexism in early childhood and provides opportunities to teach explicitly about human rights for all families. When students learn accurate, respectful language and vocabulary regarding the LGBT community, they are better able to respond to anti-LGBT perspectives.

While the selection of children's literature that depicts families headed by LGBT people is still limited, it has grown significantly in breadth and depth since 1989, when Leslea Newman wrote and self-published *Heather Has Two Mommies*.[14] For the twentieth anniversary of that book in 2009, Newman and many other authors and publishers expanded children's literature selections with texts that affirm families headed by gay and lesbian couples, single people, and LGBT parents who have separated. Some recent titles for early childhood literacy activities that discuss a more inclusive definition of family and that affirm families headed by lesbian, gay, bisexual, and transgender people are listed on the Gay, Lesbian, and Straight Education Network (GLSEN) Web site.[15]

The list of titles in children's literature that affirm LGBT identity is growing in number. Early childhood teachers and students who are engaging in the "dangerous discourse" (which we discussed in our definition of multicultural education as education for social justice) use these books and other similar resources.[16]

Dangerous discourse becomes common practice and unthreatening when these books are integrated into daily literacy activities that develop reading and listening skills, motivate class discussion, and make interdisciplinary connections. Along with books that depict many other kinds of families, a rich children's literature collection affirms diverse family structures and questions those who exclude families headed by gay, lesbian, bisexual, and transgender parents from fully participating in a democracy.

Early childhood is an essential phase of development in which to address heterosexism by integrating this literature. Children are on the cusp of what Louise Derman-Sparks calls pre-prejudice. They are asking questions that may be naïve about society's oppressions or they may be ventriloquizing social epithets without understanding the meaning behind the words. First grade is an educational stage ripe with opportunity to expand a child's world.[17]

Problem-posing teachers realize that developing a children's literature collection is an ongoing, organic process. We are not suggesting that a first-grade bookshelf or a unit about family diversity should focus only on families headed by lesbian, gay, bisexual, and transgender people. Such an approach would obviously not affirm the families of all students in the class. However, given the current sociopolitical context of the human rights struggles of the LGBT community, a critical component of a multicultural curriculum must confront the negative ways that LGBT people are depicted by the popular media. An expanding children's literature collection may act as a counternarrative to oppressive acts and highlight the positive role of LGBT-headed families in the classroom. These books broaden the scope of a curriculum that also includes quality literature depicting families with diverse ethnic and racial identities, religious practices, socioeconomic situations, disabilities and abilities, languages, and so forth, as well as the myriad ways that families are shaped through birth, adoption, foster care, extended families, and more.

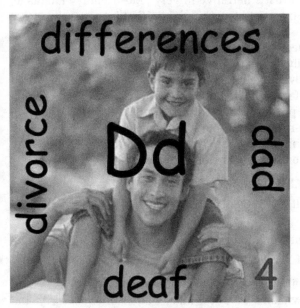

Calendar piece from Gina Simm's and Susie Secco's first-grade classrooms. Design inspired by Val Penniman's and Debbie Shumway's *Calendar Connections;* see www.calendar-connections.com.

Daily Calendar and Family Concepts

Each day in these first-grade classrooms starts with a morning meeting and calendar activity. Using a model created by teacher Val Penniman and parent Debbie Shumway, the teachers introduce alphabet skills, vocabulary, math patterns, and concepts about the current unit through the calendar activity.[18] For the family unit, the teachers designed daily calendar pieces (using clip art) to delve into concepts and vocabulary with which the children are familiar but which they may not always have the opportunity to use to develop academic knowledge.

For example, on calendar day number 4, the alphabet letter is D and the vocabulary words are *difference, dad, divorce,* and *deaf.* By including words such as *divorce, difference,* and *deaf* along with words that may be more typical of a family unit such as *dad,* the classroom curriculum is normalizing experiences so children may engage in academic skill development while some who are usually marginalized are affirmed in their family experiences. Simultaneously, other children are challenged to expand their perspective of families. Integrating vocabulary words such as *divorce* and *deaf* provides a means for students to ask questions and share stories in an emotionally safe and academically rigorous environment. Abilities, disabilities, and family change are studied through stories and new vocabulary.

All Kinds of Family Portraits

Artistic expression is honored in these classrooms as a form of sharing knowledge. Every student creates a family portrait. By studying various examples of family portraits from contemporary and historical artists, the first-graders gain a panoramic view of the multitude of ways that the concept of family can be expressed. A curriculum that expands the definition of *family* also expands the notion of what is included in a family portrait. The book *Honoring Our Ancestors: Stories and Pictures by Fourteen Artists,* edited by Harriet Rohmer, is illustrated with lively paintings by various artists who depict "ancestors" in poetic and metaphorical ways.[19] The paintings in this book represent family memories, spiritual stories, family quotes, and even a room with nobody in it to remind the viewer of the loss of a loved one. Each painting is accompanied by an artist's narrative in very "kid-friendly" language, which leads first-graders through robust literacy activities that integrate the visual image with the written word.

In another strategy to connect visual imagery and text, teachers and students study the books created by Family Diversity Projects, in which many different kinds of families are portrayed in captivating photographs with accompanying interviews of family members. Resources that use photography and interview text to depict the true stories of real families are powerful tools for developing critical thinking. In addition to using the books as curriculum resources, many teachers and schools display the touring photo-text exhibits, which can be rented from the Family Diversity Projects collection. Currently there are four traveling exhibits:[20]

- In Our Family: Portraits of All Kinds of Families
- Love Makes a Family: Portraits of Lesbian, Gay, Bisexual and Transgender People and Their Families
- Nothing to Hide: Mental Illness in the Family
- Of Many Colors: Portraits of Multiracial Families

Throughout the study of family, first-graders see images and hear stories of families that remind them of their own families. These images and stories also serve the purpose of stretching their understanding of what other families are like. The work of multicultural education for social justice begins in the earliest grades with the most elemental of human experience to help students imagine a fair world for "all kinds of families."

I like to play sports with my family. I like when my dad plays baseball with me. I like it when my mom tucks me in bed.

Michael Warren, in Gina Simm's class. *Family portrait.*

Middle School Interdisciplinary Curriculum on the Theme of Family

The exhibits and books of the Family Diversity Projects also serve as anchors for the integrated middle school curriculum about family. The middle school teachers developed big ideas to expand skills and inquiry across all content areas. The enduring understanding is that *oppression and resistance are experienced and acted upon in diverse ways by families in our society.* The essential questions that emerge from this idea are:

- How do we create an inclusive definition of family?
- What is family?
- Where do I belong?

Bearing in mind the difficulties that some students may encounter with a curriculum about families, the teachers did not ask students to bring in family photographs. They knew that many children would not have family photos and that some children would feel uncomfortably exposed by a requirement to share family photos. Instead, the team focused on the materials in the Family Diversity Projects phototext exhibit called In Our Family and on books, as well as discussions about the teachers and staff members' families, as points of departure for research. Thus, all

■ ■ ■ ■ ■ ■   **What You Can Do**
Make Your School a "Welcoming School"

You can make your school a "Welcoming School" with reliable, well-researched resources. When elementary school teachers have concerns about how to address family diversity, gender stereotyping, and bullying in the curriculum, they need curriculum materials to support their work and that support their students' academic achievement. The teachers in this curriculum case, Gina Simm and Susie Secco, developed their first-grade curriculum long before such products and Web resources were available, but now the Human Rights Campaign Foundation provides a curriculum for teachers, administrators, and families. It is one of the few resources available to elementary schools that are inclusive of LGBT families and individuals. In addition to lesson plans, lists of books, and documentation of research, the Welcoming Schools Web site at http://www .welcomingschools. org/ also provides educators with laws and policies that support Welcoming Schools work.

Form coalitions with other teachers, administrators, curriculum directors, parents/guardians, and community organizers. Follow the advice of the Welcoming Schools Web site about getting started, as quoted below:

> Laying groundwork is one of the keys to success when embracing family diversity,

avoiding gender stereotyping, and ending bullying and name-calling in K–5 learning environments.

Before you begin, consider the level of support among the parent/guardian community, the administration and the educators. Building the foundation for a welcoming school requires community support and much effort to build this support.

When beginning this work, ask yourself these questions:

- Do you need to hold events in your school community on family diversity or bullying and name-calling?

- Do you need to plan social events with the goal of building community where everyone feels welcome?

- Do you need to have more one-on-one conversations with parents and guardians? Teachers? Administrators?

Creating a safe and welcoming school for all children and families takes many people— from administrators to educators and staff to parents and guardians. You don't have to— and shouldn't—do this work alone.*

*Human Rights Campaign Foundation, 1640 Rhode Island Ave., N.W., Washington, D.C. 20036, phone 202/628-4160, TTY 202/216-1572, fax 866/304-3257, website www. welcomingschools. org, e-mail welcomingschools@hrc.org.

teachers brought their own family photos to share with the students at the beginning of the unit. These family photos provided opportunities to discuss the various ways of defining family and to share with the middle school students some aspects of the teachers' lives beyond the classroom walls.[21]

Diversity Within Groups

At first glance, it would appear that the team of teachers who undertook this unit was a group of middle-class White people. This is true, but it is not the whole story. The teachers were critically aware of the dominance of their identities and believed that their students deserved to see many different kinds of families modeled in class discussions. So the team presented their family photos to the students, and the classroom community discussions pointed out the many ways in which the teachers' families were different.

In this case, one female teacher was married to a man who had children from a previous union, so she had stepchildren. One male teacher was married to a woman and had no children. One female teacher had three sons: one from her first marriage, one from her second marriage in which she was still partnered, and one foster son who was different racially from her other family members. One female teacher lived with her lesbian partner and was adopting a child of a different race. One White male teacher was married to a White woman and they had two biological children—the only "nuclear" or "traditional" family among the teaching team.

These differences opened up opportunities for considering other kinds of diversity. Teachers invited other school faculty and staff members to visit their classrooms and bring some of their family photos. The faculty and staff visitors included a Jewish woman who told the story of her parents' surviving the Holocaust and the loss of her husband to cancer, as well as the triumph of her niece over cancer; an African American man who is married to a woman and raising their grandson; and a biracial gay man who had been adopted by a white family and had adopted two African American sons.

These conversations about the families in which the adults live provided models for students' consideration of the topic of family as an academic subject, rich with research possibilities. The students saw the teachers as full participants in the unit of study rather than simply as "deliverers" of information. The unintended consequence of this activity was that students witnessed different adults sharing their family experiences at varying levels of disclosure with distinct styles of storytelling. It gave students a range of models from which to embark on their academic work.

Studying Our Own Assumptions

The social studies teacher launched the study by bringing each class to the Family Diversity Projects photo exhibit before the accompanying text was installed in the display. (A similar activity could be designed by looking at books and photocopies of pictures of families.) The students examined each photograph and wrote responses to prompts such as:

- Find a family with whom you think you have something in common.
- Find a family with whom you think you have nothing in common.
- Pick a photo that makes you curious; write your questions.
- Pick a photo that makes you smile; tell us why you smiled.
- Pick a photo that makes you sad; tell us why it made you sad.

The social studies students compared each other's responses to the photos. They began to look critically at assumptions they were making on the basis of a photograph. Then the teachers added the companion text to each photograph, and the students revisited the exhibit, with plenty of time to read the text.

The reading and analysis of the text pointed to the sociological objectives of the unit. Students uncovered ways in which they made assumptions about some families and how those assumptions may stem from, or lead to, stereotypes. Students also learned ways in which they made accurate guesses about some of the families. For example, Jeffrey pointed out a family of four—comprised of a mom, a dad, and two sons who were both wearing baseball caps—as one that was similar to his own family because the family structure and love of baseball were similar to his family. Upon reading the text, Jeffrey learned that all four people in the photo are deaf and communicate in American Sign Language, which is different from Jeffrey's family's hearing and language abilities.

Group Membership and Responsibility

The activities that we have discussed so far eventually led to a study of how people group themselves and how society groups people. The students started with examining their membership roles in family and then moved on to examining their membership in other groups such as basketball teams, lunch-table groups, after-school clubs, religious communities, racial groups, ability groups, and so forth. This examination included analyzing group behavior and social influences on groups. When juxtaposed with the histories of various groups, these analyses helped to flesh out stories of historical oppression and resistance in the minds of these middle school students. Rather than demonizing one group or romanticizing another, students began to see the links of social power, social position, and group power. Ultimately, the students critically analyzed their own group membership and their social responsibilities within groups. They worked cooperatively to develop strategies to take responsibility when these groups dominate other groups in the microcosm of the middle school as well as in the larger society.

Reading, Writing, Researching, and Reflecting

The language arts curriculum explored the experiences of diverse families through literature. Like photo-text exhibits, literature offers students an opportunity to engage in other families' experiences, some that may resonate with their own and some that may open new worldviews to their early adolescent minds.

The middle school students selected books from an array of titles and genres. Poetry was a central vehicle for expression and questioning in the English class. Building on the curriculum advanced by Linda Christensen in *Reading, Writing and Rising Up*, each student composed a poem called "I Am From" to articulate the multiple dimensions of identity within family.[22]

While the work of poetry writing and literature circles was evolving in the English classroom, the students embarked on homework research projects to investigate their family histories. Again, if such a project is undertaken, it is advisable to provide a menu of assignments from which each student may choose to find meaningful, affirming work that also expands his or her academic skills. For example, a common project may be to ask students to research and report on when their family immigrated to this country. But when a teacher approaches the curriculum with the big idea in mind (*oppression and resistance are experienced and acted upon in diverse ways by families in our society*), the exclusion of Native American children in an assignment about immigration becomes more obvious. When teachers approach the big ideas with critical pedagogy, the students in the classroom consider multiple views of what immigration means to various families. This array of perspectives may include the forced migration and extermination of Native Americans, the forced immigration of enslaved people, immigration to escape war and political oppression, refugee experiences, the circular migration/immigration families in U.S. territories (called colonies by some) such as Puerto Rico, and the ongoing political oppression and resistance of families caught in the crossfire of U.S. immigration restrictions. When research findings based on each student's family's perspectives are integrated in a critical classroom context, voice is given to stories that have been silenced, encouraging students to question narratives that exclude some family experiences.

Measuring, Reflecting, and Representing

In math class, the middle school students spent a two-week period that the math teacher called A Day in the Life carefully measuring how their time was spent. They created circle graphs (pie charts) and bar graphs to analyze the percentage of time spent with family, comparing this percentage to time spent on homework, in extracurricular events, with friends, and other details such as grooming. (Grooming was a substantial piece of most middle school students' pie charts and graphs!) Students learned critical time management skills as well as gained an understanding of the diverse ways that their peers' families spend time.

Genetics, Probability, and Critical Pedagogy

Starting with two essential questions—"What is family?" and "Where do I belong?"—the science curriculum was integrated with math to study probability equations related to genetics and human traits such as eye color. By studying the science of genetic structure and the mathematical strategies to predict human traits, students of all family backgrounds and configurations are affirmed. Rather than starting with what each student knows about her or his heritage, teachers can start with what they do *not* know and what they are curious about to form hypotheses about their ancestors' genetic composition. Science teachers can present a variety of examples from which students may choose to develop their equations and predictions. This activity is more welcoming to children of adoption and others who may have no information about their biological heredity. The students learn academic skills for analyzing data and pursuing deeply personal questions.

Old Arguments, New Knowledge, and Social Justice

A scientifically grounded study of genetics also provides well-informed arguments against racism and ethnic oppression. A critical pedagogy examines misinformation about intelligence and ability and replaces it with methodologically rigorous academic knowledge. With race-based and ethnic-based hate crimes and genocides around the globe, students can develop accurate, rational, and scientifically sound refutations to historically and ethnically rooted oppressions. By integrating their sociological research findings on group membership and group behavior with scientific and mathematical skills, middle school students can make informed choices

■ ■ ■ ■ ■ ■ ## What You Can Do
Use Technology to Expand Multicultural Curriculum

Every teacher knows that technology tools have the potential to engage students, expand understanding, boost achievement, and bring new perspectives to what counts as knowledge. The reach of technology in our students' lives is a powerful incentive to bring these fluencies into academic relevance. While no computer or software can replace the influence of great teaching, the broad array of current instruments, applications, and networks can serve our students' academic engagement and provide them with knowledge and skills to apply in their future scholastic and career endeavors. The implementation of technology in schools is a *multicultural issue* when you consider the digital divide in access and also the confidence that students develop as they prepare for college or the workplace. But in this ever-changing world of gizmos, gadgets, and "apps," where does a teacher begin to make decisions about using technology for rigorous classroom relevance?

We have gleaned a plethora of resources to make three specific book recommendations. These can be found in old-fashioned print-on-paper or in electronic formats.

Teaching with tools kids really use: Learning with Web and mobile technologies **by Susan Brooks-Young.*** This book is dedicated to expanding students' twenty-first-century skills. It provides teachers with very practical, hands-on advice on how to engage with resource staff members in schools as well as how to enhance classroom practice with specific tools. Many of these tools are typically banned from classrooms, yet Brooks-Young rejects the notion of tools as gimmicks by providing robust curriculum with devices and activities such as cell phones, MP3 players (iPods), notebooks, virtual worlds, and gaming. Teachers will find her approach do-able and empowering. She concludes with chapters titled "Digital

about human rights issues that affect their own families. They can become activists about global concerns.

Research Questions

The development of students as activist scholars was woven throughout each subject, and social studies objectives were evident in all content areas. In one of the final social studies assignments, students chose a research question to pursue through a variety of methods. For example, one student's question was "What gets families through hard times?" She practiced social science research methodologies such as reading the photo-text exhibit, interviewing her own family members, and interviewing friends and neighbors. She contrasted these real-life families' experiences with those of families she saw on television. Many students were compelled to compare their research data with the representation of families in the media. Students learned how to organize their data by themes and write essays with a critical eye toward the media's representation of family.

Visual Art and Visual Culture

To address the many messages regarding what families look like in visual culture, the interdisciplinary art curriculum was integrated with the social studies skills the

Citizenship" and "A Decision Making and Implementation Model."

***Literacy, technology, and diversity: Teaching for success in changing times* by Jim Cummins, Kristin Brown, and Dennis Sayers.**[†] Based on rigorous research using longitudinal studies of classroom practices, this book provides various teaching approaches that address literacy from a multicultural perspective. Cummins and colleagues provide background on concerns regarding literacy, technology use, classroom instruction, and testing practices specifically aimed at the needs of students from economically depressed communities and English language learners. They present design principles for technology-supported instruction that are critical components of effective teaching. By examining six cases of classrooms that employ a range of technologies as tools for learning, the book gives teachers an understanding of the promises of these pedagogical techniques. They close with a plan of literacy instruction for the information age as an alternative to many current practices.

***Curriculum 21: Essential education for a changing world* by Heidi Hayes Jacobs.**[‡] Building on her work in curriculum design, Jacobs makes the case for students being realistically prepared for the globalized world of today and the future. With attention to technology woven throughout the book, her organizational structure and clear-minded approach cover the entire school environment with discussion of content and assessment; program structures; media literacy; globalization; sustainability; and the habits of mind that students, teachers, and administrators need to develop and practice to succeed in school, work, and life.

*Brooks-Young, S. (2010). *Teaching with tools kids really use: Learning with Web and mobile technologies*. Thousand Oaks, CA: Corwin/Sage.

[†]Cummins, J., K. Brown, and D. Sayers. (2007). *Literacy, technology, and diversity: Teaching for success in changing times*. Boston: Allyn & Bacon/Pearson.

[‡]Jacobs, H. H. (Ed.). (2009). *Curriculum 21: Essential education for a changing world*. Alexandria, VA: Association for Supervision and Curriculum Development.

students had developed. By examining images of families in film, Web media, print media, fine art, and various expressions of popular culture, students can develop skills in critical and visual literacy. Within this dialogue, the middle school students drew self-portraits in the context of family portraits. By developing confidence in art-making skills, this lesson encouraged student expressions about diverse families while expanding concepts about art and the powerful role of visual culture.

Identity and Beauty

Critical understanding of facial features and value systems was underscored in the context of a visual arts drawing lesson stemming from the big idea of the unit. The art teacher and social studies teacher integrated concepts surrounding physical anthropology that also drew upon the math and science research in genetics. They studied skin color and other various traits. They asked why certain groups in specific geographic locations developed unique adaptations that we see today in the diversity of the human form, which is most obvious in facial features, hair texture, and skin color. Exploring these concepts in the process of drawing self-portraits deepened students' critical perceptions. The class discussion sharpened analytical questions about who gets to define *beauty* and how judgments about physical appearance in U.S. society may be shaped by commercially driven aims and conformist values. The works of art created by the students communicated many messages that stemmed from their understanding of oppression and resistance based on discussions throughout the unit. Students used layers of collage, glue, papers, paint, and oil pastel to express academic research, scientific and mathematical skills, poetic insights, and socially active engagement with their multiple and inclusive definitions of family.

A Family Celebration

As a culminating event, a celebration of the students' accomplishments and a demonstration of their knowledge was held, and every student on the team invited their families to school for the event. A huge art and text display was mounted, and each student exhibited a collaged frame of three items: a self-portrait, a family portrait, and an "I Am From" poem. Every social studies essay, mathematical graph, and scientific research project was on display. Parents, grandparents, caregivers, guardians, and siblings listened intently as students read poetry and excerpts of essays. Many family members who had never before entered the school building attended the event. Students grabbed the hands of loved ones to escort them to each exhibit. The teachers noticed how students proudly showed off their work to their visitors but, on a surprising note, many students were eager to point out the work of their classmates, too. Teachers overheard students telling the stories of their peers' families and how they related to the research assignments.

The most popular display was the dessert table; every family had contributed a favorite family dessert! Excited students urged peers and teachers to taste the snacks such as Jalissa's grandmother's flan or Ari's uncle's favorite chocolate-chip concoction. After the families and children went home and the last paper plates were cleaned up, teachers reported a feeling of transformation precipitated by the Family Dessert and Demonstration Day that closed the unit. Teachers described knowing their students more deeply and intimately, as well as witnessing soaring academic engagement across the team of seventh-graders.

Students wrote self-assessments of their work and told of making connections with teachers and peers in unexpected ways, "wanting to work [their] hardest," and feeling that the project was "awesome." The sense of accomplishment and community bond among the teachers and students on the team continued to grow throughout the school year. Teachers talked about developing knowledge about oppression and resistance as well as their expanding definitions of family, and students and teachers cultivated an enduring sense of belonging while documenting rigorous academic achievement.

Curricular Adaptation 3: Gay and Lesbian Literature: Expanding Topics for Inclusive High School Content

This case presents another example for multicultural changes in the curriculum. The deliberate antibias work that we saw in the curriculum adaptation case of Expanding Definitions of Family in first grade and middle school paves the way for students to engage in this inclusive high school curriculum. The following example is the curriculum for a high school English literature course called Gay and Lesbian Literature.[23]

The course was conceived and designed by an English teacher, Ms. Sara Barber-Just. Initially, it was Ms. Barber-Just's research, creativity, and commitment to education for social justice—backed by supportive department chair, principal, and superintendent—that brought the curriculum to the classroom. Eventually the English department at the high school and the school board approved this course as an integral part of the school curriculum.

Imagining Possibilities

Ms. Barber-Just was teaching in the English department of a high school that offered a range of familiar high school literature courses such as Foundations of American Literature, Masterpieces of Ancient and Medieval Worlds, and Masterpieces of the Renaissance and Modern Worlds, as well as more consciously multicultural courses such as Women in Literature and African American Literature. Teachers in the department had developed these courses over the years, and the courses had become integrated into the school's course offerings. Ms. Barber-Just imagined that the models in place for the African American Literature and Women in Literature courses could be applied to a course called Gay and Lesbian Literature because both of the former courses dealt with identity issues.

Ms. Barber-Just developed a proposal for a course combining a wealth of research from her graduate studies and her experiences as a teacher. Her research portfolio reflected an extensive review of gay and lesbian literature with a theoretical grounding in social justice education. In planning the Gay and Lesbian Literature course, she used a course structure that paralleled those of the two courses that were already offered, focusing on group-specific content from a social justice perspective. Her course mirrored the high academic standards within the department, with expectations for students to read thoroughly and critically, write expressively and analytically, and discuss the work passionately and fairly. The following is an excerpt from the proposal she wrote, which became part of the course description:

> Students in public schools have been reading literary classics by gay, lesbian, and bisexual authors for more than a century; however, gay authors' lives are often concealed rather than rightfully explored. This course closely examines the struggles and triumphs of these artists—as well as the historical periods during which they wrote—allowing readers to more deeply analyze their diverse literary contributions. *Gay and Lesbian Literature* is split into five major sections, moving in chronological order from the early 1900s to the 1990s. Class readings include works written by gay and lesbian authors during eras of severe legal and social oppression; conformity and self-loathing; anger, activism, and radicalism; and, finally, pride and acceptance. The course focuses on renowned modern and contemporary American authors such as Willa Cather, James Baldwin, Rita Mae Brown, and Michael Cunningham, and concludes with an examination of Sri Lankan author Shyam Selvadurai and a study of short stories from around the world. Each unit includes a combination of critical essays, poetry, short story, and/or film, providing a rich cultural and historical context for the featured literature.[24]

Sara Barber-Just explained that, for purposes of this course, she would base the definition of gay and lesbian literature on two criteria: (1) literature written by LBGT people and (2) literature including gay themes in the content. (A list of some texts, films, and Web sites from the course is included in the resource section on this book's Web site at www.xxx.xxx.)

With several caveats, the curriculum director and the principal quietly agreed to offer this course as a pilot model for independent study credit only. Students could sign up for the course if their schedules allowed, and they would acquire credit for it, but the credit would not count toward the English credits required to graduate. To teach the course, Ms. Barber-Just would need to fit it into her free period and continue to carry a regular English teacher's course load. She would not earn any additional pay. As a matter of fact, Ms. Barber-Just dropped her teaching contract down to less than full-time to make space for the Gay and Lesbian Literature course in her schedule. As a result, she was teaching the same number of courses and number of students for less pay.

Student Requests and Requirements

Word spread like wildfire among the student body about the new Gay and Lesbian Literature course, and the class quickly filled up, with a waiting list of students eager to take the course. During the first term that the course was offered, the students were excited and engaged in the work. They began to question why they were not gaining English department credit for the rigorous academic work. When the course was offered for a second term, the students urged Ms. Barber-Just to appeal for English credit on their behalf. It did not seem fair to them that they were reading five major novels, producing high-level writing, and attending all the classes, and yet not being awarded department credit. After reviewing the syllabus and the impressive academic accomplishments of the students in the class, the English department voted unanimously to award English department credit for the course.

A vote by the school board was needed to add a new class to the program of studies. Ms. Barber-Just compiled portfolios of student work to be reviewed by the school board. The student portfolios included analytical and reflective writing about the five major units of study and the accompanying five books, short stories, poetry, essays, films, and course discussions. The board approved the addition of the course to the official English department's study program.

Student Voices

The literary products in the student portfolios were superior according to many standards. The knowledge of historical events, social influences on literature, and writing techniques that they reflected were remarkable. But the most compelling facet of the students' work was the consistency with which they mentioned the power of giving voice to unspoken realities. Students wrote about their own biases and their own sexual orientations: gay, straight, and bisexual. They reflected on the importance of this course to support LGBT and questioning youth and to build understanding among heterosexual teens. They spoke of lack of information about the LGBT community and critiqued the misinformation of the mass media. Consistently, student reflections mentioned the safety of their classroom community and their commitment to be engaged in social justice. In some of the most moving pieces, students wrote their reflections in the form of letters to their parents.

As established throughout this book, the structural and organizational issues in schools greatly influence student learning. Educational researcher Jeannie Oakes has consistently reported evidence that the practice of tracking negatively influences most students. Her research findings, especially on how tracking in schools stratifies students by race and social class, have been confirmed by many other researchers and evident in thousands of students' lives. This Multicultural Teaching Story illustrates how the work of some determined teachers can transform the groupings of students for math classes. Bill Blatner's story points to four components that make his efforts successful: (1) dedication to students, academic identities, (2) access to robust curriculum resources, (3) respect for colleagues, and (4) a supportive administration.

Multicultural Teaching Story

Bill Blatner: Teaching Math with A Belief in Every Kid

When I spoke with Bill, he had been a high school math teacher for 14 years. In his previous career he had worked as a civil engineer, and made the transition to teaching because he wanted a connection with service to the community and because "it feels so rewarding." In the high school where Bill works, students have two possible pathways through the math curriculum. One pathway is considered a more traditional model in which students get sorted into math ability groups in seventh or eighth grade (and even earlier in some school districts) to travel a set trajectory of courses throughout high school with determined implications for their college course and life career choices. The other pathway in this school offers coursework in the Interactive Mathematics Program (IMP) which is explained on the IMP Web site:

> The IMP curriculum integrates traditional material with additional topics recommended by the NCTM Standards, such as statistics, probability, curve fitting, and matrix algebra. IMP units are generally structured around a complex central problem. Although each unit has a specific mathematical focus, other topics are brought in as needed to solve the central problem, rather than narrowly restricting the mathematical content. Ideas that are developed in one unit are usually revisited and deepened in one or more later units.*

This approach is intended for completely untracked teaching; Bill explained that "IMP was designed for heterogeneous classes," but in many schools, the structures in place do not allow for all-school heterogeneous math programming. An alternative method is to provide these two different pathways through math simultaneously: either the traditional approach or the heterogeneous. Bill expressed that he was "very happy we have made some progress on this whole concept of heterogeneous versus homogeneous classes. I feel we're at a delicate time in our school as we make a concerted effort to work through the difficult issues involved in the traditional-versus-reform approaches." He expressed deep respect for his colleagues who are working together to try to balance these two approaches. He maintains a broad understanding of the rationale that drives math department structures. Weaving these two math programs into the fabric of a high school math department requires esteem for one's colleagues and fair-minded strategies for working within a department that practices two different philosophical visions. Bill expressed overriding concern that all colleagues' perspectives be respected as the department moves forward with implementing both pedagogical structures. His high opinion of his administrator was palpable and it was apparent that strong leadership in his school provided avenues for collaborative change.

Bill simultaneously puts the needs of his students and his concerns for their overall academic identities front and center. "In IMP everybody is in the same room working on the same thing....this allows for activities that are designed to be accessible on a number of levels. It is an approach to group work that seeks to eliminate dominance and it works." He explained that students may enroll in IMP courses at the Honors level, but it differs from traditional math scheduling because the honors students are in the same room, working on the same problems with all students in IMP, with some curricular advances when appropriate for students enrolled in honors level. He pointed out the limits of the two parallel math programs in reflecting on the demographics of the IMP classes: "We never get the full spectrum of kids. ...so we have these two cultures in the school." Bill stated with conviction,

> There are good things we've accomplished for kids.... It is very hard to tell people why IMP is a good thing without it being compared. We should be doing heterogeneous classes. It is not right that we separate people in school in ways that reinforce all the divisions among people in society. A lot of people have figured that out and agree with it. So let's do heterogeneous classes! But guess what? It is hard...we do not have a lot of good models on how to do this. You cannot just throw all the kids together and say it's going to work. IMP is a good model that shows you it can be done. I have seen it work for so many kids.
>
> There was a girl who last year was in my year-1 class, who is a student with special education services, who *specifically* told me that she had problems with math. She turned out to be a really *great* thinker and *really* good problem solver. She was pretty fearless about coming up with her own ways of thinking about problems. We do these things called "Problems of the Week," and the idea is that there is a big complicated problem that can be approached in a number of different ways. The method of solution is not at all obvious when you first look at the problem...you can't say to yourself, "Well let's see, we are studying this concept this week, so I must have to use this to solve the problem." It is not like that. These problems of the week are often intentionally disconnected from what we are doing in class, so kids actually have to read a problem, understand it from wherever they are at, find a way into it, crash around with it, think about it, put it down, crash around some more. After a week and a half they have to go through a whole write-up discussing the process they went through and whatever solutions they came up with, justified in explanation.
>
> This ended up being one of her great strengths. She would do these really *long*, involved investigations of these things, and get up in class and present her work. She started to build up this confidence and I would go down and check on her now and then in her academic support class. She never would say she needed help. She would always have something to show me.
>
> This year, I looked over my roster and I was really happy she was going to be in my class again, and this year—she is taking it for honors! This was a special education student who was supposedly having problems with math.
>
> We just finished our first unit, and I am in the process of going through their portfolios. The way I assess them is we have a bunch of goals that students are supposed to obtain: things they are supposed to learn and know how to do, demonstrate perseverance, problem solving...as well as the content understandings and skills. They put together a portfolio of their work, with some things I tell them to include, some things that they decide on. Then I go through it with "Where's the evidence that you can do all these things?"

She has totally cleaned it—the WHOLE rubric—of items that needed to be mastered, skills to have, problem solving, putting together complicated problems, connecting a lot of different ideas, making decisions about which method to use—she just cleaned it! If she had been in our traditional course and had taken traditional algebra to geometry— she would have to take the jump from the traditional algebra to honors in the traditional program.... The jump is just a culture shock in the traditional model. There are so many topics covered in a short period of time...so for some kids, it is very difficult to make that transition. The further you go along, the harder it is to make that transition. By the time you get to algebra II or pre-calculus it is really hard to switch from one to the other. Whereas in IMP, I see the opposite. As we go along, I see more and more kids in the later years, after they've been going along, taking IMP for honors. As we go along, I see more and more kids saying, "I think I can do this—switch to honors."

Bill has been at this particular school teaching the IMP courses for over seven years, and he is witnessing some change in school culture regarding the stigma that was sometimes associated with students enrolled in IMP compared with the traditional path in mathematics.

I do not want to polarize people around this idea of IMP versus traditional. In our department we are striving to meet everything in the Common Core standards—in both programs. Everybody agrees we've got to do these standards, and we know what kids need to meet these. We are making progress in that direction.

We have students going from IMP to calculus and we've got kids doing various activities we have in our school like Math Olympiads and things like that. Kids from IMP are joining those. The kids are becoming much more confident about what they are doing now, despite the fact that people who don't know or understand IMP continue to characterize it as something other than "real math." There are significant differences in emphasis between IMP and the traditional program but I can tell you as a civil engineer who used math everyday and was on the hook for the solutions that IMP is very real math. I think our students are getting a better sense of how they are benefiting from IMP, how they can moved flexibly from the real and concrete to the symbolic and abstract. We do that really well and that ability to contextualize and decontextualize is fundamental to mathematical practice.

Bill Blatner and his colleagues' dedication to cultivating their students' academic identities was buttressed by a supportive administration willing to wrestle with the knotty and divisive issue of tracking in one school's mathematics department. In spite of divergent philosophical approaches in the two math pathways, and confounding issues with student scheduling, they respectfully collaborated to preserve access to robust curriculum resources for all students. He concluded his reflection:

What is important is giving kids that opportunity—not just allowing them to be in the same room, but doing it in a way that moves their thinking forward. They do not feel like they have to explain their choice to enroll in IMP to everybody. They know what they know.

IMP is a model that helps make this happen. But this isn't really about IMP. IMP is a package of curriculum resources and professional development that schools can use to advance a more equitable approach to math education. You have to have a number of elements in place-dedicated staff, the curriculum, professional development and administrative support.

You've also got to have the will and the belief that it should be done and it can be done.

*http://www.mathimp.org/ For more information about the Interactive Mathematics Program and its implementation, contact the IMP National Outreach Coordinator at 1-888-MATH-IMP (1-888-628-4467).

SNAPSHOT
Eugene Crocket

Usually I think of my family as an adoptive family more than a gay family.

Eugene Crocket,[1] a soft-spoken Irish American ninth-grader, carries himself in a poised manner that commands respect. He has a slight build and longish brown hair that falls into his eyes, which become animated and sparkle as he speaks. Eugene grew up in the rural New England community of Hilton and attends a regional high school in nearby Howardstown, with students from a variety of backgrounds. Eugene spoke at length about his best friend, a Tibetan student, and described how they are both active in an after-school club, Students for a Free Tibet.[2] In this snapshot, Eugene focuses on his experience of being adopted and raised by two gay dads, both of whom are European American.

There are six people in my family. I have three brothers and two dads. One of my dads, Tom, lives in Puerto Rico right now and sells real estate. My other dad, Ted, cleans houses. I call Tom **Dad** and Ted **Poppy,** like **Pop** but **Poppy**.

I am the youngest in the family. My oldest brother Ronnie is 21. Then there's Michael. He's 19. Mark, he's 17, and I'm 15. Ronnie lives in Howardstown and has his own apartment. Michael is getting his own apartment soon. Mark is going away to college, so pretty soon it's going to be just me at home. Ronnie and Mark are more into sports, but me and Michael like to play video games more.

Most people, if they look at my family, they might think it's weird or something. They might think it's odd because it's not the so-called ordinary family. Personally, I don't see being in my family as too much different because it's my family and I've known them my whole life. It's just regular to me, being in my family.

All four of [us] are biological brothers. My dads adopted all of us at the same time. I was six months old, and the others were three years old, four, and six. Ronnie probably remembers it most. Basically, our parents were getting into drugs and not able to take care of us. My oldest brother Ronnie was pretty much, like, he would feed me the bottle and change my diaper and stuff. My parents just weren't able to take care of us. I'm

not really sure if they sought the adoption agency, or if they were reported by a neighbor or something. We were foster kids and then we got adopted. There was a whole controversial thing in the community because my dads were in the newspaper a lot. They had to argue for being two gay men to get us. I guess they got threatened sometimes. I know they were in the newspaper a lot. This was in the early 1990s.

These days, I'm pretty comfortable talking about it. Not too many people ask, but my close friends pretty much already know about my two dads. I've told them why we were adopted. If I make friends with someone, and they get to know my family, then they might ask questions.

When I was around the age of 11 or 12, I would notice people looking at us. They could probably put together what our family is, like, "Huh, look at that." I felt different, and I didn't like it. Now if that happens, I don't really care.

Usually I think of my family as an adoptive family more than a gay family. In Hilton, there were three adoptive families in my grade, including me. I did feel different because the three of us were adopted, but I was the only one that had two dads. I didn't really mind that people knew I was adopted and stuff. But sometimes it was a little awkward telling them about my parents. So I felt different, and I didn't like having both my parents come to school. I wasn't ashamed, but more embarrassed. I don't know; I didn't want people to think of me as different. Now, my dad Tom, he lives in Puerto Rico, and Ted, he's not really involved with school or the PTA or whatever. Usually Ted is the one who goes to parent night. I know one other kid at my school now who has two moms, and I know this other girl who was adopted who also has lesbian moms.

At home everything is normal, like everyone else's family. Going out in public is a little more different. I was going to have a class get-together one time, in seventh grade. I wanted to have a bunch of friends over, but I was, like, "How about not at my house, guys," just because I didn't want them to see pictures or something. The sense of stress was only for that moment, so I just kept it to myself. If we're ever talking about family, I usually just say "my dad," rather than "my dads." Usually I try to get to know people well before I tell them that I have two dads, so I already know what their opinions are and stuff. I have to be pretty sure I can trust them before I can tell them. I did have one friend who was Christian. I used to be better friends with him, but now I'm not as good friends with him. I made sure not to tell him because of the Bible and all that. I don't know what he would have done, so I thought it best not to tell him.

At my high school, there's lots of using the word gay and the f-a-g word, like, "That's so gay." They don't actually mean it, but it's become like an insult or something. So homophobia isn't that bad in our school. It doesn't make me too uncomfortable, but it bothers me a little bit, though. If I know the person saying it, I might say something. It matters who says it.

At our school, we have a gay and lesbian literature class. We also have a Gay/Straight Alliance.[3] I think it's a good idea. I know some people in it. People might assume you were gay or lesbian if you joined it. I don't really know what the GSA does. It has maybe ten people in it, maybe more.

One time in Spanish class, we were doing the family words. My teacher was asking everyone about their mother and their father, and I didn't want to get called on. I didn't want her to be, like, "Oh, what does your mom do?" "I don't have a mom. I don't know." I didn't get called on; I lucked out. I probably would have just said, "I don't have a mom." Another time in high school, we had to do a family tree. The teacher said we didn't have to do our parents, we could do our grandparents and our aunts and stuff. I only put in one of my parents. But in fourth grade, when we had to do a family tree, I did put in both my dads. I always felt more comfortable in elementary school. We were doing the family tree on our heritage, and I did it based on my adoptive parents because they're the parents that I know.

Being in this family, I have learned to, if I see someone who is different, to not think of them as odd or weird, but to accept people for who they are. I try not to make stereotypes, like not ask people about their mom's name and their dad's name, because I know that not everyone has a mom and a dad. Stuff like that. If I have to fill out a form at school and it says "mother's name," I just cross that out and write "father's name." I haven't ever seen a teacher react to that.

My sixth-grade teacher, Ms. Kamp, she really helped me a lot. She made me more comfortable. I was really shy and she made me a lot more comfortable speaking to groups. Academically, I got better. If we had a topic like this, she would ask me if I felt comfortable with it, like if we talked about gay/lesbian stuff. She would ask me in private—like when people were talking, she would come over and whisper it to me. She was also my neighbor.

Commentary

Eugene's snapshot raises the issue of how children of gay and lesbian parents must negotiate "outing" themselves—and their parents—as members of families headed by gay parents. Even in liberal Howardstown, with its GSA and gay and lesbian literature class, issues of homophobia and limited understanding of what makes a family arise in school, causing students like Eugene to feel uncomfortable, if not unsafe. At the same time, Eugene reported feeling particularly supported by one teacher, Ms. Kamp, who perhaps knew him better than most because she was also his neighbor in their small town.

As one of four brothers who were all adopted as a sibling group, Eugene benefited from built-in emotional support at home. Other adopted children may feel more isolated, particularly if they are the only adopted child in their family. Even with his family support and his relatively tolerant school environment, Eugene's anecdotes about offensive putdowns and questions from insensitive teachers and classmates sharpen the discussion of homophobia in schools. Teachers can do a better job of monitoring the school environment for offensive language that sets students apart by being flexible, open, and inclusive in their approaches to both the pedagogy and curriculum.

Finally, Eugene's participation in the Tibetan club underscores the importance of choice. Concerned adults might assume that students like Eugene would be better served by joining the Gay/Straight Alliance or even a group specifically for children of gay/lesbian parents.[4] In this case, Eugene took comfort in his close friendship with a Tibetan student and preferred to join Students for a Free Tibet as one of only two white students in the group. Perhaps as he progresses through high school, Eugene may be drawn to GSA or another student group. The important note for school officials is making certain that schools provide a variety of outlets that address diverse student interests and various comfort levels.

(continued)

Notes

1. We appreciate the work of our friend and colleague Dr. John Raible, who interviewed Eugene and developed the introduction and commentary for the Snapshot.

2. Students for a Free Tibet is an international organization on college and high school campuses committed to nonviolent direct action in solidarity with the Tibetan people. For more information, go to www.studentsforafreetibet.org/.

3. The Gay/Straight Alliance Network provides resources and information on how to start a Gay/Straight Alliance in your school or community group; go to www.gsanetwork.org/index.html.

4. One such group for children of gay and lesbian parents is Gay, Lesbian, Straight Education Network (GLSEN).

Evolution of Curriculum

Multicultural curriculum is a process, as we described in Chapter 3; it grows organically along with the needs and struggles of the community. This is true of the Gay and Lesbian Literature course launched by Ms. Barber-Just. In response to student demands, the school added an extra section of the course each year. Advanced placement recognition (AP credit) may now be achieved through the Gay and Lesbian Literature course. What started out as an independent study offering became socially sanctioned knowledge—a school course—as English department credit, and optional AP credit, through the determination of high school students and the courage of a teacher.

One teacher and her students could not have made these changes in isolation, however. As Christine Sleeter points out, "While teachers have varying degrees of agency to construct multicultural curriculum, teachers also work in systems that institutionalize particular concepts of curriculum, learning, teaching and relationships."[25] While maintaining high academic standards, a stalwart department chair, a supportive principal, and ultimately a visionary school board recognized the needs of a community and acted with resolve to reshape the school curriculum, which continues to become more just and inclusive.

The Gay and Lesbian Literature course, now one of the most popular at the high school, reflects the needs and identities of students and families in the immediate community of the school, including LGBT and their straight allies. Perhaps more significantly, the curriculum is responding to the urgency of nationwide social change. Melinda Miceli's statement affirms this reality: "Today, LGBT and straight ally students are in a position to imagine the possibilities of change that they can accomplish by capitalizing on the progress made by the gay rights movement."[26] The "imagine[d] . . . possibilities of change" accomplished by Sara Barber-Just with so many students, families, colleagues, administrators, and school board members provides a model of fierce hopefulness in the ongoing process of making school curriculum—and society—more inclusive and just.

Conclusion

The determination to adapt curricula for multicultural classrooms is demonstrated by Bill Blatner's Multicultural Classroom Story as well as by the practice of the other teachers highlighted in the examples in this chapter. These teachers exemplify the multifaceted, complex process of meeting the needs of a diverse classroom. While considering the sociopolitical context of schooling, they illustrate how social justice and equity can be achieved while simultaneously meeting rigorous academic standards.

▰▰▰▰ To Think About

1. When you hear a student use the word *gay* as a putdown (or pejorative term sometimes invoked to insult LGBT identity), what is your response? What does that student learn from your response? What do other students learn from your response? How can you make it a teachable moment about vocabulary, human rights, and courage?

2. Many school structures that divide students by so-called ability appear to be impenetrable to a single teacher's efforts. If such structures are in place in your school, how can you adapt your curriculum to challenge those structures? Do you have to do it alone? What will be the long-term effects of the changes you make to your approach, your classroom, and your curriculum?

3. Do you call on families to participate in the curriculum? When does it happen? Is it around holiday celebrations? Heritage festivals? How can you expand the role of families in your classroom while including and honoring the families who may not be able to participate, or may feel uncomfortable doing so, in school activities?

▰▰▰▰ Activities *for Personal, School, and Community Change*

1. Study the demographics of your classroom, grade level, team, or school. Think about students' heritages and cultural backgrounds. Take note of a specific group about which you may have little knowledge or experience and commit to implementing some curriculum about it. How might you create a unit of study to deepen the understanding of this group's experience? How can you do this so that you do not "exoticize" the group or create greater isolation for the members of that group? The teachers of the unit about Cambodia started by educating themselves; they also realized that they would learn more by diving in, researching, and teaching with their students. Where will you begin in your own classroom? Draw in colleagues for support, co-teaching, content integration, and expansion of this idea.

2. Many teachers are challenged by the notion of implementing multicultural curriculum in the current standards-based climate. Start a teacher book-discussion group based on Christine Sleeter's book *Un-Standardizing Curriculum: Multicultural Teaching in the Standards-Based Classroom* (see note 18). Ask your principal, superintendent, curriculum director, parent–teacher organization, or local business to purchase the books. Meet at least once a month throughout the school year with the goal of each teacher designing a new unit, or redesigning a former curriculum unit with fresh ideas inspired by Sleeter's practical, yet revolutionary, approach.

3. LGBT identity continues to be a target of institutional and individual oppression. Collaborate with colleagues to make your school a safe zone for LGBT students and their families. Collect resources from GLSEN and PFLAG (see appendix) and create an action plan in your school for students to feel affirmed and protected. Educate yourself, colleagues, students, and administrators. Plan curriculum and community events to welcome, affirm, and express solidarity with LGBT students, family, and community members.

10

Affirming Diversity: Implications for Teachers, Schools, Families, and Communities

In spite of the fact that Manuel Gomes, whose case study appears at the end of Chapter 6, came from a large immigrant family that was struggling to make ends meet and survive in a new country, he had great faith in education. The youngest of 11 siblings and the first to graduate from high school, Manuel was facing the future with determination and hope. His story can serve as a lesson that students who live in even the most difficult circumstances can succeed academically.

> "I think [teachers] could help students, try to influence them, that they can do whatever they want to do, that they can be whatever they want to be, that they got opportunities out there. . . . Most schools don't encourage kids to be all they can be."
>
> —Manuel Gomes (interviewee, Chapter 6)

The case studies and snapshots you have read throughout this text provide concrete evidence that academic success and failure defy easy categorization and the conventional expectations that teachers, schools, and society may have of students from particular backgrounds. The experiences of these young people also point to specific home, school, community, and societal contexts that may contribute to learning. In reality, students do not achieve academic success on their own, but in conjunction with family, peers, teachers, schools, communities, and the larger society. Thus, in this chapter, we discuss how supportive learning environments, particularly in schools, can be promoted. This chapter also considers what it means to be an American and suggests a model of multicultural education that emerges from the seven characteristics defined in Chapter 2.

Lessons from Students: Maintaining and Affirming Identity

The racism and other forms of discrimination to which students are subjected in school and society are evident in several of the case studies. Discrimination is either overt—for example, when Kaval Sethi felt singled out for wearing a turban—or more subtle, for example, when James Karam's culture was invisible in school activities or when Gamini Padmaperuma felt intimidated about speaking Singhalese in public when he was younger. Rashaud Kates, Nini Rostland, and Latrell Elton expressed the weight of low expectations felt by many African American and multiracial students. In spite of overpowering and sometimes demoralizing attitudes, behaviors, policies, and practices, however, most of these students chose not to deny or abandon their culture or language. Instead, they tended to rely on them even more firmly, although with more nuanced and dynamic ideas about identity, and not necessarily in the school setting. These young people's reliance on their culture and language may shield them from the devaluation of their identities by schools and society.

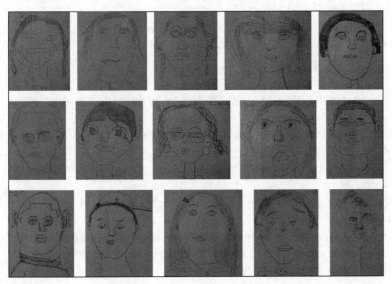

Luis Alvarado, Rodrigo Avila, Ella Banham, LaSonya R. Carson, Angelica Ariel Chavez, Stephanie E. Cobas, Isaiah Garcia, Jonathan Garcia, Mateo Lopez-Ortiz, Aleah Manning, Anaya Amanda Mateo, Breona Mitchell, Pamela Peraha, Louis Rosano, Ta'Nari Russell in Alicia Toro's visual arts class, Bronx Charter School for the Arts, The Bronx, NY. *Self-portraits*. Pencil drawings. 2007.

A few of the students had supportive school environments that accepted and built on their identities. In Savoun's case, teachers in his elementary schools supported his language through what he called *culture lessons*. Manuel felt that his bilingual program was an oasis of cultural support. Liane felt supported by her school in her effort to learn Chinese, her mother's native language. Their experiences reinforce the findings of extensive research that a pervasive and positive sense of cultural heritage is unmistakably related to mental health and social well-being.[1] The first lesson for schools seems to be that bilingual and multicultural programs can be a positive and integral component of the learning environment.

Supporting Native Language Approaches

Native language instruction has been a vital part of the educational landscape in the United States for many generations. In spite of growing linguistic diversity, however, approaches that use students' native languages have always been accompanied by great controversy, as we saw in Chapter 6. Too often, bilingual programs have been relegated, metaphorically speaking, to the space next to the boiler room in the basement or to a large unused closet.[2] In addition, bilingual teachers have been segregated programmatically and physically from other staff members, making both teachers and students feel isolated from the school community.

There needs to be a rethinking of the place for native-language use for language minority students. Promoting students' native language—whether through bilingual or English as a Second Language (ESL) programs, or even in nonbilingual settings in which teachers encourage students to use it among their peers and in their learning in general—helps make language minority students visible and respected in the school environment. Valuing their language made a difference for the young people in our case studies and snapshots, as they mentioned time and again. The seeming conversational English fluency of some students often misleads teachers into believing that these students can handle the academic rigors of cognitively demanding work in English. This is not always the case. For example, a major finding of researchers K. Tsianina Lomawaima and Teresa McCarty on Navajo bilingual programs found that students in grades K–6 who had the benefit of cumulative, uninterrupted initial literacy experiences in the Navajo language made the greatest gains on local and national measures of achievement.[3]

Some ways in which teachers and schools can support students for whom English is not a native language include the following:

- Encouraging parents to use the native language at home, by both speaking and reading it to their children.
- Allowing students to work in same-language groups for some cooperative learning activities.
- Encouraging students to use words in their native language when they don't know the equivalent words in English and to explain what they mean.
- Stocking the classroom with books and other reading materials in students' native languages.
- Asking students who are learning English to teach other students some of their home language.
- Making multilingual word charts in the classroom of commonly used words and phrases such as *pencil, crayon, book, please,* and *thank you* and asking students to bring in translations from their home language.
- Encouraging and allowing students to use their native language in the classroom and on the playground and school grounds.
- Promoting the learning of second languages among staff members by providing language classes for them in the school.

The case studies and snapshots make abundantly clear the positive results of maintaining native-language fluency in promoting the academic success of students, but bilingualism is also a worthy goal on its own and a valuable resource that should be supported. Programs promoting bilingualism are in constant jeopardy, yet it is foolhardy to do away with precisely the kinds of programs needed in a society with growing linguistic and cultural diversity and international interdependence. Certainly, the events of September 11, 2001, and subsequent wars and other events since then, are powerful reminders that we need to understand people in the international community. Language is one significant way to achieve this understanding.

Developing Comprehensive Multicultural Programs

Another key lesson from the case studies and snapshots is that multicultural education must be an integral part of the school experience of all students. This is not to imply that the interviewed students themselves recommended multicultural education. On the contrary, if they mentioned it at all, it was usually in the context of fairs, cookbooks, or other more superficial aspects and was certainly not in the comprehensive way it has been defined in this text. Given their experiences, this is all they knew about multicultural education. Yet when students are asked about the importance of addressing diversity in the schools, they tend to be supportive of such efforts. In the same way, the yearning in the voices of the students in our case studies and snapshots makes it clear that they wanted closer connections with their cultural identities, from Rebecca Florentina's gratitude for some of her teachers' support of the Gay/Straight Alliance (GSA) in her school, to Savoun Nouch's wish for continued "reading groups" in his language, to the case of David Weiss, whose snapshot follows. David longed to learn Spanish, the language of his ancestry.

Multicultural education can help new students adjust to the community and school and can also address the interethnic prejudice and hostility that are obvious in many schools. With the influx of large numbers of new immigrants, and with few appropriate programs to prepare either communities or schools for them, the problem is a serious one. Students' lack of understanding of cultures different from their own, false preconceptions about diverse groups of people they and their families may have brought from other countries, their internalizing of the negative ways in which differences are treated in our society, and the lack of information provided in the schools all serve to magnify the problem. Add to this the pecking order established in schools among different social and cultural groups, and the general reluctance of schools to deal with such knotty issues, and we are left with unresolved but chronic interethnic hostility.[4] This was poignantly illustrated by Savoun's descriptions of the violent racial tensions at his former school and his astonishment at the absence of gangs and feuding among different racial groups at his new school.

As we've discussed throughout this text, a growing body of research on multicultural education suggests that only by reforming the entire school environment can substantive changes in attitudes, behaviors, and achievement take place. Most schools have not undertaken such a comprehensive approach. When they do, they find that they need to modify the school culture itself, for example, by including strategies such as conflict resolution, cooperative learning, multicultural curriculum development, parent and community outreach, and the elimination of tracking. Such a comprehensive approach is needed, but it may also be fraught with potential conflict because it challenges traditions and ideologies that are at the very heart of schooling in the

SNAPSHOT
David Weiss

When he was interviewed, David Weiss* was 13 years old and a student in middle school. Adopted from Chile by a White Jewish family in the United States when he was just a few months old, he talked about what it meant to be adopted, biethnic, and bicultural. David was from the Mapuche Nation of Indigenous Americans, the largest indigenous group in Chile. He spoke English as his native language and learned to read Hebrew for his bar mitzvah. But he identified as Latino and he also wanted to learn Spanish, which he planned to take in school the following year because, as he said, "I was born in Chile, and I should know Spanish." David described some of the dilemmas and complexities of his hybrid identity.

My birth mother left a letter for me, which I have in the bank. I saw a picture of her. She said she didn't have enough money to raise two children and couldn't take care of me. That's why I was adopted.

Most people don't recognize me as Latino or Native American. They think I'm American and White. In looks, I am White, but inside, no: my blood is Chilean and Native American.

A teacher at school told me about another boy who's also from Chile and also adopted. Now we're friends. At first, I was surprised. It's kind of a coincidence because we were in Santiago at the same time. At first I didn't tell him I was from Chile. I got to know him, and then I told him. He said I didn't look like it. We used to talk about being adopted.

Most people know I'm adopted. I tell them. People think I look different from my mom. People notice my older brother's color more than mine. [His brother, also adopted, is darker.] One time in Health class, the teacher asked kids if they had any stories about their birth. Most kids had something to say. I didn't—I wouldn't share it, anyway. . . . Well, it depends.

If I could, I would join a school club for adopted kids and for different racial people. That way, I'd know more adopted people.

Commentary

David's snapshot presents a poignant example of the dilemmas inherent in issues of both hybrid identities and adoption. For example, David was clear about the fact that race and ethnicity are not so easy to determine. He said that what he looks like is not necessarily who he is inside or how he feels. This is an important insight, and it is especially crucial in the case of adopted children, who may not have any information about their ethnic backgrounds or birth parents. David's statement about joining a school club for adopted kids if one existed is a reminder that not all school clubs should be based on ethnicity, race, or hobbies. Having a place to "belong" is a need for all young people.

*We thank John Raible for interviewing David and helping to craft the snapshot.

United States. But this kind of comprehensive approach is, in the long run, the best guarantee that schools will become welcoming environments for all our students.

 **Support Beyond Academics**

As the case studies and snapshots make clear, when young people are involved in meaningful activities outside an academic context, whether in the school or community or in a combination of activities, including school clubs and sports, religious groups, and out-of-school hobbies, they find support that helps protect them from negative peer pressure and helps develop and reinforce their leadership and critical thinking skills. All schools, but particularly those at the secondary level, need to provide inclusive and meaningful activities that attract a wide range of students. Given the renewed emphasis on "the basics" that resulted from the educational reform movement that began in the 1980s and continues today, many schools have drastically cut or eliminated arts programs and minimized extracurricular activities.

Some reforms, particularly those focusing on "raising standards"—such as longer school days and fewer so-called frills such as music and art—have been felt most profoundly at schools serving economically deprived and culturally marginalized students. The negative results of eliminating arts programs in urban schools in the most economically strapped communities have been thoroughly documented in a position paper authored by The Arts Education Working Group and endorsed by more than 60 national arts and arts education advocacy organizations. This paper asserts that a child's education is not complete unless it includes the arts. Despite the fact that No Child Left Behind (NCLB) listed the arts among core academic subjects, the position paper points to the severe erosion of arts in schools in the decade following NCLB legislation and suggests: "Our nation needs schools to prepare students to meet the demands of the 21st century both for the students' sake and for the sake of our economy and our society. These demands cannot be met without comprehensive arts education in our nation's schools."[5]

Even in schools that provide extracurricular activities, a majority of students are not involved—for many reasons, ranging from lack of funds to schedule conflicts. For example, some sports programs, although presumably open to all, are in effect restricted to the students most able to afford them. Other programs meet after school and, because they provide no transportation, are available only to those who can get home on their own or who can rely on family or friends for transportation. Students who work after school are also unable to take part in these activities. In some cases, extracurricular activities reflect only one culture or language—although that may not be the intent of the programs—leading students of other backgrounds to perceive that they are not welcome. For example, Cambodian students who are interested in joining the soccer team may feel excluded because there are no other Cambodian students on the team, or Mexican American students in a bilingual program may want to work on the school newspaper but may not even attempt to join if the newspaper is written entirely in English. The main issue here is equal access. A school may claim that its activities are open to all students, but a policy statement is meaningless unless it is backed up in practice. Equal conditions of participation need to be established for all students.

Creating Affirming Environments for Learning

The students in our case studies and snapshots participated in environments in which they would fit in. These environments can be positive, as in the case of Yahaira Leon's work with the Mock Trial Club that led to engagement in the Junior Statesman Foundation, or the GSA for Rebecca Florentina, or they can be negative, as in the case of gang involvement for Savoun Nouch and Paul Chavez. There are several implications concerning what schools can do to provide positive environments that promote the achievement of all students. The following section explores what educational researchers have called mutual accommodation.[6]

Mutual Accommodation

A key question teachers and schools must ask themselves in their interactions with students—particularly those from diverse racial, ethnic, and linguistic backgrounds— is this: Who does the accommodating? This question gets to the very heart of how students from nondominant groups experience school every day. Dominant-group students rarely have to consider learning a new language to communicate with their teachers because they already speak the acceptable school language. The same is true of culture. Dominant-group students generally do not have to think about their parents' lifestyles and values because their families are the norm, as we saw in Vanessa Mattison's case. Students from other groups, however, have to consider such issues every day.

Some accommodation is, of course, necessary. If students and teachers spoke different languages at all times, operated under different goals and assumptions, and in general had varying expectations from those of the school, chaos would result. Students from nondominant groups and their families always expect to make some accommodations, which is clear in their willingness to learn English, their eagerness to participate in school life, and their general agreement with the rules of the game implicit in their social contract with the schools. But when does accommodation become acquiescence? Although nonmainstream students acknowledge the need to do some accommodating, they also recognize the benefits that accompany the affirmation of their languages and cultures.

The perspective of mutual accommodation allows schools and teachers to use the resources all students already have to work toward academic success. In this model, neither the student nor the teacher expects complete accommodation. Rather, they work together, using the best strategies at the disposition of each and, as a result, teachers and students are equally enriched. Using students' language, identities, and experiences as the basis for student learning might mean that teachers have to expand their own repertoires of teaching. Reorganizing the social structure of classrooms can facilitate significant improvements in prosocial development, academic achievement, and interethnic relations. Even students' attitudes and behaviors toward one another can be influenced in a positive way. Providing alternative means for learning is an essentially equitable endeavor, and it strengthens the democratic purposes of schooling.

An important lesson for teachers and schools is that, contrary to conventional wisdom and practice, it is not students and their families who must always do the accommodating. Mutual accommodation means that teachers and schools accept and build on students' experiences and identities, including their language, culture, and family knowledge, as legitimate expressions of intelligence and as the basis for learning. For students and families, mutual accommodation means accepting the culture of the school in areas such as expectations about attendance and homework and learning the necessary skills for academic achievement. Through this process, students, their families, teachers, and schools all benefit.

Teachers' Relationships with Students

Most teachers enter the teaching profession because of a sincere belief in young people and an eagerness to help them learn. However, many obstacles—including teachers' limited power, unresponsive administrators, classes that are too large, and the challenges of reaching students from a dizzying array of backgrounds—make teaching a very difficult job indeed. In spite of these challenges, developing healthy relationships with students is the best way to maintain the hope and joy that drew teachers to education in the first place.

Students in our case studies talked at length about teachers who made a difference in their attitudes toward school and their engagement with learning. Sometimes these teachers were from the same racial or ethnic background as the students themselves. Linda Howard spoke emphatically about the support she got from both her first-grade teacher, who was Black, and Mr. Benson, who was "mixed" like her. Given the general invisibility of many students' cultures and languages in the school environment, this kind of connection is healthy. One implication is that schools need to recruit teachers who share the cultural background of their students.

Teachers from students' racial, cultural, and ethnic backgrounds can make a significant contribution to the school, enriching both the environment and the curriculum, but an undue burden is sometimes placed on these teachers when they are seen as the representatives of their entire racial, ethnic, or linguistic group. Not only are they expected to be role models, but also they are increasingly called on to solve problems of cultural misunderstanding, translate letters, visit homes, chair the school's multicultural committee, and so on—usually with no extra compensation or recognition. The situation not only is unfair to these teachers but also may result in absolving the rest of the school staff of its responsibility for meeting the needs of all its students.

Schools have an obligation to aggressively recruit teachers who are as diverse as the student body, but this is something that, until now, has not been given national priority. When faculty members are from a variety of cultural backgrounds and are multilingual, students are more likely to perceive the significance of intellectual pursuits in their own lives. Nevertheless, all teachers, regardless of background, need to develop skills in multicultural communication and understanding. Their cultural knowledge and awareness, and their curricular and instructional accommodations, can make a major difference in student learning and engagement.

All teachers can become role models for all students as long as they are caring and knowledgeable about their students. One way in which teachers can build substantial relationships with students is by offering help to those who do not seek their aid. This issue arose numerous times during our case study interviews. The number of students who had absolutely no guidance in school was astonishing. For students who are the first in their families to go to college or even to graduate from high school, such help is indispensable because their families often have no prior experience from which to draw on when it comes to guiding their children. Students who are most vulnerable in terms of having access to college frequently receive the least help in schools, even when they are successful and have high aspirations for continued schooling. Research has confirmed the significance of teachers' support of their students' aspirations and goals. In a study using longitudinal data of a cohort of 11,000 adolescents, Robert Croninger and Valerie Lee investigated the benefits of teachers' guidance and support for students at risk for dropping out of high school. The researchers concluded that positive relations with teachers reduce the odds of dropping out, as do informal interactions with teachers outside the classroom. Even more significant, Croninger and Lee found that such guidance was especially crucial for students who have a history of difficulties at school.[7]

In contrast, the young people in our case studies and snapshots frequently pointed out the negative impact of low expectations. They said that they and their classmates were treated like babies; that the work teachers gave them was undemanding; and that any work, no matter how poor, was accepted. The attitude that students are incapable of performing adequately because they happen to be Black, speak a language other than English, or live in poverty may be widespread, but lowered expectations are not always conscious or based on negative intentions. Sometimes, lowering expectations is a teacher's way of adapting instruction to address student differences. Good intentions, however, do not always lead to positive results. Because such accommodations are based on the presumption that particular students are incapable of high-quality work due to language and cultural differences, they are patronizing at best.

The key lesson is that teachers and schools need to *raise,* rather than lower, expectations and standards for all students. High standards can be achieved in a great variety of ways, and not only through the standardized tests that are increasingly being used as the sole way to measure student learning. Multicultural education means finding and using culturally and linguistically relevant materials to develop students' cognitive skills. It also means using a variety of approaches in instruction. Raising standards and expectations does not require homogenizing instruction, but rather creating new and different opportunities for learning for all students.

Working with Families to Promote Student Learning

Very few of the parents and other family members mentioned in the case studies and snapshots were involved in school in any but the most superficial way, at least according to how parent involvement is generally defined. Few of them volunteered their time in school, went to meetings, or even visited the school on a consistent basis. The reasons for this lack of involvement were many, ranging from an inability to speak English to an inability to leave work during the day, to limited funds, to lack of previous experience with such activities, and to their own negative experiences with schooling.

If schools and teachers perceive parent involvement as simply involvement in what occurs in the school, the vital role families have in their children's academic success is overlooked. Educators must be concerned not just with the kinds of activities traditionally equated with school success, that is, having many books and toys in the home or attending cultural centers such as museums or going to plays. These are worthwhile activities, of course, but not all families have access to them, nor are they part of every family's repertoire. All families, however, *are* capable of providing intangibles such as consistent communication, high expectations, pride, understanding, and enthusiasm for their children's school experiences.

How did the parents of our case study students support their children's learning, and what can teachers learn from these examples? Although most did not help with homework, they monitored it and asked questions that demonstrated an interest in what their children were doing in school. They also provided support in other ways. For example, according to the students, the parents stressed the importance of going to school and going to college. Many of the students mentioned that their parents wanted them to have a better chance, to do better than they had done, and to have the opportunity for a good job. James talked about how his mother removed his brother from a class because she was unhappy with the way the teacher was treating him. Yahaira explained her mother's tenacious efforts to move the family into a better school district. Most of the families also continued to use their native language at home and to emphasize their family's cultural values, whether through religious observance; important family rituals; or deep-seated values such as family responsibility, respect for elders, and high academic aspirations. Rather than obstructing academic success, reliance on native language and culture helped promote it.

Teachers need to understand and support the kinds of activities in which these parents and other family members *were* involved in order to develop a more hopeful and democratic model of parent involvement, one that is within the reach of all students, despite the level of the schooling of their families, their socioeconomic background, or the language spoken at home. The Multicultural Teaching Story about the Boston Teachers Union School in Chapter 4 provides a robust example of second-grade teachers collaborating with family members to support children's literacy development. Unfortunately, however, the experiences and talents of families are not always taken into account, particularly in the case of families living in poverty and those who speak another language or come from a nondominant culture. The view that such families are unable to provide environments that promote learning can lead to condescending practices that reject the skills and resources that these families already have. These might include parenting classes that are patronizing, or nutrition and hygiene classes taught by "experts" that do not take into account the abilities of families.

A humorous example of patronizing attitudes such as these can be found in Esmeralda Santiago's novel *When I Was Puerto Rican* (a worthwhile book for adolescents, by the way, on the adaptation process faced by immigrants, in this case, a Puerto Rican girl). Santiago recounts how the mothers of the children in Miss Jiménez's class were asked to attend a meeting with experts from the United States who would teach them "all about proper nutrition and hygiene, so that we would grow up as tall and strong as Dick, Jane, and Sally, the *Americanitos* in our primers." At the meeting, the experts brought charts with foods, most of which, at the time, were unknown in the tropics, such as carrots, broccoli, iceberg lettuce, apples, pears, and peaches. On the other hand, the so-called experts did not bring any of the staples with which the mothers were familiar. "There was no rice on the chart, no beans, no salted codfish. There were big white eggs, not at all like the small round ones our hens gave us. . . . There were bananas but no plantains, potatoes but no *batatas* [sweet potatoes], cereal flakes but no oatmeal, bacon but no sausages." At the end of the meeting, the mothers received peanut butter, cornflakes, fruit cocktail, peaches in heavy syrup, beets, tuna fish, grape jelly, and pickles—none of which formed part of the Puerto Rican diet—and the mother of the protagonist, Negi, concluded, "I don't understand why they didn't just give us a sack of rice and a bag of beans. It would keep this family fed for a month."[8]

Such scenes, although humorous, are not uncommon. On the other hand, when parents are perceived to have resources that can aid their children's learning, the results are different. There is nothing wrong with information to help parents with the upbringing and education of their children when it is given with mutual respect, dialogue, and exchange. Parenting is hard work, and any help that teachers and schools can give parents is valuable, but it needs to be offered through two-way communication that inspires confidence and trust.

Expanding Definitions: What It Means to Be American

What it means to be an American is, in many ways, the quintessential American dilemma, yet historically it has not invited a deep or sustained critical conversation. Throughout our history, with successive generations of newcomers and conflicts with old-timers, either easy speculation or pat answers have been offered because there is an unstated assumption of what being an American means. When we question the assumed definition, a number of troubling contradictions emerge, particularly about questions of equality and social justice.

As movingly expressed by students in some of the case studies and snapshots, a number of young people have great difficulty accepting a split concept of self (what has commonly been called the hyphenated American). In our society, this dichotomy is common: one is either American or foreign, English-speaking or Spanish-speaking, Black or White. The possibility that one could, at the same time, be Spanish-speaking and English-speaking, Vietnamese and American, or Black and White is hardly considered. This is graphically illustrated in the constant media references to Barack Obama as the first African American, or Black, president. Rarely is he referred to as the first "mixed" or "multiracial" president. The chronic questions about his citizenship and whether he is a "real American" are even more illustrative, despite the fact that he was born in Hawaii to a White woman who hailed from Kansas, where he spent many of his formative years and where his White grandparents played a big part in his upbringing.

The designation of American has generally been reserved for those who are White and English-speaking. Others, even if they have been here for many years, have still been seen as separate. For example, no matter how many generations of an Asian family have been here and regardless of whether they speak only English and have little contact with their native heritage, they are not automatically considered American. Conversely, the same is usually *not* true for European Americans, even recent arrivals. Even Blacks who have been in this country for hundreds of years are sometimes seen as quite separate. Racism has always been implicated in the acceptance or rejection of particular groups in U.S. society.

Challenging "Heartbreaking Dilemmas"

As we can see, then, for a variety of reasons, the definition of *American*, as currently used, may effectively exclude those who are least powerful. As such, it legitimates the cultural, economic, and political control and hegemony of those who are already dominant in U.S. society. Our present and future diversity demands an expanded and inclusive definition—not hyphenated Americans, implying split and confused identities. *African-American* might imply a bifurcated identity, whereas *African American* signifies that a new definition is possible—one that emphasizes not confusion or denial, but acceptance and inclusion.

In the past, to become Americanized meant not only learning English but also rejecting one's native language, not only learning the culture but also learning to eat, dress, talk, and even behave like the European American model. As so poignantly expressed by a writer describing the experience of Jews in New York about 100 years ago, "The world that we faced on the East Side at the turn of the [20th] century presented a series of heartbreaking dilemmas."[9] To go through the process of Americanization too often meant the inevitable loss of a great part of oneself in the bargain. These heartbreaking dilemmas still exist today, as we have seen in the case studies and snapshots. A hundred years ago, the choice was generally made in favor of assimilation. Although no less difficult today, the choices are not as limited as they once were. There are two major reasons for this. First, the civil rights movement and related movements for women's ethnic and lesbian, gay, bisexual, and transgender (LGBT) rights, among others, have led to more freedom in asserting one's identity because they have transformed the sociopolitical and historical contexts in which such decisions are made. Second, the number and diversity of immigrants in the United States in the past three decades has been unequaled in our history. These changes are profoundly affecting the meaning of assimilation.

Toward Additive Multiculturalism

In some ways, the students currently enrolled in our schools are more fortunate than previous generations of students because they have more freedom to determine what to do about their language and culture, but the choice may still be a painful one. On one hand, if they choose to identify with their ethnic background, they may feel alienated from this society; on the other hand, if they identify with U.S. culture, they may feel like traitors to their family and community.

These choices are quite rigid: one is either true to oneself and family, or one is an American. This can be compared to what Wallace Lambert has called *subtractive bilingualism*, that is, the kind of bilingualism that develops at the expense of one's native language.[10] This kind of bilingualism means that one does not really become bilingual at all but rather goes from being monolingual in one language to being monolingual in another, although sometimes vestiges of the original language may remain. Multiculturalism, too, is subtractive if it allows only a transition from being monocultural in one culture to being so in another. Ned Seelye described this dilemma: "One can escape appearing culturally different by forfeiting one of the two cultures—and there is always considerable pressure on economically and politically

subservient groups to make this sacrifice—but trading one brand of monoculturalism for another seems an unnecessarily pallid business."[11]

The opposite of subtractive multiculturalism can be called *additive multiculturalism*. We have seen that children who achieve fuller bilingual development enjoy
cognitive advantages over monolinguals, so it makes sense that those who reach a
state of additive multiculturalism also enjoy advantages over monoculturals, including a broader view of reality, feeling comfortable in a variety of settings, and multicultural flexibility.

Expanding the definition of *American* may help students and others facing the
dilemma of fitting into a multicultural society by providing alternatives to self-
identification, as well as social and national identification. The students in our case
studies and snapshots, as well as many others, would have more choices than before
and would no longer face such "heartbreaking dilemmas" to the same extent that
they currently do. European Americans would no longer be considered the only true
Americans. *E pluribus unum* can no longer mean that cultural differences have to
be denied in order to foster a false unity. Neither is complete cultural maintenance
a realistic choice because it implies that native traditions should be preserved in a
pure and idealized state without the interdependence that is both necessary and
inevitable in a pluralistic society.

No longer a choice between assimilating or not, the question now is "How far
can society, and the institutions of society such as schools, accommodate the changing definition of *American*?" It is probably the first time in our history that this question has been asked in more than a rhetorical way. The view of the United States as
a monolithic, monocultural, and monolingual society is being challenged daily, as
seen in the wide use of languages other than English by an increasing percentage
of the population, and by the ease and conviction with which growing numbers of
people are claiming their identities as vital resources to be nurtured and maintained.
The fact that this question can even be posed places us in a unique historical
moment; in the past, such possibilities could not be seriously considered. Therefore,
the view that schools must be the obligatory assimilators of students is being disputed.

The boundaries of pluralism, formerly delimited by an Anglocentric definition,
were being vigorously questioned during the last quarter of the twentieth century.
Since September 11, 2001, there has been some backsliding on the issue of what it
means to be an American, with more rigid views expressed than we have seen in
some time. Policies such as "English Only" and anti-immigrant sentiments are gaining strength, and there is less patience with diversity in some quarters. Because of
the social and historical global context in which we are living, however, these perspectives and policies are, in the long run, ineffective.

In an insightful essay on assimilation written nearly four decades ago, William
Greenbaum proposed two reasons why assimilation occurred so quickly in the past:
one was *hope*, and the other was *shame*. Hope contributed in a major way by holding out the promise of equality, economic security, and a safe haven from war and
devastation. Nonetheless, according to Greenbaum, shame was the "main fuel" for
the American melting pot: "The immigrants were best instructed in how to repulse
themselves; millions of people were taught to be ashamed of their faces, their

family names, their parents and grandparents, and their class patterns, histories and life outlooks."[12]

Shame is no longer acceptable to a growing number of people, and it should not be acceptable in schools either. The students in the snapshots and case studies challenge what it means to be an American. Not content to accept past limitations, they provide evidence that an evolution is taking place. They are still caught in the conflict and uncertainties of how to expand their possibilities, but these young people are increasingly sure of who they are. They are determined to define their own identities—identities that are different from their parents but not restricted to the old, static definition of *American* that has been available up to now. They are, in a word, determined to become "true Americans," a broader conception of this term as defined in a recent book by legal scholar Rosemary Salomone.[13] As long as there are newcomers and as long as there are those who refuse to be included in a definition that denies them both their individual and group identities, the question of what it means to become American will be with us. The challenge for us as a society is to make room for everyone.

Levels of Multicultural Education

If, indeed, we reject past limits on what it means to be an American, we need to consider how multicultural education can be incorporated in a natural and inclusive way into curricula and instruction.

Starting Out

How does a school or a teacher achieve a multicultural perspective? To say that multicultural education must be comprehensively defined, pervasive, and inclusive is not to imply that only a full-blown program qualifies. Because multicultural education is a process, it is always changing and never quite finished. Multicultural education is also critical pedagogy, meaning that it is necessarily dynamic. A static program-in-place or a slick, packaged program is contrary to the very definition of multicultural education.

We illustrate with an example from Susan Barrett, who was a talented high school English teacher in a community of European American (primarily Irish, French, and Polish) and Puerto Rican students. Many years ago, when asked how she included a multicultural perspective in her teaching, Susan replied that she had not yet reached that level; rather, she said, her classroom had what she called *bicultural moments*. As a proponent of multicultural education, she used inclusive curriculum and instructional strategies that emerged from this perspective. However, she felt that the children in her classes did not even know about their own or one another's backgrounds, let alone about the world outside their communities, so her curriculum focused on exploring the "little world" of her students' community before venturing beyond it.

In their enthusiasm to incorporate a multicultural philosophy in their teaching, teachers can sometimes forget that their classrooms are a rich source of cultural knowledge. Yet students often know very little about their own culture or those of their classmates. *Starting out small,* then, means being sensitive to bicultural moments and using them as a beginning for more wide-ranging multicultural education.

Becoming a Multicultural Person

Developing truly comprehensive multicultural education takes many years, in part because of our own monocultural education. Most of us, in spite of our distinct cultural or linguistic backgrounds, were educated in monocultural environments. We seldom have the necessary models for developing a multicultural perspective. We have only our own experiences, and no matter what our background, these have been overwhelmingly Eurocentric and English-speaking.

Becoming a multicultural teacher, therefore, means first becoming a multicultural person. Without this transformation of ourselves, any attempts at developing a multicultural perspective will be superficial and incomplete. However, becoming a multicultural person in a society that values monoculturalism is not easy. It means reeducating ourselves in several ways.

First, *we simply need to learn more.* We need to be involved in activities that emphasize pluralism. We also need to look for books and other materials that inform us about people and events we may know little about. Because of the multicultural nature of our society, these materials are widely available, although sometimes we have "learned" not to see them.

Second, *we need to confront our own racism and biases.* It is impossible to be a teacher with a multicultural perspective without going through this process. Because we are all products of a society stratified by race, gender, class, and language, among other differences, we have all internalized some negative messages in one way or another. Sometimes, our biases are unconscious, as in the case of a former student who referred to Africans as *slaves* and Europeans as *people* but was horrified when this was pointed out to her. Sometimes the words we use convey deep-seated stereotypes, as when students who do not yet speak English are characterized as "not having language," as if they did not speak any language. Our actions also carry the messages we have learned, for example, when we automatically expect that our female students will not do as well in math as our male students. Our own reeducation means not only learning new things but also *un*learning some of the old. In the case of LGBT students, for example, it is common for both teachers and students to make statements such as "I don't care what they are, as long as they don't bring it into the classroom," as if the identities of LGBT students should be erased because they make other people uncomfortable. In all these cases, the process of confronting our own racism and biases can be difficult and painful, but it is a necessary part of becoming multicultural.

Third, *becoming a multicultural person means learning to see reality from a variety of perspectives.* Because traditional education has frequently reinforced the message that there is only one "right answer," we have developed only one way of seeing things. A multicultural perspective demands just the opposite. Reorienting ourselves in this way can be exhausting and difficult because it requires a dramatic shift in our worldview. Although the transformation of individuals from monocultural to multicultural will not, by itself, guarantee that education will become multicultural, it will lay the groundwork.

A Model of Multicultural Education

A monocultural perspective reflects a fundamentally different framework for understanding diversity than does a multicultural one. Even multicultural education, however, has a variety of levels of support for pluralism. We classify them into at least four levels: *tolerance*; *acceptance*; *respect*; and *affirmation, solidarity, and critique*. In the process of becoming multicultural, we need to consider these levels of multicultural education and how they might look in schools. These categories should be viewed as dynamic and permeable. Our purpose in creating this model is to demonstrate the various ways in which multicultural education can be implemented in schools. Please keep in mind, however, that whenever we classify and categorize reality, as we do in this model, we run the risk that it will be viewed as static and arbitrary rather than as messy, complex, and contradictory, which we know it to be.

In what follows, we propose a model, ranging from monocultural education to comprehensive multicultural education, based on the seven characteristics of multicultural education described in Chapter 2. This model explores how multicultural education pays attention to many components of the school environment and takes different forms in different settings.[14]

1. *Tolerance* is the first level of support for pluralism. To be tolerant means to have the capacity to bear something, although at times it may be unpleasant. To tolerate differences means to endure them, although not necessarily to embrace them. We may learn to tolerate differences, but this level of acceptance can be shaky because what is tolerated today can be rejected tomorrow. Therefore, tolerance represents the lowest level of multicultural education in a school setting, yet many schools have what they consider very comprehensive mission statements that stress tolerance in striving for diversity. Although the schools may believe that these mission statements are adequate expressions of support, they do not suffice. In terms of school policies and practices, tolerance may be viewed as having to bear linguistic and cultural differences as the inevitable burden of a culturally pluralistic society. When this is the perspective, programs that do not build on differences but rather replace them—for example, ELL programs—may be superficial at best. Black History Month might be commemorated with an assembly program and a bulletin board, but the acknowledgment of African Americans would stop there. The lifestyles and values of students' families, if different from the majority, may be considered by schools to require modification.

2. *Acceptance* is the next level of support for diversity. If we accept differences, at the very least, we recognize their significance. In concrete terms, programs that acknowledge students' languages and cultures are visible in the school if diversity is accepted. These programs might include a transitional bilingual program that uses the students' primary language, at least until they are "mainstreamed" into an English-language environment. Acceptance of diversity might also be reflected in the celebration of some differences through activities such as multicultural fairs and cookbooks. In a school with this level of support for diversity, time might be set aside weekly for "multicultural programs," and parents' native languages might be used for communicating with them through newsletters.

3. *Respect* is the third level of multicultural education. *To respect* means to admire and hold in high esteem. When diversity is respected, it is used as the basis for much of the education offered. This might mean offering programs of bilingual education that employ students' native language not only as a bridge to English but also throughout their schooling. Frequent and positive interactions with parents would take place. In the curriculum, students' values and experiences would be used as the basis for their literacy development. Students would be exposed to different ways of approaching the same reality and, as a result, they would expand their way of looking at the world. *Additive multiculturalism* would be the ultimate goal for everybody.

4. *Affirmation, solidarity, and critique,* which we consider the highest level of support for diversity, is based on the premise that the most powerful learning happens when students work through their differences, even if it is sometimes difficult and challenging. This means accepting the various cultures and languages of students and their families as legitimate and embracing them as valid vehicles for learning. It also means understanding that culture is not fixed or unchangeable and that it can be held up to scrutiny and criticized. Because multicultural education is concerned with equity and social justice for all people, and because basic values of different groups are sometimes diametrically opposed, conflict is inevitable. What makes this level different from the others is that conflict is not avoided but accepted as an inescapable part of learning. Passively accepting the status quo of any culture is inconsistent with multicultural education. Simply substituting one cultural myth for another contradicts the basic tenets of multicultural education because no group is inherently superior or more heroic than any other. At this level, students not only "celebrate" diversity, but also they reflect on and challenge it. As expressed by Mary Kalantzis and Bill Cope, multicultural education "needs to consider not just the pleasure of diversity but more fundamental issues that arise as different groups negotiate community and the basic issues of material life in the same space—a process that equally might generate conflict and pain."[15] Such fundamental issues may be difficult and even impossible to reconcile, and they might include different values about respect, authority, family, and gender roles, to name just a few.

Multicultural education without critique keeps cultural understanding at the romantic or exotic stage. If we are unable to transcend our own cultural experience through reflection and critique, we cannot hope to understand and critique that of others. For students, this process begins with a strong sense of solidarity with others who are different from themselves. When based on deep respect, critique is not only necessary but also, in fact, healthy. Without critique, the danger that multicultural education might be used to glorify myths into static "truth" is very real.

In the school, affirmation, solidarity, and critique means using students' identities in a consistent, critical, comprehensive, and inclusive way. This goes beyond creating ethnic enclaves, which can become exclusionary and selective, although for disenfranchised communities, this might certainly be a step in the process of implementing multicultural education. To achieve the highest level of support for diversity (affirmation, solidarity, and critique), schools must develop multicultural settings in which all students feel reflected and visible, for example, through two-way bilingual programs in which two languages are used and maintained meaningfully in the academic setting. The curriculum would be characterized by inclusiveness, offering a wide variety of content and perspectives. Teachers' attitudes and behaviors would reflect only the very highest expectations for all students. Instructional strategies would also include a range of means to teach students. Families would be welcomed and supported in the school as students' first and most important teachers. Their experiences, viewpoints, and suggestions would be sought and incorporated into classroom and school programs and activities. In turn, families would be exposed to a variety of experiences and viewpoints different from their own, which would help them expand their horizons, too. Other ways in which these four levels might be developed in schools are listed in Table 10.1.

Of course, multicultural education cannot be categorized as neatly as this table would suggest. This model simply represents a theoretical way of understanding how different levels of multicultural education might be visible in a school. It also highlights that, to be most effective, multicultural education needs to be a pervasive philosophy and practice. Although any level of multicultural education is preferable to the education offered by a monocultural perspective, each level more vigorously challenges a monolithic and ethnocentric view of society and education.

The fourth level—affirmation, solidarity, and critique—is also the most difficult to achieve for some of the reasons mentioned previously, including the lack of models of multicultural education in our own schooling and experiences. It is here that we educators are most confronted by values and lifestyles different from our own and with situations that severely test the limits of our tolerance. Interacting with people who are different from us in hygienic practices, food preferences, and religious rites can be trying. It is also extremely difficult, and at times impossible, to understand and reconcile cultural beliefs and practices that run counter to our most deeply held beliefs. For example, suppose we believe strongly in equality of the sexes and have in our classroom children whose families value males more highly than females, or who believe that education is a frill and not suitable for their children, or we have children in our classes whose religion forbids them to take part in any school activities except academics—all of these situations test our capacity for affirmation and solidarity.

Culture is not static, nor is it necessarily positive or negative. The cultural values and practices of a group of people reflect their best strategies for negotiating their environment and circumstances at a particular historical moment. What some groups have worked out as appropriate strategies may be considered unsuitable or even barbaric and uncivilized by others. Because each cultural group has developed in a different context, we can never reach total agreement on the best or most appropriate ways in which to lead our lives.

One way to tackle this dilemma is to emphasize the indisputable human and civil rights of all people. These rights guarantee that all human beings be treated with dignity, respect, and equality. Sometimes the values and behaviors of a group so seriously challenge these values that we cannot accept or tolerate them. If the values we, as human beings, hold most dear are based on extending rather than negating rights, we must decide on the side of these more universal values.

TABLE 10.1 Levels of Multicultural Education

Characteristics of Multicultural Education		
	Monocultural Education	**Tolerance**
Antiracist/ antidiscriminatory	Racism is unacknowledged. Policies and practices that support discrimination are left in place. These include low expectations and refusal to use students' natural resources (such as language and culture) in instruction. Only a sanitized and "safe" curriculum is in place.	Policies and practices that challenge racism and discrimination are initiated. No overt signs of discrimination are acceptable (e.g., name calling, graffiti, blatantly racist and sexist textbooks or curriculum). English as a second language (ESL) programs are in place for students who speak other languages.
Basic	Defines education as the 3 Rs and the "canon." "Cultural literacy" is understood within a monocultural framework. All important knowledge is essentially European American. This Eurocentric view is reflected throughout the curriculum, instructional strategies, and environment for learning.	Education is defined more expansively and includes attention to selected information about other groups.
Pervasive	No attention is paid to student diversity.	A multicultural perspective is evident in some activities, such as Black History Month and Cinco de Mayo, and in some curriculum and materials. There may be an itinerant "multicultural teacher."
Important for all students	Ethnic and/or women's studies, if available, are only for students from that group. This is a frill that is not important for other students to know.	Ethnic and women's studies are only offered as isolated courses.
Education for social justice	Education supports the status quo. Thinking and acting are separate.	Education is somewhat, although tenuously, linked to community projects and activities.
Process	Education is primarily content: "who," "what," "where," "when." The "great White men" version of history is propagated.	Education is both content and process. "Why" and "how" questions are tentatively broached.
Critical pedagogy	Education is domesticating. Reality is represented as static, finished, and flat.	Students and teachers begin to question the status quo.

Characteristics of Multicultural Education		
Acceptance	**Respect**	**Affirmation, Solidarity, and Critique**
Policies and practices that acknowledge differences are in place. Textbooks reflect some diversity. Transitional bilingual programs are available. Curriculum is more inclusive of the histories and perspectives of a broader range of people.	Policies and practices that respect diversity are more evident, including maintenance bilingual education. Ability grouping is not permitted. Curriculum is more explicitly antiracist and honest. It is "safe" to talk about racism, sexism, and other examples of discrimination.	Policies and practices that affirm diversity and challenge racism are developed. There are high expectations for all students; students' language and culture are used in instruction and curriculum. Two-way bilingual programs are in place wherever possible. Everyone takes responsibility for challenging racism and discrimination.
The diversity of lifestyles and values of groups other than the dominant one are acknowledged in some content, as can be seen in some courses and school activities.	Education is defined as knowledge that is necessary for living in a complex and pluralistic society. As such, it includes much content that is multicultural. *Additive multiculturalism* is the goal.	Basic education *is* multicultural education. All students learn to speak a second language and are familiar with a broad range of knowledge.
Student diversity is acknowledged, as can be seen not only in "Holidays and Heroes" but also in consideration of different learning preferences, values, and languages. A "multicultural program" may be in place.	The learning environment is imbued with multicultural education. It can be seen in classroom interactions, materials, and the culture of the school.	Multicultural education pervades the curriculum, instructional strategies, and interactions among teachers, students, and the community. It can be seen everywhere: bulletin boards, the lunchroom, assemblies, and so on.
Many students are expected to take part in curriculum that stresses diversity. A variety of languages are taught.	All students take part in courses that reflect diversity. Teachers are involved in overhauling the curriculum to be more open to such diversity.	All courses are completely multicultural in essence. Students of all backgrounds are visible in all aspects of the school, curricular, co-curricular and extra-curricular.
The role of the schools in social change is acknowledged. Some changes that reflect this attitude begin to be felt: students take part in community service.	Students take part in extensive community activities that reflect their social concerns.	The curriculum and instructional techniques are based on an understanding of social justice as central to education. Reflection and action are important components of learning. The community's concerns are evident in school activities.
Education is both content and process. "Why" and "how" questions are stressed more. Knowledge of, and sensitivity to, students of all backgrounds are more apparent.	Education is both content and process. Students and teachers begin to ask, "What if?" Teachers build strong relationships with students and their families.	Education is an equal mix of content and process. It is dynamic. Teachers and students are empowered. Everyone in the school is becoming a multicultural person.
Students and teachers are beginning a dialogue. Students' experiences, cultures, and languages are used as one source of their learning.	Students and teachers use critical dialogue as the primary basis for their education. They see and understand different perspectives.	Students and teachers are involved in the "subversive activity of real learning." Decision-making and social action skills are the basis of the curriculum.

This brings us to a final consideration: *Multicultural education is not easy. If it were, everyone would be doing it.* Resolving conflicts about cultural differences is difficult and sometimes impossible. The extent to which our particular cultural lenses may keep us from appreciating differences can be very great. Also, some values are simply irreconcilable, and we need to accept this fact. Usually, however, accommodations that respect both cultural values and basic human rights can be found. Because societies have generally resolved such conflicts in only one way, that is, favoring the dominant culture, few avenues for negotiating differences have been in place. Multicultural education, although at times difficult, painful, and time consuming, can provide one way of attempting such negotiations.

Balancing Hope and Despair

Anything less than a program of comprehensive multicultural education will continue to shortchange students in our schools. Beginning with the Common School Movement in the late nineteenth century and stretching into the present, our society has promised all students an equal and high-quality education, but teachers who began teaching after the civil rights movement came to an end have not heard this message proclaimed very loudly. Educational results have belied the promise of educational equality. Students most victimized by society, that is, those from economically poor and culturally and linguistically dominated groups, are also the most vulnerable in our schools. Their societal status tends to be replicated in the schools. Unless our educational system confronts inequity at all levels and through all school policies and practices, we will simply be proceeding with "business as usual."

The case studies and snapshots in this book underscore the central role of schools in promoting academic success for all students and multicultural education as a promising means to achieve this goal. *Affirming Diversity,* the title of this book, is at the core of multicultural education. It implies that cultural, linguistic, and other differences can and should be accepted, respected, and used as a basis for learning and teaching. Rather than maladies to be cured or problems to be confronted, differences are a necessary starting point for learning and teaching, and they can enrich the experiences of students and teachers.

Affirming diversity is not enough unless we also challenge inequitable policies and practices that grant unfair advantages to some students over others, and that is the point of the subtitle of this book, *The Sociopolitical Context of Multicultural Education.*[16] Simply tackling issues of racism and discrimination at the school level does little to change the broader context. Although improvement in education must take place at the school level, changing the school alone will not lead to substantive changes in society. Schools have often been sites of protest, resistance, and change, and their role in influencing public policy has sometimes been significant. However, racism, classism, ethnocentrism, sexism, linguicism, ableism, heterosexism, religious oppression, and other forms of discrimination exist in schools because they exist in society. To divorce schools from society is impossible. Although schools may, with all good intentions, attempt to provide learning environments free from bias, after students leave the classroom and building, they are again confronted with an unequal society.

Teachers, schools, and students engaged in challenging social inequities need to understand that they are involved in a struggle that critiques and questions the status quo not only of schools but also of society. They will inevitably be involved in what Mildred Dickeman, nearly four decades ago, described as "a subversive task" if they are serious about facing issues of cultural pluralism in schools.[17] Her perspective defies the simple definition of multicultural education as celebratory, implying a more complex understanding of differences.

A balance between hope and despair is difficult to maintain, yet that is precisely what is required. Multicultural education is not a remedy for social inequality, and it cannot guarantee academic success. At the same time, if one of the primary purposes of education is to teach young people the skills, knowledge, and critical awareness to become productive members of a diverse and democratic society, a broadly conceptualized multicultural education can have a decisive influence. Although racism cannot be wiped out by schools, the role that schools can play should not be underestimated. By developing antiracist and affirming policies and practices, schools can make a genuine difference in the lives of many students.

Final Thoughts

The student body in U.S. schools is becoming more diverse than ever before, reflecting more racial, cultural, linguistic, and social class differences. But our ability to understand these differences and to use them in constructive ways is still quite limited. Multicultural education is one significant way to address diversity, but we should not think of it as a superficial set of activities, materials, or approaches. Although it would have been easy to do in this book, we have resisted presenting cookie-cutter lesson plans or activities because such an approach can overlook or downplay the school conditions that produce and sustain unequal academic outcomes in the first place. In fact, we would go so far as to say that a prepackaged series of lesson plans is in direct conflict with the goals of a comprehensive multicultural education. If the purpose of education is to prepare young people for productive and critical participation in a democratic and pluralistic society, then the activities, strategies, and approaches we use in their instruction need to echo these concerns. Thus, in addition to recognizing the growing diversity of the student body, educators cannot overlook the stratification of society, which profoundly affects the schooling of students. The cultural and linguistic differences that students bring to school, along with how these differences are perceived, also need to be addressed through the curriculum and instruction. To act as if race, social class, ethnicity, religion, native language, sexual orientation, and other differences are immaterial to schooling is disingenuous. It is only by addressing all these issues in a systematic way through the curriculum, instruction, and other practices that real change will happen.

In the final analysis, multicultural education is a moral and ethical issue. The current conditions in our world call for critical thinkers who can face and resolve complex issues—problems such as war, ethnic polarization, poverty, contamination of our natural resources, and rampant racism—in sensitive and ethical ways. We need all the help we can get to solve these problems, and using the talents and strengths of all young people is crucial. If we believe that all students are capable of brilliance; that they can learn at high levels of achievement; and that the cultural and linguistic resources they bring to school are worthy of respect, affirmation, and solidarity, then multicultural education represents a far more principled approach for our schools than does monocultural education.

To Think About

1. Three different models for understanding pluralism (or the lack of it) are the following:

    *   *Anglo-conformity:* All newcomers need to conform to the dominant European American, middle-class, and English-speaking model.
    *   *"Melting pot":* All newcomers "melt" to form an amalgam that becomes American.
    *   *"Salad bowl":* All newcomers maintain their languages and cultures while combining with others to form a "salad," which is our unique U.S. society.

    Form three groups, with each group taking one of the previous options and arguing that it represents the dominant ideology in U.S. society. Have each group give concrete examples. Afterward, in a large group, decide if one of these ideologies is really the most apparent and successful. Give reasons for your conclusions. How would you critique each of these ideologies? What are the advantages and disadvantages of each?

2. What are schools for? To determine the *function* of schools, investigate the *structure* of schools. Given the following objectives of education, work in small groups to design a school to achieve each one.

    *   The purpose of schools is to "Americanize" or assimilate all students to the American way of life.
    *   The purpose of schools is to prepare a few good managers and a lot of good workers.
    *   The purpose of schools is to develop critical thinkers.
    *   The purpose of schools is to prepare citizens of all backgrounds for active participation in a democratic society.

    Explore how a school founded on one of these goals might function. Describe the curriculum, materials, administration, community outreach, and structure in the school you design. Working together in the groups, compare the differences among the four hypothetical schools. Then compare each of these schools to schools with which you are familiar. What can we learn from these comparisons?

3. Define *American.*

4. Mildred Dickeman (see note 17) has suggested that teachers are engaged in "a subversive task" if they challenge the monocultural curriculum and other inequities of schools. What does she mean? Do you agree?

Activities *for Personal, School, and Community Change*

1. With a group of colleagues, think about some of the ways extracurricular activities in your school limit the participation of students. Consider sports, the newspaper, the student government, and other activities. How can your school become more inclusive? Share your ideas with the parent–teacher organization (PTO) and ask for input and advice. Then present your suggestions to your principal.

2. Ask your principal to set up a study group to determine how well your school is fulfilling its responsibility to educate a diverse population. Use the guidelines in *Diversity Within Unity: Essential Principles for Teaching and Learning in a Multicultural Society* by James A. Banks et al.[18] Evaluate your school to see how effective it is in meeting these guidelines. Consider the curriculum; materials; interactions among staff members, students, and community residents; and the entire environment for living and learning in the school.

Notes

CHAPTER 1

1. Lake Research Partners and the Tarrance Group (2006).
2. Myslinski (2010).
3. Kymlicka (2007).
4. Lee (2004).
5. Moses (2002, 2010b).
6. Banks (2010b).
7. National Center for Education Statistics (2009a); Edwards (2006).
8. Vanneman, Hamilton, Anderson & Rahman (2009).
9. Gándara (2008); Gándara & Contreras (2010).
10. Edwards (2006).
11. Ladson-Billings (2006a) p. 3.
12. D'Amico (2001).
13. Chenoweth (2009). Also see Karen Chenoweth's summary in *Phi Delta Kappan* (2009, September, vol. 91).
14. Zurawsky (2004).
15. Barton and Coley (2009).
16. Anyon (2005), p. 2.
17. Berliner (2009), p. 7.
18. Berliner (2009), pp. 1-2.
19. Rothstein (2006).
20. D'Amico, op. cit.
21. Orfield (2004), p. 9.
22. Orfield (2009).
23. Carey & Roza (2008).
24. Support Our Law Enforcement and Safe Neighborhoods Act, AZ. SB 1070 (2010).
25. Obama (2010).
26. United Nations High Commission for Refugees (2000).
27. Howe (1983). See also Wyman, Greenfield & Gill (1993).
28. Rothstein (1998).
29. Tatum (2003), p.6.
30. Hall & Ushomirsky (2010).
31. Carey & Roza, op. cit.
32. Huh (2005).
33. U.S. Census Bureau (2010a). All the information in this paragraph is derived from the U.S. Census Bureau. See statistics available from U.S. Census Bureau Table NST-EST2009.xls. and "An Older and more Diverse Nation by Mid-Century" also "USA People Quick Facts" at http://quickfacts.census.gov/qfd/states/00000.html
34. U.S. Census Bureau (2010b). All the information in this paragraph is derived from the U.S. Census Bureau. See statistics available from U.S. Census Bureau Table Table 7-H. Projected Change in Population Size by Race and Hispanic Origin for the United States: 2000 to 2050 High Net International Migration Series (NP2009-T7-H) Source: U.S. Census Bureau, Population Division Release Date: December 16, 2009 . See also "An Older and more Diverse Nation by Mid-Century."
35. Monger (2010) for U.S. Department of Homeland Security Office of Immigration Statistics. LPR-fr-2009.
36. Monger, op. cit.
37. Grieco (2010) for U.S. Department of Commerce Economics and Statistical Administration, U.S. Census Bureau. ACS-11.
38. U.S. Department of Commerce (2010). See U.S. Census Bureau News, *Facts for Features: Back to School: 2010-2011*. CB10-FF14. June 15, 2010. Also see U.S. National Center for Education Statistics as cited in the *Statistical Abstract of the United States: 2010*, Table 214; U.S. Census Bureau (2008). See School Enrollment: Social and Economic Characteristics of Students: October 2008.
39. U.S. Census Bureau (2008; 2010c). See School Enrollment: Social and Economic Characteristics of Students: October 2008; U.S. Census Bureau News, *Facts for Features: Back to School: 2010-2011*. CB10-FF14.
40. Orfield (2004, 2009).
41. Kugler (2002).

42. All the data in this paragraph drew from the statistics and analysis of these two sources: Wight, Chau & Aratani. (2010). *Who America's Poor Children? The Official Story*. National Center for Children in Poverty. New York: Columbia University; DeNavas-Walt, C.; Proctor, B. D.; Smith, J. C. (2008). *Income, Poverty, and Health Insurance Coverage in the United States: 2007*, Washington, DC: U.S. Government Printing Office, p.13.

43. National Collaborative on Diversity in the Teaching Force (2004).

44. National Commission on Excellence in Education (1983).

45. Hirsch, E. D. (1987).

46. Buras (2008).

47. Provenzo (2005).

48. Birnbaum (2010).

49. Arizona (2010). See also *Los Angeles Times* article by Santa Cruz (2010).

50. No Child Left Behind Act of 2001, Public Law 107-110 (2001).

51. U.S. Department of Education, ESEA Blueprint for Reform. (2010). Also see Department of Education web page (ED.gov) (2010).

52. Kober, Jennings & Peltason (2010) for Center on Education Policy.

53. Forum for Education and Democracy (2010).

54. Forum for Education and Democracy, op. cit.

55. Ibid.

56. Mintrop & Sunderman (2009). For The Civil Rights Project/Proyecto Derechos Civiles.

57. Meyer & Zucker (1989).

58. Mintrop & Sunderman, op. cit.

59. American Recovery and Reinvestment Act (ARRA) of 2009 (Public Law 111-5), (2009). See also U.S. Department of Education web site for *Race to The Top* (2010).

60. FairTest (2009).

61. Center on Education Policy (2006).

62. Common Core (2009), p. iv.

63. Common Core (2009), p.iii.

64. Ibid.

65. Common Core, op. cit.; Forum for Education and Democracy, op. cit.

66. Sleeter (2005).

67. Cowhey (2006).

68. Merriam (2009), p. 43.

69. Fine (1991).

CHAPTER 2

1. A comprehensive resource on the history, goals, and concerns of multicultural education is Banks & Banks (Eds.) (2004), *Handbook of research on multicultural education*. See also Nieto (2009), Multicultural education in the United States: Historical realities, ongoing challenges, and transformative possibilities, In Banks (2009).

2. Weinberg (1982), p. 7.

3. Fine (1991).

4. Kozol (1975), pp. 16-20.

5. Geary (2009).

6. Tatum (2003).

7. Donaldson (2001).

8. Published by Delta beginning in 1994, these texts include the so-called "core" knowledge that children are supposed to know at different grade levels in order to do well in school. As an example, see Hirsch, E. D. (1994), *What your fourth grader needs to know: Fundamentals of a good fourth-grade education* (*The core knowledge*).

9. Provenzo (2005).

10. Banks (2004), p. 291.

11. Nieto (2003a).

12. See, for example, Roughgarden (2004); Ayres & Brown (2005).

13. Derman-Sparks, Ramsey & Edwards (2006).

14. Freire (1970).

15. Dewey (1966), p. 153.

16. Giroux (2002).

17. John S. and James L. Knight Foundation (2005).

18. Bhabha (1994), p. 172.

19. Freire (1985).

20. Comber (2001), p. 271.

21. Janks (2010).

22. See, for instance, Woodson (1933); DuBois (1935). For a historical analysis of multicultural education and critical pedagogy, see Banks (2009); and Nieto (2009).

23. Ashton-Warner (1963).

24. Loewen (2005, 2009).

25. Boston Children's Museum (2002); see also Bigelow & Peterson (2003).

26. Zinn (2010). For excellent classroom materials based on this important work, see http://www.zinnedproject.org

27. Halford (1999).

28. Shor (1996).

29. Vasquez (2004); Cowhey (2006); Dozier, Johnston & Rogers (2006); Christensen (2009).

30. See, for example, Derman-Sparks and the A.B.C. Task Force (1989); Compton-Lilly (2004); Au, Bigelow & Karp (2007); Bigelow, Harvey, Karp & Miller (2001); Lee, Menkart & Okazawa-Rey (2006); Menkart, Murray & View (2004); May & Sleeter (2010).

CHAPTER 3

1. According to Tove Skutnabb-Kangas, *linguicism* can be defined as "ideologies and structures which are used to legitimate, effectuate and reproduce an unequal division of power and resources (both material and non-material) between groups which are defined on the basis of language (on the basis of their mother tongues)." Skutnabb-Kangas (1988).

2. Allport (1954), p. 52.

3. See, for example, Delgado & Stefancic (2001); Ladson-Billings (2004).
4. See, for example, Gould (1981), *The mismeasure of man* (revised and expanded ed., 1996), for a history of racism in intelligence measurement; Selden (1999) for a comprehensive treatment of the eugenics movement.
5. Tatum (1992), p. 6.
6. Weinberg (1990), pp. xii–xiii.
7. See, for example, Williams (2005); Spring (2010b). For educational discrimination against Latinos, see MacDonald (2004). For the history of educational discrimination against Native Americans, see Lomawaima & McCarty (2006). For the history of gender-segregated schooling, see Sadker & Zitttleman (2010).
8. For example, Gary Orfield and his associates found that the past four decades have seen the largest backward movement toward segregation for Blacks since the 1954 *Brown v. Topeka Board of Education* decision. They also reported that Latino students have become the most segregated of all groups. See Orfield (2009).
9. On the subject of rigid tracking, see Oakes (2005); on the impact of high-stakes testing on students of color, see Au (2009).
10. Gándara (1995), p. 89.
11. See Harry & Klingner (2006); Gándara & Contreras (2010).
12. GLSEN (2009b).
13. D'Amico (2001).
14. Anyon (2005).
15. Bowles & Gintis (1976).
16. See, for instance, Anyon (2005); Berliner (2006); Rothstein (2004).
17. Schofield (2010).
18. Kozol (2005).
19. Orfield & Lee (2005).
20. Yearwood (2003), p. 110.
21. Donaldson (1996).
22. See, for example, Fine (1991); Sleeter (1994). In addition, Beverly Daniel Tatum's simple but eloquent question in the title of her latest book, *Can we talk about race?* (2007) is an admonition that too often such discussions have been silenced.
23. Rosenberg (2004), p. 257, p. 262.
24. Pollock (2004), p. 2.
25. Van Ausdale & Feagin (2001).
26. Merton (1948).
27. Rosenthal & Jacobson (1968).
28. See, for instance, Snow (1969); Wineburg (1987); Rosenthal (1998); Jussim & Eccles (1992).
29. Rist (1971).
30. See the review of this research in Anyon (2003).
31. Rist (2000), p. 259.
32. Rist, op. cit., p. 260.
33. Pizarro (2005), p. 240.
34. Rumbaut (1996).
35. Steele (1992), p.77.
36. Cohen, Garcia, Apfel & Master (2006).
37. McLaughlin & Talbert (2001).
38. Sleeter (2005), p. 128.
39. Zeichner (2003).
40. Haberman (1995).
41. Sheets (1995).
42. Ballenger (1999), p. 3.
43. Rosenthal & Jacobson, op. cit.
44. González (2002), para. 10-11.
45. See, for example, Mantsios (2010); Rothstein (2004).
46. For a review of the research on this issue, see Darling-Hammond (2010).
47. Katz (1975); see also Spring (2008).
48. Dewey (1916).
49. Tyack (1995), p. 4.
50. Giroux (2006), p. 68.
51. Morin (2006).

Case Studies

Linda Howard

1. We appreciate the work of Paula Elliott in conducting and analyzing the extensive interviews that were the basis for this case study. Currently contracted by Boston Public Schools, Paula is an educator, researcher, teacher professional development specialist as well as an arts education advocate and musician/vocalist. Her work addresses social, cultural and political forces structuring the educational experiences and equitable inclusion of urban school students and families.
2. For photographs and text that document this reality, see Introduction by Rebecca Walker in Tauber & Singh (Eds.) (2009), *Blended nation: Portraits and interviews of mixed-race America*. See also the work of Family Diversity Projects, Inc., especially Kaeser & Gillespie (2007).
3. Miller & Rotheram-Borus (1994).
4. Williamson (1980).
5. Passel, Wang & Taylor (2010).
6. Root (2004), p. 112.
7. Walker (2009), n.p.

Rashaud Kates

1. We would like to thank Joan Nichols, a high school art teacher in Georgia, who assisted us in arranging Rashaud's interview.
2. For more information on Future Business Leaders of America, visit their national website: http://www.fbla-pbl.org
3. For more information on the American Educational Research Association Commission on Research in Black Education, see the website www.aera.net.
4. King (2005).
5. Ferguson (2001).
6. Love & Kruger (2005).

7. Carter (2005).
8. Love & Kruger, op. cit.
9. See, for example, Stanton-Salazar (2001); Conchas (2006); Carter, op. cit.
10. Carter, op. cit.

Vanessa Mattison

1. We are grateful to Maya Gillingham for the interviews and the background for Vanessa's case study. Maya is a therapeutic body worker and holistic health educator, diversity trainer, and group facilitator. She lives with her partner, Chino, and their daughter, in Oakland, California.
2. Pollock (2004).
3. See McIntosh (1988).
4. For a helpful discussion about the kinds of actions Whites can take to fight racism, see Ayvazian (2010).
5. See, for example, Thiessen & Cook-Sather (2007).

CHAPTER 4

1. Dewey (1966).
2. National Working Group on Funding Student Learning (2008).
3. For the purpose of consistency, the term *tracking* rather than *ability grouping* will be generally used in the discussion in this chapter.
4. Tatum (2007), p. 41.
5. Oakes updated the 1985 research in the 2nd edition. See Oakes (2005); see also Oakes & Saunders (2008).
6. McLaughlin & Talbert (2001).
7. Krigman (2010).
8. This research is reviewed in the second edition of *Keeping Track,* Oakes (2005). See Note 5.
9. Yonezawa, Wells & Serna (2002), p. 40.
10. Burris, Welner & Bezoza (2009).
11. Black (2004).
12. Hong & Raudenbush (2005).
13. For example, see Selden (1999).
14. Terman (1916).
15. See examples of the connection between IQ testing and eugenics in Selden, *Inheriting Shame: The story of eugenics and racism in America* and in Gould (1996, revised and expanded edition), *The Mismeasure of man.*
16. For a more contemporary example of how IQ tests are used to "prove" the social and intellectual inferiority of some groups, see Herrnstein & Murray (first edition1994 and updated 2010), *The bell curve: Intelligence and class structure in American life.* In a recent iteration of the arguments made by him and his co-author, Charles Murray indicts America's schools for believing what he views as the "romantic myth" that all children can learn to high levels. In contrast, he claims that America's future depends on the gifted. See Murray (2008), *Real Education: Four simple truths for bringing America's schools back to reality.*

17. Spring (2010a).
18. Neill (personal communication, July 2010).
19. Koyama (2010).
20. Elmore (2002), para. 2.
21. Advancement Project (2010), p. 3.
22. Nichols & Berliner (2007).
23. Marklein (2009).
24. Kaplan (2005).
25. Geiser & Santelices (2007).
26. Pedula, Abrams, Madaus, Russell, Ramos & Miao (2003).
27. Darling-Hammond (2010), p. 70
28. Many books and monographs in the past decade and a half, in addition to those already cited, have weighed in on the debate about standardized tests. Most have pointed out the connection between a loss of equity and the overuse and misuse of standardized tests. See, for example, McNeil (2000), *Contradictions of school reform: Educational costs of standardized testing*; Meier, Kohn, Darling-Hammond, Sizer & Wood (2005), *Many children left behind: How the No Child Left Behind Act is damaging our children and our schools*; Noddings (2007), *When school reform goes wrong*; and Au (2009), *Unequal by design: High-stakes testing and the standardization of inequality.*
29. Dewey (1966), p. 172.
30. Apple (2004), p. 6.
31. Fecho (2003). See also Delpit & Doudy (2008).
32. Banks (2010a), p. 242.
33. Fine (1991), p. 33.
34. Fine (1991), p. 37.
35. Hughes & Bigler (2007).
36. Levin (2001), *'Teach me!' Kids will learn when oppression is the lesson.* A recent book that connects social justice with community service learning for young people also engages students in meaningful and responsible activities. See Cipolle (2010), *Service-learning and social justice: Engaging students in social change.*
37. Mack & Picower (2010).
38. Darling-Hammond, op. cit.
39. Sleeter (2005).
40. Loewen (2009). See also Loewen (2005), *Lies my teacher told me: Everything your American history textbook got wrong* and Loewen (2000), *Lies across America: What our historic sites got wrong.*
41. Goodlad (2004).
42. Wilson & Corbett (2001).
43. Haberman (1991).
44. Cummins (2007a).
45. Walters (2000).
46. Fosnot (2005).
47. Richardson (2003), p. 1635.
48. Bartolomé (1994).
49. Cummins (2000), p. 280.
50. Berger (2005), p. 35.
51. Cohen, Pickeral & McCloskey (2008/2009).

52. Lee & Burkam (2003).

53. Many of these ideas are addressed in an informative article by Susan Black (2002), The roots of vandalism: When students engage in wanton destruction, what can schools do? *American School Board Journal.*

54. See Perkins (2006), *Where we learn: The CUBE survey of urban school climate.* A companion survey, *Where We Teach: The CUBE Survey of Urban School Climate,* by Perkins (2007), assessed the perspectives of educators. Results showed that educators too care a great deal about the climate for learning.

55. Buckley, Schneider & Shang (2005).

56. Lee & Loeb (2000).

57. Finn, Gerber, Achilles & Byrd-Zaharias (2001).

58. Blatchford, Bassett & Brown (2008). For a contrary view, see research by Spyros Konstantopoulos as reported in Matthews (2008, March 10) B02.

59. For the benefits and potential pitfalls of small schools, see Meier (2006).

60. Wehlage & Rutter (1986).

61. Gregory, Skiba & Noguera (2010).

62. McCumber (2001), para. 4.

63. Lipman (1998).

64. Freire (1970), p. 59.

65. Cook-Sather (2009) and also Thiessen & Cook-Sather (2007) document the powerful impact that student engagement can have on learning and motivation.

66. Morrell (2008).

67. See, for example, Nieto (2003b); Lieberman & Miller (2008); and also Zemelman & Ross (2009).

68. Nieto (2011).

69. The findings were published by Harvard Family Research Project in 2007 in a series of briefs, *Family involvement makes a difference.*

70. Weiss, Bouffard, Bridglall & Gordon (2009).

71. Markow & Scheer (2003).

72. See Weiss et al., op. cit.

73. See, for example, Dantas & Manyak (2010), *Home-school connections in a multicultural society: Learning from and with culturally and linguistically diverse families*; Allen (2007), *Creating welcoming schools: A practical guide to home-school partnerships with diverse families*; Epstein and Associates (2009), *School, family, and community partnerships: Your handbook for action,* 3rd ed. For engaging families of middle and high school students, see Hill & Chao (2009), *Families, schools, and the adolescent: Connecting research, policy, and practice.*

74. Schott Foundation for Public Education (2009).

75. Olson (2009).

76. Oakes, Quartz, Ryan & Lipton (2000), p. xxi.

Case Studies

Avi Abramson

1. We appreciate Diane Sweet's work in finding and interviewing Avi and in providing extensive background information for this case study. Diane teaches courses in language and writing at the Wentworth Institute of Technology in Massachusetts.

2. Brumberg (1986), p. 2.

3. Wistrich (2010).

4. For an examination of the pressure Jews feel to become assimilated in U.S. society, see Lipset & Raab (1995).

5. For an update on Avi's life, see the *Epilogue* on the Book Resources section of *Affirming Diversity,* Sixth Edition, in the MEducationLab for your course and select "Epilogue."

Jasper and Viena Alejandro-Quinn

1. We would like to thank Dr. Kristen French who conducted this interview with Jasper, Viena and their parents. Kristen is an Assistant Professor of Elementary Education at Western Washington University in the Woodring College of Education and is also the WWU Director of Center for Education, Equity and Diversity.

2. Meyer, S. (2008).

3. Alexie (2007).

4. More information on the Office of Indian Education can be found at http://indianeducation.org

5. More information on the Bureau of Indian Education Schools can be found at http://www.bie.edu

6. Grigg, Moran, and Kuang. (2010).

7. Mead, Grigg, Moran & Kuang (2010).

8. Native Education 101. National Indian Education Association in partnership with the National Education Association. (2007). For more information on National Indian Education Association see: http://www.niea.org/index.php

9. Faircloth, Susan C., & Tippeconnic, III, John W. (2010). For the Civil Rights Project/Proyecto Derechos Civiles.

10. Anaya (1999).

11. For more information on *Native Lens,* a program of *Longhouse Media* that teaches digital filmmaking and media skills to indigenous youth as a form of self-expression, cultural preservation, and social change, see http://www.longhousemedia.org/index.html

12. Native Education 101, op. cit.

13. Deyhle, Swisher, Stevens & Galván. (2008).

14. Clearinghouse on Native Teaching and Learning . The people: CHiXapkaid (Pavel), Banks-Joseph, Englebret, McCubbin, Sievers, Bruna, Galaviz, Anderson, Egan, Brownfield, Lockhart, Grogan, & Sanyal. (2008). For more information see http://education.wsu.edu/nativeclearinghouse/

15. Clearinghouse on Native Teaching and Learning. The People, op. cit.

16. Grande (2004).

17. Lomawaima & McCarty (2006). On the topic of American Indian Boarding Schools, see the following collection of essays: Trafzer, Keller & Sisquoc. (2006). *Boarding School Blues: Revisiting American Indian Educational Experiences.*

CHAPTER 5

1. *Lau v. Nichols* (1974). See also Waugh (1974).
2. Tatum (2007); Howard, G. (2006); Wijeyesinghe & Jackson (2001).
3. Gutierrez & Rogoff (2003).
4. U.S. Census Bureau (2010b).
5. Lopez-Torkos (2003).
6. Olsen (2008).
7. Noguera (2008).
8. Yon (2000).
9. Dolby (2000).
10. Hobbel & Chapman (2009).
11. Payne (2005). See Bohn's critique of the self-publication process and self- promotion that lacks peer-review in Anita Bohn (2007), A Framework for understanding Ruby Payne. *Rethinking Schools,* 21(2), 13-15.
12. Kunjufu (2007, 2010).
13. Gorski (2008).
14. See Rothstein (2006); Anyon (2003, 2005) and Books (2006).
15. Boateng (1990). See also Spring (2010b).
16. Swisher & Schoorman (2001).
17. Coffield, Mosley, Hall & Ecclestone (2004).
18. Witkin (1962). To summarize Witkin's assertions, field-independent describes those who learn best in situations that emphasize analytical tasks and with material void of social context. Individuals who favor this learning mode generally prefer to work alone and are self-motivated. Field-dependence describes those who tend to learn best in highly social settings, according to this theory. Manuel Ramierez and Alfredo Castañeda (1974) followed up with a critical cultural perspective and applied Witkin's theory to ethnic groups. In research with children of various cultural backgrounds, they concluded that European American students tend to be the most field-independent learners. Mexican American, American Indian, and African American students by contrast, tend to be closer to the field sensitive (the term they use for dependent, which may have negative connotations), with Mexican Americans closest to this pole. The case was made that the values, attitudes, and behaviors taught at home become the basis for how children learn.
19. Stellwagen (2001), p. 266.
20. Deyhle & Swisher (1997), p 266. See also Deyhle, Swisher, Stevens & Galván (2008).
21. Manuelito (2005).
22. Gardner (2006).
23. Gardner (2008a).
24. Gardner (2008b).
25. Gay (2010), p. 79.
26. Tharp (1981).
27. Tharp & Dalton (2007). See also CREDE web site http://crede.berkeley.edu/research/crede/standards.html

28. Foster (1997).
29. Morrell & Duncan-Andrade (2008).
30. Lee, C. (2005, 2007).
31. Lee's book, *Culture, Literacy, and Learning: Taking Bloom in the Midst of the Whirlwind* elaborates on the cultural modeling framework.
32. Nine-Curt (1984).
33. Heath (1983).
34. Heath (2010).
35. Gay (2010); p. 24.
36. Philips (1993).
37. Kim (1997).
38. Lee, S. (2009). Also see Ngo & Lee, S. (2007).
39. Adams, (1995). Lomawaima & McCarty (2006).
40. Faircloth & Tippeconnic (2010).
41. Deyhle, Swisher, Stevens, & Galván (2008).
42. Howard, T. (2010).
43. Au, K. (2007); Gay (2010); Irizarry (2011a); Irizarry & Raible (in press/2011). Irvine (2003); Ladson-Billings (2009). See also Irizarry's recent book, (2011b) *The Latinization of U.S. Schools: Successful Teaching and Learning in Shifting Cultural Contexts.*
44. Vogt, Jordan & Tharp (1993).
45. Tharp, et al., (2007).
46. Maaka (2004), p. 9.
47. Keahi (2000), p. 58.
48. Tamura (2008).
49. Irvine & Fraser (1998).
50. Ladson-Billings (2009).
51. Milner (2010).
52. Irizarry (2007).
53. Ballenger (1999), p. 3.

Case Studies

Yahaira León

1. We appreciate the collaboration of Dr. Jason Irizarry who interviewed Yahaira León. Dr. Irizarry is a faculty member in the School of Education at the University of Connecticut where his research focuses on multicultural teacher education and urban teacher recruitment and retention, with emphasis on equity for Latino students.
2. Pew Hispanic Center (2008).
3. See quickfacts.census.gov/qfd/states/00000.html
4. Pew Hispanic Center, op.cit.
5. Hernandez & Rivera-Batiz (2006).
6. Guarnizo, Portes & Haller (2003).
7. Levitt (2004).
8. Ibid.
9. Sanchez (2007).
10. Pew Hispanic Center, op. cit.
11. Because Puerto Rico is under the political control of the United States, the term *migration* rather than *immigration* is ordinarily used to refer to the movement of Puerto Ricans to the United States, but this term is

not quite accurate because it refers to movement within the same cultural and political sphere. Some writers have suggested that the term *(im)migration* is more suitable. See Roberto Marquez, "Sojourners, Settlers, Castaways, and Creators: A Recollection of Puerto Rico Past and Puerto Ricans Present." *Massachusetts Review* 36, no. 1 (1995): 94–118. More recently, the term "Diasporican" has been used, reflecting as it does the diaspora of Puerto Ricans throughout the United States.

12. Rolón (2000).
13. Rolón op. cit., p.154; Antrop-González (2006).
14. Irizarry (2007).
15. Bode (2005).
16. For more information on the Junior Statesman Foundation's summer programs for high school students, see www.JSA.org

James Karam

1. We want to thank Diane Sweet for the interviews with James as well as for transcripts and other extensive information she was able to find about the Arab American community.
2. U.S. Census Bureau (2000). See also the American-Arab Institute Foundation for these and other demographics and general information about Arab Americans, as well as for a discussion of the problems in counting Arab Americans in the U.S. Census: http://www.aaiusa.org
3. Aruri (1969).
4. Ibid.
5. See http://www.aaiusa.org/pages/demographics/
6. See http://www.adc.org/education/educational-resources/ for demographic data, government and legal information, educational resources, and lesson plans. See also Arab World and Islamic Resources (AWAIR) at www.awaironline.org; AMIDEAST (www.amideast.org); and the Arab American Institute, a Washington, DC–based organization that serves as a leadership group for Americans of Arab descent at www.aaiusa.org

Hoang Vinh

1. We are grateful to Haydée Font for the interviews and transcripts for this case study. When she did these interviews, Haydée was a graduate student in multicultural education at the University of Massachusetts Amherst; she later worked in the development office at several universities.
2. The Vietnamese use family names first, given names second. The given name is used for identification. In this case, Vinh is the given name and Hoang is the family name. Accordingly, whereas in U.S. society John Jones would be known formally as Mr. Jones and informally as John, in Vietnam, Hoang Vinh would be known both formally and informally as Mr. Vinh or Vinh.
3. See Takaki (1998) and Zhou & Bankston (2000).
4. Kiang & Wai-Fun Lee (1993).

5. See the 2006 *American Community Survey* (ACS) from the U.S. Census Bureau. Available at: http://factfinder.census.gov
6. Tam (1980).
7. Chang & Au (2007/2008); Chou & Feagin (2008); Lee, S. (2009).
8. This and many related studies are documented in Portes & Rumbaut (2006).

Rebecca Florentina

1. We are grateful to John Raible who interviewed Rebecca and assisted in identifying the themes and analysis of the themes. John is Assistant Professor, Department of Teaching, Learning, and Teacher Education at the University of Nebraska-Lincoln. His interests include exploring the intersections between identities, families, schools, and communities.
2. For purposes of convenience, and because Rebecca most often identified simply as "lesbian," that is the term that is generally used in this case study. For other students who identify as lesbian, gay, bisexual, or transgender, the acronym LGBT is used.
3. GLSEN is the leading national education organization focused on ensuring safe schools for all students. For all their resources and information, see their website: http://www.GLSEN.org
4. Gibson (1989).
5. Sadowski (2006).
6. The Governor's Commission on Gay and Lesbian Youth (1993).
7. See, for example, Miceli (2005) *Standing out, standing together: The social and political impact of Gay-Straight Alliances*; Campos (2005), *Understanding gay and lesbian youth: Lessons for straight school teachers, counselors, and administrators*; Baker (2002), *How homophobia hurts children: Nurturing diversity at home, at school, and in the community.*
8. Buckel (2000).
9. See their most recent report on school safety for LGBT students: Gay, Lesbian, and Straight Education Network (GLSEN), *National school climate survey 2009.*

CHAPTER 6

1. Skutnabb-Kangas defines *linguicism* as "ideologies and structures which are used to legitimate, effectuate and reproduce an unequal division of power and resources (both material and nonmaterial) between groups which are defined on the basis of language." See Skutnabb-Kangas (1988), p. 13.
2. U.S. Census Bureau (2010b, 2010c).
3. Jost (2009).
4. For this and other relevant statistics on English Language Learners, see the National Clearinghouse for English Language Acquisition and Language Instruction website (NCELA) at www.ncela.gwu.edu.

5. Hernandez, Denton & Macartney (2008).
6. Crawford (2000).
7. As quoted in Crawford (2000), p. 8.
8. Helms (2010).
9. Crawford (2008), *Advocating for English learners: Selected essays*; Crawford (2000).
10. Spring (2010b).
11. Skutnabb-Kangas, op. cit.
12. *Lau v. Nichols,* 414 U.S. 563 (1974).
13. *Equal Educational Opportunities Act of 1974,* 20 U.S.C. ¶ 1703(f).
14. Jost, op. cit.
15. Jost, op. cit.
16. Gándara & Hopkins (2010).
17. See Crawford (2008), *Loose ends in a tattered fabric: The inconsistency of language rights in the United States.* Also available at http://www.languagepolicy.net/excerpts/loose.html
18. *Horne v. Flores,* 08-289 (2009).
19. Crawford (17 July, 2010). Personal communication via email.
20. Plyler v. Doe, 457 U.S. 202 (1982).
21. Kovács & Mehler (2009).
22. Bialystok, Craik & Freedman (2007).
23. Adesope, Lavin, Thompson & Ungerleider (2010).
24. Portes & Rumbaut (2001).
25. Callahan (2005), p. 322.
26. Bartolomé (2008), p. 377.
27. Cummins (2001), p. 73.
28. Brisk (2006); Genesee, Lindholm-Leary, Saunders & Christian (2006); Ovando, Collier & Combs (2006); Reyes & Kleyn (2010).
29. Portes & Rumbaut, op. cit.
30. Some excellent resources that focus on research as well as strategies and approaches for nonspecialist teachers who have ELLs in their classrooms are: Adger, Snow & Christian (2002), *What teachers need to know about language*; Celic (2009), *English language learners day by day, K-6*; Cloud, Genesee & Hamayan (2009), *Literacy instruction for English language learners*; Dragan (2005), *A how-to guide for teaching English language learners in the primary classroom*; Fisher, Rothenberg & Frey (2007), *Language learners in the English classroom*; Freeman & Freeman (2008), *Academic language for English language learners and struggling readers: How to help students succeed across content areas*; Fu (2009), *Writing between languages: How English language learners make the transition to fluency*; García & Frede (2010), *Young English language learners: Current research and emerging directions for practice and policy*; Li & Edwards (2010), *Best practices in ELL instruction*.
31. Krashen (1981).
32. For a more in-depth discussion of these issues, see Adger, Snow & Christian (2002); see also Merino (2007).
33. For early research on additive and subtractive bilingualism, see Lambert (1975).
34. Schwarzer, Haywood & Lorenzen (2003).
35. Freeman, Freeman & Ramirez (2008).
36. Wiley (2005).
37. See, for instance, García (2009), *Bilingual education in the 21st century: A global perspective*; Pérez & Torres-Guzmán (2006), *Learning in two worlds: An integrated Spanish/English biliteracy approach*; Martínez-Roldán & Fránquiz (2009), *Latina/o youth literacies: Hidden funds of knowledge.*
38. For a more extensive discussion of Bill Dunn's experience, see Nieto (2010).
39. For in-depth descriptions of the many program models and their implications, see Wiley (2005).
40. See Howard, Christian & Genesee (2004).
41. Lindholm-Leary & Borsato (2001).
42. See August & Shanahan (2006); Crawford & Krashen (2008); Rolstad, Mahoney & Glass (2005).
43. Slavin, Madden, Calderón, Chamberlain & Hennessy (2010).
44. Fry (2008).
45. National Comprehensive Center for Teacher Quality and Public Agenda (2008).
46. Moll & Arnot-Hopffer (2005).
47. Orfield (2009).
48. Gándara & Contreras (2010).
49.
50. Dolson & Burnham-Massey (2010).

Case Studies

Manuel Gomes

1. We are grateful to Carol Shea for the interviews and transcriptions and for many valuable insights in the development of this case study. After over 30 years in urban education, mostly at Madison Park High School in Boston as an English and theatre arts teacher and then as a school counselor, Carol is now involved in counselor training and in developing resources and support programs that assist young women in meeting their personal and educational needs.
2. See Child Trend Data. Available at http://www.childtrendsdatabank.org/?q = node/300.
3. See https://cia.gov/library/publications/the-world-factbook/geos/cv.html The 2010 U. S. Census counted Cape Verdeans as a separate category.
4. West Africa: Combating world's lowest literacy rates (2009).
5. See Portes & Rumbaut (2001), p. 53.

Alicia Montejo

1. We appreciate the work of Stephanie Schmidt, an art teacher at Bear Creek High School in Colorado, who interviewed Alicia and helped us with many details for the case study.

2. For more information about the Colorado Small Schools Initiative (CSSI), see www.coloradosmallschools.org
3. The Bill & Melinda Gates Foundation states on its website, www.gatesfoundation.org/education, that "the Bill & Melinda Gates Foundation is committed to raising the high school graduation rate and helping all students—regardless of race or family income—graduate as strong citizens ready for college and work." The Gates Foundation has made a positive impact in many urban communities, yet questions remain about the use of private money for funding public schools. For a critique of the current movement to privately fund school reform, using the "small schools" banner, and a cautionary statement about abandoning the social justice concerns of the early small schools movement, see Fine (2005).
4. To protect the participant's anonymity, the school documents are not disclosed here.
5. Fass & Cauthen (2008).
6. On the topic of unequal schooling among Latinos, especially Mexican Americans, see Gándara & Contreras (2010); see also Nieto, Rivera, Cammarota, Canella, García, González, Irizarry, Moll, Pedraza, Perez, Romo & Valenzuela (2010).
7. National Center for Education Statistics (2009a).
8. Fry (2008).
9. For more about "pushouts," see Yosso (2006); Solórzano, Ledesma, Pérez, Burciaga & Ornelas (2003).
10. Yosso (2006), op. cit., pp. 2–3.
11. Bode (2005).
12. Bridgeland, Dilulio & Morison (2006).
13. Yosso, op. cit.
14. Hildago (2005).
15. Stanton-Salazar (2001).

CHAPTER 7

1. Nodding (2005), p. xv.
2. Crabtree, (2004), p. 9.
3. Valenzuela (1999, 2004).
4. Flores-González (2002).
5. Rólon-Dow (2005).
6. Garza (2009).
7. Gibson & Bejínez (2002). See also Gibson, Gándara & Koyama (2004). *School Connections: U.S. Mexican Youth, Peers, and School Achievement.*
8. Roberts (2010).
9. Nieto (2005), p. 204.
10. Bode (2005).
11. Baratz, S. & Baratz, J. (1971).
12. Ryan, W. (1971), p. 61.
13. Ferguson (2008), p. 78. See also Ferguson (2007). *Toward Excellence and Equity: An emerging vision for closing the achievement gap.*
14. Herrnstein and Charles Murray (1994/2010).
15. For scholarly critique of Herrnstein & Murray see Steve Fraser's (1995) edited book: *The Bell Curve Wars: Race, Intelligence, and the Future of America.* Also see Newby (1995), and see *Measured Lies: The Bell Curve Examined* edited by Joe L. Kincheloe and Shirley R. Steinberg (1997).
16. Bourdieu (1986), p. 246. See also Bourdieu & Passeron (1977), *Reproduction in Education, Society and Culture.* To see how Bourdieu's work continues to influence current research see Roberts, K. (2009).
17. Bowles & Gintis (1976); Spring (1989).
18. Apple (1986).
19. Freire (2005), p. 72-73.
20. Ladson-Billings (2009); Gay (2010).
21. Faircloth & Tippeconnic (2010). For the Civil Rights Project/Proyecto Derechos Civiles, p. 30.
22. Faircloth & Tippeconnic, op. cit., p. 31.
23. Lewis (1965); Harrington (1997/1971).
24. Ladson-Billings (2006b).
25. See Chenoweth, K. (2009a). *How it's Being Done: Urgent Lessons from Unexpected Schools.* See also Bempechat (2008), Reading success: A motivational perspective in R. Fink and S.J. Samuels, eds., *Inspiring reading success: Interest and motivation in the age of high stakes testing.* See also the work of Jeff Howard and the Efficacy Institute http://www.efficacy.org
26. Rothstein (2004, 2006).
27. Berliner (2009), p. 1.
28. Ibid.
29. Harlem Children's Zone, http://www.hcz.org/ (accessed 2010).
30. Tough (2008).
31. Ladd, Noguera & Payzant (2006), http://www.boldapproach.org/ (accessed 2010).
32. Noguera (2004).
33. Ryan, J. (2010).
34. Giroux (2001); Cummins (2001); Kohl (1994).
35. Erickson (1993).
36. Kohl (1994), p. 2
37. Giroux (1996).
38. For these insights, we are grateful to Dr. John Raible of the University of Nebraska-Lincoln.
39. Children's Defense Fund (2008). See also Edelman (2007).
40. Noguera (2008). See also Wald & Thurau (2010).
41. See the collaborative report of the Advancement Project and the Civil Rights Project of Harvard University. Opportunities suspended: the devastating consequences of zero tolerance and school discipline. Proceeding from the National Summit on Zero Tolerance; 2000 Jun 15-16; Washington, D.C. http://www.civilrightsproject.ucla.edu/research/discipline/opport_suspended.php
42. Vaught (2011). See also Brown, T. (2007).

43. Raible & Irizarry (2010).
44. Wald & Losen (2003).
45. Noguera & Cannella (2006).
46. Ogbu & Simons (1998).
47. Ogbu (1987).
48. Ibid.
49. Cummins (2001).
50. Fordham & Ogbu (1986).
51. Gibson, M. (1997).
52. Gillborn (1997).
53. Carter (2005, 2006); Conchas (2006); Conchas & Rodríguez (2008). See also Jackson, D. B. (2003).
54. Conchas (2006), pp. 12-13.
55. Carter (2005), p. 8.
56. Ibid.
57. Ibid.
58. Conchas (2006), p. 115.
59. Ibid.
60. Jackson, D. B., op. cit.
61. Nieto & Raible (2010).

Case Studies

Paul Chavez

1. We are grateful to Dr. Mac Lee Morante for the interview and background information for Paul's case study. Dr. Morante is a bilingual school psychologist for the Anaheim City Schools and also works as a counselor at Santa Ana College in California.
2. *Raza* refers to the people of Mexican and Mexican American origin.
3. Rodríguez (2005), p. 250.
4. Vigil (1999, 2007).
5. Rodríguez, op. cit.
6. Advancement Project http://www.advancementproject.org
7. See Rice (2010) in Huffington Post http://www.huffingtonpost.com/constance-l-rice/las-response-to-its-gang_b_475780.html
8. Rodríguez, op. cit., p. 9.
9. Portes & Rumbaut (2001), p. 280. See also their most recent research in *Immigrant America: A Portrait,* 3rd Ed. (2006).
10. Vigil (1999).

Latrell Elton

1. We want to thank Vera Stenhouse, PhD, for conducting the interview with Latrell. Vera is currently a researcher at Emory University where her research explores how new teacher preparation programs educate teachers to work with diverse students. Vera also provided follow-up information about Latrell's school to add depth to the case study.
2. Kozol (2005).

3. Conchas (2006), p. 113–115.
4. Conchas, op. cit., p. 56.
5. Conchas, op. cit., p. 59.
6. Kozol, (2005), p. 37.

CHAPTER 8

1. Nieto, Bode, Kang & Raible (2008).
2. Bourdieu (1986); See also Halpern, D. (2005).
3. Deyhle & Swisher (1997). See also Deyhle, Swisher, Stevens & Galván. (2008).
4. Grande (2008, 2004).
5. Olsen (2008).
6. Aronowitz (2010, 1997).
7. Portes & Rumbaut (2006).
8. Blohm & Lapinsky (2006).
9. Park, Goodwin & Lee (2003).
10. Sadowski (2008).
11. Phinney, Berry, Sam & Vedder (2001), p. 12.
12. *Anglo-conformity* refers to the pressures, both expressed and hidden, to conform to the values, attitudes, and behaviors representative of the dominant group in U.S. society.
13. The excellent video *How We Feel: Hispanic Students Speak Out* was developed by Virginia Vogel Zanger and is available from Landmark Media, Falls Church, VA. The contact information is www.landmarkmedia.com and (800) 342-4336.
14. Halpern, R. (2003).
15. Hirsch, B. J. (2005).
16. Bouie (2006).
17. Mahiri (1998).
18. Miceli (2005).
19. Greene (2000).
20. Art*Show,* to be understood as "arts show how," comprises a dual package of resource guide and documentary video. See Laura Smyth and Shirley Brice Heath, *ArtShow: Youth and Community Development* (Washington, DC: Partners for Livable Communities, 1999). See also the documentary film *ArtShow* directed by Shirley Brice Heath produced for Partners for Livable Communities and for PBS, 1999. For more information see www.shirleybriceheath.com
21. See http://www.throughstudentseyes.org/TSE/Home.html See also: Kristien Zenkov & James Harmon (2009), Picturing a Writing Process: Photovoice and Teaching Writing to Urban Youth.
22. Joshi (2006).
23. Portes & Rumbaut (2006); Carter (2005). See also Drummond & Stipek (2004).
24. Comber (2000).
25. Carnes (1999).
26. Zirkel (2002, 2008).
27. Cummins (2001).

28. Tosolt (2010).
29. Stanton-Salazar (2001).
30. Carter (2005).
31. Ladson-Billings (2009).

Case Studies

Nadia Bara

1. We appreciate Dr. Carlie Tartakov, who located the Bara family and spent a day interviewing the daughters Nadia and Layla, and Sarah, their mother. Dr. Tartakov also sent information about the city in which they live and the Muslim community there. In addition, she transcribed all the interviews, going above and beyond our expectations. All of these things made the job of developing this case study a great deal easier than it might have been.
2. U.S. Census Bureau, *Census 2000*. Table DP-2. "Profile of Selected Social Characteristics: 2000." (Washington, DC: U.S. Department of Commerce, 2000).
3. Hajar (2008).
4. Eck (2001).
5. Jamal & Naber (2008).
6. Eck (2001). See also Henderson, Wood & Kristonis (2007).

Savoun Nouch

1. We appreciate the work of Keonilrath Bun, who interviewed Savoun for this case study. Keo is an alumnus of Rhode Island School of Design, currently working at the Metropolitan Museum of Art, New York.
2. St. Pierre (1995); Jo (2004).
3. Kiernan (2008).
4. Smith-Hefner (1999); See also Him (2001).
5. Kiernan (2004).
6. United Nations (2000); Robinson (1998).
7. Gutierrez & Rogoff (2003).
8. Choi, He & Harachi (2007).
9. Smith-Hefner (1999).
10. Crawford, Wright & Masten (2006).
11. Wallitt (2005, 2008).
12. Wallitt (2005), p. 296.
13. Wallitt (2008).

Christina Kamau

1. We appreciate the work of Dr. Carlie Tartakov, who interviewed Christina and provided support for this case study. Dr. Tartakov is Professor Emerita at Iowa State University.
2. U.S. Census (2010c); see www.census.gov. See also Takyi (2002).
3. U.S. Census Bureau (2010b). Available at: www.census.gov. See also Arthur (2000).
4. Mutume (2003). See also the United Nations Web page www.un.org/ecosocdev/geninfo/afrec/vol17no2/172brain.htm. See also Amadu Jack Kaba. (2009).
5. Takougang (2003).

6. Lan Do Rong & Brown (2002).
7. Lindsey (2004); Hines (2002).
8. Blohm & Lapinsky (2006).
9. See two chapters in *The New African Diaspora* (2009) Okpewho & Nkiru Nzegwu (Eds): Clark (2009), pp. 255-269 and Humphries (2009), pp. 271-301.
10. Dodson & Diouf, (2006). Available at: www.inmotionaame.org/migrations/landing.cfm?migration=13

CHAPTER 9

1. We would like to thank the teachers who worked at Amherst Regional Middle School in Amherst, Massachusetts at the time of this case study: Margarita Bonifaz, Sarah Lange Hayes, Gale Kuhn, Lynn Podesek, Sokhen P. Mao, Paul Plummer, and Maura Neverson, whose work and dedication made this unit of study about Cambodia a success for all of their students. Patty Bode also worked on this curriculum team as the art teacher.
2. Ronnie J. Booxbaum, PhD, and Sokhen P. Mao, MEd, developed this staff development course and wrote a handbook to accompany it.
3. Ung (2006a). See also Ung (2006b).
4. Go to the web site for this book at xxx for a list of resources.
5. Wiggins & McTighe (2005).
6. Bigelow, Harvey, Karp & Miller (2001).
7. See the Web site (www.cambodianmasters.org) of the Cambodian Masters Program, which supports revival of the traditional art forms of Cambodia and inspires contemporary artistic expression. They have visiting artists, lecturers and performances.
8. The Angkor Dance Troupe helps Cambodian young people navigate the balance between contemporary youth culture and their cultural heritage. See www.angkordance.org
9. *Monkey Dance* is a documentary film by Julie Mallozzi about three teens coming of age in Lowell, Massachusetts. See www.monkey-dance.com/ and www.juliemallozzi.com/monkey.html
10. The Peace Pagoda Nipponzan Myohoji Sangha Buddhist temple was created as a collaborative effort by Vietnam Veterans Against the War and the Cambodian American Community. See www.peacepagoda.org
11. See the Resources for Teaching About Cambodia on the web site for this book at XXX, which includes many of the folktales that Margarita Bonifaz used in this unit.
12. Menzel, Mann & Kennedy (1995).
13. Combs (with Hosler, illus.) (2001).
14. Newman (with Souza, illus.) (2009).
15. The Gay, Lesbian, Straight Education Network (GLSEN) is a national organization working to end anti-gay biases in schools. See GLSEN's website www.glsen.org
16. Bigler (1999).

17. Derman-Sparks (1997).
18. Val Penniman and Debbie Shumway's "Calendar-Connections," which helps teach critical thinking in a classroom curriculum, may be found at www .calendar-connections.com.
19. Rohmer (1999).
20. See www.familydiv.org
21. We are grateful to the teachers who developed this curriculum and gave it their heartfelt attention for three years when they were teaching together at Amherst Regional Middle School. They are Beth Adel Wohlleb, social studies teacher; Phil Covelli and Gale Kuhn, science teachers; Mari Hall, health teacher; Esther Haskell, English teacher; and Robert Lord, math teacher. Dr. John Raible worked as a consultant on the curriculum. Patty Bode worked as an art teacher with the team. Also, Kristen French provided feedback with a critical multicultural perspective for the unit.
22. Christensen op. cit.
23. We are grateful to Sara Barber-Just for her inspiring contributions to the field of high school English language arts teaching, and for the time she spent helping us to develop this curriculum case.
24. Sara Barber-Just, "Curriculum Proposal for Amherst Regional High School" (2001).
25. Sleeter (2005), p. 179.
26. Miceli (2005), p. 12.

CHAPTER 10

1. See the November 2005 issue of *Ethnic and Racial Studies* that presents original results from the third wave of the Children of Immigrants Longitudinal Study (CILS). See also Portes, A. & Rumbaut, R.G. (2006).
2. For further development of this idea, see Nieto, S. (2000a). Bringing bilingual education out of the basement, and other imperatives for teacher education. See also Montaño, Ulanoff, Quintanar-Sarellana & Aoki (2005).
3. Lomawaima & McCarty (2006). Also see McCarty (2006). For more on Navajo culture and education, see Manuelito (2005).
4. Olsen (2000).
5. Arts Education Working Group (2010, March). Available from Americans for the Arts at http://artsactionfund.org/news/entry/speak-up-for-the-arts-in-schools
6. Díaz, Moll & Mehan (1986).
7. Croninger & Lee (2001).
8. Santiago (1993), pp. 64, 66, 68.
9. Morris Raphael Cohen, quoted in Brumberg, S. F. (1986); p. 116.
10. Lambert & Taylor (1990).
11. Seelye (1993).
12. Greenbaum (1974), p. 431.
13. Salomone (2010).
14. See Nieto (1994) for an expansion of this model, with scenarios for each level.
15. Kalantzis & Cope (1990), p. 39.
16. I (Sonia) have written on this issue in more detail. See Nieto (2003a). Profoundly multicultural questions. *Educational Leadership 60* (4), 6–10.
17. Dickeman (1973).
18. See Banks, Cookson, Gay, Hawley, Irvine, Nieto, Schofield & Stephan (2001).

References

Adams, D. W. (1995). *Education for extinction: American Indians and the boarding school experience, 1875–1928.* Lawrence: University Press of Kansas.

Adesope, O. O., Lavin, T., Thompson, T., & Ungerleider, C. (2010). A systematic review and meta-analysis of the cognitive correlates of bilingualism. *Review of Educational Research, 80*(2), 207–245.

Adger, C. T., Snow, C. E., & Christian, D. (Eds.). (2002). *What teachers need to know about language.* Washington, DC: Center for Applied Linguistics.

Advancement Project. (2009). Retrieved from http://www.advancementproject.org/

Advancement Project. (2010). *Test, punish, and push out: How 'zero tolerance' and high-stakes testing funnel youth into the school-to-prison pipeline.* Washington, DC: Author.

Advancement Project, Civil Rights Project of Harvard University. (2000). Opportunities suspended: The devastating consequences of zero tolerance and school discipline. Paper presented at the *National Summit on Zero Tolerance,* Washington, DC. Retrieved from http://civilrightsproject.ucla.edu/research/k-12-education/school-discipline/opportunities-suspended-the-devastating-consequences-of-zero-tolerance-and-school-discipline-policies/?searchterm=Opportunities%20suspended

Africa Section, Strategic Communications Division, Department of Public Information, United Nations. (2010). *United Nations Africa Renewal.* Retrieved from http://www.un.org/ecosocdev/geninfo/afrec/vol17no2/172brain.htm

Alexie, S. (2007). *The absolutely true diary of a part-time Indian.* New York: Little, Brown & Co.

Allen, J. (2007). *Creating welcoming schools: A practical guide to home-school partnerships with diverse families.* New York: Teachers College Press.

Allport, G. W. (1954). *The nature of prejudice.* Reading, MA: Addison-Wesley.

American Educational Research Association. (2010). *American Educational Research Association Website.* Retrieved from http://www.aera.net

American Recovery and Reinvestment Act of 2009, Pub. L. No. 111-5, 14005-6, 123 Stat. 128 (2009).

Americans for the Arts. (2010). *Arts education: Creating student success in school, work, and life.* Retrieved March, 2010, from http://artsactionfund.org/news/entry/speak-up-for-the-arts-in-schools

Anaya, R. (1999). *Bless Me, Ultima.* New York: Grand Central Publishing.

Angkor Dance Troupe. (2010). *Helping Cambodian young people navigate the balance between contemporary youth culture and their cultural heritage.* Retrieved from www.angkordance.org

Antrop-González, R. (2006). Toward the school as sanctuary concept in multicultural small school urban education: Implications for small high school reform. *Curriculum Inquiry, 36*(3), 273–301.

Anyon, J. (2003). Inner cities, affluent suburbs, and unequal educational opportunity. In J. A. Banks & C. A. M. Banks (Eds.), *Multicultural education: Issues and perspectives* (4th ed., pp. 85–103). New York: John Wiley.

Anyon, J. (2005). *Radical possibilities: Public policy, urban education, and a new social movement.* New York: Routledge.

Apple, M. W. (1986). *Teachers and texts: A political economy of class and gender relations in education.* New York: Routledge.

Apple, M. W. (2004). *Ideology and curriculum* (3rd ed.). New York: Routledge.

Archibold, R. C. (2010, April 23). Arizona enacts stringent law on immigration. *New York Times,* doi:http://www.nytimes.com/2010/04/24/us/politics/24immig.html

Arizona. HB 2281 Prohibited courses; discipline; schools, (2010).

Arizona: SB: 1070. Support Our Law Enforcement and Safe Neighborhoods Act, U.S. Legal Permanent Residents. (2010).

Aronowitz, S. (1997). Between nationality and class. *Harvard Educational Review, 67*(2), 188–207.

Aronowitz, S. (2010). *Class: The anthology*. Boston, MA: Blackwell.

Arthur, J. (2000). *Invisible sojourners: African immigrant diaspora in the United States*. Westport, CT: Greenwood Press.

Aruri, N. H. (1969). The Arab-American community of Springfield, Massachusetts. In E. C. Hagopian, & A. Paden (Eds.), *The Arab-Americans: Studies in assimilation* (pp. 50–66). Wilmette, IL: Medina University Press International.

Ashton-Warner, S. (1963). *Teacher*. New York: Simon & Schuster.

Au, K. (2007). Culturally responsive instruction: Application to multiethnic classrooms. *Pedagogies, 2*(1), 1–18.

Au, W. (2009). *Unequal by design: High-stakes testing and the standardization of inequality*. New York: Routledge.

Au, W., Bigelow, B., & Karp, S. (Eds.). (2007). *Rethinking our classrooms: Teaching for equity and justice* (2nd ed.). Milwaukee: Rethinking Schools.

August, D., & Shanahan, T. (2006). *Developing literacy in second-language learners*. Mahwah, NJ: Lawrence Erlbaum; Center for Applied Linguistics.

Ayres, I., & Brown, J. G. (2005). *Straightforward: How to mobilize heterosexual support for gay rights*. Princeton, NJ: Princeton University Press.

Ayvazian, A. (2010). Interrupting the cycle of oppression: The role of allies as agents of change. In P. S. Rothenberg (Ed.), *Race, class, and gender in the United States* (8th ed., pp. 609–615). New York: Worth Publishers.

Baker, J. M. (2002). *How homophobia hurts children: Nurturing diversity at home, at school, and in the community*. San Francisco: Harrington Park Press.

Ballenger, C. (1999). *Teaching other people's children: Literacy and learning in a bilingual classroom*. New York: Teachers College Press.

Banks, J. A. (2004). Teaching for social justice, diversity, and citizenship in a global world. *The Educational Forum, 68,* 289–298.

Banks, J. A. (2009). Introduction. In J. A. Banks (Ed.), *The Routledge international companion to multicultural education* (pp. 1–5). New York: Routledge.

Banks, J. A. (2010a). Approaches to Multicultural Curriculum Reform. In J. A. Banks & C. A. M. Banks (Eds.), *Multicultural education: Issues and perspectives* (7th ed., pp. 233–256). Hoboken, NJ: John Wiley.

Banks, J. A. (2010b). Multicultural education: Characteristics and goals. In J. A. Banks & C. A. M. Banks (Eds.), *Multicultural education: Issues and perspectives* (7th ed., pp. 20–22). Hoboken, NJ: John Wiley.

Banks, J. A., & Banks, C. A. M. (Eds.). (2004). *Handbook of research on multicultural education* (2nd ed.). San Francisco: Jossey-Bass.

Banks, J. A., Cookson, P., Gay, G., Hawley, W. D., Irvine, J. J., Nieto, S., Schofield, J. W., & Stephan, W. W. (2001). *Diversity within unity: Essential principles for teaching and learning in a multicultural society*. Seattle: Center for Multicultural Education, University of Washington.

Baratz, S. S., & Baratz, J. C. (1971). Early childhood intervention: The social science base of institutional racism. *Harvard Educational Review* (Challenging the Myths: The Schools, the Blacks, and the Poor, Reprint Series no. 5).

Barber-Just, S. (2001). *Curriculum Proposal for Amherst Regional High School*. Unpublished manuscript.

Bartolomé, L. I. (1994). Beyond the methods fetish: Toward a humanizing pedagogy. *Harvard Educational Review, 64*(2), 173–195.

Bartolomé, L. I. (2008). Understanding policy for equity in teaching and learning: A critical-historical lens. *Language Arts, 85*(5), 376–381.

Barton, P. E., & Coley, R. J. (2009). *Parsing the Achievement Gap II*. Princeton, NJ: Educational Testing Service.

Bempechat, J. (2008). Reading success: A motivational perspective. In R. Fink & S. J. Samuels (Eds.), *Inspiring reading success: Interest and motivation in the age of high stakes testing* (pp. 75–97). Newark, DE: International Reading Association.

Berger, R. (2005). What is a culture of quality? In T. Hatch, D. Ahmed, A. Lieberman, D. Faigenbaum, M. E. White, & D. H. P. Mace (Eds.), *Going public with our teaching: An anthology of practice* (pp. 34–56). New York: Teachers College Press.

Berliner, D. C. (2006). Our impoverished view of educational reform. *Teachers College Record, 108*(6), 949–995.

Berliner, D. C. (2009). *Poverty and potential: Out-of-school factors and school success*. Boulder & Tempe: Education and the Public Interest Center & Educational Policy Research Unit. Retrieved from http://nepc.colorado.edu/publication/poverty-and-potential

Bhabha, H. K. (1994). *The location of culture*. London: Routledge.

Bialystok, E., Craik, F. I., & Freedman, M. (2007). Bilingualism as a protection against the onset of symptoms of dementia. *Neuropsychologia, 45*(2), 459–464.

Bigelow, B., Harvey, B., Karp, S., & Miller, L. (Eds.). (2001). *Rethinking our classrooms: Teaching for equity and justice*. Milwaukee, WI: Rethinking Schools.

Bigelow, B., & Peterson, B. (2003). *Rethinking Columbus: The next 500 years* (2nd ed.). Milwaukee, WI: Rethinking Schools.

Bigler, E. (1999). *American conversations: Puerto Ricans, White ethnics and multicultural education*. Philadelphia: Temple University Press.

Birnbaum, M. (2010, July 15). Texas board approves social studies standards that perceived liberal bias. *Washington Post,* retrieved from http://www .washingtonpost.com/wp-dyn/content/article/ 2010/05/21/AR2010052104365.html

Black, S. (2002). The roots of vandalism: When students engage in wanton destruction, what can schools do? *American School Board Journal, 189*(7), 1–7.

Black, S. (2004). Second time around. *American School Board Journal, 191*(11). Retrieved July 16, 2010, from www.asbj.com/researcharchive/index.html

Blatchford, P., Bassett, P., & Brown, P. (2008). Do low attaining and younger students benefit most from small classes? Results from a systematic observation study of class size effects on pupil classroom engagement and teacher pupil interaction. American Educational Research Association Annual Meeting, New York.

Blohm, J. M., & Lapinsky, T. (2006). *Kids like me: Voices of the immigrant experience.* Boston: Intercultural Press.

Blumenfeld, W. J., Joshi, K. Y., & Fairchild, E. E. (Eds.). (2008). *Investigating Christian privilege and religious oppression in the United States.* Boston: Sense Publishers.

Boateng, F. (1990). Combating deculturalization of the African-American child in the public school system: A multicultural approach. In K. Lomotey (Ed.), *Going to school: The African-American experience* (pp. 73–84). Albany: State University of New York Press.

Bode, P. (2005). *Multicultural art education: Voices of art teachers and students in the postmodern era.* Unpublished doctoral dissertation, University of Massachusetts, Amherst.

Bohn, A. (2006). A framework for understanding Ruby Payne. *Rethinking Schools, 21*(2), 13–15.

Books, S. (Ed.). (2006). *Invisible children in the society and its schools* (3rd ed.). Mahwah, NJ: Lawrence Earlbaum.

Booxbaum, R., & Mao, S. P. (2003). Amherst Public Schools Professional Development Workshops. *Cambodian Culture, American Soil: Conflict, Convergence and Compromise.* Amherst, MA.

Boston Children's Museum. (2002). *Many Thanksgivings: Teaching Thanksgiving—including the Wampanoag perspective.* Boston: Boston Children's Museum.

Bouie, A. (2006). *After-school success: Academic enrichment with urban youth.* New York: Teachers College Press.

Bourdieu, P. (1986). The forms of capital. In J. G. Richardson (Ed.), *Handbook of theory and research for the sociology of education* (pp. 241–258). New York: Greenwood Press.

Bourdieu, P., & Passeron, J. C. (1977). *Reproduction in education, society and culture.* London: Sage.

Bowles, S., & Gintis, H. (1976). *Schooling in capitalist America: Educational reform and the contradictions of economic life.* New York: Basic Books.

Bridgeland, J. M., DiIulio, J. J., Jr., & Morison, K. B. (2006). *The silent epidemic: Perspectives of high school dropout.* Washington, DC: Civic Enterprises.

Brisk, M. E. (2006). *Bilingual education: From compensatory to quality schooling* (2nd ed.). Mahwah, NJ: Lawrence Erlbaum.

Brooks-Young, S. (2010). Teaching with tools kids really use: Learning with web and mobile technologies. Thousand Oaks, CA: Corwin/Sage.

Brown, T. M. (2007). Lost and turned out: Academic, social and emotional experiences of students excluded from school. *Urban Education, 42*(5), 432–455.

Brumberg, S. F. (1986). *Going to America, going to school: The Jewish immigrant public school encounter in turn-of-the-century New York City.* New York: Praeger.

Buckel, D. S. (2000). Legal perspective on ensuring a safe and nondiscriminatory school environment for lesbian, gay, bisexual, and transgendered students. *Education and Urban Education, 32*(3), 390–398.

Buckley, J., Schneider, M., & Shang, Y. (2005). Fix it and they might stay: School facility quality and teacher retention in Washington, DC. *Teachers College Record, 107*(4), 1107–1123.

Buras, K. L. (2008). *Rightist multiculturalism: Core lessons on neoconservative school reform.* New York: Routledge.

Bureau of Indian Education. (2010). Retrieved from http://www.bie.edu/

Burris, C. C., Welner, K. G., & Bezoza, J. W. (2009). *Universal access to a quality education: Research and recommendations for the elimination of curricular stratification.* East Lansing, MI: Great Lakes Center for Education Research and Practice.

Byard, E. (2010). *GLSEN: Gay, Lesbian and Straight education network.* Retrieved from www.GLSEN.org

Callahan, R. M. (2005). Tracking and high school English learners: Limiting opportunity to learn. *American Educational Research Journal, 42*(2), 305–328.

Cambodian Masters Program. (2010). *Cambodian masters: Culture and art of Cambodia.* Retrieved from www.cambodianmasters.org

Campos, D. (2005). *Understanding gay and lesbian youth: Lessons for straight school teachers, counselors, and administrators.* Lanham, MD: Scarecrow Education.

Carey, K., & Roza, M. (2008). *School funding's tragic flaw.* Seattle: Center on Reinventing Public Education, University of Washington.

Carnes, J. (1999). Searching for patterns: A conversation with Carlos Cortés. *Teaching Tolerance, 16,* 10–15.

Carter, P. L. (2005). *Keepin' it real: School success beyond Black and White.* New York: Oxford University Press.

Carter, P. L. (2006). Straddling boundaries: Identity, culture, and school. *Sociology of Education, 79*(4), 304–328. doi:10.1177/003804070607900402

Celic, C. M. (2009). *English language learners day by day, K–6.* Portsmouth, NH: Heinemann.

Center on Education Policy. (2006). *From the capital to the classroom: Year 4 of the No Child Left Behind Act.* (No. 6851). Washington, DC: Center on Education Policy. Retrieved from http://www.cep-dc.org/index.cfm?fuseaction =Feature.showFeature&featureID = 7

Chang, B., & Au, W. (2007/2008). You're Asian, how could you fail math? Unmasking the myth of the model minority. *Rethinking Schools, 22*(2), 16–19.

Chenoweth, K. (2009a). *How it's being done: Urgent lessons from unexpected schools.* Cambridge, MA: Harvard Education Press.

Chenoweth, K. (2009b). It can be done, it's being done, and here's how. *Phi Delta Kappan, 91*(1), 38–43.

Children's Defense Fund. (2008). *America's cradle to prison pipeline.* Washington, DC: Children's Defense Fund. Retrieved from http://www.childrensdefense.org/child-research-data-publications/data/cradle-prison-pipeline-report-2007-full-highres.html#updates

Child Trends DataBank. (2010). Retrieved August 17, 2010, from http://www.childtrendsdatabank.org/?q = node/300

CHiXapkaid (Pavel, Michael), Banks-Joseph, S. R., Inglebret, E., McCubbin, L. L., Sievers, J., Bruna, L., Galaviz, S., Anderson, A., Egan, E., Brownfield, S., Lockhart, M., Grogan, G., & Sanyal, N. (2008). *From where the sun rises: Addressing the educational achievement of Native Americans in Washington State.* Pullman, WA: Clearinghouse on Native Teaching and Learning.

Choi, Y., He, M., & Harachi, T. W. (2007). Intergenerational cultural dissonance, parent–child conflict and bonding, and youth problem behaviors among Vietnamese and Cambodian immigrant families. *Journal of Youth and Adolescence, 37*(1), 85–96. doi:10.1007/s10964-007-9217-z

Chou, R. S., & Feagin, J. R. (2008). *The myth of the model minority: Asian Americans facing racism.* Boulder, CO: Paradigm Publishers.

Christensen, L. (2000). *Reading, writing and rising up.* Milwaukee, WI: Rethinking Schools.

Christensen, L. (2009). *Teaching for joy and justice.* Milwaukee, WI: Rethinking Schools.

Cipolle, S. B. (2010). *Service-learning and social justice: Engaging students in social change.* Lanham, MD: Rowman & Littlefield Publishers.

Clark, M. K. (2009). Questions of identity among African immigrants. In I. Okpewho & N. Nzegwu (Eds.), *The new African diaspora* (pp. 255–269). Bloomington: Indiana University Press.

Cloud, N., Genesee, F., & Hamayan, E. (2009). *Literacy instruction for English language learners.* Portsmouth, NH: Heinemann.

Coffield, F., Mosely, D., Hall, E., & Ecclestone, K. (2004). *Learning styles and pedagogy in post-16 learning: A systematic and critical review.* London: Learning Skills and Research Center/Cromwell Press.

Cohen, G. L., Garcia, J., Apfel, N., & Master, A. (2006). Reducing the racial achievement gap: A social-psychological intervention. *Science, 313*(5791), 1307–1310. doi:10.1126/science.1128317

Cohen, J., Pickeral, T., & McCloskey, M. (2008/2009). The challenge of assessing school climate. *Educational Leadership, 66*(4) Retrieved from www.ascd.org/publications/educational_leadership/dec08/vol66/num0/The_Challenge_of_Assessing_School_Climate.aspx.

Colorado Small Schools. (2010). Retrieved from www.coloradosmallschools.org

Comber, B. (2000). What *really* counts in early literacy lessons. *Language Arts, 78*(1), 29–39.

Comber, B. (2001). Critical literacies and local action: Teacher knowledge and a "new" research agenda. In B. Comber & A. Simpson (Eds.), *Negotiating critical literacies in classrooms* (pp. 301–314). Mahwah, NJ: Lawrence Erlbaum.

Combs, B. (2001). *1,2,3: A family counting book.* Ridley Park, PA: Two Lives.

Common Core. (2009). *Why we're behind: What top nations teach their students but we don't.* Washington, DC: Common Core. Retrieved from http://www.commoncore.org/ourreports.php

Compton-Lilly, C. (2004). *Confronting racism, poverty, and power: Classroom strategies to change the world.* Portsmouth, NH: Heinemann.

Conchas, G. Q. (2006). *The color of success: Race and high-achieving urban youth.* New York: Teachers College Press.

Conchas, G. Q., & Rodriguez, L. F. (2008). *Small schools and urban youth: Using the power of school culture to engage students.* Newbury Park, CA: Corwin Press.

Cook-Sather, A. (Ed.). (2009). *Learning from the student's perspective: A sourcebook for effective teaching.* Boulder, CO: Paradigm.

Cowhey, M. (2006). *Black ants and Buddhists: Thinking critically and teaching differently in the primary grades.* Portland, ME: Stenhouse.

Crabtree, S. (2004, June 4), Teachers who care get the most from kids. *Detroit News.* Retrieved from www.detnews.com/2004/schools/0406/04/a09173712htm

Crawford, E., Wright, M. O., & Masten, A. S. (2006). Resilience and spirituality in youth. In E. Roehlkepartain, P. E. King, L. Wagener, & P. L. Benson (Eds.), *The handbook of spiritual development in childhood and adolescence* (pp. 355–370). Thousand Oaks, CA: Sage.

Crawford, J. (2000). *At war with diversity: U.S. language policy in an age of anxiety.* Tonawanda, NY: Multilingual Matters.

Crawford, J. (2008a). *Advocating for English learners: Selected essays.* Bristol, UK: Multilingual Matters.

Crawford, J. (2008b). Loose ends in a tattered fabric: The inconsistency of language rights in the United States. In J. Magnet (Ed.), *Language rights in comparative perspective* (np). Markham, ON: LexisNexis Butterworths.

Crawford, J., & Krashen, S. (2008). *English learners in American classrooms: 101 questions, 101 answers.* New York: Scholastic.

Croninger, R. G., & Lee, V. E. (2001). Social capital and dropping out of high school: Benefits to at-risk students of teachers' support and guidance. *Teachers College Record, 103*(4), 548–581.

CSPAN2 Book TV. (2001). *In Depth: Ronald Takaki.* Retrieved from http://www.booktv.org/Watch/ 10271/In + Depth + Ronald + Takaki.aspx

Cummins, J. (2000). *Language, power, and pedagogy: Bilingual children in the crossfire.* Clevedon, UK: Multilingual Matters.

Cummins, J. (2001). *Negotiating identities: Education for empowerment in a diverse society* (2nd ed.). Ontario, CA: California Association for Bilingual Education.

Cummins, J. (2007a). Pedagogies for the poor? Realigning reading instruction for low-income students with scien-tifically-based reading research. *Educational Researcher, 36*(9), 564–572.

Cummins, J. (2007b). *Literacy, technology, and diversity: Teaching for success in changing times.* Boston: Allyn & Bacon/Pearson.

D'Amico, J. J. (2001). A closer look at the minority achievement gap. *Educational Research Service ERS Spectrum, 19*(2), 4–10.

Dantas, M. L., & Manyak, P. C. (Eds.). (2010). *Home-school connections in a multicultural society: Learning from and with culturally and linguistically diverse families.* New York: Routledge.

Darling-Hammond, L. (2010). *The flat world and education: How America's commitment to equity will determine our future.* New York: Teachers College Press.

David, G. C., & Ayouby, K. K. (2005). Studying the exotic other in the classroom: The portrayal of Arab Americans in educational source materials. *Multicultural Perspectives 7*(4), 13–20.

Delgado, R., & Stefancic, J. (2001). *Critical race theory: An introduction.* New York: New York University Press.

Delpit, L., & Doudy, J. K. (Eds.). (2008). *The skin that we speak: Thoughts on language and culture in the classroom.* New York: The New Press.

DeNavas-Walt, C., Proctor, B. D., & Smith, J. C. (2008). *Current population reports, income, poverty, and health insurance coverage in the United States: 2008* (No. P60-238). Washington, DC: U.S. Census Bureau. Retrieved from www.census.gov/prod/2010pubs/ p60-238.pdf

Derman-Sparks, L. (1997). *Teaching/learning anti-racism: A developmental approach.* New York: Teachers College Press.

Derman-Sparks, L., & the A.B.C. Task Force. (1989). *Anti-bias curriculum: Tools for empowering young children.* Washington, DC: National Association for the Education of Young Children.

Derman-Sparks, L., Ramsey, P. G., & Edwards, J. O. (2006). *What if all the kids are White? Anti-bias multicultural education with young children and families.* New York: Teachers College Press.

Dewey, J. (1966). *Democracy and education.* New York: Free Press.

Deyhle, D., & Swisher, K. (1997). Research in American Indian and Alaska Native education: From assimilation to self-determination. *Review of Research in Education, 22,* 113–194.

Deyhle, D., Swisher, K., Stevens, T., & Galván, R. T. (2008). Indigenous resistance and renewal: From colonizing practices to self-determination. In F. M. Connelly, M. Fang He, & J. Phillion (Eds.), *The Sage handbook of curriculum and instruction* (pp. 329–348). Los Angeles: Sage.

Díaz, S., Moll, L. C., & Mehan, H. (1986). Sociocultural resources in instruction: A context-specific approach. In Los Angeles Office of Bilingual Education (Ed.), *Beyond language: Social and cultural factors in schooling language minority students* (pp. 187–230). Los Angeles: California State Department of Education, Evaluation, Dissemination and Assessment Center.

Dickeman, M. (1973). Teaching cultural pluralism. In J. A. Banks (Ed.), *Teaching ethnic studies: Concepts and strategies* (43rd yearbook ed.). Washington, D.C.: National Council for the Social Studies.

Dodson, H., & Diouf, S. A. (Eds.). (2006). *In motion: The African-American migration experience.* New York: The New York Public Library Schomburg Center for Research in Black Culture.

Dolby, N. (2000). Changing selves: Multicultural education and the challenge of new identities. *Teachers College Record, 102*(5), 898–912.

Dolson, D., & Burnham-Massey, L. (Eds.). (2010). *Improving education for English learners: Research-based approaches.* Sacramento: California Department of Education.

Donaldson, K. B. M. (1996). *Through students' eyes: Combating racism in United States schools.* Westport, CT: Praeger.

Donaldson, K. B. M. (2001). *Shattering the denial: Protocols for the classrooms and beyond.* Westport, CT: Bergin & Garvey.

Dozier, C., Johnston, P., & Rogers, R. (2006). *Critical literacy, critical teaching: Tools for preparing responsive teachers.* New York: Teachers College Press.

Dragan, P. B. (2005). *A how-to guide for teaching English language learners in the primary classroom.* Portsmouth, NH: Heinemann.

Drummond, K. V., & Stipek, D. (2004). Low income parents' beliefs about their role in their children's academic learning. *The Elementary School Journal, 104*(3), 197–213.

DuBois, W. E. B. (1935). Does the Negro need separate schools? *Journal of Negro Education, 4*(3), 328–335.

Eck, D. L. (2001). *A new religious America: How a "Christian Country" has become the world's most religiously diverse nation*. New York: Harper Collins.

Edelman, M. W. (2007, July). The cradle to prison pipeline: An American health crisis. *Preventing Chronic Disease, 4*(3). Retrieved from http://www.ncbi.nlm.nih.gov/pmc/articles/PMC1955386/

Edwards, V. B. (2006). Quality Counts at 10: A Decade of Standards-Based Education. *Education Week, 25*(17). Retrieved July 14, 2010 from http://www.edweek.org/ew/toc/2006/01/05/index.html.

Elmore, R. F. (2002). Testing trap. *Harvard Magazine, 105*(1), 35 + . Retrieved from http://harvardmagazine.com/magazine/issues

El Rassi, T. (2007). *Arab in America* (Graphic novel). San Francisco: Last Gasp Publications.

Epstein, J. L., Sanders, M. G., Sheldon, S. B., Simon, B. S., Salinas, K. C., Jansorn, N. R., Van Voorhis, F. L., Martin, C. S., Thomas, B. G., Greenfeld, M. D., Hutchins, D. J., & Williams, K. J. (2009). *School, family, and community partnerships: Your handbook for action* (3rd ed.). New York: Corwin Press.

Equal Educational Opportunity Act, 20 U.S.C. § 1703 (1974).

Erickson, F. (1993). Transformation and school success: The politics and culture of educational achievement. In E. Jacob & C. Jordan (Eds.), *Minority education: Anthropological perspectives* (pp. 27–51). New York: Ablex.

Faircloth, S. C., & Tippeconnic, J. W., III. (2010). *The dropout/graduation rate crisis among American Indian and Alaska Native students: Failure to respond places the future of native peoples at risk*. Los Angeles: The Civil Rights Project/Proyecto Derechos Civiles at UCLA. Retrieved from http://civilrightsproject.ucla.edu/research/k-12-education/school-dropouts/the-dropout-graduation-crisis-among-american-indian-and-alaska-native-students-failure-to-respond-places-the-future-of-native-peoples-at-risk

FairTest: The National Center for Fair and Open Testing. (2009). *FairTest critical comments on US Education Department's "Race to the Top Fund" guidelines*. Retrieved from http://www.fairtest.org/fairtest-critical-comments-us-education-department

Fass, S., & Cauthen, N. K. (2008). *Who are America's poor children? The official story*. New York: National Center for Children in Poverty, Mailman School of Public Health at Columbia University. Retrieved from http://nccp.org/publications/pub_684.html

Fecho, B. (2003). *Is this English? Race, language, and culture in the classroom*. New York: Teachers College Press.

Ferguson, A. A. (2001). *Bad boys: Public school in the making of Black masculinity*. Ann Arbor: University of Michigan Press.

Ferguson, R. F. (2007). *Toward excellence with equity: An emerging vision for closing the achievement gap*. Cambridge, MA: Harvard Education Press.

Ferguson, R. F. (2008). Helping students of color meet high standards. In M. Pollock (Ed.), *Everyday antiracism: Getting real about race in school* (pp. 78–81). New York: New Press.

Fine, M. (1991). *Framing dropouts: Notes on the politics of an urban high school*. Albany: State University of New York Press.

Fine, M. (2005). Not in our name: Reclaiming the democratic vision on small school reform. *Rethinking Schools, 19*(4), 11–14.

Finn, J. D., Gerber, S. B., Achilles, C. M., & Byrd-Zaharias, J. (2001). The enduring effects of small classes. *Teachers College Record, 103*(2), 145–183.

Fisher, D., Rothenberg, C., & Frey, N. (2007). *Language learners in the English classroom*. Urbana, IL: National Council of Teachers of English.

Flores-González, N. (2002). *School kids, street kids: Identity and high school completion among Latinos*. New York: Teachers College Press.

Fordham, S., & Ogbu, J. U. (1986). Black students' school success: Coping with the burden of acting White. *Urban Review, 18*(3), 176–206.

Fontánez, E. (2010). *Exit studio*. Retrieved from http://www.exitstudio.com/

Forum for Education and Democracy. (2010). *Creating a national culture of learning: The forum for education and democracy's recommendation for the reauthorization of ESEA*. Retrieved from www.forumforeducation.org

Fosnot, C. T. (Ed.). (2005). *Constructivism: Theory, perspectives, and practice* (2nd ed.). New York: Teachers College Press.

Foster, M. (1997). *Black teachers on teaching*. New York: The New Press.

Fraser, S. (Ed.). (1995). *The bell curve wars: Race, intelligence, and the future of America*. New York: Basic Books.

Freeman, Y. S., & Freeman, D. E. (2008). *Academic language for English language learners and struggling readers: How to help students succeed across content areas*. Portsmouth, NH: Heinemann.

Freeman, Y. S., Freeman, D. E., & Ramirez, R. (2008). *Diverse learners in the mainstream classroom*. Portsmouth, NH: Heinemann.

Freire, P. (1970). *Pedagogy of the oppressed*. New York: Seabury Press.

Freire, P. (1985). *The politics of education: Culture, power, and liberation*. South Hadley, MA: Bergen & Garvey.

Freire, P. (2005). *Teachers as cultural workers: Letters to those who dare teach* (expanded ed.). Boulder, CO: Westview Press.

Fry, R. (2008). *The role of schools in the English language learner achievement gap.* Washington, DC: Pew Hispanic Center. Retrieved from pewhispanic.org/reports/report.php?ReportID=89

Fu, D. (2009). *Writing between languages: How English language learners make the transition to fluency, grades 4–12.* Portsmouth, NH: Heinemann.

Future Business Leaders of America. (2010). *Future Business Leaders of America website.* Retrieved from http://www.fbla-pbl.org

Gándara, P. (1995). *Over the ivy walls: The educational mobility of low-income Chicanos.* Albany: State University of New York Press.

Gándara, P. (2008). *The crisis in the education of Latino students* (Research Brief. vol. 1a). University of California–Los Angeles: Civil Rights Project/Proyecto Derechos Civiles. Retrieved from http://www.nea.org/home/17404.htm

Gándara, P., & Contreras, F. (2010). *The Latino education crisis: The consequences of failed social policies.* Cambridge, MA: Harvard University Press.

Gándara, P., & Hopkins, M. (2010). *Forbidden language: English learners and restrictive language policies.* New York: Teachers College Press.

García, E. E., & Frede, E. C. (Eds.). (2010). *Young English language learners: Current research and emerging directions for practice and policy.* New York: Teachers College Press.

García, O. (2009). *Bilingual education in the 21st century: A global perspective.* Indianapolis, IN: Wiley-Blackwell.

Gardner, H. (2006). *Multiple intelligences: New horizons.* New York: Basic Books.

Gardner, H. (2008a). The 25th anniversary of the publication of Howard Gardner's *Frames of Mind: The Theory of Multiple Intelligences* [Online forum comment]. Retrieved from http://www.pz.harvard.edu/pis/hg.htm

Gardner, H. (2008b). *Five minds for the future.* Cambridge, MA: Harvard Business School Press.

Garza, R. (2009). Latino and White high school students' perceptions of caring behaviors: Are we culturally responsive to our students? *Urban Education, 44*(3), 297–321. doi:10.1177/0042085908318714

Gates Foundation, Bill & Melinda. (2010). Retrieved from www.gatesfoundation.org/education

Gay, G. (2010). *Culturally responsive teaching: Theory, research, and practice* (2nd ed.). New York: Teachers College Press.

Geary, R. (2009). *Multicultural education and global education: Preparing the next generation of world citizens* (Unpublished master's thesis). Lesley University, Cambridge, MA.

Geiser, S., & Santelices, M. V. (2007). *Validity of high school grades in predicting student success beyond the freshman year: High-school record vs. standardized tests as indicators of four-year college outcomes.* Berkeley: Center for Studies in Higher Education; University of California, Berkeley. Retrieved from http://cshe.berkeley.edu/publications/publications.php?id=265

Genesee, F., Lindholm-Leary, K., Saunders, W. M., & Christian, D. (2006). *Educating English language learners: A synthesis of research evidence.* New York: Cambridge University Press.

Gibson, M. (1997). Conclusion: Complicating the immigrant/involuntary minority typology. *Anthropology and Education Quarterly, 28*(3), 431–454.

Gibson, M., & Bejínez, L. F. (2002). Dropout prevention: How migrant education supports Mexican youth. *Journal of Latinos and Education, 1*(3), 155–175.

Gibson, M., Gándara, P., & Koyama, J. P. (Eds.). (2004). *School connections: U.S. Mexican youth, peers, and school achievement.* New York: Teachers College Press.

Gibson, P. (1989). *Gay male and lesbian youth suicide. Report of the Secretary's task force on youth suicide.* Washington, DC: U.S. Department of Health and Human Services.

Gillborn, D. (1997). Ethnicity and educational performance in the United Kingdom: Racism, ethnicity, and variability in achievement. *Anthropology & Education Quarterly, 28*(3), 375–393.

Gillespie, P., & Kaeser, G. (2010). *Family diversity projects.* Retrieved from http://www.familydiv.org/

Giroux, H. (1996). *Fugitive cultures: Race, violence and youth.* New York: Routledge.

Giroux, H. A. (2001). *Theory and resistance in education: Towards a pedagogy for the opposition.* Westport, CT: Bergen & Garvey.

Giroux, H. A. (2002). Democracy, freedom, and justice after September 11th: Rethinking the role of educators and the politics of schooling. *Teachers College Record, 104*(6), 1138–1162.

Giroux, H. A. (2006). Spectacles of race and pedagogies of denial: Antiblack racist pedagogy. In D. Macedo, & P. Gounari (Eds.), *The globalization of racism* (pp. 68–93). Boulder, CO: Paradigm.

GLSEN. (2009a). *The experiences of lesbian, gay, bisexual and transgender middle school students* (GLSEN research brief). New York: Gay, Lesbian and Straight Education Network.

GLSEN. (2009b). *National school climate survey 2009* (GLSEN research brief). New York: Gay, Lesbian and Straight Education Network.

González, J. (2002, June 27). Schools ruling defies logic. *New York Daily News.* Retrieved from www.nydailynews.com/.../2002-06-27_schools_ruling_defies_logic.html

Gonzalez, N., Moll, L. & Amanti, C. (2005). *Funds of knowledge: Theorizing practices in households, communities, and classrooms.* Mahwah, NJ: Lawrence Erlbaum.

Goodlad, J. I. (2004). *A place called school* (20th anniversary ed.). New York: McGraw-Hill.

Gorski, P. (2006/2007). Savage inequalities: Uncovering classism in Ruby Payne's framework. *Rethinking Schools, 21*(2), 16–19

Gorski, P. (2008). Peddling poverty for profit: Elements of oppression in Ruby Payne's framework. *Equity & Excellence in Education, 41*(1), 130–148. doi:10.1080/10665680701761854

Gould, S. J. (1996, revised and expanded from 1981). *The mismeasure of man* (2nd ed.). New York: W. W. Norton.

Governor's Commission on Gay and Lesbian Youth. (1993). *Making schools safe for gay and lesbian youth: Breaking the silence in schools and in families.* Boston: Massachusetts Department of Education.

Grande, S. (2004). *Red pedagogy: Native American social and political thought.* Lanham, MD: Rowman & Littlefield.

Grande, S. (2008). Red pedagogy: The un-methodology. In N. Denzin, Y. S. Lincoln, & L. T. Smith (Eds.), *Handbook of critical and indigenous methodologies* (pp. 233–254). Thousand Oaks, CA: Sage.

Grant-Thomas, A., & Orfield, G. (2009). *Twenty-first century color lines: Multiracial change in contemporary America.* Philadelphia: Temple University Press.

Gray, M. W. (2010). *AMIDEAST.* Retrieved from www.amideast.org

Greenbaum, W. (1974). America in search of a new ideal: An essay on the rise of pluralism. *Harvard Educational Review, 44*(3), 411–440.

Greene, M. (2000). *Releasing the imagination: Essays on education, the arts, and social change.* San Francisco: Jossey-Bass.

Gregory, A., Skiba, R. J., & Noguera, P. A. (2010). The achievement gap and the discipline gap: Two sides of the same coin? *Educational Researcher, 39*(1), 59–68.

Grieco, E. (2010). *Race and Hispanic origin of foreign-born population in the United States: 2007* (American community survey reports). Washington, DC: U. S. Census Bureau. Retrieved from www.census.gov/prod/2010pubs/acs-11.pdf

Grigg, W., Moran, R., & Kuang, M. (2010). *National Indian education study—Part I: Performance of American Indian and Alaska Native students at grades 4 and 8 on NAEP 2009 reading and mathematics assessments* (Report No. NCES 2010–462). Washington, DC: National Center for Education Statistics; Institute of Education Sciences; U.S. Department of Education. Retrieved from nces.ed.gov/nationsreportcard/nies/

Guarnizo, L., Portes, A., & Haller, W. (2003). Assimilation and transnationalism: Determinants of transnational political action among contemporary migrants. *American Journal of Sociology, 108*(6), 1211–1248.

Gutierrez, K., & Rogoff, B. (2003). Cultural ways of learning: Individual traits or repertoires of practice. *Educational Researcher, 32*(5), 19–25.

Haberman, M. (1991). The pedagogy of poverty versus good teaching. *Phi Delta Kappan, 73*(4), 290–294.

Haberman, M. (1995). Selecting "star" teachers for children and youth in urban poverty. *Phi Delta Kappan, 76*(10), 777–781.

Hajar, P. (2008). Arab Americans: Concepts, strategies, and materials. In J. A. Banks (Ed.), *Teaching strategies for ethnic studies* (8th ed., pp. 489–508). Boston: Allyn & Bacon.

Halford, J. M. (1999). A different mirror: A conversation with Ronald Takaki. *Educational Leadership, 56*(7), 9–13.

Hall, D., & Ushomirsky, N. (2010). *Close the hidden funding gaps in our schools.* Washington, DC: The Education Trust.

Halpern, D. (2005). *Social capital.* Cambridge, England: Polity Press.

Halpern, R. (2003). *Making play work: The promise of after-school programs for low-income children.* New York: Teachers College Press.

Hancock, Markie (Producer), & Fine, M. (Director). (1998). *Off track: Classroom privilege for all* [DVD]. Available from Teachers College Press at www.tcpress.com

Harlem Children's Zone. (2009). Retrieved from http://www.hcz.org/

Harmon, J., Zenkov, K., van Lier, P. & Reid, H. (2009). *Through students' eyes.* Retrieved September, 15, 2010, from http://www.throughstudentseyes.org/TSE/Home.html

Harrington, M. (1997/1971). *The other America: Poverty in the United States.* New York: Scribner.

Harry, B., & Klingner, J. (2006). *Why are so many minority students in special education? Understanding race and disability in schools.* New York: Teachers College Press.

Harvard Family Research Project. (2007). *Family involvement makes a difference.* Cambridge, MA: Harvard Graduate School of Education. Retrieved from http://www.hfrp.org/

Heath, S. B. (1983). *Ways with words.* New York: Cambridge University Press.

Heath, S. B. (2010). Family literacy or community learning? Some critical questions on perspective. In K. Dunsmore & D. Fisher (Eds.), *Bringing literacy home* (pp. 15–41). Newark, DE: International Reading Association.

Helms, A. D. (2010, February 7). Worker: School banned Spanish. *The Charlotte Observer.* Retrieved from http://www.charlotteobserver.com/2010/02/07/1230320/worker-school-banned-spanish.html

Henderson, N., Wood, J. A., & Kristonis, W. A. (2007). Muslims in America. *National Forum of Multicultural Issues Journal, 4*(2), 1–8.

Hernandez, D. J., Denton, N. A., & Macartney, S. E. (2008). Children in immigrant families: Looking to America's future. *Social Policy Report: Giving Child and Youth Development Knowledge Away, 22*(3), 3–13 Society for Research in Child Development. Retrieved from https://www.srcd.org/index.php

Hernandez, R., & Rivera-Batiz, F. L. (2006). *Dominicans in the United States: A socioeconomic profile, 2000*. New York: CUNY Dominican Studies Institute.

Herrara, S. (2010). *Biography-driven culturally responsive teaching*. New York: Teachers College Press.

Herrnstein, R. J., & Murray, C. (1994/2010). *The bell curve: Intelligence and class structure in American life*. New York: Simon & Schuster.

Hildago, N. M. (2005). Latino/a families' epistemology. In P. Pedraza, & M. Rivera (Eds.), *Latino/a education: An agenda for community action research* (pp. 375–402). Mahwah, NJ: Lawrence Erlbaum.

Hill, N. E., & Chao, R. K. (Eds.). (2009). *Families, schools, and the adolescent: Connecting research, policy, and practice*. New York: Teachers College Press.

Him, C. (2001). *When broken glass floats: Growing up under the Khmer Rouge*. New York: W.W. Norton.

Hines, M. S. (2002). Remembering Amadou Diallo: The response of the New Teachers Network. *Phi Delta Kappan, 84*(4), 303–306.

Hirsch, B. J. (2005). *A place to call home: After-school programs for urban youth*. New York: Teachers College Press.

Hirsch, E. D. (1987). *Cultural literacy: What every American needs to know*. New York: Houghton-Mifflin.

Hirsch, E. D., Jr. (Ed.). (1994). *What your fourth grader needs to know: Fundamentals of a good fourth-grade education (the core knowledge)*. New York: Delta.

Hobbel, N., & Chapman, T. K. (2009). Beyond the sole category of race: Using a CRT intersectional framework to map identity projects. *The Journal of Curriculum Theorizing, 25*(2), 76–89.

Hollins, E. (2008). *Culture in school learning: Revealing the deep meaning* (2nd ed.). New York: Routledge.

Hong, G., & Raudenbush, S. W. (2005). Effects of kindergarten retention policy on children's cognitive growth in reading and mathematics. *Educational Evaluation and Policy Analysis, 27*(3), 205–224.

Horne v. Flores, 516 S. Ct. 3d 1140 (2009).

Howard, E. R., Christian, D., & Genesee, F. (2004). *The development of bilingualism and biliteracy from grade 3 to 5: A summary of findings from the CAL/CREDE study of two-way immersion education* (Report No. 13). Santa Cruz: Center for Research on Education, Diversity, and Excellence at the University of California, Santa Cruz. Retrieved from www.cal.org/crede/pdfs /rr13.pdf

Howard, G. (2006). *"We can't teach what we don't know": White teachers, multiracial schools* (2nd ed.). New York: Teachers College Press.

Howard, J. (2010). *The Efficacy Institute*. Retrieved from http://www.efficacy.org/

Howard, T. C. (2010). *Why race and culture matter in schools: Closing the achievement gap in America's classrooms*. New York: Teachers College Press.

Howe, I. (1983). *World of our fathers*. New York: Simon & Schuster.

Hughes, J. M., & Bigler, R. S. (2007). Addressing race and racism in the classroom. In E. Frankenberg & G. Orfield (Eds.), *Lessons in integration: Realizing the promise of racial diversity in American schools* (pp. 190–206). Charlottesville: University of Virginia Press.

Huh, N. Y. (2005, August 9). Does money transform schools? *The Christian Science Monitor,* Retrieved from www.csmonitor.com/2005/0809/p01.S03-ussc.html

Humphries, J. M. (2009). Resisting "race": Organizing African transnational identities in the United States. In I. Okpewho & N. Nzegwu (Eds.), *The New African Diaspora* (pp. 271–301). Bloomington: Indiana University Press.

Independent Television Service, the Center for Asian American Media, & WGBH Boston (Producer), & Mallozzi, J. (Director). (2006). *Monkey dance* [Video/DVD] Quincy, MA: American Public Television (APT).

IRIN a service of the UN Office for the Coordination of Humanitarian Affairs. (2009, April 22). West Africa: Combating world's lowest literacy rates. *IRIN Humanitarian News and Analysis.* Retrieved from http://www.irinnews.org/Report.aspx?ReportId=84052

Irizarry, J. (2007). Ethnic and urban intersections in the classroom: Latino students, hybrid identities, and culturally responsive pedagogy. *Multicultural Perspectives, 9*(3), 1–7.

Irizarry, J. G. (2011a). Culturally responsive pedagogy. In J. M. Cooper (Ed.), *Classroom teaching skills* (9th ed., pp. 188–214. Boston: Houghton Mifflin.

Irizarry, J. G. (2011b). *The Latinization of U.S. schools: Successful teaching and learning in shifting cultural contexts*. Boulder, CO: Paradigm.

Irizarry, J. G., & Raible, J. (In press). Beginning with El Barrio: Learning from exemplary teachers of Latino students. *Journal of Latinos and Education.*

Irvine, J. J. (2003). *Educating teachers for a diverse society: Seeing with the cultural eye*. New York: Teachers College Press.

Irvine, J. J., & Fraser, J. W. (1998). Warm demanders. *Education Week, 17*(35), 56–57.

Jacobs, H. H. (2009). (Ed.). *Curriculum 21: Essential education for a changing world*. Alexandria, VA: Association for Supervision and Curriculum Development.

Jackson, D. B. (2003). Education reform as if student agency mattered: Academic microcultures and student identity. *Phi Delta Kappan, 84*(8), 579–585.

Jamal, A., & Naber, N. (2008). *Race and Arab Americans before and after 9/11: From invisible citizens to visible subjects*. Syracuse, NY: Syracuse University Press.

Janks, H. (2010). *Literacy and power*. New York: Routledge.

Jo, J. O. (2004). Neglected voices in the multicultural America: Asian American racial politics and its implication for multicultural education. *Multicultural Perspectives, 6*(1), 19–25.

John, S., and James L. Knight Foundation. (2005). *Future of the First Amendment.* Author. Retrieved from www.firstamendmentfuture.org/

Johnson, M. K., Crosnoe, R., & Elder, G. H. J. (2001). Students' attachment and academic engagement: The role of race and ethnicity. *Sociology of Education, 74*(4), 318–334.

Joshi, K. Y. (2006). *New roots in America's sacred ground: religion, race, and ethnicity in Indian America.* New Brunswick, NJ: Rutgers University Press.

Jost, K. (2009). Bilingual education vs. English immersion: Which is better for students with limited English? *CQ Researcher, 19*(43), 1029–1052.

JSA. (2010). *Junior Statesman Foundation.* Retrieved from www.JSA.org

Jussim, L., & Eccles, J. S. (1992). Teacher expectations II: Construction and reflection of student achievement. *Journal of Personality and Social Psychology, 63*(6), 947–961.

Kaba, A. J. (2009). Africa's migration brain drain: Factors contributing to the mass emigration of Africa's elite to the West. In I. Okpewho & N. Nzegwu (Eds.), *The New African Diaspora* (pp. 109–125). Bloomington: Indiana University Press.

Kaeser, G., & Gillespie, P. (1997). *Of many colors: Portraits of multiracial families.* Amherst: University of Massachusetts Press.

Kalzantzis, M., & Cope, B. (1990). *The experience of multi-cultural education in Australia: Six case studies.* Sydney: Wollongong University, Center for Multicultural Studies.

Kaplan, J. (2005). The effectiveness of SAT coaching on math SAT scores. *Chance, 18*(2), 25–34.

Katz, M. B. (1975). *Class, bureaucracy, and the schools: The illusion of educational change in America.* New York: Praeger.

Kaur Foundation. (Producer & Director). (2008). *Cultural Safari* [DVD]. Available from: http://www.kaurfoundation.org

Keahi, S. (2000). Advocating for a stimulating and language-based education: "If you don't learn your language, where can you go home to?" In M. K. P. A. Nee-Benham & J. E. Cooper (Eds.), *Indigenous educational models for contemporary practice: In our mother's voice* (pp. 55–60). Mahwah, NJ: Lawrence Erlbaum.

Kiang, P. N., & Wai-Fun Lee, V. (1993). Exclusion or contribution? Education K–12 policy. In *The State of Asian Pacific America: Policy issues to the year 2020* (pp. 25–48). Los Angeles: Asian Pacific American Public Policy Institute & the UCLA Asian American Studies Center.

Kiernan, B. (2004). *How Pol Pot came to power: Colonialism, nationalism, and communism in Cambodia* (2nd ed.). New Haven, CT: Yale University Press.

Kiernan, B. (2008). *The Pol Pot regime: Race, power, and genocide in Cambodia under the Khmer Rouge, 1975–79* (3rd ed.). New Haven, CT: Yale University Press.

Kim, H. (1997). *Diversity among Asian American high school students.* Princeton, NJ: Policy Information Center, Educational Testing Service. Retrieved from http://www.ets.org/research/pic/asian.htm

Kincheloe, J. L., & Steinberg, S. R. (Eds.). (1997). *Measured lies: The bell curve examined.* New York: Palgrave McMillan.

King, J. E. (Ed.). (2005). *Black education: A transformative research and action agenda for the new century.* Mahwah, NJ: Lawrence Erlbaum.

Kober, N., Jennings, J., & Peltason, J. (2010). *Better federal policies leading to better schools.* Washington, DC: Center on Education Policy. Retrieved from http://www.cep-dc.org/index.cfm?fuseaction=Page.viewPage&pageId=536&parentID=481

Kohl, H. (1994). *"I won't learn from you" and other thoughts on creative maladjustment.* New York: New Press.

Kovács, Á. M., & Mehler, J. (2009). Cognitive gains in 7-month-old bilingual infants. *Proceedings of the National Academy of Sciences, 106*(16), 6556–6560.

Koyama, J. P. (2010). *Making failure pay: For-profit tutoring, high-stakes testing and public schools.* Chicago: University Of Chicago Press.

Kozol, J. (1975). Great men and women (tailored for school use). *Learning Magazine, 4*(4), 16–20.

Kozol, J. (2005). *The shame of the nation: Restoration of apartheid schooling in America.* New York: Crown.

Krashen, S. (1981). *Second language acquisition and second language learning.* New York: Pergamon Press.

Krigman, E. (2010). Education tracking continues to stir debate. *NationalJournal.com.* Retrieved from http://www.nationaljournal.com.ezproxy.library.tufts.edu/njonline/no_20091214_5320.php

Kugler, E. G. (2002). *Debunking the middle-class myth: Why diverse schools are good for all kids.* Lanham, MD: Scarecrow Press.

Kunjufu, J. (2007). *An African centered response to Ruby Payne's poverty theory.* Sauk Village, IL: African American Images.

Kunjufu, J. (2010). *Reducing the Black male dropout rate.* Sauk Village, IL: African American Images.

Kymlicka, W. (2007). Foreword. In J. A. Banks (Ed.), *Diversity and citizenship in education: Global perspectives* (pp. xiii–xviii). San Francisco: Jossey-Bass.

Ladd, H., Noguera, P. A., & Payzant, T. (2010). *A broader, bolder approach to education.* Retrieved September 1, 2010, from http://www.boldapproach.org/

Ladson-Billings, G. (2004). New directions in multicultural education: Complexities, boundaries, and critical race theory. In J. A. Banks & C. A. M. Banks (Eds.),

Handbook of research on multicultural education (2nd ed., pp. 50–65). San Francisco: Jossey-Bass.

Ladson-Billings, G. (2006a). From the achievement gap to the education debt: Understanding achievement in U.S. schools. *Educational Researcher, 35*(7), 3–12.

Ladson-Billings, G. (2006b). It's not the culture of poverty, it's the poverty of culture: The problem with teacher education. *Anthropology and Education Quarterly, 37*(2), 104–109.

Ladson-Billings, G. (2009). *The dreamkeepers: Successful teachers of African American children* (2nd ed.). San Francisco: Jossey-Bass.

Lake Research Partners and The Tarrance Group. (2006). *PEN: Give Kids Good Schools Launch.* Retrieved from http://www.publiceducation.org/

Lambert, W., & Taylor, D. (1990). *Coping with cultural and racial diversity in urban America.* Westport, CT: Praeger.

Lambert, W. E. (1975). Culture and language as factors in learning and education. In A. Wolfgang (Ed.), *Education of immigrant students: Issues and answers* (pp. 55–83). Toronto, Canada: Ontario Institute for Studies in Education.

Lau v. Nichols, 414 U.S. 563 (1974).

Lee, C. (2005). Intervention research based on current views of cognition and learning. In J. E. King (Ed.), *Black education: A transformative research and action agenda for the new century* (pp. 45–71). Washington, DC: American Educational Research Association.

Lee, C. (2007). *Culture, literacy, and learning: Taking bloom in the midst of the whirlwind.* New York: Teachers College Press.

Lee, E. (2004). Connecticut National Association for Multicultural Education (NAME). *Equity and Equality.* Hartford, CT.

Lee, E., Menkart, D., & Okazawa-Rey, M. (Eds.). (2006). *Beyond heroes and holidays: A practical guide to K–12 anti-racist, multicultural education and staff development* (3rd ed.). Washington, DC: Teaching for Change.

Lee, S. (2009). *Unraveling the "model minority" stereotype: Listening to Asian American students.* New York: Teachers College Press.

Lee, S., & Ngo, B. (2007). Complicating the image of model minority success: A review of Southeast Asian American education. *Review of Educational Research, 77*(4), 415–453.

Lee, V. E., & Burkam, D. T. (2003). Dropping out of high school: The role of school organization and structure. *American Educational Research Journal, 40*(2), 353–393.

Lee, V. E., & Loeb, S. (2000). School size in Chicago elementary schools: Effects on teachers' attitudes and students' achievement. *American Educational Research Journal, 37*(1), 3–31.

Levin, M. (2001). *"Teach me!" Kids will learn when oppression is the lesson.* Lanham, MD: Rowman & Littlefield.

Levitt, P. (2004). Salsa and ketchup: Transnational migrants straddle two worlds. *Contexts, 3*(2), 20–26.

Lewis, O. (1965). *La Vida: A Puerto Rican family in the culture of poverty—San Juan and New York.* New York: Random House.

Li, G., & Edwards, P. A. (Eds.). (2010). *Best practices in ELL instruction.* New York: Guilford Press.

Lieberman, A., & Miller, L. (Eds.). (2008). *Teachers in professional communities: Improving teaching and learning.* New York: Teachers College Press.

Lindholm-Leary, K., & Borsato, G. (2001). *Impact of two-way bilingual elementary programs on students' attitudes toward school and college* (Report No. 10). Santa Barbara, CA: Center for Research on Education, Diversity, and Excellence.

Lindsey, D. (2004). To build a more "Perfect Discipline": Ideologies of the normative and the social control of the criminal innocent in the policing of New York City. *Critical Sociology, 30*(2), 321–353.

Lipman, P. (1998). *Class, race, and power in school restructuring.* Albany: State University of New York Press.

Lipset, S. M., & Raab, E. (1995). *Jews and the new American scene.* Cambridge, MA: Harvard University Press.

Loewen, J. W. (2000). *Lies across America: What our historic sites got wrong.* New York: The New Press.

Loewen, J. W. (2005). *Lies my teacher told me: Everything your American history textbook got wrong.* New York: The New Press.

Loewen, J. W. (2009). *Teaching what really happened: How to avoid the tyranny of textbooks and get students excited about doing history.* New York: Teachers College Press.

Lomawaima, K. T., & McCarty, T. L. (2006). *To remain an Indian: Lessons in democracy from a century of Native American education.* New York: Teachers College Press.

Longhouse Media: Native Lens. (2010). Retrieved from http://www.longhousemedia.org/

Lopez-Torkos, A. M. (2003). Mixed-race school-age children: A summary of census 2000 data. *Educational Researcher, 32*(6), 25–37.

Love, A., & Kruger, A. C. (2005). Teacher beliefs and student achievement in urban schools serving African American students. *Journal of Educational Research, 99*(2), 87–98.

Maaka, M. J. (2004). E kua takoto te mānuka t~utahi: Decolonization, self-determination, and education. *Educational Perspectives, 37*(1), 3–13.

MacDonald, V. (2004). *Latino education in the United States: A narrated history.* New York: Palgrave Macmillan.

Mack, T., & Picower, B. (2010). *Planning to change the world: A plan book for social justice teachers.* New York: NYCoRE and the Education for Liberation Network.

Mahiri, J. (1998). *Shooting for excellence: African American and youth culture in new century schools*. New York: Teachers College Press.

Mantsios, G. (2010). Class in America: Myths and realities. In P. S. Rothenberg (Ed.), *Race, class and gender in the United States* (8th ed., pp. 168–182). New York: Worth.

Manuelito, K. (2005). The role of education in American Indian self-determination: Lessons from the Ramah Navajo Community School. *Anthropology & Education Quarterly, 36*(1), 73–87.

Marklein, M. B. (2009, August 25). SAT scores show disparities by race, gender, family income. *USA Today*. Retrieved from http://www.usatoday.com/

Markow, D., & Scheer, M. (2003). *The MetLife Survey of the American Teacher: An examination of school leadership* (Report No. 20). Rochester, NY: Harris Interactive, Inc. Retrieved from http://www.metlife.com/about/corporate-profile/citizenship/metlife-foundation/metlife-survey-of-the-american-teacher.html?WT.mc_id=vu1101

Marquez, R. (1995). Sojourners, settlers, castaways, and creators: A recollection of Puerto Rico past and Puerto Ricans present. *Massachusetts Review, 36*(1), 94–118.

Martínez-Roldán, C. M., & Fránquiz, M. E. (2009). Latina/o youth literacies: Hidden funds of knowledge. In L. Christenbury, R. Bomer, & P. Smagorinsky (Eds.), *Handbook of adolescent literacy research* (pp. 323–342). New York: Guilford Press.

Matthews, J. (2008, March 10). Smaller classes don't close learning gap, study finds. *The New York Times*. Retrieved from http://www.nytimes.com/

May, S., & Sleeter, C. (2010). *Critical multiculturalism: Theory and praxis*. New York: Routledge.

McCarty, T. L. (2006). Reclaiming the gift: Indigenous youth counter-narratives on native language loss and revitalization. *American Indian Quarterly, 30*(1 & 2), 28–48.

McCumber, D. (2001, July, 1). School discipline: An uneven hand. *Seattle Post-Intelligencer*. Retrieved from www.seattlepi.nwsource.com/disciplinegap/

McIntosh, P. (1988). *White privilege and male privilege: A personal account of coming to see correspondences through work in women's studies* (Report No. 189). Wellesley, MA: Wellesley College Center for Research on Women.

McLaughlin, M. W., & Talbert, J. E. (2001). *Professional communities and the work of high school teaching*. Chicago: University of Chicago Press.

McNeil, L. (2000). *Contradictions of school reform: Educational costs of standardized testing*. New York: Routledge.

Mead, N., Grigg, W., Moran, R., & Kuang, M. (2010). *National Indian Education Study 2009—Part II: The educational experiences of American Indian and Alaska Native Students in grades 4 and 8*. (Report No. NCES 2010–463). Washington, DC: National Center for Education Statistics; Institute of Education Sciences; U.S. Department of Education. Retrieved from nces.ed.gov/pubsearch/pubsinfo.asp?pubid=2007454

Meier, D. (2006). "As though they owned the place": Small schools as membership communities. *Phi Delta Kappan, 87*, 657–662.

Meier, D., Kohn, A., Darling-Hammond, L., Sizer, T. R., & Wood, G. (2005). In D. Meier & G. Wood (Eds.), *Many children left behind: How the No Child Left Behind Act is damaging our children and our schools*. Boston: Beacon Press.

Menkart, D. (1999). Deepening the meaning of heritage months. *Educational Leadership, 56*(7), 19–21.

Menkart, D., Murray, A. D., & View, J. L. (Eds.). (2004). *Putting the movement back into civil rights teaching*. Washington, DC: Teaching for Change.

Menzel, P., Mann, C., & Kennedy, P. (1995). *Material world: A global family portrait*. San Francisco: Sierra Club.

Merino, B. (2007). Identifying critical competencies for teachers of English learners. *University of California Language Minority Research Institute Newsletter, 16*(4), 1–7.

Merriam, S. B. (2009). *Qualitative research: A guide to design and implementation*. Hoboken, NJ: Jossey-Bass.

Merton, R. K. (1948). The self-fulfilling prophecy. *Antioch Review, 8*, 193–210.

Meyer, M., & Zucker, L. (1989). *Permanently failing organizations*. Thousand Oaks, CA: Sage.

Meyer, S. (2008). *The twilight saga collection*. New York: Little, Brown.

Miceli, M. (2005). *Standing out, standing together: The social and political impact of gay-straight alliances*. New York: Routledge.

Miller, R. L., & Rotheram-Borus, M. J. (1994). Growing up biracial in the United States. In E. P. Salett & D. R. Koslow (Eds.), *Race, ethnicity, and self: Identity in multicultural perspective* (pp. 143–169). Washington, DC: National Multicultural Institute.

Milner, H. R. (Ed.). (2010). *Culture, curriculum and identity in education*. New York: Palgrave MacMillan.

Mintrop, H., & Sunderman, G. (2009). *Why high stakes accountability sounds good but doesn't work—and why we keep doing it anyway*. Los Angeles: The Civil Rights Project Provecto Derechos Civiles at UCLA.

Moll, L. C., & Arnot-Hopffer, E. (2005). Sociocultural competence in teacher education. *Journal of Teacher Education, 56*(3), 242–247.

Monger, R. (2010). *Annual flow report U.S. permanent legal residents: 2009*. Washington, DC: Department of Homeland Security Office of Immigration Statistics.

Montaño, T., Ulanoff, S. H., Quintanar-Sarellana, R., & Aoki, L. (2005). The debilingualization of California's prospective bilingual teachers. *Social Justice, 32*(3), 103–119.

Morin, R. (2006, June 9). The color of disaster assistance. *The Washington Post*, p. A02.

Morrell, E. (2008). *Critical literacy and urban youth: Pedagogies of access, dissent and liberation*. New York: Routledge.

Morrell, E., & Duncan-Andrade, J. (2008). "Comin' from the school of hard knocks": Hip-hop and the revolution of English classrooms in city schools. In W. Ayers, G. Ladson-Billings, G. Michie, & P. A. Noguera (Eds.), *City kids, city schools* (pp. 197–206). New York: The New Press.

Moses, R. P. (2002). Quality education is a civil rights issue. In D. T. Gordon (Ed.), *Harvard Education Letter Focus Series 7* (pp. 26–27).

Moses, R. P. (2010). Constitutional property vs. constitutional people. In T. Perry, R. Moses, J. T. Wynne, E. Cortes, & L. Delpit (Eds.), *Quality education as a constitutional right: Creating a grassroots movement to transform public schools* (pp. 70–92). Boston: Beacon Press.

Moses, R. P., & Cob, C. E. (2001). *Radical equations: Civil rights from Mississippi to the algebra project*. Boston: Beacon Press.

Murillo, E. G., Villenas, S. A., Galvan, R. T., Muñoz, J. S., Martinez, C., & Machado-Casas, M. (Eds.). (2010). *Handbook of Latinos in education: Theory, research and practice*. New York: Routledge.

Murray, C. (2008). *Real education: Four simple truths for bringing America's schools back to reality*. New York: Random House.

Mutume, G. (2003). Reversing Africa's "brain drain": New initiatives tap skills of African expatriates. *Africa Recovery, 17*(2), 1.

Myslinski, M. (2010, June). Election shows voters back candidates, measures that support students and public schools. *California Teachers Association Magazine, 1* Retrieved from http://www.cta.org/About-CTA/News-Room/Press-Releases/2010/06/20100609_1.aspx

National Center for Education Statistics. (2009a). The Condition of Education, 2009 (Report No. NCES 2009-082). Washington, DC: U.S. Department of Education.

National Center for Education Statistics. (2009b). U. S. Department of Education, Institute of Education Sciences, National Assessment of Educational Progress (NAEP). Washington, DC: U.S. Department of Education.

National Clearinghouse for English Language Acquisition & Language Instruction Educational Programs. Retrieved August 17, 2010, from www.ncela.gwu.edu

National Collaborative on Diversity in the Teaching Force. (2004). *Assessment of diversity in America's teaching force: A call to action*. Washington, DC: National Collaborative on Diversity in the Teaching Force.

National Commission on Excellence in Education. (1983). *A nation at risk: The imperative for education reform*. Washington, DC: U.S. Government Printing Office.

National Comprehensive Center for Teacher Quality and Public Agenda. (2008). *Lessons learned: New teachers talk about their jobs, challenges and long-range plans* (Report No. 1). Washington, DC: National Comprehensive Center for Teacher Quality and Public Agenda.

National Working Group on Funding Student Learning. (2008). *Funding student learning: How to align education resources with student learning goals*. Bothell: Center on Reinventing Public Education at University of Washington–Bothell.

Native Education 101: Basic facts about American Indian, Alaska Native, and Native Hawaiian education. (2007). Washington, DC: The National Indian Education Association & NEA.

Newby, R. (1995). The bell curve: Laying bare the resurgence of scientific racism. *American Behavioral Scientist, 39*(1), 12–24.

Newman, L., & Souza, D. (2009). *Heather has two mommies* (20th anniversary ed.). Boston: Alyson Books.

Nichols, S. L., & Berliner, D. C. (2007). *Collateral damage: How high-stakes testing corrupts America's schools*. Cambridge, MA: Harvard Education Press.

Nieto, S. (1994). Affirmation, solidarity and critique: Moving beyond tolerance in multicultural education. *Multicultural Education, 103*(4), 9–12, 35–38.

Nieto, S. (2000a). Bringing bilingual education out of the basement, and other imperatives for teacher education. In Z. Beykont (Ed.), *Lifting every voice: Pedagogy and politics of bilingual education* (pp. 187–207). Cambridge, MA: Harvard Educational Review.

Nieto, S. (Ed.). (2000b). *Puerto Rican students in U.S. schools*. Mahwah, NJ: Lawrence Erlbaum.

Nieto, S. (2003a). Profoundly multicultural questions. *Educational Leadership, 60*(4), 6–10.

Nieto, S. (2003b). *What keeps teachers going?* New York: Teachers College Press.

Nieto, S. (2005). *Why we teach*. New York: Teachers College Press.

Nieto, S. (2009). Multicultural education in the United States: Historical realities, ongoing challenges, and transformative possibilities. In J. A. Banks (Ed.), *The Routledge international companion to multicultural education* (pp. 79–95). New York: Routledge.

Nieto, S. (2010). *The light in their eyes: Creating multicultural learning communities* (10th anniversary ed.). New York: Teachers College Press.

Nieto, S. (2011). *From surviving to thriving: Finding joy in teaching students of diverse backgrounds*. Portsmouth, NH: Heinemann.

Nieto, S., Bode, P., Kang, E., & Raible, J. (2008). Pushing the boundaries of multicultural education: Retheorizing identity, community and curriculum. In F. M. Connelly, M. F. He, & J. Phillion (Eds.), *Handbook of curriculum and instruction* (pp. 176–197). Thousand Oaks, CA: Sage.

Nieto, S., & Raible, J. (2010). Beyond categories: The complex identities of adolescents. In S. Nieto (Ed.),

Language, culture, and teaching: Critical perspectives (2nd ed., pp. 199–213). New York: Routledge.

Nieto, S., Rivera, M., Cammarota, J., Cannella, C., García, E., Gonzalez, M., Irizarry, J., Moll, L. C., Pedraza, P., Perez, P. B., Romo, H., & Valenzuela A. (2010). *Charting a new course: Understanding the sociocultural, political, and economic context of Latino/a education in the United States.* Synthesis paper funded by the Spencer Foundation.

Nine-Curt, C. J. (1984). *Nonverbal communication* (2nd ed.). Cambridge, MA: Evaluation, Dissemination, and Assessment Center.

No Child Left Behind Act of 2001, Pub. L. No. 107-110, 115 Stat. 1425 (2001).

Noddings, N. (2005). *The challenge to care in schools: An alternative approach to education* (2nd ed.). New York: Teachers College Press.

Noddings, N. (2007). *When school reform goes wrong.* New York: Teachers College Press.

Noguera, P. (2008). Joaquín's dilemma: Understanding the link between racial identity and school-related behaviors. In P. Noguera (Ed.), *The trouble with Black boys . . . and other reflections on race, equity, and the future of public education* (pp. 1–16). San Francisco: John Wiley.

Noguera, P. A. (2004). Social class, but what about schools? *Poverty & Race, 13*(5), 11–12.

Noguera, P. A. (2008). Schools, prisons, and social implications of punishment: Rethinking disciplinary practices. In P. A. Noguera (Ed.), *The trouble with Black boys . . . and other reflections on race, equity, and the future of public education* (pp. 111–130). San Francisco: Jossey-Bass.

Noguera, P. A., & Cannella, C. M. (2006). Conclusion—youth agency, resistance and public activism: The public commitment to social justice. In P. A. Noguera, S. Gilwright, & J. Cammarota (Eds.), *Beyond resistance! Youth activism and community change: New democratic possibilities for practice and policy for America's youth* (pp. 333–347). New York: Routledge.

Oakes, J. (2005). *Keeping track: How schools structure inequality* (2nd ed.). New Haven, CT: Yale University Press.

Oakes, J., Quartz, K. H., Ryan, S., & Lipton, M. (2000). *Becoming good American schools: The struggle for civic virtue in education reform.* San Francisco: Jossey-Bass.

Oakes, J., & Saunders, M. (Eds.). (2008). *Beyond tracking: Multiple pathways to college, career, and civic participation.* Cambridge, MA: Harvard Education Press.

Obama, B. (2010). *Remarks by the president on comprehensive immigration reform.* American University School of International Service.

Office of Indian Education. (2010). Retrieved from http://indianeducation.org/

Ogbu, J. U. (1987). Variability in minority school performance: A problem in search of an explanation. *Anthropology and Education Quarterly, 18*(4), 312–334.

Ogbu, J. U., & Simons, H. D. (1998). Voluntary and involuntary minorities: A cultural-ecological theory of school performance with some implications for education. *Anthropology & Education Quarterly, 29*(2), 155–188.

Olsen, L. (2000). Learning English and learning America: Immigrants in the center of a storm. *Theory into Practice, 39*(4), 196–202.

Olsen, L. (2008). *Made in America: Immigrant students in our public schools* (10th anniversary ed.). New York: New Press.

Olson, K. (2009). *Wounded by school: Recapturing the joy in learning and standing up to old school culture.* New York: Teachers College Press.

Orfield, G. (2004). Losing our future: Minority youth left out. In G. Orfield (Ed.), *Dropouts in America: Confronting the graduate rate crisis* (pp. 1–11). Cambridge, MA: Harvard Education Press.

Orfield, G. (2009). *Reviving the goal of an integrated society: A 21st century challenge.* Los Angeles: The Civil Rights Project/Proyecto Derechos Civiles at UCLA. Retrieved from http://civilrightsproject.ucla.edu/

Orfield, G., & Lee, C. (2005). *Why segregation matters: Poverty and educational inequality.* Cambridge, MA: The Civil Rights Project at Harvard University. Retrieved from http://civilrightsproject.ucla.edu/research/k-12-education/integration-and-diversity/why-segregation-matters-poverty-and-educational-inequality/

Ovando, C. J., Collier, V. P., & Combs, M. C. (2006). *Bilingual and ESL classrooms: Teaching in multicultural contexts* (4th ed.). New York: McGraw-Hill.

Park, C. C., Goodwin, A. L., & Lee, S. J. (2003). *Asian American identities, families, and schooling: Research on the education of Asian and Pacific Americans.* Charlotte, NC: Information Age.

Partners for Livable Communities (Producer), & Heath, S. B. (Director). (1999). *ArtShow* [Video/DVD] Arlington, VA: PBS.

Passel, J. S., Wang, W., & Taylor, P. (2010). *Marrying out: One-in-seven new U. S. marriages is interracial or interethnic.* Washington, DC: Pew Research Center.

Payne, R. (2005). *A framework for understanding poverty* (4th ed.). Highlands, TX: Aha! Process.

Pedraza, P. & Rivera, M. (Eds.) (2005). *Latino education: An agenda for community action research.* Mahwah, NJ: Lawrence Erlbaum.

Pedula, J. J., Abrams, L. M., Madaus, G. F., Russell, M. K., Ramos, M. A., & Miao, J. (2003). *Perceived effects of state-mandated testing programs on teaching and learning: Findings from a national survey of teachers.* Chestnut Hill, MA: National Board on Educational Testing and Public Policy, Boston College.

Penniman, V., & Shumway, D. (2010). *Calendar-connections: Thinking critical thinking skills in elementary schools.* Retrieved from http://www.calendar-connections.com/

Pérez, B., & Torres-Guzmán, M. E. (2006). *Learning in two worlds: An integrated Spanish/English biliteracy approach* (3rd ed.). Boston: Allyn & Bacon.

Perkins, B. K. (2006). *Where we learn: The CUBE survey of urban school climate.* Washington, DC: The Urban Student Achievement Task Force, Council of Urban Boards of Education, National School Boards Association.

Perkins, B. K. (2007). *Where we teach: The CUBE survey of urban school climate.* Alexandria, VA: Urban Achievement Task Force, Council of Urban Boards of Education, National School Boards Association.

Pew Hispanic Center. (2008). *Fact sheet: Hispanics of Dominican origin in the United States, 2008.* Washington, DC: Pew Research Center.

Philips, S. U. (1993). *The invisible culture: Communication in classroom and community on the Warm Springs Indian Reservation* (reissued with changes ed.). Prospect Heights, IL: Waveland Press.

Phinney, J. S., Berry, J. W., Sam, D. L., & Vedder, P. (2001). Understanding immigrant youth: Conclusion and implications. In J. S. Phinney, J. W. Berry, D. L. Sam, & P. Vedder (Eds.), *Immigrant youth in cultural transition: Acculturation, identity, and adaptation across national contexts* (pp. 211–233). Mahwah, NJ: Lawrence Erlbaum.

Pizarro, M. (2005). *Chicanas and Chicanos in school: Racial profiling, identity battles, and empowerment.* Austin: University of Texas Press.

Plyler v. Doe, 457 U.S. 202 (1982).

Pollard, A. (2000). *African-centered schooling in theory and practice.* Westport, CT: Bergin & Garvey.

Pollock, M. (2004). *Colormute: Race talk dilemmas in an American school.* Princeton, NJ: Princeton University Press.

Portes, A., & Rumbaut, R. G. (2001). *Legacies: The story of the immigrant second generation.* Berkeley/New York: University of California Press and Russell Sage Foundation.

Portes, A., & Rumbaut, R. G. (2005). The second generation in early adulthood [Special issue]. *Ethnic and Racial Studies, 28*(6), 983–1214.

Portes, A., & Rumbaut, R. G. (2006). *Immigrant America: A portrait* (3rd ed.). Berkeley: University of California Press.

Provenzo, E. F., Jr. (2005). *Critical literacy: What every American ought to know.* Boulder, CO: Paradigm.

Raible, J., & Irizarry, J. G. (2010). Redirecting the teacher's gaze: Teacher education, youth surveillance and the school-to-prison pipeline. *Teaching and Teacher Education, 26*(5), 1196–1203. doi:10.1016/j.tate.2010.02.006

Ramirez, M., & Castañeda, A. (1974). *Cultural democracy, Bicognitive development and education.* New York: Academic Press.

Rice, C. L. (2010, February 24). LA's response to its gang epidemic. *Huffington Post,* Retrieved from http://www.huffingtonpost.com/constance-l-rice/las-response-to-its-gang_b_475780.html

Richardson, V. (2003). Constructivist pedagogy. *Teachers College Record, 105*(9), 1623–1640.

Rifka, S. (2010). *American-Arab anti-discrimination committee.* Retrieved from www.adc.org/education/educational-resources/

Rist, R. C. (1971). Student social class and teacher expectations: The self-fulfilling prophecy in ghetto education. In S. Stodolsky (Ed.), *Challenging the myths: The schools, the Blacks, and the poor* (Reprint series No. 5). Cambridge, MA: Harvard Educational Review.

Rist, R. C. (2000). Author's introduction: The enduring dilemmas of class and color in American education. *Harvard Educational Review,* HER Classic Reprint, *70*(3), 257–302.

Roberts, K. (2009). Socio-economic reproduction. In A. Furlong (Ed.), *Handbook of youth and young adulthood: New perspectives and agendas* (pp. 14–21). New York: Routledge.

Roberts, M. A. (2010). Toward a theory of culturally relevant critical teacher care: African American teachers' definitions and perceptions of care for African American students. *Journal of Moral Education, 39*(4), 449–467.

Robinson, W. C. (1998). *Terms of refuge: The Indochinese exodus and the international response.* London, England: Zed Books.

Rodríguez, L. (2005). *Always running, la vida loca: Gang days in L.A.* New York: Simon & Schuster.

Rohmer, H. (Ed.). (1999). *Honoring our ancestors: Stories and pictures by fourteen artists.* San Francisco: Children's Book Press.

Rolón, C. (2000). Puerto Rican female narratives about self, school and success. In S. Nieto (Ed.), *Puerto Rican students in U.S. schools* (pp. 141–165). Mahwah, NJ: Lawrence Erlbaum.

Rólon-Dow, R. (2005). Critical care: A color(ful) analysis of care narratives in the schooling experiences of Puerto Rican girls. *American Educational Research Journal, 42*(1), 77–111.

Rolstad, K., Mahoney, K., & Glass, G. V. (2005). The big picture: A meta-analysis of program effectiveness research on English language learners. *Educational Policy, 19*(4), 572–594.

Rong, X. L. D., & Brown, F. (2002). Socialization, culture, and identities of Black immigrant children: What educators need to know and do. *Education and Urban Society, 34*(2), 247–273.

Root, M. P. P. (2004). Multiracial families and children: Implications for educational research and practice. In J. A. Banks, & C. A. M. Banks (Eds.), *Handbook of research on multicultural education* (pp. 110–124). San Francisco: Jossey-Bass.

Rosenberg, P. M. (2004). Color blindness in teacher education: An optical illusion. In M. Fine, L. Weis, L. P. Pruitt, & A. Burns (Eds.), *Off White: Readings on power, privilege, and resistance* (2nd ed., pp. 257–272). New York: Routledge.

Rosenthal, R. (1998). Pygmalion effects: Existence, magnitude, and social importance. *Educational Researcher, 16*(9), 37–44.

Rosenthal, R., & Jacobson, L. (1968). *Pygmalion in the classroom.* New York: Holt, Rinehart and Winston.

Rothstein, R. (1998). Bilingual education: The controversy. *Phi Delta Kappan, 79*(9), 672–678

Rothstein, R. (2004). *Class and schools: Using social, economic, and educational reform to close the Black-White achievement gap.* Washington, DC/New York: Economic Policy Institute and Teachers College Press.

Rothstein, R. (2006). *Reforms that could help narrow the achievement gap. Policy perspective.* San Francisco: WestEd.

Roughgarden, J. (2004). *Evolution's rainbow: Diversity, gender, and sexuality in nature and people.* Berkeley: University of California Press.

Rumbaut, R. G. (1996). The crucible within: Ethnic identity, self-esteem, and segmented assimilation among children of immigrants. In A. Portes (Ed.), *The new second generation* (pp. 119–170). New York: Russell Sage Foundation.

Ryan, J. E. (2010). *Five miles away, A world apart: One city, two schools, and the story of educational opportunity in modern America.* Oxford: Oxford University Press.

Ryan, W. (1971). *Blaming the victim.* New York: Vintage Books.

Sadker, D., & Zittleman, K. R. (2010). Gender bias: From colonial America to today's classrooms. In J. A. Banks & C. A. M. Banks (Eds.), *Multicultural education: Issues and perspectives* (7th ed., pp. 137–156). New York: John Wiley.

Sadowski, M. (2006). Making schools safer for LGBT youth. *Harvard Education Letter, 22*(3), 1–3.

Sadowski, M. (Ed.). (2008). *Adolescents at school: Perspectives on youth, identity, and education* (2nd ed.). Cambridge, MA: Harvard Education Press.

St. Pierre, S. (1995). *Teenage refugees from Cambodia speak out: In their own voices.* New York: Rosen.

Salomone, R. (2010). *True American: Language, identity and the education of immigrant children.* Cambridge, MA: Harvard University Press.

Sanchez, J. R. (2007). *Boricua power: A political history of Puerto Ricans in the United States.* New York: New York University Press.

Santa Cruz, N. (2010, May 12). Arizona bill targeting ethnic studies signed into law. *Los Angeles Times,* doi:http://articles.latimes.com/2010/may/12/nation/la-na-ethnic-studies-20100512

Santiago, E. (1993). *When I was Puerto Rican.* Cambridge, MA: Da Capo.

Satrapi, M. (2003). *Persepolis: The story of a childhood* (Graphic novel). Pantheon: New York.

Schofield, J. W. (2010). The colorblind perspective in school: Causes and consequences. In J. Banks & C. A. M. Banks (Eds.), *Multicultural education: Issues and perspectives* (7th ed., pp. 259–283). Hoboken, NJ: John Wiley.

Schott Foundation for Public Education. (2009). *Lost opportunity: A 50 state report on the opportunity to learn in America.* Cambridge, MA: Schott Foundation for Public Education. Retrieved from www.OTLstatereport.org

Schwarzer, D., Haywood, A., & Lorenzen, C. (2003). Fostering multiliteracy in a linguistically diverse classroom. *Language Arts, 80*(6), 453–460.

Seelye, H. N. (1993). *Teaching culture: Strategies for intercultural communication.* Lincolnwood, IL: National Textbooks.

Selden, S. (1999). *Inheriting shame: The story of eugenics and racism in America.* New York: Teachers College Press.

Sesoy, Ö., & Stonebanks, C. D. (2009). *Muslim voices in school: Narratives of identity and pluralism.* Rotterdam/Boston: Sense Publishers.

Shabbas, A. (2007). *Arab World and Islamic Resources (AWAIR).* Retrieved from www.awaironline.org

Sheets, R. H. (1995). From remedial to gifted: Effects of culturally centered pedagogy. *Theory into Practice, 34*(3), 186–193.

Shor, I. (1996). *When students have power: Negotiating authority in a critical pedagogy.* Chicago: University of Chicago Press.

Skutnabb-Kangas, T. (1988). Multilingualism and the education of minority children. In T. Skutnabb-Kangas & J. Cummins (Eds.), *Minority education: From shame to struggle* (pp. 9–44). Clevedon, England: Multilingual Matters.

Slavin, R. E., Madden, N., Calderón, M., Chamberlain, A., & Hennessy, M. (2010). *Reading and language outcomes of a five-year randomized evaluation of transitional bilingual education.* Baltimore, MD: Johns Hopkins University and Success for All Foundation.

Sleeter, C. E. (1994). White racism. *Multicultural Education, 1*(4), 5–8, 39.

Sleeter, C. E. (2005). *Un-standardizing curriculum: Multicultural teaching in the standards-based classroom.* New York: Teachers College Press.

Smith-Hefner, N. (1999). *Khmer American: Identity and moral education in a diasporic community.* Berkeley: University of California Press.

Smyth, L., & Heath, S. B. (1999). *ArtShow: Youth and community development*. Washington, DC: Partners for Livable Communities.

Snow, R. E. (1969). Unfinished Pygmalion. *Contemporary Psychology, 14,* 197–200.

Solórzano, D. G., Ledesma, M. C., Pérez, J., Burciaga, M. R., & Ornelas, A. (2003). *Latina equity in education: Gaining access to academic enrichment programs* (Report No. 4). Los Angeles: UCLA Chicano Studies Research Center.

Spring, J. H. (1989). *The sorting machine revisited: National educational policy since 1945*. New York: Longman.

Spring, J. H. (2008). *The American school: From the Puritans to No Child Left Behind* (7th ed.). New York: McGraw-Hill.

Spring, J. H. (2010a). *American education* (14th ed.). New York: McGraw-Hill Higher Education.

Spring, J. H. (2010b). *Deculturalization and the struggle for equality: A brief history of the education of dominated cultures in the United States* (6th ed.). Boston: McGraw-Hill.

Stanton-Salazar, R. D. (2001). *Manufacturing hope and despair: The school and kin support networks of U.S.-Mexican youth*. New York: Teachers College Press.

Steele, C. M. (1992). Race and the schooling of Black Americans. *The Atlantic Monthly, April,* 68–78.

Stellwagen, J. B. (2001). A challenge to the learning style advocates. *The Clearing House, 74*(5), 265–268.

Swisher, K., & Schoorman, D. (2001). Learning styles: Implications for teachers. In C. F. Diaz (Ed.), *Multicultural education in the 21st century* (1st ed., pp. 55–70). Reading, MA: Addison-Wesley.

Szymusiak, M. (1999). *The stones cry out: A Cambodian childhood, 1975–1980* (J. Hamilton-Merritt, L. Coverdale, Trans.). Bloomington: Indiana University Press.

Takaki, R. (1998). *Strangers from a different shore: A History of Asian Americans*. New York: Penguin Books.

Takaki, R. (2008). *A Different mirror: A history of multicultural America*. New York: Bay Back Books.

Takougang, J. (2003). Contemporary African immigrants to the United States. *Irinkerindo: A Journal of African Migration, December 2003*(2). Retrieved from http://www.africamigration.com/

Takyi, B. (2002). The making of the second diaspora: On the recent African immigrant community in the United States of America. *Western Journal of Black Studies, 26*(1), 32–43.

Tam, T. D. W. (1980). *Vietnamese refugee students: A handbook for school personnel*. Cambridge, MA: National Assessment and Dissemination Center.

Tamura, E. H. (2008). Hawai'i Creole (Pidgin), local identity, and schooling [Special issue]. *Educational Perspectives: Journal of the College of Education, 41*(1 & 2), 3–66.

Tanenbaum Center for Interreligious Understanding. (2010). *Religions in my neighborhood: Preparing students for a multicultural and multireligious world*. New York: Tanenbaum Center for Interreligious Understanding.

Tatum, B. D. (1992). Talking about race, learning about racism: The application of racial identity development theory in the classroom. *Harvard Educational Review, 62*(1), 1–8.

Tatum, B. D. (2003). *"Why are all the Black kids sitting together in the cafeteria?" and other conversations about race*. New York: Harper Collins.

Tatum, B. D. (2007). *Can we talk about race? And other conversations in an era of school resegregation*. Boston: Beacon Press.

Teaching for Change and Rethinking Schools. (2010). *The Zinn Education Project*. Retrieved from http://zinnedproject.org/

Terman, L. (1916). *The measurement of intelligence*. Boston: Houghton Mifflin.

Tharp, R. G. (1981). Psychocultural variables and constants: Effects on teaching and learning in schools. *American Psychologist, 44*(2), 211–220.

Tharp, R. G., & Dalton, S. S. (2007). Orthodoxy, cultural compatibility, and universals in education. *Comparative Education, 43*(1), 53–70.

Tharp, R. G., Jordan, C., Speidel, G. E., Au, K. H., Klein, T. W., Calkins, R. P., Sloat, K. C. M., & Gallimore, R. (2007). Education and native Hawaiian children: Revisiting KEEP. *Hūlili: Multidisciplinary Research on Hawaiian Well-being, 4*(1), 269–317.

Thiessen, D., & Cook-Sather, A. (Eds.). (2007). *The international handbook of student experience in elementary and secondary school*. Dordrecht, The Netherlands: Springer.

Tosolt, B. (2010). Gender and race differences in middle school students' perceptions of caring teacher behaviors. *Multicultural Perspectives, 12*(3), 149–150.

Tough, P. (2008). *Whatever it takes: Geoffrey Canada's quest to change Harlem and America*. New York: Houghton Mifflin.

Trafzer, C., Keller, J. A., & Sisquoc, L. (Eds.). (2006). *Boarding school blues: revisiting American Indian educational experiences*. Lincoln: University of Nebraska Press.

Tyack, D. B. (1995). Schooling and social diversity: Historical reflections. In W. D. Hawley & A. W. Jackson (Eds.), *Toward a common destiny: Improving race and ethnic relations in America* (pp. 3–38). San Francisco: Jossey-Bass.

Ung, L. (2006a). *First they killed my father*. New York: Harper Collins.

Ung, L. (2006b). *Lucky child: A daughter of Cambodia reunites with the sister she left behind*. New York: Harper Collins.

United Nations, High Commission for Refugees. (2000). Chapter 4: Flight from Indochina. *United Nations, High Commission for Refugees Report* (pp. 79–103). Geneva, Switzerland: United Nations.

U.S. Census Bureau. (2000). *Table DP-2. Profile of selected social characteristics.* Washington, DC: U.S. Census Bureau.

U. S. Census Bureau. (2006). *2006 American community survey.* Washington, DC: U.S. Census Bureau. Retrieved from http://factfinder.census.gov

U.S. Census Bureau. (2007). *Language use in the United States, 2007.* Washington, DC: U.S. Census Bureau.

U.S. Census Bureau. (2009). *The 2010 statistical abstract national data book: Education.* Retrieved July 15, 2010, from http://www.census.gov/compendia/statab/cats/education.html

U.S. Census Bureau. (2010a). *An older and more diverse nation by midcentury.* Retrieved July 28, 2010, from http://www.census.gov.ezproxy.library.tufts.edu/mp/www/cpu/2010_06.html

U.S. Census Bureau. (2010b). *U.S. Census Bureau.* Retrieved from http://www.census.gov

U.S. Census Bureau. (2010c). *USA people quick facts.* Retrieved July 15, 2010, from http://quickfacts.census.gov

U.S. Census Bureau, Housing and Household Economic Statistics Division. (2008). *School enrollment—social and economic characteristics of students: October 2008.* Retrieved from http://www.census.gov.ezproxy.library.tufts.edu/population/www/socdemo/school/cps2008.html

U.S. Department of Commerce. (2010). *Back to school: 2010–2011* (Report No. CB10-FF.14). Washington, DC: U.S. Census Bureau.

U.S. Department of Education. (2010a). *Elementary and secondary education: Reauthorization of the Elementary and Secondary Education Act.* Retrieved July 15, 2010, from http://www2.ed.gov/policy/elsec/leg/blueprint/index.html

U.S. Department of Education. (2010). *ESEA blueprint for reform: The reauthorization of the Elementary and Secondary Education Act.* Washington, DC: Office of Planning, Evaluation and Policy Development. doi:http://www2.ed.gov/policy/elsec/leg/blueprint/

U.S. Department of Education. (2010b). *Race to the Top Fund.* Retrieved July 15, 2010, from http://www2.ed.gov/programs/racetothetop/legislation.htm

Valenzuela, A. (1999). *Subtractive schooling: U.S.-Mexican youth and the politics of caring.* Albany: State University of New York Press.

Valenzuela, A. (2004). *Leaving children behind: How "Texas style" accountability fails Latino youth.* Albany: State University of New York Press.

Van Ausdale, D., & Feagin, J. R. (2001). *The first r: How children learn race and racism.* Lanham, MD: Rowman & Littlefield.

Vanneman, A., Hamilton, L., Anderson, J. B., & Rahman, T. (2009). *Achievement gaps: How Black and White students in public schools perform in mathematics and reading on the National Assessment of Educational Progress* (Report No. NCES 2009-455). Washington, DC: U.S. Department of Education, National Center for Education Statistics.

Vasquez, V. M. (2004). *Negotiating critical literacies with young children.* Mahwah, NJ: Lawrence Erlbaum.

Vaught, S. (2011). Juvenile prison schooling and re-entry: Disciplining young men of Color. In F. Sherman & F. Jacobs (Eds.), *Health and well-being in the juvenile justice system* (In press). Hoboken, NJ: John Wiley.

Vietnam Veterans against the War and the Cambodian American Community. (2009). *Peace Pagoda Nipponzan Myohoji Sangha Buddhist temple.* Retrieved from www.peacepagoda.org

Vigil, J. D. (1999). Streets and schools: How educators can help Chicano marginalized gang youth. *Harvard Educational Review, 69*(3), 270–288.

Vigil, J. D. (2007). *The projects: Gang and non-gang families in East Los Angeles.* Austin: University of Texas Press.

Vogt, L. A., Jordan, C., & Tharp, R. G. (1993). Explaining school failure, producing school success: Two cases. In E. Jacob & C. Jordan (Eds.), *Minority education: Anthropological perspectives* (pp. 276–286). Norwood, NJ: Ablex.

Wald, J., & Losen, D. J. (2003). Defining and redirecting the school-to-prison pipeline [Special issue: Deconstructing the school to prison pipeline]. *New Directions for Youth Development: Theory, Practice, Research, 99,* 9–15.

Wald, J., & Thurau, L. (2010). Taking school safety too far? The ill-defined role police play in schools. *Education Week, 29*(22), 24–26.

Walker, R. (2009). Introduction. In M. Tauber & P. Singh (Eds.), *Blended nation: Portraits and interviews of mixed-race America* (n.p.). San Rafael, CA: Channel Photographics.

Wallitt, R. (2005). *Breaking the silence: Cambodian students speak out about school, success, and shifting identities.* Unpublished doctoral dissertation. University of Massachusetts, Amherst, MA.

Wallitt, R. (2008). Cambodian invisibility: Students lost between the "Achievement Gap" and the "Model Minority." *Multicultural Perspectives, 10*(1), 3–9.

Walters, L. S. (2000). Putting cooperative learning to the test. *Harvard Education Letter, 16*(3), 1–7.

Waugh, D. (1974). *Breakthrough for bilingual education: Lau v. Nichols and the San Francisco school system.* Washington, DC: U.S. Commission on Civil Rights.

Wehlage, G. G., & Rutter, R. A. (1987). Dropping out: How much do schools contribute to the problem? In G. Natriello (Ed.), *School dropouts: Patterns and policies* (pp. 70–88). New York: Teachers College Press.

Weinberg, M. (1982). Notes from the editor. *Chronicle of Equal Education, 4*(3), 7.

Weinberg, M. (1990). *Racism in the United States: A comprehensive classified bibliography.* New York: Greenwood Press.

Weiss, H. B., Bouffard, S. M., Bridglall, B. L., & Gordon, E. W. (2009). *Reframing family involvement in education: Supporting families to support educational equity.* (Report No. 5). New York: Campaign for Educational Equity, Teachers College, Columbia University.

Welcoming Schools: Human Rights Campaign. (2010). *Welcoming Schools guide.* Retrieved from http://www.welcomingschools.org/

Wiggins, G., & McTighe, J. (2005). *Understanding by Design* (2nd ed.). Alexandria, VA: Association for Supervision and Curriculum Development.

Wight, V. R., Chau, M., & Aratani, Y. (2010). *Who are America's poor children? The official story.* New York: National Center for Children in Poverty.

Wijeyesinghe, C. L., & Jackson, B. W. (Eds.). (2001). *New perspectives on racial identity development: A theoretical and practical anthology.* New York: New York University Press.

Wiley, T. G. (2005). *Literacy and language diversity in the United States* (2nd ed.). Washington, DC: Center for Applied Linguistics.

Williams, H. A. (2005). *Self-taught: African American education in slavery and freedom.* Chapel Hill: University of North Carolina Press.

Williamson, J. (1980). *New people: Miscegenation and mulattos in the United States.* New York: Free Press.

Wilson, B. L., & Corbett, H. D. (2001). *Listening to urban kids: School reform and the teachers they want.* Albany: State University of New York Press.

Wineburg, S. S. (1987). The self-fulfillment of the self-fulfilling prophecy: A critical appraisal. *Educational Researcher, 16*(9), 28–37.

Wistrich, R. S. (2010). *A lethal obsession: Anti-Semitism from antiquity to the global jihad.* New York: Random House.

Witkin, H. A. (1962). *Psychological differentiation.* New York: Wiley.

Woodson, C. G. (1933). *The mis-education of the Negro.* Washington, DC: The Associated Publishers.

World Factbook, The. (2010). Retrieved August 17, 2010, from https://www.cia.gov/library/publications/the-world-factbook/geos/cv.html

Wyman, M., Greenfield, P. J., & Gill, F. B. (1993). *Round-trip to America: The immigrants return to Europe, 1880–1930.* Ithaca, NY: Cornell Paperbacks.

Yearwood, J. (2003). Words that kill. In S. Nieto (Ed.), *What keeps teachers going?* (pp. 109–112). New York: Teachers College Press.

Yon, D. A. (2000). *Elusive culture: Schooling, race, and identity in global times.* Albany: State University of New York Press.

Yonezawa, S., Wells, A. S., & Serna, I. (2002). Choosing tracks: "Freedom of choice" in detracking schools. *American Educational Research Journal, 39*(1), 37–67.

Yosso, T. J. (2006). *Critical race counterstories along the Chicana/Chicano educational pipeline.* New York: Routledge.

Zanger, M. (2003). *The American history cookbook.* Westport, CT: Greenwood.

Zanger, V. V. (Director), & Landmark Media (Producer). (1991). *How we feel: Hispanic students speak out* [Video/DVD]. Falls Church, VA: Landmark Media.

Zeichner, K. M. (2003). Pedagogy, knowledge, and teacher preparation. In B. Williams (Ed.), *Closing the achievement gap: A vision for changing beliefs and practices* (2nd ed., pp. 99–114). Washington, DC: Association for Supervision and Curriculum Development.

Zemelman, S., & Ross, H. (2009). *13 Steps to teacher empowerment.* Portsmouth, NH: Heinemann.

Zenkov, K., & Harmon, J. (2009). Picturing a writing process: Photovoice and teaching writing to urban youth. *Journal of Adolescent & Adult Literacy, 52*(7), 575–584. doi:10.1598/JAAL.52.7.3

Zhou, M., & Bankston III, C. L. (2000). *The biculturalism of the Vietnamese student.* (Report No. 152). New York: ERIC Clearinghouse on Urban Education Digest.

Zinn, H. (2010). *A people's history of the United States.* New York: Harper Perennial Modern Classics.

Zirkel, S. (2002). "Is there a place for me?" Role models and academic identity among White students and students of color. *Teachers College Record, 104*(2), 357–376.

Zirkel, S. (2008). Creating more effective multiethnic schools. *Social Issues and Policy Review, 2*(1), 187–241.

Zogby, J. (2010). *Arab American Institute.* Retrieved from www.aaiusa.org

Zurawsky, C. (2004). Closing the gap: High achievement for students of color. *Research Points, 2*(3). Washington, DC: American Educational Research Association.

Index